Centuries of Genocide

The fourth edition of *Centuries of Genocide: Essays and Eyewitness Accounts* addresses examples of genocides perpetrated in the nineteenth, twentieth, and twenty-first centuries. Each chapter of the book is written by a recognized expert in the field, collectively demonstrating a wide range of disciplinary perspectives. The book is framed by an introductory essay that spells out definitional issues, as well as the promises, complexities, and barriers to the prevention and intervention of genocide.

To help the reader learn about the similarities and differences among the various cases, each case is structured around specific leading questions. In every chapter authors address: Who committed the genocide? How was the genocide committed? Why was the genocide committed? Who were the victims? What were the outstanding historical forces? What was the long-range impact? What were the responses? How do scholars interpret this genocide? How does learning about this genocide contribute to the field of study?

While the material in each chapter is based on sterling scholarship and wide-ranging expertise of the authors, eyewitness accounts give voice to the victims. This book is an attempt to provoke the reader into understanding that learning about genocide is important and that we all have a responsibility not to become immune to acts of genocide, especially in the interdependent world in which we live today.

Samuel Totten is a Professor at the University of Arkansas, Fayetteville, and co-founding editor of *Genocide Studies and Prevention: An International Journal*. He has also been a Fulbright Fellow at the Centre for Conflict Management, National University of Rwanda.

William S. Parsons is Chief of Staff for the United States Holocaust Memorial Museum in Washington, D.C.

Centuries of Genocide

Essays and Eyewitness Accounts

Fourth Edition

Edited by Samuel Totten and William S. Parsons

Routledge
Taylor & Francis Group

NEW YORK AND LONDON

Fourth edition published 2013
by Routledge
711 Third Avenue, New York, NY 10017

Simultaneously published in the UK
by Routledge
2 Park Square, Milton Park, Abingdon, Oxon OX14 4RN

Routledge is an imprint of the Taylor & Francis Group, an informa business

First edition published by Routledge 1997

Library of Congress Cataloging in Publication Data
Centuries of genocide : essays and eyewitness accounts / edited by Samuel Totten and William S. Parsons.
    p. cm.
    Rev. ed. of: Century of genocide. 3rd ed. 2009.
    Includes index.
    1. Genocide–History–20th century. 2. Crimes against humanity–
    History–20th century. I. Totten, Samuel. II. Parsons, William S.
    (William Spencer), 1945– III. Title: Century of genocide.
    HV6322.7.C46 2012
    909.82–dc23   2012001507

ISBN: 978-0-415-87191-4 (hbk)
ISBN: 978-0-415-87192-1 (pbk)
ISBN: 978-0-203-86781-5 (ebk)

Typeset in Minion
by Wearset Ltd, Boldon, Tyne and Wear

Printed and bound in the United States of America by Sheridan Books, Inc. (a Sheridan Group Company).

Contents

Acknowledgments

We wish to sincerely thank all of the contributors to *Centuries of Genocide*, all of whom are extremely busy scholars. We offer a special thank you to Dr. Donald Niewyk for taking on the Herculean task of addressing three different cases (that of the Jews, the handicapped, and Roma and Sinti) in a single chapter.

We also wish to acknowledge and thank our acquisitions editor, Michael Kerns, for his ongoing support of our efforts to radically revise and update this book, now in its fourth edition. A warm thank you is also due to Ms. Darcy Bullock, Editorial Assistant (Political Science) at Routledge, for her hard work and, in particular, her attention to detail.

We wish to offer a huge thank you to Dr. George F. McCleary, Jr. in the Geography Department at the University of Kansas, and his colleagues and students for the research, thought, and hard work that they put into the development of the maps that accompany the case studies of genocide in this new edition. More specifically, genuine thanks are due to: Darin Grauberger, Director of Cartographic and GIS Services, University of Kansas; Karen S. Cook, cartographer and librarian; Michael K. Steinberg, The New College and Department of Geography, University of Alabama, Tuscaloosa; George Lovell, Professor of Geography at Queen's University, Kingston, Ontario and Visiting Professor in Latin American History at Universidad Pablo de Olavide in Seville, Spain; and the Centre for Development and Environment (CDE) of the University of Bern for helping create the map of the Nuba Mountains.

We also wish to acknowledge and offer thanks to two University of Kansas students for the painstaking work they put into the creation of various maps: John R. Granger, who developed the inset-handling design for Australia, and Lauren James who worked on maps that appeared in the third edition and now this fourth edition.

With Rouben Adalian, we heartily thank Donald E. Miller and Lorna Touryan Miller for granting us permission to publish several of the interviews they conducted with survivors of the Armenian genocide.

Finally, we greatly appreciate all of the publishers and organizations that provided us with permission to use excerpts of various eyewitness accounts that appeared initially in their publications.

Maps

Editors and Contributors

Editors

Samuel Totten is a genocide scholar based at the University of Arkansas, Fayetteville. In 2008 he served as a Fulbright Scholar at the Center for Conflict Management at the National University of Rwanda.

In July and August of 2004, Totten served as one of 24 investigators on the U.S. State Department's Darfur Atrocities Documentation Project, whose express purpose was to conduct interviews with refugees from Darfur in order to ascertain whether genocide had been perpetrated or not in Darfur. Based upon the data collected by the team of investigators, U.S. Secretary of State Colin Powell declared on September 9, 2004, that genocide had been perpetrated in Darfur, Sudan, by Government of Sudan troops and the *Janjaweed*.

For the past seven years he has conducted research into the Darfur genocide (2003 to present) and the Nuba Mountains genocide (late 1980s into the 1990s) in refugee camps along the Chad/Darfur border and in the Nuba Mountains, respectively.

Since 2003 Totten has served as the Managing Editor of a series entitled *Genocide: A Critical Bibliographic Review* (Transaction Publishers). The two most recent volumes in the series are *Fate and Plight of Women During and Following Genocide* (2009) and *The Genocide of Indigenous Peoples* (with Robert Hitchcock) (2011). The forthcoming volume in the series is *Impediments to the Prevention and Intervention of Genocide* (scheduled for publication in 2012).

Since 2005 he has served as founding Co-editor of *Genocide Studies and Prevention: An International Journal*, the official journal of the International Association of Genocide Scholars (University of Toronto Press).

Among the books he has authored, co-authored, and co-edited on genocide are: *Dictionary of Genocide* (Greenwood Publishers, 2008); *Century of Genocide: Critical Essays and Eyewitness Accounts* (Routledge, 2009); *Genocide in Darfur: Investigating Atrocities in the Sudan* (Routledge,

2006); *An Oral and Documentary History of the Darfur Genocide* (Praeger Security International, 2010); and *We Cannot Forget: Interviews with Survivors of the 1994 Genocide in Rwanda* (with Rafiki Ubaldo) (Rutgers University Press, 2011). Totten is currently completing a book on Darfur, *The Unequivocal Genocide in Darfur*, and a book on the genocidal actions perpetrated in the Nuba Mountains, *Genocide by Attrition: Nuba Mountains, Sudan.*

William S. Parsons is Chief of Staff of the United States Holocaust Memorial Museum in Washington, DC. Before becoming Chief of Staff, he served as the Museum's Director of Education and was responsible for developing educational programs both in Washington and throughout the nation. For the past 40 years he has been involved in writing, speaking, and creating programs that advance public awareness and knowledge about the Holocaust and genocide and the implications of this history for the world we live in today.

He is a co-founder of the Massachusetts-based Facing History and Ourselves National Foundation, Inc., and his published works include: *Facing History and Ourselves: Holocaust and Human Behavior* (coauthor, *Facing History & Ourselves*, 1982), and *Century of Genocide: Eyewitness Accounts and Critical Views* (co-editor, Garland Publishing, revised for 2004 publication and again in 2009 under the title of *Century of Genocide: Critical Essays and Eyewitness Accounts*).

Parsons holds a BA in History from Cornell College and an MA in Teaching from the University of Wisconsin. In 2002 he received the *Distinguished Achievement Award* from Cornell College for his career work in Holocaust and genocide education.

Contributors

Rouben P. Adalian, who earned his PhD in history from the University of California, Los Angeles (UCLA), is the Director of the Armenian National Institute (ANI) and the Armenian Genocide Museum of America project in Washington, DC.

A specialist on the Caucasus and the Middle East, Adalian has taught at a number of universities, including The School of Foreign Service at Georgetown University and The School of Advanced International Studies at Johns Hopkins University.

In 1993 he completed a project to document the Armenian genocide in the United States National Archives, which resulted in Chadwyck-Healey Inc. publishing 37,000 pages of American evidence on microfiche. The accompanying 476-page *Guide to the Armenian Genocide in the U.S. Archives 1915–1918* was issued in 1994.

Adalian is the Associate Editor of the *Encyclopedia of Genocide* (ABC-CLIO Ltd, 1999) and has contributed to numerous publications, including *Genocide in Our Time* (Pierian Press, 1992), *Genocide in the Twentieth Century* (Garland, 1995, 1997, 2004, 2009), *Studies in Comparative Genocide* (Palgrave Macmillan, 1999), *Genocide: Essays Toward Understanding, Early-Warning, and Prevention* (Association of Genocide Scholars, 1999), *Actualité du genocide des Arméniens* (Edipol, 1999), *America and the Armenian Genocide* (Cambridge University Press, 2003), and *Defining the Horrific: Readings on Genocide and Holocaust in the Twentieth Century* (Prentice Hall, 2004).

He is the author of *From Humanism to Rationalism: Armenian Scholarship in the Nineteenth Century* (Scholars Press, 1992) and the *Historical Dictionary of Armenia* (Scarecrow Press, 2002, 2010). Adalian is also the compiler and editor of the ANI website (www.armenian-genocide.org), which holds extensive information on the Armenian genocide.

Gerald Caplan has an MA in Canadian history and a PhD in African history from the School of Oriental and African Studies at the University of London. He is an author, teacher, media commentator, and social and political activist with a life-long commitment to African development.

Caplan, who has traveled extensively in Rwanda, is preoccupied with genocide and genocide prevention, particularly as it relates to the 1994 genocide in Rwanda. He is the author of the report *Rwanda: The Preventable Genocide* (2000), which was issued by the International Panel of Eminent Personalities appointed by the Organization of Unity to investigate the genocide.

He has been a consultant on African development issues to many United Nations agencies, as well as to the African Union. His latest book is called *The Betrayal of Africa*. He writes a weekly online column for the *Globe and Mail*. He has also studied and written about genocide denial.

Alex de Waal is Executive Director of the World Peace Foundation and Research Professor at the Fletcher School, Tufts University. During 2009–2011 he served as Senior Advisor to the African Union High Level Implementation Panel for Sudan. He was also Program Director at the Social Science Research Council, with responsibilities for research programs on humanitarian issues and HIV/AIDS and social transformation.

His academic research has focused on issues of famine, conflict, and human rights in Africa. He was on the *Prospect/Foreign Policy* list of 100 public intellectuals in 2008, and the *Atlantic Monthly* list of 27 'brave thinkers' in 2009.

His major publications include: *Darfur: A New History of a Long War* (with Julie Flint) (Zed Books, 2008); *War in Darfur and the Search for*

Peace (Harvard University Press, 2007); *Famine that Kills: Darfur, Sudan* (Oxford University Press, 1989) (revised edition in 2004 and a U.S. edition in 2005); *Islamism and Its Enemies in the Horn of Africa* (Indiana University Press, 2004); and *Famine Crimes: Politics and the Disaster Relief Industry in Africa* (Indiana University Press, 1997).

James Dunn has degrees in political science and Asian studies from Melbourne University and the Australian National University. Initially, he served as a defense analyst specializing in Asian affairs, then as a diplomat in Western and Eastern Europe, and finally as an Australian Consul to Portuguese Timor. In 1974 he was a member of a two-man fact-finding mission sent to Timor by the Australian government; and in 1975, at the beginning of Indonesian military intervention in East Timor, he led an aid mission. For the 10 years prior to his retirement he was senior foreign affairs advisor to the Australian parliament, with a specialization in Soviet affairs, Southeast Asia, and human rights issues. In 2001 Dunn carried out an investigation of crimes against humanity in East Timor for UNTAET. Dunn is the author of *Timor: A People Betrayed* (Jacaranda-Wiley, 1983).

Rounaq Jahan has a PhD in political science from Harvard University and is a Distinguished Fellow at the Centre for Policy Dialogue, Bangladesh (2010–). She was Senior Research Scholar and Adjunct Professor of International Affairs at the School of International and Public Affairs at Columbia University 1990–2009. She was Professor of Political Science at Dhaka University (1970–1982); Coordinator of the Women in Development Programme at the UN Asia-Pacific Development Centre, Kuala Lumpur (1982–1984); and Head of the Programme on Rural Women at the International Labour Office, Geneva, Switzerland (1985–1989).

She is the author of several books and numerous articles. Her books include: *Bangladesh Politics: Problems and Issues* (University Press Ltd., 1980, 2005); *Bangladesh: Promise and Performance* (editor; Zed Books, 2000); *Women and Development: Perspectives from South and South East Asia* (co-editor; Bangladesh Institute of Law and International Affairs, 1979); and *Pakistan: Failure in National Integration* (New York: Columbia University Press, 1972).

She is the founder of *Women for Women*, a research and study group in Bangladesh; serves on the advisory board of Human Rights Watch: Asia, and is the Convener of the Advisory Board of *Bangladesh Health Watch*, a civil society network. Professor Jahan lives and works both in Bangladesh and the United States.

Susanne Jonas has been a scholar and expert on Central America, particularly Guatemala, for 45 years, and taught Latin American & Latino Studies at the University of California, Santa Cruz for 24 years.

In 2000 she published *Of Centaurs and Doves: Guatemala's Peace Process* (Westview Press, 2000), an in-depth study of the Guatemalan peace process, which was designated a Choice "Outstanding Academic Book" for 2001; it was also published in Spanish by FLACSO/Guatemala in 2000. She is also the author of *The Battle for Guatemala: Rebels, Death Squads, and U.S. Power* (Westview Press, 1991; and, in Spanish, Nueva Sociedad and FLACSO/Guatemala in 1994).

Jonas also co-edited and contributed to *Globalization on the Ground: Postbellum Guatemalan Democracy and Development* (Rowman & Littlefield, 2001). In 1996 *Foreign Policy* published her essay, "Dangerous liaisons: The U.S. in Guatemala." She is currently working on a co-authored book on Guatemalan migration to the United States.

Ben Kiernan is A. Whitney Griswold Professor of History and Director of the Genocide Studies Program at Yale University, and Convener of the Yale East Timor Project. Kiernan is author of *How Pol Pot Came to Power* (Verso Books, 1985), *The Pol Pot Regime: Race, Power and Genocide in Cambodia Under the Khmer Rouge, 1975–1999* (Yale University Press, 2002), and the award-winning *Blood and Soil: A World History of Genocide and Extermination from Sparta to Darfur* (Yale University Press, 2007). He is also editor of *Genocide and Democracy in Cambodia: The Khmer Rouge, the United Nations, and the International Community* (Yale University Press, 1993).

From 1994 to 1999 Kiernan was Founding and Managing Director of Yale University's Cambodian Genocide Program, which he established with grants from the U.S. and other governments. He founded Yale's Genocide Studies Program in 1998. Kiernan is a member of the editorial boards of *Critical Asian Studies*, *Human Rights Review*, the *Journal of Human Rights*, and the *Journal of Genocide Research*.

Michiel Leezenberg is Associate Professor in the Department of Philosophy of the Faculty of Humanities at the University of Amsterdam. He has conducted extensive research on the *Anfal* operations and subsequent developments in Iraqi Kurdistan, and made several field trips to the region.

Among his main publications relevant to the *Anfal* operations are "Between assimilation and deportation: History of the Shabak and the Kakais in northern Iraq" in B. Kellner-Heinkele and K. Kehl-Bodrogi's *Syncretistic Religious Communities in the Near East* (Brill, 1997); "De Anfaloperaties in Iraaks Koerdistan: tien jaar straffeloosheid" ("The

Anfal preparations in Iraqi Kurdistan: Ten years of impunity") in *Soera*, June 1998; "Politischer Islam bei den Kurden" in *Kurdische Studien* (2001); "Iraqi Kurdistan: Contours of a post-civil war society," *Third World Quarterly* (2005); and "Political Islam among the Kurds" in F. Abdul-Jabar and H. Dawod's *The Kurds: Nationalism and Politics* (Saqi Books, 2006).

James E. Mace was born in 1952 in Oklahoma, and died in 2004 in Kyiv, Ukraine. He was Professor of Political Science at Kiev-Mohyla Academy National University.

Mace was Staff Director of the U.S. Commission on the Ukraine Famine, created by the U.S. Congress. Prior to his work with the Commission on the Ukraine Famine, he had been affiliated with the Russian and European Center at the University of Illinois at Champaign and the Ukrainian Research Institute of Harvard University.

His publications included, among many others: *Communism and the Dilemmas of National Liberation: National Communism in Soviet Ukraine, 1918–1933* (Harvard University Press, 1983); "The man-made-famine of 1933 in the Soviet Ukraine: What happened and why" in Israel W. Charny's *Toward the Understanding and Prevention of Genocide: Proceedings of the International Conference on the Holocaust and Genocide* (Westview Press, 1984); and "The Ukrainian genocide" in *The Encyclopedia of Genocide* (ABC CLIO Publishers, 1999).

Ben Madley is Andrew Mellon Postdoctoral Fellow in the History Department and Native American Studies Program at Dartmouth. Educated at Yale and Oxford, his scholarship largely focuses on the United States and Native America, but he has also written about colonial genocides in Africa, Australia, and Europe, often applying a transnational and comparative approach.

Among Madley's many publications are: "Tactics of nineteenth-century colonial massacre: Tasmania, California and beyond" in Philip Dwyer and Lyndall Ryan's *Theatres of Violence: Massacre, Mass Killing and Atrocity throughout History* (Berghahn Books, 2012); "When 'the world was turned upside down': California & Oregon's Tolowa Indian genocide, 1851–1856" in Adam Jones' *New Directions in Genocide Research* (Routledge, 2011); "California's Yuki Indians: Defining genocide in Native American history" in *The Western Historical Quarterly* (2008); "From terror to genocide: Britain's Tasmanian penal colony and Australia's history wars" in the *Journal of British Studies* (2008); "From Africa to Auschwitz: How German south west Africa incubated ideas and methods adopted and developed by the Nazis in Eastern Europe" in *European History Quarterly* (2005); and "Patterns of frontier genocide,

1803–1910: The Aboriginal Tasmanians, the Yuki of California, and the Herero of Namibia," in the *Journal of Genocide Research* (2004).

Madley's first book, *American Genocide: The California Indian Catastrophe, 1846–1873*, is scheduled for publication by Yale University Press.

Martin Mennecke is Assistant Professor of International Law at the University of Copenhagen, Denmark, and Visiting Lecturer at the University of Greenland in Nuuk, Greenland. He holds an LLM in public international law from the University of Edinburgh and a PhD in international criminal law from the University of Frankfurt, Germany. His current research interests include the International Criminal Court, the responsibility to protect and the role of international law in the Arctic. Mennecke is a member of the Danish delegations to the Assembly of State Parties to the International Criminal Court. He participates as an academic advisor in meetings at the United Nations and the European Union.

Donald L. Niewyk is Professor Emeritus of Modern European History at Southern Methodist University. A specialist in the history of anti-Semitism, he is the author of five books on German and Jewish history, including *Fresh Wounds: Early Narratives of Holocaust Survival* (University of North Carolina Press, 1998); *The Jews in Weimar Germany* (Transaction Publishers, 2000); and *The Holocaust: Problems and Perspectives of Interpretation* (Houghton Mifflin, 2003).

Dominik J. Schaller teaches modern history at Ruprecht-Karls-University Heidelberg, Germany. His main fields of research are African history, genocide research, and colonial and global history.

Schaller served as Editor of the *Journal of Genocide Research* from 2005 to 2009. He has written numerous articles and book chapters on the Armenian genocide, German colonialism in Africa and the Rwandan genocide.

His major publications include: *The Armenian Genocide and the Shoah* (Chronos, 2002), *Enteignet-Vertrieben-Ermordet: Beiträge zur Genozidforschung* (Chronos, 2004), *The Origins of Genocide: Raphael Lemkin as a Historian of Mass Violence* (Routledge, 2009), *Late Ottoman Genocides: Young Turkish Population and Destruction Policies* (Routledge, 2009).

Colin Tatz has held Chairs of Politics positions at the University of New England and Macquarie University. He is Co-director of the Australian Institute for Holocaust and Genocide Studies in Sydney; Visiting Fellow in Politics and International Relations, School of Arts and Social

Sciences, at the Australian National University in Canberra; and Honorary Visiting Fellow at the Australian Institute of Aboriginal and Torres Strait Islander Studies.

He has written extensively about race relations in Canada, South Africa, Australia, and New Zealand, Aboriginal studies, and genocide and Holocaust studies. He is the author of *With Intent to Destroy: Reflecting on Genocide* (Verso, 2003).

Introduction

SAMUEL TOTTEN AND WILLIAM S. PARSONS

"Will the killing ever stop? Will the scourge of genocide ever be eradicated? Will humanity ever be wise enough to prevent the deaths of potential genocidal victims *before* they become yet another set of statistics in the welter of statistics?"

We posited those questions in the introduction of the first paperback edition of *Century of Genocide*, which was published in 1997. We followed the questions up with the following comments and observations:

> These and similar thoughts continue to weigh heavily on our minds.... How could they not? In the not-too-distant past, daily broadcasts and reams of print journalism issued terrible news about the genocide taking place in Bosnia-Herzegovina; the genocide of Tutsis and moderate Hutus by Rwandan government forces and paramilitary extremists; the Indonesian army-"sponsored" killings in East Timor in the late 1990s; the sporadic and ongoing mass killings in Burundi; the continuing conflict and killing in [southern] Sudan; and the horrific violence and killings that have recently erupted in the Congo. That's not to mention the insidious and incremental destruction of indigenous peoples' ways of life across the globe; and the ubiquitous deprivation of various peoples' human rights which sometimes explodes into genocide.

In the years since we wrote those words, the world has faced yet another genocide: the Government of Sudan's (GoS) and *Janjaweed*'s (Arab militia) genocide of the black Africans of Darfur. Reliable estimates set the number of dead at over 400,000. And, as we write today (late December 2011), the crisis in Darfur continues unabated.

Alarmingly, the GoS is also currently carrying out ground and aerial attacks against other groups of people in Sudan—those residing in the

Nuba Mountains and the Blue Nile. As we go to press in January 2012 it appears that the fighting between rebel groups in each area and the GoS is not likely to end anytime soon, thus placing civilians in the desperate situation of being horribly injured and killed. Over and above that, the Nuba Mountains people are facing potential starvation as they huddle in the mountains, away from their farms where they had ready access to food.

The point is, while genocide is an ancient crime, it is one that continues to plague humanity. And while humanity has made incredible progress on a variety of fronts (health, space exploration, communication technology, and so on), at one and the same time it is also true that the constant outbreak of crimes against humanity and genocide makes it seem as though humanity is still in the Stone Age when it comes to behaving peaceably.

Although most people express horror at the perpetration of crimes against humanity and genocide, such repugnance seldom leads to prevention. Sadly, time and again, far too many individuals, groups, and nations seem to find reasons not to act to prevent the slaughter of innocent people.

It is painfully clear that we—humanity and members of the international community—more often than not do not care enough, and/or lack the political will, to prevent genocide. In chapter after chapter in this book one reads about the excuses and compromises offered by outside governments as to why they choose not to intervene to prevent acts of genocide from being perpetrated.

What humanity is in most need of in this respect is how to cast off addiction to *realpolitik*, the lack of political will to act, and, ultimately, the lack of real care about "others" who face annihilation at the hands of mass murderers. In other words, we, humanity (all members of the international community), have not truly found the humanity that is needed to prevent genocide from reappearing, time and again, like a horrific nightmare.

So, why are we taking the time, effort, and thought to revise and update this book yet again? A key reason is to inform, educate, cajole, prod, and encourage people to break out of their mold of silence, to collectively reach out to the victims and the voiceless, and to demand that such atrocities be halted!

The challenge for humanity is whether individuals can become knowledgeable about these matters and then find a collective voice strong enough to convince leaders in society, along with the public at large, to prevent and/or stanch such crimes early on.

Definitional Issues vis-à-vis the Term "Genocide"

Raphael Lemkin, a Polish Jewish émigré and noted scholar who taught law at Yale and Duke Universities, coined the term *genocide* in 1944. To do so, he combined the Greek *genos* (race, tribe) and *cide* (killing).

After lengthy debate over the definition of genocide and ample compromise on how it should be defined, the international community adopted the UN Genocide Convention on the Prevention and Punishment of Genocide (UNCG) on December 9, 1948, and in doing so defined genocide in the following manner:

> In the present Convention, genocide means any of the following acts committed with the intent to destroy, in whole or in part, a national, ethnical, racial, or religious group, as such:
>
> a. Killing members of the group
> b. Causing serious bodily or mental harm to members of the group
> c. Deliberately inflicting on the group conditions of life calculated to bring about its physical destruction in whole or in part
> d. Imposing measures intended to prevent births within the group
> e. Forcibly transferring children of the group to another group.

Even though debate continues over the definition used in the UNCG—for example, there is ample dissension over the fact that it does not include "political groups" in its list of protected groups—it is *the* definition that the international community adheres to, and thus it is the one used by attorneys and judges in trying cases at ad hoc tribunals (e.g., the International Criminal Tribunal for Rwanda and the International Criminal Tribunal for the Former Yugoslavia), and the International Criminal Court (ICC).

While various scholars might not label some of the cases included in this book as genocide, we, the editors, believe that each of the victim groups was, in fact, targeted in whole or in part for destruction, as such. And because of that we believe each case is critical to developing a solid understanding as to the different ways in which genocide can be initiated and perpetrated.

Focus of the Book

In 1995, when we, along with Israel W. Charny, completed the first edition of *Century of Genocide*, it focused solely on genocides perpetrated in the 20th century. In 2009, while preparing the third edition of *Century of Genocide*, we decided it was important to add a chapter on the first *genocide* perpetrated in the 21st century, the Darfur *genocide*. In the years since the third edition was published, we have come to the conclusion that it would be valuable to extend the focus of the book even more, and thus this, the fourth edition, includes two cases of genocide that were perpetrated in the 19th century (the Native Americans and the Aboriginals of Australia).

As a result of the most recent changes, *Centuries of Genocide* is significantly different from the three earlier editions entitled *Century of Genocide*. It now spans three centuries—the 19th, 20th, and 21st. As in each of its earlier iterations, *Centuries of Genocide* is comprised of critical chapters by some of the most noted scholars in the field of genocide studies about various genocidal acts committed over the last three centuries. Each chapter on a particular genocide is accompanied by oral testimony.

We chose to expand the focus of the book for three main reasons. First, it is always our goal to strengthen each and every new edition.

Second, many readers of earlier editions have called for a chapter on the plight and fate of the Native Americans. The author of the chapter on the Native Americans, Benjamin Madley, a Yale University-educated historian, has, through meticulous work, become the expert on *the* genocide of various Native Americans groups during the 19th century.

Third, we wished to emphasize the critical issue of impunity; that is, those situations where alleged perpetrators are not brought to trial and held accountable for the crimes they allegedly committed. In that regard, we chose to add a chapter on the genocidal actions of the GoS against the Nuba Mountains people in the 1990s, which adds plenty of food for thought when read in conjunction with the chapter on the Darfur genocide perpetrated by the GoS a decade later (beginning in 2003). The author of the chapter on the Nuba Mountains, Alex de Waal, is the premier scholar/ expert on the Nuba Mountains genocide, and we believe readers will find his insights about the case to be fascinating, instructive, and disturbing.

In addition to adding the new cases/chapters to this edition, every author represented in the book was also asked to revise and update his/ her chapter vis-à-vis the sociopolitical situation in the post-genocide period; attempts at reconstruction and reconciliation; the consideration of and/or actual payment of reparations; issues of immunity and impunity; the holding of trials and the fairness and comprehensive nature of such; the state of the lives of the survivors in the post-genocide period; and so on. Unfortunately, and sadly, several of our original contributors have passed away, and thus we needed to bring in new authors to address the cases they wrote about, and in one case a contributor retired and had no interest in revising his chapters; thus we invited a highly respected author to write a new and up-to-date chapter. These instances will be discussed shortly.

Due to space constraints and our desire to add three new chapters (Native Americans, Australian Aboriginals, and Nuba Mountains genocides) to this edition, we made the difficult decision to collapse what, previously, were three chapters on the Holocaust (the fate of the physically and mentally handicapped by Hugh Gallagher [deceased]; the fate of the Jews by Donald Niewyk; and the fate of the Roma and Sinti by Sybil Milton [deceased]) into a single chapter. Ultimately, we asked Dr. Donald Niewyk, the author of the original chapter on the fate of the Jews, if he would tackle a new and more inclusive chapter, and he readily agreed to do so. He did a remarkable job, and we believe readers will find the chapter extremely informative and highly engaging.

The original chapter on the Hereros by Jon Bridgman and Leslie Worley was also replaced. Bridgman had retired and was unable to update the chapter, and thus we invited Dr. Dominik Schaller, a highly respected German scholar and expert on the Hereros, to write a new chapter. His well-written and extremely detailed chapter greatly benefits from the latest research into the case as well as his unique insights based on his own research.

Three other chapters from earlier editions of *Century of Genocide* did not make it into this edition: the massacre of communists and suspected communists in Indonesia; the genocide in Burundi; and the genocide of indigenous peoples. It was a tough decision to exclude these chapters but space constraints precluded their inclusion. Be that as it may, Routledge has kindly suggested and agreed to place these chapters online so that those who purchase *Centuries of Genocide* will have access to those chapters (see www.routledge.com/books/details/9780415871914).

Ultimately, then, the cases of genocide addressed in *Centuries of Genocide* are: genocide of the Yana (Native Americans) in California; genocide of the Aboriginals in Australia; the German genocide of the Hereros; the Ottoman Turk genocide of the Armenians; the Soviet man-made famine in Ukraine; the Nazi genocide of the Jews, Gypsies, and mentally and physically handicapped; the Bangladesh genocide; the Indonesian genocide of the East Timorese; the Khmer Rouge genocide of their fellow Cambodians; the genocide of the Mayans in Guatemala; the Iraqi gassing and genocide of the Kurds in the late 1980s; the genocidal actions against the Nuba Mountains people in Sudan; the 1994 Rwandan genocide; the genocide of some 8,000 Muslim boys and men in Srebrenica; and the genocide of the black Africans in Darfur, Sudan.

In order to assure some semblance of continuity, each author was asked to address a series of questions posited by the editors: Who committed the genocide? How was the genocide committed? Why was the genocide committed? Who were the victims? Who was involved (e.g., state, societal institutions, various peoples, ethnic groups, individuals with certain job roles/professions, bystanders, etc.)? What were the out-standing historical forces and trends at work that led to the genocide? What was the long-range impact of the genocide on the victim group? What have been the responses of individuals, groups, and nations to this particular genocide? Is there agreement or disagreement among "legitimate scholars" as to the interpretation of this particular genocide (e.g., preconditions, implementation, ramifications)? Do people care about this genocide today? If so, how is that concern manifested? And what does a study of this genocide contribute to the field of genocide studies?

Since the intent of this book is to highlight a range of genocides, readers need to keep in mind that the chapters provide only a basic overview, detailed though they are, of the various historical events.

Each of the contributing authors was also asked to include one to four highly informative and powerful eyewitness accounts vis-à-vis the case of genocide they discuss in their chapter. As readers will see, a couple of the authors were hard-pressed to locate much at all in the way of eyewit-ness accounts. This is an acute problem, and one that will be discussed in more detail elsewhere in this introduction.

Value and Limitation of Eyewitness Accounts

Time and again, scholars have noted the unique contribution that such eyewitness accounts make in regard to providing a more thorough understanding of the genocidal process. In speaking about eyewitness accounts of the Armenian genocide, Richard Hovannisian (1973), pro-fessor of history and director of the Near Eastern Center at the Univer-sity of California at Los Angeles, asserted: "Eyewitness accounts of decisive events may be as valuable as official dispatches and reports. It is in such versions especially that the human element becomes manifest, affording insights not to be found in documents" (p. xxiii).

In regard to this same issue, Totten (1991b, p. xi) commented:

> First-person accounts by victims and others are capable of break-ing through the numbing mass of numbers in that they provide the thoughts, the passions and the voices of those who experi-enced and/or witnessed the terrible calamity now referred to as genocide. And while first-person accounts serve many purposes among the most significant is the fact that authentic accounts constitute valuable testimony as to what it means to be caught up in the maelstrom of hatred and savagery that is genocide.

Oral accounts also remind scholars, educators, and students who record or study statistics, examine documents, and argue over definitions of genocide and interpretations of genocidal actions that the victims are human beings just as they and their family members are—that is, innocent men, women, and children. Not numbers, not statistics, but human beings with feelings, aspirations, fears, family members, and, it should not be forgotten, fundamental human rights guaranteed to every single individual on earth by the UN Declaration of Human Rights (1948).

Although eyewitness accounts are a valuable means of documenting historical events, their validity as a primary source is only as good as the procedures by which they are collected as well as the accuracy of the witnesses whose accounts are documented. The same research standards used to develop historical works need to be applied to gathering, recording, authenticating, and interpreting eyewitness accounts.

Dearth of Oral Testimony

There are numerous reasons as to why there is a dearth of first-person accounts of various genocidal acts, but among the main ones are the following: The survivors may not have been literate, and thus did not have the means to develop a written record; in the aftermath of the genocide, the survivors may have had to struggle simply to survive, thus documenting their tragedy was not foremost on their minds; the survivors may not have had the financial means to take the time to record and collect testimony; the survivors may not have had a constituency that was interested in their plight, and thus no one collected or supported documentation of their tragedy; the survivors may have been (or continue to be) leery of people who question them about their plight; and some survivors may have continued to live under the very regime that perpetrated the genocide, which, in turn, prevented (through censorship, coercion, or threats of violence) the survivors or others from documenting the atrocities (Totten, 1991b, pp. xliii–liii).

Despite the aforementioned impediments and difficulties that scholars, human rights organizations, and others face in collecting eyewitness accounts of certain genocidal acts, it is still disturbing that there has not been more of a concerted and collective effort by both the scholarly and human rights communities to collect as many accounts as possible of the least-documented genocides over the last couple of centuries. While not wishing to appear cynical, it seems that by not assisting those who have largely remained voiceless, we (the scholars, human rights organizations, and others) have contributed to, rather than ameliorated, the problem. Instead of locating the survivors and other witnesses in order to "return" the voices to the voiceless, we have remained on the sidelines. Certainly, a place to begin the collection of such testimony would be many of the refugee camps located across the globe. Other places are those communities and enclaves in various parts of the globe where relatively large numbers of survivors of the same genocide now reside and where censorship and political constraints do not pose a problem to the researchers or the witnesses.

In regard to those genocidal acts where survivors and witnesses to the genocide are still alive, it is incumbent upon scholars and activists to collect as many accounts as possible. Not to do so leaves the historical record bereft of what could prove to be invaluable information. It also constitutes a further injustice to the victims.

Issues of Prevention and Intervention

Over the past decade a remarkable amount of attention has been focused on the issues of the prevention and intervention of genocide. A mere listing of names of the projects/positions/reports provide the reader with a solid sense of the eclectic and broad nature of such activity:

- the International Commission on Intervention and State Sovereignty's creation of the concept of "Responsibility to Protect";
- the United Nation's establishment of a new office and position, UN Special Advisor on the Prevention of Genocide;
- the creation of a Genocide Prevention Task Force by the U.S. Holocaust Memorial Museum, the American Academy of Diplomacy and the U.S. Institute of Peace, which published a major report entitled *Preventing Genocide, A Blueprint for US Policymakers*;
- the Montreal Institute for Genocide and Human Rights Studies' (Concordia University) The Will to Intervene Project;
- the Kennedy School's Carr Center for Human Rights Policy's (Harvard University) The Mass Atrocity Response Operation (MARO) Project.

What these efforts will result in is anyone's guess. That is, when it comes right down to it, only time will tell if the various efforts, ideas, plans, promises, and words will actually contribute to the stanching of crimes against humanity and genocide in a timely and effective manner or not.

While some scholars praise such efforts and suggest that they indicate that an ever-increasing number of scholars, organizations, and individuals care deeply about the need to prevent genocide, other scholars take a much more critical, and somewhat cynical, approach, asserting that many of the aforementioned efforts are either naïve in their approach to politics, are run-of-the-mill approaches that have not worked in the past and are not likely to work today or in the future, and are not as forward-thinking or revolutionary as their founders/creators deem them to be.

The sad fact is, as long as individual nations, individually and collectively (i.e., as part of the United Nations), continue to allow *realpolitik* to dictate their policies when it comes to the issues of the intervention and prevention of genocide, then the 21st century is more than likely to experience the same sort of pusillanimous responses from the UN and individual states that were so apparent in the latter half of the 20th century. Still, the recent attention to preventing genocide does provide some hope that sooner or later there may be a *real* breakthrough in combating genocide in an effective and timely manner.

Individuals, NGOs, and the International Community: The Need for a Well-organized, Collective, and Concerted Effort to Intervene or Prevent Genocide

Individually, a person can only do so much to protest genocidal actions or to work on behalf of oppressed individuals. Collectively, people have a much better chance of effecting positive change.

To be more effective, those working on the issue of genocide need to begin to initiate campaigns against genocide with an eye toward influencing international public opinion as well as the decisions and actions of governmental organizations. They also need to establish themselves as a main source of documentation for investigating the perpetration of genocide. As it now stands, most individuals and organizations dealing with the issue of genocide are putting more time into working on the scholarly examination of genocide (including issues of intervention and prevention) than the actual prevention of or intervention in genocide. There are, though, several major exceptions to this rule, and among the most notable are the Germany-based *Gesellschaft fur Bedrohte Volker* (Society for Threatened Peoples); Human Rights Watch; the London-based International Alert (IA) Standing International Forum on Ethnic Conflict, Genocide and Human Rights; the International Crisis Group (ICG), the Denmark-based International Work Group for Indigenous Affairs (IWGIA); STAND: A Student Anti-Genocide Coalition; and the U.S. Holocaust Memorial Museum's Committee on Conscience.

Educating about Genocide

In his hard-hitting and perspicacious report, *Revised and Updated Report on the Question of Prevention and Punishment of the Crime of Genocide*, Ben Whitaker argued as follows:

The results of research [on the causes of genocide] could help form one part of a wide educational programme throughout the world against such aberrations (e.g., genocide), starting at an early age in schools. Without a strong basis of international public support, even the most perfectly redrafted [U.N.] Convention [on Genocide] will be of little value. Conventions and good governments can give a lead, but the mobilization of public awareness and vigilance is essential to guard against any recurrence of genocide and other crimes against humanity and human rights.... As a further safeguard, public awareness should be developed internationally to reinforce the individual's responsibility, based on the knowledge that it is illegal to obey a superior order or law that violates human rights. (1985, p. 42)

We agree with Whitaker that it is crucial for educational institutions across the globe to teach their students about the causes and ramifications of genocide as well as the fact that it is each person's responsibility to act in a moral manner when human rights infractions (including genocide) rear their ugly heads. As for the goal of Holocaust and genocide education, Israel Charny (1993) makes the perceptive point that the goal

must be to make awareness of Holocaust and genocide part of human culture, so that more and more people are helped to grow out of killing and from being accomplices to killers, or from being bystanders who allow the torture and killing of others. (p. 3)

The sort of study that we advocate is one that is immersed in both the cognitive and the affective domains (values and feelings). More specifically, it is one that: (1) engages the students in a study of accurate and in-depth theories, research, and facts; (2) contextualizes the history; (3) avoids simple answers to complex history; and (4) addresses issues of personal and societal responsibility both from a historical as well as a contemporary perspective. (For a more in-depth discussion of such concerns, see Totten's (2004) *Teaching About Genocide: Issues, Approaches and Resources.*

More Specifics vis-à-vis Teaching and Learning about Genocide

Over the years we, the two editors, have given innumerable talks to educators on teaching about genocide, co-authored the U.S. Holocaust Memorial Museum's *Guidelines for Teaching the Holocaust* (many of the guidelines are equally applicable to teaching about any case of genocide), and co-published numerous articles on teaching about genocide. What we delineate here is simply a fraction of our thoughts in this arena; nevertheless, they constitute what we consider some key thoughts as individuals prepare to teach and learn about genocide.

First, it is absolutely essential to help students understand the difference between crimes against humanity, war crimes, ethnic cleansing, and genocide. A key way to do that is to provide them with solid definitions of each and then have them, in an assessment and follow-up discussions, delineate the key differences between and among the various crimes. Here it is essential to provide the students with, and make use of, the UN Convention on the Prevention and Punishment of the Crime of Genocide (UNCG). And that is exactly why we've included a copy of the UNCG in the book.

Second, many have no idea where the vast majority of genocides have taken place and little to no sense as to where the regions/countries are located. For this reason, at the outset of any study it is imperative to provide students with a map of the world and to carefully point out key locations vis-à-vis the genocide under study (continent, region, country, major cities/towns, detention centers, etc.). Students should be required to bring the maps to each class session for easy referral, and instructors should assign in-class and out-of-class assignments tied to the maps. Only in this way will students gain a solid sense of the significance of the "geography of the genocide."

Third, time and again students have commented that among the more moving and meaningful aspect of learning about genocide are the words of the survivors (what they personally witnessed, their trials and tribulations, etc.). For this reason, it is absolutely essential to find time for the students to read the testimonies tied to each genocide under study and to discuss them in class. The testimonies will provide students with insights they will never glean from reading historical essays, and the accounts are likely to resonate with them like very few other resources.

Fourth, the best courses on genocide allow for ample student discussion. Obviously, genocide is complex and a dark topic, and students will, naturally, have innumerable questions about why certain populations were targeted, how one group of people could harm another group of people in such vicious ways, why the international community did not act to save the targeted population, and so on. Encouraging students to raise questions and discuss and debate issues in class that are important to them will contribute to making the study just that much more meaningful for them and help to deepen their understanding of such torturously complex and horrific events and issues.

Fifth, in order to avoid leaving students with the sense that nothing can be done to prevent genocide, it is valuable to address the many and different efforts that have been undertaken to attempt to prevent genocide (classic examples are the cases of both Kosovo and East Timor in 1999). Concomitantly, it is worthwhile to avail the students of the various organizations and individuals who have worked assiduously to develop a critical mass to speak out about the need to halt genocide and/or to stanch it early on and effectively. Here we are thinking of such organizations as the U.S. Holocaust Memorial Museum's Committee on Conscience, Genocide Watch, The International Crisis Group, and Human Rights Watch, among others. By gleaning information about and insights into such efforts, students will come to appreciate that both individuals and people working collectively can make a difference.

Denial of Genocide

It is, to say the least, disconcerting that we live in a world in which various parties and nations perpetuate the denial of certain genocides that have occurred. Generally, such denial is undertaken by those who either harbor animosity or hatred against the victim group, wish to avoid culpability for the crimes they or their nation committed, or due to sheer ignorance. Scholars often arrive at different historical interpretations, but those who purposely distort the historical record and disregard vast amounts of historical documentation know exactly the game they play. As every attorney knows, it is often easier to create doubt in order to win than it is to prove what actually took place. Indeed, such deniers, minimizers, and obfuscators (Hawk, 1988, p. 151) seem to gain some sort of bizarre satisfaction from the fact that they drain the energy and limited resources of legitimate scholars who are compelled to repudiate the distortions in order to keep the historical record intact.

By minimizing or distorting a particular genocide, deniers assault survivors one more time. In fact, one of the key rationales for including accounts by survivors and other eyewitnesses in this book is to send a message that no matter how hard deniers try to manipulate history, accounts of the genocide will be recorded and remembered.

Conclusion

At times it is difficult not to be disheartened, especially when the international community and individual governments do little to nothing when new genocides erupt somewhere across the globe. Indeed, at times it is difficult not to wonder whether all the scholarship, all the words, and all the pledges to "Never Forget" are simply some type of anodyne to ease the pain of the survivors or soothe the conscience of those who deeply care about such tragedies but feel impotent to stanch genocide early on. And at times it is difficult not to wonder whether those of us who hold out hope that genocide can, at a minimum, be halted early on are doing so more out of desperation than any sense of objectivity or reality.

We recognize that these were bleak words and thoughts with which to introduce a book, but we believe that they are apropos. Certain situations demand bluntness and anger, and the continued perpetration of genocide, in our minds, is one of them.

Paradoxically, while genocide continues largely unabated, at no other time in the history of humanity have so many (individual citizens, social activists, scholars, non-governmental organizations, individual nations, the United Nations) voiced their concern about genocide and the critical need to halt it before it begins—and if it does break out then to stanch it as quickly as possible. Be that as it may, it is also true that while humanity has eradicated smallpox, developed vaccinations to prevent various diseases (including chicken pox, diphtheria, and polio), explored the heavens, sent a man to the moon, and invented such mind-boggling inventions as the internet, humanity has not, when all is said and done, figured out how to prevent genocide from being perpetrated, or committed itself to establishing and implementing the most effective mechanisms for stanching it once it has erupted. In part, that speaks clearly and loudly to both the sheer complexity of the issue of preventing genocide as well as the fact that something is seriously flawed at the core of the international system. But it is also true that unlike many major problems facing humanity, halting genocide is not one that can be solved with a technical fix—such as creating a safe vaccine that results in an immune response to deadly disease. Rather, it is a problem that is, at one and the same time, social, political, geopolitical, and technical in nature, each of which is daunting in and of itself. Furthermore, unlike a vaccine found to be effective, preventing and halting genocide is protean in nature as it continually emerges in different parts of the world due to different causes, involving completely different actors and sociopolitical situations, etc. And, the prevention and intervention of genocide also faces such daunting impediments as *realpolitik*, the lack of political will, and a "simple" but profound lack of caring.

The scholars who have contributed chapters to this volume are doing vitally significant and, in many cases, groundbreaking work in regard to assisting humanity to gain a clearer understanding as to how, why, and when genocide is perpetrated. They, and others like them, are to be commended. At the same time, what is still needed is the development of a critical mass of humanity across the globe to work for the intervention and prevention of genocide. To develop such a critical mass, individuals, communities, and states need to undertake an effort to educate themselves and their young about genocide; speak out against injustices anywhere against anybody; remain vigilant; and finally, encourage and prod one's family, friends, community, and nation to be vigilant.

In that vein, we agree with Charny (1988, p. 23) when he argues that:

> There needs to be a growing consensus on the part of human beings and organized society that penetrates the very basis of human culture that mass killing is unacceptable to civilized peoples, otherwise the prevailing momentum of historical experience will continue to confirm for generation after generation that genocide is a phenomenon of nature, like other disasters, and this view of the inevitability of genocide as an almost natural event will continue to justify it in the sense of convincing people that nothing can be done.

Further, as Totten (1991a, pp. 334–335) has written:

> it is easy to call for the prevention of genocide. In fact, far too often in [books] of this sort, as well as at commemorative ceremonies for the victims and survivors, well-intentioned people almost perfunctorily recall Santayana's admonition, "Those who do not remember the past are condemned to repeat it." Through its repeated use, this finely wrought and powerful notion has become not much more than a cliché. The past must be remembered, yes; but humanity must go beyond merely remembering a particular genocidal act. Inherent in authentic remembrance is vigilance and action. More often than not, remembrance has been bereft of such crucial components. As Elie Wiesel has eloquently and powerfully stated: "Memory can be a graveyard, but it also can be the true kingdom of man." The choice is before humanity.

The greatest hope that exists in regard to preventing future genocides is that those who care deeply about the issue will continue to explore and devise potential ways to halt it. We firmly believe that where there is a will there is a way, and thus while genocide may never be totally eradicated we believe it can be stanched to a much greater degree than it has been in the past.

References

Charny, Israel W. (1988). Intervention and prevention of genocide. In Israel W. Charny (Ed.) *Genocide: A critical bibliographic review* (pp. 20–38). New York: Facts on File.

Charny, Israel W. (1993). Editorial comment. *Internet on the Holocaust and Genocide, 43,* 3.

Hawk, David (1988). The Cambodian genocide. In Israel W. Charny (Ed.) *Genocide: A critical bibliographic review* (pp. 20–38). New York: Facts on File.

Hovannisian, Richard (1973). Introduction. In Stanley E. Kerr's *The lions of Marash: Personal experiences with Near East relief, 1919–1922* (pp. xix–xxv). Albany: State University of New York Press.

Lemkin, Raphael (1944). *Axis rule in occupied Europe: Laws of occupation, analysis of government, and proposals for redress.* Washington, DC: Carnegie Foundation for International Peace. [Reprint, New York: Howard Fertig, 1973.]

Totten, Samuel (1991a). First-person accounts of genocidal acts. In Israel W. Charny (Ed.) *Genocide: A critical bibliographic review* (Vol. 2, pp. 321–362). London and New York: Mansell Publishers and Facts on File.

Totten, Samuel (1991b). *First-person accounts of genocidal acts committed in the twentieth century: An annotated bibliography.* Westport, CT: Greenwood Press.

Totten, Samuel (2004). *Teaching about genocide: Issues, approaches and resources.* Greenwich, CT: Information Age Publishing.

Whitaker, Ben (1985). *Revised and updated report on the question of the prevention and punishment of the crime of genocide.* 62 pp. (E/CN.4/Sub.2/1985/6, July 2, 1985).

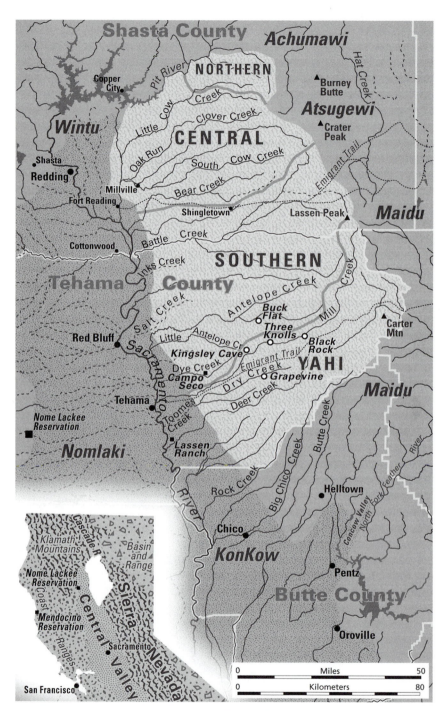

Map 1.1 California

CHAPTER **1**

The Genocide of California's Yana Indians

BENJAMIN MADLEY

On August 28, 1911, a Yahi Yana man emerged from the Sierra Nevada Mountains at a slaughterhouse corral in Oroville, California (*Oroville Daily Register*, August 29, 1911, p. 1). He was alone, having lost his family and his tribe (Waterman, 1918, p. 64). Scholars studied him intensively and he soon became famous as Ishi, "the last of the Yanas" and "the last wild Indian in North America" (Pope, 1932; Kroeber, 1961). He was, in fact, a genocide survivor. Before 1847 the Yana may have numbered more than 3,000 people;[1] by 1872, when Ishi was about 10 years old, perhaps a few dozen survived (Kroeber, 1961, p. 43). Despite an extensive Yana ethnography and many books about Ishi, there exists no comprehensive narrative of this cataclysm.[2]

In 1918 anthropologist T.T. Waterman outlined the tribe's demographic decline. Author Theodora Kroeber and others then enhanced his narrative, and in 1987 anthropologist Russell Thornton asserted—in a brief summary of the Yana population decline—that they "were destroyed virtually overnight ... in large part because of their genocide by settlers in north-central California during the mid-1850s" (Waterman, 1918; Kroeber, 1961, pp. 56–78; Thornton, 1987, pp. 110, 109–114). Using varied sources—including many new to Yana studies—this chapter builds on previous scholarship and expands upon information provided in *American Genocide: The California Indian Catastrophe, 1846–1873* to create the most detailed history yet of the Yana's near-extermination by individuals, groups, and California state militiamen (Madley, forthcoming).

Why did the Genocide Happen?

The motives driving immigrants to destroy the Yana changed over time, as did the organization of their killing operations. From 1850 to 1858, immigrants' violence and destruction of traditional Yana food sources precipitated Yana stock raids to which small, volunteer groups responded with retaliatory massacres. In 1858 immigrants articulated a new goal: removing the Yana by any means necessary, including extermination. State-sanctioned killing and capturing operations—including a state militia operation—unfolded in 1859. Finally, from 1860 to 1871, volunteer death squads hunted surviving Yana in order to punish them for raids, obtain their wealth, and eliminate them as a potential threat. The genocide thus began as disproportionate retaliation, escalated to state-sanctioned mass killing and removal, and concluded with small operations bent on total extermination. All of this violence took place within the context of state and federal decision-makers' support or acquiescence.

The Yana Before Contact

Before contact with non-Indians, the Yana lived in an ecologically varied, almost Delaware-sized region between the Sacramento River and the southern Cascades of northern California.[3] Near the Sacramento, the hills of Yana territory are low, grassy, and oak-studded. Climbing east, canyons deepen and the boulder-strewn land gives way to conifers, alpine meadows, and 10,462-foot-high Lassen Peak. Yana land was rugged but bountiful. Streams supplied salmon and other fish. Oaks yielded acorns. Meadows and grasslands provided grasses and tubers as well as antelope, bear, deer, elk, and small game (Johnson, 1978, p. 361).

They referred to themselves as Yana, meaning "person" (Kroeber, 1925, p. 337; 1961, p. 30). Ethnologists categorized them into four groups, based upon their dialects: Northern Yana, Central Yana, Southern Yana, and the southernmost Yahi Yana, who were Ishi's people (Kroeber, 1925, p. 338). These groups were linguistically but probably not politically united, as Yana political organization centered around "bands, each of which consisted of a principal village and a number of smaller surrounding settlements" (Waterman, 1918, p. 35; Malinowski, Sheets, Lehman, & Doig, 1998, vol. 4, p. 227).

Yana communities participated in a regional economy. Although sometimes at odds with their California Indian neighbors, they traded with them, often facilitating transactions with dentalia, or seashell currency. "Obsidian was obtained from the Achumawi and Shasta"; "arrows, buckskin, wildcat quivers, and woodpecker scalps were secured from the Atsugewi; clam disc beads and magnesite cylinders, from the

Maidu or [Nomlaki] Wintun; dentalium shells, from the Wintu" and "barbed obsidian arrow points, from the north. In return the Yana supplied buckeye fire drills, deer hides, dentalia, salt, and buckskin to the Atsugewi; baskets to the Nomlaki; and salt to the Wintu" (Johnson, 1978, p. 363). Trade connected the Yana to the wider world for centuries, but they were nearly obliterated in 21 years.

Invasion, Raids, and Massacres, 1850–1859

Yana people probably first encountered non-Indians in 1821, but the California Gold Rush transformed their world (Johnson, 1978, p. 362). "By 1848 the California–Oregon trail crossed Northern and Central Yana territory" and from 1848 to 1850 "as many as nine thousand emigrants" traversed the Lassen Cutoff, ripping "a bloody gash through the heart of the Yahi homeland." Immigrants depleted game and grasses while perhaps engaging in violent conflict (Johnson, 1978, p. 362; Dornin, 1922, pp. 160–164; Stillson, 2006, p. 110; Heizer & Kroeber, 1979, p. 2). As early as 1849 they killed two Yahi Yana people in "Deer Creek cañon" after their camp was robbed (Martin, 1883, p. 80). By 1850, immigrants—some of whom colonized the western edge of Yana territory—were brutalizing and killing Yana people. One of these newcomers was West Point-trained J. Goldsborough Bruff. In the summer of 1850 Bruff reached Lassen's Ranch and recorded Native Americans—likely Yana given the location—held as forced laborers, tortured, and sometimes killed while their villages were plundered. In a July 11 journal entry, he reported one Indian whipped and another beaten. On August 15, "Battis whipped his squaw in the night." On November 4,

> McBride has very severely whipped a poor indian, and afterwards wounded him with buckshot. I was informed that a year ago, one of Davis' sons attempted to chastise this very indian, who resisted: and the young man then ordered the indian's brother to hold him, while he whipped him: this, of course, the Indian refused, when Young Davis shot him dead, on the spot.

Bruff also described the August and September plundering of nearby villages (Bruff, Read, & Gaines, 1949, pp. 365, 382–383, 384, 403, 449). Sexual attacks likely generated further Yana resentment. As Bruff theorized, after recording the August gang rape of a Native American woman, "it is such enormities which often bring about collisions between the whites & Indians" (Bruff et al., 1949, p. 382).

To protect themselves, Yana people had three choices. They could seek protection from the newcomers (by becoming servants, concubines, wives, and laborers), fight them, or retreat into the mountains. All three options were hazardous. Living among immigrants posed numerous dangers because Native Americans had almost no legal rights under California law. Meanwhile, fighting was perilous, given the range and firepower disparity between immigrant rifles and Yana bows and arrows. Thus, most Yana chose the mountains.

Throughout the 1850s, immigrants made mountain life increasingly difficult. Few settled deep in the hills, but gold mining elsewhere, coupled with local ranching and hunting, increased hunger and exposure. Hydraulic mining spilled dirt, debris, and toxic mercury into the Sacramento, killing spawning salmon before they reached Yana territory. Newcomers and their stock further depleted hunting, fishing, and harvesting areas while denying the Yana access to what remained (for more on this process, see Kroeber, 1961, p. 49). Finally, the threat of violence and capture forced many Yana into higher, colder, snowier altitudes where food was scarce and survival difficult.

To eat, and perhaps to retaliate, some Yana began raiding ranchers' stock and property. Immigrants responded with punitive massacres, beginning in 1850. Theodora Kroeber believed that an April 5, 1850 newspaper report describing the retaliatory killing of 22 or 23 Indians near Deer Creek referred to the Yahi Yana. Yet because the same newspaper described Indian killing on the Deer Creek in Maidu territory one week later, it is not clear that this article referred to Yana people (Kroeber, 1961, p. 58; *Sacramento Transcript*, April 5, 1850, p. 2; April 12, 1850, p. 2). An attack that undisputedly did target the Yana took place later that year. On December 14, 1850, two of Bruff's Lassen's Ranch acquaintances told him that after cattle and oxen went missing from a mountain pasture, they tracked the lost stock up Mill Creek. Coming upon a Yahi Yana hamlet, they killed the inhabitants and burned it to the ground (Bruff et al., 1949, vol. 2, p. 937).

Soon thereafter, California legislators imposed anti-Indian measures that created a framework for Yana killing. In a January 1851 speech, California's first civilian United States governor, Peter Burnett, helped set the course of the state's Indian policies by declaring "that a war of extermination will continue to be waged ... until the Indian race becomes extinct," while warning that what he called "the inevitable destiny of the race is beyond the power or wisdom of man to avert" (California, 1851a, p. 15). State legislators then put the power of the purse behind Governor Burnett's declaration. In 1851 they appropriated $500,000 to pay for past and future Indian-hunting campaigns by volunteer California state militia units (California, 1851b, pp. 520–521). The following year they raised another $600,000 for additional volunteer state militia campaigns (California Legislature,

1852, p. 59). Policy-makers thus communicated their support for Indian-killing both by militiamen as well as individuals and unofficial groups.

In August 1851 local men responded to the killing of "a boy" at "Dye's rancho" by setting out after local Indians. They soon "charged upon … Indians" located "north of the head of Salt creek, about 30 miles from Dye's," in Southern Yana territory, "killed two chiefs and captur[ed] fifty-three men, women and children." Immigrants now issued their first recorded threat to annihilate local Indian people. The prisoners were to "make a treaty with the whites and live peaceably in the valley [or] be slain" (Letter from Mr. Dye summarized in *Sacramento Union*, August 16, 1851, p. 2)[4]

Records for the Yana in the early 1850s are thin, but indicate massacres in 1853, 1854, and 1855. When "Tiger Indians [probably Yahi Yana] stole cattle," in Butte County in 1853, seven men led by Manoah Pence caught and lynched "Express Bill" before attacking "a camp of about thirty warriors." According to an 1891 history, "The Indians had nothing but bows and arrows and could do but little damage." Thus, "Twenty-five redskins were killed" (Anonymous, 1891, pp. 113–114). Locals committed two more recorded massacres the following year. The *Shasta Courier* reported that on January 17, 1854:

> nineteen white men started from Mr. Casey's on Clover Creek for the purpose of whipping a number of Indians, who, the day previous, had stolen some stock from Hooper's ranch on Oak Run [in or on the margin of Central Yana territory]. The first rancheria they attacked contained but one Indian man, whom they killed. They next fell upon a rancherie [*sic*] of the tribe headed by "Whitossa" killing eight men and seriously wounding five others. (Gardiner Brooks in the *Shasta Courier*, February 25, 1854, p. 2)

In March, after stock were stolen near Tehama, "whites started in pursuit, and … killed twenty-three" Indians (probably Yana) "among the rocks of Dry Creek canyon" (*Butte Weekly Record*, March 11, 1854, p. 2). Then, in about May 1855, whites assaulted a village "less than half a mile from Cow Creek flouring mills"—that is Harrill's Mill—"on Suspicion" of harboring an Achumawi leader who they claimed was planning "to burn the mill." One participant counted 13 dead Indian men on the ground while indicating that others may have died of gunshot wounds or immolation (P.A. Chalfant in *The Morning Call*, January 4, 1885, p. 1).[5]

Massacres became more frequent in 1856. On March 8, the *Shasta Republican* reported that Antelope Creek and Cow Creek [Yanas] stole "seven head of cattle from a ranch near Shingletown." Whites followed, overtook them, and killed six. Several days later, "about thirty hogs were driven off." Another massacre followed: "The Indians were soon overtaken [and] all killed on the spot, and the white men then fell upon the rancherias, sacrificing to their vengeance men, women and children! About thirty Indians in all were killed" (*Shasta Republican*, March 8, 1856, p. 2).

Sometimes the mere possibility of theft precipitated atrocity. On April 19, 1856, the *Shasta Republican* reported that "During the past week a large number of the Cow Creek Indians went to Harrill's mill [Millville], on Cow Creek ... and insisted on being presented with a sack of flour a-piece." The *Republican* suggested that these Central Yanas wanted flour for "one of their most important pow-wows." More likely, they simply needed food, as acorns, game, fish, tubers, and grasses were diminishing under the triple onslaught of ranching, hunting, and mining, even as immigrants denied them access to what remained. Nevertheless, "the three or four men in charge of the mill" refused to provide any flour, the Yana allegedly made "hostile threats," and "a fight" broke out. When the smoke cleared "About twenty Indians were killed" and their "[r]ancherias ... burned" while two mill workers were injured (*Shasta Republican*, April 19, 1856, p. 2; T.J. Moorman in *Sacramento Daily Union*, April 22, 1856, p. 2).

Rumors now spread—which later proved false (*Shasta Republican*, April 26, 1856, p. 2)—that the Cow Creek Yana "were gathering all the forces they could musteri [muster] with the intention of attacking and burning the mill." Thus, "about a dozen [Shasta] citizens left town" on April 16, "fully armed, in order to garrison the mill." Reinforcements swelled their number to 42 and on April 17 they divided "into two parties." Meanwhile, "On [April] 16th ... a company of men from Oak Run killed an Indian and wounded one other." Then, on April 17 or 18, the Clover Creek "party discovered and attacked a *rancheria*, killing thirteen Indians," without suffering a single casualty (*Shasta Republican*, April 19, 1856, p. 2; italics in original).

By the summer of 1856, retaliatory massacres were coalescing into an ominous pattern. A North Cow Creek rancher reported that, following livestock thefts, "Parties have been or are out of course, on another 'digger hunt.'" He then predicted that: "A few years and the like depredations and excursions will not be heard of. Neither will the Indians. They ere [*sic*] fast wasting away." He explained: "With them stealing is as natural as breathing, and shooting them for the same, by the whites, equally so" (Geo. to Editor, August 18, 1856 in *Shasta Republican*, August 23, 1856, p. 2).

The following year, the United States Army intervened. According to Theodora Kroeber,

> in 1857 … a company of cavalry, dispatched from Sacramento in
> response to clamor up valley, is said to have tried a frontal attack
> against the Yana, and to have been surprised by the unseen red-
> skins, who sent the soldiers scrambling down bluffs and through
> chaparral in disorderly retreat to the valley floor. (Kroeber, 1961,
> p. 61)[6]

This was the first of several army operations that failed to successfully
engage the Yana (Kroeber, 1961, p. 62).

Local colonizers, for whom massacres were increasingly common, thus
took matters into their own hands with catastrophic consequences for
Yana people. For example, on or about June 10, 1857, Indians killed a "Mr.
Loree, near Antelope Mills." The perpetrators were "supposed to be of the
Pitt [sic] or Feather River tribe." They were not reportedly Yana. Yet, on
June 12, 15 Red Bluff men "started for the scene of the murder with the
intention of chastising the Indians." Two days later they "encountered
about two hundred Indians about four miles above Lassen's cabin … in
Mill creek cañon, where they had a rancheria." To maximize the death toll,
the 15 waited until "about daylight" on the morning of June 15 to attack.
Despite the element of surprise, the Yahi "stood their ground." "Armed
with rifles," they advanced and a running fight ensued as the Red Bluff
posse retreated down-canyon. Still, the attackers wrought terrible destruction at little cost to themselves. One participant reported two whites
injured while "at least 50 Indians were killed and wounded" (*Red Bluff
Beacon*; Mr. Chaffee in *Shasta Republican*, June 20, 1857, p. 2).

Despite the threat of overwhelming retaliatory massacres, Yana desperation fueled continuing raids.[7] According to Deer Creek resident
Robert Anderson's 1909 recollection: "During the winter of 1857 they
caused much uneasiness among the settlers. Many raids were made into
the valley, followed always by swift retreats into the hills" (Anderson,
1909, p. 3). Desperation inspired new daring: "These depredations
occurred usually along the edge of the valley, but extended on some
occasions as far as the Sacramento River" (Anderson, 1909, p. 4).

Immigrants predictably responded with more violence in 1858. On
March 6, 17 "persons" attacked "a rancheria about a mile from Deer
Creek [in Yahi territory], and fifteen from the Sacramento Valley." They
were "victorious, without [suffering] either killed or wounded," suggesting another massacre (*Red Bluff Beacon*, March 10, 1858, p. 2). Years
later, Dan Delaney recollected that after "a family living on Antelope
creek … was murdered" that spring, Harmon Good and five others surrounded a village and attacked at dawn. "Not one of the Indian hunters
was touched, whilst every dusky devil that had occupied the camp was a
ghastly corpse" (Delaney, 1872, p. 1)

To help pay for continuing sorties against the Yana, local immigrants now began appealing to the state of California for financial support. "In the vicinity of Red Bluff" they circulated "[a] petition ... asking the Legislature to assist, by an appropriation of small means, in chastising the Indians on Antelope and Deer Creeks" (*Sacramento Daily Union*, March 15, 1858, p. 3). Legislators did not make the appropriation but nor did they stop the killing. On May 3, 1858, a correspondent reported a rumor

> that a company of fifteen or twenty white men, who have had stock stolen and other depredations committed by the Indians near "Lassen's Peak," joined together lately for the purpose of extinguishing the small tribe, attacked them at their rancheria, and killed nearly everyone, men, women and children, to the number of forty or fifty. (May 3, 1858 letter in *Sacramento Daily Union*, May 6, 1858, p. 1)

Two days later, the *Red Bluff Beacon* reported another atrocity. After several thefts and the escape of "George Lane's squaw," who took "his Indian boy and a good revolver, a lot of ammunition, &c.," volunteers sought out Native Americans, and when they "came upon them somewhere on Battle Creek [probably in Southern Yana territory], [they] killed some fifteen" (E.W. Inskeep to Editors, April 28, 1858 and editor in *Red Bluff Beacon*, May 5, 1858, p. 2). Soon thereafter, the *Beacon* described how a posse searching for stock rustlers in "Antelope Canyon" wounded and then executed an Indian man there before announcing matter-of-factly: "Another Indian was killed on Battle Creek yesterday" (*Red Bluff Beacon*, May 19, 1858, p. 2).

Clearing the Land, 1858–1859

Colonizers' intentions now shifted dramatically. On May 25, 1858, some 39 "citizens at Antelope District" proclaimed a new goal. No longer interested in punishing Yana raids with massacres, they demanded an Indian-free environment. To their neighbors and to the local federal Indian agent they announced that unless all nearby "Indians ... are soon removed to the Reservation, we are determined to remove them out of the country ourselves, even if we should have to exterminate them in doing so." The threat was unmistakable: "We are not merely going to give them a slight chastising, but we are resolved to continue the search for them until we have exterminated the last one of them, and leave nothing in the shape of an Indian in the country" (*Red Bluff Beacon*, May 26, 1858, p. 2).

Meanwhile, the army and Indian Affairs Office commenced a forced removal operation and 23 soldiers arrived "to induce [the Yana and perhaps others] to go to the Reservation" (*Red Bluff Beacon*, May 19, 1858, p. 2). By May 26, Nome Lackee Reservation employee W.S. Knott was deporting "175 Indians, from Major Readings, Jelly's, Loye's, and other ranches on Battle Creek [to] the Reservation" (*Red Bluff Beacon*, May 26, 1858, p. 2). Many Yana people probably died during this and other removals. Indeed, according to Theodora Kroeber, "Forced migrations account for some hundreds of Yana deaths" (Kroeber, 1961, p. 47).

To the south, immigrants continued punitive attacks against the "Mill Creeks," who by this point likely included both Yahi and/or other California Indian refugees who had retreated to Mill Creek.[8] On August 25, 1858, the *Red Bluff Beacon* reported that after "Mill creek Indians" stole food near Red Bluff "and committed depredations at various other places ... citizens went out in pursuit," and killed at least one "near Antelope mills" (*Red Bluff Beacon*, August 25, 1858, p. 2). Indian hunters also targeted Yana to the north early the next year. On January 22, "Rudolph Klotz discovered a party of Indians endeavoring to steal stock from a ranch on Battle creek" and "the day following ... suddenly came upon them," opened fire and killed "ten or twelve Indians" who "are supposed to be a portion of the Antelope Indians." As was common in such attacks, "[n]one of the whites were injured" (*Shasta Courier*, January 29, 1859, p. 2; *Red Bluff Beacon*, February 2, 1859, p. 2). Then, in March 1859 a cowboy was murdered and Harmon Good—already a "celebrated" Yana killer—led a night ambush at the "Grapevine," massacring 14 "Mill Creeks" (Sauber, 1897, pp. 123, 127).

That spring, immigrants modified their strategy for clearing the land. First, they institutionalized killing. On April 6, 1859, the *Red Bluff Beacon* reported that

> [a] new plan has been adopted by our neighbors opposite this place to chastise the Indians.... Some men are hired to hunt them, who are compensated by receiving so much for each scalp, or some other satisfactory evidence that they have been killed. The money has been raised by subscription. (*Red Bluff Beacon*, April 6, 1859 in *Sacramento Daily Union*, April 9, 1859, p. 4)

The new policy soon yielded results. On April 21, "citizens left Antelope" searching for horse thieves and that night "commence[d] an indiscriminate slaughter," killing 14 people, most of whom, according to "some of the party ... were women and children, only one 'buck' having been killed, and two wounded" (*Red Bluff Beacon*, April 27, 1859 in *Nevada Democrat*, May 4, 1859, p. 4). Still, piecemeal killing was not fast enough for many immigrants. The next month they organized a two-month-long campaign against the Yahi Yana. It was the most ambitious Yana-killing operation yet.

On May 9, 48 immigrants living in "the vicinity of Antelope and Deer Creeks" petitioned California Governor John Weller for "assistance and relief" in dealing with "frequent depredations committed by the Indians inhabiting the mountains on the eastern border of this county,"—that is the Yana (Amos Figel and others to Gov. John B. Weller, May 9, 1859 in Kibbe, 1860, pp. 13–14). Three days later, 240 Red Bluff residents petitioned Governor Weller for "relief," claiming that "[o]n the night of the eleventh instant [May 12th] the house of Col. E.A. Stevenson was fired by the Indians and burned, causing the death of two women and four children, and probably that of one man" (James W. Smith and others to Gov. John B. Weller, May 14, 1859 in Kibbe, 1860, pp. 14–16). The press later reported seven people killed (*Red Bluff Beacon*, May 18, 1859, p. 2). Three more local petitions to the governor followed over the next two days (Hon. Newell Hall and others to Gov. John B. Weller, May 15, 1859; Thomas James and others to Gov. John B. Weller, May 15, 1859; and Messrs. Harrison and Bradley to Gov. J.B. Weller, May 16, 1859 in Kibbe, 1860, pp. 17–19). Then, on May 21, men took "the Indian boy of Col. Stevenson, who was confined on the charge of having set fire to the latter's house" and lynched him (*Shasta Republican*, May 28, 1859, p. 2; Red Bluff telegram dated May 22, 1859 in *Daily Alta California*, May 24, 1859, p. 1).

Extant primary source documents do not record why the "Mill Creeks" burned Stevenson's house. It may have been revenge. Or, they may have come for food but burned the house to cover their retreat. The arson could also have been a desperate but calculated strategic gambit. Realizing the impossibility of surviving indefinitely in an ever-shrinking mountain refuge, yet not knowing of the vast population that could replace fallen colonizers, arson may have been an attempt to drive immigrants away.

Whatever the arsonist's motives, the army now took action at the request of the governor (*Red Bluff Beacon*, May 25, 1859, p. 3). On May 19, Brigadier-General Clark ordered Captain F.F. Flint, with Company A of the 6th Infantry, to Red Bluff to arrest Indian "marauders" and turn them over to "civil authorities" (Order of Gen. Clark to Capt. F.F. Flint, May 19, 1859 in Kibbe, 1860, p. 21). They arrived in town on May 26 and Flint's 60 men soon began patrolling Yana territory "between Battle and Mill Creeks" but made no contacts (Shover, 1999, p. 11; F.F. Flint to Gen. Kibbe, July 12, 1859 in Kibbe, 1860, p. 26). Flint would remain in the field until June 19 but many local immigrants soon saw the operation for what it was: another failed army pacification campaign (Shover, 1999, p. 20).

In late May "fifteen hundred dollars was subscribed for the purpose of paying the expenses of an Indian hunt" and John Breckenridge led "about ten" men into the hills (Mr. Davis in *Shasta Republican*, May 28, 1859, p. 2). Their intentions were clear. On May 25 the *Beacon* proclaimed "The Indians *must* be chastised;—that sort of chastisement they most merit is a *total extermination* of the fragment of their tribe" (*Red Bluff Beacon*, May 25, 1859, p. 2; italics in original). Then, in the second week of June, local immigrants "resolved to petition the Governor again for authority to raise a volunteer force … to drive the Indians from their fastness, or exterminate the tribe" (*Shasta Herald*, June 11, 1859, p. 2). Like the Antelope District residents before them, they sought to clear the land of Native Americans by any means necessary. Ultimately, they raised some $3,000 "for the purpose of paying a volunteer company to go out under the direction of John Breckenridge, to chastise the Indians on the head-waters of Deer, Mill, and Antelope Creeks" (*Red Bluff Beacon*, June 15, 1859, p. 2; see also Anderson, 1909, p. 10). According to Anderson "Hi [*sic*] Good, John Breckenridge, and myself, together with [four others] were selected and engaged to hunt the red men for two months" (Anderson, 1909, p. 10).

Before departing, the squad received state recognition and federal leadership. California state militia Adjutant "General [William] Kibbe sent Captain Burns of the army to take command of our party. He arrived in good time and we started on June 15th." The mission continued to enjoy state approval, but Burns soon "became completely exhausted, and … ended his participation." Two new recruits then joined and ten men continued the operation (Anderson, 1909, pp. 11, 13).

Moving south, they crossed Chico Creek into Konkow Maidu country and located a presumably Konkow Maidu camp (Anderson, 1909, p. 22; Waterman, 1918, p. 44; Kroeber, 1961, p. 67). While studying the terrain, Anderson and Good encountered and killed an Indian man: "We carried the scalp to camp with us, this being the first trophy we had taken in the campaign." The killing was the first of three instances Anderson reported in which expedition members summarily shot or killed Indian men (Anderson, 1909, pp. 21, 27, 37). It also highlighted another pattern: scalping. In 1923 the Indian-hunter Sim Moak recalled that "At one time Good had forty hanging in the poplar tree by his house" and described Good wearing scalps from his belt: "you can imagine a great tall man with a string of scalps from his belt to his ankle" (Moak, 1923, pp. 31, 23).[9] Good was not alone. In 1917 Waterman described a Butte County man "who had on his bed even in recent years a blanket lined with Indian scalps" (Waterman, 1917, p. 530). Perhaps with thoughts of adding to their collections, Breckenridge surrounded the encampment and attacked at dawn. Anderson recollected: "Soon we were in possession of the camp. There was not a bad Indian to be found, but about forty good ones lay scattered about" (Anderson, 1909, pp. 21, 23). In contrast, the *Red Bluff Beacon* reported that during the last week of July the posse "killed fifteen Indians and one white man" in two incidents near "the headwaters of Butte and Deer Creek" (*Red Bluff Beacon*, August 3, 1859, p. 2).

Breckenridge now swung north into indisputably Yahi territory and located a camp "on the head waters of Deer Creek" (*Red Bluff Beacon*, August 24, 1859, p. 2). Again, he attacked at dawn and "killed a number, but many escaped up that brushy, boulder-strewn canyon." Anderson followed and captured a group of "mostly squaws and children." Posse members immediately executed "a young man called 'Billy'" when he admitted killing a white person, before shooting another man dead for attempting to liberate his wife (Anderson, 1909, pp. 38, 39–40, 42). Thus, a newspaper reported that "Breckenridge's party … killed all the bucks, and took the squaws and children to the Reservation" (*Red Bluff Beacon*, August 24, 1859, p. 2). In sum, according to historian Steve Schoonover, "about a dozen" people were killed in this attack (Schoonover, 1994, p. 11).

Following "a long talk with Captain Breckenridge" on August 31, the *Red Bluff Beacon* summarized the expedition: "they killed twenty-nine Indians, wounded about twenty more, a great portion of them severely [and] took thirteen women and children to the [Nome Lackee] Reservation" (*Red Bluff Beacon*, August 31, 1859, p. 2). These deportees presumably joined the Central Yana sent there in 1858 (Waterman, 1918, p. 46). However, if Anderson's recollections are accurate, the Breckenridge posse killed over 42 Indians, presumably including both Maidu and Yana victims. Either way, a militia campaign now absorbed most of the Breckenridge posse.[10]

State-sanctioned Killing and Removal, 1859

California's governor magnified the size, scope, and lethality of these operations by ordering volunteer state militiamen into the field against all Yana people. On Independence Day, 1859, Governor Weller ordered General Kibbe north to determine whether or not a militia unit should be raised to fight Tehama county Indians (Gov. John B. Weller to Gen. W.C. Kibbe, July 4, 1859 in Kibbe, 1860, p. 24). Kibbe reported back that

> there are from one hundred and seventy-five to two hundred and fifty Indian warriors belonging to several different tribes, banded together through feelings of revenge against the whites, armed with guns, and bows, and arrows, occupying a section of country extending from Butte Creek, on the south, to Little Cow Creek, on the north. (Kibbe to Weller, no date, in Kibbe, 1860, p. 26)

Kibbe thus described most of Yana territory as hostile, marking it for attack by the state.

On August 2, 1859, Weller responded by ordering Kibbe to enroll up to 80 volunteer militiamen. He cautioned Kibbe: "There must be no indiscriminate slaughter of the Indians" and warned that "women and children must be spared." Still, he also ordered that "Those of the tribes who have been engaged in these murders, arsons, and robberies ... should be punished" (Weller to Kibbe, August 2, 1859 in Kibbe, 1860, p. 28). Weller thus provided himself with political insurance against future criticism while commanding Kibbe to punish at a time when punishing California Indians routinely meant massacring them. Kibbe "proceeded to Tehama County, and on the sixteenth of [August] organized a company of volunteers" (Kibbe, 1860, p. 5). At Red Bluff, 93 men—including Anderson and his group—enlisted for a three-month campaign (Potter, n.d., p. 8; Anderson, 1909, p. 43; www.militarymuseum.org/KibbeRangers.html).

In his self-congratulatory 1860 report, Kibbe sought to justify his request for $69,486.43 to pay for the expedition. His report is thus suspect. Anderson deemed the portion of the campaign that took place in his region "a complete failure" that "did not get a single Mill Creek" (Anderson, 1909, p. 44). Kibbe, in contrast, styled his campaign a triumph. He reported trying to kill or capture all Indians threatening "the white population of that tract of country extending from Butte Creek on the south, to the head of Pitt [sic] River on the north." His plan was ambitious. It covered a huge area of steep and rugged terrain, extending from northern Maidu territory, through Yana country, and north and east into Achumawi and Astugewi lands. To cover this region with 93 men, Kibbe divided them into three detachments. Each entered the campaign area at a different point, but they all moved south to north, in three sub-campaigns (Kibbe, 1860, pp. 5–7).

One week after enrolling volunteers, Kibbe's Yana operation was underway. On August 24 the *Red Bluff Beacon* reported that Lieutenant "Baily, with a portion of the company, went to Antelope Mills; Captain Burns, with another detachment, went up ... the south side of Mill Creek" (*Red Bluff Beacon*, August 24, 1859, p. 2). A week later Agent Geiger reported "An Indian war, under the auspices of the State government, is now being waged against the Indians east of the Sacramento river" (Indian Agent Vincent E. Geiger to Sup't Indian Affairs J.Y. McDuffie, August 31, 1859 in U.S. Office of Indian Affairs, 1860, pp. 440–441). By September 3 Kibbe had a Battle Creek headquarters in Southern Yana territory and Captain Burnes was capturing those who lived on the stream (E.A. to Editor, September 3, 1859 in *Shasta Herald*, September 17, 1859, p. 2).

Kibbe's militiamen took hundreds of prisoners, but also engaged in one-sided annihilationist killing. Indeed, he apparently spoke of both options. In early October he boasted that "in six weeks" he would "have all the Indians in the mountains, east of [Red Bluff] on the Reservation or exterminated" (*Red Bluff Beacon*, October 12, 1859, p. 2). Others saw his campaign simply as one of extermination. On October 15, the *Shasta Herald* reported that, "GEN. KIBBE still continues to wage a war of extermination against the hostile Indians, in the eastern portion of Shasta and Tehama counties," explaining that "small detachments of men" operating under "relaxed ... military discipline ... can move more rapidly from one point to another—penetrating to the Indian's hiding places—visiting on them swift and certain destruction." The newspaper also hinted at the indiscriminate nature of the killing by attempting to rationalize it: "in the event some squaws and children fall unavoidable victims, it cannot be helped." The *Shasta Herald* concluded ominously: "A chastisement must be inflicted on them that will forever put an end to their atrocities" (*Shasta Herald*, October 15, 1859, p. 2). Three days later, the *Sacramento Daily Union* added, "It has not been much of a war ... the truth being that nobody has been hurt [except Indians] 'being skinned'" (*Sacramento Daily Union*, October 18, 1859, p. 2).

Kibbe's operation was a large-scale version of Breckenridge's and employed similar tactics. He reported: "The plan of moving upon, and attacking, the rancherias of the Indians at night, I had learned by experience, was the best and only one calculated to be attended with happy results." Kibbe aimed to clear the land by capturing and killing:

> From time to time small parties of Indians were captured, until the southern portion of the country operated in [presumably Maidu lands] contained not a warrior to offer resistance. The intermediate section was next visited [presumably Yana lands], and the Indians occupying it, after several severe skirmishes, compelled to flee for safety to the country occupied by the Pit River [Achumawi] and Hat Creek [Atsugewi] Indians.

Kibbe concluded his campaign by moving into the Pit River and Hat Creek regions. Here he

> attacked the Indian stronghold with forty men, completely routing those who defended it, killing several of their number and taking others prisoners; those who escaped were pursued. A number of engagements subsequently occurred with them, in which a great number were killed or captured.

Kibbe then reported a mass surrender of "four hundred and fifty" followed by many "different skirmishes" (Kibbe, 1860, pp. 6–7).

The expedition was both a forced removal operation and an extermination campaign. On December 15 Kibbe brought some 450 prisoners to San Francisco, en route to the Mendocino Reservation. The next day a *New York Times* correspondent there concluded of white Californians' attitudes toward the Kibbe campaign, "They wanted the Indians exterminated, and to all intents and purposes they have been" (Glaucus, December 16, 1860 in *New York Times*, January 12, 1861, p. 2). Kibbe himself reported: "Out of the whole number of Indians fought about two hundred were killed, and twelve hundred taken prisoner" (Kibbe, 1860, p. 7; *Shasta Herald*, January 21, 1860, p. 2 agreed with these estimates). Despite his admission of surrounding and attacking sleeping villages, Kibbe improbably claimed that "No children were killed, and but one woman, during the whole campaign." In contrast: "Not a single [militiaman's] life was lost, and the wounded all recovered" (Kibbe, 1860, pp. 7, 9).

It is difficult to know how many Yana people Kibbe's campaign killed because he did not identify his victims by tribe. He reported "several severe skirmishes" in what was likely Yana territory but did not provide related death-toll estimates. Nor did he identify the Yana refugees he may have killed in Atsugewi and Achumawi lands. However, on September 30, 1859 he reported that "we have taken about two hundred Indians ... who belong to, or are connected with, the Deer Creek and Antelope [Yana] Indians" (Kibbe to Weller, September 30, 1859 in Kibbe, 1860, p. 30). According to a December 7 issue of the pro-Kibbe *Red Bluff Beacon*, "In the south, about three hundred [Indians] were captured, without loss of a single life on either side, and sent to the Mendocino Reservation" (*Red Bluff Beacon*, December 7, 1859, p. 2). While the paper's report that Kibbe killed not a single Indian in the southern portion of the campaign seems improbable, some of the 200 people the paper reported killed in the north were probably Yana refugees, while some Yana prisoners likely died en route to reservations as high mortality rates often accompanied 19th-century forced removals of Native Americans. Other Yana people likely starved to death as a result of Kibbe's campaign. By keeping them running and "hemmed in," denying them "time to gather acorns or seeds sufficient for winter," or to fish, he used the coming winter to force survivors of his campaign to surrender or face possible starvation. For people who had suffered massacres and had little faith in whites, it was likely an agonizing choice. According to local historian May Southern, "It was said 50 starved to death in the mountains that winter" (Southern, *c.*1942, p. 81).

Legislators in Sacramento and Washington sanctioned Kibbe's operation ex post facto. Indeed, Kibbe received most of the $69,486.43 he requested (Kibbe, 1860, p. 9). On March 20, 1860 state legislators passed an "Act for Payment of Expenses incurred in the Suppression of Indian Hostilities," allocating $60,475.85 "for the payment of the indebtedness incurred by the expedition against the Indians in the counties of Tehama, Shasta, Plumas, and Butte."[11] One year later U.S. congressmen voted to reimburse California for related expenses, ultimately paying the state $41,761.54 (*Congressional Globe*, March 1, 1861 in Rives, 1861, p. 1278; "Pitt River Expedition, 1859" in Comptroller of California (n.d.)).

Annihilation Campaigns, 1860–1872

Following Kibbe's operation, Yana people in the mountains had less food than ever. To flee Kibbe's militiamen, they likely abandoned crucial hunting, fishing, harvesting, and food-processing implements, as well as houses and crucial food stores. The campaign also drove them higher into the mountains and farther from most traditional fishing, hunting, and harvesting areas.[12] Thus, "During the winter of '59 and '60 the raids [by] the Indians followed one another with startling swiftness and regularity" (Anderson, 1909, pp. 44–45). These raids precipitated a new phase of the Yana genocide, in which small volunteer death squads sought out and destroyed surviving Yana in order to punish raids, obtain their wealth, and eliminate them as a potential threat.

Never resorting to conciliation or diplomacy, Anderson, Good, and others launched new search-and-destroy missions in Yahi territory during 1860. According to Anderson, "Finally, they [the Yahi] grew so bold as to pay a visit to Hi [*sic*] Good's rock corral on Deer Creek and to drive off some work cattle that belonged to Good and me." Good, Anderson, and "a young man named Bownman [aka Bully] at once set out after the cattle thieves." The three "trailed them," "located [a] camp near the head of" Dry Creek and opened fire. Anderson did not record any killed but Delaney described "many" dead (Anderson, 1909, p. 45; Delaney, 1872. p. 1; Delaney mistakenly placed these events in 1865). Anderson also boasted of his participation in subsequent routine killing sorties: "During these times Hi [*sic*] Good and I, sometimes with 'Bully' and sometimes by ourselves, made many scouting trips into the hills and managed to reduce the number of bad Indians on almost every trip" (Anderson, 1909, pp. 45, 47). C.F. Kauffman also recollected that "Hi. [*sic*] Good, Sandy Young and Bill. [*sic*] Sublette made frequent raids … and killed [a] great number." They were not alone. Kauffman remembered helping to attack a Mill Creek camp near Black Rock, where his group killed perhaps 17 people that February (Kauffman, *c.*1882).[13]

Shasta county "citizens" institutionalized similar small-scale killing operations the following year. On May 7 or 8, 1861 they met and raised "a fund to be disbursed in payment of Indian scalps for which a bounty was offered." Their intent was obvious. As the *Shasta Herald* explained, "The initial steps have been taken, and it is safe to assert that the extinction of the tribes ... will be the result." On May 9, the *Shasta Herald* reported that following the loss of some stock a group went to "Mill Creek ... and succeeded in killing four." Three days later, the *Marysville Appeal* warned: "The Diggers can be saved from forcible extermination only by the intervention of Uncle Sam" (*Shasta Herald*, May 9, 1861; editor in *Marysville Appeal*, May 12, 1861, p. 2). Unfortunately, the U.S. government failed to protect the Yana. That fall, after "Mrs. Moore ... was killed by the Indians on Singer creek, near to Oak Grove ... Good, with his trusty Indian hunters" apparently "killed about eight of them" (Delaney, 1872, p. 1).

In 1862—"the probable year of Ishi's birth"—large numbers of immigrant men joined Anderson and Good in the first of seven loosely connected annihilation campaigns spread over nine years (Kroeber, 1961, p. 68). In June, California Indians—who may or may not have been Yahi—killed a teamster and three white children near "Rock Creek Cañon" and furious immigrants began advocating total annihilation (*Sacramento Daily Union*, June 26, 1862, p. 2; *Red Bluff Semi-weekly Independent*, July 1, 1862, p. 2). According to Anderson, "the feeling against the Indians was so bitter that it was proposed to make a general cleanup, even of the friendly Indians" (Anderson, 1909, p. 55). On July 1, the *Red Bluff Semi-weekly Independent* reported, "the general expression is, that the prowling savages must be effectually wiped out." Continuing, it asserted that "There should be a general turnout from all sections, and every Indian exterminated that can be found in the mountains east of us ... the only way to deal with these rascals is to shoot them down upon sight" (*Red Bluff Semi-weekly Independent*, July 1, 1862, p. 2). That night volunteers attacked an Indian camp, "killing several" (*Butte Union Record*, July 5, 1862, p. 2). Three days later, the *Independent* reported the "breaking up of an Indian camp some four miles from [Dye's] mill," probably in Yana territory, before concluding, "Companies should be raised to hunt down ... and punish them, and that punishment should be extermination" (*Red Bluff Semi-weekly Independent*, July 4, 1862, p. 2). On July 22, Good began soliciting funds to campaign until "the guilty are extinct" (Harmon Good, July 22, 1862 in *Red Bluff Beacon*, July 31, 1862, p. 2). The next month the *Independent* insisted "that the extermination of the red devils will have to be resorted to before ... the people will be safe" (*Red Bluff Semi-weekly Independent*, August 4, 1862, in Heizer, 1974, p. 56).

Good was already heeding that call. The *Independent* gloated over the operations of "Captain Harmon Good, with his company of volunteer scouts ... who have been out on the trail for some two weeks, hunting Indians." The paper reported that "fifteen or twenty miles east of Red Bluff" one of the scouts "'drew a bead' on [a] red skin, and shot him through" on August 3. Later that day, upon locating a "Big Antelope" Creek village, Good "ordered his men to surround the camp and wait for daylight" (*Red Bluff Semi-weekly Independent*, August 8, 1862, p. 2).[14] According to Marysville's *Daily Appeal*, "Seventeen of the Indians were killed *and scalped* (*Daily Appeal*, August 9, 1862, p. 2; emphasis in original).[15] Meanwhile, six children were captured while, of the wounded, "six or eight died."[16] The *Appeal* concluded that "They are determined to drive off or exterminate the Indians," while Anderson recollected: "The whites made a pretty good clean-up on this occasion. A day or two later I was sitting on my porch when Hi [Good] and Sandy [Young] rode past on their way home. Hi showed me eight fresh scalps that he had tied to his saddle" (*Daily Appeal*, August 9, 1862, p. 2; Anderson, 1909, p. 55).

Good's posse returned to the field on August 12, and two days later attacked a Mill Creek camp, killing four men and capturing 11 women and 10 children (Harmon A. Good, August 18, 1862 in *Red Bluff Beacon*, August 21, 1862, p. 3). The Yale scientist William Brewer visited the Rock Creek area on October 11, 1862 and wrote that following the murders of the white children, "'volunteers' ... killed indiscriminately all the wild Indians they could find, male or female" (Brewer, 1974, p. 338).

The U.S. Army arrived in September, once most killing had ceased. They traversed the region between Battle Creek and Deer Creek in search of the Yana but failed to find, let alone engage, any Yana people (Kroeber, 1961, p. 69; see also Kauffman, *c*.1882, p. 27).

The cycle of 1862 repeated itself the next year. On June 7 or 8, 1863 whites lynched five Native Americans of unknown tribal affiliation—probably not Yana—at Helltown, northeast of Chico, in Konkow Maidu territory (Correspondent to the Union, Sand Rock, Butte County, June 8, 1863 in *Sacramento Daily Union*, June 11, 1863, p. 2). Likely in response, Indians again kidnapped white children, killing two.[17] These murders comprised just one of several attacks on Anglo-Americans in Konkow Maidu territory that July (Wells & Chandler, 1882, vol. 2, p. 219; Carson, 1915, p. 2). No recorded Indian voices from this period explain the motives behind these assaults, but vengeance likely played a role.

At the same time, killing women and at least five children suggests a last-ditch effort. Evidence indicates that a variety of Indian peoples had retreated into the mountains. Thankful Lewis, for example—who escaped Indian kidnappers—believed one of them "was not a Mill Creek Indian, but was supposed to have been one from the Rancheria" (Carson, 1915, p. 6). If people from various tribes were gathering in the remote upper reaches of Yahi territory as a multi-tribal guerilla resistance, the group would have been comprised of people backed into a corner with nowhere to flee, little to lose, and dwindling options. These attacks may have been their last, desperate bid to drive immigrants away.

Whatever the killers' motives, the attacks catalyzed a fresh wave of annihilationist violence. On July 21, Oroville Guards Captain H.B. Hunt telegraphed Governor Leland Stanford: "The Indians are killing white men within fifteen miles Oroville[.] Give us power to fight them or permission for the citizens to use our arms" (HB Hunt, Capt Comdg Oroville Guards to Gov Stanford, July 21, 1863. BANC MSS, C-A 120, Pt. 3, [University of California] Bancroft Library, Berkeley, California). Soon thereafter

> [a] proclamation [was] issued, threatening all Indians who did not come in by Saturday night and deliver themselves up, with extermination. One hundred and three came in to Chico, on Saturday morning and expressed willingness to put themselves in charge of the Sub-Indian Agent. (*Marysville Appeal*, July 28, 1863, p. 3)

Indian Agent G.M. Hanson rushed to the scene "by steamer, railroad, and stage," arriving "at Chico about 10p.m." on July 26. He arrived too late: "Just before my arrival they tied two up to a tree, and shot and scalped them; no proof against them whatever" (G.M. HANSON, Superintending Agent to WILLIAM P. DOLE, Commissioner of Indian Affairs, August 4, in U.S. Office of Indian Affairs, 1864, p. 96).

The following day, Hanson attended a meeting of 300–500 "infuriated" whites "at the Pentz Ranch" (HANSON to DOLE, August 4, 1863 in U.S. Office of Indian Affairs, 1864, p. 95; Moak, 1923, p. 14). He reported that despite his intervention, attendees "passed a resolution that the superintending agent should be requested to remove every Indian in the county of Butte within thirty days, to the reservation, and any left after that time should be killed" (HANSON to DOLE, August 4, 1863 in U.S. Office of Indian Affairs, 1864, p. 95).[18] Moak recollected: "Some wanted to kill all the Indians in the valley and in the hills (Moak, 1923, p. 14). According to Wells and Chambers, "The excitement was so intense that it was determined to make an indiscriminate slaughter of Indians." Indeed, "A war of extermination was evidently about to be commenced, and the blood of the savages would flow freely if some measures were not adopted to have the whole of them removed" (Wells & Chambers, 1882, vol. 2, p. 219).

After the meeting, Thankful Lewis reviewed a line-up of surrendered Indians. "She finally stopped and took a good look at one of the Indians and said, 'He looks just like the one that left the others the morning they killed Johnny.'" Others identified another "bad one," "quickly tied" the hands of both men and killed them. Moak concluded "It did not take more than suspicion to shoot an Indian in those days" (Moak, 1923, p. 14).[19]

The *Oroville Union* stoked the inferno of exterminationist hatred. On July 25, the paper described "outrages" before asking: "What will those say to this catalogue of outrages, who are opposed to killing off these 'devils of the forest'?" The paper enthused that whites had already "sent several to the 'big hunting ground'" before offering a malevolent benediction: "May unbounded success attend them, and may they never take one male prisoner" (*Oroville Union*, July 25, 1863, p. 3). By July 29 the *Marysville Appeal* reported at least "six Indians killed" (*Marysville Appeal*, July 29, 1863, p. 3).

The number of Yana people killed in this second campaign is unclear. Delaney recollected that Good "never ceased until he slew the last Indian connected with the [Lewis] tragedy." Were the victims Yanas? Anderson did remember that in June he and two companions attacked a camp near "the breaks of Mill Creek," killing seven and leaving "two badly wounded," while Delaney recalled that after "Indians stole" stock from a Deer Creek ranch Anderson and Good killed three (Anderson, 1909, pp. 66, 70). Yet, while there were shootings and lynchings in Maidu territory, it is difficult to know if the victims were Yana. Thankful Lewis, however, thought her captors were mainly "Mill Creeks" and recalled "[g]reat numbers of Indians," including some of her captors, "captured and killed" that year (Carson, 1915, p. 15).

In 1864 the third and most devastating wave of annihilationist killing broke upon the upper Sacramento River plains, where many Yana lived on white-owned farms and ranches. As the ethnographer Stephen Powers euphemistically wrote in 1874, "They adapted themselves early to the necessities of labor and the usages of civilization" (Powers, 1874, p. 417). Yet, in a single summer, death squads murdered all but a handful.

Living in "civilization" made these Yana particularly vulnerable. Some employers respected and trusted them. Thus, Powers noted, "[t]hey have a reputation for honesty" and "[a] ranchman states that he has frequently known them to bring in strayed cattle on their own motion" while "John Love had sometimes a hundred Nozes [Yana] in his employment at once. And they wrought faithfully, as they do to-day" (Powers, 1874, p. 417). Other farmers and ranchers harbored colder feelings. Agent Geiger pointed out in 1858 that "whites are divided in sentiment relative to [Indian] removal: those who have good Indian house and farm servants oppose their removal, while their less favored neighbors urge it" (Geiger to Henley, July 1858 in U.S. Office of Indian Affairs. 1858, p. 289). White farmers and ranchers were similarly divided over Yana laborers. Those without Yana workers may have wanted an excuse to level the social and economic playing field by killing their rivals' employees. Others may have wished to do away with the Yana, as we shall see, to obtain their money.

As in 1862 and 1863, an assault on white children triggered the killing. Linguist and author Jeremiah Curtin visited northern California in 1884 and interviewed both white and Yana locals. He believed the attack emanated from Yahi territory, but did not blame the Yahi:

> Certain Indians lived, or rather lurked, around Mill Creek [and] These Mill Creeks were fugitives; outlaws from various tribes, among others from the Yanas. To injure the latter, they went to the Yana country about the middle of August 1864, and killed two white women, Mrs. Allen and Mrs. Jones. Four children were also left for dead by them, but the children recovered. (Curtin, 1898, p. 517)

Who attacked the Jones family and why? In 1886 Irvin Ayres recalled what was likely the same attack. Though never before cited to explain these events, Ayres may have answered these questions. A "Mr David Matlock informed" Ayres

> that he knew who the Indian was who had committed the murders. He said it was a man whose brother, together with another Indian, while peacefully engaged plowing in the fields, working for white men, some months previously, had been shot by the very settler whose house was visited and whose family was killed; that, in fact, it was an act of vengeance. (Ayres, 1886, pp. 2–3)

In response, ranchers, farmers, and miners raised two volunteer companies and initiated what, if Curtin's data is accurate, was the most lethal extermination campaign ever launched against the Yana. It was so deadly both because of the large number of men involved and because whereas prior killing operations had targeted Yana in the mountains, this campaign also targeted Yana people working for and living with whites in the lowlands of the upper Sacramento River Valley.

Ayres recalled that soon after a "mass meeting" volunteers killed "two or three Indian lads who had been brought up in white families on Oak

Run and who were living with these families at the time" and shot "an Indian about two miles above the mill on Cow Creek" (Ayres, 1886, p. 3). On September 10, the *Copper City Pioneer* announced that

> Mr. Worley, who has just returned from our Volunteer Company, reports that a party of semi-civilized men, numbering some sixty odd, organized on Cow Creek ... are killing the domesticated Diggers indiscriminately [and] have confined their attacks to tame and friendly Indians. (*The Copper City Pioneer*, September 10, 1864 in *Shasta Courier*, September 17, 1864, p. 2)

By September 17, "some 40" Copper City men and "30 to 50" others from "Millville and the tributaries of Cow Creek" had been out for about a week. The *Shasta Courier* continued: "The Millville Company, it is reported, are bent on extermination and are killing indiscriminately all of Indian blood, wherever found." The paper lamented:

> Many of the domesticated Indians who had for years been living in peace on the ranches on the opposite sides of the river, molesting nobody, have been exterminated, and at our present writing no one can tell where the bloody business will end. (*Shasta Courier*, September 17, 1864, p. 2)

By September 24 "the Copper City and Millville companies [had] united," raised $100, and recently killed at least 12 "Antelope Indians," or Southern Yanas (*Shasta Courier*, September 24, 1864, p. 2; *Red Bluff Independent*, September 26, 1864 in *Marysville Appeal*, September 30, 1864, p. 3). Two days later, the *Red Bluff Independent* asserted that "the Millville party are exterminating the whole race of Diggers in that section" (*Red Bluff Independent*, September 26, 1864 in *Marysville Appeal*, September 30, 1864, p. 3). Then, in early October, a 30-man posse killed perhaps eight Indians who had "fled" to the Sacramento's west side "for safety" (*Shasta Courier* in *Sacramento Daily Union*, October 10, 1864, p. 5). Four days after that, Millville settlers resolved that any Indians found between the Pit River, Antelope Creek, the Sacramento River, and the Cascade crest—that is most of Yana territory—would have 10 days to leave after which "it shall be the privilege of our company ... to exterminate or expel said Indians" (*Shasta Courier*, October 15, 1864, p. 2).

Curtin turned his interviews with Yana survivors and others into a detailed, if fragmented, narrative of the campaign. According to him, "Two parties of white men were formed at once to avenge the women and four children. Without trying in any way to learn who the guilty were, they fell upon the Yanas immediately, sparing neither sex nor age."

Indeed, "They had resolved to exterminate the whole nation." Curtin's interviews yielded harrowing descriptions of unadorned slaughter:

> At Millville, twelve miles east of Redding, white men seized two Yana girls and a man. These they shot about fifty yards from the village hotel. At another place they came to the house of a white woman who had a Yana girl, seven or eight years of age. They seized this child, in spite of the woman, and shot her through the head.

"We must kill them, big and little," said the leader, "nits will be lice." In another instance: "A few miles north of Millville lived a Yana girl named Eliza, industrious and much liked by those who knew her. She was working for a farmer at the time." When the death squad arrived, Eliza recognized them. She pleaded: "Don't kill me; when you were here I cooked for you, I washed for you, I was kind to you; I never asked pay of you; don't kill me now." Her pleas were in vain. The killers "took Eliza, with her aunt and uncle, a short distance from the house and shot the three." According to Curtin, "My informant counted eleven bullets in Eliza's breast [and] saw her after [her] skull was broken" (Curtin, 1898, pp. 517–518).

Death squads searched methodically for Yana people on farms, but not everyone complied. "Another party went to a farm on Little Cow Creek where they found three Yana men threshing hayseed in a barn." After murdering the trio, the death squad entered the house and found "the three wives of the men killed in the barn." The women were screaming. Preparing to murder them, the killers encountered unexpected resistance:

> The [pregnant] farmer's wife hurried out with a quilt, threw it around the three women, and stood in front of them, holding the ends of the quilt. "If you kill them you will kill me" she said, facing the party.

According to Curtin, "To kill, or attempt to kill, under such conditions, would be a deed too ghastly for even such heroes; so they went away, swearing that they would kill the 'squaws' later." Yet, "these three Indian women were saved [and] taken beyond the reach of danger by two white men." Ultimately, "[a]bout twelve [others] were saved by Mr. Oliver and Mr. Disselhorst, both of Redding" (Curtin, 1898, pp. 518–519). Regrettably, Curtin recorded few other tales of such courage and heroism.

Small-scale slayings, such as a "killing" on Bear Creek, were punctuated by massacres ("A Private Informant" in Waterman, 1918, p. 51). "At one place they killed an Indian woman and her infant, at another three women. In the town of Cottonwood they killed twenty Yanas of both sexes." According to Curtin, "The most terrible slaughter in any place was near the head of Oak Run, where three hundred Yanas had met at a religious dance. These were attacked in force, and not a soul escaped." Still, "The slaughter went on day after day till the entire land of the Yanas was cleared." When the killing ended, "the whole number of surviving Yanas of pure and mixed blood was not far from fifty" (Curtin, 1898, p. 519).

In evaluating the killers' motives, Curtin identified three factors: "an intense feeling of indignation at the murder" of the two white women; "an unspeakable contempt for Indians"; and "plundering." Accordingly,

> it was not uncommon for a single [Yana] person of them to have from $40 to $60. One informant told me that a man showed a friend of his $400 which he had taken from murdered Indians. Money and everything of value that the Yanas had was snatched up by these robbers. (Curtin, 1898, pp. 519, 520)

Thus, greed apparently helped motivate some killers.

To the south, attacks on Yahi people continued the following year. In July 1865, a "Lieutenant Elliott went out after the Indians who made the raid on Bacon's barn lately" and killed one before others escaped "for Mill Creek Canyon" (*Red Bluff Independent* in *Sacramento Union*, July 24, 1865, p. 2). The next month, after raiders killed two whites in Concow Valley, south of Yahi territory, locals pursued them. On August 12 the *Union Record* reported, "There is an intense excitement among the people, and if found a terrible retribution will be visited upon these savages." The article concluded: "Quite a number of Indians have been killed at Con Cow and other places" (*Butte Union Record*, August 12, 1865, p. 3; see also Moak, 1923, p. 18; Wells & Chambers, 1882, vol. 2, p. 221). In an August 20 letter, Daniel Klauberg described how his group set out on August 9 and solicited Anderson's "company to hunt the raiders, which he readily agreed to." They then recruited "Hiram [sic] Goode [sic] who took command" and "seventeen men" headed into the hills on August 12 (Daniel Klauberg, August 20, 1865 letter in *Union Record*, August 26, 1865, p. 3).[20] When the posse told Anderson "We're after Bidwell's Indians!" (Maidu people), he convinced them that the real perpetrators were "The Mill Creeks." Locating a camp of some 50 people "about sixteen miles from" Red Bluff "in the region of the three knolls" in a Mill Creek gorge on August 13 or 14, Anderson and Good maneuvered using familiar tactics, surrounding "the camp … before break of day" (Anderson, 1909, pp. 71, 72, 76; August 15, 1865 Tehama dispatch in *Sacramento Daily Union*, August 16, 1865, p. 2). Good, "with six men ... advance[d]" from downstream, while Anderson "took [nine men and approached] from the up-stream side" (Anderson, 1909, pp. 78–79). The steep canyon walls, in combination with the pincer movement, made escape difficult.

The assault began when Good shot an early-rising man in the back. Anderson then "shouted, 'Down the creek boys, down the creek.'" (Anderson quoted in Moak, 1923, p. 21). "We crowded forward and poured a hot fire into the Indians from upstream, while Good's men hammered them from below." Desperate men, women, and children leaped "into the stream ... but few got out alive. Instead, many dead bodies floated down the rapid current" (Anderson, 1909, p. 79). Ultimately, "The Indians broke through the ranks and fled," leaving 5–9 dead while one attacker noted that "as many as six or seven who will surely die" and that the victims carried "off a great number of wounded," while the dead who floated downstream apparently remained uncounted.[21] The attackers, meanwhile, were unscathed (*Union Record*, August 26, 1865, p. 3). They did, however, murder a wounded woman prisoner for being "sullen" and refusing "to go a step further" (Anderson, 1909, p. 81).

Moak, who participated in the massacre, concluded, "The Mill Creeks were so thoroughly punished that they never committed any more murders" (Moak, 1923, pp. 23, 24). Anderson concurred: "This battle practically ended the scourge of the Mill Creeks" (Anderson, 1909, p. 80). According to Alfred Kroeber, "If there were known to be survivors, they were so few and so terrified that they were obviously harmless; and no further attention was paid to them. General opinion reckoned the tribe as extinct" (Kroeber, 1925, p. 342).

Still, sporadic killings continued. Delaney wrote that after Good encountered Indians on Deer Creek in 1866, Good and three others set out and "Ten victims bit the dust" (Delaney, 1872, p. 1). That same year, after "the robbing of the Silva home by the Mill Creek Indians" on April 24, Moak recalled that six men—including Anderson—attacked a Deer Creek village, "badly wounding" some people while killing at least two others. He concluded, "This was the last time we had to punish those Indians" (Moak, 1923, pp. 24–27).

Despite the Yana's waning numbers, some whites felt that killing should cease only with total extermination. That July the *Chico Courant* proclaimed:

It has become a question of extermination, now. The man who takes a prisoner should himself be shot. It is a mercy to the red devils to exterminate them, and a saving of many white lives. Treaties are played out—there is only one kind of treaty that is effective—cold lead. (*The Chico Courant*, July 28, 1866, p. 2)

In light of such attitudes, it was hardly surprising that an August 20, 1866 raid "resulted in the uprising of the settlers to exterminate the Indians" (Southern *c*.1942, p. 93).[22] According to Fred Dersch, 15 Indians raided his family's Bear Creek homestead, near Fort Reading (Southern, *c*.1942, pp. 92, 96). The raiders stole, destroyed property, and killed his mother (Southern, *c*.1942, pp. 92–94; *Red Bluff Independent*, September 5, 1866, p. 2). Veteran Yana-killer Rudolph Klotz now organized an 11-man posse (Southern, *c*.1942, p. 94; see also Waterman, 1918, p. 51). They followed the raiders for days and found them on August 29 near the headwaters of Antelope Creek and "a high palisade of rocks" about "two miles [from] the Antelope Flour mill, five miles from Red Bluff" (*Red Bluff Independent*, September 5, 1866, p. 2).

Employing typical tactics, Klotz enveloped the camp and struck at dawn. According to the *Red Bluff Independent*, "Four Indians, two bucks and two squaws, lay dead, while three more had limped off, one of the eight being unhurt." Scouts later found evidence that one of the wounded died (*Red Bluff Independent*, September 5, 1866, p. 2). Describing what was probably a separate assault, Dersch and Waterman believed that following the attack on the Dersch homestead some 30 Indians were massacred at a cave north of Dye Creek, in the Campo Seco vicinity (Waterman, 1918, p. 51; F. Dersch in Southern, *c*.1942, pp. 94–95). According to Dersch, "All were killed with the exception of a few women who got through the lines" (F. Dersch in Southern, *c*.1942, p. 95). Waterman added that, as of 1917, "the marks of the bullets are still to be seen on the rocks," and that, "In 1869 the side hill (visited at the time by Mr. Norvall) was still covered with skeletons." Waterman concluded: "At this point we may consider the history of the Yana closed, excepting only the Yahi division" (Waterman, 1918, p. 51).

Still, some locals continued baying for Yana blood. After reporting this massacre, the *Red Bluff Independent* proclaimed: "The settlers are up in arms, and we hope they will shoot, hang or burn every black rascal they find, that cannot give a good clear account of himself." The paper insisted "Extermination is the only safeguard for life and property" (*Red Bluff Independent*, September 5, 1866, p. 2). Red Bluff citizens also raised $70 and gave two Henry rifles to two members of the Klotz party (*Red Bluff Independent*, September 19, 1866, p. 2).

Soon thereafter, "Indians hunters" found some Dersch family possessions "in a rancheria on the Gerke grant." Thus, "the work of vengeance and slaughter commenced" once again and the *Red Bluff Independent* announced "It cannot be helped, and it must be done. We believe that a white man's life is worth a hundred Indians" (*Red Bluff Independent*, October 10, 1866, p. 2). Meanwhile, the *Shasta Courier* reported "four or five" Indians—presumably Yana—killed by Millville men "at a cave on the head of Antelope Creek" (*Shasta Courier*, September 22, 1866, p. 2;

October 6, 1866, p. 2). Interviewed in mid-October 1866—as he and a man named Sheridan were raising thousands of dollars in donations to support such operations—the group's commander, Captain John Boyce, explained, "Well, we have planted a few of them and keep pretty steady to work" (Captain John Boyce in *Red Bluff Independent*, October 17, 1866, p. 2).

Such men carried out at least four massacres in Yana territory during 1867. In mid-May, a death squad attacked seven Indians at "Buck's Flat, on Little Antelope Creek" killing five and mortally wounding two, "it is believed" (*Red Bluff Independent*, May 22, 1867, p. 3). The following month "Several men" killed "two bucks" on Antelope Creek (*Shasta Courier*, June 22, 1867, p. 2). Others "came upon a party of ten Indians [probably Yana] encamped on Ink's creek ... and killed seven of them, wounding two more." In response the *Red Bluff Independent* shrieked "We hope that a war of extermination will be waged upon the dirty, saddle-colored dogs" (*Red Bluff Independent*, July 3, 1867, p. 3). That fall, "Indian hunters" again attacked "Antelope Indians" killing "eight or nine bucks" and by early 1868 the *Shasta Courier* estimated that "the tribe is now supposed to be reduced to about four bucks and five or six squaws" (*Shasta Courier*, May 23, 1868, p. 2). Still, D.B. Lyon told Waterman that "thirty-three wild Indians" (presumably Yahi) were "killed at Campo Seco" in 1868, although this may have been a retelling of Dersch's report of 30 people massacred in a Campo Seco-area cave in 1866.

Regardless, Yana hunting continued. Delaney wrote that "In spring of 1869," after "Indians robbed some sheep herders, and killed some cattle, on or near Deer Creek, Capt. Good, with two followers" set out, surrounded an Indian camp at night, and "killed several," taking two female prisoners (Delaney, 1872, p. 1). The following year Good assailed a Mill Creek village that one attacker thought was Ishi's, murdering an elderly man there (D.B. Lyon and W.J. Segraves in Waterman, 1918, p. 57). That May, Good—who "devoted his time to hunting and killing Indians"—was found "pierced with twelve bullets and his head smashed with rocks," reportedly, "by Indians" (*Sacramento Daily Union*, May 7, 1870, p. 4).

Immigrants carried out their last major Yana massacre in April 1871. After losing a steer in Morgan Valley, near the headwaters of Mill Creek, ranchers "J. J. Bogard, Jim Baker, Scott Wellman, and Norman Kingsley" tracked the missing animal. After finding it they "trail[ed] the Indians with dogs" to "a cave." There, the four managed to "corner" a group of Indian people and "kill about thirty." Mr. Novall, who reported these events, attempted to justify the atrocity as a response to suspected theft, noting that "In this cave there [was] 'about a ton' of dried meat." Yet his description eliminated any possible justification: "In the cave with the meat were some Indian children. Kingsley could not bear to kill these children with his 56-calibre Spencer rifle. 'It tore them up so bad.' *So he did it with his 38-calibre Smith and Wesson revolver*" (Novall in Waterman, 1918, p. 59; italics in original).[23]

By 1874 Powers deemed "the Nozes ... nearly extinct." According to him, only five "Mill Creek Indians"—"two men, two women, and a child," presumably including Ishi—remained alive. Still, "There are men in and around Chico who have sworn a great oath of vengeance that these Indians shall die a bloody death" (Powers, 1874, pp. 417–418). Ultimately, the drive to destroy the Yana became an ideology of total annihilation that fueled the near obliteration of an entire people (Table 1.1).

Despite 21 years of Yana-killing—often carried out with fanatical zeal—some Yana people survived. Through skill, luck, and sheer defiance they evaded death squads, moved and intermarried into neighboring tribes such as the Achumawi and Wintu, or found ways to accommodate themselves to the invaders' new order (Speaker, 2003, p. 82).[24] Some of their descendents—who generously shared information for this chapter—are enrolled members of the federally recognized multi-tribal, 270-member Redding Rancheria, in Redding, California (Redding Rancheria Cultural Resources Program Manager James Hayward, Sr. to author, August 22, 2011). They are rejuvenating their cultural practices but describe their history, in part, as "the tragic and devastating story of genocide."[25]

Direct acts of violence accounted for a substantial portion of the Yana population cataclysm. According to Theodora Kroeber, records reveal "some six hundred Yana deaths by violence from white settlers" between 1850 and 1872 (Kroeber, 1961, p. 46). She probably underestimated. Reports of killings usually failed to identify California Indians by tribe, so it is impossible to identify all of the victims of the killings presented in this chapter as definitively Yana. Still, evidence suggests that, during these years, recorded acts of immigrant violence killed as many as 800–915 Yana or more, to say nothing of the unrecorded killings alluded

TABLE 1.1 Yana population estimates, 1847–1885[a]

Year	Estimated total Yana population
Before 1847	2,000–3,000+
1848	1,900
1852	1,800
1880	20
1885	30+

Note

a For "precontact" see: Kroeber (1961, p. 15) and Thornton (1987, p. 111). For 1848, 1852, and 1880, see Cook (1943, p. 105). For 1885, see Waterman (1918, p. 40).

to by Robert Anderson, John Boyce, Jeremiah Curtin, and Thankful Lewis in their references to extended killing campaigns. Nor do these numbers include the victims of Kibbe's campaign, the "hundreds" that Theodora Kroeber thought died during forced removals, those who may have perished on reservations, or those who died from starvation or exposure related to killing campaigns.

In contrast, Yana people killed relatively few immigrants, even while defending themselves and their families from genocide. D.F. Crowder, who settled near Chico in 1856, recollected of operations by Anderson, Good, Young, and others that, "It is a noticeable fact that no one was killed or wounded in any of these attacks upon the Indians" (D.F. Crowder in *Chico Daily Enterprise*, December 28, 1917, pp. 1, 8; January 21, 1918, p. 6; January 22, 1918, p. 6). Meanwhile, Yana aggression caused relatively few casualties. Theodora Kroeber estimated that Yana people killed not more than 20 whites, while Johnson argued that "the deaths of fewer than 50 settlers can be directly attributed to them with any degree of certainty" (Kroeber, 1961, p. 45; Johnson, 1978, pp. 362–363).

With their superior numbers and firepower, the state of California, the U.S. government, or immigrant communities could have negotiated with the Yana and avoided genocide. Diplomacy might have generated a very different outcome. Instead, the state's major effort to pacify the Yana, during Kibbe's 1859 campaign, was as much about annihilationist killing as taking prisoners, and both Sacramento and Washington sanctioned it after the fact. Meanwhile, despite repeatedly bringing U.S. soldiers to the scene and the presence of nearby Indian Office agents, federal officials never seriously attempted to negotiate with the Yana. Finally, Yana-hunters like Anderson, Good, and Klotz could have negotiated the surrender of surprised and surrounded Yana encampments. Instead, because their communities rewarded scalping and articulated the intent to destroy the Yana, they routinely massacred Yana villages and frequently failed to take prisoners. Finally, sustained and systematic killing would have been impossible had the state not supported atrocities or turned a blind eye to them (Table 1.2).

Accounts: The Genocide of the Yana

Editors' note: Due to the fact that the vast majority of the first-person accounts of the genocidal acts perpetrated against the Yana are extremely succinct (ranging from one line to four or five lines) and because Dr. Madley has woven such accounts/statements throughout his essay above, we requested that herein he include newspaper articles from the late 1800s that address the treatment of the Yana at the hands of the white citizens residing in northern California between Sacramento and Chico.

TABLE 1.2 Reported killings in Yana territory, 1850–1871

Year	Location	Reported number of Native Americans killed (Yana or likely Yana)	Reported number of immigrants killed
1850	Near Deer Creek	22–23 (possibly not Yana)	2(?)
1850	Mill Creek	2+	0
1851	North of the head of Salt Creek	2 (likely Yana)	0
1853	Unknown	1 (likely Yana)	0
1853	Unknown	25 (likely Yana)	0
1854	Unknown	1 (likely Yana)	0
1854	Unknown	1 (likely Yana)	0
1854	Near Oak Run	8 (likely Yana)	0
1854	Dry Creek canyon	23 (likely Yana)	0
1855	Near Cow Creek Mills (Harrill's Mill)	13–14+	0
1856	Near Shingletown	6	0
1856	Possibly near Cold Springs Valley	~30	0
1856	Harrill's mill, on Cow Creek	~20	0
1856	Unknown	1	0
1856	Unknown	13	0
1857	Mill Creek Canyon	10+ (50 killed and wounded)	0
1858	Near Lassen's Peak	40–50	0
1858	Unknown	10+ (entire village, likely Yana)	0
1858	Battle Creek	~15 (likely Yana)	0
1858	Antelope Canyon	1 (likely Yana)	0
1858	Battle Creek	1 (likely Yana)	0
1858	Near Antelope Mills	1	0
1859	Near Battle Creek	10–12 (likely Yana)	0
1859	Grapevine near Mill Creek	14 (likely Yana)	0
1859	Near Antelope	14 (likely Yana)	0
1859	Unknown	1 (likely Yana)	0
1859	Headwaters of Deer Creek	~12	0
1860	Near Headwaters of Dry Creek	0–10+ (likely Yana)	0
1860	Black Rock, Mill Creek	3–17	0
1861	Mill Creek	4 (likely Yana)	0
1861	Near Oak Grove?	8 (likely Yana)	0
1862	Unknown	3+ (several)	0

Year	Location		Count
1862	15–20 miles east of Red Bluff	0	1
1862	Big Antelope Creek	0	20–25
1862	Mill Creek	0	4 (likely Yana)
1863	Near the Pentz Ranch	0	2 (likely Yana)
1863	Mill Creek	0	7
1863	Deer Creek?	0	3 (likely Yana)
1864	Oak Run	0	2–3
1864	Above the mill on Cow Creek	0	1
1864	Antelope Creek region	0	12+
1864	West of the Sacramento River	0	8 (likely Yana)
1864	Millville	0	3
1864	A few miles north of Millville	0	3
1864	Little Cow Creek	0	3
1864	Unknown	0	2
1864	Unknown	0	3
1864	Cottonwood	0	20
1864	Near the head of Oak Run	0	300
1865	Near Bacon's barn	0	1
1865	Three Knolls, Mill Creek Gorge	0	5–16+ (likely Yana)
1865	Near Three Knolls	0	1 (likely Yana)
1866	Deer Creek?	0	10
1866	Deer Creek	0	2+
1866	Antelope Creek headwaters	0	4–5
1866	Cave north of Dye Creek, Campo Seco	0	30
1866	Cave on the head of Antelope Creek	0	4–5
1867	Buck's Flat, on Little Antelope Creek	0	5–7
1867	Antelope Creek	0	2
1867	Ink's Creek	0	7 (likely Yana)
1868	Antelope Creek region	0	8–9
1868	Campo Seco	0	33 (a retelling of the 1866 cave massacre?)
1869	Deer Creek Region?	0	3+
1870	Mill Creek	0	1 (likely Yana)
1871	Kingsley Cave	0	~30 (likely Yana)
TOTAL		2(?)	~800–915

Note

Low-end total does not include the 1850 near Deer Creek or 1868 Campo Seco killings. A value of 10+ has been assigned to estimates of "many" and a value of 3+ to estimates of "several."

Selected Newspaper Articles

Extant 19th- and early 20th-century sources contain no quoted Yana accounts of the genocide that they suffered. Linguist and author Jeremiah Curtin did interview Yana survivors in 1884, but he, like other journalists and scholars, either did not receive or failed to quote Yana recollections of the ordeal. This absence may have been imposed, in part, by Yana cultural norms. For example, Ishi never broke the Yahi taboo against speaking of the dead (Kroeber, 1961, p. 93). Still, bystanders' and perpetrators' reports and recollections, quoted in this chapter, do shed light on the killers' intense racism and on their ruthless, often exterminatory, tactics.

Historian James J. Rawls has argued that some California whites "advocated and carried out a program of genocide that was popularly called 'extermination'" (Rawls, 1984, p. 171). Using Rawl's equation of the 19th-century term "extermination" with the 20th-century term "genocide," the following three newspaper articles highlight how publicly some whites advocated genocide against the Yana.

"Sowing the Wind and Reaping the Whirlwind"

Red Bluff Beacon, May 25, 1859, p. 2

Under the above caption, we noticed in the Sacramento *Bee* of the 13th inst., quite a lengthy article, deprecating, in the most unmeasured terms, the treatment by the people of this County of the Antelope Indians. We suppose the remarks of the *Bee* were superinduced by several articles that have recently appeared in this paper, coupled with the call made upon the Governor for aid in suppressing Indian depredations in this neighborhood. It is an easy matter for the editor of a newspaper, whose locality places him beyond harm's way, to sit down and write a long article in defence of the *"poor Indian."* But to those of us who have been made to feel the pangs of adversity by having our little all destroyed, time and again, by these ruthless and barbarous savages, the task is not quite so easy. Perhaps the people of no locality in the State have borne with more Christian fortitude, without complaining, the many wrongs inflicted upon themselves and property, by the brutality of these same Indians, than have the people residing on the east side of the Sacramento river. That fairest portion of our county has been, within the last few years, almost despoiled of its beauty by the heartless and fiendish operations of the tribe of Indians living in the foot-hills, and mountains adjacent, and forming the eastern boundary of the valley. The citizens, unable to protect themselves from their nightly incursions, have repeatedly sought the aid of both the Federal and State authorities, in bringing them to punishment. Hitherto their repeated petitions for aid in punishing them properly, have been answered in *fair promises*. In the meantime the work of destruction has steadily progressed. The people, suffering and smarting under their many wrongs, in one or two instances, have associated themselves together for the purpose of ridding themselves of their tormentors. A few Indians have been killed, and, in the excitement of the moment, we regret to say, some of them were women and children. But we can readily appreciate the feelings that actuated those of our citizens who composed the various expeditions of a private character sent out to punish them. Nearly all of them were sufferers from Indian depredations. The Indians were the aggressors—they threw the first stone. The whites were only acting upon the principle of *"lex talionis,"* the only salutary rule that can be applied to Indians over whom the government has no control and who compose a mere fragment of a tribe that live by plundering and murdering defenceless persons. Under this state of things, will the *philanthropic* editor of the *Bee*, who is entirely out of danger, suggest some more proper mode of punishment? Or does his sympathy for the *"poor Indian"* forbid his information on the subject coming to light? The editor of the *Bee* has grossly mistaken the character of the population that have suffered by outrages of these Indians, if he thinks they have mistreated them. They have heretofore contented themselves with protecting, upon their own premises, the lives of their families. The time has now come for some other sort of action. The Indians *must* be chastised;—that sort of chastisement they most merit is a *total extermination* of the fragment of their tribe. (Italics in original.)

"Indian Massacre"

Red Bluff Semi Weekly Independent *on July 1, 1862, p. 2*

The cruel murders perpetrated at Rock Creek last week, has created a general feeling of indignation among our citizens, and the general expression is, that the prowling savages must be effectually wiped out. We have received a letter from J. W. Lemons, of Deer Creek, giving the particulars of the sad affair, a portion of which has been heretofore published. From this letter we learn that the Indians, after killing and scalping Thomas Allen, and wounding the Indian boy, attacked a party of young people, out blackberrying in Rock Creek Cañon, and captured Miss Ida Heacock, aged seventeen years, her sister, aged thirteen, and a brother aged ten. A party who went in pursuit of the Indian found the bodies of the two girls, pierced with arrows and scalped, and stripped of their clothing. The boy has not yet been found. Men all along the valley are turning out in pursuit of the murderous savages. Dr. S. M. Sproule, of Chico, has gone below for arms and ammunition, and assistance.

There should be a general turnout from all sections, and every Indian exterminated that can be found in the mountains east of us. No person is safe along this valley as long as the savages are permitted to prowl around unmolested. It was only last spring that Mr. Meador was chased by Indians near Antelope, and the only way to deal with the rascals is to shoot them down upon sight.

"Fight with the Indians"

Marysville Daily Appeal, *August 9, 1862, p. 2*

From private information, we learn that Capt. Good's company of volunteers overtook a party of Indians near the site of the late massacre in Butte county, near Chico, and gave them battle. Seventeen of the Indians were killed *and scalped* by the volunteers, who, being from the immediate vicinity of the former massacre, are highly exasperated at the redskins. None were killed on the side of the whites. They are determined to drive off or exterminate the Indians, it is said. (Italics in original.)

Notes

The author thanks Jeff Diamant, Johnny Faragher, James Hayward, Sr., Ben Kiernan, Timothy Macholz, Susan Madley, Carol Maga, Christopher O'Brien, Jesse Philips, Sam Redman, Scott Sherman, Susan Snyder, and the Redding Rancheria community for their help.

1. For pre-1847 population estimates, see Curtin (1898, p. 517); Kroeber (1925, p. 339); Cook (1943, p. 90); Kroeber (1961, p. 15); Thornton (1987, p. 111).
2. Publications bearing Ishi's name include: Kroeber (1961; 1972); Pope (1920; 1932); Apperson (1971); Heizer and Kroeber (1979); Burrill (1990, 2001); Collins and Bergen (2000); Kroeber and Kroeber (2003); Starn (2004).
3. Yana territory covered 2,000–2,400 square miles. See: Waterman (1918, p. 36); Kroeber (1961, pp. 42–43); Cook (1976, p. 16). For borders see: Dixon (1905, p. 124, plate 38); Waterman (1918, map 1, 40); Kroeber (1925, pp. 337–338); Johnson (1978, p. 361); McCarthy (1998, vol. 4, pp. 227).
4. Dye noted: "There is some doubt whether the Indians captured are of the 'Millcreek' or 'Valley' tribe."
5. Chalfant stipulated: "I won't be positive as the exact month, or even certain as to the year, though every incident herein stated is given as a literal occurrence." For Harrill's Mill location, see Gudde (1974, p. 202).
6. Anderson (1909, p. 10) recalled: "The soldiers finally gave it up as a bad job and quit the game."
7. Waterman wrote:

> I strongly suspect that the unreconstructed belligerency of the Yahi during this period was largely due to the increased difficulty of their life. Hemmed in more and more in their lava hills, and cut off more and more from acorn grounds and fishing places, they probably visited the valley and stole livestock to escape famine and actual starvation. (Waterman, 1918, p. 43)

8. H.H. Sauber, who arrived in the region in 1859, recollected: "perhaps from half a dozen of the Indian bands of Northern California, parties of renegades had drifted into the dark, wild canon of Mill Creek" and Waterman later noted: "It has always been supposed that

remnants of several tribes made up these Mill Creek renegades" (Sauber, 1897, p. 122; Waterman, 1915, p. 235).

9. Sauber recollected "the strings of black-haired scalps that adorned" Good's house (Sauber, 1897, p. 123).

10. Breckenridge joined a volunteer unit "under the command of Coon Gardner" that "captured twelve or fourteen Indians lately near Centerville, and were obliged to kill or wound three who were trying to escape" (Red Bluff Beacon in Daily Alta California, September 5, 1859, p. 1).

11. "Act for Payment of Expenses incurred in the Suppression of Indian Hostilities, March 20, 1860" in www.militarymuseum.org/KibbeRangers.html.

12. After 1859, men hunting Yana usually found them high in the mountains; see, for example, Anderson (1909, p. 45).

13. Scott Sherman kindly provided a photocopy of this article.

14. Anderson located the massacre at "the head of Antelope Creek" (1909, p. 55). The Daily Appeal erroneously placed it "near Chico" (August 9, 1862, p. 2).

15. The Red Bluff Semi-weekly Independent also reported 17 people massacred (August 8, 1862, p. 2).

16. For the number of children captured, see VOLUNTEER, Mill Creek, August 11, 1862 in Sacramento Daily Union, August 15, 1862, p. 2; Correspondent to the Union, Sacramento Daily Union, August 21, 1862, p. 2. Delaney (1872, p. 1) later reported a total of 20 killed. Delaney noted, incorrectly, that the massacre took place in 1861. In fact it occurred in 1862, as did the "Heacock" killings.

17. Northern California Indian Affairs Superintendent George Hanson later argued that the murder "could be traced to an outrage committed upon that same tribe of Indians a few days previously, wherein some bad white men had hanged five of their tribe to a tree without any proof whatever" (G.M. HANSON, Superintending Agent to WILLIAM P. DOLE, Commissioner of Indian Affairs, August 4, 1863 in U.S. Office of Indian Affairs, 1864, pp. 95–96).

18. For more on this resolution, see Oroville Union in Sacramento Daily Union, August 3, 1863, p. 4.

19. Carson (1915, p. 15) recalled: "My father, with a posse, came to Chico and killed two who were known to be bad ones." This seems to refer to the two killings mentioned by Moak.

20. Anderson (1909, p. 74) recalled being "captain" and Good "second in command."

21. The August 15, 1865 Tehama dispatch in Sacramento Daily Union, August 16, 1865, p. 2 and the Union Record, August 19, 1865, p. 3 reported nine dead. Klauberg reported five "killed on the spot" and "as many as six or seven who will surely die" (Union Record, August 26, 1865, p. 3).

22. Waterman thought this happened "probably in the year 1867," but Southern's information came from the victim's son, Fred Dersch, and the inscription on Marie Dersch's Parkville cemetery tombstone.

23. Theodora Kroeber thought that this happened in "1870, 1871, or 1872" (1961, p. 239). Archeologists later located the remains of 30 people—only one of which they could positively identify as an adult male—at a site they called Kingsley Cave (Baumhoff, 1955, pp. 40–73). In 2004 the Phoebe Hearst Museum repatriated the remains of 59 human beings taken from a place they called Kingsley Cave (Conversations with James Hayward, Sr. and Dr. Christopher O'Brien).

24. For an example of Yana/Achumawi intermarriage, see Barbara Murphy in Russell (2008).

25. Back matter summary on cover of Russell (2008).

References

Anderson, Robert A. (1909). *Fighting the Mill Creeks: Being a personal account of campaigns against Indians of the Northern Sierras.* Chico, CA: The Chico Record Press.

Anonymous (1891). *Memorial and biographical history of northern California illustrated.* Chicago, IL: The Lewis Publishing Company.

Apperson, Eva M. (1971). *We knew Ishi.* Red Bluff, CA: Walker Lithograph Company.

52 • B. Madley

Ayres, Irvin (1886). *NOTES furnished by and concerning IRVIN AYRES, ESQ're.* Berkeley, CA: University of California, Bancroft Library.

Baumhoff, Martin A. (1955). Excavation of site Teh-1: Kingsley Cave. *University of California Archaeological Survey Reports, 30*, 40–73.

Brewer, William H. (1974). *Up and down California in 1860–1864: The journal of William H. Brewer.* Ed. Francis P. Farquhar. Berkeley, CA: University of California Press.

Bruff, J. Goldsborough, Read, Georgia Willis, & Gaines, Ruth (Eds.) (1949). *Gold rush: The journals, drawings and other papers of J. Goldsborough Bruff, April 2, 1849–July 20, 1851.* New York: Columbia University Press.

Burrill, Richard (1990). *Ishi: America's last stone age Indian.* Sacramento, CA: The Anthro Company.

Burrill, Richard (2001). *Ishi Rediscovered.* Sacramento, CA: The Anthro Company.

California (1851a). *Journals of the Legislature of the State of California, at its Second Session.* n.p.: Eugene Casserly.

California (1851b). *The Statutes of California.* Sacramento, CA: Eugene Casserly.

California Legislature (1852). *The Statutes of California passed at The Third Session of the Legislature begun on the fifth of January, 1852 and ended on the fourth day of May, 1852, at the cities of Vallejo and Sacramento.* San Francisco, CA: G.K. Fitsch & Co.

Carson, A. Thankful (1915). *Captured by the Mill Creek Indians: A true story of the capture of the Sam Lewis children in the year 1863.* Chico, CA: Author.

Collins, David, & Bergen, Kristin (2000). *Ishi: The last of his people.* Greensboro, NC: Morgan Reynolds.

Comptroller of California (n.d.). *Expenditures for military expeditions against Indians, 1851–1859.* Sacramento, CA: California State Archives.

Cook, Sherburne F. (1943). *The conflict between the California Indian and White civilization, III: The American invasion 1848–1870.* Berkeley, CA: University of California Press.

Cook, Sherburne F. (1976). *Population of the California Indians, 1769–1970.* Berkeley, CA: University of California Press.

Curtin, Jeremiah (1898). *Creation myths of primitive America in relation to the religious history and mental development of mankind.* Boston, MA: Little, Brown, and Company.

Delaney, Dan (1872, June 7). The adventures of Captain Hi Good. *The Northern Enterprise*, p. 1.

Dixon, Roland (1905). *The northern Maidu.* New York: Knickerbocker Press.

Dornin, May (1922). *The emigrant trails into California.* (Unpublished MA Thesis). Berkeley, CA: University of California at Berkeley.

Gudde, Erwin K. (1974). *California place names: The origin and etymology of current geographical names.* Berkeley, CA: University of California Press.

Heizer, Robert F. (1974). *They were only diggers: A collection of articles from California newspapers, 1851–1866, on Indian and white relations.* Ramona, CA: Ballena Press.

Heizer, Robert F., & Kroeber, Theodora (1979). *Ishi the last Yahi: A documentary history.* Berkeley, CA: University of California Press.

Johnson, Jerald Jay (1978). Yana. In William C. Sturtevant, (Ed.) *Handbook of North American Indians, Volume 8: California* (pp. 361–369). Washington, DC: Smithsonian Institution.

Kauffman, C.F. (*c.*1882). The Nosea Indians: A reminiscence of Sierra Township, Tehama County. In *Judge Herbert South Gans Scrapbook*, Tehama County Library, Red Bluff, California.

Kibbe, William (1860). *Report of the expedition against the Indians in the northern part of this state.* Sacramento, CA: Chas. T. Botts, State Printer.

Kroeber, Alfred (1925). *Handbook of the Indians of California.* Washington, DC: Government Printing Office.

Kroeber, Alfred (1972). *The Mill Creek Indians and Ishi.* Berkeley, CA: University of California Press.

Kroeber, Clifton, & Kroeber, Karl (Eds.) (2003). *Ishi in three centuries.* Lincoln, NE: University of Nebraska Press.

Kroeber, Theodora (1961). *Ishi in two worlds: A biography of the last wild Indian in North America.* Berkeley, CA: University of California Press.

McCarthy, Amanda (1998). Yana. In Sharon Malinowski, Anna Sheets, Jeffrey Lehman, & Melissa Doig (Eds.) *The Gale encyclopedia of Native American Tribes, Volume IV: California, Pacific Northwest, Pacific Islands.* Detroit, MI: Gale Research.

Madley, Benjamin (forthcoming). *American Genocide: The California Indian Catastrophe, 1846–1873*. New Haven, CT: Yale University Press.

Malinowski, Sharon, Sheets, Anna, Lehman, Jeffrey, & Doig, Melissa Walsh (Eds.) (1998). *The Gale encyclopedia of Native American tribes, Volume IV: California, Pacific Northwest, Pacific Islands*. Detroit, MI: Gale Research.

Martin, Oscar F. (1883). Pioneer sketches I: The Old Lassen Trail. *Overland Monthly and Out West Magazine, 2*(7), 74–82.

Moak, Sim (1923). *The last of the Mill Creeks and early life in northern California*. Chico, CA: no publisher.

Pope, Saxton (1920). The medical history of Ishi. *University of California Publications in Archaeology and Ethnology, 13*, 175–213.

Pope, Saxton (1932). *Ishi, the last of the Yanas*. Berkeley, CA: University of California Press.

Potter, Elijah Renshaw (n.d.). *Reminiscences of the early history of northern California and of the Indian troubles*. Berkeley, CA: University of California, Bancroft Library.

Powers, Stephen (1874). The California Indians, No. XI. *Overland Monthly and Out West Magazine, 12*, 412–424.

Rawls, James J. (1984). *Indians of California: The changing image*. Norman, OK: University of Oklahoma Press.

Rives, John (1861). *Congressional Globe ... Second Session of the Thirty-Sixth Congress*. Washington, DC: Blair and Rives.

Russell, Kent (dir.) (2008). *With the strength of our ancestors: The story of the Redding Rancheria* [Motion picture]. Redwood City, CA: Fat Box Films.

Sauber, H.H. (1897). True tales of the Old West, XV: Hi Good and the "Mill Creeks". *Overland Monthly and Out West Magazine, 30*, 122–127.

Schoonover, Steve (1994). Kibbe's campaign. *Dogtown Territorial Quarterly, 20*, 10–12, 45–49.

Shover, Michele (1999). The politics of the 1859 Bidwell–Kibbe campaign: Northern California Indian–settler conflicts of the 1850s. *Dogtown Territorial Quarterly, 38*, 4–37.

Southern, May Hazel (*c*.1942). *Our storied landmarks, Shasta County, California*. San Francisco, CA: P. Balakshin Printing Company.

Speaker, Stuart (2003). Repatriating the remains of Ishi. In Clifton Kroeber & Karl Kroeber (Eds.) *Ishi in three centuries* (pp. 73–86). Lincoln, NE: University of Nebraska Press.

Starn, Orin (2004). *Ishi's brain: In search of America's last "wild" Indian*. New York: W.W. Norton.

Stillson, Richard (2006). *Spreading the word: A history of information in the California Gold Rush*. Lincoln, NE: University of Nebraska Press.

Thornton, Russell (1987). *American Indian holocaust and survival: A population history since 1492*. Norman, OK: University of Oklahoma Press.

U.S. Office of Indian Affairs (1858). *Report of the Commissioner of Indian Affairs, accompanying the Annual Report of the Secretary of the Interior, for the year 1858*. Washington, DC: W.M.A. Harris, Printer.

U.S. Office of Indian Affairs (1860). *Report of the Commissioner of Indian Affairs, accompanying the Annual Report of the Secretary of the Interior, for the year 1859*. Washington, DC: George W. Bowman, Printer.

U.S. Office of Indian Affairs (1864). *Report of the Commissioner of Indian Affairs for the year 1863*. Washington, DC: Government Printing Office.

Waterman, T.T. (1915). The last wild tribe of California. *Popular Science Monthly*, March, 233–243.

Waterman, T.T. (1917). Ishi, the last Yahi Indian. *The Southern Workman, 46*, 528–537.

Waterman, T.T. (1918). The Yana Indians. *University of California Publications in American Archaeology and Ethnology, 13*(2), 35–102.

Wells, H.L., & Chandler, W.L. (1882). *The history of Butte County, California, in two volumes*. San Francisco, CA: Harry L. Wells.

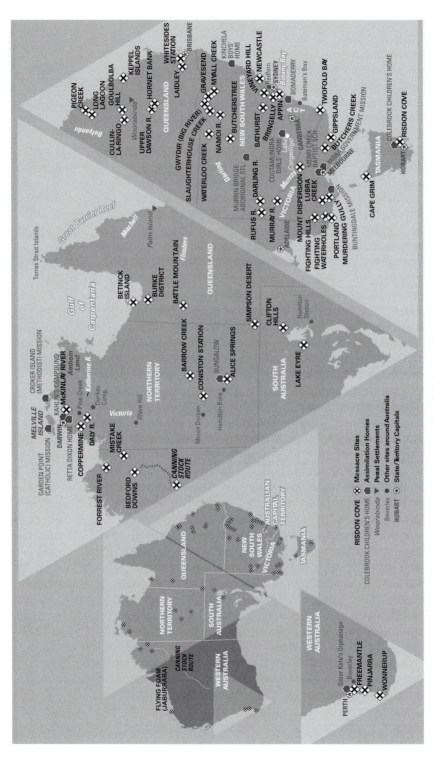

Map 2.1 Australia

CHAPTER 2

Genocide in Australia

COLIN TATZ

Australia has differed in more than a dozen ways from the more conventional cases of genocide—in its historical context, its system of governance, in time span, scale, pace, methods, nature of the perpetrators, the almost total absence of trials (apart from a few cases of murder), the defense of good intent motivating forcible child removals, the late admissions of responsibility, the even later apologies, the refusal (except in Tasmania) to consider reparations, and the nature of the denialism. This case also tells us something about the criminal acts defined in Article(s) II(b) and II(c) of the Convention on the Prevention and Punishment of the Crime of Genocide, and touches on complicity and conspiracy in genocide (Article III).

The Victims

Murdering individuals and eliminating small clans of Aborigines occurred between the early 1800s and the late 1920s, at first in dribs and drabs by private settlers who engaged in weekend massacres, and later by state police and special Native Police Forces, which, euphemistically, "dispersed kangaroos" (Article IIa). The forcible removal of Aboriginal children from their families and their ostensible assimilation into the mainstream began in the late 1830s and ended only in the late 1980s (Article IIe). Legal and geographic fences protected Aborigines by segregating them—usually on isolated reserves and remote church-run mission stations—from predators who wanted to kill them, or take their women, or abduct their children, or sell them opium when they needed labor or wanted sex. Protection-by-segregation began in Victoria in the late 1860s and continued across the continent from the turn of the century until 1973 (in theory). Raphael Lemkin, the coiner of the term "genocide" and the man who was largely responsible for pushing through the United Nations Convention on the Prevention and Punishment of the Crime of Genocide, would have judged such incarceration as a systematic "destruction of the essential foundations" of Aboriginal societies, and certainly as the "destruction of personal security, liberty, health, dignity and even the lives of individuals belonging to such groups" (Article(s) II(b), II(c); Lemkin, 1944, p. 79). The Aboriginal genocide is not one short, sharp, dramatic episode and no easily definable historical forces led to their attempted destruction.

The Victims: As Nuisance

Dehumanization of victims is common in most genocides. In Australia it has been more a matter of non- or un-humanization, more an enduring "insectification" and animalization of a people.

Visiting New Holland (Australia) in 1697, the English buccaneer and circumnavigator William Dampier noted that "the inhabitants of this country are the miserablest people in the World." When Captain Arthur Phillip's First Fleet arrived at Botany Bay [Sydney] in January 1788 to take possession for King George III, they adopted the noble savage view of a people [the Aborigines], between 500,000 and 750,000 in number, who had inhabited the continent for 60,000 years.

Despite early official efforts "to open an intercourse with the natives and to conciliate their goodwill," to "live in amity and kindness with them," relations were not good. The land was treated as a wasteland but for flora and fauna, of which the "natives" were deemed a part. The First-Fleeters could see no visible kings or tribal chiefs among the nomadic hunter-gatherers, no obvious reign of law, no judicial system, and worse, no John Lockean sense of property ownership or a capacity to till the soil—and so Australia was categorized, in the language of political anthropology, as a stateless society, peopled but with no [apparent] equivalent organs of governance.[1] Australia was thus regarded as a land of settlement rather than as a colony gained by conquest.

The killing era was as much about the removal of non-human pests as it was warfare resulting from a traditional colonial invasion and resistance to it. All layers of society regarded Aborigines as a separate species. For settlers, their targets were "troublesome wild animal[s] to be shot and hunted down," "vermin," "*ferae naturâ*," "creatures scarcely human," "hideous scandals to humanity," "loathsome," and "a nuisance," regarded as fair game for white "sportsmen" (Evans, Saunders, & Cronin, 1988, pp. 75–78).

In 1861 a select committee of the Queensland Legislative Assembly concluded that while there were "some excesses" of killing by police, there was credible evidence that the native people were "addicted to cannibalism," "had no idea of a future state," and "were sunk in the lowest depths of barbarism" (Loos, 1982, pp. 22–23). More than a few missionaries described these potential Christians as less than human, more as children of darkness. In the 1870s, a Queensland clergyman wrote that "if our instincts are true we must loathe the Aborigines as they are now because they are less estimable than the mongrels that prowl like them in the offal of a station [cattle ranch]" (Evans et al., 1988, p. 85). A Northern Territory Lutheran missionary defended locking up Aboriginal youth in dormitories due to their "utter rottenness in things sexual," he declared. "No white man has any conception ... what depths of infamy these blacks are steeped in" (DeMayo, 1990, p. 97). Not all mission views were as odious; some regarded Aborigines as human, albeit heathen, and as perpetual children in need of supervision, even as late as the 1970s.

The Victims: As Embarrassment and Menace

The colony of Victoria began programs of forced assimilation, child "retention" and separation as early as the 1830s.[2] After the Victorian Aborigines Act of 1869, jurisdictions across Australia assumed the power to remove children of mixed descent to absorb them either culturally or physically into the general population and thus end their Aboriginality. The movement gained momentum after the 1920s and lasted a further three generations. New South Wales closed Kinchela Boys' Home in 1970; South Australia closed Colebrook Children's Home in 1972; the Retta Dixon Home in the Northern Territory ceased in 1980; Western Australia closed its major "assimilation home," Sister Kate's Orphanage, in 1987; and the last such mission institution in New South Wales, Bomaderry, shut down in 1988. For over a century, between 20,000 and 35,000 children—often the progeny of Aboriginal women and white cattle station workers, crop-growers, miners, and adventurers—were taken away. In Northern Australia, "yellafellas" [as mixed-race Aborigines were called] were embarrassments to white society and were quickly taken to institutions to be weaned of their Aboriginality. Private shame became a cornerstone of state and federal administrators. White Australians always assumed that their culture and color genes were the stronger of the two groups, and that any degree of "white blood" made Aboriginal children more likely to survive biologically and more salvageable for cleanliness, Christianity, and civilization. In southern Australia, children of part-descent Aboriginal parents were removed from their homes.

In 1909 the Chief Protector in Western Australia, Charles F. Gale, quoted one of his traveling Protectors, Inspector James Isdell, as follows:

> The half-caste is intellectually above the aborigine, and it is the duty of the State that they be given a chance to lead a better and purer life than their brothers. I would not hesitate for one moment to separate any half-caste from its Aboriginal mother, no matter how frantic her momentary grief might be at the time. They soon forget their offspring. (Quoted in Haebich, 2000, p. 233)

Continuing, Isdell noted, it was but "maudlin sentiment" to leave children with their Aboriginal mothers: "They forget their children in twenty-four hours and as a rule [were] glad to be rid of them" (quoted in Haebich, 2000, p. 233).

Cameron Raynes (2009) cites an "unequivocal statement" by the South Australian State Children's Council in 1911 of the intent to "put an end to Aboriginality" or at least significant manifestations of it—the kinship relationships, communality and reciprocity systems, birth, circumcision and mourning rituals, earlier than "normal" sexual development, and color (if possible). It proposed removal of "half-caste, quadroon and octoroon" children, paying "special attention" to the girls: "prompt action [is needed] in order to prevent the growth of a race that would rapidly increase in numbers, attain a maturity without education or religion, and become a menace to the morals and health of the community" (Raynes, 2009, pp. 2–13).

The Perpetrators: As Killers

Nineteenth-century killing was so rampant and eliminationist in intent that the colony of Queensland was pressed to introduce the world's first statute to protect a people from genocide: The Aboriginals Protection and Restriction of the Sale of Opium Act of 1897. The British High Commissioner for New Zealand and the Pacific, Arthur Hamilton Gordon, was a reliable witness as to what was taking place in Australia. In 1883 he wrote to his friend, the British Prime Minister William Gladstone:

> The habit of regarding the natives as vermin, to be cleared off the face of the earth, has given the average Queenslander a tone of brutality and cruelty in dealing with "blacks" which it is very difficult to anyone who does not *know* it, as I do, to realize ... men of culture and refinement, of the greatest humanity and kindness

> to their fellow whites ... talk not only of the *wholesale* butchery
> ... but of the *individual* murder of natives, exactly as they would
> talk of a day's sport, or having to kill some troublesome animal.
> (Evans et al., 1988, p. 78)

The mass killings were committed initially by private settlers, squatters, and former convicts, with the colonial [later, state] authorities complicit as bystanders. Native Police Forces, described by historian Henry Reynolds as "the most violent organization[s] in Australian history," had white officers and black troops (Moore, 1993, p. 92). The Native Police Force system was introduced into colony Victoria in 1837 and disbanded in 1853. New South Wales initiated such a force in 1848, and massacres ensued. Queensland followed suit in 1859: the Black Police, with 22 white officers and 120 Aboriginal troops, were disbanded in 1900 following its record of butchery. The Northern Territory force, headed by William Willshire, also began systematic attacks, but following Willshire's acquittal of murder, it was disarmed in 1891. Such forces may have been essential as a buffer between ruthless (and frightened) settlers and Aboriginal clans, but their dedication to butchery rather than to mere reprisal, to killing rather than to "refereeing," led to their disbandment.

Not every settler was like Gordon's cruel and brutal "average Queenslander." There was a small humanitarian minority, illustrated by the work of a few men like Archibald Meston. In 1896 the Queensland Colonial Secretary appointed him as Special Commissioner to investigate the Aboriginal condition. "Men and women [were] hunted like wild beasts," he wrote; "kidnapping of women and nameless outrages were reported"; in 25 years, one tribe of 3,000 "was down to 100 survivors" as a result of "the old style of 'dispersal'"; "boys and girls were frequently taken from their parents ... with no chance of returning"; and "the Mosman [district] blacks had been exterminated [all of which, he wrote was] a reproach to our common humanity" (Meston, 1896, pp. 722–735). The "only way to arrest their destruction," to "save any part of the race from extinction," was to abolish the Native Police Force, ban opium ("this detestable drug") and ensure the "absolute isolation" from the whites who, "coloured by prejudice, distorted by ignorance," committed "shameful deeds" (Meston, 1896, pp. 733–735).

Despite Queensland's new strict isolation policy, a Scot named McKenzie obtained a government lease over Bentinck Island in the Gulf of Carpentaria in 1911. The Kaiadilt population was probably 100, yet by 1918 McKenzie and his posse had eliminated the tribe by gun, rape, and the use of galloping horses to drive people into the sea (Elder, 1998, pp. 203–206; Kelly & Evans, 1985, pp. 44–52).

Between 1860 and 1895 there was massive population loss in Central Australia, then administered by South Australia. Possibly 20% of Aborigines may have died from diseases not previously encountered, but some 1,750 people, or 40% of the Aboriginal population in the Alice Springs region, were mostly shot in what was called "dispersal" (Kimber, 1997, pp. 43–44). Native Police were now among the perpetrators. Giving evidence in 1861, a Queensland Native Police lieutenant was asked what he meant by dispersing. "Firing at them," was his reply, but "I gave strict orders not to shoot any gins [Aboriginal women].... It is a general order that, whenever there are large assemblages of blacks, it is the duty of an officer to disperse them" (Kimber, 1997, p. 43).

In 1928 Aborigines killed a white bushman, Fred Brooks, near Coniston Station in Central Australia. A punitive expedition, under Mounted Constable William Murray and his cattleman friend William John Morton, killed a great number of Aborigines, certainly between 60 and 70, but the police, who were exonerated on the grounds of self-defense, admitted to killing "only 17" (Elder, 1998, pp. 177–191). A three-man Board of Enquiry was initiated only because reports of the massacres had appeared in the British press. One member was J.C. Cawood, Resident Governor and Police Commissioner in Central Australia and the man who had given Murray a free hand to deal with Brooks' killers. The Board "almost by chance" found that 31 had died (Cribbin, 1984, p. 156). While there was critical reaction to this episode in Southern Australia, popular sentiment was with Murray; he was "the hero of Central Australia.... He rides alone and always gets his man," proclaimed an Adelaide paper (Cribbin, 1984, p. 165).

Western Australia was little different, except that it had no Native Police Force. There were numerous private massacres between the first colonial settlement and the 1920s; the last of the official punitive expeditions, the Forrest River killings in 1926, was the only episode to result in a Royal Commission. The outcome was typical for the most part—the acquittal (and the promotion) of the two (regular) police officers allegedly involved in the shooting of perhaps 100 people and the burning of many corpses (Elder, 1998, pp. 168–176; Green, 1995).

Frontier massacres were episodic and sporadic, resulting in between a dozen and ten dozen dead at a time—more eliminationist than simply punitive in intent—for stealing livestock or spearing cattle ranchers, bushmen, miners, and men who took Aboriginal women.[3] Loos (2007) cites the *Cooktown Courier* in 1878 as reporting on "our present fitful scheme of haphazard little massacres [in] north Queensland" (p. 24). The Battle of Pinjarra in Western Australia in 1834 was designated a punitive expedition, one of 10 such at the time in Western Australia, with some 80 Aboriginal men killed and eight women and children captured (Horton, 1994, p. 111). In the Burke district of north Queensland, Sub-inspector Uhr, in charge of both the regular and Native Police, won applause for his ruthless reprisals for Aboriginal stock theft. In 1868 he killed 59 Aborigines in retaliation for the slaughter of several horses (Loos, 1982, pp. 36–37). In 1884 Aborigines in the Northern Territory killed four miners in retaliation for the taking of their women, in what were known as the Coppermine Murders or Daly River Murders. The death toll at the hands of a private party was 150 Aborigines; despite an outcry from the southern-based press, the local Palmerston [Darwin] press applauded the actions and a local board of inquiry said it could find no proof that anyone was killed (Horton, 1994, p. 229).

Very rarely did a colony (or state) prosecute white killers. John Kirby, a convict, was hanged in 1820 for the murder of Burragong ("King Jack"), an important leader, in Newcastle. Twelve stockmen and hut keepers murdered 28 Aborigines at Myall Creek in New South Wales in 1838. After the intervention of Governor Gipps, seven of the accused were retried after their initial acquittal and then hanged. This drama and the ensuing executions caused a huge uproar in Sydney (Reece, 1974, pp. 140–174; Millis, 1995, pp. 322–371). Emotional responses to the seven executions are still evident, as shown in anger at the unveiling in June 2000 of a memorial to the Myall Creek Aboriginal victims (rather than to their killers) and the vandalizing of the boulder and plaque in 2005.

Another vengeful Scot, Angus McMillan, "decided to teach the Kurnai a lesson in frontier law." He and his posse of stockmen killed 50–60 Kurnai [Aborigines] in Victoria's Gippsland. With something more than irony, McMillan later became a member of the Victorian Legislative Assembly and a Protector of Aborigines, a man the *Australian Dictionary of Biography*[4] describes as taking "a sympathetic interest in the welfare of the Aborigines."

The Tasmanian story is legendary, though not always accurate. Most texts regard Truganini, who died in 1876, as the last Tasmanian. Truganini's mother was killed and one of her sisters was abducted by sealhunters who, together with whaling men, were the major perpetrators of massacres in that colony. That there was genocidal intent, which sometimes failed to come to fruition, and that there was genocidal massacre, is not in scholarly dispute, except by Keith Windschuttle (2000, 2002, 2010), whose two volumes on denial have been described by accredited historians as naïve, filtered, manipulated, biased, and "an exercise in incomprehension." There was certainly acknowledged conspiracy in Tasmania, much government complicity, and a serious attempt at extermination: fruition or completion of the intent is not the issue. There was some rescue, there were survivors, and today there are 17,000 descendants of that era.

The Perpetrators: As Eugenicists

The protection-segregation era (the late 1890s to the mid-1970s) stopped much of the killing phase, but it gave momentum to child removal. Several key state bureaucrats—C.F. Gale, Dr. W.E. Roth in the early years of the 20th century, followed by A.O. Neville in the West, J.W. Bleakley in Queensland and Dr. Cecil Cook in the Northern Territory, and a few years later William Penhall in South Australia—were educated men and doubtless aware of the eugenicist principles prevalent in Europe and the United States. Ultimately, they consummated their ideas at a national summit in Canberra in 1937: "The destiny of the natives of Aboriginal origin, but not of full blood, lies in their ultimate absorption by the people of the Commonwealth and it is therefore recommended that all efforts shall be directed to this end" (Tatz, 2003, pp. 88–94). These men never defined absorption, but the kernel of their ideas was physical distance from tribal kin and, hopefully, disappearance of color.

Neville presented a three-point plan. First, keep "full-bloods" in reserves where they were destined to die out. Second, take all "half-castes" away from their mothers. Third, control marriages so that "pleasant, placid, complacent, strikingly attractive, auburn-haired and rosy-freckled" quarter- and half-blood Aboriginal maidens would marry into the white community. It would then be possible to "eventually forget that there were ever any Aborigines in Australia" (Beresford & Omaji, 1998, pp. 30–34, 47–52). "The native," Neville concluded,

> must be helped in spite of himself! … Even if a measure of discipline is necessary it must be applied, but it can be applied in such a way as to appear to be gentle persuasion … the end in view will justify the means employed. (quoted in Haebich, 2000, p. 259)

Dr. Cecil Bryan made the following recommendation to the 1934 Moseley Royal Commission regarding the treatment of Western Australian Aborigines: "I am come to the Commission to ask that steps be taken to breed out the half-caste, not in a moment, but in a few generations, and not by force but by science" (quoted in Haebich, 1988, p. 320).

Some of these ideas/suggestions became official practices. When the "full-blood" people in isolated reserves didn't die out, some reserves after 1937 were phased out but dozens of new ones were established and older ones reinforced by tougher regulations. Coaxed (or even coerced) Christian marriages were never going to succeed but child removal by policemen and other officials became the order of the day. Run by government staff and by mission agencies, "assimilation homes"—in the form of residential schools, dormitories, hostels, and welfare institutions—flourished. Several were in urban domains, some in settled rural areas, but most were in remote Australia.

Whatever justifications were offered before 1949, there can be no exoneration of forcible child removal once Australia ratified the UN Genocide Convention in June 1949. Ultimately, the saga of the stolen generations (the term now in regular use) came into some public discussion in the 1980s, but in 1981 historian Peter Read brought the phrase into Australia's political vocabulary. That "dissociating the children from [native] camp life must eventually solve the Aboriginal problem" was official New South Wales practice (quoted in Read, 1981, p. 7). To leave them where they were, "in comparative idleness in the midst of more or less vicious surroundings," the government claimed, would be "an injustice to the children themselves, and a positive menace to the State" (quoted in Read, 1981, p. 7). Read found 5,625 removals in that jurisdiction between 1883 and 1969. Until 1939 there was never any investigation of individual children or families, only wholesale generalization. In the columns headed, "Reasons for [Aborigines Welfare] Board Taking Control of the Child," the great majority carried this standard, handwritten entry: "For being Aboriginal" (Read, 1981, p. 6). After 1939, removals in that state required a hearing before a magistrate.

The Long-term Consequences and Impacts

Given that an estimated 500,000 people in 1788 had been reduced by various means to an official figure of only 30,758 (or 83,588 according to some sources) at the 1911 census, protection was crucial (Tatz, 2003, pp. 74–76). Settler-introduced diseases—particularly chickenpox, influenza, measles, syphilis, smallpox, and tuberculosis—radically reduced native populations, but guns and poisons, arsenic in particular, were certainly major causes of death. Historian Richard Broome warned that while "the statistics of frontier violence are certain to be inaccurate," it is likely that 20,000 Aborigines were killed Australia-wide (quoted in Attwood & Foster, 2003, pp. 96–97).

Elementary protection began in New South Wales as early as 1814, Victoria in 1837, South Australia in 1850, and Western Australia in 1844 and again in 1886. Queensland's 1897 statute spurred protection by segregation in other colonies: Western Australia (1905), New South Wales (1909), South Australia and the Northern Territory (1911), and Tasmania (1912). When legal cocoons were insufficient, some attempts were made to deal with Aborigines in their own domains, but all too often they were administered on remote and large reservations, or confined to government-run settlements and church-run mission stations, some of which began as early as 1820 in New South Wales, 1839 in South Australia and Victoria, 1845 in Western Australia, 1866 in Queensland, and 1886 in the Northern Territory. Often enough these almost inaccessible domains were not Aboriginal choices or places of their natural habitation. Many sites in North Queensland, Central Australia, Arnhem Land, and the Kimberley region of Western Australia were, to use one mission society's phrase, "splendidly secluded" or, as Meston noted, "foolishly selected situations" (DeMayo, 1990, p. 53; Meston, 1896, p. 734). They were seen as places where "the Christian Church and the Government can but play the part of physicians and nurses in a hospital for incurables" (DeMayo, 1990, pp. 31–32). The reality was that few of these "hospices"—also said to be refuges for "the untouched natives"— were places of continuing kindness and gentleness. They certainly arrested population decline but their general thrust was cultural suppression and harsh discipline.

Following federation of the six colonies in 1901, Aborigines were essentially a state matter, and policies and practices were not uniform. Queensland's rigid control began in 1897 and only ended in 1985 after national condemnation (Nettheim, 1981). The Northern Territory, the only specifically federal jurisdiction, introduced special laws in 1911 and repealed most of them by 1971. Emancipatory policy ideals about assimilation and equality were announced in 1951, and again in 1961 and 1965, but it took another two to three decades for the "protection" statutes to be abolished. Until then, Aborigines, as defined, were under legal guardianship, wards of the state, minors in law, specifically denied civil rights, social welfare entitlements, and most of the benefits inherent and explicit in the rule of law (Tatz, 1963, 1964a, 1964b, 1966).

Quintessentially nomadic hunter-gatherers became sedentary and stationary. Usually, they couldn't leave without permission, or sell their labor in free markets. They couldn't work for the minimum wage prescribed by the wage arbitration system. In the Northern Territory, one-third of the Aboriginal population were born, lived, and worked on cattle stations in a labor-for-rations symbiosis typical of British colonial systems; the other two-thirds on settlements and missions received rations and a "pocket-money" component of their "special" wage allocation (Tatz, 1964a, 1966; Rowse, 1998). Where actual remuneration was paid, these monies went into state-run trust funds, much of which disappeared, as in Queensland. (In 2002 that state initiated a "stolen wages" reparations program.) Nor could "full-blood" people join essentially racist trade unions.

In most jurisdictions Aborigines couldn't marry non-Aborigines without permission; nor could they have sex (at least lawfully) across the color line. Pubescent girls were locked in dormitories to circumvent the traditional bride-promissory system. The power of elders to settle disputes or administer tribal punishments was limited or prohibited. Queensland officials sent "trouble-makers" to even more remote penal settlements like Palm Island and Woorabinda, most often without wives and children, with no rights of appeal and no time limits on their exile (Tatz, 1963, pp. 33–49).

Aborigines couldn't vote in federal elections until 1962, or in some state elections (for example, Queensland) until 1965. They couldn't drink or have access to alcohol. In Queensland they could be imprisoned—for up to three weeks at a time—on settlements and missions for crimes no other Australian could commit, such as playing cards, being cheeky, refusing to work, committing adultery, or refusing to give fecal samples (Tatz, 1963). In Western Australia Aborigines were punished for being untidy, chopping down trees, or wasting water. There were no appeals and there was no outside oversight mechanisms in place. Eligible in theory, Aborigines were not paid their social welfare entitlements; instead, such monies were plowed into state treasuries, mission societies, or to cattlemen who "maintained" the Aborigines on their properties (Tatz, 1963, 1964a).

Remote populations had no access to, and no involvement with, normal civic institutions. Generally, administrators were under-educated and untrained people who could obtain employment (and status) only where the clients were Aboriginal. Missionaries worked in locations where governments would not and so they became agencies of government. In most states they were delegated the same draconian powers as government officials, and given authority to act as civic authorities normally do, providing employment, food, education, housing, health services, roads, airstrips, buildings, sewage and garbage-disposal facilities, safe water, electricity—and justice. They had license to govern in a way not found in mission work anywhere else in the world and they were, to put it mildly, way out of their pastoral depths.

Here, indeed, was another universe for "inmates" who had committed no crimes, a separated, inferior legal class of people, perpetual wards of the state (and church), geographically remote, under special laws that prescribed codes of conduct, with special private "courts" in some domains; the "missions" were administered by officials, priests, and police in secrecy, with visitors unwelcome and required to have a good reason, written permission, and recent chest X-rays for entry. This system of a separate, secretive, and mistrustful Aboriginal administration certainly saved people from murder and it did arrest the decline of Aboriginal populations. But, with bitter irony, saving lives did not stop the removal of mixed-race children from their families and it destroyed much of the fabric of Aboriginal societies.

Over the years, Aborigines have survived almost every conceivable depredation, and today number some 455,028 people.[5] But the impacts of these strict policies, their sudden cessation in the 1970s with very little administrative support or guidance, left many communities floundering. This all too sudden "autonomy" now manifests daily in abnormally high rates of family and social breakdown, internal (and external) violence, disease prevalence and incidence, early deaths, educational deficit, astounding youth suicide rates, and grossly disproportionate incarceration in state institutions such as prisons (Tatz, 1990, 2005).

Responses and Reactions: The Aborigines

The Link-Up movement to find lost children, siblings, and parents began in 1981. By then, finding and reuniting removed family members with their families had become the single-most important issue in Aboriginal life. Strident Aboriginal voices persuaded the federal Labor government to initiate an inquiry into "the separation by compulsion" of Aboriginal children from their families. "Separation" in the terms of reference inferred that some reuniting was envisaged. That was never the intention of most of the removers: Children were to be separated forever from their Aboriginality.

The Australian government report, *Bringing Them Home* (HREOC, 1997), was something of a bestseller: "A finding of genocide was presented: the essence of the crime was acting with the intention of destroying the group, not the extent to which that intention was achieved" (pp. 270–275). The removals were intended to "absorb," "merge," and "assimilate" the children "so that Aborigines as a distinct group would disappear" (HREOC, 1997, pp. 270–275). Much of the ongoing hostility to these findings has arisen from people who insist that genocide is, and can only be, the footage we see of the Bergen-Belsen bulldozing of corpses, striped "creatures" hanging on the wire at Auschwitz, and serried skulls in the Tuol Sleng Genocide Museum in Cambodia.

Several former officials involved in the removals have admitted that while the practices were based on the notion of the rescuability of "half-caste" children, the removals were "for their own good" and not done heartlessly: "Many of the children taken away were being given a chance to live and not die, to have a life beyond childhood without being permanently maimed" (Macleod, 1997, pp. 165–176). A widespread fallacy, even among scholars, is that *motive* is synonymous with *intent*. Given the proximity of the Holocaust to the UN Convention on Genocide, "with intent to destroy" is often incorrectly assumed as meaning intent with *male fides*, bad faith, evil intent. But nowhere does the UN Convention on Genocide distinguish or define the kind of intent needed to commit acts of genocide. A pertinent legal view is that "it can be (mis-guidedly) committed 'in the interests' of a protected population" (Storey, 1997, pp. 11–14). Or, as the moral philosopher Raimond Gaita (1997, p. 21) contends, "the concept of good intention cannot be relativized indefinitely to an agent's perception of it as good." If we could, he argues, then we would have to say that Nazi murderers had good, but radically benighted, intentions, because most of them believed they had a sacred duty to the world to rid the world of the "race" that polluted it.

That some purported "good" has come out of these practices, and that many removed children have made outstanding contributions to society as activists, professionals, writers, artists, and sportspeople, is not really an issue in this context. Hindsight speculations are, in reality, pleas about the need to understand the times, the places, and the deeds, about mitigation, leavening the negatives with positives, and a seeking of alle-viation of both responsibility and accountability, none of which is acceptable.

Responses and Reactions: The Denialists

In genocide studies the terms denialism and denialist are not used as a polemical category or as shorthand for disordered personalities. Denial(ism), as sociologist Stanley Cohen argues (2001), is about "the politics of ethnic amnesia," essentially assertion (rather than demonstra-tion) that "it didn't happen; it happened too long ago to prove; the facts are open to different interpretations; what happened was not genocide" (pp. 12–13). Australia is a curious case. From time to time, one or another specific massacre—such as at Forrest River—is denied. Keith Windschuttle (2002, 2010) has written extensively (in his privately owned Macleay Press) about "the fabrication of Aboriginal history" in Tasmania and elsewhere, concentrating his efforts on what he calls the lack of integrity and the mistaken or dubious footnotes of several histo-rians in order to sustain his case. If genocide occurred, he argues, it was somehow warranted by the behavior of the natives in attacking settlers or killing livestock for food.

More commonly, denialism focuses on child removal. Windschuttle (2002, 2010), anthropologist Ron Brunton (1998), businessman John Dawson (2004), a handful of retired civil servants and politicians, and an ardent but small coterie of senior newspaper journalists and commercial radio talkback comperes contend, inter alia, that removal "was good for them"; "it was just like boarding school"; "look how many Aborigines from that kind of background are successful"; "it was all a case of false memory syndrome and it never happened in the first place"; and that the national enquiry report was nothing but "unsupported hyperbole," a document that "well and truly took the quality media for a ride" (McGuinness, 2001; Sheehan, 2010).

Political scientist Robert Manne (2003) sees this small coterie engaging in a "right-wing and populist" resistance campaign to counter "discussions of historical injustice" (p. 134). Separation of mother and child "deeply captured the national imagination" (Manne, 2003, p. 134). The stolen generations story had the power to change forever the way they saw their country's history—hence, the imperative by some to destroy that story (Manne, 2001, p. 134; 2003). He is right, in the main. The "debate" is very much about the inclusiveness of Australia's ethnic nationalism, its egalitarian virtues and heroic deeds; it is a brazen attempt at an affirmation of Australian decency and morality in the face of the judicial injustices that transported them from Britain in the first instance. In short, the denialists argue, democratic colonists don't have a dark side and simply didn't and don't do things like this.

Responses and Reactions: Governments, Apologies, and Law Suits

The prevailing tenor in the 1990s and early 2000s was that the present generation cannot be held guilty or responsible for the misdeeds (if any) of our forebears. The first public admission by a senior government figure was made in 1992 when Prime Minister Paul Keating's speech in the Sydney suburb of Redfern admitted the taking of their traditional lands, the murders, dispossessions, the introduction of alcohol, diseases, the taking of children from their mothers, the smashing of traditional life and their exclusion from society and its benefits (Moores, 1995, pp. 377–382). Between 1997 and 2000, state and territory governments (except the Northern Territory), most police forces, almost all churches and mission societies, many city and shire councils, proclaimed both sorrow and apology for general treatment of Aborigines and, on occasion, for specific forcible removals of children.

The outstanding exception was John Howard's federal coalition (conservative) government (1996–2007). Howard was adamant that for the nation to say sorry was to open the way for costly compensation claims. Nor, he said, could he apologize on behalf of migrant groups who had nothing to do with these events. He wanted Australians to "feel relaxed and comfortable about their past," he didn't wish to wake up each day to hear that Australia has had "a racist, bigoted past," and, accordingly, he would attempt a national school history program that accentuated "positive achievements." Despite his offer of a personal apology, his government was steadfast about any official acknowledgment of these events (Tatz, 2003, pp. 164–170).

But then, in November 2007, the Australian Labor Party won the election and Prime Minister Kevin Rudd set about issuing a national apology. On February 13, 2008, the nation came close to a standstill as the national apology was televised from federal Parliament for several hours (Hansard, February 13, 2008):

> We apologise for the laws and policies of successive Parliaments and governments that have inflicted profound grief, suffering and loss on these our fellow Australians.
>
> We apologise especially for the removal of Aboriginal and Torres Strait Islander children from their families, their communities and their country.
>
> For the pain, suffering and hurt of these Stolen Generations, their descendants and for their families left behind, we say sorry.
>
> To the mothers and the fathers, the brothers and the sisters, for the breaking up of families and communities, we say sorry.
>
> And for the indignity and degradation thus inflicted on a proud people and a proud culture, we say sorry.

Such theater was made all the grander by the strident intransigence of the former government. When state and local governments apologized years earlier, the press notices were there, recognized but somewhat muted. The delayed and therefore much-awaited national apology was climactic and, in a real sense, a *tremendum* in the national psyche.

A dramatic day—yet everyone (with the exception of the Aboriginal community, of course) was happy enough that the rider to the apology was that there would be no reparations. That kind of money, said the government, could be better spent elsewhere. Ironically, Tasmania alone has initiated financial restitution. In January 2008, the then Premier Paul Lennon declared that the lives of 106 claimants had been "deeply affected by this flawed policy of separation." Of the 106 claimants, 84 were paid approximately $A55,000 each and each family of deceased claimants received approximately $A4,700.

The Australian public were more generous. Many more people accepted the *Bringing Them Home* (HREOC, 1997) findings than rejected them (HREOC, 1999, pp. 27–47). Hundreds of thousands were prompted to sign "sorry books" located in public places; thousands stood in lines to listen to removed children telling their stories; many more thousands planted small wooden hands on lawns and beaches, signifying guilt or sorrow; and even more thousands marched in solidarity across major city bridges.

Several of the stolen generations have resorted to civil law in search of recognition of their experience and compensation for their usually troubled lives. Two dozen cases have been heard in various jurisdictions.

Most have focused on sexual assaults while incarcerated, or on breaches of fiduciary care, arguing that state or territory administrations had, by removing them, not cared for them appropriately. Most have lost on technicalities and several have cost enormous sums (Cunneen & Grix, 2004). But it is important to note that not one case has sought to establish *directly* that forcible child transfer is the essence of Article II(e).

The federal government spent $A15–$A20 million defending one case alone (brought by Lorna Cubillo and Peter Gunner, both removed at eight years of age) in the Northern Territory (Rush, 2008, p. 30). In 2007 South Australia's Supreme Court awarded Bruce Trevorrow $A525,000 for being treated unlawfully and falsely imprisoned when he was removed from his mother at the age of 13 months, and handed to a white family in 1957. Unsurprisingly, following his death soon after, the South Australian government has appealed the verdict "vigorously."

Lessons and Judgments

The genocide issue in Australia has come a long way in a very short time. In 1873 a visiting English writer, Anthony Trollope, observed that "we have massacred them [the Aborigines] when they defended themselves," "and taught them by hard warfare to acknowledge us as their master" (Trollope, 1873, pp. 134–142). It took exactly another 100 years for local historians to begin to deal with massacres and the inglorious past.

Genocide (and genocide in Australia) is now in the political lexicon in Australia, causing anger, dismay, and, inevitably, some denialism. Historian Geoffrey Blainey (1993) coined the phrase "the Black Armband view of history" in 1993, meaning that "the pendulum has swung too far" in the direction of the "decidedly jaundiced," that is, those who now vilify those who once vilified Aborigines and who make "mischievous statements" that Aboriginal numbers were drastically reduced primarily by slaughter (rather than by disease) (pp. 11, 15). There was no historical clock and no pendulum before the 1970s. That there was no desire, let alone a need, to look at the hard facts in regard to how the Aboriginals were treated was partly because of a strong belief that Australian-ness is an inherent prophylactic against, or an antidote to, such bad, homicidal, let alone genocidal, behavior. Breaches of human rights are strongly denied on this ground.

Facing UN criticism, a recent foreign minister, Alexander Downer, argued that Australia can't possibly breach international treaties on child, sex, and race discrimination *because* we are Australians. Australians inhabit "the land of the fair go," the continent of mateship and egalitarianism, people who regard themselves as decent colonists and quintessential democrats (Australian Broadcast Corporation, 2000).

Leslie Haylen, a Labor member of federal parliament, was indignant about ratifying the Genocide Convention in June 1949:

> the horrible crime of genocide is unthinkable in Australia.... That we detest all forms of genocide ... arises from the fact that we are a moral people.... The fact that we have a clean record allows us to take such an attitude. (cited in Hansard, 1949, p. 1871)

His conservative Liberal Party colleague, Archie Cameron, said: "No one in his right senses believes that the Commonwealth of Australia will be called before the bar of public opinion ... and asked to answer for any of the things which are enumerated in this convention" (cited in Hansard, 1949, p. 1876).

Haylen and Cameron were wrong. Australia's behavior is now before the bar of public opinion, on the international conference table, in a growing number of museums, in a small raft of university courses, in the high-school syllabi, and in books such as this one. Genocide is now so much more than thinkable.

Eyewitness Accounts

Direct survivor testimony of the early killing eras in Australia is rare. We have to rely on comments by a handful of perpetrators, a few sympathetic whites, official investigators like Archibald Meston, memoirs of early settlers and squatters, and newspaper correspondents. There was no strict chronology of killing, no systematic or schematic violence within short time frames, and so the excerpts here indicate the haphazard nature of Australia's little and not so little massacres.

Nineteenth-century Aboriginal societies had no written language and provided no evidence of their lives in English. Some drawings and paintings attest to events. Aborigines had, and still have, an extraordinary oral history tradition. A vigorous emancipatory identity movement in the late 1960s led Aborigines who had been removed, incarcerated, adopted, or fostered to reclaim their lives and families. From the 1970s, people began to speak on their own behalf, and by the 1990s there was a sufficient body of Aboriginal writing to constitute a powerful literature on their specific removal experience.

The Frontiers: 1816 to 1897

Account 1

Indiscriminate killing was occasionally mixed with regret and apology. In his journal dated April 17, 1816, Captain James Wallis of the 46th

Regiment, discussed the massacres in the Appin-Cow Pastures, Bringelly district south of Sydney (quoted in Elder, 1998, pp. 24–25):

> A little after one o'clock a.m. we marched. Noble joined us, and led us where he had seen the natives encamped. The fires were burning, but deserted. We feared they had heard us and were fled.
>
> A few of my men who wandered on heard a child cry. I formed line ranks ... the dogs gave the alarm and the natives fled over the cliffs. A smart firing now ensued. It was moonlight. The grey dawn of the moon appearing so dark as to be able early to discover their figures bounding from rock to rock.
>
> Before marching from Quarters I had ordered my men to take as many prisoners as possible, and to be careful in sparing and saving the women and children. My principal efforts were now directed to this purpose. I regret to say some had been shot and others met their fate by rushing in despair over the precipice. I was however partly successful—I led up two women and three children. They were all that remained, to whom death would not be a blessing.
>
> Twas a melancholy but necessary duty I was employed upon. Fourteen dead bodies were counted in different directions....

Account 2

This succinct comment appeared in the *Colonial Times and Tasmanian Advertiser* in June 1832 (Elder, 1998, p. 41):

> [T]he custom that has been almost universal among certain Settlers and their servants whenever the Natives have visited their neighbourhood, to consider the men as wild beasts whom it was praiseworthy to hunt down and destroy and the women as only fit to be used for the worst of purposes. The shooting of blacks is spoken of as a matter of levity.

Account 3

The next excerpt is taken from the journals and papers of George Augustus Robinson, the controversial Englishman who attempted to conciliate the Tasmanian Aboriginal–settler "Black War of 1827–1830" (quoted by Reynolds (1982, p. 83):

> They [the Aboriginals] have a tradition amongst them that white men have usurped their territory, have driven them into the

forests, have killed their game ... have ravished their wives and daughters, have murdered and butchered their fellow country-men; and are wont whilst brooding over these complicated ills in the dense part of the forest, to goad each other on to acts of bloodshed and revenge for the injuries done to their ancestors and the persecutions offered to themselves through their white enemies.

Account 4

Henry Melville, a respected author and editor, published *The History of Van Diemen's Land* [Tasmania] *from the Year 1824 to 1835, Inclusive, During the Administration of Lieutenant-Governor George Arthur*, in 1835. In the following excerpt he summarizes the plight of the Tasmanian Aborigines (quoted by Elder, 1998, p. 29):

> These poor bewildered creatures have been treated worse than were any of the American tribes by the Spaniards. Easy, quiet, good-natured and well-disposed toward the white population they could no longer brook the treatment they received from the invaders of their country. Their hunting grounds were taken from them, and they themselves were driven like trespassers from the favourite spots for which their ancestors had bled and had claimed by conquest.... The stock-keepers may be considered as the destroyers of nearly the whole of the Aborigines—the proper, legitimate owners of the soil: these miscreants so imposed upon their docility, that at length they thought little or nothing of destroying the men for the sake of carrying to their huts the females of the tribes; and if it were possible ... to record but little of the murders committed on these poor harmless creatures it would make the reader's blood run cold at their recital.

Account 5

In May 1836, Major Thomas Mitchell, Surveyor-General of New South Wales, together with his convict retainers, met with Aborigines along the Murray and Darling Rivers. Mitchell had a reputation as a brutal man; and despite orders from the government not to use arms against the Aborigines, he did so, openly, as reported in his 1839 *Three Expeditions into the Interior of Eastern Australia: With Descriptions of the Recently Explored Region of Australia Felix and of the Present Colony of New South Wales* (quoted in Reece, 1974, p. 120):

Attacked simultaneously by both parties ... [Aborigines] betook themselves to the river; my men pursuing them and shooting as many as they could. Numbers were shot in swimming across the Murray, and some even after they had reached the opposite shore, as they ascended the bank. Amongst those shot was the chief (recognised by a particular kind of cloak he wore, which floated after he went down). Thus, in a very short time, the usual silence of the desert prevailed on the banks of the Murray, and we pursued our journey unmolested.

Some years later Mitchell's feelings on the massacres were recorded in *Thomas Mitchell: Surveyor-General and Explorer*, by J.H.L. Cumpston (quoted in Elder, 1998, pp. 67–68): "I still look back upon that eventful day with entire satisfaction." Elder notes that Mitchell's "satisfaction" was enhanced by his naming of a nearby hill—Mount Dispersion. Mitchell was subsequently rebuked by Governor Bourke for his undue aggression.

Account 6

William Hobbs, an overseer at Henry Dangar's Myall Creek Station in northern New South Wales, stated that

the Aborigines at Myall Creek were harmless and would have been allowed to live but success having attended the first two massacres, the murderers grew bold; and in order that their cattle might never more be "rushed" it was resolved to exterminate the whole race of blacks in that quarter. (Reece, 1974, pp. 42–43)

Hobbs wrote a letter to Police Magistrate Edward Day on July 9, 1838 (a document discovered in 1988, now in the NSW State Archive, quoted by Millis, 1995, p. 322):

Sir, I beg to acquaint you that about a month since I had occasion to leave Mr Dangar's Station on the Big River for a few days on my return I saw near the Hut the remains of about thirty Blacks principally Women and Children. I recognised them as part of a tribe that had been at the Station for some time and who had since they first came conducted themselves in a quiet and proper manner, on making inquiry I was informed that a party of white men had come to the Station who after securing them had taken them a short distance from the Hut and destroyed nearly the whole of them.

Police Magistrate Edward Day investigated the murders and captured 11 of the 12 murderers. In 1839 he reported to the *Committee on Police and Gaols, Votes and Proceedings, 1839*, Vol. II, p. 224 (quoted in Reece, 1974, p. 43):

> It was represented to me, and I believe truly, that the blacks had repeatedly been pursued by parties of mounted and armed stockmen, assembled for the purpose [of killing Aborigines], and that great numbers of them had been killed at various spots, particularly at Vineyard Hill, Slaughterhouse Creek, and Gravesend, places so called by the stockmen, in commemoration of the deeds enacted there.

Account 7

In 1846 Henry Meyrick traveled in South Gippsland, Victoria, a journey described in *Life in the Bush: A Memoir of Henry Howard Meyrick* by Frederick James Meyrick, London, Thomas Nelson, 1939. It records the massacres of the Kurnai tribe, which began in 1840. Henry Meyrick protested at every station he visited "but these things are kept very secret as the penalty would certainly be hanging [a reference to the execution of the Myall Creek murderers two years earlier] (quoted in Gardner, 1993, p. 34):

> The blacks are quiet here now poor wretches. No wild beast of the forest was ever hunted down with such perseverance as they. Men, women and children are shot whenever they can be met with.... They will shortly be extinct. It is impossible to say how many have been shot, but I am convinced that not less than 450 have been murdered altogether ... now I am become so familiarized with scenes of horror from having murder made a topic of everyday conversation.

Gardner suggests that 450 was too high a number for this particular event but concludes that 700–800 Kurnai were killed between 1840 and 1846.

Account 8

In the 1840s, some squatters (men who, without permit or lease, grazed stock on Crown land) came to call their gifts of rations to Aborigines "death puddings," a mix of flour and arsenic or strychnine. The following excerpt is from *Advance Australia: An Account of Eight Years' Work, Wandering and Amusement* by Harold Finch-Hatton, 1885 (quoted by Evans et al., 1988, p. 49):

The rations contained about as much strychnine as anything else and not one of the mob escaped. When they woke up in the morning they were all dead corpses. More than a hundred Blacks were stretched out by this ruse of the owner of Long Lagoon.

Account 9

In 1857, 11 whites, including eight members of the Fraser family, were killed by Yeeman tribes-people in the Upper Dawson River area of Queensland. The chief avenger was Billy Fraser, away from home at the time of the killings. By March 1858 some 150 Aborigines had been killed in retaliation. In his very short and unpublished autobiography, George Pearce-Serocold, a retired naval officer who became a cattleman, wrote (Elder, 1998, p. 145):

When the news of the Hornet Bank massacre went around the district, all the squatters turned out and the Native Police from different tribes acted with us, and a considerable number were shot. It was necessary to make a severe example of the leaders of the tribe, and about a dozen of them were taken into the open country and shot. They were complete savages ... and were so much alike that no evidence could ever be produced to enable them to be tried by our laws. These men were allowed to run and they were shot at about thirty or forty yards distant.

The Frontiers: 1900 to 1928

Account 10

Roma Kelly and Nicholas Evans—in "The McKenzie Massacre on Bentinck Island," (*Aboriginal History, 9*, 1985, pp. 44–52)—relate that during his time on Bentinck Island, a man named McKenzie "systematically tried to eliminate the Kaiadilt, riding across the island on horseback, and shooting down everyone but the girls he intended to rape." In this excerpt, Roma Kelly, born a year before the 1918 events, has set down in her dialect (with English translations) the stories she heard from her surviving parents:

[They] drowned, [they] didn't like that thing [gun], might get shot by it ... didn't like that gun, didn't like that warlike mob [McKenzie and his men] ... and drowned. Some went to the sandhills, some went high up, some drowned ... robbed, robbed of their women ... [McKenzie's men] took the nubile girls back [to their camp] … the nubile girls were taken [sexually] … [McKenzie's mob] shot them out into the sea and killed, killed, mothers ran away, fathers ran away.

Account 11

This excerpt relates to the Forrest River massacres in the northwest of Western Australia in June 1926. In his 1998 *Blood on the Wattle: Massacres and Maltreatment of Aboriginal Australians Since 1788*, Bruce Elder includes the following quotes related to the killing of Aborigines (p. 171):

> No-one knew how many were killed. Professor [A.P.] Elkin, who travelled through the area two years later, said "20 or more." The Reverend E.R. Gribble [Protector and head of the Forrest River Mission] wrote, "There are some thirty native men and women missing." [Aboriginal] Daniel Evans said, "So many hundred … women, men and children." And old Grant Ngabidj, who was twenty-two at the time, and who really knew, said, "They shootim that lot now, picaninny, old old woman, blackfeller, old old man, somewhere about hundred."

George Wood, a senior Perth stipendiary magistrate, was appointed as royal commissioner to investigate the matter. In the report of *The Royal Commission into Alleged Killing and Burning of Bodies of Aborigines in East Kimberley and Use of Police Methods When Effecting Arrests, 1927*, Wood concluded that 11 Aboriginal people in police custody had been shot and their bodies burned in the three sites he was allowed to investigate. The punitive expedition had been moving through the reserve, shooting Aborigines when they could before Reverend Gribble, a Justice of the Peace, stopped them. Wood could not find responsibility for seven of the deaths, but held that Constables Dennis Regan and James St. Jack were responsible for four killings.

Account 12

Constable Murray was the central figure in the Darwin trial of Padygar and Arkirkra for the murder of Fred Brooks at Coniston Station. He gave evidence as the perpetrator of the massacre and as the key witness on what had occurred after Brooks' death. At one point, Justice Mallam engaged him (Cribbin, 1984, p. 114):

> "Constable Murray, was it really necessary to shoot to kill in every case? Could you not occasionally have shot to wound?"

"No, Your Honour. What use is a wounded black feller a
hundred miles from civilization?"
"How many did you kill?"
"Seventeen, Your Honour."...
"You mowed them down wholesale!"

Several survivors of the same massacre have given interviews to historians, including Johnny Nelson Jupurrulu to Peter Read in 1977 (quoted
in Cribbin, 1984, pp. 162–163):

Police came long this way ... shooting all the way...
Was that your father? Yeah. My father got shot there...
*They wanted to get your father to show them where all the
soaks* [water holes] *were, so they'd know where those people were
hiding?* Yeah. And he [Murray] shootem. That's the last. They
comen there now, chasem them round now, some all run away.
Right, prisoners whole lot, everyone. Tie em longa trees. All little
boys, oh, lotta tracker, some stockmen too. And shootem whole
lot.
Just the men, or women too? Oh, woman and all. Not young
girls, no, lettem go.
What about little fellers? Oh Yeah, some fellers.... Some
running away. Lettem go, some of them.

The Forcible Removal of Children

There is quite a debate about stolen generations testimony (Kennedy,
2001, pp. 116–131). There are the abnegators who dismiss the whole
issue and call into question the facts; those who claim that for a very
short time span there had been a period that resulted in "collective hys-
teria"; those individuals who are not sure of the facts; those who insist
on forensic-quality evidence before they will believe anything happened;
those who seek the "scientific" data, and take the clinical view that is
devoid of emotion; those who perceive (and sometimes disdain) the
stories as chronicalist, or as literary, or metaphorical, or symbolic, or
simply interpretive. What matters is establishing that various official
administrations, including the police, forcibly removed children because
they were Aboriginal and did so with the intention of eliminating their
ethnic Aboriginality by incorporating them, permanently, into mainstream society and values. There are ample enough institutional archives
that attest to the reality of premeditated action (MacDonald, 1995;
HREOC, 1997; Mellor & Haebich, 2002).

Account 13

The late Burnum Burnum (Harry Penrith)—activist, actor, writer, sportsman—gave this somewhat kindly account of at least one of the institutions to which he was removed. This excerpt appears in Moores (1995, pp. 422–423):

> Soon after my mother died, my brother, sister and I were seized and taken to the care and protection of the United Aboriginal Mission at Bomaderry in southern New South Wales. I was well cared for by the Baptist missionaries, who were quite extraordinary.... They put all their spiritual, emotional and physical energy into raising us. I was then declared a Ward of the State but the State Government was a highly negligent parent.... We were deprived and cooped up [at Kinchela Boys' Home] and had almost no identity. It was as if we were numbers in a prison ... [they were all known by their numbers].

Account 14

Rosalie Fraser, an Aboriginal child of just over two years old, was taken from her parents, brothers, and sisters. In her memoir, Fraser (1988, pp. 10–12) wrote:

> The date was 13 March 1961, the place was Beverley [East of Perth] in Western Australia. On that day, my brothers and sisters Terry aged eight, Stuart aged six, Karen aged four-and-a-half, Beverley aged eight months, and myself, were all made Wards of the State through action taken by the Child Welfare Department of Western Australia.

The boys and girls were sent to separate institutions and Rosalie was later "collected" by her foster mother, Mrs Kelly.

> When we first went to the Kellys', we had no idea where our parents were, we never saw or heard from them and we were unaware of what efforts they might be making to get us back. The Welfare communicated not with us but with the Kellys. The separation was total; our new life was the only one we knew.

Account 15

Bill Simon is a church pastor working in Redfern, a suburb of Sydney. In his chronicle—*Back on the Block: Bill Simon's Story* by Bill Simon, Des Montgomerie and Jo Tuscano (2009, pp. xii–xiii)—he relates that as a young boy he was taken from his parents (on the grounds of neglect), sent to Kinchela Boys' Home in northern New South Wales for eight years, was repeatedly told that he was "the scum of the earth," and that his mother didn't want him:

> Telling this story has not been easy. There were times when speaking about my memories caused me great pain. I still have nightmares about the day I was stolen. I didn't see my mother again until well into my thirties, and by that time I had turned into someone that not many mothers would have wanted for a son.... I am one of the "Stolen Generations" and my life has been directly affected by that fact right up to the present day.... Any semblance of normal childhood was cut short at the age of ten and I didn't really start to get back on track until I was in my thirties.... To say that Aboriginal children were taken away from their parents for their own good is a lie. I was taken over forty years ago, and nothing good has ever come out of that decision.

Account 16

Alec Kruger was born in 1924 at a place called Donkey Camp on the Katherine River in the Northern Territory. In his memoir—*Alone on the Soaks: The Life and Times of Alec Kruger* by Alec Kruger and Gerard Waterford (2007, p. 1, pp. 25–27)—he wrote:

> I have been to the High Court in Australia as part of a test case for us kids taken away. The court rejected our claims for compensation.... The papers had got lost.... Without supporting records we were stuck.... The police faced a mob of Aboriginal women. We were snatched from our mother's arms before anyone could raise the alarm. My mother and the other women were taken by surprise. Us kids couldn't be hidden ... I was not much more than a toddler and my sister had just turned six. We were taken and locked up at the police station, waiting with the kids from the West to be taken on the train to Darwin.... When the train stopped for the night at Pine Creek us kids were locked up in the Pine Creek jail. My mother was on the train. She stood at the Kahlin's [Compound] wire fence waiting to catch sight of us. Having kids taken had happened to Polly before with her first baby, Ada. Now it was happening again. Like all the other Aboriginal mothers, she didn't get to take us back.

Account 17

In his *The Wailing: A National Black Oral History* (1993), Stuart Rintoul interviewed Jean Ingram. Born in Bateman's Bay, New South Wales, she recalls what happened to her cousins (Rintoul, 1993, p. 20):

> My cousin, she had six or seven kiddies, she lived in Hugo Street, and the Aboriginal Welfare Board came after her kiddies and they were running ... I think it was back in the Forties. The police was with them and I seen my cousins were running, like scared rabbits. They'd go in the house and they went under the bed and into the cupboards, and the police went in behind them and hauled them out and put them in the car there screaming for their mother. The eldest girl, she got in between two mattresses, one on top of the other. She got in between them and she laid there and they couldn't find her.... They all finished up in Cootamundra [Girls' Home, established in 1912] and the boys in Kinchela. All that split the family. The closeness and the relationship of the family was broken.

Account 18

Maria Tomlins, daughter of a Walbiri woman, was born at Mount Doreen, a cattle station west of Alice Springs. Her memory is vivid, as recorded by Peg Havnen in *Under the Mango Tree: Oral Histories with Indigenous People from the Top End* (2001, p. 25):

> I was seven when I was taken away, but I remember. I remember that day very clearly. Oh, yes, very very clearly. It was just me and my brother Ted and my two cousins Jackie and Tommy Cusack. We were all playing and a man came in the truck and he said he was taking us for a ride. So we all got in. We thought it was fun. We thought we were just going for a ride.

They were taken first to the Bungalow, an institution for Aboriginal children in Alice Springs, then evacuated down south: "When we moved to Adelaide, they changed my name. My name was Laura and they changed my name to Maria because Laura wasn't a saint's name."

Account 19

Mona Tur grew up at Hamilton Station, about 100 km from Oodnadatta, in remote South Australia. One day, at Hamilton Bore, her mother tried frantically to hide her from a white man who arrived unannounced. In

Many Voices: Reflections on Experiences of Indigenous Child Separation,
edited by Doreen Mellor and Anna Haebich (2002, pp. 38–39), Mona
recalls the following:

> All of a sudden we could hear our people screaming out in our
> language *"Walkatjara, walkatjara, walkatjara,"* and I under-
> stood that the *walkatajara* would have been a policeman. So
> Mother said to me, "Ngitji Ngitji"—I have a traditional name
> called Ngitji Ngitji which is like a noise made by a cicada—she
> said, "Ngitji Ngitji, I haven't got time to run away with you
> because the policeman will see me running away with you." So
> she said, "I'm going to dig a hole inside the *ngura*. She dug a
> hole inside the *ngura* [a home made of sticks and spinifex
> grass], she put me in and she covered me right up to my neck
> in red desert sand and just let my neck stick out and shooed the
> dogs on top of me, and remember it's very hot outside. She said
> to me, "You mustn't make any noise whatsoever because you'll
> be taken away forever," and once again she reminded me about
> my relatives that had been taken away. I was six years old, I
> found out.... Finally they came to our *ngura* and he asked
> mother, in the language, *"Nyuntu tji tji apkatja kanyini?"* (Have
> you got a "half-caste" kid?), and mother said *"Wiya"* ("No"),
> and that seemed to satisfy the policeman and then he went
> away. That left me claustrophobic and really, really scared of
> police throughout my life.

Account 20

In her memoir—*Long Time Coming Home* (2001, pp. 10, 12)—Marjorie Woodrow explains that she "was born under a big tree at Carowra
Tank" near Lake Cargelligo in New South Wales. Told that her
mother was dead, she was sent to Cootamundra Girls' Training
Home:

> We were all Aboriginal, we were never called by our names. It
> was always "number 108, step forward!" We had numbers sewn
> on our uniforms. Everyone could see that we were from the Girls'
> Home. We were branded just like cattle.

It took Marjorie 60 years to discover that her mother might be alive.

> It took only a short, but very determined effort before I found her
> and we met. We were reunited at Murrin Bridge Aboriginal set-
> tlement near Lake Cargelligo in Central New South Wales, and

we had had eighteen months together before my mother, Ethel Johnson, died in 1994.

Account 21

Ted Evans devoted his life to Aboriginal administration. He began his career as a patrol officer in the Northern Territory, and later became Chief Welfare Officer in the unit called the Welfare Branch, the organization in which this author (Tatz) worked and studied for his doctorate on Aboriginal administration. A devout Catholic, Ted wrote this report in December 1949, addressed to the Administrator of the Territory (quoted in *Between Two Worlds: The Commonwealth Government and the Removal of Aboriginal Children of Part Descent in the Northern Territory* by Roweena MacDonald, 1995, pp. 55–56). At that time, 163 "colored" boys and 194 such girls were in three institutions specifically for removed children—the Retta Dixon Home in Darwin, Croker Island (Methodist) Mission, and Garden Point (Catholic) Mission on Melville Island. Evans wrote:

> The removal of the children from Wave Hill by MacRobertson Miller aircraft was accompanied by distressing scenes the like of which I wish never to experience again.... I endeavoured to assuage the grief of the mothers by taking photographs of each of the children prior to their departure and these have been distributed amongst the mothers. Also a dress length was given the five mothers. Gifts of sweets to the children helped break down a lot of their fear.

Evans recommended that "an itinerant female welfare worker" be appointed to "assist mothers on cattle stations and to help in the gentler removal of part-aboriginal children." He felt that "a native mother would be far readier to hand over her offspring to the care of a white woman than to the mercies of a male." He concluded:

> I cannot imagine any practice which is more likely to involve the Government in criticism for violation of the present day conception of "human rights." Apart from that aspect of the matter, I go further and say that superficially, at least, it is difficult to imagine any practice which is more likely to outrage the feelings of the average observer.

Interviewed in 1982, Evans stated: "I was unfortunately involved in the removal of 'half-caste' kiddies" (Mellor & Haebich, 2002, p. 158):

Oh, I gave it away. I refused to obey the instruction and this is what brought things to a head. The matter was stopped. It was traumatic, really traumatic from all sides, me included. Much more so for the mothers of course.

Notes

1. That legal fallacy—which by the 20th century came to be called the doctrine of *terra nullius*—was finally put to rest by the High Court in 1992 when it recognized the prior occupation of land by the Murray Island people (*Mabo* v. *Queensland* (2), CLR 175 (1) (1992).

2. Yarra Government Mission (1837–1839), Buntingdale Mission (1838–1848), and Merri Creek Baptist School (1845–1851).

3. Across the continent, and across a century, the following events evoke and memorialize some of the many killing eras: Risdon Cove (Tasmania, 1804); Twofold Bay (New South Wales, 1806); Appin-Bringelly (New South Wales, 1816); Bathurst (New South Wales, 1824); Cape Grim (Tasmania, 1824); Fremantle (Western Australia, 1830); Portland (Victoria, 1833–1834); Pinjarra (Western Australia, 1834); Darling River massacres (New South Wales, 1835–1865); Myall Creek (New South Wales, 1838); Gwydir and Namoi Rivers massacres (New South Wales, 1838); Waterloo Creek (New South Wales, 1838); Murdering Gully Massacre (Victoria, 1839); Gippsland (Victoria, 1840–1851); Fighting Hills and Fighting Waterholes massacres (Victoria, 1840); Long Lagoon (Queensland, 1840); Butchers Creek (Victoria, 1841); Rufus River (South Australia, 1841); Wonnerup (Western Australia, 1841); Lubra Creek massacre (Victoria, 1842); Butchers Tree (New South Wales, 1849); Hornet Bank and Upper Dawson (Queensland, 1857); Cullin-la-Ringo (Queensland, 1861); Pigeon Creek (Queensland, 1862); Flying Foam massacre, also known as Jaburrara (Western Australia, 1868); Barrow Creek (Northern Territory, 1874); Goulbolba Hill (Queensland, 1876); Lake Eyre and Simpson Desert massacres and Clifton Hills massacres (South Australia, 1880s); Keppel Islands (Queensland, 1880s); Battle Mountain (Queensland, 1884); McKinlay River (Northern Territory, 1884); Canning Stock Route (Western Australia, 1906–1907); Mistake Creek (Western Australia, 1915); Bentinck Island (Queensland, 1918); Bedford Downs (Western Australia, 1924); Forrest River (Western Australia, 1926); Coniston Station (Northern Territory, 1928).

4. See www.adb.online.anu.edu.au.

5. In the late 1960s the federal government led the way in establishing a much wider definition of "Aborigines" than the traditional method of color which tried to define "full-bloods," "half-castes," "quadroons," and "octoroons." With improvements in the national census questions on identity, many more hitherto "unidentified" Aborigines of varying descent began to define themselves.

References

Attwood, Bain, & Foster, S.G. (Eds.) (2003). *Frontier conflict: The Australian experience*. Canberra, ACT: National Museum of Australia.

Australian Broadcast Corporation (2000, March 30). *7.30 Report*.

Beresford, Quentin, & Omaji, Paul (1998). *Our state of mind: Racial planning and the stolen generations*. Fremantle, Western Australia: Fremantle Arts Centre Press.

Blainey, Geoffrey (1993). Balance sheet on our history. *Quadrant, XXVII*(7–8), 10–15.

Broome, Richard (2003). The statistics of frontier conflict. In Bain Attwood & S.G. Foster (Eds.) *Frontier conflict: The Australian experience* (pp. 88–98). Canberra, ACT: National Museum of Australia.

Brunton, Ronald (1998). Genocide, the "stolen generations" and the "unconceived generations". *Quadrant, XLII*(5), 19–24.

Cohen, Stanley (2001). *States of denial: Knowing about atrocities and suffering*. Cambridge: Polity Press.

Cribbin, John (1984). *The killing times: The Coniston Massacre 1928*. Sydney, NSW: Fontana Books.

Cuneen, Chris, & Grix, Julia (2004). *The limitations of litigation in stolen generations cases*. Research Discussion Paper No. 15. Canberra, ACT: Aboriginal Studies Press.

Dawson, John (2004). *Washout: On the Academic response to the fabrication of Aboriginal history*. Sydney, NSW: Macleay Press.

DeMayo, Catherine (1990). *Splendidly secluded: The location of Aboriginal mission sites in Australia*. (Unpublished Master of Arts Thesis). Politics Department, Macquarie University, Sydney.

Elder, Bruce (1998). *Blood on the wattle: Massacres and maltreatment of Aboriginal Australians since 1788*. Sydney, NSW: New Holland Publishers.

Evans, Raymond, Saunders, Kay, & Cronin, Kathryn (1988). *Race relations in colonial Queensland: Exclusion, exploitation and extermination*. Brisbane: University of Queensland Press.

Fraser, Rosalie (1998). *Shadow child: A memoir of the stolen generation*. Sydney, NSW: Hale & Iremonger Pty. Ltd.

Gaita, Raimond (1997). Genocide: The Holocaust and the Aborigines. *Quadrant, XLI*(11), 17–22.

Gale, C.F. (1909). *Report of the Chief Protector* (Vol. 2). Perth: Western Australia Parliament, Votes and Proceedings.

Gardner, Peter (1993). *Gippsland massacres: The destruction of the Kurnai tribes 1800–1860*. Ensay, Victoria: Ngarak Press.

Green, Neville (1995). *The Forrest River massacres*. Fremantle, Western Australia: Fremantle Arts Centre Press.

Haebich, Anna (1988). *For their own good: Aborigines and government in the southwest of Western Australia*. Perth: University of Western Australia Press.

Haebich, Anna (2000). *Broken circles: Fragmenting indigenous families 1800–2000*. Fremantle, Western Australia: Fremantle Arts Centre Press.

Hansard, House of Representatives (1949). Genocide Convention Bill, June 30, 1949, Vol. 203, pp. 1869–1876.

Hansard, House of Representatives (2008). Apology to Australia's Indigenous People, February 13, 2008, pp. 167–173.

Havnen, Peg (collector) (2001). *Under the mango tree: Oral histories with indigenous people from the top end*. Darwin: Northern Territory Government.

Horton, David (Ed.) (1994). *The encyclopaedia of Aboriginal Australia: Aboriginal and Torres Strait Islander history, culture and society*. Two volumes. Canberra, NSW: Aboriginal Studies Press.

HREOC (Human Rights and Equal Opportunity Commission) (1997). *Bringing them home: Report of the National Inquiry into the Separation of Aboriginal and Torres Strait Islander Children from their Families*. Sydney, NSW: Author.

HREOC (Human Rights and Equal Opportunity Commission) (1999). *Social justice report 1998*, Sydney, NSW: Author.

Kelly, Roma, & Evans, Nicholas (1985). The McKenzie massacre on Bentinck Island. *Aboriginal History, 9*, 44–52.

Kennedy, Roseanne (2001). Stolen generation testimony: Trauma. historiography and the question of "truth". *Aboriginal History, 25*, 116–131.

Kimber, Richard (1997). Genocide or not? The situation in Central Australia, 1860–1895. In Colin Tatz, Peter Arnold, & Sandra Tatz (Eds.) *Genocide perspectives I: Essays in comparative genocide* (pp. 33–65). Sydney, NSW: Centre for Comparative Genocide Studies, Macquarie University.

Kruger, Alec, & Waterford, Gerard (2007). *Alone on the soaks: The life and times of Alec Kruger*. Alice Springs, Northern Territory: IAD Press.

Lemkin, Raphael (1944). *Axis rule in occupied Europe: Laws of occupation, analysis of government, and proposals for redress*. Washington, DC: Carnegie Foundation for International Peace.

Loos, Noel (1982). *Invasion and resistance: Aboriginal–European relations on the North Queensland frontier 1861–1897*. Canberra, NSW: Australian National University Press.

Loos, Noel (2007). *White Christ black cross: The emergence of a black church.* Canberra, ACT: Aboriginal Studies Press.

MacDonald, Roweena (1995). *Between two worlds: The Commonwealth government and the removal of Aboriginal children of part descent in the Northern Territory.* Alice Springs, Northern Territory: IAD Press.

McGuinness, Padraic (2001). The erosion of the "stolen generations" slogan. *Quadrant, XLV*(4), 2–4.

Macleod, Colin (1997). *Patrol in the dreamtime.* Sydney, NSW: Random House.

Manne, Robert (2001). *Quarterly essay: In denial—The stolen generations and the right.* Melbourne, Victoria: Morry Schwartz, Black Inc.

Manne, Robert (Ed.) (2003). *Whitewash: On Keith Windschuttle's fabrication of Aboriginal history.* Melbourne, Victoria: Black Inc. Agenda.

Mellor, Doreen, & Haebich, Anna (Eds.) (2002). *Many voices: Reflections on experiences of indigenous child separation.* Canberra, NSW: National Library of Australia.

Meston, Archibald (1896). Report on the Aborigines of North Queensland. *Queensland Parliament Votes and Proceedings, 4*(85): 1–18.

Millis, Roger (1995). *Waterloo Creek: The Australia Day Massacre of 1838, George Gipps and the British conquest of New South Wales.* Ringwood, Victoria: McPhee Gribble.

Moore, Clive (1993). "Restraining their savage propensities": The South Kennedy and North Leichhardt districts in the 1860s and 1870s. In Henry Reynolds (Ed.) *Race relations in North Queensland* (pp. 83–114). Townsville, Queensland: Department of History and Politics, James Cook University.

Moores, Irene (Ed.) (1995). *Voices of Aboriginal Australia: Past, present, future.* Springwood, NSW: Butterfly Books.

Nettheim, Garth (1981). *Victims of the law: Black Queenslanders today.* Sydney, NSW: George Allen and Unwin.

Raynes, Cameron (2009). *The last protector: The illegal removal of Aboriginal children from their parents in South Australia.* Kent Town, South Australia: Wakefield Press.

Read, Peter (1981). *The stolen generations: The removal of Aboriginal children in New South Wales 1883 to 1969.* Sydney: NSW Ministry of Aboriginal Affairs.

Reece (1974). *Aborigines and colonists: Aborigines and colonial society in New South Wales in the 1830s and 1840s.* Sydney, NSW: Sydney University Press.

Reynolds, Henry (1982). *The other side of the frontier: Aboriginal resistance to the European invasion of Australia.* Melbourne, Victoria: Penguin Books.

Reynolds, Henry (Ed.) (1993). *Race relations in North Queensland.* Townsville, Queensland: Department of History and Politics, James Cook University.

Rintoul, Stuart (1993). *The wailing: A national black oral history.* Melbourne, Victoria: William Heinemann Australia.

Rowse, Tim (1998). *White flour, white power: From rations to citizenship in Central Australia.* Cambridge: Cambridge University Press.

Rush, John (2008). *Cubillo and Gunner* revisited: A question of national character. *Australian Indigenous Law Review, 12,* 25–31.

Sheehan, Paul (2010, June 9). Rudd's electoral cracks. *National Times,* n.p.

Simon, Bill, Montgomerie, Des, & Tuscano, Jo (2009). *Back on the block: Bill Simon's story.* Canberra, ACT: Aboriginal Studies Press.

Storey, Matthew (1997). Kruger v the Commonwealth: Does genocide require malice? *University of New South Wales Law Journal Forum, 21*(1), 11–14.

Tatz, Colin (1963). Queensland's Aborigines: Natural justice and the rule of law. *Australian Quarterly, XXXV*(3), 33–49.

Tatz, Colin (1964a). *Aboriginal administration in the Northern Territory of Australia.* (Unpublished doctoral thesis). Australian National University.

Tatz, Colin (1964b). Commonwealth Aboriginal policy. *Australian Quarterly, XXXVI*(4), 49–63.

Tatz, Colin (1966). Aborigines: Equality or inequality? *Australian Quarterly, XXXVIII*(1), 73–90.

Tatz, Colin (1990). Aboriginal violence: A return to pessimism. *Australian Journal of Social Issues, 25*(4), 245–260.

Tatz, Colin (2003). *With intent to destroy: Reflecting on genocide.* London: Verso.

Tatz, Colin (2005). *Aboriginal suicide is different: A portrait of life and self-destruction.* Canberra, ACT: Aboriginal Studies Press.

Trollope, Anthony ([1873] 1966). *Trollope's Australia: A selection from the Australian passages in Australia and New Zealand by Anthony Trollope*. London: Nelson.

Windschuttle, Keith (2000). The myths of frontier massacres in Australian history: Part I. *Quadrant*, *XLIV*(10), 8–21; Part II. *Quadrant*, *XLIV*(11), 17–24; Part III. *Quadrant*, *XLIV*(12), 6–20.

Windschuttle, Keith (2002). *The fabrication of Aboriginal history: Van Diemen's land 1803–1847*. Sydney, NSW: Macleay Press.

Windschuttle, Keith (2010). *The fabrication of Aboriginal history: The stolen generations*. Sydney, NSW: Macleay Press.

Woodrow, Marjorie (2001). *Long time coming home*. Lake Haven, NSW: Marjorie Woodrow.

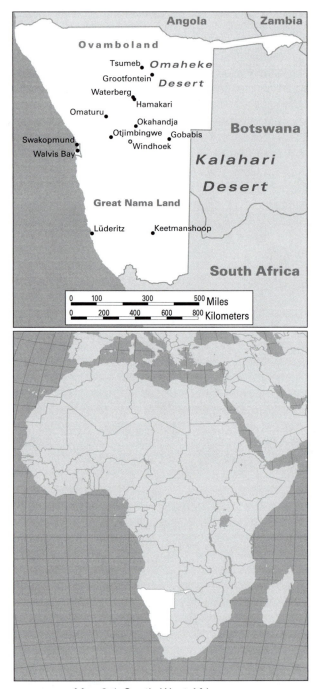

Map 3.1 South-West Africa

CHAPTER 3

The Genocide of the Herero and Nama in German South-West Africa, 1904–1907

DOMINIK J. SCHALLER

On October 2, 1904, Lothar von Trotha (1848–1920), the military commander of the German troops in colonial South-West Africa (present-day Namibia) issued his infamous shooting order:

> I the great General of the German troops send this letter to the Herero people. The Hereros are no longer German subjects.... All the Hereros must leave the land. If the people do not do this, then I will force them to do it with the great guns. Any Herero found within the German borders with or without a gun, with or without cattle, will be shot. I shall no longer receive any women or children. I will drive them back to their people or I will shoot them. This is my decision for the Herero people.

In a supplement designated only for his officers, Lothar von Trotha added:

> And the shooting of women and children is to be understood to mean that one can shoot over them to force them to run faster. I definitely mean that this order will be carried out and that no male prisoners will be taken, but it should not degenerate into killing women and children. This will be accomplished if one shoots over their heads a couple of times. The soldiers will remain conscious of the good reputation of German soldiers. (Drechsler, 1980, p. 156)

The German general's supplement was far from being an act of mercy. His aim was rather perfidious: He did not want to spare Herero women and children at all. "Make them run away" meant nothing else than driving them back into the waterless Omaheke desert where they had to face death from starvation and exhaustion (Drechsler, 1980, p. 185).

Lothar von Trotha's order marked the transition of a colonial war to a colonial genocide. Colonial warfare usually resulted in massacres of non-combatants. However, Lothar von Trotha's extremism was excessive in that he left no doubt that he aimed at annihilating the revolting Herero completely. In a letter to the chief of the German general staff in Berlin, he declared:

> To accept women and children who are for the most part sick, poses a great risk to the force, and to feed them is out of the question. For this reason, I deem it wiser for the entire nation to perish than to infect our soldiers into the bargain and to make inroads into our water and food supplies. (Drechsler, 1980, p. 161)

The outcome of the German war against the Herero and Nama in South-West Africa was disastrous: Up to 60,000 Herero and 10,000 Nama lost their lives. The political and socioeconomic structures of the indigenous societies were laid waste. Their reconstruction took several decades. In Germany, politicians complained about the huge costs of the war in South-West Africa: 14,000 German soldiers were necessary to suppress the African resistance. Almost 2,000 of them died, mainly due to epidemics. The military campaign swallowed 585 million Reichsmark (Bley, 1968, p. 197). A few politicians condemned the genocidal warfare because of its economic consequences for the colony. Paul Rohrbach (1869–1956), commissioner on settler affairs in South-West Africa and one of the most influential intellectuals in Germany at the time, deplored the destruction of indigenous manpower: "South-West Africa with natives was of much more value ... than without" (Rohrbach, 1953, p. 64). But only a minority of German politicians and opinion leaders were afraid that the slaughter of the Africans might damage Germany's reputation as a leading *Kulturnation* (nation of culture) (Sobich, 2006, pp. 73–78).

But why did hostilities between the Herero and the German colonizers start in January 1904 and why did this war degenerate into genocide? The war had not been preplanned by the Africans and its beginning was rather spontaneous and surprised both Germans and Herero. European settlers had been waiting for the elimination of the Africans as autonomous actors for almost 20 years, but they were well aware that their military power and the colonial infrastructure had not been sufficient. Therefore, German settlers were afraid that a major African uprising could hamper the positive political and economic development in the colony. There was a constant fear of a Herero rebellion among German settlers and colonial authorities. It was exactly this paranoid fear in combination with an accumulation of misunderstandings that triggered the war on January 12 in the Central Namibian town of Okahandja: A gathering of important Herero chiefs in this town made the German officer Zürn believe the Herero were planning a war against the colonizers. Zürn's fear was fueled by the fact that Theodor Leutwein, Germany's Civil Governor of South-West Africa, and the bulk of the German colonial army were in the south of the colony to wage war against the Bondelswarts, a small Nama group that had not been ready to accept the Germans' claim of power. Zürn's panicked reactions, in turn, led the Herero to believe that the Germans wanted to kill their self-proclaimed paramount-chief Samuel Maharero (1856–1923). Therefore, the outbreak of the war in South-West Africa can be understood as a self-fulfilling prophecy (Gewald, 1999, pp. 142–156).

In the first months of the war, about 8,000 Herero faced some 2,000 German soldiers and reservists (Krüger, 1999, p. 47). The Africans took the initiative, plundered remote farms, killed European settlers, and besieged German villages. German reactions were rather helpless at the beginning. But reinforcements from Europe and the colonial army's efficient weapons, such as machine guns, soon turned the tide.

The Herero had gathered with their families and herds in the Waterberg region, hoping to negotiate peace with Governor Leutwein. However, a diplomatic solution was no longer an option. German politicians and settlers had blamed Leutwein for the humiliating military setbacks, and so, although Leutwein officially remained civil governor of South-West Africa, he was deprived of influence and lost all his executive power to the new extremist supreme commander Lothar von Trotha.

On August 11, 1904, the German general attacked the Herero at Hamakari (Waterberg). The Germans' military superiority and Lothar von Trotha's radical methods of warfare resulted in a massacre. Nevertheless, the battle at Hamakari was a failure for the Germans. Most Herero managed to flee from the battle of encirclement and hid in the neighboring Omaheke desert. The paths through the desert to British Bechuanaland were known to the Herero as traditional trade routes (Gewald, 1999, pp. 15–181). However, the capacity of the water holes was not sufficient to ensure the survival of all the refugees. To finish the Hereros off, the Germans established a cordon of the Omaheke. To drive the Herero into the desert and let them die of thirst had not been planned in advance by Lothar von Trotha (Hull, 2005, p. 37). It was the failure of his original plan to annihilate the Africans at Hamakari that made him develop this new strategy of extermination and proclaim the above-mentioned genocide order.

The military defeat of the Herero did not mark the end of war in colonial South-West Africa. The Nama chief Hendrik Witbooi had been a close and important ally of the German governor. His troops supported the suppression of the Herero revolt. Therefore, the Germans were more than surprised when Witbooi initiated hostilities against them. The Namas' motives were to some extent religious. Shepherd Stuurman, a preacher of the so-called Ethiopian movement, motivated Hendrik Witbooi to get rid of European religious, cultural, and political influence. But the fear of Lothar von Trotha treating the Nama the same way as the Herero was doubtlessly more decisive (Bühler, 2003, pp. 157–181). The German war against the Nama lasted another three years and varied significantly from the previous struggle against the Herero. The Nama avoided open battles and resorted to highly efficient guerilla warfare. They launched systematic attacks against German military posts and lines of communication. Furthermore, the Germans suffered from the harsh climate conditions and the inaccessible terrain in Southern Namibia. In order to defeat the Nama, Lothar von Trotha pursued a scorched-earth policy. African villages and granaries were systematically burned. The civilian population and prisoners of war were deported to concentration camps along the Atlantic coast (Hillebrecht, 2008, p. 153). On March 31, 1907, the German governor Friedrich von Lindequist officially declared the end of the war. Although military resistance by the Africans had been completely suppressed, the genocidal policy of the German colonizers continued in the form of forced labor and the gradual destruction of indigenous culture.

Who were the Victims?

South-West Africa was most likely initially inhabited solely by San (often referred to as "Bushmen" in the literature) and Mountain-Damara before Bantu-speaking groups immigrated to the region in the 11th century. The ancestors of the Namibian Herero and Ovambo soon marginalized the indigenous populations, who ended up withdrawing to inaccessible regions such as the Kalahari Desert. The southern part of Namibia was inhabited by Khoisan-speaking Orlam or Nama groups. The peoples of South-West Africa established a complex tribute economy that was not exclusively organized along ethnic lines; changing trans-ethnic alliances were not unusual.

In the second half of the 19th century, the Herero managed to overthrow the hegemony of the Orlam and became the leading power in Central Namibia (Lau, 1978; Krüger, 2008). This event caused a remarkable socioeconomic and political change among the Herero: Although the Herero were originally pastoralists, they depended almost solely on hunter-gathering and horticulture in the first half of the 19th century. But while the Herero fought successful trade wars and secured their position of power in Namibia, they established huge cattle herds and soon came to be known as *the* outstanding cattle-breeders in South-West Africa (Gewald, 1999, pp. 10–26). The economy of the Nama peoples in Southern and Central Namibia relied likewise on cattle, but mainly on trade with farmers from the Cape Colony. Northern Namibia—inhabited by the Ovambo—remained for the most part untouched by the European colonizers. The Ovambo lived in centralized and highly stratified kingdoms that depended economically on agriculture, fishery, and trade with other Ovambo groups in Portuguese Angola (Siiskonen, 1990). At the turn of the century (from the 19th to the 20th), about 80,000 Herero, 20,000 Nama, and up to 450,000 Ovambo lived in South-West Africa. Even before the advent of the German colonizers, Namibia had not been an isolated corner of the world: The region had been connected economically and politically to the emerging frontier society of the Cape Colony. Therefore, the Herero and Nama had been in touch with European goods and ideas. The Nama chiefs used modern rifles and wore Western clothes. Missionaries were the most important intermediaries of European culture. Nama chiefs like Hendrik Witbooi converted and lived according to Christian values. Both Herero and Nama practiced intensive animal husbandry and managed to build up impressive herds and accumulate wealth. In a nutshell: The African societies of South-West Africa were rather strong and independent and, therefore, not at all ready to give up their self-sustaining economies.

The German conquest of Namibia was rather difficult. Although the Germans welcomed the acquisition of huge territories in Africa, Chancellor Bismarck and his successors were not ready to spend much money for the colonial project. They had hoped that land and concession companies would contribute to the development of colonial infrastructure in the African colonies. However, these hopes were in vain. As a result, colonial authorities did not have many financial or personnel resources at their disposal. They were expected to conquer South-West Africa by peaceful and inexpensive means. Nevertheless, hasty colonial officials and soldiers started hostilities against the Herero and Nama and almost lost control over South-West Africa more than once.

The German governor, Theodor Leutwein, established a complex system of indirect rule in the colony. He had realized that South-West Africa could only be conquered by cooperating with indigenous chiefs. Samuel Maharero was the ideal partner as his claim to the position of paramount chief of all Herero was contested. His alliance with the

Germans helped him to get rid of his rivals. Leutwein's strategy of *divide et impera* worked very well and resulted in the Germans becoming more and more powerful in Namibia.

Leutwein and his superiors in Berlin, however, saw the cooperation with African leaders only as a provisional and temporary measure. Total German control, they believed, ought to be established in the medium term. The final aim was the creation of a European settler colony and the political and cultural dissolution of the indigenous societies. Africans were expected to become cheap laborers without any "tribal" identity. In the first decade of German presence in South-West Africa, these plans seemed rather utopian because of the Africans' economic and military strength.

Natural disasters have often facilitated the European penetration of large parts of the world in the age of imperialism. Rinderpest (cattle disease) reached Namibia in 1897. It changed the balance of power in South-West Africa dramatically: whereas German settlers managed to vaccinate their herds, the Herero lost approximately 90% of their cattle. Moreover, the Herero, enfeebled through a lack of milk, fell victim to a malaria epidemic. The German missionary Jakob Irle estimated that up to 10,000 Herero died due to malaria (Irle, 1906, p. 127). These events led to a far-reaching economic and cultural crisis of Herero society. To secure their livelihood, the Herero had to sell their land to European settlers, traders, and land companies. Furthermore, many Herero were forced into wage labor for the first time ever. Many chiefs encountered difficulty in maintaining their extravagant lifestyles and therefore sold large parts of their communities' ancestral land at very low prices to German settlers. A large number of Herero were thus transformed from once proud and autonomous pastoralists to weak and dependent proletarians. This significant transformation took place within a few months, yet it turned the hierarchy of power between Africans and Europeans upside down (Gewald, 1999, p. 133).

Whereas the Herero were deprived and suffered from a crisis of collective self-esteem, the European settler community expanded and prospered. Before the outbreak of the war in January 1904, almost 5,000 Germans, English, and Boers inhabited South-West Africa (Kaulich, 2001, p. 353). Their new power strengthened their racist arrogance and tempted them into maltreating African workers.

How was the Genocide Committed?

The genocide against the Namibian Herero and Nama had three phases. Massacring non-combatants, driving the Herero into the Omaheke desert, and implementing a scorched-earth strategy in the fight against the Nama all characterized the first phase.

Although many German settlers supported Lothar von Trotha's radical approach to warfare, they did not agree with his plan to annihilate all the Africans. They had a profound interest in forced laborers. Their lobbyists in Berlin, as well as representatives of mission societies, urged the German government to interfere in South-West Africa. Consequently, the supreme commander of the German forces in Namibia had to repeal his genocidal shooting order. Chancellor von Bülow ordered the establishment of concentration camps. Missionaries were entrusted with the gathering of the African survivors. However, this decision did not mean that the German policy of genocide had come to an end. Rather, the German treatment of the Herero and Nama has to be understood as the continuation of von Trotha's policy of extermination, and thus as the second phase of this genocide (Zimmerer, 1999, p. 292).

The conditions in the concentration camps were horrible. In March 1907 the command of the German forces in South-West Africa reported that 7,682 out of a total of 17,000 inmates in German concentration camps had died within a period of two-and-a-half years (Schaller, 2004, pp. 220–221). The inmates of the camps suffered from torture, insufficient sanitary equipment, and malnutrition. The camps in Swakopmund and on Shark Island near Lüderitz were notorious. The harsh and cold climate along the Atlantic coast contributed to the high mortality among the inmates (Erichsen, 2008; Zeller, 2008). The incarceration of the people in the concentration camps served two main purposes. First, colonial officials understood the ill-treatment of the Africans as a punishment for the revolt, as the following statement by Deputy Governor Tecklenburg reveals:

> The more the Herero people now feel physically the consequences of the uprising the less they will yearn after a repetition of the experience for generations to come. Our actual successes in battle have made only a limited impression on them. I expect that the period of suffering they are now experiencing will have a more lasting effect. (Quoted in Zimmerer, 2008a, p. 53)

The second and more important purpose of the concentration camps was economic. Settlers and politicians understood the availability of thousands of African prisoners as the perfect solution to overcome the shortage of labor in the colony. The concentration camps served as work camps providing public companies and private entrepreneurs with forced laborers. African men, women, and children were subjected to slave labor. The construction of the Otavi railroad was a particularly deadly task, and constantly needed an influx of new workers: The mortality among the forced laborers was about 30%.

German colonial authorities believed that slave labor had an educational value and a salutary effect on the Africans. In a letter to his superiors in Berlin, the new governor, Lindequist, stated:

> Setting the Herero to work while they are held prisoner is very salutary for them, one could even say that they are fortunate, because they learn to work before regaining complete freedom. Otherwise, as far as one can tell, they would just wander work-shy around the country and eke out a miserable life having lost all their cattle. (quoted in Zimmerer, 2008a, p. 53)

This cynical statement reminds one of the infamous and inhuman slogan, "Arbeit macht frei," that the Nazis placed at the entrances to several concentration camps.

The Africans also suffered from regular flogging and sexual violence committed by German guards.

Herero and Nama were officially released from captivity after the state of war had been terminated in March 1907. The systematic destruction of the African societies in Namibia continued, however. The following measures can be understood as the third phase of the genocide against the indigenous populations of South-West Africa: The Germans aimed at transforming the Africans into a class of proletarians or helots without any specific "tribal" identity. Therefore, the colonizers regarded the destruction of traditional cultures and lifestyles as crucial. This process started before the end of war: In July 1905, Deputy Governor Tecklenburg stated that all "tribal organization" ought to come to an end (Schaller, 2004, p. 183). Both Herero and Nama were dispossessed and all their land was officially seized by the colonial power. Moreover, the Germans wanted to control the Africans *totally*. What the Africans faced was basically a totalitarian situation. All Africans were compelled to compulsory work. The so-called native decrees of 1907 restricted the Africans' freedom of movement gravely and forced them to carry a tiny identity badge around the neck.

The German obsession with control over the Herero and Nama gradually became more radical. Since Africans often escaped from their brutal employers and got rid of their identity badges, German farmers demanded all Herero and Nama be tattooed (Zimmerer, 2001, pp. 68–109). Although Herero and Nama were militarily defeated and enslaved, colonial authorities in South-West Africa still feared possible uprisings, and thus the colonial government considered the deportation of the Africans to the German colonies in Cameroon and Papua New Guinea. However, the Germans were not able to implement their plans of large-scale deportations because of the outbreak of World War I (Schaller, 2004, pp. 189–195).

The nomadic San were also targeted by the German policy of cultural genocide. Colonial troops and police forces regularly hunted the San and forced them to live as forced laborers in permanent settlements or camps. The consequences of this forced assimilation were often lethal. A German doctor realized that the "domestication" of the San was impossible: "I believe that the capture of the San will result in the deaths of a great number of them due to the different living conditions" (quoted in Schaller, 2008, p. 314). However, this statement did not result in a different policy toward the San. Their extermination was willingly accepted.

Outstanding Historical Forces at Work that Led to the Genocide

Any examination of the genocide against the Herero and Nama has to take the racist and social-Darwinist worldview of German soldiers and settlers into account. The supreme commander of the German forces in South-West Africa was an experienced colonial soldier and left no doubt about his racist attitudes. Lothar von Trotha did not agree with Governor Leutwein and most settlers that the prosperity of the colony depended on African manpower. In a letter to his superior in Berlin, he made clear that there was only one way to end the war with the Herero:

> There is only one question to me: how to end the war? The ideas of the governor and the other old African hands and my ideas are diametrically opposed. For a long time they have wanted to negotiate and have insisted that the Hereros are a necessary raw material for the future of the land. I totally oppose this view. I believe that the nation as such must be annihilated or if this is not possible from a military standpoint then they must be driven from the land. (quoted in Drechsler, 1980, p. 161)

In an article for a local newspaper in South-West Africa, Lothar von Trotha expressed how much his thinking was influenced by social-Darwinism: "At the outset, we cannot do without the natives. But they finally have to melt away. Where the climate allows the white man to work, philanthropic views cannot banish Darwin's law 'Survival of the Fittest'" (quoted in Krüger, 1999, p. 66).

Social-Darwinist theories were very popular at the time. However, Lothar von Trotha's fanaticism was extreme. The German chancellor, von Bülow, had disagreed with the appointment of von Trotha as supreme commander for South-West Africa as he feared that it would be difficult to control the stubborn general. It was only the pressure coming from the German military high command that made von Trotha's appointment possible. The German kaiser had a personal affection for adventurous and laddish "war heroes." Furthermore, Alfred von Schlieffen, the head of the German army, shared von Trotha's worldview and approved his war aims in the colony, as a letter to the chancellor reveals:

> One can agree with his plan of annihilating the whole people or driving them from the land. The possibility of whites living peacefully together with blacks after what has happened is very slight unless at first the blacks are reduced to forced labor, that is, a sort of slavery. An enflamed racial war can be ended only through the annihilation or complete subjugation of one of the parties. (Quoted in Drechsler, 1980, p. 162)

Lothar von Trotha's and Alfred von Schlieffen's racist worldview was particularly extreme in that they regarded Africans as a "dying race." Most colonial politicians and experts agreed that South-West Africa ought to become a European settler colony inhabited by whites; however, they considered Africans to be fit enough for labor. Therefore, a majority of German settlers condemned the physical extermination of the Herero and Nama as counterproductive and preferred the establishment of a kind of apartheid system based on the destruction of indigenous cultures and customs.

Why is the Case of the Herero and Nama Important to Understanding the Complexities of Genocide?

Ideological motives alone cannot explain the genocidal outcome of the war against the Herero and Nama. The colonial war in Namibia is a typical example of how a war degenerated into genocide. Several situational factors contributed to a process of cumulative radicalization: The political peculiarities of the German Empire have already been mentioned: The *Kaiser* and his generals wanted to wage the war in South-West Africa according to their own extremist views. The imperial and military elite of the German Empire adhered to a specific military culture favoring radical and final solutions (Hull, 2005).

Social-psychological literature on the development of soldiers' readiness to commit atrocities has shown that stress and fear are decisive factors for genocidal behavior. European soldiers in Africa were usually under extreme pressure: They suffered from the harsh climate and from tropical diseases. Moreover, many colonial soldiers were not familiar with the geography and topography of the region and they had little knowledge about their enemies.

Paranoid fantasies and constant fear of ambushes were the result. Rumors about African atrocities further radicalized European soldiers. The German troops in Namibia believed that the Africans would torture white women and violate the corpses of Europeans. In the eyes of German soldiers, the alleged brutality of the African enemies justified atrocities against non-combatants (Schaller, 2010, p. 360). In a nutshell, colonial mass violence was fueled by racist ideas, but genocidal violence—for example the murder and incarceration of the Namibian Herero and Nama—was often the result of a radicalization process (Kuss, 2010).

The Impact of the Genocide on the Victim Groups

To a great extent, the Germans managed to destroy the foundations of the indigenous societies in South-West Africa. In 1944 the South African politician Willem Petrus Steenkamp stated that the Herero of Namibia had never recovered from German rule and, therefore, had committed "race suicide":

> There exists in South-West Africa a widespread belief that the declining birthrate amongst the Herero is due to a nation-wide determination for committing national or race suicide. This resolution was soon taken after the German conquest, because as a race they could not reconcile themselves to the idea of subjection to Germany and thus loss of independence.... Having nothing left to exist for as a nation any longer, national suicide was started by birth control of a rigorous nature and artificial abortion. (Steenkamp, 1944, p. 8)

Steenkamp's theory has been adopted by historians and cultural anthropologists alike (Poewe, 1985). The Herero were thus portrayed as helpless victims of German colonialism. The post-war situation in South-West Africa has often been described as "the silence of the graveyard" (Drechsler, 1980, p. 230). Only in recent years have historians paid more attention to the survival strategies of the Africans (Gewald, 1999; Krüger, 1999).

Herero and Nama regularly fled from German farms, stole cattle, and started to rebuild small herds. Moreover, the Africans did not abandon their identities and preserved the memory of their past. Herero servants of the German army promoted the social reorganization of their people.

They established a broad social support system for Herero dispersed all over Namibia.

An important step in the history of the Hereros' social reconstruction was the funeral of Samuel Maharero in Okahandja on August 26, 1923. Thousands of Herero from all corners of Namibia attended this event. For the first time since the German genocide against their people, the Herero demonstrated publicly that they perceived themselves as a self-administering community with their own national identity. Every last weekend in August, the Herero gather in Okahandja to celebrate "Herero Day." They march to the graves of their former chiefs and remember the genocidal killing of their ancestors by the Germans.

Responses to the Genocide and Scholarly Perceptions

Although newspapers all around the world reported on the atrocities in South-West Africa and criticized Lothar von Trotha's policy of extermination, there was no official protest from other imperial powers. Rather, British politicians hoped the Germans would manage to quickly suppress the African resistance in Namibia since they feared the battles with the Herero and Nama could motivate the African populations in the Cape Colony and Botswana to revolt against British rule.

The mass murder of the Herero and Nama became a political issue only during World War I when British politicians were gathering arguments that could justify the seizure of the German colonies. The genocide in South-West Africa served as the prime example of Germany's inability to rule colonies for the benefit of the indigenous societies. After the conquest of Namibia by South African troops in 1915, British Major Thomas Leslie O'Reilly was instructed to collect information on German massacres and to compile them in a report. Ultimately, O'Reilly interviewed 50 survivors of the colonial war 1904–1908. His *Report on the Natives of South-West Africa and their Treatment by Germany*, which was published in 1918, constitutes one of the most important sources for the reconstruction of the Africans' experiences during the German genocide.

Raphael Lemkin, the international lawyer who coined the term genocide in 1944, was also interested in German rule in Africa. Lemkin's (unpublished) manuscripts on the war against the Herero and Nama were mainly based on O'Reilly's report. Lemkin had no doubt that the German policy against the African inhabitants of Namibia was an unambiguous genocide (Schaller, 2009).

After the horrors of World War II and the Holocaust, the fate of the Herero and Nama was almost completely forgotten outside Namibia. In the 1960s, most Germans did not even know that their country had been a major colonial power through 1918.

Only a few experts and historians such as Horst Drechsler and Helmut Bley examined Germany's colonial past. Historians from the former German Democratic Republic were especially interested in German imperialism and its fatal consequences for the Africans. Most of these historians were politically biased because of their overt sympathy for the liberation movements in the so-called third world. Nevertheless, their studies were based on rich empirical material and provided researchers and students with many important insights about the genocidal dynamics of the colonial war in Namibia (Zimmerer, 2008b).

The genocide of the Herero and Nama attracted increased awareness after the end of the Cold War and Namibia's independence from South Africa in 1990. Motivated by the success of the Holocaust restitution movement in the late 1990s, representatives of the Herero filed a lawsuit against the government of the Federal Republic of Germany and three German enterprises in the U.S. Federal Court in September 2001.[1] It was the first time that an ethnic group demanded reparation for colonial policies that fit the legal definition of genocide (Cooper, 2007). Because of many legal and political obstacles to the case, the Herero and their lawyers tried to attract public attention for their cause by emphasizing causal connections between the German genocide in South-West Africa and the Nazi genocide against the Jews. In fact, in recent years the study of the colonial war in Namibia has been dominated by this question. Historians have examined and debated whether the murder of the Herero and Nama can be seen as a kind of precursor of the Nazis' policy of extermination in Eastern Europe during World War II (Zimmerer, 2005; Madley, 2005; Gerwarth & Malinowski 2007). Whereas this debate is highly contested, genocide scholars agree that the killing of the Namibian Herero and Nama is the first genocide of the 20th century. The efforts of human rights activists and historians have finally paid off: 100 years after the outbreak of the colonial war, Heidemarie Wieczoreck-Zeul, the German minister of economic cooperation and development, visited Namibia in August 2004 and apologized officially for the German genocide in South-West Africa.

Eyewitness Accounts

In their memoirs and diaries, German soldiers and officials described their experiences during the colonial war against the Herero and Nama. They glorified their actions during the war and reported on the German army's "heroic deeds." In the aftermath, many participants of the war published their memoirs or diaries as books or newspaper articles. The German public showed great interest in such reports, and because of that the authors did not include reports of the violence committed against helpless women and children. Rather, they reflected on the murder of the Herero in a pseudo-philosophical way. That is, violence against the Africans was explained by referring to social-Darwinist ideas. The soldiers claimed that their actions supported an alleged natural process that would unavoidably lead to the disappearance of "inferior races." However, these explanations merely served as retrospective rationalizations. The memoirs and diaries also reveal how stress, fear, and rumors about alleged African atrocities radicalized the soldiers' behavior.

Whereas German soldiers and officials did not overtly report on violence against African women and children, African members of the German auxiliary corps told unreservedly how they witnessed massacres and sadistic excesses when they were interviewed after the British conquest of South-West Africa in 1915. Their statements were compiled in the *British Report on the Natives of South-West Africa and their Treatment by Germany* (Union of South Africa, 1918). The so-called *Blue Book* is an important and indispensable source. It sheds light on the experiences of Africans during the colonial war. It needs to be remembered, however, that the interviews with survivors and German collaborators were conducted more than 10 years after the events. Moreover, the intention of the British was to demonstrate Germany's failure as a "civilized" colonial power. The motives of the editors were thus political (Kössler, 2004). Nevertheless, the accounts in the *Blue Book* reveal the dimensions of violence against women and children.

Manuel Timbu, who worked for Lothar von Trotha, reported the following (excerpted from Union of South Africa, 1918, pp. 63–64):

> I was sent to Okahandja and appointed groom to the German commander, General von Trotha. I had to look after his horses and to do odd jobs at his headquarters. We followed the retreating Hereros from Okahandja to Waterberg, and from there to the borders of the Kalahari Desert. When leaving Okahandja, General von Trotha issued orders to his troops that no quarter was to be given to the enemy. No prisoners were to be taken, but all, regardless of age or sex, were to be killed. General von Trotha said, "We must exterminate them, so that we won't be bothered with rebellions in the future." As a result of this order the soldiers shot all natives we came across. It did not matter who they were. Some were peaceful people who had not gone into rebellion; others, such as old men and old women, had never left their homes; yet these were all shot. I often saw this done.
>
> Once while on the march near Hamakari beyond the Waterberg, we came to some water-holes. It was winter time and very

cold. We came on two very old Herero women. They had made a small fire and were warming themselves. They had dropped back from the main body of Hereros owing to exhaustion. Von Trotha and his staff were present. A German soldier dismounted, walked up to the old women and shot them both as they lay there. Riding along we got to a *vlei*, where we camped. While we were there a Herero woman came walking up to us from the bush. I was the Herero interpreter. I was told to take the woman to the general to see if she could give information as to the whereabouts of the enemy. I took her to General von Trotha; she was quite a young woman and looked tired and hungry. Von Trotha asked her several questions, but she did not seem inclined to give information. She said her people had all gone towards the east, but as she was a weak woman she could not keep up with them. Von Trotha then ordered that she should be taken aside and bayoneted. I took the woman away and a soldier came up with his bayonet in his hand. He offered it to me and said I had better stab the woman. I said I would never dream of doing such a thing and asked why the poor woman could not be allowed to live. The soldier laughed and said, "If you won't do it, I will show you what a German soldier can do." He took the woman aside a few paces and drove the bayonet through her body. He then withdrew the bayonet and brought it, all dripping with blood, and poked it under my nose in a jeering way, saying, "You see, I have done it." Officers and soldiers were standing around looking on, but no one interfered to save the woman. Her body was not buried, but, like all others they killed, simply allowed to lie and rot and be eaten by wild animals.

A little further ahead we came to a place where the Hereros had abandoned some goats which were too weak to go further. There was not water to be had for miles around. There we found a young Herero, a boy of about 10 years of age. He had apparently lost his people. As we passed he called out to us that he was hungry and very thirsty. I would have given him something, but was forbidden to do so. The Germans discussed the advisability of killing him, and someone said that he would die of thirst in a day or so and it was not worthwhile bothering, so they passed on and left him there.

On our return journey we again halted at Hamakari. There, near a hut, we saw an old Herero woman of about 50 or 60 years digging in the ground for wild onions. Von Trotha and his staff were present. A soldier named König jumped off his horse and shot the woman through the forehead at point blank range.

Before he shot her, he said, "I am going to kill you." She simply looked up and said, "I thank you."

That night we slept at Hamakari. The next day we moved off again and came across another woman of about 30. She was also busy digging for wild onions and took no notice of us. A soldier named Schilling walked up behind her and shot her through the back. I was an eyewitness of everything I have related.

In addition I saw the bleeding bodies of hundreds of men, women and children, old and young, lying along the roads as we passed. They had all been killed by our advance guards. I was for nearly two years with the German troops and always with General von Trotha. I know of no instance in which prisoners were spared.

Jan Cloete worked as a guide for the German colonial troops and saw how soldiers massacred Africans and killed a baby in a sadistic manner (excerpted from Union of South Africa, 1918, pp. 64–65):

I was in Omaruru in 1904. I was commandeered by the Germans to act as a guide for them to the Waterberg district, as I knew the country well. I was with the 4th Field Company under Hauptmann Richardt. The commander of the troops was General von Trotha. I was present at Hamakari, near Waterberg when the Hereros were defeated in a battle. After the battle, all men, women and children, wounded and unwounded, who fell into the hands of the Germans were killed without mercy. The Germans then pursued the others, and all stragglers on the roadside and in the veld were shot down and bayoneted. The great majority of the Herero men were unarmed and could make no fight. They were merely trying to get away with their cattle.

Some distance beyond Hamakari we camped at a water-hole. While there, a German soldier found a little Herero baby boy about nine months old lying in the bush. The child was crying. He brought it into the camp where I was. The soldiers formed a ring and started throwing the child to one another and catching it as if it were a ball. The child was terrified and hurt and was crying very much. After a time they got tired of this and one of the soldiers fixed his bayonet on his rifle and said he would catch the baby. The child was tossed into the air towards him and as it fell he caught it and transfixed the body with the bayonet. The child died in a few minutes and the incident was greeted with roars of laughter by the Germans, who seemed to think it was a great joke. I felt quite ill and turned away in disgust because, although I knew they had orders to kill all, I thought they would have pity on the child.

I decided to go no further, as the horrible things I saw upset me, so I pretended that I was ill, and as the Captain got ill too and had to return, I was ordered to go back with him as guide. After I got home I flatly refused to go out with soldiers again.

Daniel Esma Dixon was working as a transport driver for the Germans. He indicated that the Germans took no prisoners after the battle of Hamakari in August 1904 and executed Herero by hanging (excerpted from Union of South Africa, 1918, pp. 66):

In August 1904, I was taking a convoy of provisions to the troops at the front line. At a place called Ouparakane, in the Waterberg district, we were outspanned for breakfast when two Hereros, a man and his wife, came walking to us out of the bush. Under-officer Wolff and a few German soldiers were escort to the wagons and were with me. The Herero man was a cripple, and walked with difficulty, leaning on a stick and on his wife's arm. He had a bullet wound through the leg. They came to my wagon, and I spoke to them in Herero. The man said he had decided to return to Omaruru and surrender to the authorities, as he could not possibly keep up with his people who were retreating to the desert, and that his wife had decided to accompany him. He was quite unarmed and famished. I gave them some food and coffee and they sat there for over an hour telling me of their hardships and privations. The German soldiers looked on, but did not interfere. I then gave the two natives a little food for their journey. They thanked me and then started to walk along the road slowly to Omaruru. When they had gone about 60 yards away from us I saw Wolff, the under-officer, and a soldier taking aim at them. I called out, but it was too late. They shot both of them. I said to Wolff, "How on earth did you have the heart to do such a thing? It is nothing but cruel murder." He merely laughed and said, "Oh! These swine must all be killed; we are not going to spare a single one."

I spent a great part of my time during the rebellion at Oka-handja, loading stores at the depot. There the hanging of natives was a common occurrence. A German officer had the right to order a native to be hanged. No trial or court was necessary. Many were hanged merely on suspicion. One day alone I saw seven Hereros hanged in a row, and on other days twos and threes. The Germans did not worry about rope. They used ordinary fencing wire, and the unfortunate native was hoisted up by the neck and allowed to die of slow strangulation. This was all done in public, and the bodies were always allowed to hang for a day or so as an example to the other natives. Natives who were placed in gaol at that time never came out alive. Many died of sheer starvation and brutality.

Hendrik Fraser's testimony confirms that the Germans killed prisoners systematically. Fraser also mentions that the Germans poisoned the water holes in order to exterminate the fleeing Herero (excerpted from Union of South Africa, 1918, pp. 66–67):

In March 1905 I was sent from Karibib and accompanied the troops of Hauptmann Kuhne to the Waterberg. I then saw that the Germans no longer took any prisoners. They killed all men, women and children whom they came across. Hereros who were exhausted and were unable to go any further were captured and killed. At one place near Waterberg, in the direction of Gogabis, after the fight at Okokadi, a large number (I should say about 50) men, women and children and little babies fell into the hands of the Germans. They killed all the prisoners, bayoneted them.

On one occasion I saw about 25 prisoners placed in a small enclosure of thorn bushes. They were confined in a very small space, and the soldiers cut dry branches and piled dry logs all round them—men, women and children and little girls were there—when dry branches had been thickly piled up all round them the soldiers threw branches on the top of them. The prisoners were all alive and unwounded, but half starved. Having piled up the branches, lamp oil was sprinkled on the heap and it was set on fire. The prisoners were burnt to a cinder. I saw this personally. The Germans said, we should burn all these dogs and baboons in this fashion. The officers saw this and made no attempt to prevent it.

From that time to the end of the rising the killing and hanging of Hereros was practically a daily occurrence. There was no more fighting. The Hereros were merely fugitives in the bush. All the water-holes on the desert border were poisoned by the Germans before they returned. The result was that fugitives who came to drink the water either died of poisoning or, if they did not taste the water, they died of thirst.

In the following testimony, a German officer, Ludwig von Estorff, speaks about being entrusted with the persecution of the Herero in the desert (excerpt is from Gewald, 1999, p. 174):

I followed their spoor and found numerous wells which presented a terrifying sight. Cattle which had died of thirst lay scattered around the wells. These cattle had reached the wells but there had not been enough time to water them. The Herero fled ahead of us into the Sandveld. Again and again this terrible scene kept repeating itself. With feverish energy the men had worked at opening the wells, however the water became ever sparser, and wells evermore rare. They fled from one well to the next and lost virtually all their cattle and a large number of their people. The people shrunk into small remnants who continually fell into our hands. Sections of the people escaped now and later through the Sandveld into English territory. It was a policy which was equally gruesome as senseless, to hammer the people so much. We could have still saved many of them and their rich herds if we had pardoned and taken them up again. They had been punished enough. I suggested this to General von Trotha but he wanted their total extermination.

In this testimony, Hendrik Fraser, a Rehobother[2] from Keetmanshoop, speaks about the conditions for prisoners in Swakopmund, which were extremely harsh (excerpted from Union of South Africa, 1918, p. 100):

When I got to Swakopmund I saw very many Herero prisoners of war who had been captured in the rebellion which was still going on in the country [These were prisoners captured before von Trotha's arrival]. There must have been 600 men, women and children prisoners. They were in an enclosure on the beach, fenced in with barbed wire. The women were made to do hard labour just like the men. The sand is very deep and heavy there. The women had to load and unload carts and trolleys, and also to draw Scotch-cart loads of goods to Nonidas [9–10 km away] where there was a depot. The women were put in spans of eight to each Scotch-cart and were made to pull like draught animals. Many were half-starved and weak, and died of sheer exhaustion. Those who did not work well were brutally flogged with sjamboks. I even saw women knocked down with pick handles. The German soldiers did this.

I personally saw six women [Herero girls] murdered by German soldiers. They were ripped open with bayonets. I saw the bodies.

I was there for six months, and the Hereros died daily in large numbers as a result of exhaustion, ill-treatment and exposure.

They were poorly fed, and often begged me and other Cape boys for a little food.... The soldiers used the young Herero girls to satisfy their passions. Prisoners continued to come in while I was there; but I don't think half of them survived the treatment they received.

After six months at Swakopmund I was sent to Karibib towards the end of September 1904.... There, I also saw an enclosure with Hereros waiting for transport to Swakopmund. Many were dying of starvation and exhaustion. They were all very thin and worn out.

The inmates of the concentration camps in Swakopmund and Lüderitzbucht were subject to permanent maltreatment and forced labor. In the following testimony Samuel Kariko, a Herero, recalls such illtreatment (excerpted from Union of South Africa, 1918, p. 101):

When von Trotha left, we were advised of a circular which the new Governor, von Lindequist, had issued, in which he promised to spare the lives of our people if we came in from the bush and mountains where we lived like hunted game. We then began to come in. I went to Okambahe, near my old home, and surrendered. We then had no cattle left, and more than three-quarters of our people had perished, far more. There were only a few thousand of us left, and we were walking skeletons, with no flesh, only skin and bones. They collected us in groups and made us work for the little food we got. I was sent down with others to an island far in the south, at Luderitzbucht. There, on that island, were thousands of Herero and Hottentot prisoners. We had to live there. Men, women and children were all huddled together. We had no proper clothing, no blankets, and the night air on the sea was bitterly cold. The wet sea fogs drenched us and made our teeth chatter. The people died there like flies that had been poisoned. The great majority died there. The little children and the old people died first, and then the women and the weaker men. No day passed without many deaths. We begged and prayed and appealed for leave to go back to our own country, which is warmer, but the Germans refused. Those men who were fit had to work during the day in the harbor and railway depots. The younger women were selected by the soldiers and taken to their camps as concubines.

The following is a statement by a German missionary, Heinrich Vedder, who confirms the terrible and inhuman conditions in the concentration camps (excerpt from Zeller, 2008, p. 64):

[Large] transports of prisoners of war arrived. These were accommodated in miserable spaces made only of sackcloth and laths and set up behind double barbed wire which enclosed the whole area of the port authority dockyard. They were forced to live 30 to 50 people to a room without distinction of age or sex. On Sundays and holidays as well as workdays, from the early morning until late in the evening, they had to work till they dropped under the cudgels of brutal overseers. Their food was worse than meager: for bodies weakened by life in the field and used to the hot sun of the interior, rice with nothing added was not sufficient to stand the cold and the unceasing exertion of all their energies in Swakopmund captivity. Hundreds were driven to their deaths like cattle and like cattle they were buried.

Herein, Herero chief Hosea Mungunda speaks about how female prisoners fell victim to sexual violence in the concentration camps (excerpted from Union of South Africa, 1918, p. 101):

Those who were left after the rebellion were put into compounds and made to work for their food. They were sent to farms, and also to the railways and elsewhere. Many were sent to Luderitzbucht and Swakopmund and died in captivity; and many were hanged and flogged nearly to death and died as the result of ill-treatment. Many were mere skeletons when they came in and surrendered, and they could not stand bad food and ill-treatment.... The young girls were selected and taken as concubines for soldiers; but even the married women were assaulted and interfered with.... It was one continuous ill-treatment.... When the railways were completed and the harbor works, we were sent out to towns and to farms to work. We were distributed and allocated to farmers, whether we liked them or not.

Herein, Traugott Tjienda, a survivor of the German genocide against the Herero, recalls the forced labor he suffered at the hands of the Germans (excerpted from Union of South Africa, 1918, pp. 101–102):

I was made to work on the Otavi [railway] line which was being built. We were not paid for our work, we were regarded as prisoners. I worked for two years without pay.... As our people came in from the bush they were made to work at once. They were merely skin and bone. They were so thin that one could see through their bones. They looked like broomsticks.... Bad as they were, they were made to work; and whether they worked or were lazy they were repeatedly sjambokked by the German overseers. The soldiers guarded us at night in big compounds made of thorn bushes. I was a kind of foreman over the labourers. I had 528 people, all Hereros, in my work party. Of these 148 died while working on the line.

The Herero women were compounded with the men. They were made to do manual labour as well. They did not carry the heavy rails, but they had to load and unload wagons and trucks and to work with picks and shovels. The totals above given include women and children....

When our women were prisoners on the railway work they were compelled to cohabit with soldiers and white railways labourers. The fact that a woman was married was no protection. Young girls were raped and very badly used. They were taken out of the compounds into the bush and there assaulted. I don't think any of them escaped this, except the older ones.

Leslie Cruikshank Bartlet from England comments herein that the Germans perceived the ill-treatment of the African prisoners as a form of just punishment (excerpted from Union of South Africa, 1918, p. 102):

I came to German South-West Africa with the first transport during the Hottentot war in 1905. The prisoners, Hereros and Hottentots, mostly women, and all in a terribly emaciated condition, were imprisoned on an island adjoining Luderitzbucht. The mortality amongst the prisoners was excessive, funerals taking place at the rate of ten to fifteen daily. Many were said to have attempted escape by swimming, and I have seen corpses of women prisoners washed up on the beach between Luderitzbucht and the cemetery. One corpse I remember was that of a young woman with practically fleshless limbs whose breasts had been eaten by jackals. This I reported at the German Police Station, but on passing the same way three or four days later the body was still where I saw it first. The German soldiery spoke freely of atrocities committed by Hereros and Hottentots during the war, and seemed to take a pride in wreaking vengeance on those unfortunate women. When the railway from Luderitzbucht to Keetmanshoop was started gangs of prisoners, mostly women, scarcely able to walk from weakness and starvation, were employed as labourers. They were brutally treated. I personally saw a gang of these prisoners, all women, carrying a heavy double line of rails with iron sleepers attached on their shoulders, and unable to bear the weight they fell. One woman fell under the rails which broke her leg and held it fast. The Schachtmeister [ganger], without causing the rail to be lifted, dragged the woman under and threw her on one side, where she died untended. The general treatment was cruel, and many instances were told me, but that which I have stated I personally saw.

Herero and Nama were officially released from captivity in March 1907. The concentration camps were shut down. But the Africans were far from being free. Here, Hosea Mugunda, a Herero headman from Windhoek, speaks about the lack of freedom (excerpted from Union of South Africa, 1918, p. 114):

When the railways and the harbor works were completed, we were sent out to towns and to farms to work. We were distributed and allocated to farmers whether we liked them or not. The farmers could do as they liked; many trashed and ill-treated us and fed us badly. If we ran away the police gave 25 lashes or even 30, and then sent us back to the farmer. The courts gave us no protection, the evidence of a native was never accepted against that of a white man. No regard was had for family relationships. Often a man was sent to one place to work, his wife to quite another district or farm, and the children elsewhere. All children over seven years had to work, and were taken by force from the parents and sent away to work. Many men never saw their wives again, many wives lost their husbands, and the children often disappeared forever.

German officials and farmers resorted to flogging and torture in order to secure their despotic rule over the Africans. Herein, Richard Kainzo, a Herero who served as a so-called police-boy, describes his tasks and the colonial regime for which he served (excerpted from Union of South Africa, 1918, pp. 114–115):

In 1905 the Germans made me chief police-boy at Omaruru to do the floggings. That was the sole work of the chief police-boy.... The custom was for the sergeant-in-charge of the police to decide on all complaints made by or against natives. If the charge was made by a German master and it was a very serious charge, such as theft, the sergeant would send natives accused to the District Chief [Bezirksamtmann] for trial. Petty cases were dealt with summarily by the sergeant merely on verbal information by the white master. For instance, if a German brought his native servant to the sergeant and said the native had been idle or negligent or cheeky, the sergeant would immediately order me to take the native and prepare him for flogging. I and my assistant had then to take the native to the kraal near the police station, strip him and make him lie over a tub or a box. We generally used a tub. The sergeant would then come along and in his presence and that of the German master I was ordered to give the native 15, 20, or 25 lashes with a heavy sjambok. The sergeant counted and generally told me when to stop beating. We nearly always kept on beating until the blood began to flow. I often had to beat men whom I knew well; I used to feel sorry for them and tried to hit as lightly as possible. When the sergeant noticed this he would swear at me and promise me 25 lashes for myself if I did not do my duty. Therefore I had to hit hard. These German police sergeants were nearly all ex-soldiers who had helped General von Trotha to exterminate our nation, and they had no mercy for us. They hated the Hereros. I remained in service as a police-boy only because it gave me some sort of protection. I was not treated like the rest of our natives as I had to help the German police.

Very often innocent people were badly flogged in this way merely to satisfy the spite of their masters. When a complaint was made by a white man the native was not allowed to speak or to give any evidence. We natives were always told that we did not know what was meant by truth, and that a white man could never lie....

Many prisoners were also kept in heavy chains fastened to the walls of their cells. Most prisoners were placed in chains. Although a white man was always believed, a native's complaint was never accepted by the police. I have seen dozens of natives who had been badly flogged by their own masters, and who came to complain of their treatment, kicked away and ordered to go back at once and resume work. In fact, some of the complainants were flogged over again by the police for the offence of leaving their master's farm [which they had to do to complain] without his permission.

Notes

1. The Herero claimants resorted to the Alien Torts Claim Act of 1789 that grants jurisdiction to U.S. Federal Courts over "any civil action by an alien for a tort only, committed in violation of the law of nations or a treaty of the United States." The U.S. legal culture provided the Herero with convenient conditions for their cause. See Bazyler (2004).
2. An ethnic group in Namibia.

References

Bazyler, Michael J. (2004). Lex Americana: Holocaust litigation as a restitution model for other massive human rights abuses. In Dominik J. Schaller, Rupen Boyadjian, & Vivianne Berg (Eds.) *Enteignet-Vertrieben-Ermordet: Beiträge zur Genozidforschung* (pp. 349–394). Zürich: Chronos.

Bley, Helmut (1968). *Kolonialherrschaft und Sozialstruktur in Deutsch-Südwestafrika 1894–1914*. Hamburg: Leibniz.

Bühler, Andreas Heinrich (2003). *Der Namaaufstand gegen die deutsche Kolonialherrschaft in Namibia von 1904–1913*. Frankfurt am Main: IKO-Verlag.

Cooper, Allan D. (2007). Reparations for the Herero genocide: Defining the limits of international litigation. *African Affairs, 106*(422), 113–126.

Drechsler, Horst (1980). *Let us die fighting. The struggle of the Herero and Nama against German imperialism*. London: Zed Press.

Erichsen, Casper W. (2008). Forced labour in the concentration camp on Shark Island. In Jürgen Zimmerer & Joachim Zeller (Eds.) *Genocide in German south-west Africa: The colonial war of 1904–1908 and its aftermath* (pp. 84–99). Monmouth: Merlin Press.

Gerwarth, Robert, & Malinowski, Stephan (2007). Der Holocaust als "genozidale Kolonialkrieg"? Europäische Kolonialgewalt und nationalsozialistische Vernichtungskrieg. *Geschichte und Gesellschaft, 33*(3), 439–466.

Gewald, Jan-Bart (1999). *Herero heroes. A socio-political history of the Herero of Namibia 1890–1923*. Oxford: John Currey.

Hillebrecht, Werner (2008). The Nama and the war in the south. In Jürgen Zimmerer & Joachim Zeller (Eds.) *Genocide in German south-west Africa: The colonial war of 1904–1908 and its aftermath* (pp. 143–158). Monmouth: Merlin Press.

Hull, Isabel V. (2005). *Absolute destruction: Military culture and the practices of war in Imperial Germany*. Ithaca, NY: Cornell University Press.

Irle, Jakob (1906). *Die Herer: Ein Beitrag zur Landes-, Volks- und Missionskunde*. Gütersloh: C. Bertelsmann.

Kaulich, Udo (2001). *Die Geschichte der ehemaligen Kolonie Deutsch-Südwestafrika (1884–1914): Eine Gesamtdarstellung*. Frankfurt am Main: Peter Lang.

Kössler, Reinhart (2004). Sjambok or Cane? Reading the *Blue Book*. *Journal of Southern African Studies, 30*(3), 703–708.

Krüger, Gesine (1999). *Kriegsbewältigung und Geschichtsbewusstsein: Realität, Deutung und Verarbeitung des deutschen Kolonialkriegs in Namibia 1904 bis 1907*. Göttingen: Vandenhoeck und Ruprecht.

Krüger, Gesine (2008). The golden age of the pastoralists. In Jürgen Zimmerer & Joachim Zeller (Eds.) *Genocide in German south-west Africa: The colonial war of 1904–1908 and its aftermath* (pp. 3–18). Monmouth: Merlin Press.

Kuss, Susanne (2010). *Deutsches Militär auf kolonialen Kriegsschauplätzen: Eskalation von Gewalt zu Beginn des 20. Jahrhunderts*. Berlin: Ch. Links.

Lau, Brigitte (1978). *Namibia in Jonker Afrikaner's time*. Windhoek: National Archives of Namibia.

Leutwein, Theodor (1906). *Elf Jahre Gouverneur in Deutsch-Südwestafrika*. Berlin: Mittler und Sohn.

Madley, Benjamin (2005). From Africa to Auschwitz: How German south west Africa incubated ideas and methods adopted and developed by the Nazis in Eastern Europe. *European History Quarterly, 35*(3), 429–464.

Poewe, Karla (1985). *The Namibian Herero: A history of their psychological disintegration and survival*. Lewinston, ME: Edwin Mellen.

Rohrbach, Paul (1953). *Um des Teufels Handschrift: Zwei Menschenalter erlebter Weltgeschichte*. Hamburg: Hans Dulk.

Schaller, Dominik J. (2004). Kolonialkrieg, Völkermord und Zwangsarbeit in Deutsch-Südwestafrika. In Dominik J. Schaller, Rupen Boyadjian, & Vivianne Berg (Eds.) *Enteignet-Vertrieben-Ermordet: Beiträge zur Genozidforschung* (pp. 147–232). Zürich: Chronos.

Schaller, Dominik J. (2008). From conquest to genocide: Colonial rule in German Southwest Africa and German East Africa. In A. Dirk Moses (Ed.) *Empire, colony, genocide: Conquest, occupation, and subaltern resistance in world history* (pp. 296–324). New York: Berghahn.

Schaller, Dominik J. (2009). Raphael Lemkin's view of European colonial rule in Africa: Between condemnation and admiration. In Dominik J. Schaller & Jürgen Zimmerer (Eds.) *The origins of genocide: Raphael Lemkin as a historian of mass violence* (pp. 87–94). London: Routledge.

Schaller, Dominik J. (2010). Genocide and mass violence in the 'Heart of Darkness': Africa in the colonial period. In Donald Bloxham & A. Dirk Moses (Eds.) *The Oxford handbook of genocide studies* (pp. 345–364). Oxford: Oxford University Press.

Siiskonen, Harri (1990). *Trade and socioeconomic change in Ovamboland, 1850–1906.* Helsinki: Suomen Historiallinen Seura.

Sobich, Frank Oliver (2006). *Schwarze Bestien: Rote Gefahr. Rassismus und Antisozialismus im deutschen Kaiserreich.* Frankfurt am Main: Campus.

Steenkamp, Willem Petrus (1944). *Is the south-west African Herero committing race suicide?* Cape Town: Unie-Volkspers.

Union of South Africa (1918). *Report on the natives of South-West Africa and their treatment by Germany: Prepared in the Administrator's Office, Windhuk, south-west Africa, January 1918.* London: H.M. Stationery Office.

Zeller, Joachim (2008). "Ombepera i koza—The cold is killing me": A history of the concentration camp on Shark Island. In Jürgen Zimmerer & Joachim Zeller (Eds.) *Genocide in German south-west Africa: The colonial war of 1904–1908 and its aftermath* (pp. 64–83). Monmouth: Merlin Press.

Zimmerer, Jürgen (1999). Kriegsgefangene im Kolonialkrieg: Der Krieg gegen die Herero und Nama in Deutsch-Südwestafrika (1904–1907). In Rüdiger Overmans (Ed.) *In der Hand des Feindes: Kriegsgefangenschaft von der Antike bis zum Zweiten Weltkrieg* (pp. 277–294). Köln: Böhlau.

Zimmerer, Jürgen (2001). *Deutsche Herrschaft über Afrikaner: Staatlicher Machtanspruch und Wirklichkeit im kolonialen Namibia.* Münster: Lit-Verlag.

Zimmerer, Jürgen (2005). The birth of the 'Ostland' out of the spirit of colonialism: A postcolonial perspective on Nazi policy of conquest and extermination. *Patterns of Prejudice, 39*(2), 197–219.

Zimmerer, Jürgen (2008a). War, concentration camps and genocide in south-west Africa: The first German genocide. In Jürgen Zimmerer & Joachim Zeller (Eds.) *Genocide in German south-west Africa: The colonial war of 1904–1908 and its aftermath* (pp. 41–63). Monmouth: Merlin Press.

Zimmerer, Jürgen (2008b). Colonial genocide: The Herero and Nama War (1904–8) in German south west Africa and its significance. In Dan Stone (Ed.) *The historiography of genocide* (pp. 323–343). Basingstoke: Palgrave Macmillan.

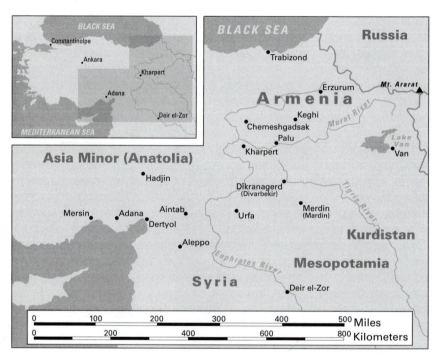

Map 4.1 Armenia

CHAPTER **4**

The Armenian Genocide

ROUBEN P. ADALIAN

Between the years 1915 and 1923 the vast majority of the Armenian population of Anatolia and historical West Armenia was eliminated. The Armenians had lived in the area for some 3,000 years. Since the 11th century, when Central Asian tribal armies prevailed over them, Armenians had lived as subjects of various Turkish dynasties. The last and longest-lived of these dynasties were the Ottomans, who created a vast empire stretching from Eastern Europe to Western Asia and North Africa. To govern this immense country, the Ottomans imposed a strictly hierarchical social system that subordinated non-Muslims as second-class subjects deprived of basic rights. In its waning days, with the empire in decline and territorially confined to the Middle East, the Ottoman leaders decided that the only way to save the Turkish state was to reduce the Christian populations. Beginning in April 1915, the Armenians of Anatolia were deported to Syria and the Armenian population of West Armenia was driven to Mesopotamia. Described euphemistically as a "resettlement policy" by the perpetrators, the deportations, in fact, constituted and resulted in genocide. In the end, after eight years of turmoil in the region, the Armenians had disappeared from their homeland.

Who Committed the Genocide?

In 1915 the Ottoman Empire was governed by a dictatorial triumvirate. Enver was Minister of War. Talaat was Minister of the Interior. Jemal was Minister of the Navy and military governor of Syria. All were members of the Committee of Union and Progress (CUP), called

117

Unionists for short. They were known in the West as the Young Turks. They had started out as members of a clandestine political organization that staged a revolution in 1908, replaced the ruler of the country in 1909, and finally seized power by a coup in 1913 (Ramsaur, 1957; Zürcher, 1998; Charny, 1999).

When World War I started, the Young Turk Committee exercised near total control in the government. Party functionaries had been appointed to posts all across the empire. Unionist cells had been organized in every major town and city. Unionist officers commanded virtually all of the Ottoman army. The cabinet was entirely beholden to the CUP. Key decisions were made by the triumviri in consultation with their party ideologues and in conformity with overt and covert party objectives. As heads of government and leaders of the CUP, Enver, Talaat, and Jemal had at their disposal immense resources of power and an arsenal of formal and informal instruments of coercion (Libaridian, 1985, pp. 37–49).

Organized in reaction to the autocratic regime of the sultan Abdul-Hamid II (1876–1909), the Young Turks originally advocated a platform of constitutionalism, egalitarianism, and liberalism. They attributed the weakness of the Ottoman Empire to its retrograde system of government. They hoped to reform the state along the progressive and modernizing course of the Western European countries. However, after the revolution, they were surprised by the strength of conservative and reactionary forces in Ottoman society and were just as quickly disillusioned by the posture of the European powers, which vied with one another for influence in the Ottoman Empire. Their realization that the problems of the Ottoman Empire were systemic and endemic became the source of their own retrenchment and growing intransigence. Also, suspicious of British, French, and Russian colonialist designs, defeated in war by the Italians, and challenged militarily by neighboring Greece, Serbia, and Bulgaria, countries which were formerly subject states of the empire, the Young Turks increasingly looked toward Germany as an ally and as the model nation-state to emulate. By 1913 the advocates of liberalism had lost out to radicals in the party who promoted a program of forcible Turkification.

By the time the first shots of World War I were fired in August 1914, the CUP had become a dictatorial, xenophobic, intolerant clique intent on pursuing a policy of racial exclusivity. Emboldened by its alliance with Imperial Germany, the CUP also prepared to embark on a parallel course of militarism. German war materiel poured into the country, and Turkish officers trained at military schools in Germany. German army and navy officers drilled the Ottoman forces, drew their battle plans, built fortifications, and when war erupted, stayed on as advisors whose influence often exceeded that of local commanders (Sachar, 1969, pp. 5–31; Trumpener, 1968, pp. 62–107; Dinkel, 1991, pp. 77–133).

Because of the preponderance of the Germans in Ottoman military affairs, the lurking question of the degree of their involvement in either advising or permitting the deportation of the Armenians has been asked many times (Dadrian, 1996). Ultimate responsibility for the Armenian genocide, however, must rest with those who considered and took the decision to deport and massacre the Armenian population of the Ottoman Empire. It also rests with those who implemented the policy of the central government, and, finally, with those who personally carried out the acts that extinguished Armenian society in its birthplace. In this equation, the heaviest burden falls on the members of the CUP. At every level of the operation against the Armenians, party functionaries relayed, received, and enforced the orders of the government. The state's responsibility to protect its citizens was disregarded by the CUP. The Ministries of the Interior and of War were charged with the task of expelling the Armenians from their homes and driving them into the Syrian desert (Dadrian, 1986). The army assigned soldiers and officers to oversee the deportation process (Toynbee, 1916, pp. 637–653; Ternon, 1981, pp. 221–239). Killing units were organized to slaughter the Armenians (Dadrian, 1989, pp. 274–277). By withholding from them the protection of the state and by exposing them to all the vagaries of nature, the Young Turk government also disposed of large numbers of Armenians through starvation (Ternon, 1981, pp. 249–260). In the absence of even minimal sanitation, let alone health care, epidemics broke out in the concentration camps and augmented the death toll.

How was the Genocide Committed?

The genocide of the Armenians involved a three-part plan conceived with secrecy and deliberation and implemented with organization and efficiency. The plan consisted of deportation, execution, and starvation. Each part of the plan had a specific purpose.

The most thoroughly implemented part of the plan was the deportation of Armenians in historical Armenia in the east, in Anatolia to the west, and even in European Turkey. Beginning in April 1915 and continuing through the summer and fall, the vast majority of the Armenians in the Ottoman Empire were deported. Upon the orders of the Ottoman government, often with only three days' notice, village after village and town after town was emptied of its Armenian inhabitants.

Many were moved by train (Toynbee, 1916, pp. 407–463). Some relied on horse-drawn wagons. A few farmers took their mules and were able to carry some belongings part of the way. Most Armenians walked. As more and more people were displaced, long convoys of deportees, comprised mostly of women and children, formed along the roads of

Anatolia and Armenia, all headed in one direction—south to the Syrian desert. Many never made it that far. Only one-quarter of all deportees survived the hundreds of miles and weeks of walking. Exhaustion, exposure, and fear took a heavy toll, especially on the old and the very young (Hairapetian, 1984, pp. 41–145).

The Ottoman government had made no provisions for the feeding and the housing of the hundreds of thousands of Armenian deportees on the road (Toynbee, 1916, pp. 545–569). Indeed, local authorities went to great length to make travel an ordeal from which there was little chance of survival (Davis, 1989, pp. 69–70). At every turn, Armenians were robbed of their possessions, had their loved ones held to ransom, and even had their clothing taken off their backs. In some areas Kurdish horsemen given to marauding and kidnapping were let loose upon the helpless caravans of deportees (Hairapetian, 1984, p. 96; Kloian, 1985, p. 8). Apart from the sheer bedlam of their raids and the killing that accompanied it, they carried away the goods they snatched and frequently seized Armenian children and women.

The Armenians were brought to the Syrian desert for their termination (Walker, 1980, pp. 227–230). Tens of thousands died from exposure to the scorching heat of the summer days and the cold of the night in the open. Men and women dying of thirst were shot for approaching the Euphrates River. Women were stripped naked, abused, and murdered. Others despairing of their fate threw themselves into the river and drowned. Mothers gave their children away to Arab Bedouins to spare them from certain death. The killing units completed their task at a place called Deir el-Zor. In this final carnage, children were smashed against rocks, women torn apart with swords, men were mutilated, others thrown into flames alive. Every cruelty was inflicted on the remnants of the Armenian people.

Thus, the fact is, deportations were not intended to be an orderly relocation process (Walker, 1980, pp. 227–230). Rather, they were meant to drive the Armenians into the open and expose them to every conceivable abuse (Hovannisian, 1967, pp. 50–51). At remote sites along the routes traversed by the convoys of deportees, the killing units slaughtered the Armenians with sword and bayonet (Dadrian, 1989, p. 272; Walker, 1980, p. 213). In a random frenzy of butchering, they cut down persons of all ages and of both genders. These periodic attacks upon the unarmed and starving Armenians continued until they reached the Syrian desert.

The Ottoman government had taken precautionary measures to minimize resistance to the deportations. The most lethal of these measures consisted of the execution of the able-bodied men in the Armenian population. The men conscripted into the Turkish armies were the first group in Armenian society targeted for collective execution. Upon the instruction of the War Ministry, these men were disarmed, forced into labor battalions, and either worked to death or outright murdered (Morgenthau, 1918, p. 302; Kuper, 1986, pp. 46–47; Sachar, 1969, p. 98).

Subsequently, the older males who had stayed behind to till the fields and run the stores were summoned by the government and ordered to prepare themselves for removal from their places of habitation. Virtually all the men turned themselves over without an inkling that their government contemplated their murder. They were immediately imprisoned, many were tortured, and all of them were taken away, sometimes in chains, and felled in mass executions (Toynbee, 1916, pp. 640–641).

To assure the complete subservience of the Armenian people to the government's deportation edicts and to eliminate the possibility of protestation, prominent leaders were specially selected for swift excision from their communities (Davis, 1989, p. 51). Although the wholesale measures against the Armenians were already in the process of implementation by late April, the symbolic beginning of the Armenian genocide is dated to the evening of April 24, 1915. That night, the most gifted men of letters, the most notable jurists, the most respected educators, and many others, including high-ranking clergy, were summarily arrested in Constantinople, the capital of the Ottoman Empire and sent to the interior—many never to be heard from again (Ternon, 1981, pp. 216–219; Balakian, 2009, pp. 56–73).

Why was the Genocide Committed?

The Armenian genocide was committed to solve the "Armenian Question" in the Ottoman Empire. There were at the very least five basic reasons for the emergence of this question. The first had to do with the decline of the Ottoman empire and internal demographic and economic pressures created upon the non-Muslim minority communities that began to experience ever-increasing and violent competition for the land resources they historically controlled. The government's failure to guarantee security of life and property led the Armenians to seek internal reforms that would improve their living conditions. These demands only invited resistance and intransigence from the government, which convinced many Armenians that the Ottoman regime was not interested in providing them the protection they needed and the civil rights they desired (Nalbandian, 1963, pp. 67–89).

Second, great-power diplomacy that offered the hope of redressing the iniquities of the Ottoman system proved inadequate to the task. The greater interest in maintaining the balance of power in Europe compromised half-hearted measures at humanitarian intervention in response to crises and atrocities. As the Armenians turned to the European powers to invite attention to their plight, the Ottomans only grew more suspicious of the intentions of the Armenians. European designs on the Ottoman Empire left the latter's government in a state of perpetual anxiety concerning its defense. Thus, the appeal of the Armenians to the Christian countries of Europe was viewed as seditious by the Ottomans. On earlier occasions European powers had exploited the tensions in Ottoman society to intervene on behalf of Christian populations. With the passage of time the Ottomans became more resolved to prevent the recurrence of such intervention by quickly and violently suppressing expressions of social and political discontent (Dadrian, 1989, pp. 242–255; 1995, pp. 61–97).

Third, the military weakness of the Ottoman Empire left it exposed to external threats and therefore made it prone to resorting to brutality as a method of containing domestic dissent, especially with disaffected non-Muslim minorities. In fact, a cycle of escalating violence against the Armenians had set in by the late 1800s (Dadrian, 1989, pp. 232–242; Kirakossian, 2004, pp. 23–33).

Fourth, the reform measures introduced in the 19th century to modernize the Turkish state had initially encouraged increased expectations from Armenians that better government and even representation were imminent possibilities. The periodic massacre of large numbers of Armenians, however, undermined the confidence of the community in its government and in the prevailing international order. This disaffection became the source of a growing Armenian national consciousness, which in turn contributed to the formation of political organizations seeking emancipation from lawlessness and discrimination (Levene, 1998, pp. 393–433).

Lastly, the rapid modernization experienced by Armenians who were more open to European concepts of progress through education resulted in great resentment among the Muslim populations of the Ottoman Empire who saw the interests of Armenians more in line with countries they regarded as infidel than with the state ruling over them.

By the early 20th century, the Ottomans had been forced out of southeastern Europe. Having relinquished the mostly Christian and Slavic regions of the Balkans, the Young Turks sought to restore the empire on new foundations. They found their justification in the concepts of Turkism and Pan-Turanism. Turkism fundamentally altered Ottoman self-perceptions based on religious precepts by promoting a national identity emphasizing the ethnicity of the Turks of Anatolia to the exclusion of other populations. Turkism also promoted the idea that the region should be the exclusive domain of the Turkish nation (Üngör, 2008, pp. 15–39). Pan-Turanism advanced the idea of conquering lands stretching into Central Asia inhabited by other Turkic-speaking peoples. Many of these Turkic peoples were living under Russian rule, and the Young Turks believed that advancing Ottoman armies would be received as liberators (Walker, 1980, pp. 189–191). The Pan-Turanian goal was to unify all the Turkic peoples into a single empire led by the Ottoman Turks (Parla, 1985).

In this formulation, the Armenians presented an ethno-religious anomaly. They were an indigenous Christian people of the Middle East who, despite more than 14 centuries of Muslim domination, had avoided Islamification. When the CUP began to implement its policy of Turkification, the Armenians resisted the CUP's plans. For example, Armenians had worked hard to build up the infrastructure of their communities, including an extensive network of elementary and secondary schools. Through education, they hoped to preserve their culture and identity and to obtain participation in the government. The new emphasis on Turkism and the heightened suspicion of the subject nationalities by the Turks was warning enough for the Armenians to redouble their effort to gain a say in at least the governance of regions where Armenians were concentrated (Libaridian, 1987, pp. 219–223).

In the increasing tension between the assimilationist policies of the Young Turk government and Armenian hopes for administrative reforms and aspirations for a measure of local self-government, the coincidence of resistance to CUP policies and the beginning of World War I proved fatal for the Armenians. As German forces were prevailing against Russia in Europe, a second front in Asia seemed to guarantee success for the Ottomans. Confident of their strength and witness to the early military victories of the German army, the Young Turks chose to enter the war. They believed that the great conflict among the imperial powers of Europe offered the Ottoman Empire an opportunity to regain a position of dominance in the region. However, that was not to be.

The fate of the Armenians was sealed in early 1915 with the defeat of the Ottoman offensive into Russian territory. The Russians not only stopped the Ottoman advance but slowly moved into Ottoman territory. The failure of the campaign was principally the fault of Enver, the Minister of War, who had taken personal command of the eastern front and chosen to fight a major battle in the dead of winter in rugged and snowbound terrain. With his ambitions dashed, this would-be conqueror and self-styled liberator exacted vengeance from the Armenian population.

Instead of accepting responsibility for their ill-conceived invasion plans and the consequential defeat of their armies, the Young Turks placed the blame on the Armenians by accusing them of collaboration with the enemy (Morgenthau, 1918, pp. 293–300). Charging the entire Armenian population with treason and sedition, the Young Turks decided to kill the innocent for the actions of those who had chosen to put a stop to their planned conquests. That was the reason, at least, given by the Minister of the Interior when asked about the CUP policy of deporting the Armenians (Morgenthau, 1918, p. 327; Trumpener, 1968, pp. 207–210). World War I, in effect, provided the opportunity to implement the Turkification of the Ottoman Empire by methods that exceeded legislation, intimidation, and expropriation. Under the cover of war, with no obligation to uphold international agreements and in an atmosphere of heightened tensions, the Unionists found their justification and opportunity to resort to extreme measures. The Turkish state now could be created internally. With the Armenians eradicated, one less racial grouping would be living on Ottoman territory. One less disenchanted group would have to be tolerated. The problems with the Armenians would be automatically resolved by eliminating the Armenians. In a country of 20 million people, the Armenians constituted only about 10% of the population. It was easily within the reach of the Ottoman government to displace and kill that many people.

For all the historical, political, and military reasons that may be cited to explain the Young Turk policy of destroying the Armenians, it must be understood that ultimately the decision to commit genocide was taken consciously. Genocide is not explained by circumstance. Mass murder is an act deliberately conceived. Decision-makers can always exercise other options in dealing with serious conflicts. The real cause of genocide lies in the self-licensing of those in charge of government with irresponsibility toward human life and amorality in the conception of their social policies. Genocide is the fulfillment of absolute tyranny. In the new social order conceived by the Young Turks, there was no room for the Armenians. They had become that excess population of which tyrants are prone to dispose.

Who were the Victims?

The Armenians were an ancient people who from the first millennium BC lived in a mountainous plateau in Asia Minor, a country to which they gave their name. This was their homeland. The area was absorbed by the Ottomans and became the eastern provinces of the Ottoman Empire in the 16th century. Two thousand years earlier the Armenians had formed one of the more durable states in the region. A series of monarchical dynasties and princely families had been at the head of the Armenian nation. Early in the 4th century, the king of Armenia accepted Christianity, making his country the first to formally recognize the new faith. Armenians developed their own culture and spoke a unique language. A distinct alphabet, native poetry, original folk music, an authentic architectural style, and centuries-old traditions characterized their separate civilization (Lang, 1970; 1981; Bournoutian, 2002; Adalian, 2010).

The remoteness of Armenia from the centers of urban life in the ancient world kept the Armenians on the periphery of the empires of Antiquity. Their distinctiveness was reinforced by the mountainous country and the harsh and long winters which discouraged new settlers. Their own armies fought off many invaders; but through the course of the centuries, Armenia proved too small a country to withstand the continued menace of outside aggression. The strength of its armies was sapped. Its leaders were defeated in battle, and its kings were exiled and never returned. Increasingly exposed to invasions, the Armenians finally succumbed to the occupying forces of a new people that emerged from the east.

Persians, Greeks, Romans, Arabs, Byzantines, and Mongols, each in turn lorded over the Armenians; however, only the Turks made permanent settlements in Armenia. The seeds of a mortal conflict were planted as the Turks grew in number and periodically displaced the Armenians. Beginning from the 11th century, towns, cities, and sometimes entire districts of Armenia were abandoned by the Armenians as they fled from the exactions of their new rulers. Unlike all the other conquerors of Armenia, the Turks never left. In time, Armenia became Turkey. The genocide of 1915 brought to a brutal culmination a 1,000-year struggle of the Armenian people to hold on to their homeland and of the Turks to take it away from them.

The Ottoman Turks who built an empire around the city of Constantinople after conquering it in 1453, and who eventually seized the areas of historical Armenia, developed a hierarchically organized society. Non-Muslims were relegated to second-class status and were subjected to discriminatory laws. The constant pressure on the Armenian population resulted in the further dispersion of the Armenians. Yet, despite the difficulties they endured and the disadvantages they faced, Armenian communities throughout the cities of the Ottoman Empire attained a tolerable living standard. By the 19th century a prosperous middle-class emerged which became the envy of the Turkish population and a source of distrust for the Ottoman government (Barsoumian, 1982, pp. 171–184).

As the Armenians recovered their national confidence, they increased their demands for reforms in Armenia, where conditions continued to deteriorate. The government, however, was opposed to the idea of introducing measures and policies that would have enhanced the progress of an industrious minority which already managed a sizable portion of Ottoman commerce and industry. This reluctance only contributed to the alienation of the Armenians from the Ottoman regime. The more the Armenians complained, objected, and dissented, the more the Ottoman government grew annoyed, resistant, and impatient. By refusing to introduce significant reform to its autocratic form of government and to restrain the arbitrariness of local administration, the Ottoman rulers placed the Armenian and the Turkish peoples on a collision course (Astourian, 1992, 1998).

Who was Involved in the Genocide?

The Armenian genocide was organized in secret but carried out in the open (Dadrian, 1989, p. 299; 1991, p. 558). The public proclamations ordering the removal of the Armenians from their homes alerted all of Ottoman society that its government had chosen a course of action specifically targeting this one minority for unusual treatment. At no time throughout its existence had the Ottoman state taken such a step against an entire population. The manner in which the deportations were carried out notified the rest of society that the measures were intended to yield a permanent outcome.

Although the decision to proceed with genocide was taken by the CUP, the entire Ottoman state became implicated in its implementation. First, cabinet decisions were taken to deport and massacre the Armenians (Dadrian, 1989, pp. 265–267). Disguised as a relocation policy, their purpose was understood by all concerned. Second, the Ottoman parliament avowedly enacted legislation legalizing the decisions of the cabinet (Dadrian, 1989, pp. 267–274). Third, the Ministry of the Interior was delegated the responsibility of overseeing the displacement, deportation, and relocation process. This ministry, in turn, instructed local authorities on procedure, the timing of deportation, and the routing of the convoys of exiles (Dadrian, 1986, pp. 326–328). The Ministry of War was charged with the disarming of the Armenian population, the posting of officers and soldiers to herd the deportees into the desert, and the execution of the Armenian conscripts. The agencies in charge of transport were also inducted into service. To expedite the transfer of the Armenians of western Anatolia, the deportees were loaded on cattle cars and shipped en masse by train to points in the east. The telegraph service encoded and decoded the orders of the ministers and governors. The governors of the provinces relayed the orders to the district governors who in turn entrusted the local authorities, courts, and constabularies to proceed with instructions. The chain of command that put the Armenian genocide into motion joined every link in the administration of the Ottoman state.

To implement the various aspects of its policy, the CUP cabinet had to go so far as to establish new agencies. One of these was a secret extra-legal body called the Special Organization. Its mission was mass-murder (Dadrian, 1989, pp. 274–277; Akçam, 2006, pp. 149–204). It was mainly composed of convicted criminals released from prisons who were divided into units stationed at critical sites along the deportation routes and near the concentration camps in Syria. Their assignment consisted solely of reducing the number of the Armenians by carrying out massacres. Sparing bullets, which were needed for the war effort, the slaughter of the Armenians was frequently carried out with medieval weaponry—scimitars and daggers. The physical proximity with which the butchering went on left a terrifying image of the Turk among those who happened to survive an attack by squads of the Special Organization.

Additionally, the government set up a Commission on Immigrants, whose stated purpose was to facilitate the "resettlement" process. In fact, the Commission served as an on-site committee to report on the progress of the destruction of the Armenians as they were further and further removed from the inhabitable regions of Anatolia and Syria. As for the Commission on Abandoned Goods, which impounded, logged, and auctioned off Armenian possessions, this was the government's method of disposing of the immovable property of the Armenians by means that rewarded its supporters. Generally, the local CUP officials pocketed the profit. It is not known what sums might have been transferred to party coffers (Baghdjian, 1987, pp. 64–87).

The same impulse motivated the Special Organization and the Kurdish tribesmen who were given license to raid the convoys of deportees. In their case, the booty included human beings as well. It was a form of enslavement limited to younger boys and girls, who, separated from their kinsmen, would be converted to Islam and either Kurdified or Turkified in language and custom. Lastly, the public auction of Armenian girls revived a form of human bondage that was, for the most part, erased elsewhere in the world. The auctioneer made money. The purchaser had a slave servant and a harem woman added to his household. This kind of brutalization scarred countless Armenian females—girls and women. Many, incapable of bearing the shame of giving birth out of wedlock to children conceived from rape and abuse by their Kurdish and Turkish owners, chose to forgo Armenian society after the war and remained with their Muslim families. Some were rescued and a few escaped, some taking their children with them, while others, fearing reprisal, abandoned them. Armenian women taken into harems against their will were often tattooed on their arms, chest, or face as signs of their ownership and as a way to discourage escape (Sanasarian, 1989, pp. 449–461; Derderian, 2005, pp. 1–25; Bjørlund, 2009, pp. 16–58; Shemmassian, 2006, pp. 113–140).

The gender, age, occupational, and regional differences in the treatment of the Armenians reflected the varying operative value systems prevailing in Ottoman society. The Young Turk ideologues in Constantinople conceived and implemented genocide, a total destruction of Armenian society. Military officers and soldiers regarded the policy as a security measure. Others in Ottoman society saw it as a convenient way of ridding themselves of effective economic competitors, not to mention creditors. Others justified the slaughter of the Armenians as religious duty called upon by the concept of jihad or warfare against infidels or non-believers in Islam. All essentially aimed at eliminating the Armenian male population. Traditional society in the Middle East still looked upon women and children as chattel, persons lacking political personality and of transmutable ethnic identity. The cultural values of children and of females could be erased or reprogrammed. Genetic continuity was a male proposition. For many, but not the CUP, the annihilation of Armenian males would have been sufficient to block or impede the perpetuation of the Armenian people (Davis, 1989, pp. 54–63).

What were the Outstanding Historical Forces/Trends at Work that Led to the Genocide?

The Armenian genocide was the result of the intensifying differences between two societies inhabiting the territories of a single state. One society was dominant, the other subordinate; one Muslim, the other Christian; one in the majority, the other in the minority. At its source, the conflict stemmed from two divergent views of the world. The Turks had established their state as a world empire. They had always ruled over lands and peoples they conquered. The receding of their empire from its far-flung provinces challenged their image of themselves. Virtually undefeated in war before 1700, in the 18th and 19th centuries the Ottomans lost battle after battle as their once-mighty armies were no longer a match for the modern tactics and weaponry of the European states. New empires taking form on the European continent began to carve away Ottoman territory. France, England, Austria, and Russia, each in turn, imposed its demands on the weakening Turkish state. By the second half of the 19th century, however, these European powers, soon joined by a Germany unified by Prussian arms, balanced out each other in their competition for global influence, and this too had a dramatic impact on the Ottoman Empire.

A new type of challenge arose to force the Ottomans into retreating further. Whereas the Ottomans were in part successful in checking the territorial aggrandizement of their neighbors by relying on the balance-of-power system, the rise of nationalist movements among the subject peoples of the empire posed a different predicament. As imperial states are wont to do, the Ottomans resorted to brutal methods of suppressing national liberation and other separatist movements. The response of the Ottomans to the uprisings in Greece, Serbia, Bulgaria, and elsewhere was mass action against the affected population. These tactics only invited European intervention, and the settlement often resulted in the formation of a small autonomous state from a former Ottoman province as a way of providing a national territory to the subject people.

Unlike the Greeks, Serbians, or Bulgarians, the case of the Armenians was more complicated. They had long been ruled by the Turks and by the early 20th century they were widely dispersed. In historical Armenia, the Armenians only formed a majority of the population in certain provinces. This was due to the fact that a substantial Kurdish and Turkish population lived in these lands. When the Armenians also began to aspire to a national home, the Ottomans regarded it as a far more serious threat than earlier and similar nationalist movements, for they had come to regard historical Armenia as part of their permanent patrimony.

The fracturing of the status of the Armenians in the Ottoman Empire has a complicated diplomatic history. The Russo-Turkish War of 1877–1878 was concluded with the signing of the Treaty of San Stefano, which ceded the Russians considerable Ottoman territory. The European powers vehemently opposed the sudden expansion of Russian influence in the Balkans and the Middle East, and compelled the Russian monarch to agree to terms more favorable to the Ottomans in the Treaty of Berlin. All the European powers became signatories to this treaty. One of the terms in the Treaty of Berlin promised reforms in the Armenian provinces of the Ottoman Empire. Armenians saw hope in this treaty. They thought an international covenant would have greater force in compelling the Ottomans to consider reorganizing the ramshackle administration of their remote provinces. When the European powers failed to persist in requiring the Ottoman sultan to abide by the terms of the treaty, the Armenians faced a rude awakening. Not only were they disappointed with a government that did not keep its promises, but they also realized that the European powers had little interest in devoting time to the problems of the Armenians (Hovannisian, 1986a, pp. 19–41).

The fundamental issue separating Armenians and Ottomans was their diametrically opposed definitions of equality. Empires are inherently unequal systems. They divide the people into the rulers and the ruled. The Islamic empires, including the Ottoman state, compounded this system of inequality because the legal and judicial precepts of Islam also subordinated non-Muslim subjects to second-class status. Not only was the Ottoman system unequal, Ottoman society was unaccustomed to a concept of equality among men irrespective of their racial or religious background. Although laws were issued accepting the principle of equality among the various confessional groups (Christians, Jews, Muslims) in the Ottoman Empire, the Muslim populace remained unconvinced that they should accept these secular ideas. Instead of leading to a new adjustment in Ottoman society, these laws became the source of consternation among Muslims, who believed these notions upset the established social order. The hierarchy of faiths had never been reconsidered in an Islamic society since the religion was founded in the 7th century. On the contrary, the combination of European states sponsoring reforms on behalf of Christian minorities who were aspiring for equal treatment under the law was perceived by the Muslims as a bid by the Ottoman Christians for power over the Muslims (Dadrian, 1999, pp. 5–26).

Islamic law disenfranchised Christians and Jews. The testimony by each was inadmissible in court, thus frequently denying them fair treatment by the justice system. Christians and Jews were also required to pay additional levies, such as a poll tax. For a peasantry eking out a living on the farm, the extra taxes often became an obligation that could not be met in a difficult year. The end result was commonly foreclosure and eviction. Disallowed from bearing arms, non-Muslims had no means for self-defense. They could protect neither their persons and families nor their properties. In certain places, dress codes restricting types of fabric for use by the Christians helped differentiate them from the population at large, exposing them to further discrimination and intimidation. At times, a language restriction meant speaking a language other than Turkish risked having one's tongue cut out. As a result, in many areas of the Ottoman Empire Armenians had lost the use of their native language (Ye'or, 1985, pp. 51–77).

These disabilities would have been debilitating under normal circumstances. In areas closer to the capital, competent governors oversaw the administration of the provinces, and Armenians flocked to these safer parts of the empire. In the remoter provinces, such as the areas of historical Armenia, the hardships faced by the ordinary people were insurmountable. Avaricious officials exacted legal and illegal taxes. Furthermore, the justice system was hopelessly rigged. The maintenance of law and order was entrusted to men who only saw in their positions the opportunity for reckless exploitation. Extortion and bribery were the custom. In the countryside, the army demanded quartering in the houses of Armenian peasants, which made their families hostages in their own homes. Unable to defend themselves, these people were also at the mercy of tribesmen who descended upon their villages and carried off goods, flocks, and women. With no recourse left, Armenians were being driven to desperation.

The disappointment over the failure of the European powers to intervene effectively, combined with the dismay over the delays of reform of the Ottoman government, continued to fuel the crisis in the Armenian provinces. Some Armenians decided to take matters into their own hands. In certain parts of Armenia, during the 1880s and 1890s, individuals began arming themselves and forming bands which, for instance, resisted Kurdish incursions on Armenian villages. Others joined political organizations advocating revolutionary changes at all levels of society. They demanded equal treatment, an adequate justice system, fair taxation, and the appointment of officials prepared to act responsibly (Nalbandian, 1963, pp. 167–168).

The Ottoman authorities refused to consider the demands. In response to the rise of nationalist sentiment among the subject peoples, and other internal and external security concerns, the Ottoman sultans had been striving to centralize power in their hands and had been creating a modernized bureaucracy which would help expand the authority of the government in all areas of Ottoman society. Among the measures introduced by the sultan Abdul-Hamid was the formation of a secret police and special cavalry regiments, called in his honor the Hamidiye corps, to act both as border guards and local gendarmerie. They became his instrument for suppression. In 1894, at a time of increasing tension between the Armenian population and the Ottoman government, which also coincided with increased political activism by Armenians and inadequate efforts at intervention by some of the European powers, the sultan unleashed his forces. Over the next three years a series of massacres were staged throughout Armenia. Anywhere between 100,000 to 300,000 people were killed; others were wounded, robbed, thrown out of their homes, or kidnapped. Many also fled the country (Bliss, 1896, pp. 368–501; Greene, 1896, pp. 185–242; Walker, 1980, pp. 156–173).

The Armenian massacres of 1894–1896 made headline news around the world. They engendered international awareness of the plight of the Armenians, and the horrendous treatment Armenians faced at the hands of the sultan's regiments resulted in condemnation of the Ottoman system (Nassibian, 1984, pp. 33–57). The European powers were compelled by public clamor in their own countries to urge the sultan to show restraint. The massacres were halted, but nothing was done to punish the perpetrators or to remedy the damage incurred by the Armenians (Deringil, 2009, pp. 344–371).

This cycle of violence against the Armenian population repeated itself in 1909 in the province of Adana, a region along the Mediterranean coast densely settled by Armenians, where again the Armenian neighborhoods were raided and burned. The estimate of the number of victims runs between 10,000 and 30,000 (Walker, 1980, pp. 182–188). The Adana massacre coincided with an event known as the Hamidian counter-revolution. The Young Turks had achieved political prominence by staging a military revolution in 1908. They had compelled the sultan, Abdul-Hamid, to restore the Ottoman Constitution which he himself had issued in 1876 and soon after suspended. The sultan was suspected of having plotted to recover his despotic powers by dislodging the Young Turks from Constantinople. The Adana massacre erupted in the ensuing climate of tension and suspicion. The Young Turks blamed the Hamidian supporters for igniting strife in order to embarrass the progressive forces in Ottoman society, but the Young Turks themselves were also implicated in the atrocities. It augured badly for the Armenians. The Adana massacre demonstrated that even in a power struggle within Turkish society, the Armenians could be scapegoated by the disaffected and made the object of violence. In this context Enver's embarrassment at his defeat in early 1915 and the government's casting of blame on the Armenians had a precedent. In this chain of events, the genocide of 1915 was the final, and mortal, blow dealt to the Armenians by their Ottoman masters (Libaridian, 1987, pp. 203–235).

What was the Long-range Impact of the Genocide on the Victim Group?

The Armenians in the Ottoman Empire never achieved equality and were never guaranteed security of life and property. They entered the Ottoman Empire as a subject people and left it as a murdered or exiled population. It is estimated that the Armenian genocide between 1915 and 1923 resulted in the death of 1.5 million people. Beyond the demographic demise of the Armenians in the larger part of historical Armenia, the Armenian genocide brought to a conclusion the transfer of the Armenian homeland to the Turkish people. The Young Turks had planned not only to deprive the Armenians of life and property, but also conspired to deny to the Armenians the possibility of ever recovering their dignity and liberty in their own country.

Whole communities and towns were wiped off the map. The massive loss in population threatened the very existence of the Armenian people. Hardly a family was left intact. The 500,000 survivors consisted mostly of orphans, widows, and widowers. The Armenian nation was saved only through the direct delivery of American relief aid to the "starving Armenians." Millions of dollars were collected in the United States to feed and house the destitute Armenians, both in the Middle East and in Russia, where tens of thousands took refuge. Hundreds of thousands eventually received some sort of aid, be it food, clothing, shelter, employment, resettlement, or emigration to the United States and elsewhere (Peterson, 2004, pp. 51–88).

The tremendous difficulty faced by the Armenians in recovering from the devastating impact of the genocide had much to do with the fact that they, as a collectivity, had been robbed of all their wealth. They were forced to abandon their fixed assets and they received no compensation for any of their confiscated property. As deportees, Armenians were unable to carry with them anything beside some clothing or bedding. All their businesses were lost. All their farms were left untended. Schools, churches, hospitals, orphanages, monasteries, graveyards, and other communal holdings became Turkish state property (Kouymjian, 1985, pp. 173–183; Payaslian, 2006, pp. 149–171). The genocide left the Armenians penniless.

Those who survived and returned to reclaim their homes and properties after the end of World War I were driven out again by the Nationalist Turks who had risen to power in Turkey (Kerr, 1973, pp. 214–254). For the Armenians, the only choice was reconciliation with their status as exiles and resettlement wherever they could find a means of earning a living. With the inability to recongregate as a people in their homeland, the Armenians dispersed to the four corners of the world (Adalian, 1989, pp. 81–114; 2002; Tachjian, 2009, pp. 60–80).

Lastly, the genocide shattered the historical bond of the Armenian people with their homeland. The record of their millennial existence in that country turned to dust. Libraries, archives, registries, the entire recorded memory of the Armenians as accumulated in their country was lost for all time (Adalian, 1999a; Bevan, 2006, pp. 53–60).

What were the Responses to this Particular Genocide?

At the time, the horror story of the Armenian genocide shocked the world. The Allies threatened to hold the Young Turks responsible for the massacres (Dadrian, 1989, p. 262), but the warning had no effect. The Allies were preoccupied with the war in Europe and did not commit resources to deliver the Armenians from their fate. Locally, however, humanitarian intervention by individual Turks, Kurds, and Arabs saved many lives (Hovannisian, 1992, pp. 173–207).

While some Turks robbed their Armenian neighbors, others helped by hiding them in safe dwellings. While some Kurds willingly participated in the massacres, others guided groups of Armenians through mountain passes to refuge in Russian territory. And while some Arabs only saw the Armenians as hopeless victims, others shared their food.

Among the first persons to see the deplorable condition of the mass of Armenians were the American missionaries and diplomats stationed in Turkey. Their appeals to their government, religious institutions in the United States, and the general public were the earliest of the active responses to the predicament of genocide. They strove to deliver aid even during the war (Sachar, 1969, p. 343; Winter, 2002; Adalian, 2003).

After the war, the European nations were little disposed to help the Armenians as they themselves were trying to recover from their losses. Nevertheless, Britain and France, which had occupied Ottoman territory in the Middle East, were more strongly positioned to influence the political outcome in the region, but neither chose to do so on behalf of the Armenians. Their interest in retaining control of these lands also conflicted with the wider goals of U.S. President Woodrow Wilson in establishing a stable world order. The American president's laudable policies were welcomed by the peoples of Europe and Asia, such as the Poles, Czechs, Arabs, and Indians, who saw in his principles for self-determination and international reconciliation the possibility of attaining their national independence. He, too, however, was unable to deliver more than words. The U.S. Congress was disinclined to involve the United States in foreign lands. Consequently, many territorial issues were solved through the pure exercise of might. Diplomacy had little chance of extending help to the Armenian refugees (Payaslian, 2005).

For the Turks, the failure of diplomacy provided an opportunity to regroup under new leadership and to begin their own national effort at building a new state upon the ruins of the Ottoman Empire. With Mustafa Kemal at their head, the Nationalist Turks forged a new government and secured the boundaries of modern-day Turkey. Their policy of national consolidation excluded despised minorities (Dadrian, 1989, pp. 327–333; Akçam, 2004, pp. 115–157). The Armenians, the weakest element, headed the list. By 1923, when the Republic of Turkey was formally recognized as a sovereign state, with the exception of those in Constantinople, the Armenians remaining in the territories of that state had been driven out. For many survivors of the deportations who had returned to their former homes, this was their second expulsion.

Before the Turkish borders were finally sealed and Armenians conclusively denied the right to their former homes, the absence of moral resolve in Turkish governmental circles to confront the consequences of the Armenian genocide was made abundantly clear. The post-war government proved reluctant to put on trial the Young Turk officials suspected of organizing the massacres. Only upon the insistence of the Allies were a series of tribunals initiated. Some dramatic evidence was given in testimony, and verdicts were handed down explicitly charging those found guilty of pursuing a course of action that resulted in the destruction of the Armenian population. Even so, popular sentiment in Turkish society did not support the punishment of the guilty, and the government chose to forgo the sentences of the court. The triumviri—Talaat, Enver, and Jemal—were condemned to death, but their trials were held in absentia since they had fled the country and their extradition was not a matter of priority (Dadrian, 1989, pp. 221–334; Bass, 2000, pp. 106–146).

Is there Agreement or Disagreement among "Legitimate Scholars" as to the Interpretation of this Particular Genocide (e.g., Preconditions, Implementation, and Ramifications?)

Two schools of thought have emerged over the years. Scholars who study the Armenian genocide look at the phenomenon as either an exceptionally catastrophic occurrence coinciding with a global conflict such as World War I (Fein, 1979, pp. 10–18; Horowitz, 1982, pp. 46–51) or as the final chapter in the peculiar fate of the Armenians as a people who lost their independence many centuries earlier (Kuper, 1981, pp. 101–119; Walker, 1980, pp. 169, 236–237).

All agree that the preconditions to the genocide were consistent with other examples where a dominant group targets a minority. They also agree on the structural inequalities of Ottoman society and how it disadvantaged the Armenians. They differ on their interpretation of the causes and consequences of Armenian nationalism. Some think that the appearance of political organization among the Armenians can be regarded as the critical breaking point. Others see these developments as inevitable and entirely consistent with global trends and not particular to the Armenians. Two questions are often debated: whether the massacres during the reign of Abdul-Hamid were a sufficient precedent to be regarded as the beginning of the Armenian catastrophe; and whether the Young Turks aggravated conditions in ways that exceeded the designs of Abdul-Hamid (Kuper, 1981, pp. 101–119; Horowitz, 1982, pp. 46–51).

In the implementation of the genocide, one thing is clear. The earlier massacres were episodic and affected select communities. The genocide was comprehensive and directed practically against everyone. The sultan's policy did not aim for the extermination of the Armenians—rather it was brutal punishment for aspiring to gain charge of their political destiny. As many scholars have pointed out, at one time the Ottoman system extended a considerable measure of security to its minorities. Although for the most part they were excluded from government and at a disadvantage in holding large-scale property, Christians and Jews were allowed to practice their faiths and distinguish themselves in commerce and finance. Therefore, it was not in the interest of the sultan to dismantle his imperial inheritance. His objective remained the continuance of his autocratic power and his rule over the lands bequeathed him by his conquering forebears.

Those studying the Young Turks have pointed out that the CUP organized its committees and conducted its activities outside this system. They were opponents of imperial autocracy. Their own political radicalism also meant that they were predisposed to think in exclusionary terms. Some of these scholars contend that the Young Turk period can be seen as a transitional phase in Turkish society, where the pluralistic construct of the multi-ethnic and multi-confessional Ottoman system was violently smashed and the ground was prepared for the emergence of a state based on ethnic singularism (Ahmad, 1982, pp. 418–425; Staub, 1989, pp. 173–187; Melson, 1986, pp. 61–84).

As with all genocides, because they are planned in secret and, at least at first, are frequently carried out surreptitiously, with the most damning orders typically issued verbally, the initial triggering events are often obscure. In the Armenian case, with so much of the incriminating evidence deliberately destroyed by those who implemented the atrocities, the question continues to be debated whether the Armenian genocide was carried out according to a preconceived plan or improvised as circumstances and conditions emerged, permitting license to proceed with the ultimate goal of ridding the country of its Armenian population (Bloxham, 2005).

A question with broader implications concerns the extent of German involvement with the Armenian genocide. Whether they condoned the deportations or not, or whether they might have prevented the atrocities or not, certainly many German officials were fully aware of the Armenian situation. The case has been made that with this knowledge, and awareness of the lack of consequences for the authorities responsible for the Armenian genocide, post-war German leaders drew their own lessons about impunity. Adolf Hitler, as well as a number of high-ranking Nazis, were aware of the demise of the Armenians, and came to the conclusion that their own policies of persecution and extermination would go unpunished. While historical evidence points in that direction, the suggestion that the Holocaust of the Jews might have been prevented had there been a stronger condemnation of the Armenian genocide and a more thorough prosecution of its organizers remains a theoretical proposition (Bardakjian, 1985, pp. 24–29).

Perhaps the issue debated most frequently about the Armenian genocide revolves around the matter of post-genocide responsibility. There is a wide divergence of opinion on the question of whether modern Turkey is liable to the Armenians for their losses, or whether it is absolved of such liability because the crime was committed under the jurisdiction of prior state authorities (Libaridian, 1985, pp. 211–227). The Turkish government dismisses all such claims since it denies that the policies implemented in 1915 constitute genocide. Some in the academic and legal community are supportive of the Turkish position (Gürün, 1985). On the other hand, that stance raises a more complex problem. Who exactly should be held responsible for genocide: the government, the state, society? (Aktar, 2007, pp. 240–270). If governments put the blame on prior regimes, all they have done is merely certify the former policy by disregarding the consequences of genocide. The reluctance by a successor state to shoulder responsibility is only another form of reaping the benefits of mass murder.

Do People Care about this Genocide Today? If so, how is that Concern Manifested? If not, why not?

For a period of about 50 years, the world fell into an apathetic silence over the Armenian genocide. Its results had been so grievous for the Armenians, and the failure of the international community to redress the consequent problems was so thorough, that the world chose to ignore the legacy of the Armenian genocide. With the consolidation of Communist rule in Russia and of nationalist rule in Turkey, the chapter on the Armenians was considered closed. People wanted to forget about the Great War and its misery. As for the Armenians, they were too few, too widely dispersed, and too preoccupied with their own survival to know how to respond.

The concern over the fate of the Armenians manifested mostly in literature as various authors wrote about the massacres and memorialized the rare instances of resistance (Lepsius, 1987; Gibbons, 1916; Werfel, 1934). After a life of struggle in foreign lands, upon reaching retirement age, survivors also began to write down their memoirs. Slowly a small corpus of literature emerged documenting in personal accounts the genocide and its consequences for individuals, their families, and communities (Hovannisian, 1978; Totten, 1991). This body of work began to serve as evidence for the study of the Armenian genocide. In the 1960s, as government archives holding vast collections of diplomatic correspondence on the deportations and massacres were opened, a significant amount of contemporaneous documentation also became available (Hovannisian, 1978; Beylerian, 1983; Ohandjanian, 1988; Adalian, 1991–1993; Dadrian, 1994). This further encouraged research in the subject. Interest in the Armenian genocide has since been growing as more researchers, writers, and educators examine the evidence and attempt to understand what happened in 1915 (Adalian, 1999b).

Commensurate to this interest, however, has been a phenomenon growing at an even faster pace. This is the denial of the Armenian genocide. For many Turks the reminder of the Ottoman past is offensive. The Turkish government's stated policy has been a complete denial (Foreign Policy Institute, 1982). The denial ranges beyond the question of political responsibility. This type of denial questions the very historical fact of the occurrence of genocide, and even of atrocities. A whole body of revisionist historiography has been generated to explain, excuse, or dismiss the Armenian genocide (Hovannisian, 1986b, pp. 111–133; Dobkin, 1986, pp. 97–109; Adalian, 1992, pp. 85–105). Some authors have gone so far as to place the blame for the genocide on the victims themselves, describing the deportations and massacres as self-inflicted, since, they say, the deportations were only counter-measures taken by the Ottoman government against a disobedient and disloyal population (Uras, 1988, pp. 855–886; Gürün, 1985). Such arguments do not convince serious scholars (Guroian, 1986, pp. 135–152; Smith, 1989, pp. 1–38). Others, regrettably, are more prone to listening to revisionist argumentation (Shaw & Shaw, 1977, pp. 314–317; McCarthy, 1983, pp. 47–81, 117–130). These kinds of debates fail to address, however, the central questions about the Young Turk policy toward the Armenian population. Was every Armenian, young and old, man or woman, disloyal? How does one explain the deportation of Armenians from places that were nowhere near the war zones, if removing them from high-risk areas was the purpose of the policy? And always, one must ask about the treatment of children. What chance did they stand of surviving deportation, starvation, and dehydration in the desert? (Göçek, 2006, pp. 101–127; Theriault, 2003, pp. 231–261; Kaiser, 2003, pp. 1–24).

For the survivors and their descendants the memory of the Armenian genocide became a central feature of their identity. In the face of official denial by Turkey and the long silence of the world community, formal recognition of the most catastrophic event in their long history as a community assumed the only form of justice remaining to be obtained. To that end the trend toward international affirmation of the Armenian genocide became the method for keeping alive the memory of the events of 1915 and for reminding the world of the horrifying injustices of the Armenian genocide. For a people dispersed around the world, the call for recognition has translated into asking the government of the countries in which they ultimately took refuge to issue official acknowledgment of the brutal record of man's inhumanity toward his fellow man (Bobelian, 2009, pp. 164–206).

What does this Genocide Teach us if we Wish to Protect Others from such Horrors?

Although, ultimately, it is the exercise of political power in the absence of moral restraint that explains the occurrence of genocide, the

demographic status of a people is demonstrated by the Armenian genocide to be a significant factor in the perpetration of genocide. A dispersed people juridically designated by a state as a minority, both in the
numerical and political sense of the word, is extremely vulnerable to
abusive policy. It lacks the capacity for any coordinated action to
respond to, or resist, genocidal measures. It is evident that a government
inclined to engage in the extermination of a minority can only be
restrained by pressures and sanctions imposed by greater powers.

Geography was no less a contributing factor in exposing the Armenians to genocide. A people inhabiting a remote part of the world is all the
more at the mercy of a brutal government, especially if it is questioning
the policies of the state. Since exposure is the principal foil of crime, the
more hidden from view a people lives, the more likely it is to be
repressed. Of all the places where the Armenians in the Ottoman Empire
might have hampered the war effort, if indeed they were a seditious population, the most likely spot would have been the capital city. Yet the
government spared most of the Armenians in Constantinople because
many foreigners lived there, and they would have been alarmed to
witness mass deportations. That signal exception underscores the importance and the high likelihood of successfully monitoring the living conditions of an endangered population.

That exception also points to another lesson which is specially pro-
nounced in the Armenian case. Since many foreign communities had a
presence in Constantinople, getting the word out to the rest of the world
would not have been difficult with such corroboration. Thereby the
Armenians in this one city remained in a protected enclave. This principle applies no less to the international status extended to an entire
people, as the European powers once did for the Armenians. Their interest in the Armenians acted as a partial restraint on the Ottoman government. The sudden alteration of the international order as a result of
global conflict left the Armenians wholly exposed. Whatever the level of
international protection extended to an endangered minority, the withdrawal of those guarantees, tenuous as they might be, only acts as an
inducement for genocide. Denying opportunity to a criminal regime is
critical for the prevention of genocide.

The experience of the Armenian people in the period after the genocide teaches another important lesson. Unless the consequences of genocide are addressed in the immediate aftermath of the event, the element
of time very soon puts survivors at a serious disadvantage. Without the
attention of the international community, without the intervention of
major states seeking to stabilize the affected region, without the swift
apprehension of the guilty, and without the full exposure of the evidence, the victims stand no chance of recovering from their losses. In

the absence of a response and of universal condemnation, genocide becomes "legitimized." Following the war, the Ottoman government never gave a full account of what happened to the Armenians, and the successor state of Turkey chose to bury the matter entirely (Adalian, 1991, pp. 99–104; Akçam, 2006, pp. 349–376).

All too frequently in the past the international community was unwilling to take concerted action to save populations clearly in danger of annihilation. Whether through monitoring and reporting systems, the activation of legal and economic sanctions, or political or military intervention, the international community is presently far better equipped to respond to genocidal crises than ever before. When the Armenian genocide occurred there was no alarm and there was no rescue. Without alarm there can be no rescue. Without a strong commitment to protecting human rights, there can be no prevention. If the Armenian genocide teaches anything, it is this: Promises of protection must be followed with enforcement. Empty promises come at the cost of human lives and mighty states can erase nations without account.

Eyewitness Accounts

Eyewitness and survivor accounts of the Armenian genocide were audio-taped and video-taped more than a half-century after the events (Miller and Miller, 1993). That means the recorded testimony was provided by persons in their seventies and eighties who were reflecting upon a life which took a sudden turn when they were still children or very young adults. Hence, the problem of the great length of time passed since the events of 1915 and the fact that those events were seen through the eyes of children who were looking at the world from their very narrow frames of reference needs to be kept in mind when dealing with testimony of this type. Certainly, children have the greatest difficulty gauging an accurate measure of time. Therefore, the episodes from their personal narratives occur at approximated intervals. Their memory, for instance, preserves the first names of numerous acquaintances, but last names are less frequently known.

A contrast to these limitations is the accuracy, of virtually all survivors, in their depiction of the geography and the topography which was the setting of their life's most tragic period. Because they were deported, knowledge of where they originated and the places they saw and stopped along the way and the spots they reached at the end of their journeys became vital information not only for their physical and emotional survival, but also for their ability to reconnect with other survivors of the communities from which they were separated. Most interesting, however, and useful for the documentary record it turns out, was their very limited sense of the world around them. Whereas an adult would have attempted to understand the events he/she witnessed in terms of his/her community and society, children describe their experiences strictly from within the confines of their immediate family and circle of friends. As such, therefore, they preserve a sense of greater pathos undiluted by either fatalism or drama. Most seem to have retained their horror of genocide through their inability to offer any larger suggestion than their very incomprehension at what happened and why.

Helen Tatarian's account is an exceptionally rare one because it describes a massacre of Armenians which happened in 1909. When these records were created, very few survivors were old enough to have lived through occurrences of massacres earlier than 1915. The details of her account are also a valuable contrast to the pattern of the 1915 genocide. The Adana massacre is characterized by random mob action occurring within the perimeter of the city. Government forces are described as a party which simply stayed out of the way and, in this case, provided safe conduct where foreigners, specifically Americans, were concerned. More importantly, she verifies the significance of the protection provided by the missionary and other third-party presence. During the genocide none of these factors came into play. The missionaries were unable to protect their parishioners. The government was an active participant in the dislocation and the execution of the Armenian population. Lastly, with the exception of some towns in the farthest eastern reaches of Anatolia, little killing occurred within the towns. The other survivors all testify to a consistent pattern of separation, deportation, and subsequent mass executions in places away from urban centers during the period of the genocide.

Sarkis Agojian records the treatment of the adult male population which was never deported. He testifies that they were arrested, tortured, and murdered very early in the process. The deportations, as he recalls, occurred after the segment of the Armenian population capable of resistance was eliminated. Lastly, his memory preserves, with a powerful poignancy, the trauma of Armenian children who were spared deportation and starvation by adoption into Turkish families. The deafening silence at his last glimpse of his mother and the shattering news of her death capture the maddening grief that seized their young lives, and which marked them for all their years.

Takouhi Levonian gives an eyewitness account of an actual episode of wholesale slaughter. Her description of the physical cruelties inflicted upon the Armenian population is especially riveting. Her description of the kinds of privations endured is no less powerful. Her testimony incontrovertibly underscores the extreme vulnerability of the Armenian young female population. It would appear that the treatment they received was most abusive. The horrific sadism practiced by the perpetrators of the Armenian genocide is hereto testified in this single account.

Yevnig Adrouni's story redeems humanity through a personal narrative of survival and rescue. Too young to be mistreated sexually, her exploits are testament to the spirit of an alert child who would not submit to degradation. Spared physical torment she committed herself to escaping her fate. Clutching onto the last shreds of her Armenian identity, she proves to herself and her rescuers that determination and defiance can, sometimes, defeat evil. As she so vividly recounts, from the survival of a single human being springs forth the new hope of larger victories.

Account 1

Helen Tatarian, native of Dertyol, born *c.*1893. Audiotaped on April 17, 1977, Los Angeles, California, by Rouben Adalian (Dertyol was a town inhabited mostly by Armenians. It is located on the Mediterranean coast in the region of Adana. Adana is also the name of the largest town in the area).

There was a massacre in 1909. I was in school at Adana. Miss Webb and Miss Mary, two Americans sisters, ran the school. Miss Webb was the older, Miss Mary the younger.

In 1909, right in the month of April, we suddenly heard guns being fired and saw flames rising. The houses of the Armenians were set on fire. There was a French school right next to ours. They burned it down completely.

At first the Turks killed quite a lot of people, then they stopped for a while. Eight days later they started firing their guns again. Reverend Sisak Manoogian came running. "Do not be afraid children, a hog had gone wild," he said, "and they are shooting it." But it was a lie, nor had a hog gone wild. The Turks had gone wild. They were about to start again.

The son-in-law of our American missionary, Mr. Chambers, had climbed on the roof. He had climbed on the roof of our laundry room to look at what was going on in the city. They shot the man.

There was a window, a small window up high. We used to look from there to see that behind the school building there were people lying dead. The Turks were shooting the Armenians. This was a massacre specifically aimed at the Armenians.

During the fire those who managed to hide remained in hiding, those who did not hide were cut down. Just like Surpik Dudu, the poor woman who was going to her brother-in-law's house. Surpik Dudu was shot in the arm, great grandmother Surpik Dudu. Later they had shot dead her husband and son. This woman owned fields. She was a rich woman. She used to travel on horseback. But it so happened that she was going in the direction of her relatives, her brother-in-law's house. Fortunately she was not killed.

We could not go out and we remained in hiding in the school building. We heard the sounds of guns, and from the sounds alone we were afraid. We were children. We cried, but we had no communication with anyone outside. Across from our building there lived an American, Miss Farris. The Turks burned her building so that our school would catch on fire and the children would have to run outside and thus they could kidnap the girls. The American missionary immediately notified the government. Soldiers came from the government and while putting out the fire a soldier fell and was burned inside.

Later we opened a hole in the wall. The missionaries did this. They opened a hole big enough to go through it in order to cross from our end of the block to the other end, to Mr. Chambers' house, the missionary's house. All the girls were there, two hundred and fifty, three hundred girls. We piled up in the man's house. The Turks were going to burn this house also. The man held out a surrender flag. They had poured gas and threatened to burn us in that house. We asked him: "Reverend, if the Turks forced you, would you hand us over to them?" "If they press me hard. If they insist," said the man. What could he do? Or else they would kill him too. Later we remained there for a night. There, we cried. The girls began such a weeping. The following morning, the government soldiers took us to the train station. By train we went to Mersin.

There was no fighting [in Adana between Armenians and Turks]. The Turks knew anyway which was the house of an Armenian. They went in and cut him down and shot the people inside and they took whatever was in the house. They robbed the houses and set them on fire. They entered them since it was the property of the Armenians. They also burned the churches, but I believe a considerable crowd had gathered in a French church. They did nothing there at that time. There were those who took refuge with our American missionaries also, but it was a little difficult to cross the street. If the Turks saw you, they were ready to shoot.

Account 2

Sarkis Agojian, native of Chemeshgadsak, born 1906. Audiotaped on May 25, 1983, in Pasadena, California, by Donald and Lorna Miller (Chemeshgadsak was a town inhabited by Armenians in the region of Kharpert in the western portion of historical Armenia).

We were in school having physical education. We had lined up when the wife of our coach, Mr. Boghos, came and told her husband that the Turks had just arrested the principal, Pastor Arshag. You see, they first took the educated, the intellectuals. They took these people to a home which they had converted into a prison and tortured them in order to get them to talk. The mail man, who was Armenian, was also arrested and tortured. They pulled out his fingernails saying that while he was carrying mail he also was transporting secret letters; mail was carried in those days on horseback in large leather bags fastened to either side of the horse. He was Sarkis Mendishian. So upon the news that Pastor Arshag was arrested, they dismissed us from school and asked all of us to go home.

We went home. My father was not there. My uncle had run away. They had put a dress on my uncle's son, even though he was not young, to disguise him. My father's uncle was also in prison, for after taking the younger educated men, they also took the elderly. I was young so they used to send me to take food to him. I did this a few times. I would go in and sit with him. One day when I was taking his food, I met a lot of police who were saying that on that day we could not deliver food—that all the prisoners were going to leave. I saw them in twos, all chained together. I could not take the food, so I returned and gave the news. I told them that they were chained and they were coming this way and would pass by our house, there being no other way to leave town toward Kharpert.

By now, all the families had heard, so they were all in the streets to see their loved ones. I got on top of the roof and was yelling "uncle." There was a doctor in this procession, and when his wife saw him, she ran out to greet him, but with the butt of the rifle the police pushed her away—even though he was an elderly man. So the men marched on, leaving all the women and families crying and grieving. There was a place outside of town about twenty minutes with trees and water. There they took their names to see if anyone was missing. Then they marched them to the edge of the Euphrates and killed them. Apparently my great uncle had some red gold with him; he gave it to the police who took it and then killed him.

Now that all the men were gone, deportation orders were issued for women and children. Our town was deported in two different groups, fifteen days apart. I wish we were in the first group because they made it all the way to Aleppo. When we were to leave our home, we left our bedding and other things with the landlord so that if we returned we would get it back. Also, we threw our rugs to the people at the public bath next door so that they would keep them for us. We said that we would get them when we returned. We are still to return!

Because we could afford it, we had rented a cart to carry some of our things. It was five hours from our town to the Euphrates River. On the way we had to pass on a bridge. We were told that one of our neighbor's boys had been killed and thrown over there. In fact, I heard some Turk boys saying to each other that there was a gold piece in the pocket of our neighbor's son. We could see the injured who had been shot but were not yet dead.

The first village that we reached was one in which our landlord lived. We saw that the fruit was getting ripe. My brother, sister, uncle's son and daughter took some money to our landlord to see if he would save their lives, and they remained with him. I stayed with my mother, my uncle's wife, and her five-year-old grandchild. We left the village of Bederatil and went to the next town, Leloushaghen, which took us a day to reach. There was a Turk man who was taking Armenian boys away, and I said that I would go with him.

That night, I and two other boys slept at this Turkish agha's house. In the morning my mother brought a bundle of clothes for me and left it with a Turkish woman whose husband had worked in my father's bakery and who had lived with this agha for years. I was there when she came to the house to leave my clothes. I was sitting there and I saw her, but it was as though I was in a trance; we never talked and she never kissed me. I don't know if it was because she could not bear it from sadness. I never saw again any of those clothes or anything that my mother might have left in them for me.

The deportation caravan now went on without me; they still had two hours to make it to the Euphrates River. When they got there, they were all killed. The way we heard this was that some of the police brought to the agha a pretty young girl and her brother that this Turk wanted. These [gendarmes] police told the agha that in a matter of a few minutes they wiped them all out. But this young Armenian girl told us that she saw the gendarmes force the deportees to take off their clothes and then shove them off a cliff into the Euphrates River far below. According to this girl, when it came time for my mother, she took gold from her bundle, threw it in the river, grabbed my four-year-old brother, and jumped down with the child in her arms. When I heard this, all of a sudden I began to weep. It's the feelings you know. I was about nine years old. As soon as this girl finished telling her story, the agha's son tried to distract me and those listening by calling me a *gavour* [infidel], making fun of the cross. I covered my head with the blanket and cried and cried.

Account 3

Takouhi Levonian, native of Keghi, born 1900. Audiotaped on April 8, 1981, in Los Angeles, California by Donald and Lorna Miller (Keghi was another Armenian town in the region of Kharpert).

When the war began, I could see and sense the men of our town gathering in groups. They were talking and looking very sad. The women used to sigh. The schools shut down and their grounds, as well as the churches, became filled with soldiers. That's how winter passed. In April, there was talk that they were going to move us out. I was 15 years old then....

Between April 29 and 30 [of 1915], word came that they were going to transfer us to Kharpert. On May first, that news was confirmed and until the fourth [of May] every household began preparations by making *kete* [Armenian bread], preparing chickens, other meats, and so on. My father told my mother not to bother with any of these preparations. He said to just take our bedding on the mules and not to bother burying anything, like so many others had done who thought that they would return to them. He said that if we ever returned, he would be glad to come back to four walls. He was farsighted.

At the onset of the war he imported large amounts of oil, sugar, matches and all the things that had to be imported. When we left [on the deportation], we distributed all this to our neighbors. They arrested only a few people from our town. The rest they left unharmed. They did not do anything to my father because he was respected by all, since he was so fair with every one—regardless of nationality. He did good equally to all.

We were the first caravan to leave with much tears and anguish since it meant separation for so many. They assigned a few soldiers to us and thus we began. We used to travel by day, and in the evenings we stopped to eat and rest. In five to six days we reached Palu. There, while we were washing up, I will never, never forget, they took my father away, along with all the men down to twelve years of age. The next day our camp was filled with the Turks and Kurds of Palu, looting, dragging away whatever they could, both possessions and young women. They knocked the mules down to kill them. I was grabbing onto my six-year-old brother; my sister was holding her baby, and my two young sisters were grabbing her skirt; my mother was holding the basket of bread. There was so much confusion, and the noise of bullets shooting by us. Some people were getting shot, and the rest of us were running in the field, not knowing where to go....

Then I saw with my own eyes the Turks beating a fellow named Sahag, who had hid under his wife's dress. They were beating him with hammers, axes right in front of me and his wife. He yelled to her to run away, that we are all going to die a "donkey death." And then I saw the husband of my aunt, who was too old to have been taken previously, and he was being beaten in the head with an ax. They then threw him in the river. It finally calmed down. The Turks left some dead, took some with them, and the rest of us found each other.

At this time it was announced that anyone who would become a Turk could remain here. Otherwise, we must continue on. Many stayed. So we took off again. [We felt] much loss, that was not material loss only, but human loss. We were in tears and anguish as we left.

From Palu to Dikranagerd they tormented us a great deal. We suffered a lot. There was no water or food. Whatever my mom had in her bag, she gave us a little at a time. We walked the whole day, ten to fifteen days. No shoes remained on our feet. We finally reached Dikranagerd. There, by the water, we washed, and whatever little dry bread we had we wetted it and ate it.

Word came that the *vali* [governor] wanted from the Armenians a very pretty twelve-year-old girl.... So by night, they came with their lamps looking for such a girl. They found one, dragged her from the mother, saying to the weeping mother that they will return her. Later, they returned the child, in horrible condition, almost dead, and left her at her mother's knees.

The mother was weeping so badly, and, of course, the child could not make it and died. The women could not comfort her. Finally, several of the women tried to dig a hole with the use of a gendarme's rifle, and buried the girl and covered her. Dikranagerd had a large wall around it, so my mother and a few other women wrote on it, "Shushan buried here."

We remained under the walls [where Shushan was buried] for two to three days. Then they made us leave again. This time they assigned to us an elderly gendarme. He had tied to his horse a large container of water and the whole way he kept giving it to children and never himself rode the horse, but allowed old women to take turns on it. We went to Mardin. He also always took us near the villages so we could buy some food, and he would not allow the villagers to sell food at expensive prices. A lot of people either died on the way or stayed behind, because they could not keep up. So by the time we reached Mardin we were a lot less in number, although still a lot. They deposited us in a large field. There they gave us food.... At this point my mother was not with us.

A Kurd woman came and told my sister that two horsemen were going to kidnap me. She panicked and started looking for my mom, but she was not around. So she thought of giving the baby, who was in her arms, to the Kurd woman, so that she would help me. So she disguised me, but when we turned around, the woman was gone with the baby.

Turks used to pay high prices for babies, probably the woman sold him. My poor sister, Zarouhi, went crazy. I, too, was going crazy, feeling that I was the cause. I cried and cried. We remained in Mardin for five days and never found the baby. My poor sister was lactating, and her milk was full but there was no baby to nurse....

It came time to leave, and we had to leave the baby behind with uncontrollable tears. The journey was dreadful. With no shoes on our feet, it was so painful to walk on the paths they took us on. We used to wrap cloth on them to ease the pain, but it didn't really help much. There was no water. In fact, at one stretch, for three full days, we had no water at all. The children would cry: "Water, water, water." One of the children died.

Then toward morning one day, my sister and another woman crawled out of camp to a far place and brought some water in a tin can. Finally, they dumped us next to a small river. There my mother took me to the river to wash my face which was always covered up, except for my eyes. But one of the gendarmes, having spotted my eyes, showed up and grabbed me. My mother fainted, and, acting bravely, I shook his hand loose and ran, mingling among the people. I could hear the women yelling to my mother to wake up, that I got away. As the caravan moved again, I kept watching that man, always trying to stay behind him.

Account 4

Yevnig Adrouni, native of Hoghe, born *c.*1905. Audiotaped on August 13, 1978 by Rouben Adalian (Hoghe was an Armenian village in the Kharpert region).

My uncle, my cousin, the government took them away. Later they gathered the noteworthy people, including my father. They took him to prison, to Kharpert. After this they began to gather the men and to take them to the place called Keghvank. That place was a slaughterhouse. I remember my uncle's wife and others used to go there. My father was still in prison at this time. They used to go there and find that their men were missing. They [the Turks] had taken them and killed them with axes even then.

During the time when my father was in prison, there occurred the thing called *Emeliet Tabure*. They recalled all the Armenian soldiers. They set them to work at road construction. In this way they gathered all of them, including the Armenian soldiers, and filled them in the prisons. Later, when my father was still in prison, they set fire to the prison so that the Armenians would be killed. Already they were torturing them every day. When he escaped from prison, a Kurd saw my father. He was an acquaintance. My father fled with the Kurd to our village. But his nails were pulled out and his body was black and blue. They had tortured my father continuously. He lived but a few days. He died.

This is in 1915. My mother was deported first. A Turk was going to keep us, but he proposed that we Turkify. My mother did not accept.

Therefore, since I was young, they thought that if my mother was not with me, they might be able to convince me to Turkify. My mother was deported three months before the rest of us. This happened in spring. As for me, they would say: "Would the daughter of a tough infidel become a Muslim?"

They deported me also, thirsty and hungry, all the way to Deir el Zor. They did not even allow us to drink water. Along the way they took us by very narrow roads. Many of the old people who were hungry and thirsty could not walk. They used to strike them with stones and roll them down the slope. Pregnant women, I have seen with my own eyes … I cried a lot. Whenever I go to church, the whole thing is in front of my eyes, the scene, the deportation. They tore open the bellies of pregnant women so that the child was born. It fell free. They used to do that. I have seen such things.

There were some men. They killed them at that time. All of us, hungry, thirsty, we walked all the way to Deir el Zor. They came, Kurds, Arabs, and carried us away from the caravan. When a piece of bread fell in my hands for the first time, I chewed it but could not swallow it because I was starved.

Along the way they did not allow us to drink water. The river was there. It flowed. They did not let us go and drink. A girl, she was thirteen, fourteen perhaps … we suddenly saw that the caravan was stopped there in the field. That girl came, her face scratched, bloodied, all her clothes torn. Her mother had sent her secretly in order to fetch water. There were Kurdish boys … all the things they have done to the poor girl. The Turkish guards caught her mother. They asked: "Who is her mother, let her come forward." The caravan was seated. A woman moved her lips. The guards said: "This is her mother." The child was in her lap. They seized the woman and in front of our eyes, they shot her [daughter] dead, saying: "Because you did not have the right. We had forbidden you to send anyone to the river."

They used to take the little ones and carry them away. The Kurds carried me away as well. For eight years I remained lost among the Kurds, the Turks and the Arabs. I was among the Kurds. I forgot much of the Armenian language, but I did not forget the Lord's Prayer. Later they used to have me tend sheep. They gave me a dog with the name of Khutto. I used to write in the dirt with my finger my name, my last name, and the name of my birthplace. I used to write the alphabet in the dirt and in this way I did not forget the Armenian letters. I did not forget the Lord's Prayer and I did not forget where I was from.

First I was with an Assyrian. They took me to Merdin. Later I was placed with Muslims to be brought up as their child, but I became ill. They returned me to the Assyrians. The Assyrians helped us a great deal.

From the church, the sister of the patriarch of the Assyrians took me to her house. They were poor as well. The Assyrians used to go to the road in order to break stones and make a living, and I went along with them. We used to go there to break stones. When that finished, it seems the war was ended, I said I am going to Aleppo. Instead of going to Aleppo, Kurdish tribesmen carried me away. They took me to their villages as a servant. I knew that I had relatives in Aleppo but how would I find them, how would I get there. I was among Kurds.

They took me to the place called Tersellor. Tersellor was a village of Kurds in the environs of Aleppo at the place called Musulme. I remained there tending sheep, but I had made up my mind that I would go to Aleppo. I did not know any other Armenians. There were no Armenians. There was nobody, but I thought to myself that my cousin might be there. By night I escaped. I went down the road. I hid from the Kurds. I saw a traveler on horseback with young ones around him. They saw me.

Now the languages, Arabic, Kurdish, I spoke fluently already. They asked me: "Where are you going?" I said: "I am going to Aleppo." They looked at each other's faces. They said: "We are going to Aleppo. We will take you along." They took me with them. They were from Aleppo, but Muslims. They have villages. In the summer they go to their villages. In the winter they return to Aleppo. They took me with them, but they did not let me out of their house in Aleppo. Next door to the house I was staying in there was an Armenian girl. She was younger than I. She remembered only her name, Mary. She brought news from the outside. She is also Armenian and I am Armenian, but I acted as if I was a Kurd since I had presented myself as a Kurd to the others. I was afraid to tell the truth to that Armenian girl. She was younger than I.

One day she had fallen down the stairs and broken her foot. They took her to the hospital. At the hospital they told her: "You are Armenian." "No, my name is Fatma," she had said.

I saw that she had come back. When we were taking out the garbage, I asked her: "Where were you?" She related what had taken place. "I was at the hospital." She said that they told her: "You are Armenian." She said: "At first I denied it." After talking for a while she conceded. "Yes, I only remember that we were under a tent. My father, my mother, all, they killed and they took me. Only that much I remember." They [the hospital personnel] said: "Do not go [back to the house]. Now there are Armenians. We have an Armenia." This is at the end of 1922. After I was freed I discovered what the date was. She said [to the hospital personnel]: "No. I go back because they spent ten red gold pieces for my foot."

Look, God sent her for me. I believe that God sent her for me. "But I will escape," she said. "I will escape." I said: "Alright, we will escape together." We had a shoemaker who was Armenian. We did not know that he was Armenian. He was from Aintab. Now I regret very much that I did not take down his name. Eventually, through his assistance, we managed to escape.

I told the girl: "Tell that boy from Aintab that there is another Armenian girl." He asked her: "Does she use a veil?" At that time I had been given a small veil since I was with a Muslim. He made me work as a servant. She said: "Yes." "Do not believe that she is Armenian," he said. The girl came and told me this. I said: "Tell him I know the Lord's Prayer." She went and told him. He said: "Anyone from another race can learn that by heart just as they learn languages." It so happened that Armenian men had attempted to rescue girls from the houses of other Arabs only to discover that they were not Armenians. I said: "Tell him that I know how to read Armenian." He said: "If she knows how to read Armenian, let her write." I wrote my name, my last name, where I was from, but I wrote in Turkish with Armenian letters. When she gave him the letter, he told her: "We will not rescue you until she is ready too. Now we believe that this girl is Armenian." If I had not known how to read and write Armenian I would not be here today. The Armenian letters saved me. This letter was handed to Nishan Der-Bedrosian, a man from Kharpert. It came into his hands and he wrote me a letter which reached me through that girl. "Try in every way to escape..."

The shop of the shoemaker was close to where we lived. The first day I found that he had locked the door to the shop and left. I went the following day. He said: "You know I cannot keep the store open after a certain hour. It is against the law." Then I found the means to escape. When I was escaping, they realized that I was escaping so they locked the door with two keys. But finally I found the way. I escaped by night. A man was standing in the dark and the shoemaker had not closed his shop. They took me and we left. It was a feast day. It was Christmas day. Apparently it was December or January, perhaps the beginning of 1923. I was free.

So this is my story. But the things which the Turks did, the massacres, I never forget. In front of our eyes ... Haygaz ... on his mother's knees, they butchered him. These sort of things I have seen. And I always cry. I cannot forget.

References

Adalian, Rouben P. (1989). The historical evolution of the Armenian diasporas. *Journal of Modern Hellenism, 6*, 81–114.

Adalian, Rouben P. (1991). The Armenian genocide: context and legacy. *Social Education, 55*(2), 99–104. (Special Issue on Teaching About Genocide, edited by William S. Parsons and Samuel Totten.)

Adalian, Rouben P. (Ed.) (1991–1993). *The Armenian genocide in the U.S. Archives 1915–1918.* Alexandria, VA: Chadwyck-Healey, Inc.

Adalian, Rouben P. (1992). The Armenian genocide: Revisionism and denial. In Michael N. Dobkowski & Isidor Wallimann (Eds.) *Genocide in our time: An annotated bibliography with analytical introductions* (pp. 85–105). Ann Arbor, MI: The Pierian Press.

Adalian, Rouben P. (1999a). A conceptual method for examining the consequences of the Armenian genocide. In Levon Chorbajian & George Shirinian (Eds.) *Studies in comparative genocide* (pp. 47–59). New York: St. Martin's Press, Inc.

Adalian, Rouben P. (1999b) Evidence, source, and authority: Documenting the Armenian genocide against the background of denial. In Roger W. Smith (Ed.) *Genocide: Essays toward understanding, early-warning, and prevention* (pp. 67–77). Williamsburg,VA: Association of Genocide Scholars.

Adalian, Rouben P. (2010). *Historical dictionary of Armenia* (2nd ed.). Lanham, MD: Scarecrow Press, Inc.

Adalian, Rouben P. (2003). American diplomatic correspondence in the age of mass murder: Documents of the Armenian genocide in the U.S. Archives. In Jay Winter (Ed.) *America and the Armenian genocide of 1915* (pp. 146–184). New York: Cambridge University Press.

Ahmad, Feroz (1982). Unionist relations with the Greek, Armenian, and Jewish communities of the Ottoman Empire, 1908–1914. In Benjamin Braude & Bernard Lewis (Eds.) *Christians and Jews in the Ottoman Empire, Volume I: The central lands* (pp. 387–434). New York: Holmes & Meier Publishers Inc.

Akçam, Taner (2004). *From Empire to republic: Turkish nationalism & the Armenian genocide.* London: Zed Books.

Akçam, Taner (2006). *A shameful act: The Armenian genocide and the question of Turkish responsibility.* New York: Metropolitan Books.

Aktar, Ayhan (2007). Debating the Armenian massacres in the Last Ottoman Parliament, November–December 1918. *History Workshop Journal, 64*(1), 240–270.

Astourian, Stephan H. (1992). Genocidal process: Reflections on the Armeno-Turkish polarization. In Richard G. Hovannisian (Ed.) *The Armenian genocide: History, politics, ethics* (pp. 53–79). New York: St. Martin's Press.

Astourian, Stephan H. (1998). Modern Turkish identity and the Armenian genocide. In Richard G. Hovannisian (Ed.) *Remembrance and denial: The case of the Armenian genocide* (pp. 23–49). Detroit, MI: Wayne State University Press.

Baghdjian, Kevork K. (1987). *La Confiscation, par le Gouvernement Turc, des Biens Arméniens ... Dits Abandonnés.* Montreal: Payette & Simms Inc.

Balakian, Grigoris (2009). *Armenian Golgotha: A memoir of the Armenian genocide, 1915–1918.* (Peter Balakian with Aris Sevak, Trans.). New York: Alfred A. Knopf.

Bardakjian, Kevork B. (1985). *Hitler and the Armenian genocide.* Cambridge, MA: Zoryan Institute for Contemporary Armenian Research and Documentation.

Barsoumian, Hagop (1982). The dual role of the Amira class within the Ottoman government and the Armenian millet (1750–1850). In Benjamin Braude & Bernard Lewis (Eds.) *Christians and Jews in the Ottoman Empire, Volume I: The central lands* (pp. 171–184). New York: Holmes & Meier Publishers Inc.

Bass, Gary Jonathan (2000). *Stay the hand of vengeance.* Princeton, NJ: Princeton University Press.

Bevan, Robert (2006). *The destruction of memory: Architecture at war.* London: Reaktion Books.

Beylerian, Arthur (1983). *Les Grande Puissances l'Empire Ottoman et les Arméniens dans les Archives Françaises (1914–1918): recueil de documents.* Paris: Publications de la Sorbonne.

Bjørlund, Mattias (2009). "A fate worse than dying": Sexual violence during the Armenian genocide. In Dagmar Herzog (Ed.) *War and sexuality in Europe's twentieth century* (pp. 16–58). New York: Palgrave Macmillan.

Bliss, Edwin M. ([1896] 1982). *Turkey and the Armenian atrocities.* Fresno, CA: Meshag Publishers.

Bloxham, Donald (2005). *The great game of genocide: Imperialism, nationalism, and the destruction of the Ottoman Armenians.* New York: Oxford University Press.

Bobelian, Michael (2009*). Children of Armenia: A forgotten genocide and the century-long struggle for justice.* New York: Simon & Schuster.

Bournoutian, George A. (2002). *A concise history of the Armenian people.* Costa Mesa, CA: Mazda Publishers.

Charny, Israel W. (Ed.) (1999). *Encyclopedia of genocide*. Santa Barbara, CA: ABC-Clio.

Dadrian, Vahakn N. (1986). The Naim-Andonian documents on the World War I destruction of Ottoman Armenians: The anatomy of a genocide. *International Journal of Middle East Studies, 18*(3), 311–360.

Dadrian, Vahakn N. (1989). Genocide as a problem of national and international law: The World War I Armenian case and its contemporary legal ramifications. *Yale Journal of International Law, 14*(2), 221–334.

Dadrian, Vahakn N. (1994). Documentation of the Armenian genocide in German and Austrian sources. In Israel W. Charny (Ed.) *The widening circle of genocide: A critical bibliographic review* (Vol. 3, pp. 77–125). New Brunswick, NJ: Transaction Publishers.

Dadrian, Vahakn N. (1995). *The history of the Armenian genocide: Ethnic conflict from the Balkans to Anatolia to the Caucasus*. Providence, RI: Berghahn Books.

Dadrian, Vahakn N. (1996). *German responsibility in the Armenian genocide: A review of the historical evidence of German complicity*. Cambridge, MA: Blue Crane Books.

Dadrian, Vahakn N. (1999). *Warrant for genocide: Key elements of Turko-Armenian conflict*. New Brunswick, NJ: Transaction Publishers.

Davis, Leslie A. (1989). *The slaughterhouse province: An American diplomat's report on the Armenian genocide, 1915–1917*. New Rochelle, NY: Aristide D. Caratzas, Publisher.

Derderian, Katharine (2005). Common fate, different experience: Gender-specific aspects of the Armenian genocide, 1915–1917. *Holocaust and Genocide Studies, XIX*(1), 1–25.

Deringil, Selim (2009). The Armenian question is finally closed: Mass conversions of Armenians in Anatolia during the Hamidian massacres of 1895–1897. *Comparative Studies in Society and History, 51*(2), 344–371.

Dinkel, Christoph (1991). German officers and the Armenian genocide. *Armenian Review, 44*(1), 77–133.

Dobkin, Marjorie Housepian (1986). What genocide? What holocaust? News from Turkey, 1915–1923: A case study. In Richard Hovannisian (Ed.) *The Armenian genocide in perspective* (pp. 97–109). New Brunswick, NJ: Transaction Books.

Fein, Helen (1979). *Accounting for genocide: National responses and Jewish victimization during the Holocaust*. New York: The Free Press.

Foreign Policy Institute (1982). *The Armenian issue in nine questions and answers*. Ankara: Author.

Gibbons, Herbert Adams (1916). *The blackest page of modern history: Events in Armenia in 1915. The facts and the responsibilities*. New York and London: G.P. Putnam's Sons.

Göçek, Fatma Müge (2006). Reading genocide: Turkish historiography on the Armenian deportations and massacres of 1915. In Israel Gershoni, Amy Singer, & Hakan Erdem (Eds.) *Middle East historiographies: Narrating the twentieth century* (pp. 101–127). Seattle: University of Washington Press.

Greene, Frederick Davis (1896). *Armenian massacres and Turkish tyranny*. Philadelphia & Chicago: International Publishing Co.

Guroian, Vigen (1986). Collective responsibility and official excuse making: The case of the Turkish genocide of the Armenians. In Richard Hovannisian (Ed.) *The Armenian genocide in perspective* (pp. 135–152). New Brunswick, NJ: Transaction Books.

Gürün, Kâmuran (1985). *The Armenian file: The myth of innocence exposed*. New York: St. Martin's Press.

Hairapetian, Armen (1984). "Race problems" and the Armenian genocide: The State Department files and documents: The State Department file. *Armenian Review, 37*(1), 41–145.

Horowitz, Irving Louis (1982). *Taking lives: Genocide and state power*. New Brunswick, NJ: Transaction Books.

Hovannisian, Richard G. (1967). *Armenia on the road to independence 1918*. Berkeley, CA: University of California Press.

Hovannisian, Richard G. (1978). *The Armenian holocaust: A bibliography relating to the deportations, massacres, and dispersion of the Armenian people, 1915–1923*. Cambridge, MA: National Association for Armenian Studies and Research.

Hovannisian, Richard G. (1986a). The historical dimensions of the Armenian question, 1878–1923. In Richard G. Hovannisian (Ed.) *The Armenian genocide in perspective* (pp. 19–41). New Brunswick, NJ: Transaction Books.

Hovannisian, Richard G. (1986b). The Armenian genocide and patterns of denial. In Richard G. Hovannisian (Ed.) *The Armenian genocide in perspective* (pp. 111–133). New Brunswick, NJ: Transaction Books.

Hovannisian, Richard G. (1992). Intervention and shades of altruism during the Armenian genocide. In Richard G. Hovannisian (Ed.) *The Armenian genocide: History, politics, ethics* (pp. 173–207). New York: St. Martin's Press.

Kaiser, Hilmar (2003). From empire to republic: The continuities of Turkish denial. *Armenian Review,* 48(3–4), 1–24.

Kerr, Stanley E. (1973). *The lions of Marash: Personal experiences with American Near East Relief, 1919–1922.* Albany, NY: State University of New York Press.

Kinross, Lord (1964). *Ataturk: The birth of a nation.* London: Weidenfeld and Nicolson.

Kirakossian, Arman J. (2004). *The Armenian massacres 1894–1896: U.S. media testimony.* Detroit, MI: Wayne State University Press.

Kloian, Richard D. (1985). *The Armenian genocide: News accounts from the American press, 1915–1922.* Berkeley, CA: Anto Printing.

Kouymjian, Dickran (1985). The destruction of Armenian historical monuments as a continuation of the Turkish policy of genocide. In Gerard Libaridian (Ed.) *A crime of silence, the Armenian genocide: Permanent Peoples' Tribunal* (pp. 173–183). London: Zed Books.

Kuper, Leo (1981). *Genocide: Its political use in the twentieth century.* New Haven, CT: Yale University Press.

Kuper, Leo (1986). The Turkish genocide of Armenians, 1915–1917. In Richard G. Hovannisian (Ed.) *The Armenian genocide in perspective* (pp. 43–59). New Brunswick, NJ: Transaction Books.

Lang, David Marshall (1970). *Armenia: Cradle of civilization.* London: George Allen & Unwin.

Lang, David Marshal (1981). *The Armenians: A people in exile.* London: George Allen & Unwin.

Lepsius, Johannes (1987). *Rapport Secret sur les Massacres d'Arménie (1915–1916).* Paris: Edition Payot.

Levene, Mark (1998). Creating a modern 'zone of genocide': The impact of nation- and state-formation on Eastern Anatolia, 1878–1923. *Holocaust and Genocide Studies, 12*(3), 393–433.

Libaridian, Gerard (1985). The ideology of the Young Turk Movement. In Gerard Libaridian (Ed.) *A crime of silence, the Armenian genocide: Permanent Peoples' Tribunal* (pp. 37–49). London: Zed Books.

Libaridian, Gerard (1987). The ultimate repression: The genocide of the Armenians, 1915–1917. In Isidor Wallimann & Michael N. Dobkowski (Eds.) *Genocide and the modern age: Etiology and case studies of mass death* (pp. 203–235). Westport, CT: Greenwood Press.

McCarthy, Justin (1983). *Muslims and minorities: The population of Ottoman Anatolia and the end of the empire.* New York: New York University Press.

Melson, Robert (1986). Provocation or nationalism: A critical inquiry into the Armenian genocide of 1915. In Richard G. Hovannisian (Ed.) *The Armenian genocide in perspective* (pp. 61–84). New Brunswick, NJ: Transaction Books.

Miller, Donald E., & Miller, Lorna Touryan (1993). *Survivors: An oral history of the Armenian genocide.* Berkeley, CA and Los Angeles, CA: University of California Press.

Morgenthau, Henry (1918). *Ambassador Morgenthau's story.* Garden City, NY: Doubleday, Page and Co. [Reprinted in 2003 by Wayne State University Press, Detroit, Michigan.]

Nalbandian, Louise (1963). *The Armenian revolutionary movement.* Berkeley, CA and Los Angeles, CA: University of California Press.

Nassibian, Akaby (1984). *Britain and the Armenian question 1915–1923.* New York: St. Martin's Press.

Ohandjian, Artem (Ed.) (1988). *The Armenian genocide, Volume 2: Documentation.* Munich: Institute fur Armenische Fragen.

Parla, Taha (1985). *The social and political thought of Ziya Gökalp 1876–1924.* Leiden: E.J. Brill.

Payaslian, Simon (2005). *United States policy toward the Armenian question and the Armenian genocide.* New York: Palgrave Macmillan.

Payaslian, Simon (2006). The destruction of the Armenian Church during the genocide. *Genocide Studies and Prevention, 1*(2), 149–171.

Peterson, Merrill D. (2004). *Starving Armenians: America and the Armenian genocide, 1915–1930 and after.* Charlottesville, VA: University of Virginia Press.

Ramsaur, Jr., Ernest Edmondson (1957). *The Young Turks: Prelude to the revolution of 1908*. New York: Russell & Russell.

Sachar, Howard M. (1969). *The emergence of the Middle East 1914-1924*. New York: Alfred A. Knopf.

Sanasarian, Eliz (1989). Gender distinction in the genocide process: A preliminary study of the Armenian case. *Holocaust and Genocide Studies, 4*(4), 449–461.

Shaw, Stanford J., & Shaw, Ezel Kural (1977). *History of the Ottoman empire and modern Turkey, Volume 2: Reform, revolution, and republic. The rise of modern Turkey 1808-1975*. New York: Cambridge University Press.

Shemmassian, Vahram (2006). The reclamation of captive Armenian genocide survivors in Syria and Lebanon at the end of World War I. *Journal of the Society for Armenian Studies, 15*, 113–140.

Smith, Roger (1989). Genocide and denial: The Armenian case and its implications. *Armenian Review, 42*(1), 1–38.

Staub, Ervin (1989). *The roots of evil: The Origins of genocide and other group violence*. New York: Cambridge University Press.

Tachjian, Vahé (2009). Gender, nationalism, exclusion: The reintegration process of female survivors of the Armenian genocide. *Nations and Nationalism, 15*(1), 60–80.

Ternon, Yves (1981). *The Armenians: History of a genocide*. Delmar, NY: Caravan Books.

Theriault, Henri (2003). Denial and free speech: The case of the Armenian genocide. In Richard G. Hovannisian (Ed.) *Looking backward, moving forward: Confronting the Armenian genocide* (pp. 231–261). New Brunswick, NJ: Transaction Publishers.

Totten, Samuel (1991). The Ottoman genocide of the Armenians. In Samuel Totten (Ed.) *First-person accounts of genocidal acts committed in the twentieth century: An annotated bibliography* (pp. 7–43). Westport, CT: Greenwood Press.

Toynbee, Arnold J. (Ed.) (1916). *The treatment of Armenians in the Ottoman Empire, 1915-1916*. London: Sir Joseph Causton and Sons, Limited. [Preface by Viscount Bryce.] [Reprinted in Beirut, Lebanon by G. Doniguian & Sons, 1979.]

Trumpener, Ulrich (1968). *Germany and the Ottoman Empire 1914-1918*. Princeton, NJ: Princeton University Press. [Reprinted in 1989 by Caravan Books, Delmar, NY]

Üngör, Uğor Ümit (2008). Seeing like a nation-state: Young Turk social engineering in eastern Turkey, 1913-1950. *Journal of Genocide Research, 10*(1), 15–39.

Uras, Esat (1988). *The Armenians in history and the Armenian question*. Istanbul: Foundation for the Establishment and Promotion of Centers for Historical Research and Documentation, and Istanbul Research Center.

Walker, Christopher J. (1980). *Armenia: The survival of a nation*. New York: St. Martin's Press.

Werfel, Franz (1934). *The forty days of Musa Dagh*. New York: The Modern Library.

Winter, Jay (2003). *America and the Armenian genocide of 1915*. Cambridge: Cambridge University Press.

Ye'or, Bat (Y. Masriya) (1985). *The Dhimmi: Jews and Christians under Islam*. Teaneck, NJ: Fairleigh Dickenson University Press.

Zürcher, Erik J. (1998). *Turkey: A modern history*. London and New York: I.B. Tauris & Co Ltd.

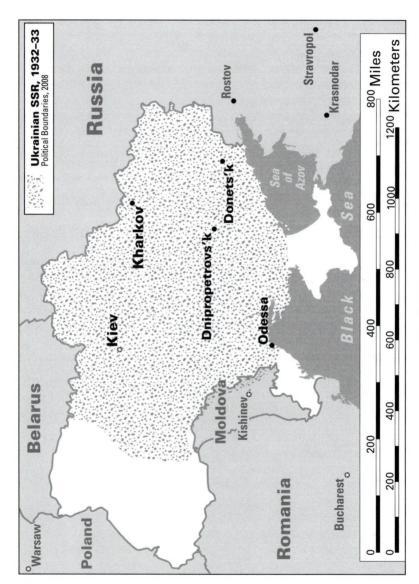

Map 5.1 Ukraine

CHAPTER 5

Soviet Man-made Famine in Ukraine

JAMES E. MACE

It is now generally accepted that in 1932–1933 several million peasants—most of them Ukrainians living in Ukraine and the traditionally Cossack territories of the North Caucasus (now the Krasnodar, Stavropol, and Rostov on the Don regions of the Russian Federation)—starved to death because the government of the Soviet Union seized with unprecedented force and thoroughness the 1932 crop and foodstuffs from the agricultural population (Mace, 1984; Conquest, 1986). After over half a century of denial, in January 1990 the Communist Party of Ukraine adopted a special resolution admitting that the Ukrainian Famine had indeed occurred, cost millions of lives, had been artificially brought about by official actions, and that Stalin and his associates bore criminal responsibility for those actions (*Holod*, 1990, pp. 3–4).

The Ukrainian Famine corresponded in time with a reversal of official policies that had hitherto permitted significant self-expression of the USSR's non-Russian nations. During and after the Famine, non-Russian national self-assertion was labeled bourgeois nationalism and suppressed. The elites who had been associated with these policies were eliminated (Mace, 1983, pp. 264–301). The authorities of the period denied that a famine was taking place at the time, sought to discredit reports on the factual situation, insofar as possible prevented the starving people from traveling to areas where food was available, and refused all offers of aid to the starving (Conquest, 1986; U.S. Commission on the Ukraine Famine, 1988: vi–xxv). They were assisted in this policy of denial by certain Western journalists, most notably Walter Duranty of the *New York Times* (Taylor, 1990, pp. 210–223).

157

In order to understand the Ukrainian Famine, a brief excursion into the period that preceded it is necessary. Despite their numerical strength as the second-largest of the Slavic-speaking nations, Ukrainians may be classed with what Czech scholar Miroslav Hroch (1985) designated the "small nations" of Europe. Such nations "were in subjection for such a long period that the relation of subjection took on a structural character"; that is, the majority of the ruling class belonged to the ruling nation, while the subjugated nation possessed an incomplete social structure partially or entirely lacking its own ruling class (Hroch, 1985, p. 9). The Ukrainians were basically a nation of peasants, their national movement being led by a numerically small intelligentsia. As in other areas occupied by subject nations in Imperial Russia and early Soviet history, the local nobility, bourgeoisie, and urban population in Ukraine were overwhelmingly Russian or Russian-speaking (Liber, 1990, pp. 12–15).

In the 19th century, Ukrainians underwent a national revival similar to that of Czechs and other "small nations"; that is, romantic scholarly excursions into the local language and history, along with the creation of a vernacular literature, brought a spreading sense of local patriotism and national identity that in turn gave way to political aspirations and, ultimately, territorial home rule. Yet, when in 1925 Stalin wrote, "The national question is, *according to its essence*, a question of the peasantry" (Stalin, 1946–1951, Vol. 7, p. 72), this held true for almost all the non-Russian peoples of the Soviet Union and certainly for Ukrainians.

The social development of Ukrainians in the Russian Empire had been retarded by extraordinarily repressive policies. In 1863, the Imperial Russian government responded to what it perceived as a nascent threat of "Ukrainian separatism" by banning education and publications (except for folk songs and historical documents) in the Ukrainian language, declaring it to be a substandard variant of Russian. This ban was broadened in 1876 to eliminate the modest exemptions in the earlier measure and remained in effect until 1905 (Savchenko, 1930). After 1905, a Ukrainian language press enjoyed a brief flowering in central Ukraine, but creeping reimposition of the old prohibitions all but eliminated it within a few years. Because repressive tsarist policies had stunted the growth of social differentiation within Ukrainian society, Ukrainian activists could expect to gain mass support only among the peasantry. Consequently, when Ukrainian political parties evolved in Imperial Russia at the turn of the century, they assumed a revolutionary socialist character, and the form in which Ukrainian political aspirations gained majority support during the Russian Revolution of 1917 was through the agrarian socialism of the Ukrainian Party of Socialist Revolutionaries (Hermaize, 1926; Khrystiuk, 1921–1922, Vol. 1, p. 35).

After the collapse of the Russian imperial authority in 1917, the national movements that attempted to establish local governments throughout the former empire's non-Russian periphery, including the Ukrainian movement, drew most of their mass support from the village, while in the cities various groups competed more or less as they did in Russia proper.

The group that seized power in the center, Lenin's Bolsheviks, mistrusted the peasants as petty property owners and relied on forced requisitions of agricultural produce in order to keep the urban population fed. Thus, the national struggle between Russians ("Red" or "White") and the subject peoples was at the same time a social struggle of the countryside versus the town, where even the working-class was drawn from the oppressor nation or had assimilated its culture. As Ukrainian Communist spokesmen recognized as early as 1920, the Russian-speaking worker, who provided the main source of support for Soviet rule in Ukraine, sneered at the Ukrainian village and wanted nothing to do with it (Mace, 1983, pp. 68–69). During the wars that followed the Russian Revolution of 1917, a Soviet regime had been imposed on Ukraine by Russia against the will of most of Ukraine's inhabitants, an absolute majority of whom had voted in free elections for groups that supported Ukrainian self-rule (Borys, 1980, p. 170, table).

In order to overcome rural resistance to the Soviet order, in 1921 Lenin proclaimed the New Economic Policy (NEP), which ended forced procurements and allowed a private market in which agricultural producers could sell what they had produced. In 1923, in order to overcome the continued national resistance of the non-Russian countryside, Lenin proclaimed a policy of indigenization (*korenizatsiia*), which attempted to give non-Russian Soviet regimes a veneer of national legitimacy by promoting the spread of the local language and culture in the cities, recruiting local people into the regime, ordering Russian officials to learn the local language, and fostering a broad range of cultural activities (Mace, 1983, pp. 87–95; Liber, 1990, pp. 33–46).

The Ukrainian Famine of 1932–1933 occurred within the context of the so-called "Stalinist Revolution from Above," a violent experiment in social transformation in which state-orchestrated paranoia about internal and external enemies was used to blame shortcomings on the machinations of class enemies. Like Nazism, Stalinism attempted to explain the world as a struggle between different categories of people, some of whom were considered inherently deleterious and whose elimination was an essential prerequisite toward the attainment of a new and better state of affairs. As a degenerated offshoot of Marxism, Stalinism attempted to explain the world by using class categories, rather than the racial ones employed by the Nazis. But what Hitler and Stalin had in common was a dualistic view of human society as composed of two implacably hostile forces: the "good" force destined for victory (Aryans for Hitler and the proletariat for Stalin), which could only liberate itself and achieve its destiny by destroying utterly the forces of evil (for Hitler, Jews and Gypsies, which he considered racially polluting elements, and for Stalin, representatives of "exploiter classes").

A major difference between Stalinism and racism (like Nazism) is that racism at least knows how to define what it hates: people who look or speak differently or have different ancestors. Class warfare, however, is a sociological concept. Sociological categories are much easier to manipulate than racial ones, especially when applied in and by a state that claims, as did Stalin's, a monopoly on truth and science thanks to its "correct" understanding and application of a theory based on claims of holistic scientism; that is, claims that it explains everything with the certainty of (pseudo) scientific laws. By redefining and manipulating such notions as class enemies and enemies of the people, and objectively serving the interests of such dark forces, Stalin was able to declare practically any group or individual worthy of destruction. This enabled Stalin to reduce Marxism, one of the great (if flawed) intellectual systems of the 19th century, to the level of a sanctioning ideology for perhaps the paradigmatic example of what Leo Kuper (1990) has called the genocide state.

Marxism views history as class struggle. It holds that modern capitalism is defined by the struggle between proletarians and capitalists, the former being destined to triumph over the latter and thereby create a new socialist stage of human history in which the economic exploitation of one person by another will be abolished. Independent small-holding peasants are viewed as peripheral in this struggle, a petty capitalist holdover of an earlier era. Leninists saw an inevitable process of class differentiation among peasants into three strata: the relatively wealthier *kulaks* (Ukrainian *kurkuls*) or village exploiters, the middle peasants or subsistence farmers who did not hire labor or depend on outside employment to get by, and the poor peasants, who could only make ends meet by working for others and thus were at least partially a rural proletarian. The middle and poor peasants were often lumped together as the *toiling peasantry* in order to mark them apart from the kulaks. However, such a division of the peasantry into such categories was arbitrary, and just who was a kulak was never defined with any precision (Lewin, 1985, pp. 121–141).

As for the national question, most varieties of Marxism reject nationalism as a species of false consciousness that reflects the interests of an exploitative bourgeois class by convincing the exploited that they owe loyalty to their capitalist-ruled nation rather than to the international working-class. Orthodox Marxists believe that only internationalism can serve the interests of the working class. There have been many conflicting policy prescriptions advocated by Marxists designed to overcome nationalistic prejudices and achieve the internationalist unity of the toiling classes.

Just as nationalism can have a variety of meanings, so can internationalism. In the pre-Stalinist period, the Soviet authorities found what they considered the "correct" internationalist approach to building socialism by attempting to combat the imperial pretensions of Russians (the dominant group) and by assisting the formerly subject peoples of the Russian Empire to overcome the legacy of colonial domination by rebuilding their various national cultures and societies—under the Party's guidance, of course. This ideological prescription actually reflected political necessity: Before the adoption of such a policy, non-Russian peasant dissatisfaction had threatened political stability in wide areas of the new Soviet Union. But there were certainly other Marxist views of internationalism. For example, Rosa Luxemburg advocated a view often criticized as "national nihilism" when she argued that national self-determination was a chimera: It was Utopian so long as capitalist exploitation survived and would be rendered irrelevant once socialism had brought about the final end of all forms of exploitation (Luxemburg, 1976, pp. 308–314).

Once an ideology comes to power, theory becomes the stuff of practical politics, influencing and being influenced by considerations of power. *Ukrainization*, the Ukrainian version of indigenization, went further than elsewhere in the Soviet Union because there were roughly 30 million Ukrainians, several times more numerous than any other single national group. On the eve of the Famine Ukrainians constituted about two-fifths of all non-Russian inhabitants of the USSR. The policies of indigenization, designed to placate the national aspirations of the non-Russian, overwhelmingly peasant nations, went hand-in-hand with the limited free-market policies of the NEP, which were designed to satisfy the economic aspirations of both Russian and non-Russian peasants.

With indigenization having legitimized national priorities among non-Russian Communists and the high politics in Moscow centering on a protracted struggle for power, throughout the 1920s national Communists in the constituent republics of the USSR accumulated a large measure of autonomy from central dictates. When, at the end of the decade, Joseph Stalin emerged victorious in the succession struggle, he abruptly changed course by announcing the crash collectivization of agriculture on the basis of the liquidation (that is, destruction) of the *kulaks* as a class.

Collectivization meant forcing millions of small farmers into large collective farms, which many peasants saw—not without reason—as a reinstitution of serfdom, the only difference being that the state was now taking the place of the nobleman who owned the peasants' grandparents. Forcing the majority of the population to restructure their lives in a way they did not wish to meant provoking a degree of hostility, which rendered concessions that had been designed to placate the non-Russian peasants on national grounds politically irrelevant.

The changed political situation enabled Stalin to pursue four objectives toward the non-Russians. Donald Treadgold (1964) has rightly summarized these as: (1) the elimination of centrifugal pressures by stifling local nationalism; (2) subversion of neighboring states by having members of a given Soviet nationality conduct propaganda among their co-nationals in neighboring areas; (3) "economic and social transformation designed to destroy native society and substitute a social system susceptible of control by Moscow"; and (4) the economic exploitation of non-Russian areas (pp. 297–298).

Transforming society by force far exceeded the capacity of any traditional authoritarian state. It required the mobilization and motivation of mass constituencies who could be called upon to do the regime's will. Starting with a phony war scare in 1927 and followed by show trials designed to point out various social groups (managers and engineers held over from the old regime, academicians, people who had been associated with national or religious movements, etc.) as nests of plotters in the pay of world capitalism, a massive propaganda campaign was carried out designed to convince people that the Soviet Union was under siege by the hostile capitalist world that encircled it. Soviet society had to catch up with the capitalist West or be crushed. The crash collectivization of agriculture was portrayed as essential in order to do this.

In order to expropriate kulaks, enforce collectivization, and take possession of agricultural produce, the authorities mobilized anyone they could. As a self-proclaimed workers' state, it was logical that the regime would turn first to the workers and trade unions for personnel to impose its will. The entire network of officially sanctioned social organizations was mobilized. The resistance they faced was interpreted in class terms as kulak terrorism, for who but a kulak or his agent could oppose the socialist transformation of the countryside? Ultimately, any problem was blamed on "kulaks" or their "agents," and repressive policies were justified by the need to combat an enemy presence that was ever more broadly defined. The village itself became an object of official mistrust as tens of thousands of factory workers were issued revolvers and sent into villages with the power to completely reorganize life as well as to circumvent or abolish village-level governmental bodies. Workers were sent from factories, and sometimes a factory would be named "patron" of a given number of villages; that is, the factory would be assigned villages in which to enforce collectivization and seize food.

Local "activists," that is, individuals whose positions gave them an active role in officially sanctioned social and political life, would also be given these responsibilities. Special peasant "tow" (*buksyr*) brigades were organized and given the task of "taking the kulaks in tow," which meant ejecting those selected by the local authorities from their houses or searching for and expropriating concealed foodstuffs. The members of these brigades did not always volunteer; sometimes county or district authorities would simply call up the able-bodied men in one village to act as a tow brigade in a neighboring village. A schoolteacher, for example, had no choice but to take part in the work of the local activists. At the height of the Famine, when most peasants were physically incapable of work, lines in front of city stores were raided from time to time, and the unfortunates rounded up were sent to weed sugar beets (U.S. Commission on the Ukraine Famine, 1988, pp. 448–449).

The essence of the collective farm system was official control over agricultural production and distribution. The state's "procurement" of agricultural produce was carried out by force such that procurements (purchases) really became forced requisitions. Since, however, the collective farm was, in theory, a private cooperative, not a state enterprise, the authorities assumed no responsibility for the welfare of the collective farmers. Whatever the state required came from the "first proceeds" of the harvest; that is, the state took its quota first. If there was anything left, it went first to what was needed to run the farm, such as seed reserves, and what was left over was then shared among the collective farmers according to the labor days (*trudodni*) they had earned (Jasny, 1949, pp. 64–85).

These "labor days" were not actual days worked. Rather, they were allocated according to a complex formula designed to calculate the different values of different kinds of labor by converting all types of labor on the farm into the Marxist concept of simple labor time. Skilled workers, like a tractor driver, might earn two labor days for each day worked, while a simple farmer without any particular skill might have to work two days in order to earn one labor day. This, however, was of no consequence if there was nothing left; in that case, of course, the labor days of the collective farmers were worthless.

At the time of the Famine, roughly 20% of the Ukrainian peasantry was still outside the collective farms. They had their own household quotas, which were imposed by local authorities. If they could not meet a given quota, they were fined, and their farms searched with the aid of metal prods.

Collectivization led to a crisis in agricultural production that the regime met sometimes with force and sometimes with promises to overcome "errors" or "excesses" or "deviations" from the Party's "Leninist general line." Such shortcomings were always blamed on subordinate officials, never on the policies of the Communist Party and Soviet state, which were held to be infallible. The first agricultural procurement campaign after crash collectivization, that of 1930, was met, thanks to a fortunate harvest. The following year, the quota was not met in spite of considerable force that succeeded only in creating pockets of starvation. In the first half of 1932, the regime announced that there had been a crop failure in parts of the Volga Basin and Asiatic Russia and sent aid there from other regions. In May, agricultural quotas for the coming crop were lowered to about the level of what had been obtained from the 1931 crop. Various officials were denounced for having used excessive force in seizing agricultural produce and promises were made that such "distortions" of the official policy would not be tolerated in the future. Some local officials who had been particularly harsh toward peasants in their charge were publicly tried and punished. For a few weeks, even Ukraine received limited food aid.

Then, in the summer of 1932, with Ukraine on the verge of mass starvation, Stalin abruptly changed course. At a Ukrainian Communist Party conference in July, amid reports that the situation in the Ukrainian countryside was growing desperate, Stalin's top assistants—Prime Minister Viacheslav Molotov and Agriculture Minister Lazar Kaganovich—announced that Ukraine's quotas for bread grain deliveries would stand at the level announced the previous May. But once the harvest was in, there simply wasn't enough grain to meet the quota. The Ukrainian authorities appealed to Moscow for an end to the grain seizures, but to no avail. Throughout the fall of 1932, Stalin sent various high officials to Ukraine to supervise the local Communists. In November, bread that had been "advanced" to the collective farmers at harvest time was declared to have been illegally distributed and was therefore seized. In order to make up for shortfalls elsewhere, those farms that met their quotas were subjected to supplementary quotas of foodstuffs that had to be delivered to the state. Local officials were ordered to determine how much bread there was in every collective farm and to put it toward the quota.

On December 14, Stalin's intimate involvement in the Ukrainian Famine became clear when he called the top leaders of Ukraine, the North Caucasus, and the Western (Smolensk) District to Moscow. The meeting produced a secret decree signed by Stalin as head of the Party and Molotov as head of the government. While the leader of the

Western District was let off with a simple admonition to meet its quotas, the Ukrainian and North Caucasus representatives were blasted for having failed to root out Ukrainian nationalism:

> As a result of the extremely weak efforts and lack of revolutionary vigilance of a number of local Party organizations in Ukraine and the North Caucasus, in a substantial portion of these organizations counterrevolutionary elements—kulaks, former officers, Petliurists, adherents of the Kuban Rada, and so forth—have been able to worm their way into the collective farms as chairmen or as influential members of their administration, bookkeepers, store managers, threshing brigade leaders, and so forth, were able to worm their way into village councils, agricultural offices, cooperatives, and attempted to direct the work of these organizations against the interests of the proletarian state and the Party's policy, attempted to organize a counterrevolutionary movement, to sabotage the grain procurements, and to sabotage the sowing, the All-Union Communist Party Central Committee and Council of Peoples Commissars of the USSR direct the Communist Party and government leadership of Ukraine and the North Caucasus to resolutely root out the counterrevolutionary elements by means of their arrest, long sentences of confinement in concentration camps, and not excluding application of the highest measure of legality (that is, execution) in the most criminal cases. (Postanova, 1991, p. 78)

The decree went on to name officials on the local level who had failed to make their quotas, mentioning the officials by name and detailing which of them were to be given prison sentences and which of them were to be shot. In addition, Ukrainian officials were condemned for their "mechanistic" (that is, overzealous) implementation of Ukrainization, and Ukrainization was ordered halted in the North Caucasus (Postanova, 1991).

A week later, Stalin's representatives in Ukraine ordered *the seizure of even the seed that had been put aside for spring planting.* In January 1933, Stalin took direct control of the Ukrainian Communist Party apparatus. His appointees, accompanied by tens of thousands of subordinates, initiated a campaign that led to the destruction of nationally self-assertive Ukrainian elites, the end of the Ukrainization policy and virtually all Ukrainian cultural self-expression, and the gradual return to the exclusive use of the Russian language in Ukraine's cities and educational institutions (U.S. Commission on the Ukraine Famine, 1988, pp. xi–xvii; *Holod*, 1990, pp. 148–235).

The food seized, people began to starve. Millions died either from starvation—an agonizingly slow process in which the body literally consumes itself until the muscles of the chest can no longer lift the rib cage to inflate the lungs and the victim suffocates—or, more commonly, from diseases that in such a weakened condition the body can no longer fend off. But to report deaths from starvation or from diseases like typhus, which are associated with famine, was considered anti-Soviet. Physicians used euphemisms like vitamin or protein deficiency (which does usually accompany caloric deficiency), heart failure (because the heart stops), diarrhea (from eating plants the body cannot digest), or "exhaustion of the organism" (Gannt, 1937, pp. 147–162).

Estimates of the number of victims in Ukraine range from three million to eight million. According to the long-suppressed 1937 census, released only in 1991, in 1937 Ukraine had one million fewer inhabitants than in 1926, three million fewer than official estimates of the early 1930s, which were probably not far off the mark (Vsesoiuznaia, 1991, p. 28, table). Using these and other long-suppressed figures, demographers in the former Soviet Union have calculated that, while the population of the USSR increased from 148.7 million in 1927 to 162.5 million in 1937, during the year 1933 the population decreased by 5.9 million. Their figures further suggest that the number of victims of famine in 1933 was 7.2–8.1 million (summarized in Ellman, 1991, pp. 375–379). Given that all but 1–2 million of these victims perished in Ukraine, the number of victims of the Ukrainian Famine would be in the range of 5–7 million.

As living conditions worsened, the authorities expanded the system of hard currency stores, the *torgsin*. The name was an abbreviation for the Russian phrase, *torgovlia s inostrantsami* (trade with foreigners), because only foreigners had the right to possess precious metals and convertible currency. In exchange for food, these stores helped extract the last valuables remaining in the countryside. Often a small piece of jewelry, a gold tooth, or a concealed silver or gold coin meant the difference between life and death.

The famine had a major long-range impact on Ukrainians. The adoption in 1932–1933 of an internal passport system from which peasants were excluded meant that the agricultural population could not leave the countryside without official permission. This meant attaching the peasantry to the land in a way not entirely different from traditional serfdom. The psychological traumatization inevitable in any situation of mass mortality was undoubtedly compounded by a policy of official denial extending to the most remote village. At the height of the Famine Stalin adopted the slogan: "Life has become better; life has become more fun," and even the starving had to repeat it. To speak openly of everyday reality meant running the risk of punishment for propagating anti-Soviet propaganda.

Children were encouraged to inform on their parents, and Pavlik Morozov, a boy who had informed on his parents and was killed by villagers after the parents' subsequent arrest, was held up as a model for Soviet young people. As a result, parents became afraid to talk openly in front of their own children. While Stalin's rapid industrialization brought millions of Ukrainian peasants to Ukraine's cities, mines, and factories, the abandonment of policies promoting the use of the Ukrainian language there often meant the rapid linguistic and cultural Russification of these new workers and city-dwellers.

As a result of the Famine and accompanying destruction of national elites, the Ukrainian nation was literally crushed. Their leadership (including the natural village leadership, the more prosperous and industrious peasants) was destroyed. Their language and culture, which had made significant inroads in the cities in the 1920s, was largely pushed back to the countryside whence it came. And in the countryside, about one out of every five people had perished. As a result, the development of Ukrainians as a nation was violently and traumatically set back.

The Ukrainians might never have recovered as a nation had it not been for Stalin's 1939 pact with Hitler, by which the Soviet Union annexed Western Ukraine as its share of the dismembered Polish Republic. Western Ukraine contained areas that had never been under Russian rule and were consequently the most developed and nationally conscious regions of Ukraine. The joining of Western Ukraine to the devastated Central and Eastern Ukrainian territories largely undermined Stalin's deconstruction of the Ukrainian nation in the 1930s, paving the way for Ukrainian independence in the 1990s.

Drawing lessons from history is always a risky business, but surely one of the principal lessons of the Ukrainian Famine has to do with the dangers of pseudo-scientific totalitarian ideologies. Such ideologies, which often claim scientific validity, explain problems within a given society by blaming them on the presence of permanent enemies that by virtue of their very existence prevent the bulk of society from achieving its destiny, living the good life, or otherwise solving its problems. Such enemies may be racial, national, political, or social, but however defined, such ideologies may easily be used as warrants for mass murder and genocide. The monopolies or near-monopolies of propaganda, reward, and coercion that totalitarian societies possess in turn make it possible for totalitarian regimes to attract sufficient mass participation to carry out such designs.

Moreover, as George Orwell demonstrated over 50 years ago in *1984*, the totalitarian monopoly of official expression allowed the Stalin regime to define and redefine concepts in order to radically change their meaning. Thus, in the Ukrainian case, class categories were manipulated in order to redefine national issues as class ones. Thus, the Ukrainian Famine further shows that the Fascist Right has no monopoly on genocide. Even ideologies espousing internationalism and social justice can be manipulated so as to target ethnic groups by redefining their terms to mean whatever might seem expedient at a given moment.

The refusal of even the moderate Left to perceive the full horror of Stalinism also carries lessons about the selective perception of evil. While it is understandable that one is more charitable to actions taken by regimes that profess adherence to "one's own" side of the political spectrum, civilized adherents of both the Left and the Right should realize that the most important issue of political life is not between continuity and change but between those who uphold such universal human values as the right of living people to remain among the living and those who do not recognize such a right for members of a given out-group. For those who profess humane values, the willingness to countenance the death of millions for their goals ceases to have anything in common with political progress: it is simply mass murder on an unspeakable scale.

Eyewitness Accounts

Account 1

S. Lozovy, "What Happened in Hadyach County" in *The Black Deeds of the Kremlin* (1953–1955, pp. 246–255). *The Black Deeds* is the classic collection of eyewitness accounts of the Famine, compiled by the Democratic Association of Ukrainians Who had Been Repressed By the Soviets (DOBRUS), which was associated with the Ukrainian Revolutionary Democratic Party, a socialist group formed after World War II by Ukrainians who had emigrated from Central and Eastern Ukraine.

Having received from comrade Kolotov, boss of the county seat, instructions to establish a commune, the chairman of the village soviet, Tereshko Myshchachenko, took great pains to carry them out. He gave them wide publicity and, as a further incentive, put his name first on the list of commune farmers. Another reason was comrade Gapon from the city of Orel who certainly would have been made chairman if Tereshko had failed in his "duties."

This was in 1930. The village of Kharkivtsi then numbered 780 individual farmers. Out of this number, only four followed his lead and joined the commune. It was easy for them to do so because they had never had places of their own, or else had sold their houses shortly before the instructions were received.

But this venture was stillborn. Even these four, having tasted commune life for one season, turned against it and began to think of leaving it.

The authorities, aware of the fact that people were reluctant to join a commune, changed their tune and began to encourage the idea of a collective farm. With this object in view, there appeared Demen Karasyuk from the city of Tambov. He spoke a Russian–Ukrainian jargon, while his family spoke only Russian. Karasyuk appropriated the house of *seredniak* [middle peasant] Brychko and sent him to Siberia, where the poor fellow was worked to death six months later. Thus began collectivization and the liquidation of *kurkuls [kulaks]* as a class.

Rallies were held in the center of the village each day, at which Communists from the county seat agitated for collectives. But people did not want to join them and said so, arguing that the government had divided the land against them. And every day GPU agents arrested two or three men.

The village soviet, seeing that people did not want to attend these rallies, hired a boy of 12 to go around with a list and ask people to sign promises that they would attend the gathering. The measure was not successful because men would hide, and their wives would sign their own names arguing that the law gave both sexes equal rights. They also caused a lot of confusion at the rallies by making a terrible noise. The GPU stopped this by sentencing Maria Treba to one year in jail.

The Communists changed their tactics. The farmers were called out individually. Under threat of reprisals they were asked to sign papers agreeing to have their property nationalized.

The farmers began to sell their livestock and horses. Their unwillingness to join the collective was stimulated by the fact that people from the neighboring counties of Komyshany and Myrhorod, from villages already collectivized a year ago, came to the village begging for bread. This was an indication as to what they could expect from a collective farm and "Communist Socialism."

The taxes had to be paid in kind and those who paid them received additional demands, sometimes even greater than the first time, to pay with their products, especially grain.

Seeing no end to this the people began to hide their grain and potatoes if they had any left. A new arrival from the Hadyach Center, comrade Shukhman, who was commissioned to collect grain in three or four counties, gave orders to form *buksyr* [tow] brigades who had authority to manhandle every farmer until he gave all his grain to the state. These brigades were supplied with special tools made in advance in some factory to facilitate the "grain hunt." These were steel rods about ⅝ inch in diameter, three to ten feet long, with one end sharpened to a point and the other equipped with an oval-shaped handle. Some had a kind of drill on the end instead of a point. The *buksyrs* would attack piles of straw, first of all sticking their rods into it to see if sacks of grain were hidden in it. The other tool was used to drill in the gardens and other likely places. The grain when found was, of course, confiscated and the owner was forbidden to remain in Ukraine and was sent to Russia [Solovky, Siberia, etc.]. The collective farmers did not hide the grain they received for their labor days [*trudodni*] because there was very little of it.

In October 1932, comrades Shukhman and Kolotov organized a "Red Column." Commandeering about 60 farm wagons, they filled them with toughs and sent them to the villages. Coming to a village, the toughs would scatter, go to the houses of the collective farmers and ask how much grain each had, pretending this was only for registration purposes. When the information was in hand, teams would come up to each house and the grain would be taken away. When all the farmers had been robbed of their grain, the wagons would be decorated with banners and slogans which proclaimed that the farmers had voluntarily, and in an organized manner, given their grain to the state.

This Red Column passed through villages to be observed, but it was always under GPU protection. When guards were absent, the columns would run into the woods or be robbed by former prisoners who escaped. Such columns took their toll from all the neighboring villages.

It should be observed here that the Communists robbed people not only of grain but also of potatoes and any other thing that could be eaten. In some cases, farmers were ordered to thresh the straw when the records showed a yield to have been poor. Combating the Communist menace, farmers would leave some grain in the straw by breaking the teeth in the cylinder of the threshing machine. Sometimes they succeeded in concealing up to 30 percent of grain which remained unthreshed in the straw. They hoped to thresh out this grain later, and thus save themselves and their families. But cases where farmers, in desperation, burned the straw together with their sheds were common.

Searches and arrests led people to despair. The indignation reached its culminating point on November 21, 1932, when great unrest in the village made the village soviet and all the *buksyrs* flee to the country seat for protection. The collective flew to pieces in half an hour. It was exclusively the work of women. They took their horses and cattle home, and the next day went to the approximate location of their former fields because all the field boundaries were destroyed.

The Communists were prompt in checking the incipient rebellion. They arrived in force in GPU cars the next night, arrested five persons and ordered that all collective farm property be returned. This order was carried out.

A stranger was now the chairman of the village soviet. Nobody knew where he came from, though he had a Ukrainian name, Boyko. He began to continue the work of his worthy predecessor, paying special attention to the Ukrainian movement for independence. "This is the work of our arch-enemy, Petlyura," he said. Then he tried to find out who had served in Petlyura's army.

Alarmed by the prospect of inevitable doom which was approaching, the people carried off one night all the grain from the collective farm stores, covering their tracks with pepper to protect themselves from detection by GPU hunting dogs. Some went to the forest to gather acorns, but this practice was soon stopped by Boyko, who declared the woods to be state property. It was forbidden to go there.

It was impossible to grind grain in the mill because the government grain quotas were not fulfilled. The farmers constructed hand mills and stampers. Boyko issued an order for the immediate arrest of the man who had built these machines, O. Khrynenko, but he was warned in time and ran away to the Donbas [industrial region of the Donets River Basin]. His wife was thrown out of the house, and it was locked by the GPU. Then she was tortured to reveal the whereabouts of her husband and where he had hidden some gold coins. She gave them 230 rubles in gold but did not know where her husband was and died in their hands.

The former chairman of the village soviet, Myshchachenko, sold his house to buy liquor. Then he took a house from Petro Yarosh and, with the assistance of Boyko, managed to have the Yarosh family exiled to the region of Sverdlovsk where all eight family members died from hard labor and ill treatment. Another case was that of F. Shobar, who did the same thing with the brothers Mykola and Stepan Nedvyha. One of them escaped and the other perished in Siberia, together with his family of ten.

A week or so later, the GPU arrested the following families: Borobavko—5 persons, V. Brychko—7 persons, Ostap Ilchenko—5 persons, Nykyfor and Zakhar Koronivsky—3 persons, O. Perepadya—4 persons, K. Riznyk—7 persons, Shyka—4 persons, Taras Elesey—6 persons, Vasyukno—4 persons, and others. All of them received life terms with hard labor and were sent 280 miles north of Sverdlovsk. In 1942, 5 of them returned and said that all the others had died from hard labor and scurvy. They were lucky to get forged papers and escaped to Donbas, where they worked in the mines. [During their terms] they had not stayed long in any one place, because as soon as they cleared a patch in the forest and built barracks and other buildings, they were sent to another place in the wilderness 18 to 24 miles away where the same thing was repeated. The direction was always further north. Their address was Sverdlovsk 5, Letter G.

"There are no *kurkuls* now and presumably no Petlyura partisans, and we can build up our collective farm in peace," said Boyko. "But you should keep in mind that there are many *sub-kurkuls* whom we have to watch and, if they are going to harm our Soviet government, we will send them after the others." He again held meetings urging people to join the collective farm. The government took away grain and meat for taxes. There were no cows or sheep in the village.

In the evening of November 2, an unknown group of farmers attacked a *buksyr brigade*. Makar Verba was killed, and three men ran away. The next day the GPU confiscated all the shotguns in the village. The attackers were not caught. Boyko then threatened that the Soviet Red Army would come and wipe out all the farmers.

The people were terrified. It was hard to find a farmer who had not served a jail term. Practically all joined the collective farm now; only 12 swore that they would not do it and did not until 1941. But these were all women and children whose husbands were in exile in Siberia.

After the fall of 1932, it became customary to go around and beg for bread or food from neighbors. These beggars were usually children and old people.

A new *buksyr* brigade appeared in the village, more cruel than the first one.

In the spring of 1933 one-third of the people in the village were starving. The others had a little food and ate once a day to keep from swelling. To save themselves and their families from starvation, men began to offer their properties for sale or in exchange for food. Some went to Kharkiv, Kiev, or Poltava [major cities of Ukraine] to buy a little food and came back disappointed. Those cities were no better than Hadyach. Then they went to Moscow, Stalingrad, Voronezh, and Orel [cities in Russia] where food could be obtained. But the GPU soon found this out and the people were searched on the trains, food confiscated, and they themselves were charged with speculation. Then an order was issued that no farmer would be allowed to travel by train without a permit from the county soviet executive.

In March 1933 all the people from the collective farm went to the authorities, asking for bread. They were not even allowed to enter the courtyard.

On March 28, 1933, we were shocked by the news that Myron Yemets and his wife, Maria, had become cannibals. Having cut off their children's heads, they salted them away for meat. The neighbors smelled meat frying in the smoke coming from their chimney and, noticing the absence of children, went into the house. When they asked about the children, the parents began to weep and told the whole story. The perpetrators of this act said that they would have children again. Otherwise, they would die in great pain and that would be the end of the family.

Chairman Boyko arrested them himself, and about six hours later the GPU began to question them. "Who has so cunningly persuaded you to do this, *kurkuls, near-kurkuls,* or Petlyura henchmen? You know that this is the work of our enemies to cast dishonor upon our country, the Soviet Union, the most advanced country in the world. You have to tell us who did it!" Hoping to save themselves in this way, the accused pointed to Pavlo Lytvynenko, who was supposed to have said: "If you have nothing to eat, butcher the children and eat them!" Lytvynenko was arrested and shot as an example to the others. Myron and Maria were sentenced to ten years in prison. However, they were shot about three months later because even the Soviet government was ashamed to let them live.

At the end of March or the beginning of April, a big department store was opened in Hadyach on Poltavska Street, by the park, across the street from Lenin's monument. It was called *Torgsin.* Stocked very well, even with goods from abroad, it had one fault, that of selling [goods] only for platinum, gold, silver, or precious stones. The prices were: For 10 gold rubles one could buy there 17 pounds of bread, 22 pounds of buckwheat cereal, 6⅔ pounds of millet, and 10 herrings.

As soon as people learned about this, all who had any gold or silver flocked to the city. There was a line eight abreast and ⅓ mile long in front of the store. There were always 50–70 people who could not get in before the store closed for the day. They spent their nights on the sidewalk disregarding cold, storm, or rain. Thefts were very common, but most died from hunger or stomach cramps after eating too much and too greedily the food they bought. The corpses were removed every morning by a GPU truck.

I also stood in line with my mother. There I saw with my own eyes ten dead bodies thrown on the truck like so many logs and, in addition, three men that were still alive. The dead were hauled to Hlyboky Yar [Deep Ravine] and dumped there.

None of the clerks in this store were Ukrainians and the store belonged to the state.

A month later, in April, this store was broken into and robbed. Half an hour before the opening an alarm was sounded that the store had been robbed at daybreak. The militia with dogs began to search the people waiting in line. All who were a little stronger, had little or no swelling and, perhaps, some gold, were arrested and taken to the building of the country executive committee which was quite close and had a large basement. The prisoners were searched and the gold coins or any other valuables they might have had were confiscated. Other GPU agents without dogs did the same.

One woman, Maria Bovt, had a gold "ship" which had been awarded her husband during the Russo-Japanese War for his bravery in saving a Russian ship. She was also arrested during this investigation and was sent to work at construction projects in Komsomolsk on the Amur River near the Pacific Ocean. All trace of her vanished. The ship must have been taken to swell the Russian treasury or went into the pocket of some GPU agent. Two weeks later, it was discovered that the real culprits had been the clerks in collusion with the militia. They were not punished because they had false documents prepared in advance, and they escaped arrest. This explanation was given out by comrades Shukhman and Kolotov.

The department store had its good and bad sides. The Russians robbed the people of practically all the gold they had. On the other hand, it saved many people's lives because 6 to 11 pounds of grain often saved one from starving to death. Those who had no gold for food died like flies or went to the cemeteries in search of corpses.

The most critical point was reached just before harvest. More and more people starved to death each day. Everything was eaten that could be swallowed: dogs, cats, frogs, mice, birds, grass, but mostly thistles, which were delicious if the plants were about 15 inches high and cleaned of spines. Many people went to graze and often died in the "grazing fields."

When rye ears began to fill out and were at least half full, the danger of death from starvation receded. The people cut ears of grain in the fields, dried them and, rubbing them down, they ate the precious green grains.

The Communists now began to combat "the grain barber menace," that is, people who cut off ears of grain with scissors. Mounted guards on watchtowers protected the grain from the "barbers." One of these watchmen, Fanasiy Hursky, killed a fellow who dared to "steal government property." But sometimes the "barbers" struck back. Some of them sawed through the props under the tower of Ivan Palchenkov when he was asleep. When the wind blew, the tower toppled down, and Ivan was killed.

In the spring of 1933, 138 people died in the village of Kharkivtsi. In comparison with some places this was very good. A great many people died from diseases caused by hunger, especially dysentery. There was only one child born at that time in the whole administrative unit to which Kharkivtsi belonged.

The 1940–1941 school year saw no beginners at all, while previously there had been about 25 each year. The new school principal, a Communist, saw the implication, and to save face made a first grade out of children a year younger if they were a little better developed than others. The same thing happened in neighboring villages.

The orphans who survived the Famine were taken to a children's home in the village. They were well cared for and most of them grew up properly and reached maturity in the years 1939–1941. The boys raised in these homes when inducted into the army in 1941 were the first to desert with arms and go back to avenge themselves on the Communists in their home villages, who deserved punishment.

Account 2

Case History SW34 (U.S. Commission on the Ukraine Famine, 1988, pp. 385–393). The interview was conducted as an oral life history in 1987 by Sue Ellen Webber and translated by Darian Diachok under the auspices of the U.S. Commission on the Ukraine Famine.

Q: Please state your year of birth.
A: 1922.

Q: Where were you born?
A: In Stavyshche, in Kiev Province.

Q: In which district?
A: The Stavyshche District.

Q: Where did you live during the 1920s and the 1930s?
A: In Stavyshche.

Q: What was your parents' profession?
A: My father worked in a bank, and my mother worked as a saleslady in a store.

Q: I see. So they weren't peasants, is that correct?
A: No, they weren't.

Q: And you had said you were born in....
A: 1922.

Q: Do you remember anything from the NEP period?
A: Well, I might have been, oh, about seven or eight years old at the time. People lived well then. But this was only for a few years. Then people were milked dry. Every single drop was wrung out of them.

Q: What can you recall about collectivization?
A: I only remember that they took away horses, farming implements, tools. Everything was taken from people against their will. And then they shoved you into a collective farm.

Q: And what social category were you given, given the fact that your family wasn't a peasant family, how were you designated?

A: Well, I come from the peasant class, but I'm not a peasant. It was a painful experience looking at all that was going on, seeing how the people were being uprooted and scattered about, how the dying were being brought in. At the time I lived close to the hospital. People were being driven in from villages near and far, as well as from Stavyshche, my native village. People were even bringing in their own children, who were already swollen. They would come to spend the night. And they would spend the night, and then they would be....

Close by, there was a park belonging to the hospital. It was quite a large park. There were yellow acacias planted in the center of the park and fenced off. Well, this is right where the cemetery was. Enormous open pits were dug and the doctors carried on stretchers the bodies of those who had died and tossed them into the pits. The process would be repeated each day until the open pit was filled and covered over with dirt shoveled over it. I know the earth over the pits has settled quite a bit since that time. But today you can still locate the exact burial spot, right by the cemetery. This was the hospital morgue where they took patients who had died. Later, they didn't bother with the morgue anymore, but took the corpses straight to the open pits on stretchers. Often nurses carried as many as ten children on stretchers and tossed them into the pit.

Q: When did people begin to die?

A: The precise time? When spring came. People were wandering about the gardens and hoping to come upon something left behind in the gardens; they would dig and dig, and examine every clump of earth. If they came upon a smelly old potato, they would clean it and take the starchy residue. They would also dry and grind acacia blossoms. Linden leaves would also be dried and made into ersatz pancakes. People dug up all sorts of roots. It was terrible, absolutely terrible. People scattered all over; they wandered here and there. Sometimes, they'd spot some small creature in the water, like a turtle and eat it as food. It was terrible. People were reduced to this state. I was right there. Some of the starving were in such a bad way that they had begun to stink already. Their feet would swell up; their wounds would open and fester. It was terrible. You would see them walking about, just walking and walking, and one would drop, and then another, and so on it went.

Q: How many were there in your family?

A: Well, there were four children, my mother, father, and grandmother, who was already quite old.

Q: And how did you survive?

A: How I survived? I'll tell you. We always had a supply of pickled cabbage, which we would prepare for the winter, as well as a supply of onions and potatoes. And that's all we had. This was the common practice. In villages, there were various ways to prepare provisions. Some people had had all their provisions, all their potato crop, seized, and they themselves had been thrown out of their houses. That's all that I remember, because I was still small then. It all began in 1929, and at that time I was only seven years old. And I can recall how they would deport people, people who never returned. And where they exiled these people, I can't say. Everything that they had was destroyed.

Q: Was there a church in your village?

A: We had three churches, in fact. One of them was called the Rozkishna Church. It belonged to a rather large town of over 10,000 inhabitants. The town was located on the other side of a dam and could be reached by taking the bridge. But for some reason Rozkishna Church was on our side. I recall going past it in 1931 when the cross was being taken down. But I was not an actual witness to the dismantling of the bells. Apparently, they needed the metal to make weapons. During the dismantling, a band of the women assembled at the church to protest what was going on. The militia was called; the women were roughed up, hit over the head. The next day, activists arrived at night and quietly cut down the bells.

The church was converted into a grain storage building. They would bring grain from Zhazhkiv, 18 miles away from our village, which was once part of Kiev Region, but which is now part of Cherkasy Region. And that's one of the places from where they were trucking the grain out. They had an enormous grain elevator there, and day and night they transported the grain from there, grain collected from the collective farms. Day and night!

This was all done at the MTS, the Machine-Tractor Station. And everywhere there were placards with the inscriptions, "MORE GRAIN!," and other similar exhortations. More grain for the government. They literally pumped the grain out of the countryside, and all for the use of the government. In the spring the Party sent in Komsomol members, who walked about the villages with pikes to which small scoops were attached. The Komsomol members searched literally everywhere to find hidden grain. They looked especially in places like hay piles in barns. They dug everywhere. And if they happened to find some grain that someone had hidden away, well, that was pretty much the end of him. He would never see the light of day again. That's how it was.

Q: And who exactly were these Komsomol members? Whose children were they?

A: The Komsomol members? Well, there were some Ukrainians among them, that's true. But the vast majority were sent from Moscow. At one point, the so-called 10,000-ers had been sent; there were supposed to have been 10,000 of them sent. Later, the government realized that this number was not enough, so it brought in the so-called 25,000-ers. And it was these groups that confiscated the grain all over the countryside. And if you happened to be a member of the Komsomol, you were forced to do these things, too. But the possibility was always open to you, that if you did find hidden grain, you could fail to report it, or you pretended you hadn't seen anything.

Q: Did the Committees of Non-Wealthy Peasants exist at this time?

A: Non-Wealthy Peasants? Yes, there were such committees; in fact, pretty much all over the countryside but they were quickly suppressed. Even though I was quite young, I remember that during the SVU [in 1930], they were branded as "enemies of the people." I myself was also considered "an enemy of the people." They took away my father in 1937.

Q: Why was he taken away?

A: Why? Well, he had been branded an "enemy of the people," and they took him away in 1937. And they also took away one of my father's brothers, and another brother, as well. And to this day, we don't know what happened to them. And when my mother went to inquire as to my father's whereabouts at the militia, they told her that he had been sentenced to ten years without the right of correspondence. It was common knowledge that this meant he had been shot. Most likely, his body is somewhere in Vinnytsia. So, the four of us were left. Yurii was the youngest, just six months old at the time. And that was how my mother was left to fend for herself. Many of the other women were sent off to Kazakhstan. It was common practice for wives of the men that had been sentenced to be sent for five years to Kazakhstan to pick cotton, or to perform similar tasks. Five years! My own Godmother was sent there and actually returned. But this was during the war. After the war, my mother came here for a visit, and told us that it became standard practice to tell the wives whose husbands had been sentenced without the right of correspondence: "Your husband was killed in 1945." This was the standard line they gave everyone during the Khrushchev era.

Q: Do you recall how many people died of hunger during the Famine? What was the percentage?

A: In our village, you mean?

Q: Yes. Would you say it was about a half of the villagers?

A: Well, there was a village not far away from us called Krasenivka, which had a population of about 10,000. It was a rather large village. They had to put up a black flag at one end of the village, and another one at the other end which indicated that absolutely no one had survived, not even a dog, or cat. The houses were all overgrown with goosefoot and other weeds. And our village? Well, what can I tell you? About ten percent of our village died of hunger. It was terrifying. Utterly terrifying.

Q: Were you yourself repressed during collectivization?

A: Well, in the beginning, you know, we had our own house, which later became my uncle's house. They evicted us and told us that they needed our house as part of the new collective farm, and they made an office out of my uncle's house. And they also confiscated 90 percent of everything we had. They took the land together with the house and all our belongings. We had had this garden there—and we lost all of this.

Q: And they didn't tell you anything?

A: At that point, they took whatever they wanted to, since technically these things were no longer ours. They would walk all over our fields, probing the latter with the sharp pikes. The pike was jammed into the ground and pulled up. If any grains of wheat were picked up, the conclusion was that grain was being hidden from the state. The men with the pikes were everywhere.

Q: Were you going to school at the time? And if so, was it a Ukrainian school?

A: Yes, it was. In our school, whenever any of the children mentioned the Famine, they were corrected by the teachers. They were told that there was no Famine, simply a year of difficulties. They confiscated all that we had and designated the year as one of difficulties!

Not far from us was a cemetery. There were many beautifully made crosses and memorials there. This was during the Famine. Every night there were two or three graves dug up. Wealthy people had been buried there, and, naturally, there were valuables in the caskets—a ring perhaps, a watch, or earring. The robbers were caught: a man by the name of Abramovich and his son. The father had forced the son into it. Well, they had been trying to break into a tomb—the rich people had all been buried in tombs. The valuables buried with them were just waiting to be taken. Nothing was done to prevent theft. The entire site was ruined and everything of value was taken.

Well, when someone like a priest was buried, a gold cross was often placed in his casket. During the Famine hundreds of graves were unearthed....

During the Famine they used to give us tea and a small piece of bread at school. The tea was made in the following fashion. It was simply over-cooked sugar and some coloring. And that was our tea. A lot of children did not go to school; they were no longer able to, because they had already reached the stage where their bodies had swelled. A large number of children died.

A few of the villagers had planted potatoes in the spring, but they had to do the plowing with shovels, because by this time, all the horses had died and no implements were left. They dug the earth with shovels and planted the potatoes. But the problem was that anyone could easily figure out where it was that you planted the potatoes, and the next day, usually at night, someone would come and dig up what you had planted. The field would again be barren. That's what went on. So, as a result, people would try to cover their tracks by raking over the newly sowed ground. We used to plant small potato cuttings which were little more than peels. Well, we planted these in our garden, and the potatoes grew beautifully. Something so simple, it could only have come from God. It was just a potato peel with some eyes on it. We planted the peels and got perfectly good potatoes that way. That's how we did it.

The greatest number of deaths from starvation actually occurred when the wheat-ears had matured. People began to steal the wheat-ears. They were starving, you understand, and all at once the wheat-ears were available. And when the people began eating great quantities of wheatears, they died even more rapidly, because their intestines would rupture. That's when the greatest number of corpses began appearing.

Q: And what did they do with the corpses?
A: What indeed! Well, they went looking for them; they collected the corpses and dumped them into pits. And if the authorities happened to come across someone who was somehow managing to stay relatively healthy, well, they gave him the job of watching over the pit that they had dug out to make sure that it wasn't used by anyone else.

Q: Are you aware of any cases of cannibalism?
A: I heard of instances, but had never witnessed anything personally. But everyone talked about it. We had our own newspaper, *The Red Collectivist*. The newspaper mentioned that someone had been apprehended in connection with the discovery of barrels of salted meat. I can't recall the entire episode. Rumors were circulating involving the activists. There were Ukrainians among them, and there may have been others as well. They

were the real activists, you know. They were involved in dekulakization, and they used to go drinking in the gardens. In fact, they didn't do much of anything else, except when it came time to dekulakize someone, they'd come and confiscate everything, throwing the children out, like unwanted puppies, into the courtyard. And this was in the dead of winter. The head of the household would go to the village soviet and request help for his seven children, and the activists would tell him something like, "Get out of here, and take those little mongrels with you!" That's how it was. And no one would help these people out. And so they would just die....

Q: Who was the head of the village soviet at the time?
A: The head of the village soviet? A man by the name of Makharynsky. I've forgotten his first name. And later they took him away as well. I don't know what the cause of that was.

Q: And what sort of man was he? Can you describe him?
A: What kind of man? Well, he did whatever they ordered him to do.

Q: I see, a bureaucrat.
A: Whatever the bureaucracy told him to do, he'd do. You know, he himself didn't actually participate in the dirty work of dekulakization; and whenever they told him to pump the grain out of a particular village, he would send in the activists, the so-called 10,000-ers, and later the 25,000-ers sent by Moscow. And these were all foreigners, outsiders.

The Famine existed only in Ukraine. There were a lot of people, a lot of people who wanted to go to Russia. People figured they could go there with the shirt on their backs and sell it for bread. On their way back everything they were carrying would be confiscated. And they would be arrested and sentenced. I myself know of several people who went there. You see, Russia was some distance away from us. The people who lived closer did try to go, but the ones who made it never returned with anything. Everything they managed to get was confiscated. By this time, the passport system had already been introduced. According to this system, you would be arrested and in great difficulties if you happened to be somewhere for nine days without reporting. So, whatever you did, you would invariably find yourself in hot water.

Q: Did you leave the village during the Famine?
A: My father was still around. I remember once we bought some coffee. The so-called coffee had actually been made out of barley. It was just overroasted barley. Well, since there was nothing to eat, we were told to mix some of this and some of that into this coffee. This mixture was awfully bitter! Yecch!

Q: Do you remember how the Famine came to an end?

A: How the Famine ended? Well, they began to provide a little something for the people; people began to go to the collective farms for soup. But as far as to how the Famine actually ended? Well, it happened gradually, in stages. How can I explain? Well, the thing is that it never really completely ended. That's the way it is over there. People were no longer dying en masse, but in a sense the Famine still continued. In fact, it recurred in 1947. Once again there was a great Famine in Ukraine. My mother recounted how there was a great migration to the cities. Life was a bit better in the cities. But even in the cities, people were dying of hunger....

Q: What sort of people joined the Party in your village?

A: There were very few Party members in our village.

Q: Well, what sort of people were the Party members?

A: What sort? There was a man by the name of Pokotylo who shot himself during the Famine. I believe he was in the District Party Committee, but I don't know what his rank was. I just know that he was a Communist and that he shot himself. There was another by the name of Nahornyi who also shot himself. This all happened during the Famine. These Communists committed suicide during the Famine, as did Mykola Khvyliovy, the writer, and Skrypnyk. Others committed suicide, too, because they saw what was actually going on. At one time they had embraced Lenin's slogans that Ukraine would be allowed to separate from the Soviet Union if it chose to. They believed the slogans, or at least I suppose they did. But later, when they understood the truth, they shot themselves. They had to. And that's how it was with our Party members.

And then came the Party purges. They were directed from Moscow. Party purges. And these were public spectacles. There was a building in our village that served as a club. And this is where the proclamations were made. When the Party purge began, they zeroed in on this fellow named Hrynchenko. They started in on him, tagging him with all sorts of accusations—that he had pumped out insufficient quantities of grain, that there was too little of this and too little of that. Although there was already nothing at all left to pump out, and they were still accusing him of falling short. "Too little!" they shouted at him.

By 1934 they were already giving out 250 grams for one labor day. This is about half a pound of bread a day. But you really had to work to earn this ration. This was a very difficult life, but people began to manage. They planted potatoes and different varieties of pumpkins, beets, and other staples. But during the Famine, a group of Soviet ruffians would come through the villages and would even pull out whatever people happened to be baking in the oven. In the markets, they would even confiscate and destroy such items as beans in jars. It was terrible. Well, this is what I myself know and saw.

Q: How did people rebuild their lives after the Famine?
A: Slowly. Before collectivization, there were still large barns around the countryside, but all these were burned as firewood. Whoever had fences for keeping in domestic livestock, these were burned also because people didn't have anything to keep themselves warm. The only housing that was left were so-called "houses on chicken legs." Reconstruction was simply awful. It was repulsive just to look at these buildings. It's probably the same way today. They say that there have been some changes, some minor changes made, that some sidewalks have been added, that electrical lines have been added, and that sort of thing....

Q: Did people ever talk about the Famine after it was over?
A: They talked about it constantly. If I knew you well, then I would feel free to talk about it; but if I didn't know you well, I wouldn't feel comfortable talking. I would be afraid of your denouncing me to the NKVD. There were so-called Judases who were capable of turning you in. Whatever you would say, they would immediately report it, and you would be in for some real trouble.

Q: You were only 11 years old during the Famine?
A: Yes.

Q: But did you hear the adults talking about the political affairs of the day? Did you know at the time who Skrypnyk was? Kaganovich? What was being said about these political figures?
A: We all knew! Kaganovich, Molotov. Except that at that time no one could speak openly about these matters. We couldn't speak openly. Let me tell you about this little song that we had from that period. I can still remember this song from my school days.

During the Famine, they sent this fellow, Postyshev, as secretary to Ukraine. And then there was this other fellow, Kossior, who was Polish. He was in the Politburo. So you can see for yourself what lovely songs we had to sing as we starved.

Hey, our harvest knows no limits or measures.
It grows, ripens, and even spills over onto the earth,
Boundless over the fields; while the patrolling pioneers
Come out to guard the ripening wheat-ears of grain.

And now here's the refrain:

> We've hardened our song in the kiln's fires
> And carry it aloft like a banner, offering it to you;
> And in this way, Comrade Postyshev, we are submitting
> Our report of the work we've done.

I remember the song as if it were yesterday. We had a very beautiful park in our village, with a stream flowing by. A gorgeous park. And in all the parks, there were loudspeakers placed, as part of this radio network, which was itself linked to the post office. And in these parks, you could always hear songs in Russian being sung, one song in particular:

> Swiftly as birds, one after another,
> Fly over our Soviet homeland
> The joyous refrains of town and country:
> Our burdens have lightened, our lives have gladdened.

They broadcast this song while people were dying in the Famine. "Our lives have gladdened." I can recall this song from my school years, when they were teaching the children to sing *The Patrolling Pioneer*. What kind of a country is this in which they keep bread from the people for the sake of a "better life"? They themselves sang, "The joyous refrains of town and country." And this song would play every day, ten times a day, and as you listened to the song, everywhere all around you people are screaming, and starving to death, while the song played on: "Our burdens have lightened."

Q: And what were you thinking?
A: What could I think?! All I could think of was where could I get some food. I didn't think anything. They let the Ukrainians have it because they had wanted to separate from Russia. That's what I think. The Ukrainian nation is still paying for that even up to this very day.

Q: Would you like to add anything to what you've said?
A: What is there that I could add? As long as you have Communism there, you will have this endless agony there. They can always institute another policy similar to NEP; they can always try something like that again. From what I hear, they want to give the people a greater share, a greater share of land as well—the primary reason being that the private plots of land yield more crops per acre than the collective farms. But people aren't going to fall for this. First of all, they don't have the implements with which to farm private land; and, secondly,

let's say, if a man does work his field, and he seeds it and plants something—potatoes, for example—then they'll tell him to pay his taxes.
And regardless whether or not something grows or doesn't grow in
your garden, you have to come up with the payment. People don't
want this system and aren't going to be taken in by it. And as long as
this system continues to exist over there, then that's how it will be over
there.

Q: Thank you very much indeed for this most interesting testimony.
A: I was quite young, but I saw a great deal. In fact, I can recall the
events of those times better than I can recall what I did yesterday.

Q: Oh, yes.
A: It was all so horrible.

Account 3

Vasyl' Pakharenko, "Holodnyi 33-yi," *Molod'* Cherkashchyny, July
18–24, 1988; translated by Vera Kaczmarskyj, *Soviet Ukrainian Affairs*,
fall 1988, pp. 14–15. The author is a schoolteacher in the city of Cher-
kassy, a regional capital in Ukraine.

Recently I was leafing through a thick notebook filled with eyewitness
accounts. I had jotted them down at various times and different villages.
They are simple narratives (I tried to record them verbatim). A surreal-
istic tragedy unfolds behind these words.

Here is Iaryna Larionivna Tiutiunyk's account of the death of her
neighbor's 6-year-old son, Myt'io [Iaryna was born in 1905 in the village
of Subotiv in the Chyhyrin region]: "He was on his way to the kindergarten one morning, where the collective farm was distributing a serving
of millet meal the size of a matchbox. And he dropped by, begging—
Auntie, give me a piece of bread. I am so hungry. I didn't give him any
because I was mad at him for eating the greens I had planted in the
garden. To the day I die I will not forgive myself for begrudging the
child a piece of bread. In the evening, on our way home from work, we
found him sitting right in the middle of the footpath—dead. He was
probably returning from the kindergarten, had got tired, sat down, and
died."

Antonina Oleksandrivna Polishchuk [born in 1925]. She lived in the
village of Buzhanka in the Lysians'kyi raion: "In 1933, our mother pretended to sew some dolls for children, filling them with grain, so that
they would not take away all the grain from us. But they found the grain

even there and seized it. They took our ox away … and killed it, taking the meat for themselves…

> Our father died from hunger, as did my 14-year-old brother, Vasia, and my twin sisters, Katia and Dunia [born in 1927]. We ate only weeds and drank water. The corpses were carted out to the cemeteries on big carts. They pushed 300 bodies into one hole…

Tetiana Iakivna Vdovychenko [born in 1911] lived in the same village: "It happened that they took people who were still alive and would throw them into the common graves. This happened with Khotyna Revenko. When they came to her house, she was still alive. They started dragging her to the cart by her feet. 'Where are you pulling me to? Give me a beet. I am hungry, I still want to live.' She was young, not yet 30.

> 'You think we are going to come back for you tomorrow?' growled the men in response, pulling her onto the cart by her feet. They brought her to the gravesite and threw her inside. She did not fall on her back, but propped up in a sitting position, her back against the side. They poked at her head and she finally fell back.
>   Motria Vdovychenko was also taken to the gravesite and buried alive with her two children [who were also still living]. Such incidents were frequent."

Denys Mykytovych Lebid' [born in 1914] from Iablunivka in Lysians'kyi raion: "I was transported to the gravesite and thrown into the common grave, but they did not cover it up that day. My friend Iaremii Stavenko was passing by and pulled me out."

Stepanida Hryhorivna [born in 1905] from the village of Zhab'ianka in the region by the same name: "In 1933, my neighbor lured my daughter to her house, killed her with a knife and ate her. My daughter was all of 6 years old at the time. When the beast was seized and taken to the *raion* [to be imprisoned], she kept taking out slices of meat and eating them, saying 'Umm, how tasty. Had I known, I would have killed her earlier.' The police could not tolerate this any longer and shot her right there on the road.…"

Account 4

Oleksandr Mishchenko, *Bezkrovna viina* (Kiev, 1991), pp. 48–49. The author, a member of the Union of Writers of Ukraine, collected 42 accounts in the Poltava region in 1990. The following account is that of Petro Ivanovych Bilous, born 1909 in the village of Andriiky, which was formed from four farmsteads (*khutirs*), including the Andreiko farmstead, in Poltava region.

In 1932–1933 the people were terrified. They no longer slept nights but sat in their houses and waited for the brigades to come for bread. In order to survive, some tried to hide some produce somewhere. For example, at Laryvon Andreiko's house the brigade leader found some buried potatoes and beneath them a few poods of wheat. Then they crawled in the attic where there were flowerpots, cast-iron pots, and jars. And in every jar and pot there were beans, dried apples, ground millet, or crab-apples, all covered with charcoal to hide it. They found it all the same. They took it down from the attic and poured it all in one sack. They found a little cask of cheese. They ate his sauerkraut and I ate some, too, because I was hungry. Old man Laryvon was left with nothing. He survived somehow, but his wife died.

In our family, both mother and father perished. Mother died when the rye was already being harvested. She went to look at how they were pouring it. Even though the rye was ripe, they wouldn't allow anyone to cut an ear. Even in their own garden. My brother was already married then. He went to live with his wife's family at Marfyna Andreiko's house. They had a cow, and he survived there. Another brother went around to the small farming communities (*khutirs*) and begged. And I was already near death, so swollen that I couldn't get out of bed, but someone remembered about my army requalification. And I was taken to the hospital. I stayed there a month and got better. I returned home. The house stood empty. All there was were the four walls. I didn't think about that then. All I thought about was going somewhere in order to earn a piece of bread and not die. But in the village there was no place to go. The dead lay in the shadows, in kitchen gardens under a tree; the people wandered sluggishly, apathetically, dazed, and no one even buried the dead.

Over there across the gully lived Kateryna Andreiko. She lost four daughters, and she also gave up her spirit to God, but her two sons, luckily, survived. One was already married, and his younger brother stayed with him. Andrii Vasyl'ovych Andreiko lost two boys and five daughters. The daughters were little, school-age. Andrii Vasyl'ovych from time to time served as chairman of the collective farm, and then they dismissed him, and then he died. His wife, too. Not only did our own people die but even outsiders who had been sent in. There was starvation in every house. At my wife's, thanks to the fact that her father had a cow, nobody died. But everybody was swollen: her mother, father, and brother. She was given a little bread in the collective farm—she didn't eat it herself but brought it home. And that's how she saved her immediate family. At Odarka Andreiko's house, not far from here, the father died, two brothers, and the sisters Mariika, Nastia, and Mylia. Odarka was already married then. She buried them in a pit. She worked on the burial detachment. Nobody made her. She came home and buried them herself. She buried Mariika, she buried Nastia, she buried her father. Before he died, her father asked for a piece of bread: "Give me some, my child, if only some crumbs, because I'm dying." She didn't have any to give him. There just wasn't any bread at all.

References

Borys, Jurij (1980). *The Sovietization of Ukraine 1917–1923: The Communist doctrine and practice of national self-determination*. Edmonton: Canadian Institute of Ukrainian Studies.

Conquest, Robert (1986). *The harvest of sorrow: Soviet collectivization and the terror-famine*. New York and Oxford: Oxford University Press.

Ellman, Michael (1991). A note on the number of 1933 famine victims. *Soviet Studies, XLIII*(2), 375–379.

Gannt, William Horsley (1937). *Russian medicine*. New York: Harper & Brothers.

Hermaize, Osyp (1926). *Narysy z istoriï revoliutsiinoho rukhu na Ukraïni (Sketches from the history of the revolutionary movement in Ukraine)*. Kharkiv: Knyhospilka.

Holod (1990). *1932–1933 rokiv na Ukraïni: Ochyma istorykiv, movoiu dokumentiv (The famine of 1932–1933 in Ukraine: In the eyes of historians and in the language of the documents)*. Kiev: Vydavnytstvo politychnoi literatury.

Hroch, Myroslav (1985). *Social conditions of national revival in Europe: A comparative analysis of the social composition of patriotic groups among the smaller European nations*. Cambridge, London, and New York: Cambridge University Press.

Jasny, Naum (1949). *The socialized agriculture of the USSR: Plans and performance*. Stanford, CA: Stanford University Press.

Khrystiuk, Pavlo (1921–1922). *Zamitky i materiialy do istoriï ukraïns'koï revoliutsiï, 1917–1920 (Notes and materials on the history of the Ukrainian revolution, 1917–1920)*. Four volumes. Prague: Ukraïns'kyi sociologychnyi instytut..

Kuper, Leo (1990). The genocidal state: An overview. In Pierre L. van den Berghe (Ed.) *State violence and ethnicity* (pp. 19–52). Niwot, CO: University of Colorado Press.

Lewin, Moshe (1985). *The making of the Soviet System: Essays in the social history of interwar Russia*. New York: Pantheon.

Liber, George O. (1990). *Soviet nationality policy, urban growth and identity change in the Ukrainian SSR, 1923–1934*. New York: Cambridge University Press.

Lozovy, S. (1953–1955). What happened in Hadyach County. In S. Pidhainy et al. (Eds.) *The black deeds of the Kremlin: A white book*. Toronto: Ukrainian Association of Victims of Russian Communist Terror.

Luxemburg, Rosa (1976). *The national question: Selected writings*. Ann Arbor, MI: Books on Demand.

Mace, James E. (1983). *Communism and the dilemmas of national liberation: National Communism in Soviet Ukraine, 1918–1933*. Cambridge, MA: Harvard University Press.

Mace, James E. (1984). The man-made famine of 1933 in the Soviet Ukraine: What happened and why. In Israel W. Charny (Ed.) *Toward the understanding and prevention of genocide* (pp. 67–83). Boulder, CO: Westview Press.

Mishchenko, Oleksandr (1991). *Bezkrovna viina*. Kiev: Vydanvnytstvo politychnoi literatury.

Postanova TsK VKP(b) ta RNK SRSR pro khlibozahotivli na Ukraïny, Pivnichnomu Kavkazi ta Zakhidnii oblasti (Decision of the All-Union Communist Party Central Committee and

USSR Council of Peoples Commissars on Grain Procurements in Ukraine, the North Caucasus, and Western District) (1991). *Zoloti vorota: Al'manakh, 1*, 78–79.

Savchenko, Fedir (1930). *Zaborone ukraïnstvo 1876 r. (The suppression of Ukrainian activities in 1876)*. Kharkiv and Kiev: Derzhavne vydavnytstvo Ukraïny.

Stalin, I.V. (1946–1951). *Sochineniia (Works)*. 14 volumes. Moscow: Gospolitizdat.

Taylor, S.J. (1990). *Stalin's apologist: Walter Duranty, the* New York Times*'s man in Moscow*. New York: Oxford University Press.

Treadgold, Donald (1964). *Twentieth century Russia* (2nd ed.). Chicago, IL: Rand McNally.

U.S. Commission on the Ukraine Famine (1988). *Report to Congress*. Washington, DC: U.S. Government Printing Office.

Vsesoiuznaia perepis' naseleniia 1937 g.: Kratkie itogi (All-Union Population Census of 1937: Summary). (1991). Moscow: Institut istorii SSSR.

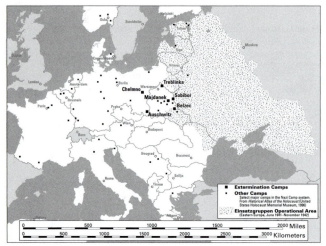

Map 6.1 Germany

Map 6.2 Western and Eastern European sites of Nazi camps

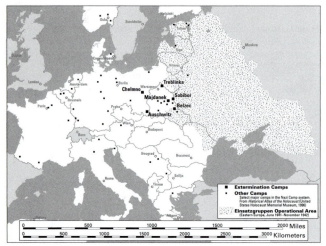

Map 6.3 Greater Germany

CHAPTER **6**

The Holocaust: Jews, Gypsies, and the Handicapped

DONALD L. NIEWYK

During World War II emerging knowledge of the Nazi slaughter of nearly six million Jews gave the world the word "genocide." At the time it seemed that only a new term could do justice to a catastrophe on such a massive scale. During the 1960s it became fashionable to use the term "Holocaust" (i.e. "devastation" or "cataclysm") to describe the Jewish catastrophe. Since then we have become aware that Nazi genocide also claimed the lives of at least 130,000 Gypsies and 275,000 handicapped people. All three groups were destined to disappear, the Jews and Gypsies because they were alien, the handicapped because they were imperfect specimens of a perfectible "master race." Nazi genocide was closely related to broader racial policies that led to the murder of millions of Soviet and Polish prisoners of war and Eastern European civilians. However, only Jews, Gypsies, and handicapped people were slated for total physical annihilation, and all three groups must be taken into account in any discussion of the Holocaust.

The Victims

The Jews, originally a Semitic tribe that settled in what is today Palestine, migrated to Europe in the 2nd and 3rd centuries and during the Middle Ages took up such occupations as the Christian majority left open to them. Making the most of their contacts with the Mediterranean world and their strengths as middlemen, many Jews achieved notoriety as merchants and money lenders. They might be valued for their economic skills, but they were also widely misunderstood as deicides ("Christ-killers") and distrusted as deliberate misbelievers. Hence their existence was often precarious until the Enlightenment introduced a liberal and secular worldview. The emancipation of the Jews in the 19th and early 20th centuries made them fully equal citizens of the countries in which they lived, and particularly in Western Europe many Jews became successful businessmen and professional people. The larger, Yiddish-speaking Jewish communities of rural Eastern Europe, on the other hand, experienced fewer opportunities to assimilate and continued to stand apart from their non-Jewish neighbors. Everywhere this partially or wholly unassimilated minority remained highly visible and controversial for its religious practices, liberal politics, and capitalist ways.

The Gypsies (or Roma and Sinti, to use the names of the principal Central European subgroups, which many Gypsies prefer) originated in northern India and entered Europe during the 15th and 16th centuries. Most moved from place to place in caravans and earned livings as horse dealers, blacksmiths, and fortunetellers, adhering to a rigid Gypsy purity code that required separation from "unclean" non-Gypsies. Their distinctiveness was accented by their dark skin, colorful clothing, exotic language (Romani, which is loosely based on Hindi), and predominantly nomadic ways. That Gypsies sometimes resorted to begging, petty thievery, and sharp practices gave rise to demands in many parts of Europe to combat the "Gypsy menace" with official discrimination and police action.

Severely handicapped people are, of course, to be found among all groups and nations. Debates about them have centered on how best to care for them and at what expense to the community. In modern times the most severely disabled were placed in state and private institutions where they were often considered costly burdens on society. Their vulnerability was heightened early in the 20th century when the vogue for "racial hygiene" introduced the notion that it was possible to improve society by sterilizing or eliminating those thought to be carriers of defective genes. Advocates of eugenics (selective breeding) sometimes added "humanitarian" arguments in favor of ending "lives not worth living."

Why did the Holocaust Happen?

Answering this question requires an imaginative leap into the mind of Adolf Hitler, the absolute master of Germany following the Nazi seizure of power in 1933. Although no one has ever pinned down the sources of Hitler's thinking, there can be no doubt that by the time he became dictator he was passionately committed to ideas about race and struggle that were fashionable in the late 19th and early 20th centuries. A visionary and a utopian, Hitler dreamed of an ethnically pure Germany that would conquer Lebensraum (living space) in Eastern Europe, unite all of continental Europe under German rule, and enslave or eliminate lesser races.

Race touched every fiber of Hitler's being, but the Jews occupied a special place in his roster of enemies. Although the Jews are not, in fact, a "race," the future dictator uncritically adopted pseudo-scientific arguments, popular a century ago, that asserted Jewish racial distinctiveness. Hitler's anti-Semitism dates from his youth in Austria before World War I, where Jew-baiting was advanced by the politicians he admired and the tabloids he read. If the psychohistorians are to be believed, it may also have been more deeply rooted in some early personal trauma (Binion, 1976; Waite, 1977).

Whatever its sources, Hitler's Judeophobia comprised all the well-established and virtually universal stereotypes: Jews were crafty, corrupt, and predatory materialists, devoid of patriotism and feelings for others, and they advocated subversive ideas such as liberalism, capitalism, Marxism, and cultural modernism. Hitler adopted this hackneyed litany in its most extreme social Darwinism form that interpreted history as an inevitable struggle between superior and inferior races. By the time he began his political career in post-war Munich, he was a convinced anti-Semite.

Doubtless, Hitler's anti-Semitism and that of many of his followers was intensified by the Bolshevik revolution in Russia, Germany's defeat in World War I, and the abortive Spartacus Revolt by German Communists in 1919. Then Hitler and his fledgling Nazi Party began associating the Jews with the alleged "stab in the back" of the German army (and hence among those responsible for the loss of the war), the liberal Weimar Republic established in Germany after the defeat, and the Communist menace. Anti-Semitism was always one of his central teachings. Occasionally during his rise to power (1920–1933) Hitler called for the emigration or deportation of the Jews, but more often he blamed problems on a Jewish world conspiracy without specifying a cure beyond inviting Germans to support his movement. Moreover, the Nazi Party tended to use anti-Jewish propaganda opportunistically, playing it up or down depending on the responses it received. Hence no one could know exactly what Hitler and his party planned to do with the Jews, and it cannot be said that the large minority of Germans who came to support him after 1930 deliberately endorsed violent racial anti-Semitism. Preoccupied as they were with economic collapse and political turmoil, Germans rarely noticed that annihilation was implicit in Hitler's ideology and that other groups, including Gypsies and handicapped people, were also potential targets of Nazi racism.

Historical Forces and Trends

A number of historical trends combined to make the Holocaust possible. These included anti-Semitism, racism, Social Darwinism, eugenics, extreme nationalism, totalitarianism, industrialism, the nature of modern war, and the bureaucratic organization of modern society. The absence of any one of these trends might well have made Nazi genocide unlikely.

Anti-Semitism has a long history in most of Europe, not just in Germany. Traditional anti-Semitism arose out of Christian rejection of the Jews as deicides and deliberate misbelievers. Once such prejudice had generated pogroms, but in modern times it inspired contempt for the Jews by providing an explanation for their alleged materialism. Having rejected the saving grace of Jesus, so the argument went, they had lost their ethical compass in the pursuit of physical wealth and secular philosophies. Religiously based Judeophobia partially merged with newer criticisms of the Jews' role in the modern economy. Having been emancipated from special laws and restrictions (extra taxes, limited civil liberties, bans from certain occupations) only in the 19th century, the Jews were still concentrated in a few highly visible economic sectors such as banking, publishing, and the metal and clothing trades. This made them convenient targets for the victims of industrialization, some of whom blamed the Jews for economic depressions, bankruptcies, and unemployment. At the same time the Jews' support for liberal political movements that had advocated Jewish emancipation generated anti-Semitism among conservative foes of individualism and representative government. The prominence of Jewish intellectuals such as Karl Marx and Leon Trotsky in the European socialist movements also sparked criticism of Jews for sacrificing patriotism to internationalism.

Although anti-Semitism was widespread before World War I, it was not a central issue. Most Judeophobes advocated solving the "Jewish Problem" through assimilation or the restoration of special laws restricting the Jews' civil and economic rights, not through violence. Only in backward Russia were there pogroms against the Jews. Racism, which implied that Jews were incapable of changing their ways, and social Darwinism, some forms of which predicted inevitable struggle between nations and races, gained adherents before 1914. But even racial anti-Semitism's most radical exponents, marginal figures without much influence, limited themselves to advocating Jewish emigration and frequently identified themselves as friends of Zionism.

World War I changed that. Anti-Semitism became entwined in the outraged nationalism of defeated Germany and in the quest for national identity by new states like Poland and Hungary and would-be states like the Ukraine and Croatia. Wherever patriotism was inflamed or contested, the Jews, as outsiders, were suspected of disloyalty. Demagogues—such as Adolf Hitler in Germany—associated the Jews with economic hard times and the foreign oppressors. The growth of threatening Communist movements, some of them led by Jews, added grist to the anti-Jewish mill. Hitler successfully claimed the mantle of Germany's savior from Communism, which, he averred, had turned Russia into a Bolshevik hell. Already a convinced racial anti-Semite and social Darwinist, Hitler advocated total solutions to Germany's staggering economic and political problems. Once in power, his totalitarian Third Reich enforced the "leadership principle" of absolute obedience to authority. Like Lenin, Hitler had learned totalitarianism from total war between 1914 and 1918. Then the belligerents had employed political centralization, economic regimentation, and thought-control to mobilize all the resources of modern industrial states in a terrible war of attrition. The Third Reich would use them to destroy domestic rivals, to mobilize the German economy for aggressive war, and ultimately to commit genocide.

The Gypsies were also victims of racial prejudice, but their social position was very different from that of the Jews. Few Gypsies were successful or even partially assimilated, and no one could convincingly argue that they enjoyed sufficient power in the world to threaten whole nations. Occasionally envied for their footloose lives but more commonly execrated for their roguish ways, the Gypsies came under increasing state pressure to become settled citizens or else depart. Even before Hitler came to power the Gypsies in Germany were subjected to special laws that placed them under police supervision as social misfits, habitual criminals, and vagabonds. The situation was much the same in other countries.

Handicapped people were targets of pseudo-science rather than simple racial prejudice. Throughout the civilized world advocates of the "science" of eugenics argued that human society could be improved by weeding out individuals with supposedly hereditary diseases, including insanity, mental retardation, deafness, blindness, and cancer. This could be achieved by sterilizing those deemed genetically flawed and, in extreme cases, euthanizing those whose lives were held to be miserable and pointless. Widely accepted by the educated elites, eugenics was adopted in the form of voluntary and compulsory sterilization programs in several European countries and 27 of the states of the United States in the years before and after World War I. In Germany the widely read 1920 book *Authorization for the Destruction of Life Unworthy of Life* by psychiatrist Alfred Hoche and legal scholar Karl Binding argued that the medical profession was morally obligated to grant a "merciful death" to severely handicapped and terminally ill patients. Among the book's most enthusiastic boosters was the rising politician Adolf Hitler. In the 1930s eugenics came under increasingly critical scrutiny in the world outside Germany, but in the Third Reich it became part of the official ideology.

Genocide: Policies and Procedures

Following Hitler's seizure of power in Germany in 1933, the Nazi state pursued eugenic policies designed to separate Jews, Gypsies, and severely handicapped Germans from the "Aryan" gene pool. The first victims of Nazi genocide were those most vulnerable, people deemed handicapped. The July 1933 "Law for the Prevention of Offspring with Hereditary Defects" resulted in the involuntary sterilization of 400,000 severely disabled and chronically mentally ill patients. With the approach of war in 1939, Hitler secretly authorized the killing of approximately 5,000 handicapped children on the pretext of granting a "merciful death" (euthanasia) to the most severely disabled youngsters. In September of that year the dictator ordered the program broadened to include all "incurables." Aware that such mass murder would not meet with popular approval, Hitler ordered that euthanasia be carried out as a covert program, informally named Operation T-4 (after the address of the unit's Berlin headquarters, Tiergartenstrasse 4), to be directed by Viktor Brack, an official from Hitler's personal chancellery. In October 1939 Hitler signed a document authorizing euthanasia killings, backdating it to September 1, the day he attacked Poland, in order to link T-4 with the demands of war. Copies of the authorization were privately shown to T-4 physicians to reassure them that they need not fear any legal repercussions.

The actual implementation of T-4 was placed in the hands of German physicians who appear to have been influenced to varying degrees by eugenics, careerism, and cost–benefit analysis—the belief that Germany's scarce health care resources should be devoted to "curables" rather than to "useless eaters." These physicians drew up questionnaires to be filled out by their colleagues in hospitals, sanitaria, and asylums in order to identify candidates for "final medical assistance." Physicians' committees reviewed the information and decided who would die. Doctors who refused to participate suffered no serious consequences. There was no shortage of health care professionals who willingly cooperated in the program.

Early T-4 killing experiments demonstrated that fatal injections and poisons were slow and impractical. Gassing proved much more efficient, and Hitler himself endorsed it as the "more humane way" of disposing of the handicapped. Starting in January 1940 the victims were bussed to one of six regional T-4 killing centers: Grafeneck, Brandenburg, Hartheim, Bernburg, Sonnenstein, and Hadamar. There they were asphyxiated with carbon monoxide in gas chambers disguised as shower rooms, following which the bodies were looted (organs removed for scientific study and gold teeth collected) and the remains cremated. Their relatives were informed that death resulted from some natural cause. Simultaneously, in occupied Poland SS execution squads both shot mental patients and smothered them with carbon monoxide in a sealed van, the first use of a "gas van" to kill Holocaust victims.

Inevitably, the truth leaked out. Too many people were involved, and hospital and asylum staff sometimes erred in misrepresenting cause of death, for example citing appendicitis in the case of someone whose appendix had been removed long before. In some cases the patients figured out what was happening for themselves and begged relatives and officials for mercy. By the summer of 1941 Protestant and Catholic church leaders were raising strong objections to Nazi euthanasia, and Hitler, desirous of maintaining public support for his war, ordered Brack to end the gassings. By that time Operation T-4 had taken the lives of more than 70,000 handicapped Germans. But Hitler's order was not intended to end T-4, which decentralized its operations and continued to kill "incurables" with fatal injections or by withholding medications. Concurrently, physicians in Operation 14f13 killed the sick and disabled in German concentration camps. This led to an additional 80,000 "euthanasia" deaths in Germany between August 1941 and the end of the war. The extension of euthanasia killings to Eastern Europe during World War II brought the total number of handicapped casualties to 275,000.

Handicapped people were the first to die in Nazi gas chambers and gas vans. It also perfected gassing techniques and provided trained personnel for the genocide of Jews and Gypsies that was to follow. T-4 was the first, but by no means the last, step in the Nazi campaign for the ethnic purification of Greater Germany.

Nazi efforts to exclude Jews and Gypsies from the German national community were, of necessity, different from those employed against the handicapped. Neither group was institutionalized, and the Jews were regarded as anything but vulnerable, having economic influence and ties to co-religionists in other countries. Hence the 600,000 German Jews always occupied center stage in Nazi thinking; the roughly 30,000 German Gypsies, regarded as poor and non-literate and hence more a nuisance than a threat, were bit-part players. This pattern of concentrating on the Jews and treating the Gypsies as an afterthought characterized what were essentially parallel policies toward the two groups from beginning to end.

During the early years of the Third Reich, the Nazi goal, more or less openly acknowledged, was to make the Jews despair of their future in Germany and emigrate, which ultimately more than half of them did. Violent attacks on Jews were uncommon, and Jews were sent to concentration camps only if they had been prominent in anti-Nazi parties. Hitler correctly assumed that legal discrimination would be more palatable to conservative Germans and foreign observers. The 1935 Nuremberg Laws, which made the Jews second-class citizens and banned sex and marriage between Jews and "Aryans," were only the most famous of many such statutes. Boycotts and the extortionate "Aryanization" of Jewish businesses, designed to deprive Jews of their livelihoods, also proceeded in orderly fashion. But violence was innate in Nazism, and impatience with the slow pace of Jewish emigration led to the "Crystal Night"

(Kristallnacht) pogrom of November 9–10, 1938, when Nazi thugs physically attacked Jews and destroyed their businesses and synagogues. Thousands of Jewish men were sent to concentration camps from which they were released only after promising to leave Germany. These actions were clearly the work of virulent anti-Semites in the Nazi Party, supported by government officials who found pogroms useful in advancing economic objectives. Most ordinary Germans ignored these atrocities out of indifference to the Jews or a sense of powerlessness to help them.

These policies aimed at forcing Jewish emigration held for more than a year after World War II began. Jews in the part of Poland conquered by Germany in 1939 were herded into ghettos; two years later the German Jews were sent to join them. The ghettos were conceived of as temporary holding pens by Nazi bureaucrats who intended to expel all the Jews in German hands farther to the east or else to the Indian Ocean island of Madagascar. Only when Hitler invaded the Soviet Union in 1941 did emigration give way to extermination.

Whereas German Jews initially were granted some leeway in determining their future, German Gypsies were branded as potentially criminal "asocials," placed under police control in municipal Gypsy camps, and disproportionately subjected to compulsory sterilization. The 1935 Nuremberg Laws were also applied to the Gypsies. Paradoxically, SS leader Heinrich Himmler was fascinated by the "Aryan" origins of the Gypsies and in 1936 assisted in founding the Eugenic and Biological Research Station of the Reich Health Office. Its team of research anthropologists was charged with identifying any remaining elements of Gypsy racial purity, but it concluded that only a tiny minority of Germany's Roma and Sinti were "of pure blood" and hence worthy of preservation and study. Most of the genealogical research findings were employed to identify Gypsies for the purpose of excluding them from German society as degenerate, criminal, and anti-social elements. A 1938 decree issued by Himmler entitled "Combating the Gypsy Plague" explicitly defined Gypsies as members of an alien and inferior race; large numbers of them were then sent to concentration camps. Following Germany's conquest of Poland in 1939, thousands of Gypsies were deported to Polish ghettos such as Lodz and Warsaw, where they shared the lot of the Jews.

The fate of both Jews and Gypsies was sealed, more than any other consideration, by the direction taken by Hitler's war. His campaign in the West had stalled in the face of British intransigence and the failure of his Luftwaffe to defeat the Royal Air Force in the Battle of Britain. By 1941 Hitler had decided to gamble on ending the war quickly by achieving a crushing victory over the USSR, which he hoped would then force Great Britain to capitulate. In his thinking, the success of his invasion of the Soviet Union (Operation Barbarossa, June 1941) required merciless racial slaughter. Believing that the German people would not understand such a ghastly policy, the Nazis carried out genocide in secrecy and under cover of war. Accordingly, responsibility for mass murder was placed in the hands of the SS (Schutzstaffel), Hitler's special guard of policemen and soldiers that had grown into the central agency of terror in Nazi-dominated Europe. Some of its officers were convinced anti-Semites who accepted the view that the Jews were Germany's most dangerous enemies. All of them were convinced and loyal Nazis who were sworn to obey orders without question.

As SS leaders prepared to participate in Hitler's invasion of the Soviet Union, they created four mobile killing squads called Einsatzgruppen (Special Action Groups) for the purpose of liquidating Jews, Gypsies, Polish and Soviet intellectuals, and Communist Party officials. The 3,000 members of these four squads shot and buried in mass graves 1–2 million people during the course of the war on the Eastern Front. Their victims also included thousands of sick and handicapped patients in Polish and Soviet hospitals and sanitaria that were then confiscated for use by the Germans. But mass shootings were found to be slow and inefficient—particularly if all 11 million European Jews were to be annihilated. Hence, Hermann Goering placed the formulation of what was to become the Nazis' "Final Solution to the Jewish Problem" in the hands of Reinhard Heydrich, the most powerful SS leader after Himmler. Heydrich's plan was submitted at a conference of top Nazi officials held in the Berlin suburb of Wannsee in January 1942. It called for concentrating all the Jews under German control in Eastern European ghettos and labor camps, where those capable of doing slave labor for the Third Reich would be kept alive as long as they were useful. Those who could not work or who were not needed would be sent to special camps for immediate extermination. The Gypsies were not mentioned at Wannsee, nor was any special plan formulated for them. In practice most Gypsies in Greater Germany were treated the same way as the Jews, whereas those in other parts of Europe were subjected to less systematic slaughter.

Genocide was too vast a process for the SS alone. The German army cooperated in the round-up and killing of victims. Volunteers from the conquered Eastern countries served as auxiliary police and as guards in the camps out of sympathy with the Nazis or the desire to escape some worse fate for themselves and their families at German hands. Occasionally local mobs in Poland, the Baltic States, and Ukraine massacred their Jewish neighbors, with German encouragement. However, unlike the Germans, none of these groups was dedicated to the systematic slaughter of every single Jew in Europe. That task was assigned principally to Hitler's elite guard, the SS.

Although the Third Reich targeted all the Jews and Gypsies in Nazi-dominated Europe, their fate varied with local conditions. Both groups were most vulnerable where their communities were large and unassimilated; where German officials managed affairs directly (and did so from the beginning of the Holocaust); and where indigenous prejudices encouraged some degree of cooperation with the murderers.

All three of these elements combined to decimate the Jews of Poland, the western USSR, and the Baltic States. There Nazi rule was most openly brutal. First under the guns of the Einsatzgruppen, and then in ghettos and labor and extermination camps, Jews from these areas were murdered or worked to death in numbers amounting to three-quarters of the total Holocaust casualties. Very few survived. Direct German control over Serbia, the Protectorate of Bohemia and Moravia, and part of Greece meant that their Jews were deported to Poland and subjected to similar atrocities. Such was also the fate of the remaining German and Austrian Jewish communities. Only small numbers of German Jews who were of mixed race, living in mixed marriages, highly decorated war veterans, or prominent persons were spared. Hungary came under direct German rule only in March 1944, following which the SS, aided by Hungarian officials, swallowed up more than half of the large Jewish population. Doubtless the losses in Hungary would have been even greater had the Germans taken control earlier.

Unlike Hungary, Germany's other Eastern European allies—Romania, Bulgaria, Slovakia, and Croatia—retained some measure of independence to the end of the war. Slovakia and Croatia, both satellites created by Nazi Germany, willingly cooperated in the Holocaust. Slovakia handed over most of its Jews to the Germans, whereas the Croatians themselves massacred their Jewish, Serbian, and Gypsy populations. Romania and Bulgaria, however, refused to comply with some German demands. Neither was a German creation, and both were fiercely protective of their national rights. Bulgaria confiscated the property of many native-born Jews and forced others into slave labor, but it would not hand them over to the Nazis. It did, however, deport Jews from lands newly acquired from Greece and Yugoslavia. In Romania, where (unlike Bulgaria) there was considerable anti-Semitism, tens of thousands of Jews in the newly reconquered eastern provinces of Bessarabia and Northern Bukovina were murdered in pogroms by Romanian forces or else deported across the Dniester River to starve or be shot by the Einsatzgruppen. Most Jews in western and central Romania, however, were spared. Hence the majority of Bulgarian and Romanian Jews survived the Holocaust.

The Jews of Western Europe, remote from the killing fields and the intense anti-Semitism of Eastern Europe, lost about 40% of their number to the Nazis. The SS gave priority to exterminating the Jews of the east, and the war ended before it could finish its work in the west. In Western

Europe, too, the pace of extermination varied with local conditions. In the Netherlands, which had been placed under direct German rule, three-quarters of the Jews perished because they were numerous, heavily concentrated in one place (Amsterdam), and led by passive community officials; they also had little opportunity to escape or hide in their heavily populated country. French Jews, too, perished as a result of the Vichy regime's collaboration with Nazi Germany. And yet, the death toll among French Jews was held to just over 20% because they seized opportunities to hide in remote villages or to flee to the nearby neutral havens of Spain and Switzerland with the help of sympathetic French Gentiles.

At the opposite extreme, almost all members of the very small Danish Jewish community were transported the short distance by boat to neutral Sweden by Danish Gentiles who had no sympathy with German occupation policies. The Italians, too, although initially German allies, were not racists. Only after Mussolini's fall and the German takeover of the country were about 16% of the Italian Jews sent to their death, and the retreating Nazis had to do most of the work themselves. Hence, in certain circumstances resistance to the German occupiers by local officials and private individuals saved lives. The fate of the different Jewish communities was determined by various concatenations of local attitudes, opportunities for flight or concealment, the size and location of the Jewish populations, and the nature of Nazi rule in the several countries (Fein, 1979).

Much the same was true for the Gypsies, although German policies on the Roma and Sinti were at first hesitant and uncertain and never approached the single-minded fanaticism that was reserved for the Jews. By 1943 Nazi efforts to distinguish between pure and hybrid Gypsies were being swept aside in the drive for ethnic purification, and the murder of Gypsies that was already underway intensified. Roma and Sinti were worked to death, shot into mass graves, and gassed alongside Jews. The German army regarded Gypsies as spies and participated in their destruction. Germany's Romanian and Croatian allies included Gypsies in their local campaigns of ethnic cleansing. The Gypsies' isolation, partially self-imposed, contributed to their vulnerability; Gentile bystanders occasionally provided Jews with food, false papers, and hiding places, but there is little evidence of such aid being extended to Gypsies. German concentration on the Jews and greater Gypsy capacity for evasion resulted in smaller percentages of deaths among the Roma and Sinti. Reliable figures for Gypsy casualties have never been established; estimates range between 135,000 and 500,000 of the approximately one million European Gypsies.

Existence for the Jews and Gypsies in ghettos and forced labor camps almost defies description. Overcrowded, overworked, and underfed, they could hope only that producing for the Nazi war machine would buy enough time to save at least a remnant of their pre-war communities.

That hope, combined with the Nazi policy of holding all the prisoners collectively responsible for any attempt at opposition or escape, kept resistance to a minimum. In 1944 the SS shut down the last of the ghettos and sent their piteous remnants to camps in Germany or to the extermination centers.

The six extermination centers, all of them situated on what had been Polish territory, ended the lives of three million Jews and Gypsies between 1941 and 1944. Four of them—Chelmno, Belzec, Sobibor, and Treblinka— were strictly killing centers where victims were gassed immediately following their arrival. Chelmno employed gas vans, whereas the other three death camps consisted of fixed installations that pumped exhaust from diesel engines into gas chambers disguised as shower rooms. Auschwitz and Majdanek were both killing and slave labor camps. In them, the able-bodied were selected for work in various military industries; the rest were consigned to the gas chambers or firing squads. Auschwitz, by far the largest of the camps, perfected use of the fast-acting pesticide Zyklon B (hydrogen cyanide gas) to kill as many as 10,000 victims per day.

To be selected for work often meant only a brief reprieve, since conditions in slave labor camps were atrocious. As the SS saw it, the victims were to die eventually anyway, and there was no reason to spare them when a steady stream of replacements kept arriving. Hence tens of thousands were literally worked to death. Others were subjected to grotesque and painful medical experiments. Survival depended on almost superhuman determination to live and often on the good fortune of securing jobs in camp kitchens, offices, and medical wards. Having, or acquiring, a skill that was useful to the Germans could be the difference between life and death.

Although most of those sent to Auschwitz were Jews, a special camp for Gypsy families was established within the larger camp in February 1943. Gypsy men, women, and children were allowed to live together, which was unusual for Auschwitz and probably reflected confused and unsettled Nazi policies concerning Roma and Sinti, which prevailed at that time. In other respects conditions in the family camp were no better than those for the Jews, and large numbers of Gypsies succumbed to hunger, disease, medical experiments, and hyperexploitation. When the Germans attempted to liquidate the surviving members of the camp in May 1944, the Gypsies fought them off with improvised weapons and their bare hands. Three months later the SS returned in force, and most of the 3,000 remaining Gypsies were gassed. Altogether about 20,000 Gypsies perished at Auschwitz.

Auschwitz was the last of the extermination centers to be shut down as Soviet forces overran Poland in the winter of 1944–1945. The SS drove the survivors of the various camps to Germany, where they were dumped in already overcrowded concentration camps and their outlying slave labor centers. Deprived of even the most elementary needs in the last days of the war, thousands died of malnutrition and disease. The liberating Allied armies found the camps littered with unburied corpses, and many of those still alive were too far gone to be saved. Of the few thousand Jews who survived the camps, the majority attempted to return to their former homes (not all successfully) while the remainder entered European displaced persons' camps and applied for permission to enter Palestine, the United States, or some other place of permanent refuge. Unknown numbers of Gypsy survivors attempted to resume lives in separate communities; their reluctance to communicate their experiences to the larger world would make it difficult to document their suffering under German rule.

Participants and Bystanders

Direct participation in the Holocaust by SS officials, T-4 doctors, Einsatz-gruppen personnel, and camp guards was required in relatively small numbers. Indirect involvement by police, civil servants, private business-men who profited from slave labor and the like was considerably broader. Moreover, fragmentary reports of the exterminations rapidly leaked out of Eastern Europe in 1942, enmeshing much of the world in the catastrophe.

German police and government bureaucrats who defined, identified, assembled, and deported the victims to their fate were not always fanatical Nazis or racists. Many were careerists and efficient professionals, dedicated to following instructions and improvising solutions to problems in the spirit of their superiors. Amorality was encouraged by specialization; each department and individual was accountable for only one small segment of the program, diffusing personal responsibility. Ordinary Germans who had nothing to do with the Holocaust might hear rumors of crimes against Gypsies and Jews in Eastern Europe, but they were preoccupied with staying alive and making ends meet in an increasingly disastrous wartime situation. Victims of racial persecution quite literally were out of sight and out of mind.

In occupied Western Europe, the Nazis were stretched thin and depended heavily on local authorities to deliver the victims for deportation. Especially in France and the Netherlands, such assistance was widespread, encouraged by careerism and fear of reprisals. Small minorities in all the Western European countries took great risks to hide Jews and Gypsies or help them escape to neutral countries. Tens of thousands were saved as a result. Equally small minorities of Nazi sympathizers turned the victims and their helpers over to the authorities. The vast majority of Western Europeans, however, were as apathetic and self-absorbed as most Germans.

Neutral countries such as Switzerland, Sweden, Spain, and Turkey accepted limited numbers of refugees, but none wanted to antagonize Hitler while his armies seemed invincible. Once the tide turned against him, however, they became more willing to aid his victims. The Vatican also held to its traditional neutrality. Pope Pius XII kept silent about the Holocaust, evidently fearing German reprisals and hoping to enhance his role as a mediator. Individual Catholic clerics and laymen, however, did intervene on behalf of the Jews, notably in France, Hungary, and Slovakia.

The nations allied against Hitler reacted to Nazi genocide in diverse ways. The Soviet Union gave refuge to significant numbers of Eastern European Jews who had fled before the German Army, but it acknowledged no special Nazi program to kill the Jews. In contrast, Great Britain and the United States warned the Germans and their allies that they would be called to account for their acts of genocide. Could more have been done? It has been charged that President Roosevelt might have saved lives had he not waited until 1944 to establish the War Refugee Board; if Germany and its satellites had been pressed to release their Jews; if the Allied air forces had bombed Auschwitz and its rail approaches more intensely in 1944; and if negotiations with the Nazis to ransom the Jews had been pursued. That these measures were not taken may reflect the presence of indifference or even covert anti-Semitism among Allied leaders.

Or it may be argued that the Allies' single-minded preoccupation with the military side of the war was responsible for their lack of action on behalf of civilians. As they saw it, the best way to help all the victims of fascism was to press for the quickest possible victory. Not everyone agrees that such measures would have altered the outcome in any significant way. In fact, no one should underestimate Nazi determination to see genocide through to the end, regardless of disruptions of the killing centers and promises held out in negotiations.

Post-Holocaust Victim Responses

Studies of Holocaust survivors have shown that virtually all suffered to some degree from a "survivor syndrome" that included acute anxiety, cognitive and memory disorders, depression, withdrawal, and hypochondria. Some became clinical cases requiring long-term professional care, but most learned to live with their trauma and rebuild old lives or start new ones (Berger, 1988.)

Nazi genocide decimated the once-thriving Jewish communities of Eastern Europe. Hundreds of thousands of Holocaust survivors from Poland, Hungary, and the Soviet Union returned to find their homes destroyed or confiscated by neighbors, governments dominated by Communists, and in some cases renewed outbreaks of anti-Semitism. Many of them gave up and became displaced persons housed in special camps in Germany and Austria. Virtually all expected to emigrate to Palestine or the United States. The U.S. government, however, limited the entry of refugees and placed heavy pressure on Great Britain to admit large numbers of Jews to Palestine. When Britain chose instead to honor its promises to the Arab majority, limiting Jewish immigration, guerrilla uprisings by militant Zionists and international pressure forced Britain to withdraw from the area. The Jewish state that emerged from the partition of Palestine by the United Nations might eventually have come into being anyway, but the creation of Israel in 1948 was greatly facilitated by the need to find a home for large numbers of Holocaust survivors and by the widespread sympathy for Zionism engendered by Hitler's murderous actions.

The genocide of the Jews also had a major impact on Jewish religious thought. For Judaism, God's covenant with the ancient Israelites bound Him and the Jewish people to the end of time. History was viewed as the expression of God's will, working out a divine plan in which the Jews occupied a special place. Judaism conceived of God as merciful, loving, and omnipotent. How, then, could the dehumanization and mass murder of God's people be explained?

For some Jewish scholars this question could not be confronted without challenging traditional Judaism. After Auschwitz, they reasoned, faith in the redeeming God of the covenant, an omnipotent and merciful deity, was no longer possible. Nor did they find it credible any longer to regard the Jews as His chosen people. Just where this reappraisal was leading remained unclear, and other Jewish theologians rushed to the defense of continuity and covenantal Judaism. One such response was to reaffirm orthodoxy by placing the Holocaust within the tradition that heard God's commanding voice in catastrophes such as the destruction of the First and Second Temples. Judaism endured then, and Jews must not hand Hitler a posthumous victory by losing faith as a result of his policies.

A second approach embraced the traditional covenant by distinguishing between God's work and man's. God, for reasons that would become evident at the end of time, voluntarily placed restraints on Himself in order to make history possible. Hence the genocide of the Jews was man's work, not God's. A third line of thought accepted that the covenant had been shattered by the Holocaust but held out the possibility of renewing it by returning to the question of redemption and redefining tradition by living authentically religious lives (Roth & Berenbaum, 1989). In all these viewpoints, the impact of genocide on Judaism and on the Jews' sense of their place in the world was unmistakable.

Gypsy survivors had few opportunities to emigrate, and it seems unlikely that many wished to do so. Like many Jewish survivors, they faced ongoing prejudice and resentment as they tried to rebuild shattered lives in post-war Europe. Public concerns about Gypsy isolation, nomadism, and low levels of social, economic, and educational development helped to perpetuate Gypsy mistreatment. The largest Gypsy populations were in Eastern Europe, where Stalinist regimes imposed by Soviet occupation officials discouraged ethnic identity and attempted to force Gypsy assimilation. For many years the new West German state denied Gypsies the monetary compensation that it made available to Jewish survivors, claiming that the Nazis had punished the former as asocials and threats to public safety rather than abused them for racial reasons. When these policies changed in the 1960s, compensation often proved to be too little, too late (Crowe, 2007; Margalit, 2002).

Other Post-Holocaust Responses

Among Christian thinkers the Holocaust induced a profound reappraisal of the traditional view of the Jews as living examples of what happens to those who reject Jesus. It is unlikely that those who advanced this view ever intended it to culminate in violence against the Jews, nor would it have done by itself. And yet, there was no explaining away the contributions made by Christian anti-Semitism to the climate of opinion that made the genocide of the Jews possible in the European heartland of ostensibly Christian Western civilization.

Some Protestant theologians demanded a critical reappraisal of traditional Christian teachings of contempt for Judaism. They called for a reinterpretation of church Christology and eschatology to affirm the authenticity of the religion of the Jews and Christianity's vital roots in Judaism. The Catholic Church repudiated Judeophobia during the reforming pontificate of John XXIII. One of the key documents that emerged from the Second Vatican Council in 1965 (*Nostra Aetate*, Latin for "In Our Age") recognized the common patrimony of Christianity and Judaism and denounced "hatred, persecutions, and displays of antisemitism, directed at Jews at any time and by anyone." In 1998 the Vatican Commission for Religious Relations with the Jews issued the document "We Remember: A Reflection on the Shoah," apologizing for the Catholic Church's failures during the Holocaust. It aroused controversy, however, because it did not link traditional Christian teachings about the Jews to Nazi genocide. Pope Benedict XVI's 2009 reinstatement of a previously excommunicated bishop who denies the Holocaust ever happened has further troubled Catholic–Jewish relations.

German church scholars of both denominations confronted the lamentable failure of German Christians to stand up for the Jews under Hitler. Germans as a whole, however, were slow to absorb the implications of Nazi genocide. Although a few called it an Allied fabrication, most repressed it and the whole memory of the now-discredited Nazi regime that had brought about their downfall. Although the new West German government in 1952 agreed to pay reparations to Jewish survivors, the West German courts were slow to pick up prosecutions of war criminals where the Allied jurists left off in 1949.

German consciousness of the Holocaust arose principally during the 1960s when a new generation began asking uncomfortable questions, primed by the sensational 1961 trial of SS Obersturmbannfuehrer Adolf Eichmann in Jerusalem. Since that time critical examinations of the Holocaust and the regime that brought it about have entered the media and the school and university curricula. Perhaps the most concrete expression of Germany's reactions to the human rights abuses of the Nazis was its liberal post-war asylum law that up until 1993 made Germany a haven for political refugees from many lands.

As was true elsewhere, however, consciousness of crimes against Gypsies and handicapped people was slow to gain recognition in Germany. For decades after the war the German medical establishment denied complicity in Nazi euthanasia, and many T-4 physicians went on to distinguished post-war medical careers. Only publication in the 1980s of well-documented studies of the genocide of disabled Germans made it possible to reassess the history of medicine in Nazi Germany (Klee, 1983; Mueller-Hill, 1988). Today, Germans engage in healthy debates about many aspects of medical ethics, but extreme sensitivity to the Nazi genocide of the handicapped has a chilling effect on discussions of eugenics, euthanasia, or assisted suicide in Germany.

The Eichmann trial's vivid documentation of Nazi atrocities also had a strong impact in the United States and especially on American Jewry. Before 1961 little attention was paid to survivors and GI liberators of the concentration camps. The effects of the trial were intensified by the Six-Day War of 1967, which strengthened the Jews' sense of solidarity with Israel and encouraged them to encounter the agony of their co-religionists under Hitler. For some American Jews that suffering imposed a special obligation to become involved in all forms of civil rights movements.

Elsewhere Nazi genocide had a much smaller impact. Austrians, who had welcomed Hitler in 1938 and perpetrated outrages against Jews and Gypsies, hid behind the cloak of having been passive objects of German aggression. Eastern Europeans, and especially Poles, saw themselves as victims of Nazism on the same level as the Gypsies and Jews. Until their downfall in the early 1990s, Communist governments reinforced that view by refusing to acknowledge that the Jews and Gypsies had been singled out for annihilation by the Nazis. Everywhere consciousness that the Gypsies were victims of Nazi genocide was slow to sink in, impeded by the emphasis on Jewish victimization in Holocaust historiography and by the Gypsies' reluctance (or inability) to relate their experiences to the wider world. Hence the widespread revulsion against anti-Semitism that ultimately emerged from the Holocaust found no counterpart for anti-Gypsy sentiment.

Debates about the Holocaust

The very definition of the Holocaust has become an issue as a result of efforts to identify a broader pool of victims. The traditional view that the Jews alone among the many victims of Nazi racism were set apart for total annihilation (Katz, 1994) has been challenged by those who would include Gypsies and handicapped people (Friedlander, 1995). The Gypsies have been the subject of unusually lively debate (Zimmermann, 2007). Those who deny that they were truly victims of genocide stress that the Nazis developed an actual plan of mass murder for the Jews alone and that they exempted many "socially adjusted" Gypsies (those having regular jobs and permanent residences) from killings and deportations (Lewy, 2000; Bauer, 2001). Scholars who assert that the fate of the Gypsies was parallel to that of the Jews admit that there were differences but minimize their significance, pointing out that all Nazi racial policies were constantly evolving in more radical directions and that in practice those regarding the Gypsies were moving toward unmistakably genocidal conclusions (Hancock, 2004; Milton, 2001).

Although there is general agreement that the key decision made by the Nazis was the one to kill all the Jews within their grasp, scholars differ about how and when it came about. According to a group of historians referred to as "intentionalists," Hitler probably planned the extermination all along and certainly gave the order no later than 1941 as he prepared to attack the USSR. Opposing this interpretation is the "functionalist" view which holds that the Nazi leadership replaced resettlement schemes with genocide only after the June 1941 attack on the USSR. Genocide, argue the functionalists, was a product of euphoria following spectacular German victories in the summer of 1941, or else of frustration over stiffening Soviet resistance in the fall and the subsequent entry of the United States into the war. Most functionalists refer to a "decision-making process" that involved two or more increasingly radical orders made over several months. Although some functionalists believe that the central decisions were made by Hitler and other top Nazi leaders, others stress initiatives by local and regional officials facing hopelessly overcrowded ghettos and believing (correctly) that Hitler would not disapprove of mass murder. Since documents have been lost and commands were often given orally (and not in writing), orders can only be inferred, not specified. The evidence is incomplete, and debates about the immediate origins of the genocide of the Jews promise to go on indefinitely (Browning, 2004).

Some Holocaust scholars have faulted the Jews for failing to offer armed resistance to the Germans or cooperating with them to some degree (Hilberg, 2003, pp. 1104–1118). Criticisms of the Jewish Councils that were forced to run the Eastern European ghettos and organize deportations from Western Europe have been particularly harsh. Other scholars have disputed this approach, stressing instead the Jews' almost total vulnerability to their tormentors and advancing a broader definition of resistance that embraces all efforts to keep Jews alive. These include measures to make Jews economically useful to the Germans, to smuggle food into the ghettos and Jews out of Nazi-dominated territory, and to provide the victims with morale-building cultural, religious, and social support (Bauer, 1979, pp. 26–40; Trunk, 1972).

What motivated the perpetrators? A popular interpretation contends that the killers were "willing executioners" conditioned by a German culture that was deeply anti-Semitic long before Hitler came to power (Goldhagen, 1996). Another stresses the immediate impact of Nazi indoctrination and ideology on the perpetrators (Bartov, 2003). A third viewpoint holds that the killers were mostly "ordinary men" who yielded to peer pressure and deferred to authority (Browning, 1992).

Controversy also surrounds the role of Holocaust bystanders, both those in German-controlled areas and those abroad. Some scholars have criticized the Poles in particular for failing to aid the Jews and even for actively betraying their Jewish neighbors (Gutman & Krakowski, 1986; Gross, 2001). The contrary view holds that the Poles were themselves so direly persecuted by the Germans that they had few opportunities to assist the Jews (Lukas, 1986). The famous silence of Pope Pius XII during the Holocaust has stimulated a great deal of commentary, both pro and con (Phayer, 2000). The United States and its allies have been condemned for doing little to rescue the Jews (Wyman, 1984). Opposing this contention is the view that, given German determination to kill all the Jews and Gypsies, there was nothing more that outsiders could have done except defeat Germany as quickly as possible (Rubenstein, 1997).

Perspectives on the Holocaust Today

The Holocaust is perhaps the one genocide of which every educated person has heard. Especially in Israel and the United States, its memory is kept alive by schools, the mass media, and the observance of national days of remembrance. A network of Holocaust memorial centers educates the public at large, although they occasionally come under pressure from groups that would vulgarize the genocide of the Jews by placing it at the service of extraneous agendas. These include heightening Jewish identity, raising funds, and promoting uncritical support for Israeli foreign policy (Novick, 1999).

Today, a third generation of post-Holocaust Germans understands Nazi genocide as history and as part of collective memory rather than as personal experience. The German media generate a constant flow of documentaries and feature stories on the subject, and they also commemorate important anniversaries, such as Auschwitz liberation day (January 27), which has been named "Memorial Day for the Victims of National Socialism." The Holocaust is featured prominently in all school curricula, which often program organized travel to museums and camp memorials. Among those memorials is one to the murdered Jews of Europe erected in the very center of Berlin in 2005. A fairly widespread inclination among German scholars and journalists to include ordinary Germans among the victims of Nazism has altered the focus on the Holocaust somewhat, but it has not prevented the recognition of very particular crimes against the Jews, Gypsies, and handicapped people. Since 1994 the denial of such crimes has been a specific offense in the German penal code (Pohl, 2004).

Public awareness of the Holocaust in the Eastern European countries where most of the murders occurred varies greatly from country to country. It is most advanced in Poland and Hungary, where memorials, museums, and research institutes have begun the process of integrating the Jewish past into national memory. Elsewhere less progress is evident. In the Baltic States, Latvia, Lithuania, and Estonia, Holocaust commemoration vies for attention with efforts to glorify volunteers from those countries who fought with the Germans in the Waffen SS. In Moscow the Russian Research and Educational Holocaust Center promotes research on all aspects of the Holocaust in the former USSR. All of these efforts at remembering and correcting the historical record by Eastern Europeans are inhibited by preoccupation with broad national tragedies under Hitler and Stalin. Ukrainians, for example, are better informed about Stalin's "Terror Famine" of 1932–1933 ("The Ukrainian Holocaust") than they are about the fate of Ukrainian Jews and Gypsies during World War II. Growing populist and right-wing nationalist movements resist Holocaust commemoration and also stress Jewish involvement in Communist parties both before and after the War. Poles, Ukrainians, Romanians, and other Eastern Europeans find it painful to come to terms with their history of anti-Semitism and collaboration under the Nazis at a time when new national identities are being forged.

Eastern Europeans are not alone in downplaying the Holocaust. Significant right-wing parties in Austria (the Austrian Freedom Party) and in France (the Popular Front) flirt with Holocaust denial. Popular Front leader Jean-Marie Le Pen has dismissed Nazi genocide as a mere "detail" of World War II history.

Lessons of the Holocaust

German history dramatizes the insidious nature of racial prejudice. Many Germans were prejudiced in varying degrees, but only a minority wanted or expected actual violence against Jews, Gypsies, and handicapped people. Although the Nazis were deliberately vague about the practical implications of their racism, they were sufficiently bold in their propaganda against the Jews that anyone supporting Hitler had at least to condone his Judeophobia. Moderate anti-Semitism made that possible and helped deliver the German nation into the hands of one of history's most malicious leaders. The Holocaust demonstrates that there is no safe level of racism. On the contrary, it teaches that any agenda that places economic and political security above human rights has the potential to result in disaster.

Once the genocide began, there was little that outsiders could do to rescue the victims. Earlier, however, many might have been saved had other countries opened their doors to refugees. The time to aid the targets of racial bigotry is before their situation becomes untenable.

Those who were called upon to carry out the extermination process found that the modern state has effective ways of securing obedience and cooperation. Although threats of coercion and reprisal were always present, compliance was more commonly assured by assigning each person only a single, highly specialized function, often not particularly significant in itself. Overall responsibility rested with someone else, and ultimately with Hitler. Unable or unwilling to answer for anything but their little spheres, well-educated and cultured individuals effectively placed themselves at the service of barbarism. Their participation made possible the bureaucratic organization of modern technology for mass extermination, this genocide's most characteristic feature. Understanding the difficulty of defining individual responsibility in a totalitarian dictatorship and the ease with which ordinary people became complicit in Nazi genocide has the capacity to heighten political awareness and challenge moral sensitivity.

Eyewitness Accounts

The Jews

Account 1

Although the Germans kept careful records of their genocide of the Jews, not all of those records survived the downfall of the Third Reich, and in any event they could never view events from the standpoint of the victims. Hence, oral histories of the Holocaust are indispensable sources. Fortunately, interviews of survivors and witnesses have been conducted in many countries. These interviews cover a wide range of topics, including Jewish life before the Holocaust, Nazi policies toward the Jews in many countries, ghettoization, slave labor, resistance, successful and unsuccessful attempts at escape, liberation, and efforts to start over. Naturally, Jewish survivors living in North America, Western Europe, and Israel are most heavily represented.

Among the first scholars to interview Holocaust survivors was the American psychologist David P. Boder (1949). During the summer of 1946 he wire-recorded interviews with 70 displaced persons, many of them Jews, at camps in France, Italy, Germany, and Switzerland. Eight of the interviews were translated and published in book form under the title *I Did Not Interview the Dead*. The interview that follows was conducted by Boder, but was not included in that volume.

The Holocaust can never be encapsulated in a single person's recollections. However, this interview with Nechama Epstein reveals a remarkable breadth of experiences, including survival in ghettos, slave labor camps, and extermination centers. Made soon after World War II ended, it has the advantages of freshness and immediacy. Epstein begins her story in 1941 when the 18-year-old native of Warsaw and her family were herded into the city's ghetto, together with 350,000 other Jews. (Note: this interview is housed in the David Boder Collection at the Simon Wiesenthal Center in Los Angeles. Acquisition # 81–992, spools 95, 96, pp. 104A/2593–2668.)

Epstein: When the ghettos began, among us began a great fight of hunger.... We began selling everything, the jewelry.... We finished at the last at the featherbed...

Q: Who bought it?
A: People who were smuggling. They had. They were earning. Christians bought it.... And then we could already see that it was very bad. We had nothing to sell any more. Eight people were living on a kilo [2.2 lbs] of beets a day.... With water. And every day, day by day, there remained less strength. We did not have any more strength to walk. My brother's 4-year-old child did not have anything to eat. He was begging for a small baked potato. There was none to give him.... And thus it lasted a year's time. Until ... the first burned offering in my home was my father who, talking and walking, said he is fading from hunger, and died. My father was 60 years old.... When my father died, there began among us a still greater hunger. A kilo of bread cost 20 zlotys.... Every day there were other dead, small children, bigger children, older people. All died of a hunger death.

Q: What was done with the dead?

A: The dead were taken ... if one fell on the street ... he was covered. A stone was put on top, and thus he lay until.... There was not enough time to collect the dead.... And then people drove around with small carts. There were no funeral coaches any more, nothing. People drove around with small carts, collected the dead, loaded them up, took them to the cemetery, and buried them—women, men, children, everybody in one grave.... And we.... It had broken out, the first deportation that was in the year 1942.... I do not remember the exact month. In the beginning of winter [Note: *sic.* Between September 5 and 12, 1942] there came down a whole ... a few thousand Germans had come down, with weapons, with machine guns, with cannons, and they ... made a blockade. They surrounded from one end of the street to the other.... They began to chase the people out of the houses.... It was terrible. Many ran into the gates. They [the Germans] saw small children. They grabbed them by the legs and knocked them against the walls.... The mothers saw what is being done to their children. They threw themselves out of windows.... They [the Germans] went into a hospital, a Jewish hospital.... And they began taking out all the sick that were there....

Q: Did you see it yourself?

A: Yes.... I was being led to the rail terminal.... The sick began jumping out the windows. So they [the Germans] ran on the roofs with machine guns and shot down at the sick. And all were shot. And we were led away to the rail terminal. There I was the whole night. That night was a terrible one....

Q: What sort of a building was it [the rail terminal]?

A: A school was there at one time.... Then a depot was made there, and the Jews of the ghetto were all concentrated there. They were led in there, and there they were a night, two nights. They led a railroad siding to the street, and in trains [Jews were] transported to Treblinka. At night Germans came in, threw hand grenades. At the people.... There were loud screams. We had no place to go out. One lay on top of the other; we had to ... eh ... relieve ourselves on the spot.... It was a frightful experience to live through that night. In the morning they began to chase us out. "Alle aus!" ... And they began to arrange in rows of five mothers with children, men, everybody together. And whoever could not ... walk straight, he was immediately shot on the spot.... We got into the railroad cars. Two hundred persons were packed into one railroad car. Riding in these wagons everyone saw death before the eyes at any instance. We lay one on top of the other. One pinched pieces from another. We were tearing pieces.

Q: Why?

A: Because everybody wanted to save oneself. Everybody wanted to catch air. One lay suffocating on top of another.... We could do nothing to help ourselves. And then real death began.... After we had traveled for four hours, it became terribly hot. But so fast did the train travel that there was nothing. We began thinking, the youths, what should we do. The mothers were telling their children they should save themselves, they should jump. Maybe in spite of all they will remain alive.

Q: Were the doors open?

A: Many had along with them files, knives, hammers.... There had begun a great thirst. It became terribly hot. Everybody undressed.... There were small children who began to cry terribly. "Water!"... So we started banging on the doors. The Germans should give water.... We were screaming. So they began to shoot inside, from all four sides.

Q: On the stations?

A: Not on the sta- ... while traveling. They were sitting on the roofs ... where one steps own, on the steps, Germans were sitting.... And they began to shoot inside. When they began to shoot inside, very many people were killed. I was sitting and looking how one gets hit by a bullet, another one gets hit by a bullet. I, too, expected to get hit in a moment.... And I saved myself by hiding under the dead. I lay down underneath the dead. The dead lay on top of me. The blood of the killed was flowing over me.... There lay a little girl of four years. She was calling to me, "Give me a little bit of water. Save me." And I could do nothing. Mothers were giving the children urine to drink....

Q: Is it really true?

A: I saw it! I did it myself, but I could not drink it. I could not stand it any more. The lips were burned from thirst I thought this is it, I am going to die. So I saw that the mother is doing it, and the child said, "Mama, but it is bitter. I cannot drink it."... So she said, "Drink, drink." And the child did not drink it, because it was bitter. And I myself imitated it, but I was not able to drink it, and I did not drink it. But what then? There were girders inside the railroad cars. From the heat, perspiration was pouring from the girders. This we ... one lifted the other one up. It was high up, and we licked the moisture off the girders. It was very stifling. There was that little window, a tiny one, so we wanted to open it. Every time we opened it, they would shoot in.... And when we wanted to open it, not minding that they were shooting, we did. There were small children, and they were all suffocating.... We could not stand it any more.

Q: And then?

A: And thus I rode all night. Early in the morning—it was about 2 in the morning, maybe 3, just before dawn—my mother began crying very much.... She begged us to save ourselves. The boys took a saw and cut a hole—it [the door] was locked with a chain from the other side.... And we took the bars off the windows. And we started to jump. No. What does "to jump" mean? One pushed out the other one...

Q: Aha. Did the Germans let them?

A: They did not let them. They immediately started shooting on the spot. When I jumped out I fell into a ditch.... And I remained lying completely unconscious. And the railroad car ... the train passed.... I came to. It was at night, around three in the morning, so I...

Q: And your mother herself did not jump.

A: No. The mother could not. With the small child she could not jump. And a woman of 60, she could not jump....

Q: And then?

A: I came to. I got back my thoughts, so I went to look for my brother.... In the meantime there arrived some sort of a Polish militia man ... and told me that I should quickly run away from here, because the Gestapo is all around here. I will be shot here. I should run away. He told me that I had jumped near Radzin and Lukow. So he told me to go to the Miedzyrzec ghetto. There is a ghetto with Jews.... I began to walk on foot toward Miedzyrzec.... When I jumped out I met a little girl. She had also jumped. She had her entire leg completely torn open. While jumping she had caught on a piece of iron, and she tore open her leg.... And the two of us started to walk. Yes, after getting up I went to look for my brother. I had gone about ten feet. He lay shot. He had a bullet here in the heart I could not move away from him, but that Christian [the militia man] said that I should go away quickly. The struggle for life was stronger than anything. I left my brother on the road. I do not know what happened to his bones. And I went on. I had walked with that little girl for about three hours. Dark it was. Through woods, through fields we crawled, crawled, crawled....

Q: That little girl was a stranger?

A: A strange little girl. I don't know at all that little girl. She was about 14 years old.... And the little girl with the bleeding leg ... for terror she did not feel the pain. After having walked thus for perhaps ten kilometers, the two of us remained sitting where the road leads into a forest. And we could not walk any more. The child said that she cannot walk any more. The leg hurts her. We don't know what will be. In the meantime I had heard gentiles saying that Germans prowl on this road looking for Jews. And I saw it is bad. With the child I cannot walk. So I took the child. I did not know what to do. I carried her perhaps ... perhaps, who knows, a kilometer or two. I myself did not have any strength. I was barefoot. My shoes had remained in the railroad car, because I had undressed. I did not have the time to put anything on. I was completely naked and barefoot. And that child remained in the field. And I went away. I could not help any more at all. The child had fallen, and I could not do anything to help any more. I went away. [A pause]

Q: Go on.
A: I had walked thus for about 20 kilometers. I do not know myself how many kilometers I had covered. I came to the Miedzyrzec ghetto.... I went in. It was a day after a large deportation. So I went in. Entering the ghetto, it became faint before my eyes. It was at night. I did not have anywhere to go. When arriving there, I regretted very much that I had jumped off the train, because at every step, wherever I went, shot people were lying. Broken windows, all stores looted. Terrible things happened there.... In that ghetto I lived eight months.

Q: Did you...?
A: ...in deathly fear.

Q: ...register with the...?
A: There was a Jewish Community Council. I registered with the Jewish Community Council, and I [just sat there and waited]. It was not worth it. Every four weeks there were new deportations. From the small towns all around and around Jews were brought in there. And there was a sort of an assembly depot for Jews. And from there all the Jews were being sent to Treblinka. There I lived through three terrible deportations. During the first deportation I hid in an open attic and lay there for four weeks. I lived just on raw beets.... I did not have anything to drink. The first snow fell then, so I made a hole in the roof and pulled in the hand a little snow. And this I licked. And this I lived on.

Q: Were you there alone?
A: No. We were about ... there were about 20 people there. There was a father with a mother with child. There were some others.... We had nothing to eat. Thus we lived four weeks. We found raw peas which we ate. I had pared the beets, and afterwards I gathered the rinds of the beets, because I had nothing more to eat. And thus I nourished myself for four weeks, till there was a deportation. It lasted four weeks, that deportation. After the deportation we came down from the attic. At that time a lot of

Jews had also been shot. Coming down from the attic, it was a terrible thing to see. We had to ... we were taken to work removing the dead.

Q: Who were the SS? Germans and who else?

A: There were a few Ukrainians, too, but not many.... All the streets were splashed with blood. In every ditch Jewish blood had been poured. We went down. We had nothing to eat. We started looking for something to eat so we...

Q: Was there no council, no Community Council?

A: At the time the chairman had been taken away. The chairman had been shot. He was taken out first. He was the first.... A very fine man. He was taken out the first—with the wife, with the child. They were told to turn around, and they were shot. There were Jewish police, too.... Jewish policemen. So they [the Jews of the ghetto] were shot little by little. During each deportation ten, twenty were taken and also transported into the railroad cars. And they were shot, sent away. Those who escaped were shot.... So there was nobody to turn to. Everybody was afraid to go out. Many were lying [in hiding] there still a few weeks after the deportation. They did not know that it is already safe.... When we came down it was sort of peaceful for about two months. For two months time we lived on that which the Jewish Council gave to those who were strangers [from other towns and waiting for deportation].... They gave them every day a kilo of potatoes and a piece of bread. The food was not important, because it was ... every day we lived in great fear. People walking in the streets were shot at.

Q: Did you have relatives there? Did you know anyone?

A: Nobody. I was all alone.... Mine had all gone away. I had remained all alone. I had to support myself. By how did I support myself? I carried water.

Q: For whom?

A: For the Jews who lived there I carried water. And for that I received a few pennies. And that is how I supported myself.... In brief, it dragged on till winter, till the Birth of Christ.

Q: That is when? Christmas?

A: Yes. Then there was a frightful night to live through. There came down drunken Gestapo from Radzin.... And in the middle of the night we were asleep in a room. There were perhaps, who knows, 30 people altogether in that house where we were.... And they entered. I was sleeping there with two little girls. These children had also escaped from the Radzin ghetto. Two girls, little ones. One was about eight years old, and one about six years. I was sleeping with them in the room. There were other girls. In our room there were about 15 persons. In the middle of the night we hear ... shooting. We lay in great deathly fear. And they were knocking on our door. And I did not know why they could not enter through the door. In the morning I got up. I opened the door. A shot person fell into ... my room, into the house where we were lying. When we came in [into the other rooms] there lay shot all who were living in those rooms. Two children with a father who were sleeping in bed, everything was shot. A man lay with his stomach completely torn open, his guts outside on the ground. And later Jewish police came in. The Germans had left, and we had to clean up the blood and all that.... During the second deportation I was not able to hide any more. I was led away to a synagogue. There was a large synagogue. There, all the Jews were assembled. In the synagogue it was terrible. They simply came in—if they heard a cry, they shot in. They threw grenades. They beat. They struck. They did not give anything to drink. We had to relieve ourselves on the same place where we slept. I was there a whole night. I saw it was bad. I did not want to go to death. I went on fighting against it. I went over to a window. It was on the first floor. We took two towels, I and another girl. We lowered the towels from the windows, and we crawled down and escaped down into a cellar, and there we again lived through the second deportation.... Again we lived [there] a few months. During the last deportation I was not able to hide any more. I was led away into a transport. It was a beautiful summer day.... It was May Day.... We were loaded on railroad cars. We were led through the streets exactly like we had been driven to Treblinka. They shot at those who did not walk in line. Many people fell, children. [We were] running fast. I myself received from a German ... a [rubber] hose over the head. I got a large bump. I did not pay attention to the pain, but I ran fast....

Q: What then?
A: We were put into the railroad cars. It was the same as to Treblinka, shooting. We had nothing to drink. We drove a day and a night. We were taken down to Majdanek. Many were saying that we were being taken to Treblinka, but the direction was toward Majdanek. We were taken off at the Majdanek camp. We were all lined up. There were many who were shot. They were taken down, those who were still alive. They were taken down on the square, and they were immediately shot to death. The mothers were put separately, the children separately, the men separately, the women separately. Everything was separated. The women, the young women, were taken to the Majdanek camp. The men were taken to another camp. The children and the mothers were led to the crematory. All were burned.... We never laid eyes on them again.... I was in

Majdanek two months. I lived through many terrible things. We had nothing to eat. We were so starved. At first we did not know yet what such a thing as a camp means. In the morning, at 6 in the morning, came in a German, an SS woman, and started to chase us with a large strap, beating everybody. We were lying on the beds, grieved, with great worries, thinking where the mothers were, where the fathers and the children were. We were crying. Then came in a German woman at 6 in the morning with a large strap and beat us over the head to go out to the inspection. At inspection it could happen that we would stand four, five hours.

Q: Why so long?
A: People were being kept so long because everybody did not know yet what ... what this was all about. Many children of about 16 years hid in the attic. They were afraid to come out. They thought they were going to be shot.... And for that, that they had hidden, we stood five hours as a punishment. Later nobody hid any more. They said whoever will hide himself will be shot. And so I was in Majdanek two months.

Q: Did you work there?
A: Yes. We were sent to do garden work. We were sent to carry the shit which.... There were no toilets there, so we carried it in buckets. We were not given anything to eat. They were hitting us over the legs. They were beating us over the heads. The food consisted of 200 grams [7 ounces] of bread a day, and a little soup of water with [leaves of] nettles. This was the food. And I was there two month's time. The hunger there was so great that when a cauldron of food was brought, we could not wait for it to be distributed, but we threw ourselves on the food, and that food would spill on the ground, and, with the mud, we ate it. After having been there two months ... they began to select the healthy, healthy children who are able to work.... They tested the heart. Whoever had the smallest blemish on the body did not come out [any more] from there. Only 600 women were picked out, and I was among them. This was in ... July.... I was taken away to Auschwitz. The conditions were then already a little better. Fewer were being packed into a railroad car. They were putting in already 60 to a wagon.... Arriving at Auschwitz, we were led into a large hall before taking us to be bathed. All the women had their hair cut off...

Q: That was the first time you had that done?
A: For the first time ... just in Auschwitz.... So I had my hair shorn off, and they tattooed numbers on us.... We had very great anguish, because we had our hair cut off. How can a woman live without hair? They took us and dressed us in long pants....

Q: Who cut off your hair?
A: Our hair was cut off by women who were working there.

Q: Yes. What then? They cut it from the whole body?
A: Completely. On the body, here [she points], everywhere, everywhere, everything.... And we were dressed in trousers and blouses. We were terribly hungry...

Q: What did you do there?
A: We went to work in a detail which was call the death detail. Why? This I will tell, too.... We went to work, the 600 women from Majdanek. It took a month, and there remained no more than 450. We died out of hunger.... We worked carrying stones on barrows, large stones. To eat they did not give us. We were beaten terribly. There were German women who were also prisoners [i.e., prisoner foremen]. They were imprisoned for prostitution.... They [the prostitutes] used to beat us terribly. They said that every day they must kill three, four Jews. And food they did not give us.... We carried stones on ... barrows. We carried sand, stones. We were building a highway—women! The work was very hard. We got heavily beaten with rubber hoses over the legs from those German women overseers, those who also were imprisoned, prisoners.... Thus I labored for three months, until I became sick. I had gotten malaria.... I went around for two weeks with a 41-degree fever [about 105 degrees F]. I was afraid to go to the sick-ward. There was such a sick-ward.... I was afraid to go, because it was said that if one goes there one does not come back any more, one is taken away to the crematory.... I saw that I cannot stand it any more. The legs were buckling under me. Each day I got more and more beaten, because I did not work. I could not eat any more.... I would accumulate bread from one day to the next. I could not eat it any more. I gave it away to other girls.... I decided to go away to the sick-ward.... There were no medicines. I lay around for about four weeks without medicine.... There was a doctor, also a prisoner, a Jewess.... She was not able to help at all. She had no medicaments. None were given to her. And in this way I pulled through the crisis....

Q: And then?
A: I lay around in such a way for four weeks. I did not have anything to drink.... I pleaded for a drink of water. They did not want to give it to me, because the water there was contaminated. It was rusty from the pipes. If one drank that water one became still more sick. I passed the

crisis, and during that time there were three such ... selections. They came to take sick [people] to the crematory. During each time I lived through much deathly fear. My whole method of saving myself was that I hid myself. Christian women were lying there, so I climbed over to the Christians, into their beds, and there I always had the good fortune to hide.

Q: Did the Christian women let you?
A: Yes. There was a Christian woman, a very fine one.... She was also very sick. She was already near death, that Christian woman.

Q: Why was she in the concentration camp?
A: She was there for political causes.... And ... she was not taken. Christians were not taken to the crematory, just Jews.... [Note: Epstein was mistaken on this point.] They had it much better. They received aid from the Red Cross. They received packages from home, and we nothing. We had to look on how they ate. If there was one, a kind one, she would occasionally give us, the sick, something. And that is how I was going on saving myself in the sick-ward. My sickness was very terrible to describe. Complications set in afterwards. I had many boils on the body. I had neglected scabies.... And I had nothing with which to cure myself. At one time I lay already completely dead, that the Christian women cried ... they made an outcry that I am already going to die. So there came up to me a doctor, and she brought some sort of an injection, and she gave it to me.

Q: A Jewish doctor?
A: Yes.... [Note: The SS routinely used Jewish doctors to treat fellow inmates who fell ill. This illustrates the tension that existed between the need to provide slave labor and the ultimate goal of genocide.] After that injection I became a little stronger, and I got out of bed. I nursed the other sick. Much strength I did not have, but I was already able to walk around a little. Three weeks had passed. There came an order to deliver the names of all the sick, everyone who had scabies.... Then one knew that he is for sure going to his death. And I had it, too. I was very worried, and I knew that now has come the moment that I have to go.... I did not sleep at night. I could not eat, because I knew that all my misery, all my suffering was for nothing, because now had come my end.... But it was not so. The same day when they had ordered to make the list of us, they came to that sick-ward where there were only typhus patients, and all were taken out, the entire sick-ward. Not one remained. It was on the night of Yom Kippur.

Q: What was done with them?

A: All were taken, undressed, nude, wrapped in blankets, thrown in the ... truck like sheep, shut the trucks, and driven away in the direction of the crematory. We all went and looked, so we saw how the women [on the trucks] were singing *Kol Nidrei*.... They were singing the *Hatikvah*. When they said good-by, they said, "We are going to death, and you take revenge for us."... They are still pleading to be left. They are young. There was a girl 18 years old, and she was crying terribly. She said that she is still so young, she wants to live, they should leave her, they should give her some medicine to heal her scabies. And nothing helped. They were all taken away.

Q: How come you were not included? You also had scabies.

A: I was not yet in the line.... Everything went according to the line....

Q: How many sick were taken?

A: Four hundred persons. An entire block....

Q: Could the crematory be seen burning?

A: Of course! When we went out at night we saw the entire sky red [from] the glow of the fire. Blood was pouring on the sky. We saw everything. We knew. When we went to the shower hall we saw the clothing of the people who were not any more lying there. The clothing was still there. We recognized the clothing of the people who had left and returned no more.... So that we knew. It was 100 percent! We saw every night the burning crematory. And the fire was so red it was gushing forth blood towards the sky. And we could not help at all. Sometimes, when we would go out at night to relieve ourselves, we saw how illuminated ... how transports were brought with mothers and children. The children were calling to the mothers.

Q: That was in Birkenau. [Note: Birkenau was the extermination division of Auschwitz.]

A: It was to Birkenau that they brought huge transports from Hungary, from Holland, from Greece ... from all over Europe.... And all that was burned in Auschwitz. The children they burned immediately, and from a certain number of people, from thousands, a hundred might be taken out, and they were brought to the camp.... And the rest were burned.... The next morning a German doctor appeared. I became very scared. All who were in the block became scared—we were all sick from malaria—because it was said that the others were taken yesterday and us they will take today.... In the meantime he came with a list, and called out my name and another 12 Jewish names, and to that another 50 Christian women.... And he said that we who are sick with malaria, who show a positive sickness—because there were positive and non-positive.... Because on me was made a ... a ... a ...

Q: A blood test?

A: ...a blood test, and it showed that I had a positive malaria. So they told us that we were going to Majdanek, back to Majdanek.... I did not believe it. In the evening all of us were taken, 70-odd people. We were put on a truck and driven to the train. Riding on the truck all of us believed that we were going to the crematory. We had thought that it will be an open truck, and we will be able to see where we are being taken to, but ultimately it turned out to be quite different. We were taken in a closed one. But [as we were driven] past the guard we heard ... "70-odd prisoners for Majdanek." ... So we already knew that we were being taken to Majdanek.... We were put ... on the station, we were led into a freight car, which is used for transporting cattle. We were all put in. Among [us] were many ethnic German women who had also been imprisoned there in the camp....

Q: Because of what?

A: They were for prostitution.

Q: How did they behave, those women?

A: Very mean. Very mean. They beat so. They hit so. One can't at all imagine.

Q: [Fighting] among themselves?

A: No they beat us, us.... And upon coming into the railroad car they made such a little piece of a ghetto. They put us into a small part of the railroad car.... And for themselves they took the bigger part. And in our part we were squeezed one on top of another. We nearly crushed ourselves to death. En route two girls died. They were very weak. We had no food. And they were full of scabies.... They could not stand it any more. En route ... they were taken down in the middle of the night in Majdanek, and they were dead.... We arrived there, 11 Jews.... When I was there the first time there were still 30,000 Jews.... A few days later we found out that there were Jews here. So one Jew sneaked away ... and came to us. She wanted to see the Jews who had arrived. From them we learned about a most sad misfortune.... On the 3rd of November it was. At 4 in the morning there came down the entire Gestapo with many policemen, with many SS men. They surrounded the entire Majdanek camp and called out all the people. There were 23,000 people.

Q: Not only Jews, everybody...

A: Just the Jews. All the Christians remained in the blocks.... The Jews were taken out and told to form rows of five. The music played very violently and....

Q: Was it Jewish music?

A: No. Polish music. German music.... And the people were told to go up [to the place where] the crematory had been installed. Two days before, 80 men had been taken out. And they were told to dig very large pits. And nobody knew what these pits were for.... Ultimately it turned out that those pits were for the people who had dug them.... They went up in rows of fives, children, mothers, old, young, all went up to the fifth sector [of the camp]. Coming to the graves, there stood sentries with Tommy guns and with machine guns. And they told them all to undress. Young women flung themselves at the sentries and began to plead that he should shoot them with good aim so that they should not suffer.... In the head ... not in the stomach or the leg so that they should suffer.... And the sentries laughed at that and said, "Yes, yes. For you such a death is too good. You have to suffer a little." And not everyone was hit by the bullet. And from them were separated 300 women, those who had remained whom we had met. And these women had to clean up next morning—all those who remained—the shot. They were doused with gasoline and were burned.

Q: In the pits?

A: In the pits. And afterwards they had to take the clothes which everybody recognized from her mother, from her sister, from her children. They cried with bloody tears. They had to take those clothes and sort them. And everybody was thinking, "Why did I not go together with them? Why did we remain alive?"...

Q: How had they been selected?

A: They came to the square where they were standing and picked out the most beautiful women ... the youngest, the healthiest women were separated.... And 55 men.... Those men were prisoners of war....

Q: Were they Christians or Jews?

A: Jews. All Jews.... And these Jews had remained there, these 55 Jews who helped us very much—[we] the women who had returned from Auschwitz.... We were completely non-human [i.e., dehumanized]. We looked like skeletons. And they [the 55 Polish-Jewish POWs] put us on our feet. They helped us very much.

Q: What could they do?

A: They had … in the things that they sorted from the dead was very much gold, very many diamonds, whole bars of gold. This they gave away. There were Christians there.… And the Christians received food packages from home, from the Red Cross. So they [the Polish-Jewish POWs] gave all that away, and they received pieces of bread, whatever one could. And with that they nourished us.

Q: Tell me, you were all searched. They looked and they searched, and one had to undress. How was it possible to find gold on the dead?

A: A Jew had it sewn in their drawers. A Jew had it in the sole of the shoes. A Jew had it concealed in the hair. On a Jew they could never … they searched and they searched, and they did not find.… With that the Jews would save themselves. They always had something on themselves…

Q: And they did not hand it over to the Gestapo?

A: No. It made no difference any more. Who wanted to go to the Gestapo? We knew today we live and tomorrow we die.… It was already all the same. At that time we were not afraid of anything any more, because we knew that our turn was coming now and now we have to perish.… Later, … when we became healthier, we were transferred to the fifth sector and we lived together in one block with these 300 women.…

Q: You had recovered from the scabies?

A: Yes, I became cured, because these men took from the Christians salves which they received from the Red Cross, stole it from them and brought to us…

Q: Why did they bring you over there?… To Majdanek, these who had positive malaria?

A: Because they … it was [just] a whim on their part. Thirty thousand they burned and 13 they led to life.… That is how it was being done by them.… And I had the luck that I was among these 13, and that I had been taken out.… And we could not believe it ourselves.… And we were in Majdanek also thinking any day we will be burned. There are no Jews. To the crematory we saw them bringing every day other … children, women.… They were brought and immediately burned, from Lublin, from all over, from the entire Lublin region. Christians.…

Q: They were not gassed?

A: Gassed first and then burned. If there was no gas, they [the SS] would shoot and then burn [them]. We even heard shots, too, because it was very near.... And we were there together with them and we lived together with them. The women told us about those tragedies. It was so frightful. They cried so terribly that it was.... They would just repeat, "Are there still Jews in the world?" We thought there were no more Jews, only we few have remained. We thought that they have already exterminated all the Jews from Europe, from all Poland. And we told them there is still a camp in Auschwitz, they are still burning Jews every day....

Q: And then?

A: After having been eight months in Majdanek, the second time, an order came: These women, the 300, the women survivors of the action, must go to Auschwitz. And we, the 13, of whom had remained 11, go someplace else, because we have been tattooed, and they [are] not. They began crying very much.... Two days later we were led out to Plaszow.... Near Cracow, a [forced labor] camp.... They had added yet 300 women from Radom.... There were little children, too. Pregnant women were there, and they led us away to Plaszow. Arriving in Plaszow, they took away the small children. They took away the pregnant women. There was a famous hill. They were taken to the top and undressed nude. There were no crematories. They were shot, and afterwards we carried boards and made a fire, and they were all burned.

Q: You yourself carried the...

A: Yes I carried the board! We carried the boards, and we saw how they shot them. If anyone had gold teeth, they pulled the teeth out.

Q: You saw that yourself?

A: Saw myself. I had afterwards still worse [experiences]. Before leaving Plaszow.... It was on the Jewish cemetery. Where the cemetery was once ... they made a camp.... We walked on the tombstones. With the tombstones they made streets. They [the SS] shot people every day at first. A Jew was pushing a barrow with stones. He struggled. So he [the guard] did not like the way he pushed it. He was instantly shot....

Q: And then?

A: While in Plaszow, a transport was brought with small children from Krasnik. I was all alone. I had it very hard, but I remedied it a little. I went to scrub floors in the blocks. People who had [something] gave me a little piece of bread to eat. When they brought the children I took a great liking to a little girl. That little girl was from Krasnik. Her name was Chaykele Wasserman.

Q: How come children were brought without mothers?

A: The mothers had been.... It was like this. They had liquidated the camp. The Russians were approaching Krasnik, so they liquidated the camp. And that child's mother had escaped, and she was shot. And that child had come alone, without a mother, to the lager. And many children—they were all without mothers, because the mothers were immediately taken away. And the children separately. And the children were ... they did not have enough time to take along the mothers. They grabbed the children and ran with them. And the children were brought to Plaszow. I took that little girl. I was with that little girl for four months. That child was very dear to me. I loved it very much. That child could not go anyplace without me. I was thinking I shall live through this war. I will be very happy with such a pretty and smart little girl, because it had hurt me very much that I had lost my brother's children. And I cheered myself up a little with that child....

Q: What did the child do there all day in the camp?

A: The child did nothing. The child went around ... on the street. It was not even called to inspection. Sometimes it went to inspection, and sometimes not.... After a time, they [the guards] came and took away from us all the children, without exception. And that child was very clever. She had a very clever head on her.

Q: How old was she?

A: She was eight years old.... She hid in a latrine, that is in a privy.... All the children were taken away. People came and told me to go there, Chaykele is calling me, she cannot crawl out from the hole. And I went and pulled out the child. The child stank very badly. I ... washed her up, dressed her in other clothes, and brought her to the block. And that child....

Q: You have to excuse me. When a child hides in a latrine ... did the other people know when they went to the latrine...

A: No. When inspection was over [and] the children were taken away, women went to the latrine. This was a women's latrine. So the child began yelling they should call me and I should take her out.... And I was instantly called, and I pulled the child out. When I pulled her out she was overjoyed with me, and she said she was a very clever little girl. "Now I shall already remain alive." You see?... But, alas, it was not so. After a time we were.... The Russians were approaching Plaszow ... and we were again dragged away. I was the second time taken to Auschwitz.... We arrived in the middle of the night.

Q: And the child with you?

A: The child I took along. What will be, will be. I kept the child with me. We came there at night. All night long the child did not sleep. She did not want to eat anything. She just kept asking me, "Does gas hurt?"... If not, [then] she is not afraid. But I cried very much. I said, "Go, you little silly one. There is a children's home. There you will be." She says, "Yes, a children's home! You see, there is the crematory. It burns. There they will burn me." It was very painful for me. I could not stand it. I could not sleep. But suddenly the child fell asleep in my arms. I left the child lying on the ground and went over to some man who worked there in the shower-bath, and I pleaded with him. I lied to him. I said it was my sister's child, and he should see to help me save the child. So he said, "You know what? Tomorrow morning you will all be undressed nude, and you will all be led before the doctor. He will make such a selection. And the child ... you will hide in your rags when you will undress." And that child was very clever. She did not even take off the shoes. She hid in the rags. And I was waiting thus—it was in the morning—till the evening, till the child will come out. And in the evening I saw the child all dressed up.... When they took away all the children ... the child got out from under the rags and came to me. The German doctor had left, and the child came to me.

Q: And who ... how did she wash herself and everything?

A: In the shower-bath there were Jewish women, there where the bath was. She was washed. Clothes there were very plentiful, from the many children [who] had been burned there, thousands, hundreds of thousands of children. She had been dressed very nicely. And the child came to me with great joy. "See," she says, "again I have remained alive. I shall again remain alive."

Q: And how ... you too were left [alive]?

A: I bathed and was sent out.... They beat badly. We were chased out. I waited. It was a huge transport of a few thousand people, so I waited till the last. Everybody had gone to the camp, to the block and I waited for the child to come out.... And together with the child I left for the block. While being in the block, not long, a short time, three days, it was very bad. It was cold. They chased us out bare to inspection. There was nothing to eat.... The cold was so cutting, one could get sick. And the child, too, had to go to inspections.... The child was counted as a grown-up person, but that child had much grief. She was not numbered.... [Note: Only those who were to be kept alive were tattooed.] After the three days there came a doctor.... And he again selected women to be sent to Germany. I was taken away. And that child cried very much. When she saw that I was being taken, she cried very much and screamed, "You are leaving me. Who will be my mother now?" But, alas, I could not help any. I could do nothing with the German. I went away and left the child....

Q: Did you ask them ... they should...
A: I asked, so he said, "If you want to go to the crematory, you can go with the child. And if not, then go away from the child."...

Q: And so you don't know what happened to the child.
A: I don't know anything [about] what happened to the child. I know only one thing: I left. The child said good-bye to me, and I was led away to Bergen-Belsen.... Arriving in Bergen-Belsen, there reigned a terrible hunger. People were dying....

Q: Do you remember in which month, in what year?
A: The last month. In the year 1944, in winter.... I was in Bergen-Belsen three months. The hunger was so great—a terror. We went to the garbage heap and picked the peels from the turnips that were cooked in the kitchen. And if one chanced to grab a turnip.... I was very daring. I did everything. I fought strongly to stay alive. So I got out through the gate, where they were shooting, and grabbed a turnip. And a minute later they shot a girl who grabbed a turnip. I ran into the block.

Q: Did the turnip lay outside the gate?
A: No. Outside the gate there was located the kitchen ... with ... with wires so one would not be able to get near.... So I opened the gate and go in. I risked it. I knew that the moment I grab it the bullet may hit me, but the hunger was stronger than [the fear of] death.... And I went and brought such a turnip. I returned to the block. People, corpses, dead ones, assaulted me, that I should give them [some] too. I shared it with them. We rejoiced. We finished the meal and went to sleep. After having been [there] three months, a German came again, and again selected Jews. I did not know where to [turn]. But I only wanted to go on, on. It always seemed to me here it is no good, there it will be better.

And again I traveled. They collected 200 Hungarian women, 300 Polish women, and we were led away to Aschersleben....

Q: What was there?
A: There was an airplane factory.... There everything had been bombed.... There was a camp commander, a very mean one. There were foreigners.... Prisoners of war ... Dutch, French, Yugoslavian. [Note: After about two months, the camp was evacuated on foot as American forces approached.]

Q: Where did you go?

A: Very terrible was the road. On the way many were shot, those who couldn't walk. We didn't get [anything] to eat. They dragged us from one village to another, from one town to another. We covered 60, 70 kilometers a day.

Q: How many people were you?

A: Five hundred.... Only women. Two hundred fell en route.... I stood and looked how the camp commander took out his revolver, and [to each] one who couldn't walk he said, "Come with me," took her aside and shot her.... We endured all that till they dragged us as far as Theresienstadt.... [Note: Theresienstadt was the model Nazi ghetto, in Czechoslovakia, about 260 km from Aschersleben.] Arriving in Theresienstadt we were completely in tatters. From the blankets we had to cover ourselves with, we made socks, we dressed ourselves. We were very dirty. We were badly treated. We were beaten. They screamed at us. "Accursed swines! You are filthy. What sort of a people are you?"... We were thinking how would they look if they were on our level.... There were only Jews, many Jews from Germany. There were very many old women who were mixed [intermarried], Germans and Jews. They had Jewish sons, SS men.... They were serving Hitler, and she was Jewish; the husband was a German. And that is the reason they remained alive. All old, grey women. And all the children with mothers had been transported to Auschwitz before.... There was very little food. And the Germans prepared a large crematory. They had heard that the front is again approaching. They prepared a large crematory, but they did not have enough time to do it.... [Note: Theresienstadt was liberated on May 8, 1945.] We heard the Russian tanks were here. And we didn't believe it ourselves. We went out, whoever was able. There were a lot of sick who couldn't go. We went out with great joy, with much crying....

Q: And then?

A: But now there began a real death. People who had been starved for so many years.... The Russians had opened all the German storehouses, all the German stores, and they said, "Take whatever you want." People who had been badly starved, they shouldn't have eaten.... And the people began to eat, to eat too much, greedily.... Hundreds of people fell a day. After the liberation, two, three days after the liberation, there had fallen very many people. In about a month, half of the camp had fallen. And nothing could be done about it.... There were stables full with dead. People crawled over the dead. It stank terribly. There was raging a severe typhus. And I, too, got sick. I lay four weeks in the hospital....

(Epstein recovered from typhus and returned to Warsaw where she married and made preparations to emigrate to Palestine.)

The Gypsies

Account 2

Gypsy survivors of the Holocaust, dependent on oral traditions, were far less likely than Jewish survivors to set down their experiences in writing. Several important interviews with Gypsies shed light on their experiences in the camps. In the first, Lani Rosenberg, a German Gypsy from Hamburg, relates his family's fate beginning with the 1938 raids targeting "asocials." This account is excerpted from Rudko Kawczynski's essay "Hamburg soll 'zigeunerfrei' werden" in *Heilen und Vernichten in Mustergau Hamburg* (1984, pp. 49–50). Translated by Sybil Milton.

The eldest in our family were arrested first. My father and older brother were arrested by the police in June 1938 at 5 A.M. In the greatest of haste, my mother asked an attorney to try to free my father and brother. Although the police had no grounds for arresting them, shrugging his shoulders the attorney reported that one couldn't do anything about it. He informed us that they had been taken to Sachsenhausen concentration camp. I wrote petitions for clemency, requesting my father's and brother's release, to Department C2 of the *Reichskriminalpolizeiamt* in Berlin and to the Führer. Eventually, I received a warning from the Hamburg-Eimsbüttel local police to stop annoying the Führer, or I too would also be arrested. Those Sinti that were still free were ordered not to leave the city limits. For starvation wages, I was compelled to do heavy physical labor.

On May 16, 1940, I, my mother, and all my other siblings still in Hamburg were arrested. I asked the police why we were being arrested. They replied that we were being resettled in Poland. We were assembled together with several hundred other Gypsies and brought to a shack near the harbor. Each of us received a red number painted on our skin. The transport to Poland began several days later. We were permitted to take only some of our clothing with us. All money and items of value were confiscated.

After several days travel we arrived in Poland at a place called Belzec. We were immediately received by an SS unit and were separated by age and gender. The SS took no great pains with many of the Gypsies, who were forced to dig their own graves; these Gypsies were then shot and buried. While being beaten we were forced to run to a shack. Later we had to put barbed wire around this hut. Early every morning we had to stand for roll call. Afterwards there were more beatings, we then received our tools, and were forced to run to "work" while again being beaten. The work place was located close to the Russian border. During the first three months of arrest, many of the younger children died of starvation and disease. There was no medical care. I often witnessed how Gypsies were shot, only because they tried to get some water. Once I observed that several 8- to 12-year-old children were compelled to lie on the ground while booted SS men marched over their bodies. It is impossible to detail everything that I experienced during five years in the concentration camps, since words are inadequate to report all of it. I lost eight brothers and sisters as well as my parents under the Nazis. My father was shot someplace near Schwerin shortly before the war ended. ...

Account 3

Like many Jewish victims of the Holocaust, some Gypsies survived by working for the Germans in slave labor and concentration camps. Hugo Franz, a Gypsy musician born in Dresden in 1913, was forced to work in a copper factory during the early part of the war. In 1942 he was deported to Sachsenhausen concentration camp and from there to a series of work camps. His interview appears in Joern-Erik Gutheil et al. *Einer muss ueberleben: Gespraeche mit Auschwitzhaeftlinge 40 Jahre danach* (1984, pp. 50–52). Translated by Sybil Milton.

At the time I was living with my parents in Hamburg. On January 7, 1942, I was arrested by the Gestapo at 5 in the morning. They told me to pack my tooth brush and other toiletries. My mother was told that I would be taken to a concentration camp. ...

At the police station, I had to countersign the protective custody order for my arrest, and I was then imprisoned for about a month until a transport for Oranienburg-Sachsenhausen could be consolidated. Beatings had already started during the transport. We wondered, "What will become of us, and where had we landed?" Everything was utterly new and strange.

We stood in the grim cold in Sachsenhausen for five hours—it was winter—and were then delivered to the Political Department. There an SS Technical Sergeant informed me that since I was a Gypsy, my transfer to this concentration camp was the end of the road for me, that it was a one-way street with no way back out. There, for the first time in my life, I saw shrunken heads like the ones made by headhunters, but these were Gypsy heads. They stood on a sideboard in the Political Department.

We were then taken to a barrack, where every hair on our bodies was shorn and shaven off. We were next taken to the bath, an ice cold shower. We were compelled to hand over all of our clothing and in return received prisoner uniforms—zebra uniforms. I wore size 39 shoes and was given size 43. By this time, we all looked a bit odd. The beating began when we arrived back in the barracks. There were already Sinti prisoners in this camp and I knew a few of them. They had connections to the clothing depot and arranged for me to get half-way decent clothing. A brown triangle had been sewn onto my prison uniform, because I had been classified an antisocial. [The inverted brown or beige triangle was the special marking used to identify Gypsy prisoners; it was frequently replaced by the more common black triangle for Roma and Sinti prisoners reclassified as "asocials" in the concentration camps.]

We were then separated into different work groups. We carried stones that were to be used in construction and had to move everything at double time. We had to carry hundred-weight sacks, two at a time. Anyone not able to do this had signed his own death warrant because SS guards kicked him mercilessly with their rubber boots. Out of a work commando of 100 men, 30 to 40 were often gone by the end of the day...

[In mid-March 1942] we were transferred to work in a rock quarry in Gross Rosen concentration camp; we often worked until midnight on the construction of the camp. We slept four men to a blanket. The windows had not yet been installed in our barracks, and when we awoke in the morning, there was often snow on our blankets.

Our rations were a piece of bread, which had at best 30 percent flour; the rest consisted of ground chestnuts and sawdust. Afternoons, turnips; evenings, coffee. We had to save some of our breakfast bread for evening, and we then got one cube of margarine for 60 people. The result of this bad food was dysentery. For medicine, there was carbon or chalk tablets, and this white substance had to be taken by spoon. The result was zero, nothing whatsoever. The majority of prisoners died. A transport of 5000 to 6000 prisoners was completely used up in eight weeks.

I, too, had typhus and at one point weighed only 78 pounds. A friend managed to have me transferred to the kitchen, where I peeled potatoes. There I did not have to work as hard, and I received a half-liter more to eat per day. That's how I recovered from that disease. Otherwise, typhus meant a death sentence. The crematorium could not keep up. We had mountains of ashes which were used to fertilize fields. Whenever a German prisoner died, the camp notified his relatives. These notices were, of course, preprinted forms. They usually stated that the cause of death was due to a generally weakened condition or heart failure. For 20 marks, the family could receive the ashes of the deceased in an urn....

At Gross Rosen, the Sinti were not housed together in a separate barracks, but you could tell who they were by their triangular marking.... As Gypsies, we could not be appointed to any prisoner posts. I was, however, the only Sinti who kept the barracks register for the *Lagerältesten* [camp elder]. It worked as follows: The block leader, a prisoner, received his assignment from the camp elder, who in turn reported to the SS. The SS appointed the prisoners to clean the barracks. The members of this work crew were responsible for order and cleanliness in the barracks, reporting to the block leader. The SS made it easy for themselves. If anything untoward occurred, punishments descended down the hierarchy; the SS would beat the camp elder, who in turn would beat the barracks elders, then the barracks elder would in turn beat the room elder, and then the room elder would beat the prisoners.

My block elder had been brought up in a juvenile care program, starting in special schools and homes and then in prison. Whenever he wanted to write home, I had to write these letters for him, but never received any benefits for doing this. A German prisoner could become a capo, a room elder, a block elder, or even a messenger to the Political Department. No Sinto could get any of these posts....

I was in Gross-Rosen until 1943 and was then transferred to a satellite camp, a chemical plant owned by BASF at Dyhrenfurth near Breslau. There were 300 prisoners in the small camp at this factory. The factory produced poisonous gas for weapons: bombs, grenades, these were the Führer's last weapons. Many prisoners became unconscious and died while filling these weapons. We were almost blinded by our work, and tiny little pills were placed in our eyes to dilate the iris so we could continue to see. Because we worked with these weapons, we were sworn to secrecy. I was not allowed to tell any of the other prisoners anything about my work. And because I knew these secrets, I had a double sense of despair and hopelessness that the Nazis would not allow me to survive.

When Lodz was liberated by the Russians on January 2, 1945, we were evacuated and had to march 70 kilometers in wooden clogs back to Gross Rosen. Prisoners too exhausted to survive the march were shot. The main camp at Gross Rosen was filled beyond capacity, since all the satellite camps had been reassembled at the main camp. After a brief stop at Gross Rosen, we were marched to Striegau.... I will never forget that march. Women standing along the road threw stones and other objects at us, calling us "pigs." At Striegau we were loaded onto open freight cars, but the locomotive did not arrive and we were forced to march back to Gross Rosen through the night. Two to three hundred prisoners were crammed into a barrack normally assigned to one hundred prisoners; we stood packed together like sardines in a box.

In the middle of the night, the barracks were lit up when the camp came under attack. The Russians had probably learned that the prisoners had been evacuated, but were unaware that the prisoners had been forced to return that night. We pushed the window panes out and sought safety from the shelling outside. We saw many wounded and dead lying everywhere. The next morning the transport to Striegau was reassembled. Every hundred prisoners were placed in open freight cars, seated adjacent to grenades that were tied together. We collected snow from the edge of the train car in order to moisten our lips, since we had not received any water all day. We travelled for six days in those open freight cars from Gross Rosen via Dresden to Litomerice in Czechoslovakia; the latter camp was located four kilometers from Theresienstadt. By then, there were only 13 prisoners left in my car.

We arrived at the camp, a former barracks already occupied by Czech and Polish prisoners. The bunk beds consisted of ten levels of boxes and since the lower tiers were already occupied, a weak prisoner could not climb that high. Our block elder from Gross Rosen arranged that we were sent to a small satellite camp called Elsabe. The prisoners worked 150 meters deep in subterranean mine tunnels completing tank motors for the Elsabe Company of Chemnitz.... After two months there, I learned from a guard that the tunnels were mined and would be blown up along with the prisoners to prevent these motors from falling into enemy hands...

Account 4

Elisabeth Guttenberger, a German Gypsy born in Stuttgart in 1926, was one of the few survivors of the Gypsy family camp in Auschwitz. Well educated, she had the advantage of being assigned to the camp offices. This account has been edited from several published sources and translated by Sybil Milton: H.G. Adler et al., *Auschwitz: Zeugnisse und Berichte* (1984, pp. 131–134); State Museum of Auschwitz-Birkenau, *Memorial Book: The Gypsies at Auschwitz-Birkenau* (1993, vol 2, pp. 1497–1503).

...We were arrested in March 1943. At 6 o'clock in the morning the police came and took us away in a truck. I was then 17. I was deported to Auschwitz together with my parents, four brothers and sisters, a 3-year-old niece, my 80-year-old grandmother, and many other relatives. My other grandmother came somewhat later with her daughter and nine grandchildren....

The first impression I had of Auschwitz was horrible. It was already dark when we arrived. A huge tract of land, although one was able to see only the lights. We had to spend the night on the floor of a huge hall. Early the next morning we had to march into the camp. There, prisoner numbers were tattooed on our arms and our hair was cut off. The clothes, shoes, and the few things we still had with us were taken away. The Gypsy camp was in the Birkenau section, located between the men's camp and the prisoners' infirmary [*Häftlingskrankenbau*]. In this section were 30 barracks which were called blocks. One block served as the toilet for the entire camp. More than 20,000 Gypsies were kept in the rest of the barracks. The barracks had no windows, only air vents. The floor was made out of clay. In one barrack, where there was enough room for perhaps 200 people, 800 or more people were lodged. This way of housing so many people was a horrible martyrdom. My aunt walked next to me. We looked at each other and tears began to roll down our faces.... It was dreadful. The people sat motionless on their plank beds and just stared at us. I thought I was dreaming. I thought I was in hell.

After about 14 days, we were divided into work gangs. With many other women, I was forced to carry heavy stones for construction work in the camp. The men were forced to build the camp road. Even old men, whether they were sick or not, had to work.... Everyone was used. My father was then 61. No one paid any attention to that.... Auschwitz was a death camp.

At that time, the construction of Birkenau had not yet been finished. The worst part was the hunger. The hygienic conditions are barely describable. There was virtually no soap or facilities for washing. When typhus broke out, the sick could not be treated, because there was no medicine. It was hell. One cannot imagine anything more horrifying. First, the children died. They cried day and night for bread. Soon they all starved to death. The children who were born in Auschwitz did not live long either. The only thing the Nazis were concerned with was that the newborn were properly tattooed and registered. Most infants died several days after their births. There was no child care, no milk, no warm water, let alone powder or diapers. The older children, above the age of ten, had to carry rocks for the camp road, despite the fact that starvation caused them to die every day....

In our labor brigade, we had to do everything while running. An SS *Blockführer* accompanied us by bicycle. If a woman tripped, because she was too frail, she was whipped. Many died from those beatings. The Blockführer in charge of the Gypsy camp was an SS Corporal [Ernst August] König; I never heard that he was tried or sentenced after the war. Even today, I could identify him immediately. [König was belatedly arraigned and indicted for murders he had committed in the Birkenau Gypsy camp and after a trial lasting nearly two years was sentenced to life imprisonment in January 1991 in the Siegen District Court. He subsequently committed suicide in prison after his appeal was rejected.]

Early morning roll calls were torture, standing at attention from 6 to 8 in the morning irrespective of weather. Everyone had to assemble for roll call, even the elderly, the children, and the sick. On Sunday, roll calls often lasted until noon, often standing in harsh heat without protective head covering. Many collapsed from heat prostration and infirmities.

After my first month in Auschwitz, a transport with 2000 Russian Gypsies arrived. These poor people were in the camp for only one night. They were sent to the crematoria and gassed the next day. Everyone, however short their stay in Birkenau, asked about the chimneys that produced smoke all night and all day. They were told that people were gassed and burned there. On the evening that the Russian Gypsies were gassed, the barracks were secured and we were forced to remain in our barracks [*Blocksperre*]. At about 9 that evening, trucks arrived at our compound and the Russian Gypsies were forcibly shoved aboard and driven to the crematoria. I secretly witnessed their departure.

I was also an eyewitness to another gassing operation. I had already been assigned to work in camp clerical office and was permitted to walk outside our barracks. The so-called sick camp [*Krankenlager*] was adjacent to our barracks. Jewish and Polish male prisoners were incarcerated there. I observed two trucks driving up to their barracks and the sick were thrown on board. Many could no longer walk and were starved skeletons. A few were naked; others had only a shirt. Before the trucks departed, a few prisoners mustered enough courage to curse their murderers.

After about a half year, I was put to work in a camp clerical office. There I had to file note cards for the transport lists, and was placed in charge of the main men's register for our camp. I had to enter the death notices brought in from the infirmary. I entered thousands of names into that book. I had been in the office for just eight days when a death notice with my father's name arrived. I was paralyzed and tears streamed down my face. At that moment, the door swung open and SS Staff Sergeant Plagge stormed in and screamed, "Why is she blubbering in the corner?" I could not answer. My friend, a clerk named Lilly Weiss, said, "Her father died." In response Plagge said, "We all have to die," and left the office....

The Gypsies also tried to defend themselves against the liquidation of the Gypsy camp. That was a very tragic story. The Gypsies made weapons out of sheet metal. They sharpened the metal into knives. With these improvised weapons and clubs, they tried to defend themselves as best they could. I know an eyewitness, a Polish woman named Zita, who worked across from us and lived through the liquidation of the Gypsy camp. Later, she told me how the Gypsies hit out and defended themselves, because they knew that they were going to be gassed. The resisters were mowed down with machine guns....

In 1944, about 2,000 Gypsies able to perform labor were deported from our compound; about 4,500 people were left behind. These were the elderly, the sick, and those no longer able to perform heavy labor. These people were "liquidated," as the SS called it, during the night of

July 31 to August 1, 1944. Of the 30,000 Gypsies deported to Auschwitz, only about 3,000 survived. I know these figures because I worked in the camp office.

I lost about 30 of my relatives in Auschwitz. Both of my grandmothers died there. An aunt with ten children was there, only two children survived.... My father literally starved to death in the first few months. My older sister contracted typhus and died in 1943. Naturally, malnutrition and hunger were significant factors. Then my youngest brother died at the age of 13. He had to carry heavy rocks until he was an emaciated skeleton. My mother died of starvation several months afterwards. Auschwitz cannot be compared to anything else. To say, "the hell of Auschwitz" is not an exaggeration....

I left the camp ill and am still sick today. I would like to remove the prisoner number tattooed on my lower left forearm. When I wear summer clothing without sleeves, I always cover this number. I have noticed that people stare at this tattooed number and often make malicious and vicious comments, thus always reminding me of the hellish camp experiences....

Account 5

There are few survivor reports about the killing fields of occupied Poland and the Soviet Union, where Jews and Gypsies were executed in forests, drowned in local rivers, and killed inside many ghettos, labor camps, and killing centers. Several eyewitness accounts by local residents are excerpted in Polish post-war regional publications as well as in the materials assembled by post-war Polish judicial authorities. These extracts provide us with some insight about the fate of Gypsies deported from various Polish ghettos to Treblinka or killed in Polish fields and forests. The narrative by Michael Chodz'ko, a former prisoner at the Treblinka labor camp, was initially published in his article "The Gypsies in Treblinka," *Rzeczpospoilta [The Republic]*, 35, (September 6, 1945) and was reproduced in Jerzy Ficowski's book, *Cyganie na polskich drogach: Wydanie trzecie poprawione i rozszerzone [Gypsies on the Roads of Poland]* (1965, pp. 125–126).

In the spring of 1942, Gypsies ... were locked up within the narrow walls of Jewish ghettos. The death penalty was threatened for leaving the ghetto and not wearing the armband with the letter Z [*Zigeuner*, Gypsy]. Until the fall of 1942, Gypsies were hauled off, along with Jews, to the killing centers at Majdanek, Treblinka, and others, where they were killed in the gas chambers, or else shot, and their bodies later burned. Despite the walls and barbed wire closing off the Jewish quarters, groups of Gypsies succeeded in temporarily getting outside the ghettos. The Germans sent Gypsies to the "labor camp" at Treblinka with assurances that they would like it in the camp especially organized for them in the forest.... They arrived in Treblinka to set up "their camp." The march was halted at the edge of the forest which was the place of execution and the grave for hundreds of thousands of people. Trustingly, the crowd sat down in a meadow; they were allowed to light a fire, over which they prepared hot meals. A few hours later the SS arrived, and the men were separated from the women and children. Their possessions and baggage were piled up in one big heap. The men were led off deeper into the forest.... They were forced into a pit a hundred at a time, and then machine-gunned. The Gypsies who were still alive were forced to bury those who had been shot—and who were often only wounded—before they, themselves, were pushed into the pit, and a hundred people more were deprived of their lives in the clatter of machine-gun fire. The bodies were covered with a shallow layer of earth.... When the men were taken away, the Gypsy women did not know what had happened to them, but when they heard the constant gunfire, they began to scream and wail. The Nazis at that point ceased to dissemble: they no longer spoke of a "Gypsy camp" and encouraged the soldiers to begin a brutal massacre. They seized babies from their mothers and killed the infants by bashing their heads against trees. With whips and cudgels the SS covered with blows the women who had been driven insane by the spectacle. The women threw themselves at the soldiers and tried to wrest their babies away. This scene was only brought to an end by salvos of gunfire from the surrounding SS and soldiers. The bodies of the executed women and children were later cleared by other prisoners specially brought in for that purpose; the corpses were taken to graves that had been prepared beforehand in an adjacent forest.

Handicapped People

Account 6

The few patients who survived Operation T-4 were in no position to understand what was happening to them. Evidence of Nazi euthanasia must be drawn from contemporary documents as well as testimony in post-war trials of euthanasia personnel. We begin with testimony in the 1946 trial in Vienna of Dr. Erwin Jekelius, given by parents who had lost children to the killing program. Source: Klamper, *Dokumentationsarchiv des Oesterreichischen Widerstandes* (1991, pp. 114–119), volume 19 of the series Archives of the Holocaust.

Testimony of Leopold Widerhofer:

My daughter, Gerta Widerhofer, was brought to the sanatorium Am Steinhof in 1933 because of schizophrenia. She remained in treatment as a psychiatric patient there.

At the beginning of August 1940, my wife and I heard a rumor during a visit to the Steinhof institution that patients at this institution were being transferred to Germany secretly at night and that they would continue to be taken away in the future. Out of concern for our daughter's life, in mid-August 1940, I personally went to see Dr. Erwin Jekelius, who was then director of the Viennese Health Office, Vienna I, Schottenring 28, in order to inquire about this. After considerable discussion, I attempted to discover whether my daughter was on the list of patients to be transferred. He denied this. I was satisfied with this.

Soon thereafter, I heard in the waiting room of the director's office of the institution Am Steinhof, that my daughter actually was on the list, and Dr. Wilhelm Podhaisky, Vienna 109, XV Baumgartnerhöhe, showed me my daughter's file, which he had already removed to his custody in order to try to save her life. This file was taken out of the records of those individuals who were to be prepared for transport; thus Dr. Podhaisky kept her file.

Dr. Podhaisky later arranged a meeting for me with the Director, Dr. Jekelius, in the waiting room of the executive offices of Am Steinhof; this would have been at the beginning of October 1940. During the nearly one hour discussion between me and the Director, Dr. Jekelius, which Dr. Podhaisky attended on behalf of the patients, Dr. Jekelius said to me twice in the presence of Dr. Podhaisky: "Your daughter must die." He tried to justify this because her disease was incurable. To my excited demand that my daughter, if she must die, would wish to die here at Am Steinhof, rather than be carried off, Dr. Jekelius replied: "Herr Direktor, you probably understand that we cannot allow our staff doctors to be implicated." I replied: "I only know that the patients will really be killed." Dr. Jekelius never responded to this.

The transports with mentally ill patients from Am Steinhof to unknown destinations continued throughout the next weeks. During this time, the two physicians from Steinhof, Dr. Unlauf and Dr. Podhaisky, routinely tried to delay the transports and they rescued my daughter by relocating her to ward 24. When this ward was evacuated at night, they moved my daughter to convalescent ward 20.

The deportations from Steinhof stopped at the end of December 1940. My daughter is still in Am Steinhof today and her condition has improved substantially.

I would also like to add, that acquaintances of mine who likewise had dependents at Am Steinhof, had already received notifications written between September and November 1940 that stated that their sick dependents, who had been transferred from Am Steinhof, had suddenly died of some disease, such as infected tonsils or pneumonia.

I would also like to state that during the subsequent months, children that were difficult to handle arrived in the vacant women's wards and that Dr. Jekelius was named director of the children's department created here.

Testimony of Anny Woedl:

I bore a handicapped child on 24 November 1934 who had difficulties walking and talking and did not develop as he should. It turned out that he understood everything, but that he couldn't speak. Also his legs were obviously too weak to carry him, so that in essence he could not walk. The doctors couldn't really determine if he actually suffered, nor could they decide the cause of his condition. I put him in the institution at Gugging when he was four years old.

I was very concerned about my child when the operation against the "incurably ill, mentally ill, and elderly" began, especially since I knew the Nazi state's position in principle about these matters. When the "operations" were carried out in Vienna, there was anxiety in the population. I was determined to appeal to Berlin in order to save my child or to stop the mechanism. I have described in detail in my petition what I achieved.

The only person who really wanted to help was Dr. Trub, who was employed at Ballhausplatz.

With the exception of Dr. Jekelius, I spoke to no other physicians about this matter. In any case, Dr. Jekelius was fully aware of what was happening and it was unambiguously clear from his remarks that he totally endorsed the entire operation against "life unworthy of life" and that he was prepared to act as the Nazi state demanded. I finally realized that I could not save my child after this conversation. Therefore, I wanted at least to stop my child from being carried off somewhere. I also wanted to spare the child any further pain, if it had to die. For these reasons, I begged Dr. Jekelius, that if the death of my child could not be stopped, that it be quick and painless. He promised me this. I never learned whether he himself carried out the deed, or whether he let someone else do it and in what manner. I saw my child's corpse. I was struck by the look of pain on his face.

On the whole, an individual could not do anything to stop these "actions," as is evident in my case. Most people did not dare try anything, since it was clear that it was much too dangerous. Meanwhile, the killing operations had spread to all sanatoriums and were carried out. I do not know the details. I only know what we heard when things leaked out and what also appeared in the press.

Account 7

As word leaked out about the genocide of the handicapped, government officials took note of its negative impact on public opinion. The following excerpt from a December, 1939 letter written by a judge in Frankfurt am Main to the Ministry of Justice in Berlin may be read as a word of warning to central officials and, perhaps, as a muted protest against extralegal executions. Source: U.S. Nuremberg War Crimes Trials, National Archives Microfilm Publications, M887, Doc 844.

People living near sanatoria and convalescent homes, as well as in adjoining regions, sometimes quite distant, for example throughout the Rhineland, are continually discussing the question whether the lives of incurable invalids should be brought to an end. The vans which take patients from the institutions they occupy to transit stations and thence to liquidation establishments are well-known to the population. I am told that whenever they pass the children call out: "There they go again for gassing." I hear that from one to three big omnibuses with blinds down go through Limburg every day on their way from Weilmünster to Hadamar, taking inmates to the Hadamar liquidation centre. The story goes that as soon as they arrive they are stripped naked, given a paper shirt and immediately taken to a gas-chamber, where they are poisoned with prussic acid and an auxiliary narcotic. The corpses are said to be transferred on a conveyor belt to an incineration chamber, where six are put into one furnace and the ashes then packed into six urns and sent to the relatives. The thick smoke of the incinerators is supposed to be visible every day over Hadamar. It is also common talk that in some cases the heads or other parts of the body are detached for anatomical investigation. The staff employed on the work of liquidation at these institutions is obtained from other parts of the country and the local inhabitants will have nothing to do with them. These employees spend their evenings in the taverns, drinking pretty heavily. Apart from the stories told by the people about these "foreigners," there is much anxiety over the question whether certain elderly persons who have worked hard all their lives and may now in their old age be somewhat feeble-minded are possibly being liquidated with the rest. It is being suggested that even old people's homes will soon be cleared. There is a general feeling here, apparently, that proper legal measures should be taken to ensure that, above all, persons of advanced age and enfeebled mentality are not included in these proceedings.

Account 8

There was nothing muted about the reaction to Operation T-4 of Clemens August Graf von Galen, the Catholic Bishop of Muenster. What follows is part of his thundering sermon of August 3, 1941, copies of which were distributed covertly all over Germany. It inspired rage among the Nazi leaders, but they knew that any reprisal against a man of Galen's moral stature would disrupt the home front in the middle of the war. Instead Galen's castigation helped to precipitate Hitler's order stopping the killing program (while in reality only disguising it more cleverly). Source: Klee, *Dokumente zur Euthanasie* (1985). Reprinted with permission.

Devout Christians! A pastoral message of the German bishops of June 26, 1941, which was read in all Catholic churches on July 6, says: "According to the Catholic moral code there are some commandments which need not be kept if their observance would involve great difficulties. But there are others, holy obligations of our moral consciousness which we have to fulfill even at the cost of our lives. Never, under any circumstances, may a human being kill an innocent person outside of war or in just self-defense." On July 6 I already had occasion to add to the words of this universal pastoral message the following explanation: For the past months we have heard reports from care and residential institutions for mental patients that patients who had been ill for a long time and who appear to be incurable have been removed forcibly on orders from Berlin. Relatives are being notified a short time afterwards that the corpse has been cremated and that they can claim the ashes. There is a suspicion bordering on definite knowledge that these numerous unexpected deaths among psychiatric patients are not due to natural causes but have been intentionally brought about. The philosophy behind this is the assumption that so-called unworthy lives can be terminated, innocent human beings killed if their lives have no value for the nation and the state. This is a terrible doctrine that seeks to justify the murder of innocent people and allows the killing of invalids who can no longer work, cripples, incurable patients, and the feeble elderly.

We have heard from reliable sources that lists have been made of such patients who will be removed from the care and residential institutions in the province of Westphalia and shortly afterwards killed. The first transport left the Marienthal institution near Münster in the course of the past week.

German men and women! Paragraph 211 of the criminal code is still in force. It states, "Whosoever intentionally kills a person will be punished for murder by death if he has done it with premeditation."

To protect those who intentionally kill those poor people, members of our families, from legal punishment, patients who have been designated to die are being removed from their home institutions to far-away facilities. Some illness is given as a cause of death. Since the corpse is immediately cremated neither relatives nor the criminal police can ascertain what the cause of death was. But I have been assured that neither the Ministry of the Interior nor the agency of Dr. Conti, the surgeon general, denies that a large number of psychiatric patients have been intentionally killed in Germany and will be killed in the future.

Paragraph 139 of the criminal code states, "Whosoever becomes aware of the plan for a capital offense and does not bring it to the attention of the authorities or the threatened person will be punished." When I heard of the plan to remove patients from Marienthal and to kill them, I filed the following charges by letter with the prosecutor of the court in Münster and the president of police in Münster: "According to reports a large number of patients, so-called unproductive citizens, of the provincial care institution of Marienthal near Münster have been transferred in the course of this week to the Eichberg institution to be intentionally killed as has happened in other institutions according to general belief. Since such a procedure is not only contrary to the divine and natural moral code but has to be punished by death according to paragraph 211, I herewith dutifully raise charges according to paragraph 139 of the criminal code and ask that the threatened citizens be immediately protected through prosecution of the agencies which organize the transport and the murder and that I be notified of whatever has been done." I have not received any information on intervention by the state prosecutor or the police.

I had previously lodged a protest on July 26 with the provincial administration of Westphalia which is responsible for the institutions to which patients have been entrusted for care and cure. It was in vain. I have heard that 300 persons have been removed from the residential care Wartstein institution.

Now we have to expect that these poor defenseless patients will be murdered in due time. Why? Not because they have committed a heinous crime, not because they attacked the caregiver in a way which would have forced him to defend his own life in justified self-defense. Are these cases in which killing is allowed and even necessary, besides killing of the enemy in a just war? No, these hapless patients have to die not for any of these reasons but because they have become unworthy to live—according to these opinions they are "unproductive citizens." The judgment holds that they cannot produce any goods; they are like an old machine which does not run anymore, they are like an old horse which has become lame and cannot be cured, they are like a cow which has ceased to give milk. What does one do with such an old machine? One wrecks it. What does one do with a lame horse, with unproductive cattle? No, I do not want to labor the comparison, justified and illuminating as it would be. We are not dealing with machines, or horses, or cows, whose only destiny is to serve people, to produce goods for human beings. They can be wrecked, they can be slaughtered when they can no longer serve their purpose. No, these are human beings, our fellow citizens, our brothers and sisters.

Poor people, sick people, unproductive people, so what. But have they forfeited their right to live? Do you, do I have a right to live only as long as we are productive, as long as others recognize us as being productive? If the principle is established and applied that "unproductive fellow citizens" can be killed, woe to all of us when we get old and feeble. If it becomes permissible to kill unproductive people, woe to the invalids who invested and sacrificed and lost their energies and sound bones during their working careers. If unproductive fellow citizens can be eliminated by force, woe to our brave soldiers who return to their homeland severely injured, as cripples, as invalids. Once it becomes legal for people to kill "unproductive" fellow citizens—even if at presently only our poor defenseless mentally ill are concerned—then the basis is laid for murder of all unproductive people, the incurable, the invalids of war and work, of all of us when we become old and feeble.

All that is necessary is another secret decree that the procedure tested with mental patients is to include other "unproductive persons," is to be applied to patients with incurable lung disease, to the feeble elderly, the disabled workers, to severely injured veterans. Nobody would be safe anymore. Some commission can put him on the list of the "unproductive." And no police will protect him and no court prosecute his murder and punish the murderer. Who could still trust his physician? Maybe he would report the patient as "unproductive" and would be ordered to kill him? It is inconceivable what depraved conduct, what suspicion will enter family life if this terrible doctrine is tolerated, adopted and carried out. Woe to humanity, woe to the German people if God's holy command "Thou shalt not kill" is not only transgressed but if this transgression is both tolerated and carried out without punishment.

I will give you an example of what happened today. In Marienthal there was a man about 55 years old, a farmer in a village in the area of

Minister—I know his name—who had been suffering from episodes of mental derangement for some years and who had been brought to the Marienthal care and residential institution. He was not really a psychiatric case; he was able to receive visitors and was always happy when his relatives came. Just two weeks ago he was visited by his wife and one of his sons who was home on leave from the front. The son dotes on his father. Saying farewell was difficult, since nobody knows if the son will return and see his father again because he may be killed fighting for his fellow citizens. The son, the soldier, will certainly not see his father again, who has meanwhile been placed on the list of "unproductive" people. A relative who wanted to visit the father this week in Marienthal was sent away with the information that the patient had been transferred on orders of the Ministry for Defense. The destination was unknown but the relatives would be informed in a few days. What will this information contain? The same as in other cases? That the person died, was cremated, and that the ashes could be claimed after payment of a fee? The soldier who fights and risks his life for fellow German citizens will not see his father again on this earth because fellow German citizens in his own country have killed him.

References

Adler, H.G., Lingens Ella, & Langbein, Hermann (1984). *Auschwitz: Zeugnisse und Berichte* (3rd edn.). Hamburg: Europäische Verlagsanstalt.

Bartov, Omer (2003). *Germany's war and the Holocaust*. Ithaca, NY: Cornell University Press.

Bauer, Yehuda (1979). *The Jewish emergence from powerlessness*. Toronto, ON: University of Toronto Press.

Bauer, Yehuda (2001). *Rethinking the Holocaust*. New Haven, CT: Yale University Press.

Berger, Leslie (1988). The long-term psychological consequences of the Holocaust on the survivors and their offspring. In Randolph L. Braham (Ed.) *The psychological perspectives of the Holocaust and of its aftermath* (pp. 175–221). Boulder, CO: Social Science Monographs.

Binion, Rudolph (1976). *Hitler among the Germans*. New York: Elsevier.

Boder, David (1949). *I did not interview the dead*. Urbana, IL: University of Illinois Press.

Browning, Christopher R. (1992). *Ordinary men: Reserve Police Battalion 101 and the final solution in Poland*. New York: HarperCollins.

Browning, Christopher R. (2004). *The origins of the final solution*. Lincoln, NE: University of Nebraska Press.

Crowe, David M. (2007). *A history of the Gypsies of Eastern Europe and Russia*. New York: Palgrave Macmillan.

Fein, Helen (1979). *Accounting for genocide: National responses and Jewish victimization during the Holocaust*. New York: Free Press.

Ficowski, Jerzy (1965). *Cyganie na polskich drogach: Wydanie trzecie poprawione i rozszerzone* (3rd edn.). Cracow and Wroclaw: Wydawnictwo Literackie.

Friedlander, Henry (1995). *The origins of Nazi genocide: From euthanasia to the final solution*. Chapel Hill, NC: University of North Carolina Press.

Goldhagen, Daniel Jonah (1996). *Hitler's willing executioners*. New York: Alfred A. Knopf.

Gross, Jan T. (2001). *Neighbors: The destruction of the Jewish community in Jedwabne, Poland*. Princeton, NJ: Princeton University Press.

Gutheil, Joern-Erik et al. (Eds.) (1984). *Einer muss ueberleben: Gespraeche mit Auschwitzhaeftlinge 40 Jahre danach*. Dusseldorf: Der Kleine Verlag.

Gutman, Yisrael, & Krakowski, Shmuel (1986). *Unequal victims: Poles and Jews during World War Two.* New York: Holocaust Library.

Hancock, Ian (2004). Romanies and the Holocaust: A Re-evaluation and overview. In Dan Stone (Ed.), *The historiography of the Holocaust* (pp. 383–396). New York: Palgrave Macmillan.

Hilberg, Raul (2003). *The destruction of the European Jews.* Three volumes. New Haven, CT and London: Yale University Press.

Katz, Steven (1994). *The Holocaust in historical context.* New York: Oxford University Press.

Kawczynski, Rudko (1984) Hamburg soll "zigeunerfrei" werden. In Angelika Ebbinghaus, Heidrun Kaupen-Haas, & Karl Heinz Roth (Eds.) *Heilen und Vernichten in Mustergau Hamburg* (pp. 49–50). Hamburg: Konkret Literatur Verlag.

Klamper, Elisabeth (Ed.) (1991). *Dokumentationsarchiv des Oesterreichischen Widerstandes.* New York and London: Garland.

Klee, Ernst (1983). *Euthanasie im NS-Statt: Die Vernichtung lebensunwerten Lebens.* Frankfurt: S. Fisher.

Klee, Ernst (Ed.) (1985). *Dokumente zur Euthanasie.* Frankfurt: Fischer Taschenbuch.

Lewy, Guenter (2000). *The Nazi persecution of the Gypsies.* Oxford: Oxford University Press.

Lukas, Richard C. (1986). *The forgotten Holocaust: The Poles under German occupation, 1939–1944.* Lexington, KY: University Press of Kentucky.

Margalit, Gilad (2002). *Germany and its Gypsies.* Madison: University of Wisconsin Press.

Milton, Sybil (2001). "Gypsies" as social outsiders in Nazi Germany. In Robert Gellately & Nathan Stoltzfus (Eds.) *Social outsiders in Nazi Germany* (pp. 212–232). Princeton, NJ and Oxford: Princeton University Press.

Mueller-Hill, Benno (1988). *Murderous science.* New York: Oxford University Press.

Novick, Peter (1999). *The Holocaust in American life.* Boston, MA: Houghton Mifflin.

Phayer, Michael (2000). *The Catholic Church and the Holocaust, 1930–1965.* Bloomington, IN: Indiana University Press.

Pohl, Dieter (2004). Contemporary responses to the Shoah in Germany and Eastern Europe. In Konrad Kwiet & Juergen Matthaeus (Eds.) *Contemporary responses to the Holocaust* (pp. 19–36). Westport, CT and London: Praeger.

Roth, John K., & Berenbaum, Michael (1989). *Holocaust: Religious and philosophical implications.* New York: Paragon House.

Rubinstein, William D. (1997). *The myth of rescue.* London: Routledge.

State Museum of Auschwitz-Birkenau (1993). *Memorial book: The Gypsies at Auschwitz-Birkenau* (2 vols.). Munich and London: K.G. Saur Verlag Gmbh & Co.

Trunk, Isaiah (1972). *Judenrat: The Jewish councils in Eastern Europe under Nazi occupation.* New York: Macmillan.

Waite, Robert G.L. (1977). *The psychopathic god, Adolf Hitler.* New York: Basic Books.

Wyman, David (1984). *The abandonment of the Jews: America and the Holocaust, 1941–1945.* New York: Pantheon.

Zimmermann, Michael (2007). Jews, Gypsies and Soviet prisoners of war: Comparing Nazi persecutions. In Roni Stauber & Raphael Vago (Eds.) *The Roma: A minority in Europe* (pp. 31–54). Budapest and New York: Central European University Press.

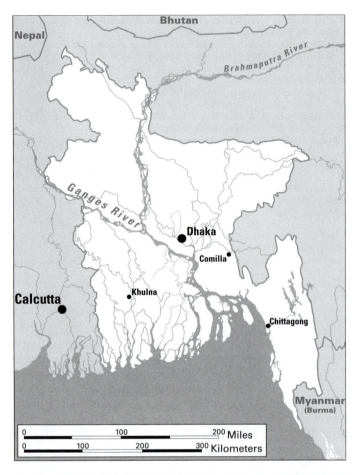

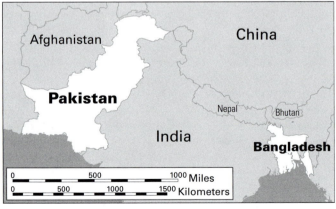

Map 7.1 Bangladesh

CHAPTER 7

Genocide in Bangladesh

ROUNAQ JAHAN

Introduction

The birth of Bangladesh in 1971 was a unique phenomenon in that it was the first nation-state to emerge after waging a successful liberation war against a postcolonial state, Pakistan. The partition of India in 1947 on the basis of religion created a single, independent state of Pakistan, carved out of two primarily Muslim majority territories in the Western and Eastern parts of India, separated by 1,600 k. However, over the years, disparities and divisions started emerging between the Eastern and Western parts of Pakistan (Jahan, 1972). The Muslims in East and West Pakistan were divided by language, ethnicity, and culture. Though the Bengali Muslims of East Pakistan comprised the majority of the population, their language and culture were threatened by the non-Bengali ruling elites who belonged to West Pakistan. The Bengalis were politically excluded as the country was ruled by either non-elected civilian leaders or military dictators from West Pakistan. East Pakistan was also economically exploited as resources were transferred from East to West Pakistan (Sobhan, 1962; Rahman, 1968).

In 1970 the Awami League (AL) led by the Bengali nationalist leader *Bangabandhu* Shiekh Mujibur Rahman (Sheikh Mujib), won an overwhelming victory in the Pakistan general election, the first free election held in the country. But the West Pakistan-based leadership refused to hand over power. Instead, on March 25, 1971, they arrested Shiekh Mujib and launched a military campaign throughout East Pakistan. This triggered the declaration of independence of Bangladesh on March 26, 1971, and the start of a national liberation war which received logistical support from India. The liberation war reached its culmination in a

249

full-scale conventional war between Pakistan and the joint forces of India and Bangladesh. Ultimately, Pakistan surrendered to the joint forces on December 16, 1971.

The nine-months-long liberation war in Bangladesh in 1971 drew world attention because of the genocide committed by the Pakistani armed forces, which, with the support of local militant groups, conducted widely documented massacres, tortures, rapes, disappearances, destruction of property, and forced displacements (Loshak, 1971; Mascarenhas 1971; Schanberg 1971; Coggin, Shepherd, & Greenway, 1971). Newspaper reports, testimonies before the U.S. Congress and other studies published during 1971 and afterwards describe in detail many of the atrocities. The declassified documents of the U.S. government show that the U.S. government officials serving in East Pakistan in 1971 used the term "genocide" to describe the events they had knowledge of at that time and/or were witnessing first-hand (Blood telegram, 1971, published in Gandhi, 2002).

The Pakistani military attacks targeted the Bengali nationalists with a particular focus on selected groups such as the students, intellectuals, and the Hindu community. Estimates of the number of victims vary. Bangladesh authorities claim that nearly three million people were killed; approximately 200,000 girls and women were raped; 10 million took refuge in India, and another 30 million were displaced within the country.

After independence, the new government in Bangladesh made attempts to bring the perpetrators of these atrocities to justice. But internal and international pressures prevented that from happening. However, the demand for justice and accountability were persistently raised by civil society groups within Bangladesh. Finally, in the 2008 parliamentary elections impunity became a major campaign issue and the AL, which won an overwhelming victory, promised to prosecute these crimes. In 2009 Bangladesh established an International Crimes Tribunal (ICT), a domestic court with a mandate to prosecute Bangladeshi collaborators involved in the 1971 atrocities. The ICT is conducting an investigation and has begun to issue arrest warrants of alleged suspects. In 2010, four suspects were arrested. These recent actions of the Bangladesh government have received international support. At the same time, the government has been advised to ensure that this justice meets international standards (ICT Briefing, July 2010).

This chapter briefly addresses the following questions: What were the historical forces and trends that led to the genocide? How was the genocide committed? Who committed the genocide? What were the responses to the genocide? What has been the impact of the genocide? What are the contestations about the genocide? And, finally, why is the Bangladesh case important to understanding the complexities of genocide?

Historical Forces and Trends Leading to the Genocide

The Pakistan government's military action and genocide in Bangladesh caught outside observers as well as the Bengali nationalists by surprise. After all, the Bengali nationalists were not involved in any armed struggle prior to March 25, 1971. They were essentially waging a peaceful constitutional movement for democracy and autonomy. Their only crime, as U.S. Senator Edward Kennedy observed, appeared to have been to win an election (Malik, 1972).

A brief analysis of Pakistan's history from 1947 till 1971 illustrates the forces and trends that led to military action and genocide in Bangladesh. Soon after the creation of Pakistan, unelected civil–military bureaucratic elites from West Pakistan monopolized state power and started behaving like colonial masters toward the Bengalis in East Pakistan. The Pakistani rulers threatened the linguistic and cultural identity of the Bengalis. They thwarted all attempts of democratic rule to keep the Bengalis, who were the majority of the population, from gaining control of political decision-making positions (Jahan, 1972). The Bengalis had little representation in the Pakistani military as the British colonialists did not recruit Bengalis in the military, considering them as a "non-martial" race. The Pakistan military, composed of mainly Punjabis and Pathans, imbibed this British colonialist image of Bengalis as "non-martial," a physically weak race not interested in serving or unable to serve in the army (Marshall, 1959). The following remarks of General Ayub Khan (1967), Pakistan's first military dictator (1958–1968), about the Bengalis in his memoirs reflect the typical attitude of the Pakistani ruling elites:

> East Bengalis probably belong to the very original Indian races... They have been and still are under considerable Hindu cultural and linguistic influence.... They have all the inhibitions of down trodden races.... Their popular complexes, exclusiveness, suspicion and ... defensive aggressiveness ... emerge from this historical background. (p. 187)

The conflict between Bengalis in East Pakistan and West Pakistan-based non-Bengali rulers first started over the issue of Bengali language and culture. Though the Bengalis comprised 54% of Pakistan's population, in 1948 the ruling elites declared their intention to make Urdu, which was the language of only 7% of the population, the sole state language. Bengali students immediately protested the decision and launched a movement that continued for the next eight years, until the Pakistan Constitution, adopted in 1956, recognized both Bengali and Urdu as state languages (Ahmad, 1967).

The Bengalis had to defend not only the right to practice their own language, but other creative expressions of their culture such as literature, music, dance, and art. The Pakistani ruling elites looked upon Bengali language and culture as too "Hindu leaning" and made repeated attempts to "cleanse" it from Hindu influence (Umar, 1966; 1967; 1969). First, in the 1950s, attempts were made to force Bengalis to substitute Bengali words with Arabic and Urdu words. Then, in the 1960s, state-controlled media such as television and radio banned songs written by Rabindra Nath Tagore, a Bengali Hindu, who won the Nobel Prize in 1913 and whose poetry and songs were equally beloved by Bengali Hindus and Muslims. The attacks on their language and culture as "Hindu leaning" alienated the Bengalis from the state-sponsored Islamic ideology of Pakistan, and as a result the Bengalis started emphasizing a more secular ideology and outlook.

The Bengali nationalist movement was also fueled by a sense of economic exploitation. Though jute, the major export-earning commodity, was produced in East Pakistan, most of the economic investments took place in West Pakistan. A systematic transfer of resources took place from East to West Pakistan, creating a growing economic disparity and a feeling among the Bengalis that they were being treated as a colony by Pakistan (Sobhan, 1962; Rahman, 1968; Jahan, 1972).

In the 1950s and 1960s, a group of Bengali economists carefully documented the process of economic disparity and marshaled arguments in favor of establishing a "two-economy" system in Pakistan (Sobhan, 1970). The movement toward autonomy initiated in the 1950s culminated in the famous Six-Point Program of 1966, which not only rejected the central government's right of taxation, but demanded that the power to tax and establish trade and commercial relations, including the establishment of separate accounts of foreign exchange earning, be placed in the hands of the two provincial governments of East and West Pakistan.

However, it was the barriers erected by the powers that be that both prevented the Bengalis from participating in the political process and resulted in their exclusion from state power that gradually drove the Bengalis to demand autonomy, and finally to demand self-determination (Jahan, 1972). From the beginning, the Bengalis demanded democracy with free and regular elections, a parliamentary form of government, and freedom of political parties and the media. But the ruling elites in Pakistan hindered every attempt at instituting democracy in the country (Callard, 1957; Sayeed, 1967). In 1954 a democratically elected government in East Bengal was dismissed within 90 days of taking power. A constitution was adopted in 1956, after nine years of protracted negotiations, only to be abrogated within two years by a military coup. In 1958, just before the first nationally scheduled election, the military took direct control of the government. This was out of fear that the Bengalis might dominate in a democratically elected federal government.

The decade of the 1960s saw the military rule of General Ayub Khan. It was eventually toppled in 1969 as a result of popular mass movements in both wings (East and West) of Pakistan. However, after the fall of Ayub, another military dictator, General Yahya Khan, who was the commander-in-chief of the armed forces, took charge of the government. The Yahya regime acceded to a number of key demands of the Bengali nationalist movement, including the holding of a free democratic national election on the basis of one person, one vote. The first free democratic national elections held in Pakistan in 1970, two decades after the birth of the country, resulted in a sweeping victory for the Bengali nationalist party, the AL. The election results gave the AL not only total control over their own province, but also a majority nationally and a right to form the federal government.

Once again, the ruling elites in Pakistan took recourse to unconstitutional measures to prevent the Bengalis assuming state power. On March 1, 1971, General Yahya postponed indefinitely the scheduled March 3 session of parliament. This, in turn, threw the country into a constitutional crisis. The AL responded by launching an unprecedented non-violent, non-cooperation movement, which resulted in the entire administration of then East Pakistan coming to a virtual standstill. Even the Bengali civil and military officials complied with the non-cooperation movement. The movement demonstrated that the Bengali nationalists had total allegiance and support of the Bengali population.

The Yahya regime initiated political negotiations with the AL, but at the same time flew thousands of armed forces in from West to East Pakistan, thus preparing for military action. On March 25, 1971, General Yahya abruptly broke off the negotiations and unleashed a massive armed strike, which was named Operation Searchlight. In two days of uninterrupted military operations, in the capital city of Dhaka, hundreds of ordinary citizens were killed; houses and property were destroyed; and the leader of the AL, *Bangabandhu* Sheikh Mujibur Rahman, was arrested. The army also launched armed attacks in Chittagong, Comilla, Khulna, and other garrison cities. Simon Dring, a reporter with the *Daily Telegraph*, London, and Michel Laurent, an Associated Press photographer, escaped the Pakistani dragnet and roamed Dhaka and the countryside. On March 28 they reported that the loss of life had reached 15,000 in the countryside. On the Dhaka University campus, 17 professors and some 200 students were killed in cold blood (Loshak, 1971, pp. 88–126).

One of the main reasons behind the atrocities was to terrorize the population into submission. The Pakistani military regime calculated that since the Bengalis had no previous experience in armed struggle, they would be frightened and crushed in the face of overwhelming fire power, mass killings, and destruction. Another factor that influenced the Pakistani military's action was their assumption, as previously noted, of racial superiority as a "martial race." Cleansing of Bengali Muslims from Hindu influence was a goal often repeated by the Pakistani military during the 1971 genocide.

The genocide in Bangladesh, which started with the Pakistani military operation against unarmed citizens on the night of March 25, continued unabated for nearly nine months until the Bengali nationalists, with the help of the Indian army, succeeded in liberating the country from Pakistani occupation forces on December 16, 1971. The atrocities committed by the Pakistani army were widely reported by the international press during 1971 (Loshak, 1971; Mascarenhas, 1971; Schanberg, 1971; Jenkins, Clifton, & Steele, 1971; Coggin et al., 1971).

From the eyewitness accounts documented during and immediately after the genocide in 1971, as well as those published over the last 40 years, it is possible to analyze the major features of the Bangladesh genocide—how it was committed and who was involved, both the perpetrators and the victims in the genocide.

How was the Genocide Committed?

On March 25, 1971, as the Pakistani government initiated military action in Bangladesh, a number of sites and groups of people were selected as targets of attack. In Dhaka, for example, the university campus, the headquarters of the police and the Bengali paramilitia, slums and squatter settlements, and Hindu-majority localities, all were selected as special targets. The Pakistani ruling elites believed that the leadership of the Bengali nationalist movement came from the intellectuals and students; that the Hindus and the urban *lumpenproletariat* were the main supporters; and that the Bengali police and army officials could be potential leaders in any armed struggle. In the first two days of army operations in Dhaka, hundreds of unarmed people were killed on the university campus, and in the slums and the old city where Hindus lived. Eyewitness accounts at the end of this chapter provide chilling insights into the killings on the Dhaka university campus.

The news of the Dhaka massacres immediately spread to the rest of the country. Instead of cowing the unarmed Bengalis into submission, which was ostensibly the intention of the Pakistani army in initiating the brutal killings, nationalist sentiments were inflamed. On March 26, 1971, within 24 hours of the armed crackdown in Dhaka, the independence of Bangladesh was declared over the radio from the city of

Chittagong on behalf of the AL and its leader, *Bangabandhu* Sheikh Mujibur Rahman.

Spontaneous resistance was organized in all the cities and towns of the country. The AL politicians, Bengali civilian administration, police, army, students, and intellectuals constituted the leadership of the resistance. This first phase of the liberation war was, however, amateurish and uncoordinated and only lasted approximately six weeks. By the middle of May, the Pakistani army was successful in bringing the cities and towns under their control, though the villages remained largely "liberated" areas.

In occupying one city after another, the Pakistani army used the superiority of its fire and air power to its advantage. These operations also involved massive killings of civilians and wanton looting and destruction of property. The leadership of the resistance generally left the scene prior to the Pakistani army's arrival. They took refuge either in India or in the villages. But, in any case, the Pakistani army engaged in killings and burnings in order to terrorize the civilian population. Again, Awami Leaguers, students and intellectuals, civilian and army officers, and Hindus were selected as targets of attack (Malik, 1972). The army's campaign against the cities and towns not only led to massive civilian casualties; it also resulted in a large-scale dislocation of people. Nearly 10 million people—Hindus as well as Muslims—took refuge in neighboring India, and approximately 30 million people from the cities took refuge in the villages. Government offices, educational institutions, and factories were virtually closed.

The second phase of the liberation war (from mid-May to September) was a period of long-term planning for both the Bengali nationalists and the Pakistani government. The Bengali nationalists established a government-in-exile and undertook external publicity campaigns in support of their cause. They also recruited nearly 100,000 young men as freedom fighters who underwent military training and undertook guerrilla operations inside Bangladesh. The Pakistani army essentially dug into their own strongholds during this time, with periodic operations in rural areas to punish the villagers for harboring freedom fighters. The army also engaged in large-scale looting and raping of girls and women.

In fact, systematic and organized rape was the special weapon of war used by the Pakistani army during the second phase of the liberation struggle. During the first phase, young able-bodied males were targeted for death; during the second phase, girls and women became the targets of Pakistani aggression. During army operations, girls and women were raped in front of close family members in order to terrorize and inflict racial slander. Girls and women were also abducted and repeatedly raped and gang-raped in special camps run by the army near army barracks. Many of the rape victims either were killed or committed suicide. Altogether, it is estimated that approximately 200,000 girls and women were raped during the 1971 genocide (Brownmiller, 1981). An eyewitness account of the rape camps organized by the Pakistani army is included in this chapter.

All through the liberation war, able-bodied young men were suspected of being actual or potential freedom fighters. Thousands were arrested, tortured, and killed. Eventually, cities and towns became bereft of young males who either took refuge in India or joined the liberation war. During the second phase, another group of Bengali men in the rural areas (those who were coerced or bribed to collaborate with the Pakistanis) fell victim to the attacks of Bengali freedom fighters.

The third phase of the liberation struggle (from October till mid-December) saw intensified guerrilla action and finally a brief conventional war between Pakistan and the combined Indian and Bangladeshi forces, which ended with the surrender of the Pakistani army on December 16, 1971 (Palit, 1972; Ayoob & Subrahmanyan, 1972). In the last week of the war, when their defeat was virtually certain, the Pakistani government engaged in its most brutal and premeditated genocidal campaign. In order to deprive the new nation of its most talented leadership, the Pakistani military decided to kill the most respected and influential intellectuals and professionals in each city and town. Between December 12 and 14, selected intellectuals and professionals were abducted from their houses and murdered. Many of their names were later found in the diary of Major-General Rao Forman Ali, advisor to the Martial Law Administrator and Governor of occupied Bangladesh (Malik, 1972).

The victims of the 1971 genocide were, thus, first and foremost Bengalis. Though Hindus were especially targeted, the majority of the victims were Bengali Muslims—ordinary villagers and slum dwellers—who were caught unprepared during the Pakistani army's spree of wanton killing, rape, and destruction. As previously mentioned, the Pakistani ruling elites identified certain groups as their special enemies—students and intellectuals, Awami Leaguers and their supporters, and Bengali members of the armed forces and the police. However, many members of these targeted groups went into hiding or into exile in India after the initial attack. As a result, the overwhelming majority of the victims were defenseless, ordinary poor people who stayed behind in their own houses and did not suspect that they would be killed, raped, taken to prison, and tortured simply for the crime of being born a Bengali.

The sheltered and protected life of women, provided by the Bengali Muslim cultural norm, was virtually shattered in 1971. Thousands of women were suddenly left defenseless and forced to fend for themselves as widows and rape victims. The rape victims were particularly vulnerable. Though they were casualties of the war, many of them were discarded by their own families as a way for the latter to avoid shame and dishonor (Brownmiller, 1981; Jahan, 1973b).

Who Committed the Genocide?

The Pakistani government (the Yahya regime) was primarily responsible for the genocide. Not only did it prevent the AL and Sheikh Mujibur Rahman from forming the federal government, but it opted for a military solution to a constitutional crisis. In doing so, it decided to unleash a brutal military operation in order to terrorize the Bengalis. Yahya's decision to put General Tikka Khan (who had earned the nickname of "Butcher of Baluchistan" for his earlier brutal suppression of Baluchi nationalists in the 1960s) in charge of the military operation in Bangladesh was an overt signal of the regime's intention to launch a genocide.

The Pakistani military leaders, however, were not the only culprits. The political parties (e.g., the Pakistan People's Party [PPP]) also played an important role in instigating the army to take military action in Bangladesh. The PPP and its leader, Zulfikar Ali Bhutto, supported the army action all through 1971 (Bhutto, 1971; Jahan, 1973a).

There were also Bengalis who collaborated with the Pakistani regime. During the second phase of the liberation war, the Pakistani government deliberately recruited Bengali collaborators. Many of the Islamist political parties and groups such as the Muslim League and the Jamaat-e-Islami (JI), who were opposed to the AL, collaborated with the army. Peace committees were formed in different cities and localities and under their auspices *rajakars* (armed volunteers) were raised and given arms to counter the freedom fighters. Two armed vigilante groups (Al Badr and Al-Shams) were trained and took the lead in the arrest and killing of the intellectuals during December 12–14, 1971. Some Bengali intellectuals were also recruited to conduct propaganda in favor of the Pakistanis.

The non-Bengali residents of Bangladesh—the Biharis—were the other group of collaborators. Many of them acted as informants and participated in riots in Dhaka and Chittagong. Biharis, however, also became victims of acts of violence committed by Bengalis.

The Response to the Genocide

The response to the genocide can be analyzed at various levels. At the official level, world response toward the 1971 genocide was determined by geopolitical interests and major power alignments. Officially, from the beginning, India took cognizance of the genocide and supported Bangladesh. The Soviet Union—India's major superpower ally at the time—and other Eastern Bloc countries were also supportive of Bangladesh (Jackson, 1975).

Predictably, Pakistan launched a propaganda campaign denying that it had committed genocide. Pakistan's allies, Islamic countries, and China supported Pakistan's stance. The official policy of the United States was to "tilt in favor of Pakistan" because Pakistan was used as an intermediary to open the door to China (Jackson, 1975).

At the non-official level, however, there was a great outpouring of sympathy for the Bangladesh cause worldwide because of the genocide. The Western media—particularly that of the United States, Britain, France, and Australia—kept Bangladesh on the global agenda all through 1971. Well-known Western artists and intellectuals also came out in support of Bangladesh. George Harrison, the former Beatle, and Ravi Shankar, master of the sitar, held a concert to support Bangladesh. André Malraux, the noted French author, volunteered to go and fight with the Bengali freedom fighters. In the United States, citizen groups and individuals lobbied Congress successfully to halt military aid to Pakistan. Despite the Nixon Administration's official support of the Pakistani government, influential senators and congressmen such as Frank Church and Edward Kennedy spoke out strongly against the genocide. Members of parliament in the United Kingdom and other Western countries were also highly critical of the Bangladesh genocide.

Both officially and unofficially, India played a critical role in mobilizing support for Bangladesh. The genocide and the resultant influx of 10 million refugees in West Bengal and neighboring states created spontaneous unofficial sympathy. The press, political parties, and voluntary organizations in India pressed Indian Prime Minister Indira Gandhi to immediately intervene in Bangladesh when the Pakistani army cracked down in March 1971. The Indian government initially refused to intervene but gave moral and financial support to the Bangladesh government-in-exile as well as the freedom fighters. It also sponsored a systematic international campaign in favor of Bangladesh. Finally, in December 1971, when the ground was well prepared, Bangladesh was liberated as a result of direct Indian army intervention (Jackson, 1975).

The world's sympathy for the Bangladesh people in the aftermath of the 1971 genocide was also demonstrated by the tremendous relief and rehabilitation efforts mounted by the United Nations and private voluntary organizations in Bangladesh. Even before the liberation of Bangladesh, large-scale relief efforts were undertaken by the world community to feed the refugees in the India-based camps. And during the first two years of the new nation's existence, "as many as 72 foreign relief groups, including UN agencies, contributed to what observers considered the largest single and most successful emergency relief endeavor of our times" (O'Donnell, 1984, p. 112). Nearly $1.3 billion of humanitarian aid was given to Bangladesh during that period.

However, despite the generous response of the international community in giving humanitarian aid, there was very little support for the war crime trials that Bangladesh proposed to hold. In the 1970s the world community was yet to embrace the human rights framework which became more universally acceptable in the 1990s. Hence Bangladesh's demands for holding war crimes trials did not receive international support. The Indian army quickly removed the 93,000 Pakistani prisoners of war (POW) from Bangladesh soil to India in order to prevent any reprisals against them. India and other friendly countries were supportive of a negotiated package deal as a way to settle all outstanding issues between Pakistan and Bangladesh, including trial of the war crimes. In 1972 Bangladesh requested that India turn over 195 Pakistani military and civilian officials out of 93,000 Pakistani POWs so they could be tried for their role in specific atrocities. In response Pakistan filed a claim against India in the International Court of Justice (ICJ), claiming that only Pakistan could try its citizens for breaches of the Genocide Convention. At the same time, Pakistan held some 250,000 Bengalis who were working and living in Pakistan, in internment camps. Known as "stranded East Pakistanis," their release was promised by Pakistan only in exchange for Pakistani POWs. After two years of persistent international pressure to drop the war crime trials, in early 1974 India, Pakistan, and Bangladesh signed a tripartite agreement which allowed the Pakistani POWs and "stranded East Pakistanis" to return to their respective homes. Pakistan withdrew its ICJ claim and promised to conduct its own trials. Pakistan also recognized the independence of Bangladesh.

Soon after the end of the liberation war, the Bangladeshi government also initiated actions to bring to trial alleged Bengali collaborators during the genocide. On January 24, 1972 the Bangladesh Collaborators (special Tribunals) Order (Collaborators Order) was promulgated by a Presidential Decree which provided for prosecution of "collaborators" before special tribunals for wide-ranging criminal acts including murder, rape, arson, and genocide. Between 1972 and 1974 some 37,400 people were arrested and investigations commenced. On July 20, 1973 the Bangladeshi parliament passed the International Crimes Tribunal Act (ICTA), which drew heavily on the International Military Tribunal (IMT) Charter used at Nuremberg. The ICTA was to serve as the basis for the establishment of a national tribunal and specialized investigation/ prosecution unit to try people for genocide, crimes against humanity, war crimes, and other crimes under international law. However, numerous clemency measures halted the plans to conduct the trials. In February 1973 the Bangladeshi government passed the Bangladesh Liberation Struggle (Indemnity) Order which granted freedom fighters immunity from prosecution for acts committed in connection with the liberation war. On May 16, 1973 clemency was granted to those who were convicted of petty offences under the Collaborators Order. On November 30, 1973 the Bangladeshi government announced a general amnesty for all collaborators, except those accused of murder, rape, arson, or genocide. As a result, 26,000 people detained under the Collaborator's Order were released; another 11,000 lower-level, local, alleged collaborators went on to face trial and approximately 750 were convicted (ICTJ Briefing, July 2010).

After the military coup and assassination of Sheikh Mujib in August 1975, the new regime adopted a policy of seeking political support from the Islamist parties and groups to counter the AL. As a result, the state policy toward the collaborators was reversed. The new government repealed the Collaborators Order, disbanded the tribunals set up under it and pardoned and released all those detained and convicted. The government also passed an Indemnity Ordinance that gave those involved in Sheikh Mujib's assassination immunity from legal action. The ICTA, however, was never repealed.

The policy aimed at rehabilitating and rewarding the collaborators continued all through the rule of two military dictators, Ziaur Rahman (1975–1981) and H.M. Ershad (1982–1990). These policies were pursued even after the restoration of democracy in 1991, when the Bangladesh Nationalist Party (BNP), founded by the military ruler Ziaur Rahman, formed the government with the support of the Jamaat-i-Islami. It was then left to civil society actors to undertake transitional justice initiatives.

In 1992 an unofficial People's Tribunal was constituted in Dhaka that conducted a mock trial of several suspected Bangladeshi collaborators and convicted and sentenced them to death in absentia. Organizations such as Gathak Dalal Nirmul Committee and Liberation War Museum began private efforts to collect documentation of the atrocities, carry out public education, memorialize mass graves, and organize national and international conferences. The issue of the trial for the perpetrators of the genocide gained a boost when the former Sector Commanders of the liberation war started a nationwide campaign during 2007–2008 to undertake such trials. The AL finally included it as one of its election pledges before the 2008 parliamentary elections.

Following the AL's landslide electoral victory in March 2009, the Bangladeshi government again announced various steps to prosecute Bangladeshi collaborators, after a silence of nearly 33 years. In late 2009 an amendment to the 1973 ICTA was passed, promising the independence of the tribunal in the exercise of its judicial function and fair trials. Three judges were appointed to the tribunal and a team of prosecutors began investigations. Funds were allocated to conduct the various activities for the preparation of the trials. On July 27, 2010, the ICT issued arrest warrants for four suspects who were all senior leaders of the Jamaat-e-Islami. The government promised that indictments and trials would proceed as of 2011.

While the recent developments in Bangladesh constitute a rare example of a national search for accountability, international observers have raised various concerns about the planned trials, including, for example, the following: the legality of the death penalty under the ICT; judicial independence during the course of the trials; the possibility of victimizing in various ways the political opposition; the potential limits placed on the rights of suspects and the accused; and the lack of specialized experience in investigation and prosecution of mass crimes committed nearly 40 years ago (ICTJ Briefing, July 2010).

The Impact of the Genocide

A major impact of the genocide was the introduction of violence in Bangladesh society, politics, and culture. Prior to 1971, Bengalis were a relatively peaceful and homogeneous community with a low level of violent crimes. They were highly faction-ridden and politicized, but differences and disputes were generally settled through negotiations, litigation, and peaceful mass movements. After the Pakistani armed attack, Bengalis took up arms and for the first time engaged in armed struggle. The genocide, looting, burning, and rapes brutalized the Bangladeshi society. After witnessing so much violence, the people seem to have developed a higher degree of tolerance toward wanton violence. A qualitative change has taken place in regard to people's attitudes towards conflict resolution. Armed violence has now become much more prevalent in Bangladesh.

The role of the Bengali collaborators in perpetrating the genocide has created deep division and mistrust in the otherwise homogeneous Bengali social fabric. In addition, the failure to hold the collaborators accountable for their atrocities because of political expediency created a culture of impunity which impeded the development of rule of law in the country. Protection and rewards given to the individuals, against whom there were allegations of committing war crimes, by post-1975 military governments and the BNP-led governments signaled that crimes would go unpunished if criminals pledge political support to the regime in power.

Additionally, the genocide has had several long-term impacts on different target groups. First, after 1971 many members of the Hindu community felt unsafe and decided not to return to Bangladesh. Furthermore, there has been a steady migration of young Hindus to India even after Bangladesh was liberated, particularly after the 1975 change of regime when the state's commitment towards secularism was abandoned and the government adopted a more Islamist stance. Second, students and youth, who became familiar with the use of arms, did not give them up after 1971. They started using sophisticated weapons in settling political scores. Continuous armed conflicts between rival student groups have resulted in destroying the academic atmosphere and the standard of educational institutions. Finally, the status of women was altered as a result of the genocide. Following the ravage of war, thousands of destitute women, for the first time, entered a variety of paid employment outside their homes, such as public works programs, rural extension work, civil administration, police work, and employment in garment industries. Surprisingly, women's participation in paid economic work did not result in commensurate empowerment of women. Violence against women has not diminished. It has become widespread and common.

Contestations about the genocide

Contestations about the genocide and the issue of Bangladeshi collaborators started soon after 1971. As noted earlier, the Pakistan government steadfastly refused to accept that acts of genocide had been committed in 1971. The Hamoodur Rahman Commission (1972), established by the government of Pakistan, acknowledged that atrocities took place but refers to a smaller number of casualties in its report. Though civil society organizations in Pakistan recognized the genocide and offered apologies to the people of Bangladesh, the Pakistan government never offered a formal apology. In 2002, on an official visit to Bangladesh, the president of Pakistan regretted the "excesses" committed by the Pakistani soldiers but the statement fell short of expressing apologies for the 1971 genocide.

In the last 40 years there has been very little academic debate about the 1971 genocide. No scholar has questioned whether the atrocities have taken place, though recently one Indian academic (Bose, 2005) posited that the number of victims were much less than what Bangladesh has claimed. Her research methodology and findings, have, however, been critiqued as flawed and biased by others (Mookherjee, 2006).

Though there is widespread acceptance that massive atrocities were committed in 1971, the issue of justice for the victims and accountability for the perpetrators became contested even within Bangladesh as a result of regime change. After the 1975 army coup and the overthrow of the AL government, many of the collaborators who had been opposed to the Awami League joined the political parties floated by the two military dictators, Ziaur Rahman and H.M. Ershad. The military dictators chose to emphasize the country's Islamic ideology, allowed religion-based parties to function, and appointed a few well-known collaborators to their cabinets. All of this was done to broaden support for their undemocratic rule.

The gradual ascendance of the Islamist forces in the country became evident when democracy was restored in 1991. After the 1991 election, the BNP, founded by Ziaur Rahman, succeeded in forming the government with the support of the Islamist party, Jamaat-e-Islami, a party which opposed the independence of Bangladesh and actively collaborated with Pakistan. However, the growing political influence of the collaborators of the 1971 genocide enraged the victims of the genocide. Several civil society groups started mass campaigns demanding that the alleged collaborators be tried in a court of law. The genocide and the collaborators' issue, which had been marginalized during the military rule (1975–1990), were again brought back to center stage of the political arena following the return of democratically elected governments in the 1990s.

During the 1996 election campaign, the AL pursued a two-pronged strategy. On the one hand, it kept Jamaat-i-Islami from forming an electoral alliance with the BNP; on the other, it successfully utilized the anti-Jamaat campaign launched by the NGOs and cultural organizations whose work with education and women's empowerment had come under attack by Jamaat. In the 1996 election, the AL was returned to power after 21 years. The ruling BNP contested the election without the support of the Jamaat and lost, while the Jamaat experienced a massive loss of seats. During the four years of the AL government (1996–2000), textbooks used in public schools and programs in state-sponsored media began to specifically refer to the genocide committed by the Pakistanis (in previous decades, reference was often made to the genocide without specifying the name of Pakistan). However, the AL did little to initiate the war crimes trials during its tenure.

The AL lost the 2001 election when the BNP was successful in forming an electoral coalition with the Jamaat and the other Islamist parties to pool anti-AL votes to win a majority in the First Past the Post (FPTP) electoral system. Thirty years after opposing the birth of Bangladesh and collaborating with Pakistan, Jamaat-e-Islami succeeded in gaining a share in state power as a partner in the BNP-led coalition. Two well-known collaborators became cabinet ministers.

Jammat's share in state power further fueled demands for the trial of the collaborators. As noted earlier, during 2007–2008, the Sector Commander's Forum, a civil society initiative of former Sector Commanders of the liberation war, initiated a nationwide campaign to press for trials. The issue acquired a level of political potency and the AL picked up on the issue in its election campaign. The party's massive electoral victory was in some measure served by the pledge. The government has finally begun the process of trying the collaborators. However, these efforts have been criticized by the opposition political parties, the BNP and the Jamaat, who claim that the government is using the trials to victimize the opposition. As of today (mid-2011), there is no consensus between the two main political parties, the AL and the BNP, about the trial of the collaborators.

Why the Bangladesh Case is Important to Understanding the Complexities of Genocide

An analysis of the Bangladesh case is important to understanding the complexities of genocide for several reasons. First, it showcases how the world's response to genocide is often determined by geopolitical interests. Super and regional powers generally recognize or ignore acts of genocide through the prism of their own national interests. In the case of Bangladesh, India and her allies recognized the Bangladesh genocide while Pakistan and her allies, Islamic bloc countries, China, and the United States refused to recognize the atrocities as acts of genocide.

Second, the Bangladesh case exemplifies the difficulties of sustaining world attention on specific cases of genocide for a prolonged period. Though the genocide received widespread international media attention during 1971, very soon after the media turned to other issues and Bangladesh became an almost forgotten case.

Third, the Bangladesh case underscores how once atrocities are started by one group, resistance is organized by the victims, who can, in turn, also commit atrocities. Atrocities committed by one group often lead to retaliatory atrocities by the other groups. The Pakistani military started killing Bengalis; the latter then initiated counter mobilization and the counter attacks were not only aimed at the Pakistani military but also against the alleged collaborators of the Pakistanis, both Bengalis and Biharis.

Finally, the Bangladesh case illustrates the complexities of instituting justice for the victims and accountability for the perpetrators of genocide. Internal as well as external pressures can be created to halt the process of justice. Changes in international and domestic political circumstances and expediency can also impede accountability, as had happened in Bangladesh.

The Bangladesh case also shows how the denial of justice and accountability can haunt generations for decades and create deep schisms in society. Despite the fact that after the military takeover of state power in 1975 there was official neglect and denial of war crimes, this could not erase the memory of the genocide and demands for accountability and justice. Civil society groups kept alive the memory of the atrocities through documentation, films, public education, and other forms of memorialization. Demands for justice and accountability were persistently raised by non-state actors. It was argued that democracy and the rule of law could not be established in the country so long as the perpetrators of atrocities of 1971 enjoyed impunity for their crimes. Sadly and tellingly, war crimes and collaborator issues continue to create deep social and political divides in the country.

Eyewitness Accounts

The following eyewitness accounts of the 1971 genocide depict different incidents. The first two eyewitness accounts describe the mass murders committed on March 25 on the Dhaka University campus. The first account is by a survivor of the killings in one of the student dormitories (Jagannath Hall) where Hindu students lived. The second account is by a university professor who witnessed and videotaped the massacres on the Dhaka University campus. The third and fourth eyewitness testimonies describe the mass rape of women by the Pakistanis. The fifth testimony describes the killings in the village of *Bangabandhu* Sheikh Mujibur Rahman, the leader of the nationalist movement. The last account describes the atrocities of the non-Bengali Biharis who collaborated with the Pakistan army.

The testimonies are taken from two sources. One is a Bengali book entitled *1971: Bhayabaha Abhignata (Terrible Experiences)* (1996), which was edited by Rashid Haider and is a collection of eyewitness accounts. Sohela Nazneen translated the accounts from Bengali to English. The other source, *The Year of the Vulture* (1972), is Indian journalist Amita Malik's account of the genocide. In Malik's book Dhaka is spelled "Dacca," which was the spelling used in 1972.

Account 1: Massacre at Jagannath Hall

This testimony is from Kali Ranjansheel's "Jagannath Hall e-Chilam" ("I was at Jagannath Hall"). In *1971: Bhayabaha Abhignata* (1989, p. 5). Reprinted with permission.

I was a student at the Dhaka University. I used to live in room number 235 (South Block) in Jagannath Hall. On the night of 25th of March, I woke up from sleep by the terrifying sound of gunfire. Sometimes the sound of gunfire would be suppressed by the sound of bomb explosions and shell-fire. I was so terrified that I could not even think of what I should do! After a while I thought about going to Shusil, assistant general secretary of the student's union. I crawled up the stairs very slowly to the third floor. I found out that some students had already taken refuge in Shusil's room, but he was not there. The students told me to go to the roof of the building where many other students had taken shelter but I decided (rather selfishly) to stay by myself. I crawled to the toilettes at the northern end of the third floor and took refuge in there. I could see the east, the south and the west from the window. I could see that the soldiers were searching for students with flashlights from room to room, were taking them near the *Shahid Minar* [Martyr's memorial] and then shooting them. Only the sound of gunfire and pleas of mercy filled the air. Sometimes the Pakistanis used mortars and were shelling the building. The tin sheds in front of Assembly and some of the rooms in North Block were set on fire....

After some time, about 40 to 50 Pakistani soldiers came to the South Block and broke down the door of the dining room. The lights were turned on and they were firing at the students who took shelter in that room.... When the soldiers came out they had Priyanath [the caretaker of the student dormitory] at gunpoint, and forced him to show the way through all the floors of the dormitory. During this time I was not able to see them as I left the toilette by climbing up the open window and took shelter on the sunshed of the third floor. But I could hear the cracking sounds of bullets, the students pleading for mercy and the sound of the soldiers rummaging and throwing things about in search of valuables. The soldiers did not see me on the sunshed....

After they left, I again took refuge in the washroom. I peeked through the window and saw that the other students' dormitory, Salimullah Hall, was on fire. The northern and the eastern parts of the city were on fire too as the north and east horizon had turned red. The whole night, the Pakistani soldiers continued their massacre and destruction.... Finally I heard the call for the morning prayer....

The curfew was announced at dawn and I thought that this merciless killing would stop. But it continued. The soldiers started killing those who had escaped their notice during the night before....

It was morning and I heard the voices of some students. I came out of the toilette, and saw that the students were carrying a body downstairs while soldiers with machine guns were accompanying them. It was the dead body of Priyanath. I was ordered to help the students and I complied. We carried bodies from the dormitory rooms and piled them up in the field outside. There were a few of us there—students, gardeners, two sons of the gateskeeper and the rest were janitors. The janitors requested the Pakistanis to let them go since they were not Bengalis. After a while the army separated the janitors from us....

All the time the soldiers were cursing and swearing at us. The soldiers said, "We will see how you get free Bangladesh! Why don't you shout '*Joy Bangla*' [Victory to Bengal]!" The soldiers also kicked us around. After we had finished carrying the bodies, we were divided into groups. They then took my group to one of the university quarters and searched almost every room on the fourth floor and looted the valuables. Downstairs we saw dead bodies piled up, obviously victims from the night before. They also brought down the flag of Bangladesh....

After we came back, we were again ordered to carry the dead bodies to the *Shahid Minar*. The soldiers had already piled up the bodies of their victims and we added other bodies to the piles. If we felt tired and slowed down, the soldiers threatened to kill us....

As my companions and I were carrying the body of Sunil (our dormitory guard), we heard screams in female voices. We found that the women from the nearby slums were screaming as the soldiers were shooting at the janitors (the husbands of the women). I realized that our turn would come too as the Pakistanis started lining up those students who were before us, and were firing at them. My companion and I barely carried the dead body of Sunil toward a pile where I saw the dead body of Dr. Dev [professor of philosophy]. I cannot explain why I did what I did next. Maybe from pure fatigue or maybe from a desperate hope to survive!

I lay down beside the dead body of Dr. Dev while still holding onto the corpse of Sunil. I kept waiting for the soldiers to shoot me. I even thought that I had died. After a long time, I heard women and children crying. I opened my eyes and saw that the army had left and the dead bodies were still lying around and women were crying. Some of the people were still alive but wounded. All I wanted to do was to get away from the field and survive.

I crawled towards the slums. First I went to the house of the electrician. I asked for water but when I asked for shelter his wife started crying aloud and I then left and took refuge in a toilette. Suddenly I heard the voice of Idu who used to sell old books. He said, "Don't be afraid. I heard you are alive. I shall escort you to safety." I went to old Dhaka city. Then I crossed the river. The boatman did not take any money. From there, I first went to Shimulia, then, Nawabganj and finally I reached my village in Barishal in the middle of April.

Account 2: Horror Documentary

This testimony is from Amita Malik's *The Year of the Vulture* (1972, pp. 79–83).

At the professors' funeral, Professor Rafiq-ul-Islam of the Bengali Department whispered to me, "At the television station you will find that there is a film record of the massacre of professors and students at Jagannath Hall. Ask them to show it to you."

This sounded so incredible that I did not really believe it. However, I wasted no time in asking Mr. Jamil Chowdhury, the station manager of TV, whether he did, indeed, have such a film with him: "Oh yes," he said, "but we have not shown it yet because it might have dreadful repercussions." He was, of course, referring to the fact that the Pakistani army was still very much in Dacca in Prisoner-of-War (POW) camps in the Cantonment, and it would have been dangerous to show them gunning down professors and students at Dacca University. The people of Dacca had shown tremendous restraint so far, but this would have been going a bit too far. However, I had it confirmed that NBC VISNEWS and other international networks had already obtained and projected the film.

"But who shot the film?" I asked in wonder.

"A professor at the University of Engineering, who had a video tape recorder and whose flat overlooks the grounds of Jagannath Hall," said Mr. Chowdhury.

It was therefore by kind courtesy of Dacca TV that I sat in their small projection room on January 5 and saw for the first time what must be a unique actuality film, something for the permanent archives of world history.

The film, lasting about 20 minutes, first shows small distant figures emerging from the hall carrying the corpses of what must be the students and professors massacred in Jagannath Hall. These are clearly civilian figures in lighter clothes and, at their back, seen strutting arrogantly even at that distance, are darker clad figures, the hoodlums of the Pakistan army. The bodies are laid down in neat, orderly rows by those forced to carry them at gunpoint. Then the same procession troops back to the Hall. All this time, with no other sound, one hears innocent birdsong and a lazy cow is seen grazing on the university lawns. The same civilians come out again and the pile of bodies grows.

But after the third grisly trip, the action changes. After the corpses are laid on the ground, the people carrying them are lined up. One of them probably has a pathetic inkling of what is going to happen. He falls on his knees and clings to the legs of the nearest soldier, obviously pleading for mercy. But there is no mercy. One sees guns being pointed, one hears the crackle of gunfire and the lined up figures fall one by one, like the proverbial house of cards or, if you prefer, puppets in a children's film. At this stage, the bird-song suddenly stops. The lazy cow, with calf, careers wildly across the lawn and is joined by a whole herd of cows fleeing in panic.

But the last man is still clinging pathetically to the jackboot of the soldier at the end of the row. The soldier then lifts his shoulder at an angle, so that the gun points almost perpendicularly downwards to the man at his feet, and shoots him. The pleading hands unlink from the soldier's legs and another corpse joins the slumped bodies in a row, some piled on top of the very corpses they had to carry out at gunpoint, their own colleagues and friends. The soldiers prod each body with their rifles or bayonets to make sure that they are dead. A few who are still wriggling in their death agony are shot twice until they stop wriggling.

At this stage, there is a gap because Professor Nurul Ullah's film probably ran out and he had to load a new one. But by the time he starts filming again, nothing much has changed except that there is a fresh pile of bodies on the left. No doubt some other students and professors had been forced at gunpoint to carry them out and then were executed in turn. Insofar as one can count the bodies, or guess roughly at their number in what is really a continuous long-shot amateur film, there are about 50 bodies by this time. And enough, one should think.

Professor Nurul Ullah's world scoop indicated that he was a remarkable individual who through his presence of mind, the instinctive reaction of a man of science, had succeeded in shooting a film with invaluable documentary evidence regardless of the risk to his life.

I immediately arranged to track him down and he very kindly asked me to come round to his flat. Professor Nurul Ullah is a professor of electricity at the University of Engineering in Dacca. I found him to be a quiet, scholarly, soft-spoken, and surprisingly young man with a charming wife. He is normally engrossed in his teaching and students. But he happened to be the proud possessor of a video tape recorder which he bought in Japan on his way back from a year at an American university. He is perhaps the only man alive who saw the massacre on the lawns of Dacca University on the first day of the Pakistani army crack-down.

It was fascinating to sit down in Professor Nurul Ullah's sitting room and see the film, twice, with him, the second time after he had shown me the bedroom window at the back of his flat which overlooked both the street along which the soldiers drove to the university and the university campus. When he realized what was happening, he slipped his microphone outside [through] the window to record the sounds of firing. The film was shot from a long distance and under impossible conditions. Professor Nurul Ullah's description of how he shot the film was as dramatic and stirring as the film itself:

On March 25, 1971, the day of the Pakistani crack-down, although I knew nothing about it at the time, my wife and I had just had breakfast and I was looking out of my back windows in the professors' block of flats in which I and my colleagues from the Engineering University live with our families. Our back windows overlook a street across which are the grounds of Jagannath Hall, one of the most famous halls of Dacca University. I saw an unusual sight, soldiers driving past my flat and going along the street which overlooks it, towards the entrance to the University. As curfew was on, they made announcements on loudspeakers from a jeep that people coming out on the streets would be shot. After a few minutes, I saw some people carrying out what were obviously dead bodies from Jagannath Hall. I immediately took out my loaded video tape recorder and decided to shoot a film through the glass of the window. It was not an ideal way to do it, but I was not sure what it was all about, and what with the curfew and all the tension, we were all being very cautious. As I started shooting the film, the people carrying out the dead bodies laid them down on the grass under the supervision of Pakistani soldiers who are distinguishable in the film, because of their dark clothes, the weapons they are carrying and the way they are strutting about contrasted with the civilians in lighter clothes who are equally obviously drooping with fright.

As soon as firing started, I carefully opened the bedroom window wide enough for me to slip my small microphone just outside the window so that I could record the sound as well. But it was not very satisfactorily done, as it was very risky. My wife now tells me that she warned me at the time: "Are you mad, do you want to get shot too? One flash from your camera and they will kill us too." But I don't remember her telling me, I must have been very absorbed in my shooting, and she says I took no notice of what she said.

It so happened that a few days earlier, from the same window I had shot some footage of student demonstrators on their way to the university. I little thought it would end this way.

Anyway, this macabre procession of students carrying out bodies and laying them down on the ground was repeated until we realized with horror that the same students were themselves being lined up to be shot.

After recording this dreadful sight on my video tape recorder, I shut it off thinking it was all over—only to realize that a fresh batch of university people were again carrying out bodies from inside. By the time I got my video tape recorder going again, I had missed this new grisly procession but you will notice in the film that the pile of bodies is higher.

I now want to show my film all over the world, because although their faces are not identifiable from that distance in what is my amateur film, one can certainly see the difference between the soldiers and their victims, one can see the shooting and hear it, one can see on film what my wife and I actually saw with our own eyes. And that is documentary evidence of the brutality of the Pak army and their massacre of the intellectuals.

Account 3: Our Mothers and Sisters

The following testimony is from M. Akhtaurzzaman Mondol's "AmaderMa Bon" ("Our Mothers and Sisters") in *1971: Bhayabaha Abhignata* (1996, p. 197). It was translated by Sohela Nazneen. Reprinted with permission.

We started our fight to liberate Vurungamari from the Pakistani occupation forces on November 11, 1971. We started attacking from West, North and East, simultaneously. The Indian air forces bombed the Pakistani stronghold on November 11 morning. On November 13 we came near the outskirts of Vurungamari, and the Indian air force intensified their air attack. On November 14 morning the guns from the Pakistani side fell silent and we entered Vurungamari with shouts of *"Joy Bangla"* [Victory to Bengal]. The whole town was quiet. We captured 50 to 60 Pakistani soldiers. They had no ammunition left. We found the captain of the Pakistan forces, Captain Ataullah Khan, dead in the bunker. He still had his arms around a woman—both died in the bomb attack in the bunker. The woman had marks of torture all over her body. We put her in a grave.

But I still did not anticipate the terrible scene I was going to witness as we were heading toward east of Vurungamari to take up our positions. I was informed by wireless to go to the Circle Officer's office. After we reached the office, we caught glimpses of several young women through the windows of the second floor. The doors were locked, so we had to break them down. After breaking down the door of the room, where the women were kept, we were dumbfounded. We found four naked young women, who had been physically tortured, raped, and battered by the Pakistani soldiers. We immediately came out of the room and threw in four *lungis* [dresses] and four bed sheets for them to cover themselves. We tried to talk to them, but all of them were still in shock. One of them was six to seven months pregnant. One was a college student from Mymensingh. They were taken to India for medical treatment in a car owned by the Indian army. We found many dead bodies and skeletons in the bushes along the road. Many of the skeletons had long hair and had on torn saris and bangles on their hands. We found 16 other women locked up in a room at Vurungamari High School. These women were brought in for the Pakistani soldiers from nearby villages. We found evidence in the rooms of the Circle Officer's office which showed that these women were tied to the window bars and were repeatedly raped by the Pakistani soldiers. The whole floor was covered with blood, torn pieces of clothing, and strands of long hair....

Account 4: The Officer's Wife

This testimony is from Amita Malik's *The Year of the Vulture* (1972, pp. 141–142).

Another pathetic case is that of a woman of about 25. Her husband was a government officer in a subdivision and she has three children. They first took away the husband, although she cried and pleaded with them. Then they returned him half-dead, after brutal torture. Then another lot of soldiers came in at 8 or 9 A.M. and raped her in front of her husband and children. They tied up the husband and hit the children when they cried.

Then another lot of soldiers came at 2.30 P.M. and took her away. They kept her in a bunker and used to rape her every night until she became senseless. When she returned after three months, she was pregnant. The villagers were very sympathetic about her but the husband refused to take her back. When the villagers kept on pressing him to take her back, he hanged himself. She is now in an advanced stage of pregnancy and we are doing all that we can do to help her. But she is inconsolable. She keeps on asking, "But why, why did they do it? It would have been better if we had both died."

Account 5: The Maulvi's Story

This testimony appears in Amita Malik's *The Year of the Vulture* (1972, pp. 102–104).

On April 19, 1971, about 35 soldiers came to our village in a launch at about 8 A.M. A couple of days earlier, I had asked the Sheikh's father and mother to leave the village, but they refused. They said, "This is our home and we shall not go away."

Soon after I heard the sound of the launch, a soldier came running and said, "Here Maulvi, stop, in which house are the father and mother of the Sheikh?" So first, I brought out his father. We placed a chair for him but they made him sit on the ground. Then Sheikh Sahib's *amma* [mother] was brought out. She took hold of my hand and I made her sit on the chair. The soldiers then held a sten-gun against the back of the Sheikh's *abba* [father] and a rifle against mine. "We will kill you in 10 minutes," said a soldier looking at his watch.

Then they picked up a diary from the Sheikh's house and some medicine bottles and asked me for the keys of the house. I gave them the bunch of keys but they were so rough in trying to open the locks that the keys would not turn. So they kicked open the trunks. There was nothing much inside except five teaspoons, which they took. They saw a framed photograph and asked me whose it was. When I said it was Sheikh Sahib's, they took it down. I tried to get up at this stage but they hit me with their rifle butts and I fell down against the chair. Finally, they picked up a very old suitcase and a small wooden box and made a servant carry them to the launch.

Then they dragged me up to where the Sheikh's father was sitting and repeated, "We shall shoot you in 10 minutes."

Pointing to the Sheikh's father, I asked: "What's the point of shooting him? He's an old man and a government pensioner."

The soldiers replied, "*Is liye, keonki wohne shaitan paida kiya hai*" ["Because he has produced a devil."].

"Why shoot me, the *imam* of the mosque?" I asked.

"*Aap kiska imam hai? Aap vote dehtehain*" ["What sort of an *imam* are you? You vote."], they replied.

I said, "The party was not banned, we were allowed to vote for it. We are not leaders, we are *janasadharan* [the masses]. Why don't you ask the leaders?"

The captain intervened to say that eight minutes were over and we would be shot in another two minutes. Just then a major came running from the launch and said we were to be let alone and not shot.

I immediately went towards the *masjid* [mosque] and saw about 50 villagers inside. Three boys had already been dragged out and shot. The soldiers asked me about a boy who, I said, was a *krishak* [cultivator]. They looked at the mud on his legs and hands and let him go. Khan Sahib, the Sheikh's uncle, had a boy servant called Ershad. They asked me about him. I said he was a servant. But a *Razakar maulvi*, who had come with them from another village, said he was the Sheikh's relative, which was a lie. The boy Ershad was taken to the lineup. He asked for water but it was refused.

Another young boy had come from Dacca, where he was employed in a mill, to enquire about his father. He produced his identity card, but they shot him all the same. They shot Ershad right in front of his mother. Ershad moved a little after falling down so they shot him again. Finally, the boy who had carried the boxes to the launch was shot. With the three shot earlier, a total of six innocent boys were shot by the Pakistani army without any provocation. They were all good-looking and therefore suspected to be relatives of the Sheikh.

After this, the Sheikh's father and mother were brought out of the house. *Amma* was almost fainting. And the house was set on fire and burnt down in front of our eyes until all that remained was the frame of the doorway which you can still see.

Altonissa, the lady with the bloodstained clothes of her son, is the mother of Tomb Yad Ali who was shot. They did not allow her to remove her son's body for burial, because they wanted the bodies to be exposed to public view to terrorize the villagers.

They also shot Mithu, the 10-year-old son of this widowed lady. She had brought him up with the greatest difficulty—they never had anything to eat except *saag-bhaat* [spinach and rice]. They shot little Mithu because he had helped the *Mukti Bahini*. You can now ask the ladies about their narrow escape.

Shaheeda Sheikh, Sheikh Mujib's niece, then added that fortunately all the women were taken away to safety across the river to a neighbouring village three days before the Pakistani soldiers came. For months they had lived in constant terror of *Razakars* pouncing on them from bushes by the village pond. Beli Begum, Mujib's niece, a strikingly lovely woman, told me how she had fled from the village when seven months pregnant and walked 25 miles to safety. Pari, a girl cousin, escaped with a temperature of 104 degrees. Otherwise they would all have been killed.

Account 6: Massacre at Foys Lake

This testimony is from Abdul Gofran's "Foys Lake—Gonohataya" ("Massacre at Faiz Lake"), which first appeared in *1971: Bhayabaha Abhignata* (1996). It was translated by Sohela Nazneen.

I own a shop near Akbar Shah mosque in Pahartali. On November 10th, 1971, at 6 A.M. about 40 to 50 Biharis came to my shop and forced me to accompany them. I had to comply as any form of resistance would have been useless against such a large number of people.

They took me to Foys Lake. As we passed through the gates of Foys Lake I saw that hundreds of non-Bengalis had assembled near the Pumphouse and wireless colony. The Bengalis who had been brought in were tied up. They were huddled by the side of the lake, which was at the north side of the Pumphouse. Many of the Biharis were carrying knives, swords and other sharp instruments. The Biharis were first kicking and beating up the Bengalis brutally and then were shoving their victims towards those carrying weapons. This other group of armed Biharis were jabbing their victims in the stomach and then severing their heads with the swords. I witnessed several groups of Bengalis being killed in such a manner.... When the Biharis came for me, one of them took away my sweater. I then punched him and jumped into the lake.... I swam to the other side and hid among the bushes.... The Biharis came to look for me but I was fortunate and barely escaped their notice. From my hiding place I witnessed the mass murder that was taking place. Many Bengalis were killed in the manner which had been described earlier.

The massacre went on till about 2 o'clock in the afternoon. After they had disposed of the last Bengali victim, the Biharis brought in a group of ten to twelve Bengali men. It was evident from their gestures that they were asking the Bengalis to dig a grave for the bodies lying around. I also understood from their gestures that the Biharis were promising the group that if they completed the task they would be allowed to go free. The group complied to their wish. After the group had finished burying the bodies, they were also killed, and the Biharis went away rejoicing. There were still many dead bodies thrown around the place.

In the afternoon many Biharis and [the] Pakistani army went along that road. But the Pakistani soldiers showed no sign of remorse. They seemed rather happy and did nothing to bury the dead.

When night fell I came back to my shop but left Chittagong the next day.

References

Ahmad, Kamruddin (1967). *A social history of East Pakistan.* Dhaka: Crescent Book Store.

Ayoob, Mohammad, & Subrahmanyan, K. (1972). *The liberation war.* New Delhi: S. Chand and Company.

Bhutto, Zulfikar All (1971). *The great tragedy!* Karachi: Pakistan Peoples Party.

Blood, Archer (2002). *The cruel birth of Bangladesh: Memories of an American diplomat.* Dhaka: University Press Limited.

Bose, Sharmila (2005, October 8). Anatomy of violence: Analysis of civil war in east Pakistan in 1971. *Economic and Political Weekly*, pp. 4463–4470.

Brownmiller, Susan (1981). *Against our will: Men, women, and rape.* New York: Simon and Schuster.

Callard, Keith (1957). *Pakistan: A political study.* New York: Macmillan.

Coggin, Dan, Shepherd, James, & Greenway, David (1971, August 2). Pakistan: The ravaging of golden Bengal. *Time*, pp. 24–29.

Gandhi, Sajit (2002). The tilt: The U.S. and the South Asian crisis of 1971. National Security Archive Electronic Briefing Book No. 79. December 16, 2002. Retrieved from: www.gwu. edu/~nsarchiv/NSAEBB/NSAEBB79.

Haider, Rashid (Ed.) (1996). *Bhayabaha Abhignata*, Shahitya Prakash. Dhaka: no publisher.

Hamoodur Rahman Commission (1972). *Hamoodur Rahman Commission report.* Retrieved December 28, 2010, from: www.pppusa.org/Acrobat/Hamoodur%20Commission%Report. pdf.

Jackson, Robert (1975). *South Asia crisis: India, Pakistan and Bangladesh.* London: Chatto and Windus.

Jahan, Rounaq (1972). *Pakistan: Failure in national integration.* New York: Columbia University Press.

Jahan, Rounaq (1973a). Elite in crisis: The failure of Mujib–Yahya–Bhutto Negotiations. *Orbis, 17*(21), 575–597.

Jahan, Rounaq (1973b). Women in Bangladesh. In Ruby Rohrlich-Leavitt (Ed.) *Women cross culturally: Change and challenge* (pp. 5–30). The Hague: Mouton Publishers.

Jenkins, Loren, Clifton, Tony, & Steele, Richard (1971, August 2). Bengal: The murder of a people. *Newsweek*, pp. 26–30.

Khan, Ayoob (1967). *Friends not masters.* London: Oxford University Press.

Loshak, David (1971). *Pakistan crisis.* New York: McGraw-Hill.

Malik, Amita (1972). *The year of the vulture.* New Delhi: Orient Longman.

Marshall, Charles B. (1959). Reflections on a revolution in Pakistan. *Foreign Affairs, 37*(2), 247–256.

Mascarenhas, Anthony (1971). *The rape of Bangladesh.* New Delhi: Vikas Publication.

Mookherjee, Nayanika (2006). Skewing the history of rape in 1971: A prescription for reconciliation? *Forum, 1*(2): n.p.

O'Donnell, Charles Peter (1984). *Bangladesh.* Boulder, CO: Westview Press.

Palit, D.K. (1972). *The Lightening Campaign: Indo-Pakistan War.* New York: Compton Press.

Rahman, Anisur (1968). *East and west Pakistan: A problem in the political economy of regional planning.* Cambridge, MA: Center for International Affairs, Harvard University.

Sayeed, K.B. (1967). *The political system of Pakistan.* Boston, MA: Houghton Mifflin.

Schanberg, Sidney (1971). Pakistan divided. *Foreign Affairs, 50*(1), 125–135.

Sobhan, Rehman (1962). The Problem of regional imbalance in the economic development of Pakistan. *Asian Survey, 2*(5), 31–37.

Sobhan, Rehman (1970, December 12). Coming to terms with Six Points. *Forum*, n.p.

Umar, Badruddin (1966). *Sampradaikata [Communalism].* Dhaka: Janamaitri Publications.

Umar, Badruddin (1967). *Sanskriti Sankat [Crisis in culture].* Dhaka: Granthana.

Umar, Badruddin (1969). *Sanskntite Sampradaikata [Communalism in culture].* Dhaka: Granthana.

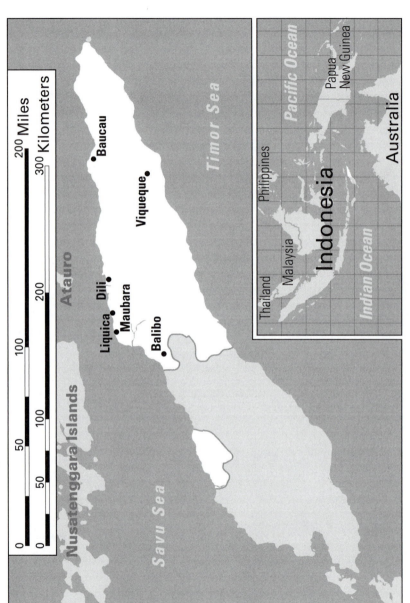

Map 8.1 East Timor

CHAPTER **8**

Genocide in East Timor

JAMES DUNN

Introduction

In 1975 Indonesian forces invaded the Portuguese colony of East Timor, which was then in the process of decolonization. The invasion provoked a spirited armed resistance, and during the subsequent five-year period, which was marked by bitter fighting in the interior and harsh oppression in occupied areas, the population of the territory underwent a substantial decline. So heavy was the loss of life that 16 years later (in 1991) the population was reported to be significantly lower than the estimate prior to the Indonesian invasion. In relative terms, therefore, the humanitarian costs of this act of forced integration reached genocidal proportions, which makes the East Timor case manifestly one of the most costly genocides in recent history.

While it should not be concluded that the Indonesian authorities embarked on a grand plan designed to bring about the systematic destruction of the Timorese people, Indonesia's occupation strategies and the behavior of the military seemed bound to achieve that end. The large influx of Indonesian settlers into the province could, in the long run, have led to ethnocide—that is, the destruction of the distinctive culture of East Timor. In the years following the invasion, however, the Timor case remained on the UN agenda, despite persistent efforts by Indonesia and its powerful Western friends. Thanks to the efforts of courageous Timorese such as Bishop Carlos Bello, by the end of the 1980s there was a growing awareness in the international community of the catastrophic consequences of this process of annexation and subjugation.

Be that as it may, until the 1990s, the international response to this very serious violation of international law was largely characterized by indifference and irresolution. Indeed, the expressions of international concern at the deteriorating humanitarian situation in the years following the invasion were so weak that Indonesian authorities had become openly defiant of world opinion. As a result, the Suharto government, despite its heavy dependence on Western economic aid, clearly did not feel the need to respond to international concerns in a positive way— that is, until the Santa Cruz massacre in November 1991.

The Santa Cruz massacre sent shock waves around the world and put the Indonesian authorities on the defensive. Still, its concessions were of little real significance, falling well short of a concession to the demands of East Timor's leaders for the removal of the Indonesian military and for an act of self-determination. And again, thanks to accommodating reactions from officials in, among others, Washington, Paris, Tokyo, and Canberra, the Suharto government appeared to regain its determination to ignore the ongoing criticisms of its annexation of East Timor. Indonesia's agreement to the holding of a plebiscite, under UN auspices, in August 1999 was, it should be understood, an outcome attributable less to international pressures than to the fall of Suharto following the Asian economic collapse. The flexible stance adopted by President Habibie and the determined efforts of Kofi Annan, the newly appointed UN Secretary General, were the key elements in the fortuitous sequence of events that led to East Timor's liberation in September 1999, after 24 years of occupation. As it happened, the Indonesian military persisted until the very end with its practice of indiscriminate killing and wanton destruction, until the International Forces in East Timor (INTERFET) intervention, authorized by the Security Council, forced its withdrawal from the territory.

On the other hand, events elsewhere in the early 1990s, the implications of the liberation of the Baltic States and the international rejection of Iraq's seizure of Kuwait, together with the awarding of the Nobel Peace Prize jointly to Jose Ramos-Horta and Bishop Bello, served to place Indonesia's occupation of East Timor under closer scrutiny. In the event, it was not international pressure but the fall of the Suharto regime that provided the catalyst for a radical change in Indonesia's Timor policy. The new president, Habibie, began a process of negotiation with East Timorese leaders, on the one hand, and UN and Portuguese officials, on the other, which led to a UN-administered plebiscite on August 30, 1999. In spite of extreme intimidation, the outcome of the plebiscite was decisive; almost 80% of voters rejected Jakarta's offer of autonomy. After a period of violence, which shocked the international community, President Habibie responded to the demands of the Security Council, and the intervention of President Clinton, and ordered the withdrawal of Indonesian troops and agreed to the transfer of the former Portuguese colony to the United Nations Transitional Administration in East Timor (UNTAET), with the task of preparing the devastated country for full independence.

The Setting

The island of Timor lies at the southeastern extremity of the Indonesian Nusatenggara island group, which was named the Lesser Sundas in Dutch colonial times. It is located at the opposite end to the island of Bali, one of Asia's best-known tourist attractions. Following a long period of rivalry and conflict, Timor came to be divided into two almost equal parts by the Dutch and Portuguese colonial administrations. The partition began to take shape about the middle of the 17th century, as Portugal's colonial power in the East Indies began to weaken in the face of the more vigorous Dutch intrusion. Boundary disputes between the two colonial powers persisted until the late 19th century; that is, until the Lisbon Convention of 1893 and the subsequent signing of the *Sentenca Arbitral* in April 1913, which demarcated the borders as they exist today. The Portuguese colony of East Timor comprised the eastern half of the island, the tiny enclave of Oecussi on the north coast of West Timor, and the small island of Atauro north of Dili.

East Timor is a small country, but it is not insignificant by the standards of smallness among today's membership of the UN. The territory has an area of about 7,300 square miles, comparable in size as well as population with Fiji and only slightly smaller in area than Israel or the state of New Jersey. On the eve of the Indonesian invasion, the Timorese population of the territory was estimated at about 680,000 people, with an annual growth rate of near 2%.

Portuguese navigators first reached Timor about 20 years after Columbus embarked on his epic trans-Atlantic crossing half a millennium ago. About 50 years later, their colonial rule of the area began in earnest. Therefore, for more than four centuries Portugal had been the dominant, almost exclusive, external influence in East Timor—except for a brief Japanese interregnum, from February 1942 until they surrendered to Allied forces in August 1945.

Within five years, the Dutch colony of the Netherlands East Indies was formally to become the Republic of Indonesia. Portuguese colonial rule over East Timor was restored, however, and until 1974 its colonial status was virtually ignored by the nationalist leaders of the new republic. This lack of interest persisted during the last seven years of Sukarno's presidency, when Indonesia embarked on an aggressive anti-colonial policy, with Jakarta vigorously asserting its own claim for the "return" of West Irian. After that objective was secured, Indonesia launched, in

1962, a costly and futile confrontation with Malaysia, which Sukarno perceived as a British neocolonial creation.

At no stage during this period did Indonesia seek to bring any real pressure to bear on the Portuguese administration in East Timor, although the Salazar regime had by that time become the chief target of the mounting campaign for decolonization. Portugal had become the only colonial power that refused to declare its colonies non-self-governing. While Dutch colonialism in West New Guinea was denounced in vitriolic terms, the more traditional form of colonial rule then being conducted by the Portuguese in neighboring East Timor scarcely rated a mention in Jakarta.

From the early 1960s until 1965 there were occasional remarks by a few leading Indonesian political and military figures, hinting that East Timor's future lay with its big neighbor, but these statements were not taken further by the government of the time, and certainly never evolved into a formal claim or political campaign.[1] After 1965 the Suharto regime, which was keen to develop closer relations with the Western nations sharing its hostility to communism and to attract economic assistance from them, was anxious to show that Indonesia no longer had territorial designs on the territories adjacent to it.

This policy appeared to prevail at the highest political level in Jakarta, right up to the point of Indonesia's military intervention in East Timor, with most official statements from Jakarta emphasizing East Timor's right to self-determination.[2] Certainly, at no stage, under either Sukarno or Suharto, was a claim to East Timor ever formally made by the government in Jakarta.[3]

The idea of an East Timor nation emerged spontaneously from the Portuguese colonial experience, just as Indonesia, Malaysia, Singapore, and the north Kalimantan states were shaped by British and Dutch colonial policies and rivalry. Although the two great empires of Srivijaya and Majapahit extended Java's influence to other parts of the archipelago for a period, there is no evidence that Timorese kingdoms were ever subjugated by the Javanese.

As a political concept, the notion of a nation of East Timor, even taking into account the arbitrary division of the island, is surely no less valid than the idea of an Indonesian state.

It could be said that the Indonesian nation was itself created not by a natural historical evolution but by colonial circumstances, determined by imperial and commercial rivalry in distant Western Europe. The legitimacy of the Indonesian state, it could therefore be argued, has its roots in Dutch colonial expansion and the political consensus—and dissent—it aroused, rather than in the natural evolution of a national political culture. In the world at large in 1974, events in East Timor aroused little interest. It was poor, undeveloped, remote, and unconnected to the global network of commercial and tourist communications. It possessed no apparent strategic value to any nation, with the possible exception of Indonesia. Its status was therefore of little consequence in perceptions of national interest, other than to Portugal, Indonesia, and Australia. By the end of that year, the Portuguese themselves, with their empire now falling apart, had turned to Europe and were little interested in the fortunes of a distant colony of very little economic value.

Australia is East Timor's nearest Western neighbor, its Northern Territory coastline lying less than 400 miles to the south, across the Timor Sea. For some years after World War II, Canberra regarded the Portuguese colony as strategically important, but by 1962 its significance had faded in the view of the Australian political establishment. In that year, it was the assessment of the Australian government that Indonesian rule over East Timor would not pose any additional external threat and was therefore not unacceptable. Significantly, in September of 1974 Prime Minister Gough Whitlam, who was attracted to the notion that East Timor's integration with Indonesia was the best solution, conveyed that view to the Indonesian leader, President Suharto, at a meeting in Java.

Based on the strong support for decolonization and self-determination declared by Whitlam after he came into office in December 1972, the Timorese had a much more optimistic view of Australia's position. Furthermore, their idea that Australia owed a debt to East Timor, because of the extensive support Australian forces received during their commando operation against the Japanese in 1942,[4] had created an unshakable belief that Australia would help them out in the end.

While Foreign Minister Adam Malik was prepared to countenance independence for East Timor, his views were not in fact shared by Indonesia's most powerful military leaders, who had, from the very outset, different plans for East Timor's future. To be fair, it was not so much a desire for additional territory that motivated them—East Timor was, in the days before the recent offshore oil discoveries, anything but an economic prize. One of their main concerns was that an independent East Timor would stimulate ambitions for independence among discontented nearby ethnic groups, such as the West Timorese and the Ambonese. Also, in the aftermath of the Vietnam War, Indonesia's military leadership was obsessed with the risk of communist infiltration and insurgency. To the military, therefore, integration was the only acceptable solution for East Timor.

As it happened, the Australian government was in a position to head off Indonesia's designs on East Timor but did not do so. From their extensive intelligence monitoring of Indonesian military activities[5] they were aware, at its very inception, that a subversive operation had been put in place with the aim of bringing about integration.[6] Before the end of 1974 this operation was set up by a group of Indonesian generals, among them Lieutenant-General Ali Murtopo, Major-General Benny Murdani (a senior intelligence officer close to the president), and Lieutenant-General Yoga Sugama, then head of the intelligence services. The existence of this operation, code-named Operasi Komodo,[7] became known to U.S. and Australian intelligence agencies before the year was out. Its aim was to bring about the integration of East Timor at any cost, though preferably by non-military means. Its first activities, which included a stream of clumsy propaganda vilifying the independence movement, the open backing of Apodeti, and some thinly disguised covert intelligence actions, had the effect not of dividing the two major parties, but of bringing them together.

Thus it was partly in reaction to this heavy-handed meddling that, early in January 1975, Fretilin[8] and UDT[9] formed a common front for independence. There is little doubt that Australia's accommodating stance, at the official level, strengthened the hands of the generals bent on the annexation of East Timor. Indeed, it is probable that the viability of this operation was predicated on the assumption that Australia would accept it. By the end of 1974, Indonesia was waging a strident propaganda campaign against Fretilin, in particular, and all Timorese in favor of independence in general. Fretilin was a party of the Left, and the Indonesian military chiefs were quite paranoid about its activities. The Fretilin leaders were accused of being communists and anti-Indonesian, and falsified accounts of links between them, Peking, and Hanoi were circulated. In reaction to the provocative propaganda outpourings from Jakarta, the Timorese themselves became increasingly hostile towards Indonesia.

In the first couple of months after April 1974, the Portuguese were rather indifferent toward the idea of independence for East Timor, with some military officers believing that joining with Indonesia made sense for such a small and undeveloped country. One senior official believed he had a responsibility to promote the idea of integration.[10] However, the apparent popular support for independence eventually convinced Lisbon and the colonial authorities that the Timorese were simply not disposed to merge with Indonesia. They saw themselves as being different, in terms of their culture, their languages, their political traditions, and their religions.[11] The aggressive approach of the Indonesians after August 1974 merely served to strengthen the East Timorese national consciousness, impelling the two major parties to form a coalition for independence. In the event, the Portuguese authorities commenced a decolonization program late in 1974, presenting the Timorese political elite with three options—full independence, continuing with Portugal under some new and more democratic arrangement, or integration with Indonesia.

The year 1975 proved to be a turbulent one for East Timor. As a result of political instability in Portugal, and the demoralization of the overseas administration, the decolonization program for Timor soon ran into difficulties. Political turmoil in Lisbon weakened the colonial power's administrative control, and the Indonesian generals heading Operasi Komodo exploited the deteriorating situation subtly and subversively. By mid-fall of that year political differences had surfaced between the two major parties, and in an Operasi Komodo operation, guided by Lieutenant-General Murtopo himself, the Indonesians sought to divide the independence movement. Their propaganda offensive against Fretilin was intensified, while the UDT leaders were invited to Jakarta—and courted. They were lectured, sometimes by Murtopo himself, on the dangers of communist subversion, were exhorted to break the coalition with Fretilin, and were sent, at Jakarta's expense, on tours of anti-communist political centers in Asia—South Korea, the Philippines, and Taiwan. Furthermore, fabricated evidence of links between the Fretilin leaders, on the one hand, and Peking and Hanoi, on the other, was passed on to them.

At least two of the conservative Timorese leaders, Lopes da Cruz and Mousinho, were actually recruited by Bakin, the powerful Indonesian military intelligence agency.[12] By the middle of 1975 relations between the two Timorese parties had become so tense that talks between them broke down completely. At this time, rumors were circulated by Bakin agents that Fretilin was planning a coup, encouraging UDT leaders to act hastily and rashly.[13]

Early in August 1975 Lieutenant-General Murtopo informed UDT leaders, who were visiting Jakarta, that his intelligence agents had uncovered a Fretilin conspiracy to launch a coup, and he encouraged them to take pre-emptive action.[14] Days after their return, these UDT leaders, with what military support they could muster, launched an abortive coup in Dili—abortive because within three weeks the party and its followers had been overwhelmed by Fretilin. They were defeated not because of external military intervention, but because most Timorese troops, who formed the majority of the colonial military establishment, favored the left-wing party. In this brief but intense conflict[15] the Portuguese, whose administrative apparatus had been reduced to a small number of officials and fewer than 100 combat troops, withdrew to the offshore island of Atauro.[16]

The Indonesian military, their plans having backfired, would have no truck with the independence movement and ignored its overtures. Operasi Komodo's military commanders sought to persuade President Suharto to authorize direct military intervention, but the president, who was unenthusiastic about any moves that would prejudice Indonesia's international standing (especially in Southeast Asia and the United States) as a nation without territorial ambitions, continued to hesitate until September when Generals Murtopo, Murdani, and Sugama (then head of Bakin) managed to secure his consent to a military operation against East Timor. They were able to assure him that the governments of greatest importance to Indonesia, among them the United States, Japan, Australia, the Netherlands, and ASEAN (Association of Southeast Asian Nations) would accommodate a military operation to secure East Timor's integration into Indonesia.

Two weeks later, Indonesia's first major military action against East Timorese territory was launched. It was carried out as a covert operation and involved an attack on the border village of Balibo. Its casualties were to include the five members of two television teams from Australia.[17]

Weeks before this assault, the victorious Fretilin leaders had sought to assuage Indonesian fears, and had encouraged the Portuguese to return and resume decolonization. But there was no response from the Portuguese, whose government in Lisbon was still in crisis. The Indonesian response was a series of military attacks over the border from West Timor. The official news agency, Antara, claimed that the "anti-Fretilin forces" had regrouped and were counter-attacking.

With the Portuguese having failed to respond to their request to return and resume decolonization, the Indonesians attacking from the west, and the international community ignoring their plight, Fretilin's unilateral decision to declare East Timor an independent republic was hardly surprising.

The Invasion and Its Aftermath

Having in a way provoked Fretilin's hasty decision to declare East Timor independent, the Indonesians lost no time in mounting a full-scale invasion—an amphibious attack on the capital, Dili. The status of East Timor was therefore changed abruptly on December 7, 1975,[18] when a combined military and naval force, under the overall command of Major-General Murdani, moved in from the sea. From the considerable evidence accumulated over the past several decades, it is clear that the invasion and subjugation of East Timor, especially in the early stages, was carried out with scant regard for the lives, let alone rights, of the Timorese people. Not only was the act of aggression itself a violation of the UN Charter, but the brutal way it was carried out over a period of several years constitutes genocide.

In the very first days of the invasion, rampaging Indonesian troops engaged in an orgy of indiscriminate killing, rape, and torture. Large-scale public executions were carried out—women being included among the victims—suggesting a systematic campaign of terror. In some villages whole communities were slaughtered, except for young children.

Outraged by these atrocities, the small but determined Timorese army bitterly contested the advance of the invading forces, and in terrain ideal for guerrilla warfare they were able to inflict heavy losses on the attackers until the early 1980s, denying the ABRI[19] effective control outside the main towns and administrative centers. The retaliation of the invading force to this stiff challenge to integration was the imposition of a harsh and oppressive occupation. In the areas under Indonesian control serious human rights violations were a daily occurrence, forcing tens of thousands of Timorese to seek refuge behind Fretilin lines.

The invasion force, which was soon to amount to more than 30,000 troops, entered the Portuguese colony from the west, where East Timor adjoins Indonesia, and in landings at major towns on the north coast, such as Baucau and Maubara. Thousands of Timorese were killed in the first weeks of the invasion when, from all accounts, troops went on a rampage, no doubt in response to the unexpectedly determined Timorese resistance to the invasion. In Dili there were a number of public executions—including along the wharf area where more than 100 were reportedly shot, at Santa Cruz, at the military police barracks, and at Tasitolo, near the airport. Also, in the small towns of Maubara and Liquica and at other villages in the interior, Indonesian military units carried out public executions, killing from 20 to more than 100 persons.

While conditions in the occupied areas were harsh and oppressive, indiscriminate killing, rape, and torture were even more widespread in the disputed areas. In their advance into the mountainous interior, especially where the advance was being hotly contested, the Indonesian forces killed many of the Timorese they encountered. The biggest single killing reported to the author by the Timorese driver of one of the Indonesian trucks occurred in 1975 at Lakmanan, near the western border, where invading troops returning from a stiff encounter with Fretilin turned their guns on a large temporary encampment of Timorese. One of these witnesses estimated that as many as 2,000 were killed over a period of several hours.[20]

As Indonesia sought to overpower the armed resistance and to suppress opposition to integration in occupied areas, tens of thousands of Timorese were to perish up to the end of 1979. During this period, East Timor was virtually sealed off from the outside world. The International Red Cross, which had been present in strength until just before the invasion, did not regain access to the territory until the second half of 1979, almost four years after the invasion.[21]

Although initially it was the intention of most townsfolk to remain in their homes and communities, the widespread killing, torture, and rape committed by the invading troops resulted in the flight of a large proportion of the population into the interior, to the comparative safety of the mountain districts under the control of Fretilin. However, it was in the mountainous interior of the island that the greatest loss of life was to occur in the following three years. Most of the deaths were from famine and related diseases, but it was the harsh treatment meted out by the Indonesians that prompted the Timorese to flee to the mountains.

Because of the absence of demographic records, whether kept by the invaders or by other authorities, no precise account of the human cost of the invasion and its aftermath exists. However, recent Indonesian census statistics provide evidence that it attained genocidal proportions. Before the invasion East Timor's population was about 690,000, and growing at about 2% per year. It follows that by 1991 there should have been more than 950,000 people; but based on Indonesian statistics, in East Timor, which had been designated the twenty-seventh province of Indonesia, there were only about 740,000 people.[22] Of this number, though, as many as 140,000 were non-Timorese who had, in recent years, moved into the territory from elsewhere in Indonesia, some of them transmigrants and others opportunistic drifters. The upshot is that, in effect, the Timorese population, some 16 years after the invasion, was 12% fewer than it was in 1975.

The annexation of East Timor had a drastic effect on all aspects of life in the community. Before the invasion, the ethnic and cultural patterns in the territory were exceedingly complex but, aside from some special characteristics, they resembled the patterns in the nearby islands of Eastern Nusatenggara.[23] The population was essentially Autronesian in character, but with a noticeable Melanesian influence. It reflected a long procession of migrations from west, north, and the east. But it would be an oversimplification to describe the territory as culturally part of Indonesia, if only because of the great ethnic and cultural diversity within this sprawling archipelagic nation. To call a Timorese "Indonesian" is rather like calling a Kurd an Iraqi or a Tibetan Chinese, labels that are imprecise and attract resentment. The Timorese were not, however, antagonistic toward people from other parts of the archipelago, at least before Indonesia began to meddle in the affairs of the island.[24] But in the past they had regarded the occasional visiting Indonesian fishing vessels with some suspicion. Perhaps this was because, unlike the Javanese or Buginese, the Timorese were not themselves a seafaring people and felt threatened by outsiders with these skills.

The rugged mountainous interior of East Timor provided excellent conditions for Fretilin's guerrilla campaign, but the resistance forces were not in a position to provide the basic needs of the tens of thousands of people who sought refuge within this territory. Food and medical supplies were inadequate, and the Timorese were subjected to constant air attacks (including, for a short period, the use of napalm). The Timorese were bombed and strafed, and once the Indonesian air force acquired Bronco anti-insurgency aircraft from the United States, these attacks intensified. In the two years following the invasion, the Timorese leaders managed to feed the people within their lines by developing the agricultural resources available to them in the rich valleys, but according to reports from Fretilin, in 1978 these farms were subject to air attacks by AURI[25] aircraft. According to one report, chemical substances were dropped on the crops, causing the plants to die. By 1978 the food situation behind Fretilin lines was desperate, and the Timorese leaders began encouraging their people to return to Indonesian-occupied areas; the resistance forces were no longer able to feed them, nor to provide even the most basic of medical treatment.

Initially, when these "refugees" moved into occupied territory, their reception was anything but humane. Some suspected Fretilin supporters were summarily executed, while many others were beaten or tortured at the slightest provocation (Amnesty International, 1985). The refugees were forced into resettlement camps, where food and medical facilities were grossly inadequate. In 1979, the first international aid workers to enter the territory reported that the basic needs of the Timorese in these centers were being seriously neglected and that thousands were dying needlessly from famine and disease.

Reports on the grim situation in East Timor began to come out of the territory as early as the end of 1976. In that year a confidential report from Catholic Church sources depicted a scene of oppression and wanton killing. Its authors suggested that in the year since the invasion as many as 60,000 Timorese might have lost their lives.[26] Was the international community aware of this very heavy loss of life and, if so, how did it react? In fact, these early reports aroused very little international attention. East Timor was remote, little known, and without any strategic or economic importance, even to the colonial power. While the UN itself promptly condemned the invasion and called on Indonesia to withdraw its forces, its pronouncements were mostly vague and irresolute.[27]

There is a more sinister aspect to this dismal situation. When the gravity of the humanitarian situation in this territory began to unfold, East Timor could easily have been made an issue of international concern by nations like the United States or Australia if their governments had chosen to do so.[28] In the 1970s, however, Indonesia had begun to assume a new importance in the eyes of the major Western powers. It was large, Muslim, and oil-producing, and the archipelago straddled the division between the strategically important Pacific and Indian Oceans. And the Suharto regime, despite its undemocratic character, fulfilled important political conditions—it was anti-communist, it was development-oriented, and it had created a facade of stability and harmony.

Under those circumstances, the Western governments with the greatest interest in Indonesia—which were also best placed to monitor events in East Timor—chose to play down the reports, most of them emanating from Church sources in Dili, that Indonesian military operations were inflicting heavy loss of life on the general population. In the Australian parliament, for example, these reports were repeatedly alluded to by official sources as being unproven, or ill-founded and exaggerated.

If the foreign missions in Jakarta were aware of just how serious the humanitarian situation was, they were careful not to disclose it in their public statements. In the case of the missions representing Australia, Canada, and the United States, the extent to which their diplomats were able to report on this situation was, in the experience of this writer, diminished by the tacit support that their governments had given to integration. According credibility to the reports from organizations such as the Catholic Church in East Timor would have been tantamount to admitting by implication a measure of responsibility.

Some of the reports made public could not have been honestly arrived at. For example, early in 1977 one U.S. State Department official told members of the U.S. Congress that only 2,000 Timorese had died as a result of the invasion. A few weeks later another U.S. official, Robert Oakley, came up with a revised figure of 10,000, which yet another official source later qualified with the comment that many of these deaths had occurred in the fighting between Fretilin and UDT.[29] Australian official responses were delivered in a similar vein. Their statements appeared to be designed to minimize the seriousness of the situation on the ground in East Timor and, in so doing, to discredit reports that Indonesian troops were responsible for widespread death and destruction. It was a blatant attempt to deflect international criticism of Indonesian actions. Thus, in 1978, when conditions in the territory were being described as nightmarish, the Australian government led by Prime Minister Fraser felt able to take the extraordinary step of recognizing de facto the annexation.[30]

By the end of 1979, however, the devastating consequences of Indonesia's military annexation of East Timor could no longer be concealed. And so, some four years after the invasion, when Indonesian authorities finally allowed a small number of international aid workers to conduct a survey of the humanitarian needs of the province, the dimensions of the tragedy began to emerge. The human misery they encountered shocked even some officials with experience in Africa and Southeast Asia. Their estimates suggested that in the preceding four years, Timor had lost between one-tenth and one-third of its population and that 200,000 of the remainder were in appalling conditions in "resettlement camps," which one official, who had previously served in Cambodia, described as among the worst he had seen.[31]

These revelations should have shocked the world into demanding that Indonesia withdraw from the former Portuguese colony, but that did not happen. Not one of the major powers was prepared to press Indonesia to reconsider its seizure of the territory and to bring any real pressure to bear on the Suharto government. The best that Washington and Canberra could come up with was to urge Indonesia to admit international humanitarian relief organizations.[32] These requests, which brought some response from Indonesia, resulted in the readmission to the province of the International Red Cross, which had been forced to leave on the eve of the invasion, in the face of Indonesia's refusal to guarantee the necessary protection.[33]

It was to be more than a decade after the invasion before Jakarta could claim to exercise administrative control over most of the island. Into the late 1990s armed resistance continued, despite annual large-scale operations by Indonesian forces, who invariably outnumbered the guerrillas by more than ten to one.[34] Thanks to the intervention of international agencies, and the work of some dedicated Indonesians, material conditions in Timor improved markedly during the 1980s. However, serious human rights abuses, mostly by the Indonesian military, continued to occur throughout the 1990s. In one annual report after another issued by Amnesty International, the authorities were accused of summary executions, "disappearances," torture, and imprisonment on the grounds of conscience.[35]

Notable examples of indiscriminate killing occurred at Creras, near Viqueque, in August 1983 and in Dili in November 1991. The Creras incident was first recounted to the author by a priest from the district some months later, and its details confirmed in 2001 by a leading East Timorese, Mario Carrascalao, who in 1983 was governor of the province. He told me that shortly after the incident he went to the area and personally investigated it. According to these accounts, rapes by Indonesian troops led to an attack by the Falintil (the military arm of Fretilin) on the Indonesian military unit to which the soldiers belonged, an attack that resulted in the killing of 16 Indonesian troops. In the following days, Indonesian forces, allegedly under the command of Major Prabowo Subianto (later Lieutenant-General), carried out severe reprisals against the population of the immediate region. According to Carrascalao, over 1,000 people, including many women and children, were massacred.

Another case of indiscriminate killing was the Dili massacre of November 1991, which cost the lives of more than 200 young Timorese.

It occurred when Indonesian troops opened fire on unarmed demonstrators, most of them students, near the Santa Cruz cemetery in Dili. The incident was widely reported in the international media, thanks to the presence of foreign observers. The Timorese were about to engage in a peaceful protest at the killing of one of their number, as well as at the forced integration of the territory. For several minutes Indonesian troops fired into the crowd of demonstrators, killing many of them. From evidence that subsequently became available, it appears that most of the killings took place after the firing had stopped. A large number of the wounded were killed in a crude fashion, some of them over the next two or three days, with their bodies being secretly disposed of at a site near Tibar.

Largely in response to an international reaction, the Indonesian government set up a Committee of Inquiry *(Komisi Penjelidik Nasional)*, which issued its Preliminary Report on December 26, 1991. While the report acknowledged some mistakes and lack of control, it absolved the authorities, including the military command in East Timor, from any responsibility for the massacre. While several senior military officers, including the East Timor and regional commanders, were removed from their posts, they were not formally charged with any offenses. Subsequently, nine junior-ranking soldiers and one policeman were to face court-martial, but the charges laid against them were of a relatively minor nature. None of the troops were charged with killing, and all received relatively light sentences. For the Timorese demonstrators, however, it was a different matter. More than a dozen trials were held and, although none were charged with carrying weapons or using violence, most received severe sentences ranging from six years to life imprisonment (Asia Watch Committee, 1992).

The Santa Cruz massacre is significant not only because it occurred 16 years after the beginning of Indonesia's military action to annex East Timor. It also happened at a time when the Suharto regime, and governments friendly to it, were seeking to assure the international community that the East Timor situation was settled, and no further action against Indonesia was therefore warranted. Government officials in, for example, the United States, Canada, and Australia were insisting that indiscriminate killing, and most other forms of mistreatment, had been ended by a more enlightened regional administration.

While the humanitarian situation in the province eased in the mid-1990s, a new crisis unfolded following the collapse of the Suharto regime in May 1998, and the launching of a more conciliatory policy toward the East Timorese by his successor, Habibie. By the middle of that year, self-determination and the possibility of independence was again on the agenda. The new president began a dialogue with both Timorese leaders and senior UN officials, including Kofi Annan himself, the new UN Secretary General, who stepped up the world body's efforts to achieve a just solution to what, at that time, was the biggest issue of its kind remaining on the agenda of the Decolonization Commission.

These new moves, and the development of a more democratic regime in Jakarta, led to two conflicting developments: on the one hand, a sharp increase in East Timorese demands for self-determination and the right to the choice of independence; and on the other, a strong reaction on the part of the Indonesian military command. These developments were of particular concern to the politically powerful Special Forces Command (Kopassus), which had played a leading role in the illegal seizure of the former Portuguese province, and in the subsequent administration of the territory. In the years of military operations against the Timorese resistance, many thousands of Indonesian troops had lost their lives, and the idea of giving up the territory was therefore anathema to the commanders.

In the event, senior Kopassus generals organized the establishment of a militia force, recruited from among the East Timorese minority who favored continuation of Indonesian rule. The structure of the militia was designed by Kopassus, while arms, military training, and other funding were provided from various government sources. Under these arrangements, each of the 13 districts had a militia unit. These troops were exhorted to wage a campaign of violence and intimidation against East Timorese who favored independence.

Early in 1999, President Habibie announced his readiness to agree to a plebiscite on his offer of autonomy, assuring the Timorese that the right to independence would be accepted should the offer be rejected. The militia campaign of violence was stepped up with TNI officers, who called on the paramilitary forces to attack and kill pro-independence supporters—in some cases, the militia were exhorted to kill supporters' families. What transpired was, in effect, a conspiracy by senior TNI generals aimed at preventing the loss of East Timor and at sabotaging UN efforts in support of what was regarded internationally as a much-delayed act of self-determination. These commanders may have operated independently, but clearly their operations were known to the Indonesian defense force commander, General Wiranto.

The presence of UNAMET after June 1999 hampered this campaign of violence, but by the time the plebiscite was held in August of that year dozens of East Timorese had been killed in attacks organized or aided by the Indonesian military, and thousands more had been dislocated by the militia terror. As the plebiscite approached, the military commanders realized that, regardless of the militia operations, they were going to lose the vote. It was then that the military command devised a campaign of killing and destruction, as a punishment of the East Timorese for their disloyalty and their humiliation of the Indonesian military. The operation, designated Operasi Guntur (Operation Thunder), was launched within hours of the announcement of the results of the plebiscite (78.5% voted against acceptance of autonomy). TNI troops, aided by their militia, swarmed over the province in a campaign of destruction. In less than three weeks 72% of all buildings and houses were destroyed or damaged, and hundreds of East Timorese were killed, many of them in massacres at Suai, Maliana, and the Oecussi enclave. More than 250,000 people were deported to West Timor. The casualty rate would have been much higher had not hundreds of thousands of Timorese fled to the mountains where they faced severe food shortages—a crisis, though, that was soon eased by UN and Australian emergency airdrops.

Unlike in 1975, this genocidal crime attracted an immediate global response, with the UN Security Council calling on Indonesia to end the rampage and allow for the implementation of the outcome of the plebiscite. A force composed of a coalition of the willing, led by Australia, was instructed by the UN to enter the territory immediately after its authorization by President Habibie. The nightmare of the previous weeks ended, but East Timor was left in a totally devastated state, and without the basic elements of a community infrastructure. The loss of life from this military operation is still not fully known (some of the bodies were disposed of in the deep-sea channel north of the island), but the author believes that it could exceed 2,000.

The following November a UN mission with a comprehensive mandate to prepare the country for independence began its mission, ending 25 years of harsh occupation. Reconstruction of the nation's destroyed towns and villages began, and after considerable delay the return of those who had been forced to go to the Indonesian part of the island was negotiated by UN authorities. The UN has been less successful in its quest to bring to justice those ultimately responsible for these atrocities. According to the findings of the International Commission of Enquiry established by CHR Resolution 1999/S-4/1, "ultimately the Indonesian Army was responsible for the intimidation, terror, killings, and other acts of violence experienced by the people of East Timor before and after the popular consultations [plebiscite]." A more damning report came from Indonesia's Human Rights Commission's special committee, implicating the military, including General Wiranto, as being responsible for these heinous actions.

The obvious answer would have been an ad hoc international tribunal, but enthusiasm for such an outcome soon wilted. That was due to several reasons. First, Indonesia came under the leadership of President Wahid, a leading reformer who insisted that Indonesia would itself establish a tribunal and bring to justice the military commanders responsible for the crimes committed. Second, Wahid encountered great difficulty in implementing his reforms, and one of the casualties was the proposed tribunal. Third, though it finally came into being some months after Megawati Sukarnoputri took office, it was a pale shadow of the intended tribunal, its terms of reference offering an escape for the generals responsible for setting up the militia. Indeed, its outcome has been a farce. The senior officer who gave orders at the Suai massacre has been acquitted. Other killers have not even been charged. More seriously, not one of the conspirators who planned the campaign of terror and killing has even appeared before the court—except to witness its proceedings! One senior officer was given a brief sentence, but his case is subject to an appeal.

In East Timor itself a number of militia were captured, and after a considerable delay several were sentenced to lengthy prison terms. Unfortunately, for several months the efforts of UNTAET's prosecutors suffered from poor direction. Then, under the new management of the prosecutor-general's office, the process was expedited, but with the office no longer being a direct UN responsibility it encountered political criticism from the leaders of the newly independent state, who were anxious to avoid a confrontation with Jakarta in the first difficult years of independence. The recent indictment of a number of Indonesian military commanders attracted an angry rejection from Jakarta and a cool response from Dili.

Responsibility for the Genocide

There can be little doubt that direct responsibility for the killing in East Timor rests with the Indonesian military forces. From the outset the invading forces had an opportunity to extend maximum protection to the non-combatant population, in accordance with the Geneva Conventions. The invaders almost totally ignored these basic rights, at huge cost to Indonesia, as it turned out.[36] A humane and disciplined occupation would have moderated the attitudes of the Timorese themselves, and the character of the resistance would have been radically different. As it turned out, the senseless killing and harsh occupation policies in general, especially under General Dading Kalbuardi, stiffened the courage, determination, and endurance of the Falintil—the military arm of Fretilin. Indeed, because the armed resistance was effectively isolated, and was able to attract little international support, their will to resist may have collapsed much earlier had it not been for the harsh nature of Indonesian military rule in East Timor.

From time to time it has been alleged that many of the Timorese casualties were caused by the civil war, or later internecine conflicts. In fact, between 1,500 and 2,000 were killed in the brief civil war of August

1975,[37] but there is no evidence that tribal conflicts occurred after Indonesia's invasion. On the other hand, it is known that the resistance forces killed several hundred collaborators over a period of 10 years.

It has been argued, especially by some apologists for the Suharto regime, that none of this killing was ordered from Jakarta and that most of the blame rests with undisciplined or impulsive troops. Following the killings at Santa Cruz cemetery, for example, officials in Washington, Canberra, and certain other Western capitals responded along these lines. Yet, governments cannot be absolved of responsibility so conveniently. Even if these killings were not ordered by the government of Indonesia, it remains the final responsible authority. Moreover, the government can hardly claim ignorance of human rights abuses of this nature, because they were so frequently reported and the focus of regular protests by organizations like Amnesty International and Asia Watch.

The Suharto government's line of defense was especially facile if we consider the Santa Cruz tragedy. The Indonesian decision to set up a commission of investigation was clearly a response to international outrage, and not a spontaneous reaction to the news of the killing. In the immediate aftermath of the massacre, the reaction from Jakarta was defensive, while the military's response was dismissive, even defiant.[38] There can be little doubt that the Indonesian authorities would have reacted differently had foreign observers not been present. It may well be that no order to kill indiscriminately has ever been issued by Jakarta—even at the highest military levels. Nevertheless, it is inconceivable that the military command had been unaware of the indiscriminate killing and summary executions perpetrated by the military during those 16 years. Yet there is no evidence that, until the Santa Cruz incident, any of the perpetrators were ever placed on trial or disciplined.

It is impossible not to conclude, therefore, that such gross violations of fundamental human rights were tolerated by the government of Indonesia. Certainly, within the military itself such killings had become acceptable behavior. In Indonesia, military and political leadership tends to merge at the top, and therefore it follows that the top-ranking responsible authorities in Indonesia had long been aware that the behavior of the military forces in East Timor had resulted in the decimation of the indigenous population.

Clearly, genocide, in the form of the destruction of a significant part of a group, can occur as the result of inhumane and irresponsible actions, without a formal intention being identified. Troops can be indoctrinated with hatred in what many might accept as the normal preparation for combat; that is, the strengthening of the soldier's will to fight.

In Timor, for example, in the early weeks of the fighting some of the Indonesian forces were told they were fighting communists, who had been the subject of hatred and indiscriminate killing after 1965 because of the PKI's alleged conspiracy to overthrow the government and set up a Marxist state.[39] Ideological hatred breeds racial hatred and intolerance. The way the annexation of East Timor was carried out inevitably provoked an irreconcilable antagonism on the Timorese side. Dislike, therefore, was mutual, causing Indonesian troops to care little about the lives of Timorese, whose language they did not speak and whose religion most of them did not share.

On the other hand, there is no evidence that the Indonesian government, or for that matter the military leadership, sought, as a matter of deliberate policy, to destroy the Timorese people as a race or ethnic group. Yet it cannot escape the charge that it was aware of the wanton human destruction, especially between 1975 and 1982, and the organized militia violence that culminated in massive destruction, wanton killing, and large-scale deportations in 1999.

There is one aspect of intention worthy of closer scrutiny. It could be argued that when it became apparent to Indonesia's highest political and military authorities that the majority of the East Timorese were opposed to integration, the Indonesian military command in the province sought to destroy the will of the people for independence. This meant destroying a key element in the Timorese identity, that is, changing their identity from that of a people seeking to shape their own political future to a radically different status, that of being a loyal component of the Indonesian state.

If they had initially aimed to achieve this end by persuasion—by winning hearts and minds—why did their invading force behave like barbarians? Why did they torture, rape, and kill indiscriminately? Was not this killing and other inhuman actions, which inevitably led to tens of thousands of deaths, part of a plan to destroy the desire for independence and the will to oppose integration?

If we accept the words of no less an authority than General Murdani,[40] the principal targets of the occupation authorities for eradication were, and, for that matter, continued to be for years to come, the independence movement leaders and their supporters. But the government's oppressive policies ensured that the vast majority of Timorese still yearned for independence, even if only a few of them were prepared to take up arms. If the Indonesian military had persisted with the idea that all support for independence must be eliminated, it would have placed the majority of the population at risk.

The Timor situation highlights an important dimension of the subject of this book—cultural genocide. In Portuguese times, foreigners made up only a small percentage of the population of East Timor. The largest minority was the Chinese. The Portuguese, even if we include their military, never amounted to more than a few thousand people.

By the early 1990s, outsiders—that is, people who had come from elsewhere in Indonesia after the invasion—made up one-fifth of the population. In terms of power, they were not a mere minority, but the successors of the colonial power. In fact, their presence was infinitely more pervasive and had a far greater impact on Timorese society. From the latter's point of view, these intruders dominated virtually all aspects of the government of the province. In the economy, as well as in government and the military, the Indonesian role was much more powerful and commanding than was the place of the Portuguese, even under the Salazar dictatorship.

The Indonesian newcomers were very much a ruling class, dominating as they did the military and the civil government. Thousands of transmigrants moved into some of the province's best agricultural lands, in some cases displacing the indigenous inhabitants. A flood of informal arrivals, mostly drifters seeking to exploit any economic opportunity, swelled the populations of the major towns. This massive intrusion of outsiders, and Jakarta's efforts to change Timorese ways and attitudes, was undermining the very identity of the Timorese, the least "Indonesian" of the communities of the archipelago.

Special Characteristics of the Timor Case

The case of East Timor presents a number of distinctive elements. First and foremost, it is a live issue, an issue of our time as distinct from being a lesson of history. The question of culpability for the crimes committed is still before the UN. It is one of the issues that had not been resolved when UNTAET's mandate ended, leaving the world body with a continuing responsibility. There has been strong pressure for the setting up of an ad hoc international tribunal, but the proposal has attracted little support from the UN Security Council, despite widespread criticism of the conduct of the Indonesian tribunal. The low level of international interest has discouraged some of East Timor's leaders from pursuing such an outcome. Hence, more emphasis has been placed on the reconciliation process than the exposure of past crimes and action against those responsible for them. Although East Timor's position has changed radically over the past 10 years, this case continues to highlight the frailty of international resolve when it comes to the small and unimportant in the global power play. It is a reminder of the vulnerability of small states outside the mainstream of global political and economic interests.

Second, while past international responses at times caused Indonesian political leaders some discomfort, they have always been able to resist such pressures. The Santa Cruz massacre illustrates this point. The official response from countries like Australia, the United States, and Japan was restrained, even non-judgmental. Most of those governments, who were quick to denounce relatively recent cases of indiscriminate killing in Iraq and Bosnia-Herzegovina, did not resort to the same kind of blunt language in their responses to the massacre of more than 200 Timorese in November 1991.

On the whole, in its seizure of East Timor, Indonesia was able to exploit the prevailing Cold War context. Indeed, the Suharto regime's Western friends to an extent encouraged the annexation by accepting as credible Jakarta's alleged fears of communist insurgency in the post-Vietnam years. Perhaps the most disturbing aspect of this case is that these crimes against humanity went virtually unchallenged at a time when acts of aggression and oppression were being challenged in almost every other part of the world.

Third, the annexation of East Timor could in fact have been averted, had Indonesia's Western friends acted responsibly in the 1974–1975 period. The Suharto regime's moves to annex the colony were carefully devised against the anticipated reactions of countries like Australia and the United States, whose intelligence agencies were familiar with the unfolding conspiracy. It is in this context that the genocide dimensions of the problem are profoundly disturbing. Most Western governments, especially those members of Indonesia's aid consortium, were aware, more than a decade before the Santa Cruz killing, of the genocidal impact of Jakarta's military operations in East Timor; that is, in the terms of Article II(c) of the Convention. The failure of the IGGI (Inter-Governmental Group on Indonesia) members, in particular, to take up the issue at a time when the Suharto regime was heavily dependent on Western aid was at best shameful. Ever since the anti-communist Suharto regime came to power it had been sensitive to the concerns of major Western powers like the United States. Despite this fact, even when the extent of loss of life in East Timor became evident in the early 1980s, the continued acceptability of Indonesia rule of the former Portuguese colony was never seriously questioned.

Fourth, although the Timor case was for more than two decades before the UN, the problem was not effectively addressed until after the fall of President Suharto, the collapse of his regime brought about by causes unrelated to the Timor problem. East Timor is arguably the only remnant of the once-extensive European empires to have been annexed by its neighbor, with the virtual collusion of many of those nations who today regard themselves as being at the forefront of the international movement to promote universal respect for human rights, including the right to self-determination.

The Timor Case as a Contributor to Genocide Studies

The case of East Timor is a significant one, particularly as a definitive case of genocide within the terms of Article II of the UN Convention on the Prevention and Punishment of the Crime of Genocide. Although the question of the denial of the right to self-determination has now been resolved, the commissioners of the serious crimes committed have yet to be appropriately dealt with by the international community. The violation against the people of East Timor has some classical characteristics, in the sense that it resulted from an act of aggression by the large power next door. However, it occurred within a contemporary historical framework; that is, an extensive body of human rights principles and laws had set down protective parameters for the international community. It also occurred at a time when acts of aggression of this kind were no longer tolerated by the UN system, as the cases of the Falklands (1982) and Kuwait (1990) dramatically demonstrated.

On the other hand, the lesson of East Timor is that some things have not changed, despite the growing intolerance of the international community toward gross human rights violations involving mass killing. The East Timorese suffered from their country's remoteness, from its lack of economic and strategic importance, and conversely, from the perceived importance of the violator, today the world's largest Islamic nation, which forms a strategically and economically important division between the Indian and Pacific Oceans. However, one of the most disturbing aspects of the case is that the perpetrators of those atrocities were in practice shielded from international scrutiny by countries like Australia and the United States, which pride themselves on their commitment to human rights.

Perhaps the most disturbing aspect of the experience of East Timor is that it highlights just how difficult it is to invoke the Genocide Convention, even in circumstances where the evidence that grave violations have occurred is substantial and persistent. Indeed, the Timor case suggests that the Convention is so difficult to invoke that it is perceived by the victims and others as being virtually irrelevant as an international legal protection or recourse against this monstrous form of crime. On a number of occasions at the United Nations, Timorese representatives and their supporters examined the possibility of invoking the Convention before the International Court of Justice, but in each case experts cast doubt on this course of action. As for the governments of Australia and the United States, "genocide" is a term that has been studiously avoided, even when there have been expressions of concern at the human rights situation in Timor.

The East Timor case also brings into focus the factor of cultural genocide, which is of crucial importance when the victims of aggression are massively outnumbered in terms of population. While this aspect is not specified in the Convention, it remains extremely important, as the Timor cases attests.

It is very likely that deliberate "Indonesianization" would have submerged Timorese culture, ultimately risking its destruction, had not unforeseen circumstances led to a radical change of policy by the Indonesian government.

Editors' note: The following update is provided by the editors. It covers the years 2002–2011.

Becoming an independent nation was, as one can imagine, a monumental event for the people of Timor-Leste, who had suffered through 400 years of Portuguese colonial rule and 24 brutal years of occupation by Indonesia. Slowly but surely the new nation has continued to crawl toward the realization of creating a democratic state. A key reason for the jittery and slow progess is that Timor-Leste has had to virtually start from the ground up in creating what are considered fundamental institutions of modern democracy. One of the key problems over the years has been the large gap between the establishment of governmental bodies and regulations and implementation of these building blocks for a society that promotes justice and human dignity for all its citizens.

In August 2001, while still under the authority of UNTAET, East Timor adopted a parliamentary form of government and established its first parliament in a UN-supervised election. Not surprisingly, the Fretilin Party won the most seats in the election. On May 20, 2002, East Timor formally became an independent republic, Timor-Leste.

In April 2002, Xanana Gusmao was elected Timor-Leste's first president. Gusmao was a beloved and legendary rebel who fought against Indonesia's rule of East Timor for some two decades. Not only did he put his life on the line fighting for the freedom of his people, but he was incarcerated and then placed under house arrest for six years by the Indonesian government.

With East Timor's independence, UNTAET's mandate came to an end. UNTAET was replaced by the UN Mission for the Support of East Timor (UNMISET), whose primary purpose was to assist the new nation in many areas, such as managing law and order and training a new police force as the government became more established. UNMISET's mandate ended on May 20, 2005, and was followed by a special political mission (UN Office in Timor-Leste or UNOTIL) aimed at assisting Timor-Leste.

In 2002 the Commission for Reception, Truth and Reconciliation was established and held its first public hearings in November of that year. The Commission delved into human rights violations committed just prior to Indonesia's invasion of East Timor in 1975 and throughout its

24-year occupation. The Commission faced a huge task as innumerable human rights violations and atrocities had been committed by Indonesia against the people of East Timor during that long, sordid period.

Timor-Leste experienced its first full year of independence in 2003. Throughout the year, the government worked at developing and/or strengthening new institutions and policies, abiding by key human rights instruments and treaties, and creating a police force that stood for law and order and justice for all citizens. These were tasks that were going to try the patience of many, be called into question in regard to their implementation, and take years to work out both small and extremely serious issues.

Throughout 2002 and 2003, efforts continued to be made to bring to justice those who had allegedly committed criminal acts during the vote on independence in 1999. According to the well-known human rights organization, Amnesty International, "by December [2003], indictments had been served against 369 individuals for serious crimes, including crimes against humanity, in connection with the independence ballot in 1999. Among those indicted were 281 people residing in Indonesia, including senior Indonesian military officials." Indonesia, however, balked at sending suspects to Timor-Leste to stand trial.

In 2004 the two governments of Timor-Leste and Indonesia agreed to establish a bilateral Truth and Friendship Commission for the purpose of establishing "the conclusive truth in regard to the events prior to and immediately after the popular consultation in 1999, with a view to promoting reconciliation and friendship, and ensuring the non-recurrence of similar events." Many, however, including citizens of Timor-Leste and international human rights organizations, feared that such an entity might end up granting impunity to alleged perpetrators of major crimes committed during the 1999 vote on whether East Timor was to remain with Indonesia or seek independence.

In June 2005 the UN-sponsored Commission of Experts (CoE) submitted a report to the UN Security Council that included an analysis of Timor-Leste's prosecution of serious violations of human rights perpetrated during the 1999 vote. It found that those who were most responsible for the crimes perpetrated during that period had not been held accountable, and its major recommendation was *not* to allow impunity for such individuals. In the same report, serious concerns were issued in regard to the focus of the Truth and Friendship Commission. Again, its major concern was that various provisions of the Commission might not be in compliance with international standards vis-à-vis the denial of impunity, and thus it called for "clarification, reassessment and revision" of such provisions. Basically ignoring the criticism and recommendations, the Truth and Friendship Commission was established in August.

In October 2005 the Commission for Reception, Truth and Reconciliation in Timor-Leste submitted its report to the president's office. The report delineated, in detail, the various human rights violations that had been perpetrated between 1974 and 1999 in East Timor. Interestingly, its recommendations largely matched those in the report issued by the CoE. In doing so, it supported the ongoing process of arresting and trying in a court of law those who allegedly committed crimes, and suggested that, if justice was not served and impunity reigned, serious thought should be given to establishing an international tribunal.

Unfortunately, as alluded to above, and as is often the case with new nations, not all went smoothly. It did not help that Timor-Leste is one of the poorest countries in the Asia-Pacific region and, for that matter, in the world. It is estimated that half of its citizens live below the poverty line. Those residing in urban areas are no better off than those in rural areas. Among the major problems faced by citizens all across the country are a lack of adequate infrastructure, such as electricity, telecommunications and roads, bridges, and transport.

Furthermore, as the new government continued to stumble along, Timor-Leste citizens alleged that the police in the newly established police force abused the laws by, for example, both detaining individuals arbitrarily and beating suspects. There also continued to be a massive shortage of judges, defense lawyers, and prosecutors, which largely undermined the efficacy of the judicial system.

In February 2006 an estimated 400 soldiers (out of some 1,400) complained to President Xanana Gusmao about the discriminatory behavior they were allegedly facing. The head of the nation's military (F-FDTL), however, summarily dismissed the complaints. On April 28 about 400 soldiers held a demonstration, which exploded into deadly violence.

Fearing for their safety, many civilians fled from their towns and villages, seeking sanctuary elsewhere. Mass chaos, fighting, and the destruction of homes and buildings ensued. As mobs and gangs virtually took over Dili, the capital of the country, and killed at will, the city became so dangerous that thousands more fled into the countryside. Ultimately, it was estimated that some 150,000 had fled from their homes. On May 28, fearing the entire nation was about to descend into anarchy, the leaders of Timor-Leste sought assistance from Australia, New Zealand, Malaysia, and Portugal to help return the nation to peace.

Due to intense criticism of how the prime minister dealt with the aforementioned conflict he resigned on July 10, which was followed by the creation of a new cabinet on July 14. On August 25, the UN Security Council passed Resolution 1704, which established the United Nations Integrated Mission in Timor-Leste (UNMIT). UNMIT's express mission was to assist the government of Timor-Leste in various ways, including but not limited to the following:

- to support the government and relevant institutions, with a view to consolidating stability, enhancing a culture of democratic governance, and facilitating political dialogue among Timorese stakeholders, in their efforts to bring about a process of national reconciliation and to foster social cohesion;
- to support Timor-Leste in all aspects of the 2007 presidential and parliamentary electoral process;
- to ensure the restoration and maintenance of public security in Timor-Leste;
- to assist in further building the capacity of state and government institutions in areas;
- to assist in further strengthening the national institutional and societal capacity and mechanisms for the monitoring, promotion, and protection of human rights and for promotion of justice and reconciliation; and
- to facilitate the provision of relief and recovery assistance and access to the Timorese people in need.

In April 2007, presidential elections were held, and, after a run-off, Jose Ramos-Horta, who had resigned as Prime Minister in order to run for president, won by 69% of the vote. In June, the country held parliamentary elections and, again, Fretilin candidates won the most seats but no party won a majority of seats in parliament. Complicating matters, the parties could not come to a consensus on forming a new government. Subsequently, in August 2007, President Ramos-Horta asked the former president of the country, Xanana Gusmao, to help form a new government. Gusmao agreed to do so and became the new prime minister.

While both of the aforementioned elections in 2007 were, for the most part, free of threats, violence, and suspect behavior, violence did break out upon the creation of the new government. Some members of Fretilin were furious that they were not asked to form the new government and during the course of their protests violence broke out. Once the protests and violence were quelled, those in Fretilin remained perturbed that they had been slighted and asserted that the current government was unconstitutional. Be that as it may, Fretilin has taken an active part in the new government and today constitutes the major opposition party in parliament.

The new government has worked diligently to address the various problems that have resulted in grievances in the recent past. For example, it addressed the complaints of the military personnel who felt discriminated against; it has tackled the difficult issue of reintegrating displaced persons back into society; and it continues to address land rights issues.

Unfortunately, violence has continued to plague Timor-Leste. For example, on February 11, 2008 an assassination attempt was carried out against President Ramos-Horta by the followers of a disenchanted former military police commander, Alfredo Reinado. Ramos-Horta was shot and suffered severe injuries but was whisked to Darwin, Australia, and underwent successful surgery.

On the very same day that Ramos-Horta was attacked, a failed assassination attempt was carried out against Prime Minister Gusmao. Due to the quick actions of his bodyguards he was not shot or harmed in any way. Ultimately, Reinado was caught and killed.

Due to the assassination attempts on the two top political leaders of the country, the government announced a "state of siege." Security forces were allowed greater freedom to carry out searches and arrests of suspects, a curfew was imposed, and freedom of assembly was limited. Not wishing to cause hardship for the society at large and wanting to avoid criticism for adopting such a tough approach, the measures were gradually removed by the government as calm was reestablished.

Upon the capture and surrender of all of Reinado's men, the state of emergency was called off on April 29. On March 3, 2010 most of Reinado's men were tried and convicted of attempting to assassinate Ramos-Horta. Magnanimously, Ramos-Horta commuted the sentences of all of the men and all were released from prison.

In July 2008, Prime Minister Xanana Gusmao and President Jose Ramos-Horta met in Bali with Indonesian President Susilo Bambang Yudhoyono in order to receive the Truth and Friendship Commission's report. The Commission asserted that attacks and abuses had been perpetrated by individuals and groups aligned with both sides of the crisis but assigned "institutional responsibility" to the Indonesian military for committing gross human rights violations. As might be imagined, the reception to the report was extremely mixed. Those who supported the report asserted that the findings and recommendations were likely to bring about reconciliation between the two nations; critics, on the other hand, decried the report's authors for failing to demand accountability for those Indonesians (military troops, members of the militia, and individuals) who killed, tortured, maimed, and created a life of misery for the people of East Timor.

In late August 2009, Amnesty International (2011) issued a report in which it asserted that the ongoing failure to try those who wreaked violence during the 1999 independence vote constituted an ongoing threat to the new nation's stability. The report noted that almost all of the suspects who perpetrated the violence had not yet been tried in independent courts in Timor-Leste or Indonesia. Those who had been tried in Indonesia had been acquitted. Not surprisingly, the court proceedings were roundly criticized as being fundamentally flawed. The Amnesty International report also asserted that

> The failure to rebuild the justice system effectively and to bring those responsible for past human rights violations to justice contributes to an environment where there is no strong deterrent to political violence and human rights violations.... The denial of justice ... has eroded key pillars of the new state: the rule of law and a strong and independent judiciary. (Amnesty International, 2011, p. 4)

The report concluded by calling on the UN Security Council to halt the ongoing impunity and to establish an international criminal tribunal to try the alleged perpetrators of the various crimes committed during East Timor's occupation by Indonesia.

Today, in January 2012, Timor-Leste's economy remains shaky. Due to its citizens' "low skill base" and the country's "weak public governance," the establishment of a strong, sustainable, and far-reaching (meaning for all citizens throughout the country) economic base is still but a dream. Real security for all citizens as well as the protection of individuals' land rights continue to plague Timor-Leste. The latter has resulted in people fighting over the same piece of land, each claiming the land as their own. All of these concerns must be addressed if Timor-Leste is to move toward a truly stable society based on law, justice, and equity.

Eyewitness Accounts

Since Indonesian troops invaded East Timor close to 30 years ago, eyewitness accounts have provided mounting evidence of gross human rights violations, including those of a genocidal character. Such testimonies have been collected by professional human rights agencies such as Amnesty International and Asia Watch and, at the time of writing, a UN-supported Truth and Reconciliation Commission. In the past, researchers, including this writer, encountered a major obstacle to the recording of these accounts—the informants invariably insisted that their identities should not be made public. A few witnesses spoke out publicly but the vast majority were extremely reluctant to be identified. Until the end of Indonesian occupation in 1999, and even in its aftermath, the reason advanced was understandable enough—fear of reprisals by the Indonesian security authorities against relatives and friends in East Timor, or against refugees remaining in West Timor under duress.

Unlike other issues of this nature, the Timor saga was not, at least for close to 25 years, a matter of past history; it was an ongoing drama. While the authorities responsible for the most serious violations may no longer have been in the territory, the regime whose policies enabled them to take place was still firmly in power. And while the way East Timor was seized had been the subject of widespread criticism, there was not a serious attempt, until 1999, by the major powers to persuade Indonesia to withdraw from East Timor and to allow a process of self-determination to take place. Indeed, for many years there was simply not enough international pressure, nor foreign or human rights presence in Timor, to discourage retaliation and victimization against advocates of self-determination. Until very recently, in fact, accounts of harassment by security authorities of the relatives of those Timorese involved in the resistance and related activities continued to filter through to outside human rights agencies.

While the penalties may have eased in the mid-1990s, the TNI-led campaign of violence, deportations, and massive destruction that occurred in 1999 demonstrated that the nature of the military-dominated administration remained unchanged. Its intolerance of opposition to integration is well recorded, including several actions by the military commander in the aftermath of the Santa Cruz incident. If anything, political oppression was intensified in 1992, especially after the appointment of Governor Abilio Osorio Soares, who had long been associated with the Indonesian intelligence network.

Between 1991 and 1999 few foreigners were able to gain free access to East Timor. In those circumstances, it was very difficult to make contact with witnesses of indiscriminate killings and torture, let alone offer some protection against reprisals from the military authorities. This problem was highlighted during the trial of Xanana Gusmao in Dili, when the defense counsel informed the court that he was having difficulty in persuading witnesses to appear on behalf of the accused. The situation changed after the UN intervention in 1999, but the massive upheaval caused by the TNI's final destructive campaign of revenge, and UN and Timorese rehabilitation priorities, led to considerable delay in addressing the atrocities perpetrated during the 24 years of Indonesian occupation. Only in 2000 were these incidents starting to be investigated.

As for the TNI perpetrators, although several of the commanders have been brought before an Indonesian tribunal in response to internal pressures, most have been acquitted. Only one officer received a light sentence, but that case was summarily dismissed by a higher court. The UN-led prosecutor-general's office in East Timor has issued a number of indictments against Indonesian officers, as well as militia members, but so far these have been ignored by the government of Indonesia. It remains a matter of grave concern that most of the indicted command-ers have been rewarded with promotions, with several of them subse-quently occupying responsible operations roles in TNI military actions in West Papua and Aceh.

The following are selections of accounts that were brought to the direct attention of the author in the aftermath of the invasion. Although much new material now being assembled is available, these testimonies are typical in character.

Account 1

The invasion of Dili. Etelvina Correia was interviewed by the author some months after the invasion. She was chosen because of her clear and unhesitating account, and because she was one of the few witnesses at the scene of the killing. The following is an abbreviated version of her account.

The attack on Dili began at about 4 a.m. on December 7. Etelvina Correia was in the church, which is located in the waterfront area. Some time later paratroops began to land (some of them dropped into the water). At 7 a.m. she saw paratroops shoot a woman in the parish garage and later three women in front of the church, although their hands were raised. The Indonesian soldiers then ordered all of the people in the vicin-ity of the church to go inside. The next day, Etelvina and the others were ordered by troops to go to the wharf area. There, 20 women—Chinese and Timorese—were taken out to the front. Some of them had children who were weeping. The soldiers tore the children from the women, who were then shot one by one, with the crowd being ordered to count after each execution. At 2 p.m. on the same day, 59 men, including Chinese and Timorese, were taken to the wharf and executed in the same way. Again the witnesses were ordered at gunpoint to count. They were told that these killings were in reprisal for the killing of a paratrooper near the Toko Lay shop in Dili.

Account 2

The following consists of extracts from a letter written in November 1977 by a Catholic priest in East Timor and sent to two Dominican nuns, Sister Natalia Granada Moreira and Sister Maria Auxiliadora Her-nandez. Its importance is that it was written during what was probably the worst period following the invasion. At the time, East Timor was securely closed off to the outside world, and communications even to other parts of Indonesia were heavily censored. This letter was smuggled out by a person who carried it to Jakarta.

The war. It continues with the same fury as it had started. Fretilin continues the struggle, in spite of famine, lack of clothing, death, and a crisis in understanding and objectives which has surfaced lately. The invaders have intensified their attacks in the three classic ways—from land, sea and air.

Between December 7 and 31, 1975, and up to February 1976, in Dili harbour there were at anchor up to 23 warships which vomited intense fire towards Dili 24 hours a day. Daily eight to twelve helicopters and four bombers flew reconnaissance and bombing runs near Dili. Numerous tanks and armoured vehicles roamed about the territory. The Indonesian armed forces in Timor must have surpassed 50,000 (I don't know for certain). In December last year there was heavy movement of ships in Dili, discharging war materials and disembarking troops. From last September (1977) the war was again intensified. The bombers did not stop all day. Hundreds of human beings died every day. The bodies of the victims became food for carnivorous birds (if we don't die of the war, we die of the plague), villages were completely destroyed, some tribes decimated.... And the war enters its third year with no promise of an early end in sight. The barbarities (understandable in the Middle Ages and justifiable in the Stone Age), the cruelties, the pillaging, the unqualified destruction of Timor, the executions without reason, in a word all the "organized" evil, has spread deep roots in Timor.

There is complete insecurity and the terror of arbitrary imprisonment is our daily bread (I am on the "persona non grata" list and any day I could disappear). Fretilin soldiers who give themselves up are disposed of—for them there is no prison. Genocide will come soon, perhaps by next December. Taking advantage of the courage of the Timorese, they are being urged to fight their brothers in the interior. It is they who march in front of the (Indonesian) battalions to intimidate the prey.

[Section on the position of the Church omitted]

The political situation. Indescribable. Sabotage and lies dominate the information sector. Integration is not the expression of the will of the people.

The people are controlled by the Indonesians and, given the character of the oppressor and the level of the Indonesian presence, it is a lamb being led to the slaughter. In the presence of such force, there is no way to resist; liberty is a word without meaning. The proclaimed liberation is synonymous with slavery. Timor is returning to the nineteen forties and anti-communism is an Islamic slogan meaning "iconoclasm." The reform of our customs means the setting up of cabarets and houses of prostitution.... In commerce, the search for basic needs dominates, and black-market is the rule. The Chinese are easily corrupted and they themselves are instruments of commercial exploitation. To travel outside of Indonesia is a dream. Mail is censored....

Please do something positive for the liberty of the Timorese people. The world ignores us and our grief.... We are on the road to complete genocide. By the end of December the war could exterminate us. All of the youth of Timor (30% of the population) are in the forests: the Indonesian control only one or two kilometres beyond the villages. We ask all justice-loving people to save Timor, and we ask God to forgive the sins of the Timorese people....

Timor, November 1977 [name withheld]

Account 3

The next item consists of extracts taken from a message, written in 1977, from a Timorese father to his son in Portugal, with whose whereabouts he was not familiar. Again, it is rather general, but it is one of the few first-hand written accounts of conditions in East Timor at that time.

Tell my son that for nothing on this earth should he return to Timor. I would rather die without seeing him again than to know that he had returned to this hell....

There are very few Timorese in the streets of Dili; most of them are in the forests, dead or in prison; the cost of living is extremely high and there is a need for the most basic foodstuffs. The suffering is indescribable, as may be affirmed by the Apostolic Nuncio in Jakarta who went to Dili in the middle of October to celebrate an open-air mass. The weeping, the tears, the laments of the orphans, widows and forsaken were such that the Mass had to be interrupted for a quarter of an hour before it could continue....

In a desperate attempt to crush by force the armed resistance which continues to exist in most of the territory, the Jakarta authorities now have sent ten more battalions to Timor. Thus, the number of Indonesian troops engaged in fighting usually cited as being over 40,000 must now be more than 50,000.... The increase in military operations has once more turned Timor into a place of arms and warfare. At the present time, with the beginning of the rainy season, land operations should have diminished but the constant air raids and the launching of incendiary bombs which have been systematically punishing the rural populations continue.

Account 4

An extract from a Letter from Timor, also in 1977.

> A continuous, increasingly violent war rages in Timor. The group of villages in which I lived have been completely destroyed. There is not one soul there. I myself am in Dili and I have gone many days without eating. These are the effects of war. But there are people who are much worse off than I. I have been sick several times and at death's door for want of medication. The cost of living in Dili is very high and the salaries are very low. One sees no one else but Indonesian soldiers and Chinese on the streets of Dili. There are very few Timorese for the majority are either in the forest, dead or in jail. The luck of Timor is to be born in tears, to live in tears and to die in tears. It would, perhaps, be more appropriate to say that one does not cry for one has no more tears to shed, for Timor is no longer Timor: it is nothing but an oppressed worm....

Account 5

The following account was conducted by Michele Turner, a well-known Australian oral historian. The subject is a former Timorese guerrilla fighter, named Laurenco, who spent much of the early years of the occupation in the eastern sector of the island. He describes conditions in a mountain area, where many Timorese lost their lives, largely through air attacks, and the consequences of famine. (Note: accounts 5 and 6 are extracts from Michele Turner's *Telling: East Timor Personal Testimonies, 1942–1992* (Sydney: University of New South Wales, 1992). Reprinted with permission.)

Our section in the east was the last to be attacked. In 1978 they started to come against us. At first we didn't resist, just watched the enemy, let them feel confident. Matebian Mountain is a big area and there were 160,000 of us, fighters and civilians, divided into small groups.

On 17 October 1978 some Indonesians got right to the bottom of Matebian Mountain and that's when we started to fight back. For those first two months, October and November, we were very successful and about 3000 Indonesians died. Then they got angry and scared to come close and started to bomb us from the air. They bombed twice a day, in the morning and in the afternoon with four black planes. Their name I know now is Broncos, but we called them scorpions because they had a tail that curves up at the back like that insect. Their bombs left a big hole about two metres deep. Then they got new supersonic planes. Our people were very frightened of those because you didn't even hear they were there until they were gone. Those supersonics would zoom along the valley so fast we couldn't shoot them.

The bombing became constant, in rotation. Three supersonics came to bomb for about forty-five minutes and then went back to reload. Half an hour later the black scorpions came, and this could go on all day. In Matebian there are a lot of caves and we hid there and only moved at night.

We knew by radio from the south zone that the Indonesians had dropped four napalm bombs there. Then they dropped two of these on us. I saw all the flames and heard people shouting and screaming. I was on another mountain but I could see well; there was a close view of it, straight across. Some of us set out straight away to help those people. By foot it took half an hour to go down and up again, and by the time we got there everything was completely burnt. We saw a whole area about fifty metres square all burnt, no grass, nothing except ash. On the rocks it was a brown reddish color and on the ground ash too, no ordinary grey ash, sort of yellow ash, like beach sand. You couldn't see where bodies had been. There was nothing except ash and burned rocks on the whole area, but we had heard those people screaming.

We could find no bones or bodies, but people near said there were about a hundred people living there who were killed by this. Those people disappeared, they were not sheltering, we never saw them again. The population was large but people were in small groups in different places and knew where each group was. The whole population was very upset—no bodies of those people left to bury. My cousin said, "If this is what they can do there is no hope for the world."

We had no food because of all the bombing and we lost radio contact. Fretilin decided they couldn't defend the people properly any more and the population should surrender, otherwise we would all be wiped out. When they announced this decision the people cried. Falintil said they couldn't force us, but this was the best thing for all. Our leader said, "You surrender and it will be better for you to get food and it will be better for us too so we can fight freely. But this doesn't mean that the war stops. We will keep fighting for our freedom and don't forget, wherever you go outside, that we are nationalists, and if ever you have a way to help us in the bush, do it." Then Falintil gave up their responsibility for the people and everyone decided for themselves to stay or go. Also the Falintil broke up into small groups to fight as guerillas.

About 2000 of us tried to stay in the mountains. We broke into three groups to escape and I was in one of these trying to get through the encirclement. In our group there were a few hundred, mostly fighters, only about a hundred ordinary people. We kept walking and walking.

The Indonesians would drop some bombs, we would hide, then walk again. We were in a valley and the Indonesians were up higher. If they shot at us our fighters did not shoot back so that the Indonesians would think we were just a normal group of people walking to surrender. We had no food, the area we were going through was mostly rocks. The enemy burnt the trees and any food growing; the animals were dead.

Account 6

The following is an extract from an account by an elderly Timorese woman, named Eloise, who was in Dili when the Indonesian invasion of the capital took place in 1975. This incident was only one of a number of mass killings carried out by Indonesian troops, following their assault on Dili.

On 7 December we woke and heard this big noise of planes and saw parachutes and planes covering the light—it became dark because of them, so many. There were shots and we went inside and kept listening to more and more shooting. In the afternoon some Timorese came and told us everyone must come to surrender at headquarters. We had to get a stick and put a piece of white material on it and come. They said, "These are orders from the Indonesian people." So we went, women and children and old men and young men.

Once we got there, they divided us: the women and children and old men to one side, and on the other young boys they wanted to help carry Fretilin things—they had taken over their store and there was ammunition and food there. We watched while they took all this stuff out from the storeroom. When they finished they were coming to join us, but the Indonesians said, "No, stay there!" Then they ordered us to form a line and wait.

Then an Indonesian screams an order and we hear machine gun running through [*sic*] the men. We see the boys and men dying right there. Some see their husbands die. We look at each other stunned. We think they are going to kill us next. All of us just turn and pick up the children and babies and run screaming, wild, everywhere.

Notes

1. Curiously, the strongest argument for such an outcome was advanced in 1966 by an American academic, Professor Donald Weatherbee, who concluded, "In a sense, Portuguese Timor is a trust territory, the Portuguese holding it in trust for Indonesia" (Weatherbee, 1966).
2. In June 1974, in contrast to most of his colleagues (who studiously avoided uttering the word "independence") Foreign Minister Adam Malik generously assured the Timorese of Indonesia's support for East Timor's independence. In a letter to Jose Ramos-Horta, a Fretilin leader, Malik wrote, inter alia: "The independence of every country is the right of every nation, with no exception for the people in Timor."

3. In 1957, for example, Indonesia told the UN First Committee, in a reference to Timor: "Indonesia has no claim to any territories which had not been part of the former Netherlands East Indies. No one should suggest otherwise or advance dangerous theories in that respect."

4. Within weeks of Pearl Harbor, Australian and some Dutch forces, ignoring the protests of the Portuguese—at that time neutral—had landed in East Timor, bringing in large Japanese forces. The Timorese gave the Australians extraordinary support until their withdrawal a year later. The Japanese then imposed a harsh occupation on the local population, which cost perhaps as many as 70,000 Timorese lives.

5. Under a special agreement (UKUSA) this intelligence surveillance was shared with the United States and formed the basis of key Defense Intelligence Agency briefings prepared for the administration in Washington.

6. The Australian relationship was not as important to Indonesia as were its links with the United States, Japan, or the Netherlands, but a firm Australian stance on the decolonization rights of the Timorese would certainly have influenced the policies of the other states and reinforced Suharto's misgivings about military intervention.

7. Named after the dragon, or giant lizard on the nearby island of Alor.

8. Frente Revolucionaria de Timor-Leste Independente—the Revolutionary Front for an Independent East Timor.

9. Uniao Democrata de Timor—the Timorese Democratic Union.

10. Based on remarks made to the writer by Major Metello, a senior representative of the Armed Forces Movement.

11. East Timor is predominantly Roman Catholic.

12. Based on talks in 1975 with two of those present at the meeting, Mousinho and Martins.

13. An example of the provocative disinformation role of Bakin at this point was the deliberate circulating of a story by Operasi Komodo agents, that a number of Vietnamese officers had been smuggled into Timor and were training a Fretilin military force.

14. In fact, at the time, most Fretilin leaders were out of the country, so it was an unlikely eventuality.

15. The humanitarian consequences of this civil war were assessed by the International Red Cross and an Australian Council for Overseas Aid (ACFOA) mission, of which I was the leader, with the former insisting that the total loss of life was about 1,500.

16. For an account of the withdrawal, see Chapter 11 of Missao Impossivel? Descolonizacao de Timor by Mario Lemos Pires (1991), the Portuguese governor at that time.

17. There is now ample evidence that these newsmen were shot by Indonesian troops, at least three of them having been executed some time after the force entered the village.

18. As an indication of Western complicity, U.S. intelligence was informed in Jakarta by their Indonesian opposite numbers that the attack would take place on December 6. However, American officials in Jakarta were shocked to discover that President Ford and Dr. Kissinger would be in the Indonesian capital on that day, and their hosts obligingly delayed the attack 24 hours.

19. Angkatan Bersenjata Republik Indonesia, Indonesian Armed Forces.

20. The Indonesian army often used Timorese drivers because of their familiarity with the difficult and sometimes dangerous road conditions in the interior.

21. The International Committee of the Red Cross team, under the leadership of Andre Pasquier, was forced to withdraw before the invasion when Indonesia refused to respect its neutrality.

22. In fact, in October 1989 Governor Carrascalao, in a briefing to visiting journalists, gave a much lower total figure—659,000, which, he said, was growing at 2.63% annually. If this figure was correct, it gives an indication of the pace of immigration from elsewhere in Indonesia.

23. I have chosen deliberately to use the past tense, because the great upheaval caused by the invasion, especially the resettlement programs, has clearly had a significant impact on cultural and settlement patterns.

24. However, their attitudes were to an extent influenced by the hostility toward Javanese that was prevalent in Indonesian Timor, especially after the widespread killings in 1965–1966.

25. Angkatan Udara Republik Indonesia, Air Force of the Republic of Indonesia.

26. A copy of this report, Notes on East Timor, is held by the writer.
27. A General Assembly was followed by Security Council Resolution 384 (December 22, 1975), which was unanimously agreed to, a rare achievement at that time.
28. Of Indonesia's major trading and aid-donor partners—the United States, Japan, West Germany, Australia, and the Netherlands—only the last-mentioned showed concern at the government level.
29. Testimony of Robert Oakley in "Human Rights in East Timor and the Question of the Use of U.S. Equipment by the Indonesian Armed Forces," before Subcommittees of the Committee on International Relations, House of Representatives, 95th Congress, March 28, 1977. Also, letter from Edward C. Ingraham, Department of State, May 13, 1977.
30. East Timor had by that time been designated Indonesia's twenty-seventh province. Canberra waited only until 1979 before according de jure status to its recognition.
31. The confidential report to which the author was given access stated that, of the 200,000, about 10% were in such bad shape that they could not be saved.
32. In fairness, it should be noted that Australia was a major provider of financial backing for the operations of the International Red Cross.
33. Indonesia imposed strict conditions on the admission of the International Red Cross, which limited its effectiveness. For example, for some years it was denied the right to carry out tracing activities. Moreover, most of its work was carried out by the Indonesian Red Cross, which was largely under military direction.
34. In fact, the last of these operations, Operasi Senjum, involving some 10,000 troops was carried out in the central mountain area in the middle of November 1996.
35. See, in particular, the annual reports published by Amnesty International, especially East Timor: Violations of Human Rights (1985). Also see the publications of Asia Watch, especially its detailed accounts of the circumstances of the Santa Cruz massacre in Dili in November 1991.
36. The spirited Timorese resistance took a heavy toll on Indonesian lives; as many as 20,000 reportedly having been killed since 1975.
37. Based on the assessment of the International Red Cross mission, as conveyed to the writer some weeks after the civil war had ended.
38. Including from General Try Sutrisno, the defense forces commander, who was elected vice president of Indonesia in 1993.
39. The slaughter of more than 500,000 "communists," including their families, in the aftermath of the 1965 Gestapu affair, most of them by the army, was perhaps the bloodiest episode in Indonesia's history.
40. In a speech to Timorese officials in Dili, in February 1990, Murdani warned that those who still sought to form a separate state "will be crushed by ABRI. ABRI may fail the first time, so it will try for a second time, and for a third time." In a reference to Fretilin and its sympathizers he said: "We will crush them all … to safeguard the unity of Indonesian territory."

References

Amnesty International (1985). *East Timor: Violations of human rights*. London: Author.
Amnesty International (2011) *Timor-Leste: Amnesty International submission to the UN Universal Periodic Review 12th session of the UPR Working Group*, October
Asia Watch Committee (1992). *East Timor: The courts-martial*. New York: Asia Watch.
Pires, Mario Lemos (1991). *Missao Impossivel? Descolonizacao de Timor*. Lisboa: Círculo de Leitores.
Weatherbee, Donald (1966). "Portuguese Timor: An Indonesian dilemma," *Asian Survey*, 6(12): 683–695.

Map 9.1 Cambodia

CHAPTER **9**

The Cambodian Genocide, 1975–1979

BEN KIERNAN

In the first few weeks after Cambodia fell to the Khmer Rouge in April 1975, the nation's cities were evacuated, hospitals emptied, schools closed, factories deserted, money and wages abolished, monasteries emptied, and libraries scattered. Freedom of the press, movement, worship, organization, association, and discussion all completely disappeared for nearly four years. So did everyday family life. A whole nation was "kidnapped," and then besieged from within. Meals had to be eaten in collective mess halls. Parents ate breakfast in sittings, and if they were lucky their sons and daughters waited their turns outside. During the years 1975–1979, Democratic Kampuchea (DK) was a prison camp state, and the eight million prisoners served most of their time in solitary confinement. In that time 1.7 million of the inmates were worked, starved, and beaten to death (Kiernan, 2003).

Pol Pot and his Circle

The shadowy leaders of DK gave few clues to their personal lives. In 1978 the first journalists into DK from Yugoslavia had to ask the prime minister, "Who are you, comrade Pol Pot?" He was evasive (Pol Pot, 1978, pp. 20–21). Subsequent information on his social background suggests its importance for his political life. How little is explained by his personality, though, remains an anomaly.

The story began in a large, red-tiled, timber house on stilts overlooking a broad, brown river, downstream from the town of Kompong Thom. The river teemed with fish, its lush banks lined by coconut and mango trees. Behind the houses along the bank stretched large ricefields. A small Chinese shop sold a few consumables.

317

On May 19, 1925, Pol Pot was born Saloth Sar, the youngest in a family of six boys and a girl. His parents owned nine hectares of rice-land, three of garden-land, and six buffalo. Pol Pot's father, Saloth, with two sons and adopted nephews, harvested enough rice for about 20 people. In later years (during the reign of the Khmer Rouge), due to their relative wealth, the family would have been deemed "class enemies." But few villagers thought so then. Rich or poor, everyone tilled the fields, fished the river, cooked tasty soups, raised children, pro-pitiated local spirits and French colonial officials, or thronged Buddhist festivities in Kompong Thom's pagoda. In 1929 a French official described Kompong Thom people as "the most deeply Cambodian and the least susceptible to our influence."

But the Saloth family were Khmer peasants with a difference. They had royal connections. Pol Pot's cousin had grown up as a palace dancer, becoming one of King Monivong's principal wives. At 15, Pol Pot's eldest sister, Saroeung, was chosen as a consort. In 1928 his eldest brother, Loth Suong, began a career in palace protocol. At the age of six, Pol Pot joined him.

The country boy Saloth Sar never worked a rice field or knew much of village life. A year in the royal monastery was followed by six years in an elite Catholic school. His upbringing was strict. The girl next door, Saksi Sbong, recalls that Suong "was very serious and would not gamble or allow children to play near his home" (Kiernan, 1985a, p. 27).

The palace compound was closeted and conservative, the old king a French puppet. Outside, Phnom Penh's 100,000 inhabitants were mostly Chinese shopkeepers and Vietnamese workers. Few Cambodian child-hoods were so removed from their vernacular culture.

At 14, Pol Pot went off to high school in a bustling Khmer market town. He missed World War II's tumultuous end in Phnom Penh. Youths forced his cousin, the new boy-king Norodom Sihanouk, to briefly declare independence from France, and Buddhist monks led Cambodian nationalists in common cause with Vietnamese commu-nists. In 1948, while back in the capital learning carpentry, Pol Pot's life changed. He received a scholarship to study radio-electricity in Paris.

Pol Pot wrote to Suong occasionally, asking for money. But one day a letter arrived asking for the official biography of King Sihanouk. Suong sent back advice: Don't get involved in politics. But Pol Pot was already a member of the Cambodian section of the French Communist Party, then in its Stalinist heyday. Those who knew him then insist that "he would not have killed a chicken," that he was self-effacing, charming. He kept company with Khieu Ponnary, eight years his senior, the first Khmer woman to get the *baccalauréat*. The couple chose Bastille Day for the day of their wedding back home in 1956.

Most of Pol Pot's Paris student friends—such as Khieu Samphan, Ieng Sary, and Son Sen—remained in his circle even long after they were overthrown. He had early disagreements with Hou Yuon, later a popular Marxist intellectual, who was to be one of the first victims after the seizure of power by the Khmer Rouge in 1975.

Pol Pot stood out in his choice of a *nom de plume:* the "Original Cambodian" *(khmaer da'em)*. Others preferred less racial, modernist codenames, like "Free Khmer" or "Khmer Worker."

Pol Pot's scholarship ended after he failed his course three years in a row. His ship arrived home in January 1953 (Kiernan, 1985a, pp. 30–32, 119–122). The day prior to his arrival home, King Sihanouk had declared martial law to suppress Cambodia's independence movement, which was becoming radicalized by French colonial force. Pol Pot's closest brother, Saloth Chhay, joined the Cambodian and Vietnamese communists, and took Pol Pot along. In this first contact, Vietnamese communists began teaching him, as one of them later put it, how to "work with the masses at the base, to build up the independence committees at the village level, member by member." It seemed a patronizing slight, like his failure to quickly rise to a position of leadership. A former Cambodian comrade claims that Pol Pot "said that everything should be done on the basis of self-reliance, independence, and mastery. The Khmers should do everything on their own [and not with the assistance of the Vietnamese]" (Kiernan, 1985a, p. 123).

In the 1960s, a group of younger, mostly French-educated communists took over the leadership of the more orthodox (pro-Vietnamese) Workers' Party of Kampuchea, which had led the struggle against French colonialism in the 1950s. In 1966, the new leadership changed the party's name to the "Communist Party of Kampuchea" and set out on their path to power by staging an uprising against Prince Norodom Sihanouk's neutralist government. After their victory over Sihanouk's successor regime, that of Marshal Lon Nol, in 1975, they proclaimed the state of Democratic Kampuchea, which, as previously noted, lasted nearly four years before being overthrown by a Vietnamese invading army in 1979.

The ruling body in DK comprised the members of the Standing Committee of the Central Committee of the Communist Party of Kampuchea (CPK). The leaders with maximum national power and responsibility for the genocide about to be perpetrated were those based in Phnom Penh and not those specifically responsible for a particular geographic area of the country. The former were known as the "Party Center." The Party Center was comprised of the following individuals: Saloth Sar (alias Pol Pot), secretary-general of the CPK since 1962, and prime minister of DK; Nuon Chea, deputy secretary-general of the CPK since 1960, and president of the Representative Assembly of DK; Ieng Sary, who was ranked number three in the Party leadership since 1963 and was one of DK's deputy prime ministers (responsible for foreign affairs); Son Sen, number 11 in the Party in 1963 and a deputy prime minister of DK (for defense and security); Khieu Samphan, a Party member since the 1950s who became DK's president; Ieng Thirith, wife of Ieng Sary and DK minister of social action; and Yun Yat, wife of Son Sen and DK minister of culture. Khieu Ponnary, the older sister of Ieng Thirith and childless wife of Pol Pot, was a provincial Party official and president of the Women's Association of Democratic Kampuchea, but reportedly suffered insanity around 1975. (Pol Pot remarried in Thailand after his overthrow and had two children.)

Two other figures were long-time members of Pol Pot's group. Though they held regional posts in 1975, they increasingly assumed responsibility for the implementation of genocidal policies throughout the country: Mok, number nine in the Party in 1963, was Party secretary of the key Southwest Zone and later chief of the general staff of the Khmer Rouge armed forces; and Ke Pauk, Party secretary of the Central Zone of DK, later became under secretary-general of the Khmer Rouge armed forces.

The Mechanics of Power

The late 20th century saw the era of mass communications, but DK endured a vicious silence. Internally and externally, Cambodia was sealed off. Its borders were closed, all neighboring countries militarily attacked, use of foreign languages banned, embassies and press agencies expelled, local newspapers and television shut down, radios and bicycles confiscated, mail and telephones suppressed. Worse, Cambodians had little to tell each other anyway. They quickly learned that any display of knowledge or skill, if "contaminated" by foreign influence (normal in modern societies), was a folly in DK. Human communications were reduced to daily instructions and orders.

The CPK Center, known as *Angkar Loeu* (the high organization), began its purges in the 1960s by assassinating CPK figures assumed to be too close to Vietnam's communists. In the early 1970s, before taking power at the national level, the Center organized the arrest and "disappearances" of nearly 900 Hanoi-trained Khmer communists who had come home from North Vietnam to join the insurgency against Lon Nol's regime. They had accounted for half of the Party's membership in 1970. Then the Center gradually exerted its totalitarian control over the population by replacing autonomous or dissident Zone administrations and Party Committees with Center-backed forces commanded by loyalist Zone leaders Mok and Ke Pauk. By 1978 purges had taken the lives of half of the members of the Party's Central Committee, although there is no evidence that this body had ever officially met.

DK was initially divided into six major zones and 32 regions, each of which in turn comprised districts, subdistricts, and villages. One aim of the CPK Center was to build larger and larger units at the local level, abolishing village life altogether in favor of "high-level cooperatives" the size of a subdistrict. At the other end of the hierarchy, the Center set about reducing the autonomy of the zones by bringing them under its own direct control.

The most common pattern was for Mok's or Ke Pauk's forces to undermine a zone from below, first purging the district, subdistrict, and village committees, then regional ones, before finally picking off the severely weakened zone Party leadership. Another tactic was to carry out purges through the regional security forces (*santesok*) in a direct chain of command from the Center, bypassing the zone leadership. Those arrested were taken to the nerve center of the system, the national security service (*santebal*) prison in Phnom Penh, code-named *Office S-21*, now preserved as the Tuol Sleng Museum of Genocide. Up to 20,000 people, mostly suspected CPK dissidents and regional officials, were tortured and killed there from 1976 to 1979. Chief of the *santebal*, Kaing Khek Iev, alias Deuch, reported directly to Son Sen, who was the Center official responsible for security.

The entire process began in the insurgent zones before victory. In 1973, with Center backing, Mok emerged supreme in a factional battle for control of the Southwest Zone Party Committee, executing his senior and rival, Prasith, who had been number seven in the 1963 Party hierarchy. The poorest region, renamed the Western Zone, was assigned to another rival, Chou Chet, who was eventually executed in 1978. After victory in 1976, Ke Pauk's forces carried out a violent purge of cadres loyal to his executed predecessor, Koy Thuon, in the Northern Zone, now enlarged and renamed the Central Zone. In 1977, Mok's Southwest Zone forces and administrators carried out a similar purge of the Northwest Zone, eventually arresting the Zone Party Secretary, Nhim Ros, number eight in the 1963 Party hierarchy. On the other side of the country, Mok also took over two of the five regions of the Eastern Zone. Finally, a May 1978 conventional military suppression campaign commanded by Son Sen, Ke Pauk, and Mok overran the rest of the Eastern Zone and abolished its Party Committee. Zone Secretary So Phim, number four in the Party hierarchy since 1963, committed suicide.

The Center's struggle for total control was complete. But it had sown the seeds of its own overthrow. Surviving officials of the Eastern Zone went into rebellion, and in late 1978 they crossed the border and requested the Vietnamese military assistance that eventually brought DK to an end.

The Ideology of Genocide

Along with Stalinist and Maoist models, an underlying theme of the political worldview of the Pol Pot group was a concern for national and racial grandiosity. Their disagreements with Vietnamese communists in Paris in the early 1950s concerned the symbolic grandeur of the medieval Khmer temple of Angkor Wat and their sensitivities over the small size of Cambodia's population. In their view, Cambodia did not need to learn or import anything from its neighbors. Rather, they would recover its pre-Buddhist glory by rebuilding the powerful economy of the medieval Angkor kingdom and regain "lost territory" from Vietnam and Thailand. DK treasured the Cambodian "race," not individuals. National impurities included the foreign-educated (except for Pol Pot's Paris-educated group) and "hereditary enemies," especially Vietnamese. To return Cambodians to their imagined origins, the Pol Pot group saw the need for war, and for "secrecy as the basis" of the revolution (Boua, Chandler, & Kiernan, 1988, pp. 214, 220). Few of the grass-roots, pragmatic Cambodian communists could be trusted to implement such plans, which Pol Pot kept secret from them, just as he never admitted to being Saloth Sar.

The Party Center, with its elite, urban background, French education, and a racial chauvinism little different from that of its predecessor (the Lon Nol regime), inhabited a different ideological world from that of the more moderate, Buddhist-educated, Vietnamese-trained peasant cadre who made up the mass of the Party's membership. The acknowledged lack of a political base for its program meant that tactics of "secrecy" and violence were considered necessary. These tactics were used first against suspected Party dissidents, and then against the people of Cambodia as a whole. Given the sacrifices from the population that the nationalist revival required, the resistance it naturally provoked, and the regime's preparedness to forge ahead "at all costs," mass murder and genocide were the results.

Who were the Victims? Who was Involved?

Genocide Against a Religious Group

Pol Pot's government tried to eradicate Buddhism from Cambodia. Eyewitnesses testify to the Khmer Rouge massacres of monks and the forcible disrobing and persecution of survivors. Out of a total of 2,680 Buddhist monks from eight of Cambodia's 3,000 monasteries, only 70 monks were found to have survived in 1979 (Boua, 1991, p. 239). There is no reason to believe these eight monasteries were atypical. If the same death toll applied to the monks from all the other monasteries, fewer than 2,000 of Cambodia's 70,000 monks could be said to have survived.

A CPK Center document dated September 1975 proclaims:

> Monks have disappeared from 90 to 95 per cent.... Monasteries ... are largely abandoned. The foundation pillars of Buddhism ... have disintegrated. In the future they will dissolve further. The political base, the economic base, the cultural base must be uprooted. (Cited in Boua, 1991, p. 235)

This clear evidence of genocidal intent was carried through. As Chanthou Boua (1991, p. 227) points out, "Buddhism was eradicated from the face of the country in just one year." By early 1977 there were no functioning monasteries and no monks to be seen in Cambodia. In 1978 Yun Yat claimed that Buddhism was "incompatible with the revolution" (Jackson, 1989, p. 191). The Cambodian people, she said, had "stopped believing" and monks had "left the temples" (Jackson, 1989, p. 191). She added: "The problem gradually becomes extinguished. Hence there is no problem" (Jackson, 1989, p. 191).

Genocide against Ethnic Groups

The largest ethnic minority groups in Cambodia before 1970 were the Vietnamese, the Chinese, and the Muslim Cham. Unlike most other communist regimes, the Pol Pot regime's view of these and the country's 20 other national minorities, who had long made up over 15% of the Cambodian population, was virtually to deny their existence. The regime officially proclaimed that they totaled only 1% of the population. Statistically, they were written off.

Their physical fate was much worse. The Vietnamese community, for example, was entirely eradicated. About half of the 450,000-strong community had been expelled by the United States-backed Lon Nol regime in 1970 (with several thousand killed in massacres). Over 100,000 more were driven out by the Pol Pot regime in the first year after its victory in 1975. The ones who remained in Cambodia were simply murdered.

In research conducted in Cambodia since 1979 it has not been possible to find a Vietnamese resident who had survived the Pol Pot years there. However, eyewitnesses from other ethnic groups, including Khmers who were married to Vietnamese, testify to the fates of their Vietnamese spouses and neighbors. What they witnessed was a campaign of systematic racial extermination (Kiernan, 2008a, pp. 296–298, 393–394, 423–427).

The Chinese under Pol Pot's regime suffered the worst disaster ever to befall any ethnic Chinese community in Southeast Asia. Of the 1975 population of 425,000, only 200,000 Chinese survived the next four years. Ethnic Chinese were nearly all urban, and they were seen by the Khmer Rouge as archetypal city dwellers, and as prisoners of war. In this case, they were not targeted for execution because of their race, but like other evacuated city dwellers they were made to work harder and under much more deplorable conditions than rural dwellers. The penalty for minor infractions was often death. This basically constituted systematic discrimination predicated on geographic or social origin.

The Chinese succumbed in particularly large numbers to hunger and diseases like malaria. The 50% of them who perished is a higher proportion even than that estimated for Cambodia's city dwellers in general (about one-third).

Further, the Chinese language, like all foreign and minority languages, was banned, and so was any tolerance of a culturally and ethnically distinguishable Chinese community. This, in essence, constituted being destroyed (Kiernan, 1986b).

The Muslim Chams numbered at least 250,000 in 1975. Their distinct religion, language and culture, large villages, and autonomous networks threatened the atomized, closely supervised society that the Pol Pot leadership planned. An early 1974 Pol Pot document records the decision to "break up" the Cham people, adding: "Do not allow too many of them to concentrate in one area." Cham women were forced to cut their hair short in the Khmer style, not permitted to wear it long as was their custom; then the traditional Cham sarong was banned, as peasants were forced to wear only black pajamas. Ultimately, restrictions were placed upon religious activity.

In 1975 the new Pol Pot government turned its attention to the Chams with a vengeance. Fierce rebellions broke out. On an island in the Mekong River, the authorities attempted to collect all copies of the Koran. The villagers staged a protest demonstration, and Khmer Rouge troops fired into the crowd. The Chams then took up swords and knives and slaughtered half a dozen troops. The retaliating armed forces massacred many and pillaged their homes. They evacuated the island and razed the village, and then turned to a neighboring village, massacring 70% of its inhabitants.

Soon after, the Pol Pot army forcibly emptied all 113 Cham villages in the country. About 100,000 Chams were massacred and the survivors were dispersed in small groups of several families. Islamic schools and religion, as well as the Cham language, were banned. Thousands of Muslims were physically forced to eat pork. Many were murdered for refusing. Of 113 Cham *hakkem*, or community leaders, only 20 survived in 1979. Only 25 of their 226 deputies survived. All but 38 of about 300 religious teachers at Cambodia's Koranic schools perished. Of more than 1,000 who had made the pilgrimage to Mecca, only about 30 survived (Kiernan, 1988).

The toll goes on. The Thai minority of 20,000 was reportedly reduced to about 8,000. Of the 1,800 families of the Lao ethnic minority, only 800 families survived. Of the 2,000 members of the Kola minority, "no trace ... has been found" (Kiernan, 1990b).

Genocide Against a Part of the Majority National Group

Finally, of the majority Khmers, 15% of the rural population perished in 1975–1979, and 25% of the urban population. DK initially divided its population into the "old citizens" (those who had lived in Khmer Rouge Zones before the 1975 victory) and "new citizens" (those who had lived in the cities, and were the last holdouts of the Lon Nol regime). All cities were evacuated in April 1975. The next year, however, the "new citizens" were rebaptized "deportees," and most failed to even qualify for the next category, "candidates," let alone "full rights citizens," a group to which only favored peasant families were admitted. But not even they were spared the mass murders of the 1977–1978 countrywide purges.

The most horrific slaughter was perpetrated in the last six months of the regime, in the politically suspect Eastern Zone bordering Vietnam. The author interviewed 87 survivors in the Eastern Zone: in just 11 villages, the Khmer Rouge carried out 1,663 killings in 1978. In another community of 350 people, there were 95 executions in 1978; 705 executions occurred in another subdistrict, 1,950 in another, 400 in another. Tens of thousands of other villagers were deported to the northwest of the country. En route through Phnom Penh they were "marked" as easterners by being forced to wear a blue scarf, reminiscent of Hitler's yellow star for Jews (Kiernan, 1989b), and later eliminated en masse.

A total 1978 murder toll of over 100,000 (more than one-seventeenth of the eastern population) can safely be regarded as a minimum estimate (Kiernan, 1986a). The real figure is probably much higher (see Table 9.1).

The Historical Forces at Work

Rural conditions were better in pre-revolutionary Cambodia than in neighboring countries like Vietnam or even Thailand. Land was more equitably distributed, and most peasant families owned some land. However, rural debt was common, and the number of landless tenants or sharecroppers increased from 4% of the farming population in 1950 to 20% in 1970 (Kiernan & Boua, 1982, p. 4). Thus, alongside a land-owning middle peasant class, a new class of rootless and destitute rural dwellers emerged. Their position was desperate enough for them to have nothing to lose in any kind of social revolution.

The gap between town and countryside has been cited as a precondition for the Khmer Rouge's march to power. Unlike the countryside, the cities were not predominantly Khmer, but included large populations of ethnic Chinese and Vietnamese. Nor was the urban manufacturing sector very significant, producing few consumer goods for the countryside. Many peasants saw cities as seats of arbitrary, even foreign, political and economic power. But none of this, of course, explains why the Pol Pot regime also turned against the peasantry in such large numbers.

Another factor was the rapid expansion of education in Cambodia in the 1960s, after long neglect of education under French colonial rule. A generation gap separated peasant parents from educated youth, who were often unable to find work after graduating from high school and drifted into political dissidence. The Khmer Rouge in the 1960s recruited disproportionately among school teachers and students.

Other historical forces at work included the increasing repression by the Sihanouk regime, which drove the grass-roots left into dissidence, enabling the French-educated Khmers of elite background, led by

TABLE 9.1 Approximate death tolls under Pol Pot, 1975–1979

Social group	1975 population	Numbers perished	%
"New Citizens"			
Urban Khmer	2,000,000	500,000	25
Rural Khmer	600,000	150,000	25
Chinese (all urban)	430,000	215,000	50
Vietnamese (urban)	10,000	10,000	100
Lao (rural)	10,000	4,000	40
TOTAL New citizens	3,050,000	879,000	29
"Base Citizens"			
Rural Khmer	4,500,000	675,000	15
Khmer Krom	5,000	2,000	40
Cham (all rural)	250,000	90,000	36
Vietnamese (rural)	10,000	10,000	100
Thai (rural)	20,000	8,000	40
Upland minorities	60,000	9,000	15
TOTAL Base citizens	4,840,000	792,000	16
Cambodia	7,890,000	1,671,000	21

Pol Pot, to harness these home-grown veterans of the independence struggle to its plans for rebellion in 1967–1968; and conflict between the Vietnamese and Chinese Communists over Cambodia gave Pol Pot's faction Chinese support and valuable maneuverability against the orthodox pro-Vietnamese Khmer Communists (Kiernan, 1985a). And although it was an indigenous political phenomenon, Pol Pot's regime would not have come to power without the massive economic and military destabilization of Cambodia by the United States, beginning in 1966.

On March 18, 1969 the U.S. Air Force began a secret B-52 bombardment of Vietnamese sanctuaries in rural Cambodia (Shawcross, 1979a, pp. 21–23, 31). Exactly one year later, Prince Norodom Sihanouk was overthrown by the U.S.-backed general, Lon Nol. The Vietnam War spilled across the Vietnam–Cambodia border, Sihanouk swore revenge, and a new civil war tore Cambodia apart.

The U.S. bombing of the countryside increased from 1970 until August 15, 1973, when the U.S. Congress imposed a halt. Up to 150,000 Cambodians had been killed in the American bombardments. Nearly half of the 540,000 tons of bombs fell in the last six-month period. Hundreds of thousands of peasants fled into the cities to escape first the bombing and then the imposition of Khmer Rouge power. In the ashes of rural Cambodia arose the CPK regime, led by Pol Pot.

Pol Pot's forces had profited greatly from the U.S. bombardment. Contemporary U.S. government documents and peasant survivors reveal that the Khmer Rouge used the bombing's devastation and massacre of civilians as recruitment propaganda, and as an excuse for their brutal, radical policies and their purge of moderate and pro-Vietnamese Khmer communists and Sihanoukists (Kiernan, 1985a, 1989a). By 1975 they had national power.

The Long-term Impact on the Victim Groups

The population of Cambodia totaled around 6.5 million in 1979. The survivors emerged from the Pol Pot period nearly 3.5 million fewer than the 1980 population that had been projected in 1970 (Migozzi, 1973, p. 269). Not all of the difference is attributable to the Pol Pot regime; much is the result of the American war and aerial bombardment of the populated areas of Cambodia from 1969–1973, and of projected population growth that was unrealized due to instability, population displacement, and harsh living conditions throughout the 1970s. But 1.7 million deaths are attributable to the Khmer Rouge regime (Table 9.1; Kiernan, 1990a; 2003).

The Cambodian population remains severely affected by psychological trauma. Post-traumatic stress syndrome is a general problem, including illnesses such as psychosomatic blindness, which has been diagnosed among survivors living in the United States.

International Responses and Current Status of the Cambodian Genocide Issue

On November 26, 1975, seven months after the Khmer Rouge takeover of Cambodia, U.S. Secretary of State Henry Kissinger told the foreign minister of neighboring Thailand: "You should also tell the Cambodians that we will be friends with them. They are murderous thugs, but we won't let that stand in our way. We are prepared to improve relations with them" (Kiernan, 2008b, p. 1).

Two weeks later, on December 6, Kissinger and U.S. President Gerald Ford visited Southeast Asia. Ford told Indonesia's President Suharto: "The United States intends to continue a strong interest in and influence in the Pacific, Southeast Asia, and Asia. As a whole, we hope to expand this influence." Continuing, Ford said:

> The unification of Vietnam has come more quickly than we antic-ipated. There is, however, resistance in Cambodia to the influence of Hanoi. We are willing to move slowly in our relations with Cambodia, hoping perhaps to slow down the North Vietnamese influence although we find the Cambodian government very difficult.

Kissinger then explained Beijing's similar strategy:

> The Chinese want to use Cambodia to balance off Vietnam. We don't like Cambodia, for the government in many ways is worse than Vietnam, but we would like it to be independent. We don't discourage Thailand or China from drawing closer to Cambodia. (Burr & Evans, 2001: n.p.)

For such geopolitical reasons, while the Cambodian genocide pro-gressed, Washington, Beijing, and Bangkok all supported the continued independent existence of the Khmer Rouge regime.

In January 1979, the Vietnamese army invaded Cambodia, driving out the Khmer Rouge. A much less repressive regime was established with Hun Sen, first as foreign minister, and then as prime minister from 1985 onward. Vietnamese troops withdrew in 1989, after training a new Cambodian army that succeeded in defending the country on its own. But most of the international community embargoed the new govern-ment and continued to recognize the "legitimacy" of the defunct Pol Pot regime, voting for it to occupy Cambodia's UN seat for another 12 years. Therefore, until 1989, the Khmer Rouge flag flew over New York, and until 1992 Pol Pot's ambassador ran Cambodia's mission there. No Western country voted against the right of the government-in-exile, dominated by the Khmer Rouge, to represent their former victims in international forums (Kiernan, 1993, pp. 191–272).

Independent commentators often followed suit. In 1979 British journalist William Shawcross, author of *Sideshow*, a good study of the pre-1975 U.S. intervention and wartime destruction of Cambodia, hung the label of "genocide" on the Khmer Rouge's opponents. He alleged that Hanoi's invasion to topple Pol Pot meant "subtle genocide" (Shawcross, 1980, pp. 25–30) by enforced starvation, and warned of "2 million dead by Christmas" (Shawcross, 1979b, n.p.). Fortunately, he was very wrong. In his second book, *The Quality of Mercy*, Shawcross conceded that "there is no evidence that large numbers of people did 'starve to death' at the hands of the Vietnamese or their Cambodian allies" (Shawcross, 1984, p. 370). He also noted, "For the overwhelming majority of the Cambodian people the invasion meant freedom" (Shawcross, 1984, p. 78). Nevertheless, most Western governments portrayed the Vietnamese invasion as the cause of the Cambodian problem.

In the decade after Pol Pot's overthrow, many reputable legal organizations also dismissed proposals to send delegations to Cambodia to investigate the crimes of the DK regime. The International Commission of Jurists, the American Bar Association, and LawAsia all refused such opportunities to report on what the UN's Special Rapporteur on genocide, Benjamin Whitaker, described in 1985 as genocide, "even under the most restricted definition."[1]

A few voluntary organizations around the world pressed on, unaided by major human rights groups. These included the U.S. Cambodia Genocide Project, which in 1980 proposed a World Court case (Stanton, 1993); the Australian section of the International Commission of Jurists, which in January 1990 called for "international trials" of the Pol Pot leadership for genocide; the Minnesota Lawyers International Human Rights Committee, which in June 1990 organized a one-day mock trial of the Khmer Rouge following the procedures of the World Court, with testimony by a dozen victims of the genocide; the Washington-based Campaign to Oppose the Return of the Khmer Rouge, supported by 45 U.S. organizations, a former Cambodian prime minister, and survivors of the Khmer Rouge period; Yale University's Cambodian Genocide Program; and the NGO Forum, an international body of private voluntary agencies working in Cambodia.

At the first Jakarta Informal Meeting of Southeast Asian diplomats, on July 28, 1988, the Indonesian chairman's final communique noted a regional consensus on preventing a return to "the genocidal policies and practices of the Pol Pot regime" (Vatikiotis, 1988, p. 29). But the November 3, 1989, United Nations General Assembly resolution watered this down to "the universally condemned policies and practices of the recent past." A February 1990 Australian proposal referred only to "the human rights abuses of a recent past" (Australian Department of Foreign Affairs and Trade, 1990, pp. v–7). The five permanent members of the UN Security Council (the United States, the United Kingdom, France, the USSR, and China) emasculated this formulation in August 1990, vaguely nodding at "the policies and practices of the past" in the peace plan they drew up and imposed on Cambodia in late 1991.

In June 1991 the co-chairs of the Paris International Conference on Cambodia, Indonesia, and France, accepted Phnom Penh's proposal that the final Agreement stipulate that the new Cambodian Constitution should be "consistent with the provisions of … the UN Convention on the Prevention and Punishment of the Crime of Genocide" (*Indochina Digest*, June 7, 1991). But the great powers rejected it and reference to the Genocide Convention disappeared from the Agreement. China and the United States insisted on appeasing the Khmer Rouge to encourage them to sign it.

In Western countries, public pressure on governments mounted. One result was the British government's disclosure on June 27, 1991 that despite repeated denials, its elite SAS military teams—from 1983 to at least 1989—had trained forces allied to the Khmer Rouge (Pilger, 1991b; 1991c; Asia Watch & Physicians for Humans Rights, 1991, pp. 25–27, 59). The UN Subcommission on Human Rights, which the previous year had quietly dropped from its agenda a draft resolution condemning the Pol Pot genocide, now passed a resolution noting "the duty of the international community to prevent the recurrence of genocide in Cambodia" and "to take all necessary preventive measures to avoid conditions that could create for the Cambodian people the risk of new crimes against humanity" (UN Subcommission on Human Rights, 1991). For the first time, the genocide was acknowledged "in an official international arena" (Jennar, 1991). The *New York Times* (1991) called on Washington to publish its "list of Khmer Rouge war criminals and insist on their exclusion from Cambodian political life," and for their trial before "an international tribunal for crimes against humanity" (n.p.). Pol Pot, Ieng Sary, and Mok announced that they would not stand in UN-sponsored elections, but would campaign for Khmer Rouge candidates (*Indochina Digest*, August 30, 1991). They continued to lead the organization from the shadows.

In September 1991, diplomats revealed that "Western nations want the former head of the notorious Khmer Rouge to leave his nation, quickly and quietly," and that the United States had approached China for help in ensuring this "or at a minimum, making sure he remains in a remote part of Cambodia." Khieu Samphan retorted that Pol Pot had no plans to leave Cambodia. U.S. pressure on China and the Khmer Rouge remained verbal. Washington's material policy involved pressure on Hanoi, "to see that Vietnam holds Hun Sen's feet to the fire" (U.S. Deputy Assistant Secretary of State Kenneth Quinn quoted in Pilger, 1991d, pp. 10–11).

In October 1991, U.S. Assistant Secretary of State Richard Solomon said Washington "would be absolutely delighted to see Pol Pot and the others brought to justice for the unspeakable violence of the 1970s." He blamed Hun Sen for the Agreement's failure to include provision for a trial: "Mr. Hun Sen had promoted the idea over the summer months of a tribunal to deal with this issue. For reasons that he would have to explain he dropped that idea at the end of the negotiations" (quoted in *Indochina Digest*, November 1, 1991). The facts show, however, that the United States had never supported the idea of a trial from the time it was broached in June 1986 by Australia's Foreign Minister Bill Hayden, and that the United States and China had forced Hun Sen to drop the demand (Kiernan, 1991a).

In Paris on October 23, 1991, as the Agreement was signed, U.S. Secretary of State James Baker stated: "Cambodia and the U.S. are both signatories to the Genocide Convention and we will support efforts to bring to justice those responsible for the mass murders of the 1970s if the new Cambodian government chooses to pursue this path" (Shenon, 1991, p. A16). Australia's new Foreign Minister Gareth Evans, who had balked at his predecessor's proposal for legal action against the Khmer Rouge, now said: "We would give strong support to an incoming Cambodian government to set in train such a war crimes process" (Murdoch, 1991, p. 1).

The struggle to bring the Khmer Rouge leaders to justice began to bear fruit after the 1993 UN-sponsored elections, when they killed peacekeepers from Bangladesh, Bulgaria, Japan, and China. Following the UN's withdrawal, in 1994, the new Cambodian coalition government outlawed the Khmer Rouge insurgency, which began to fragment (Kiernan, 2002a). In August 1996, Pol Pot's former deputy Ieng Sary defected to the government, bringing the military units under his command. Sary received a "pardon" for his opposition to Phnom Penh since 1979; he also retained autonomous authority over Pailin province. Other Khmer Rouge leaders jockeyed for similar deals. In June 1997, fearing further betrayal, Pol Pot murdered Son Sen. In the jungle of northern Cambodia, as the last military forces loyal to Pol Pot abandoned their base, they drove their trucks over the bodies of their final victims: Son Sen, his wife Yun Yat—the DK minister of culture—and a dozen of their family members. Mok turned in pursuit, arrested Pol Pot, and subjected him to a show trial in the jungle for the murder of Son Sen. But in March 1998, former deputy commander Ke Pauk led a new mutiny against Mok and also defected to the government. The next month, as the various factions slugged it out, Pol Pot died in his sleep. It is possible that he may have committed suicide in order to evade capture. U.S. officials had been negotiating to take custody of Pol Pot at the Thai border.

In December 1998, the top surviving Khmer Rouge leaders—Nuon Chea, former deputy Party secretary, and Khieu Samphan, former DK head of state—surrendered to the government. Cambodian troops captured Mok in March 1999. The next month, Kang Khek Iev, alias Deuch, the former commandant of Tuol Sleng prison, was discovered by a British journalist (Dunlop, 1999). He, too, was quickly arrested by Hun Sen's police. Phnom Penh prosecutors announced that Deuch and Mok would be charged with genocide, and that both Nuon Chea and Khieu Samphan would be summoned to testify and would also be charged with genocide. Despite the deaths of Son Sen, Pol Pot, Ke Pauk (who died in 2002), and Mok (2006), five or more DK leaders remain liable to prosecution.

Cambodia's two prime ministers, Hun Sen and King Sihanouk's son Norodom Ranariddh, had appealed in 1997 to the UN to establish an international tribunal to judge the crimes of the Khmer Rouge. In response, the UN created a Group of Experts to examine the evidence, including the documents collected by Yale's Cambodian Genocide Program and its now-independent offshoot, the Documentation Center of Cambodia. The UN experts concluded in 1999 that the Khmer Rouge should face charges "for crimes against humanity and genocide" (United Nations, 1999, pp. 19–20, 57). They reported that the events of 1975–1979 fit the definition of the crime outlawed by the United Nations Genocide Convention of 1948. In their view, the Khmer Rouge regime had

> subjected the people of Cambodia to almost all of the acts enumerated in the Convention. The more difficult task is determining whether the Khmer Rouge carried out these acts with the requisite intent and against groups protected by the Convention.

The experts' response to this challenge was affirmative:

> In the view of the group of experts, the existing historical research justifies including genocide within the jurisdiction of a tribunal to prosecute Khmer Rouge leaders. In particular, evidence suggests the need for prosecutors to investigate the commission

of genocide against the Cham, Vietnamese and other minority groups, and the Buddhist monkhood. The Khmer Rouge subjected these groups to an especially harsh and extensive measure of the acts enumerated in the Convention. The requisite intent has support in direct and indirect evidence, including Khmer Rouge statements, eyewitness accounts, and the nature and numbers of victims in each group, both in absolute terms and in proportion to each group's total population. These groups qualify as protected groups under the Convention: the Muslim Cham as an ethnic and religious group; the Vietnamese communities as an ethnic and, perhaps, a racial group; and the Buddhist monkhood as a religious group.

Specifically, in the case of the Buddhist monkhood, their intent is evidenced by the Khmer Rouge's intensely hostile statements towards religion, and the monkhood in particular; the Khmer Rouge's policies to eradicate the physical and ritualistic aspects of the Buddhist religion; the disrobing of monks and abolition of the monkhood; the number of victims; and the executions of Buddhist leaders and recalcitrant monks. Likewise, in addition to the number of victims, the intent to destroy the Cham and other ethnic minorities appears evidenced by such Khmer Rouge actions as their announced policy of homogenization, the total prohibition of these groups' distinctive cultural traits, their dispersal among the general population, and the execution of their leadership.[2]

From 1999 to 2006 the UN negotiated with the Cambodian government and established a joint tribunal in Phnom Penh to ensure legal accountability for the Khmer Rouge's crimes. In 2007 the Cambodian and international co-prosecutors of the new Extraordinary Chambers in the Courts of Cambodia (ECCC) alleged that the defunct CPK regime had committed "crimes against humanity [and] genocide." The ECCC assumed custody of the imprisoned S-21 commandant Deuch, and also jailed, pending trial, four surviving leaders of the CPK "Party Center": Nuon Chea, Khieu Samphan, Ieng Sary, and Ieng Thirith. After Deuch's 2009 trial for crimes against humanity, the ECCC announced that the other four defendants would face the additional charge of genocide for Khmer Rouge crimes against Cambodia's Cham and Vietnamese minorities. This trial began in mid-2011.

Varying Interpretations

Interpretations of the nature of the Pol Pot regime have varied widely and controversially, even among Marxists and neo-Marxists. Its enemy and successor regime, for instance, quickly claimed that Pol Potism had been a case of Maoism exported to Cambodia by China's leaders in the 1970s. The official Chinese publications, in fact, praised the Khmer Rouge rule as "the period of economic reconstruction" (Guangxi People's Publishing House, 1985; Kiernan, 2002a). The pro-Chinese neo-Marxist Samir Amin (1977) had initially welcomed DK for its "correct assessment of the hierarchy of contradictions" (p. 150) in Cambodia (by which he meant that it was a peasant society lacking a large urban working class and that its unproductive cities exploited the rural areas), and as a model for African socialists to follow in similar conditions because of its "rapid disurbanisation" (p. 147) and its economic autarchy. Amin (1977) dismissed the claim that it was "an insignificant peasant rising" (p. 147). But in a 1981 reflection Amin preferred to categorize the Khmer Rouge revolution as a Cambodian combination of Stalinist orthodoxy with what he now called "a principally peasant revolution": "The excesses, which today cannot be denied, are those which we know from the entire long history of peasant revolts. They are of the same nature and represent the same character" (pp. 4, 8–9).

In 1984 the historian Michael Vickery took up this very theme as a reason to reject DK, because, he argued, "nationalism, populism and peasantism really won out over communism" (1984, p. 289). In Vickery's (1984) view, DK was no Stalinist communist regime (which he considered a lesser evil), but "a victorious peasant revolution, perhaps the first real one in modern times" (1984, pp. 289–290, 66).

Amin's contribution to our understanding of the tragedy was limited to his analysis of pre-revolutionary Cambodia as a relatively undifferentiated peasant society, similar to others in South Asia and Africa, and quite unlike China and Vietnam with their powerful landlord classes. His sympathy with the Khmer Rouge was based on their innovativeness in adapting a communist strategy to these particular conditions. However, he later conceded, "this success itself has been the origin of the tragic difficulties," including "the well known excesses and shortcomings" (Amin, 1981, pp. 4, 8–9).

But Vickery, in explaining the outcome of the Cambodian revolution, denies the very existence of the Stalinist vanguard attractive to Amin. He sees the Pol Pot leadership, not as significantly influenced by foreign Communist models, but "pulled along" by "the peasant element" (Vickery, 1984, p. 287). Vickery's approach combines an influential post-war intellectual trend in Southeast Asian historiography with a 1970s revisionist trend evident in the historiography of Hitler's Germany. I will examine each in turn.

In his groundbreaking 1955 work *Indonesian Trade and Society*, J.C. Van Leur remarked that European historians of premodern Southeast

Asia tended to see the region as outsiders, "from the deck of the ship, the ramparts of the fortress, the high gallery of the trading house" (p. 95). Yet, Van Leur (1955) argued, at least until the 19th century the European impact on Southeast Asia had been minimal and superficial: "The sheen of the world religions and foreign cultural forms is a thin and flaking glaze; underneath it the whole of the old indigenous forms has continued to exist" (p. 95).

Vickery (1998) applies this analysis to Hinduism in early Cambodian history, stressing the "Indic facade" on the indigenous culture of the pre-Angkor period. He also applies it to communism in modern times. In *Cambodia 1975–1982*, he writes that "foreign relations and influences are very nearly irrelevant to an understanding of the internal situation" (Vickery, 1984, p. xii). He later explains: "We need investigations into autonomous development rather than superficial diffusionism, a change in emphasis which has become common in most of the social sciences and has led to important advances in the last 30 years" (Vickery, 1988, p. 17). Thus, in Vickery's view, "the only way to account for the apparent similarities between DK and the programme of Sendero Luminoso" [the Peruvian Maoist guerrilla movement] is as cases of "convergent social and political evolution out of similar backgrounds" (Vickery, 1988, p. 17). So the Cambodian and Peruvian parties' common adherence to and study of "Marxism-Leninism-Mao Zedong Thought" is seen as meaningless, if not a dangerously misleading "facade."

But in my view, DK ideology was not purely indigenous. It was an amalgam of various intellectual influences, including Khmer elite chauvinism, third world nationalism, the French Revolution, Stalinism, and some aspects of Mao Zedong's "Great Leap Forward"—which DK claimed to outdo with its own "Super Great Leap Forward." The motor of the Pol Pot program was probably Khmer racist chauvinism, but it was fueled by strategies and tactics adopted from unacknowledged revolutionary models in other countries. Such syncretism is historically common in Southeast Asia, and it suggests that in an important sense the Khmer Rouge revolution was *sui generis.*

Vickery combines his argument for the primacy of the indigenous with a separate one. This is that the peasantry as a mass dominated the Cambodian revolution and took it in a direction the Pol Pot leadership could not have "either planned or expected. It is certainly safe to assume that they did not foresee, let alone plan, the unsavory developments of 1975–79. They were petty bourgeois radicals overcome by peasant romanticism" (Vickery, 1988, p. 17; Vickery, 1984, p. 287). This argument is not unlike Hans Mommsen's analysis of Nazi Germany. Mommsen (1991) suggested, for instance, that whether or not Hitler planned the extermination of the Jews early in his career, Nazi policy was formed on an ad hoc basis over time and under the pressure of developing circumstances. It was a case of "cumulative radicalization." Mommsen's argument is that Hitler was no freak aberration, and that German history and society more broadly are also implicated in the genocide of the Jews. Similarly, Vickery considers DK a sobering illustration of what happens when a peasantry assumes power, quite different to what happened in communist China and Vietnam: "It now appears fortunate that those who predicted a predominance of agrarian nationalism over Marxism in China and Vietnam were mistaken" (Vickery, 1984, p. 290).

In Vickery's view, the Pol Pot regime, then, was made up of "middle-class intellectuals with such a romantic, idealized sympathy for the poor that they did not imagine rapid, radical restructuring of society in their favour [i.e., of the poor] would lead to such intolerable violence" (Vickery, 1988, p. 14). But, Vickery claims, these Khmer Rouge leaders simply discovered that "it would have been impossible to hold the support of their peasant army" unless political enemies were "punished" and a departure made from the 1917 Bolshevik model of maintaining a "normal administration" and urban "privilege" (Vickery, 1988, pp. 14, 20, 5). And when the urban populations were deported to the countryside, "the majority base peasants" of Cambodia allegedly participated "with some glee" in the persecution of "their class enemies" (Vickery, 1989, p. 47):

> The violence of DK was first of all—because it was such a complete peasant revolution—the victorious revolutionaries doing what peasant rebels have always wanted to do to their urban enemies.... [It] did not spring forth from the brains of Pol Pot or Khieu Samphan. (Vickery, 1984, p. 286; Vickery, 1988, p. 17)

A major problem with this analysis is lack of evidence. Vickery's *Cambodia 1975–1982* contributes much to our knowledge of the Khmer Rouge, but he did not consult peasant sources seriously. Among the 90 or more interviewees Vickery presents in his survey of DK, only one is a peasant. This interviewee hardly supports the notion of a peasant revolution, reporting "that they were fed well, but overworked and subject to 'fierce' discipline" (Vickery, 1984, p. 112). A family that Vickery (1984) describes as "half peasant-half urban," although "most of them by 1975 had long since ceased doing field work," all survived DK, but they

> said that their many cousins, aunts, uncles, etc., ... had perished, mainly of hunger and illness, although they were peasants.... In the opinion of the survivors, DK mismanagement had simply been so serious that not even peasants could survive. (p. 106)

Nearly all of Vickery's oral testimony in fact comes from male urban evacuees he met in refugee camps in Thailand in 1980. His account of DK's Southwest Zone, which he correctly calls "the 'Pol Pot' zone par excellence," is based on the testimony of four former students, a former French teacher, a former Lon Nol soldier and a medic, an agricultural engineer, "a girl from the 'new' people," and "an attractive, well-educated woman of the former urban bourgeoisie" (Vickery, 1984, pp. 98, 91, 97). These 10 accounts offer unconvincing documentation of a key zone in a "peasant revolution." None of the ten witnesses from there were peasants, and the revolution was clearly a top-down process. The few inside accounts in Vickery's book include corroboration of an initial order to "kill urban evacuees indiscriminately." This order went out to both the Southwest and the Northwest Zones (Vickery, 1984, pp. 98, 112). It clearly emanated not from the peasants of the southwest but from the central government—indeed from the very "brains of Pol Pot and Khieu Samphan."

This was probably the first major controversy in the historiography of the Cambodian revolution: the question of central control. Anthony Barnett (1983) argued that DK was "a highly centralized dictatorship" (p. 212). He also stressed its Stalinism, and its creation of "a nation of indentured labourers" (pp. 211–229). But Serge Thion (1983) contended that it was "a bloody mess," "riddled" with factional and regional divergence, so that "the state never stood on its feet" (p. 28). "Stalin, at least, was a realist. Pol Pot ... was and is an unimaginative idealist, a forest monk, lost in dreams" (Thion, 1993, p. 168). David P. Chandler (1991) also followed Vickery, asserting:

> Under the regime of DK, a million Cambodians, or one in eight, died from warfare, starvation, overwork, misdiagnosed diseases, and executions. *Most of these deaths, however, were never intended by DK.* Instead, one Cambodian in eight fell victim to the government's Utopian program of total and rapid social transformation. (p. 1, italics added)

Barnett was closest to the truth. Despite its millenarian tone, Pol Potism was not a centrifugal or a peasant ideology, but a centralizing one (Kiernan, 1983, pp. 136–211). Understating the death toll of 1.7 million, Chandler (1991) also fails to cite evidence that the regime purportedly "never" intended "most" of the deaths, and skims the issue of how many were intentional (p. 271). He does suggest (without citing a source) that in 1978, "perhaps a hundred thousand Eastern Zone people were killed," but is vague in attributing responsibility and explains it as an evacuation that "degenerated into a massacre"

(Chandler, 1991, p. 271), suggesting it was unintended despite the deliberate targeting of victims in Phnom Penh itself (Kiernan, 1989b; 1991b). The regime was able to plan such mass murders precisely because of its concentrated power. It has been noted that the Khmer Rouge leadership not only succeeded in conscripting a massive labor force to turn Cambodia's landscape into a checkerboard of irrigation works, they even communalized people's breakfasts. The regime's intent was clear and was successful.

Chandler also overlooks the second major controversy, the case for genocide. He briefly notes the abolition of religion (Chandler, 1991, pp. 263–265), but not the ban on minority languages and cultures nor the enforced dispersal of ethnic communities, and he offers no estimates of any death toll among either Buddhist monks or minorities. He concedes that "the party seems to have ... discriminated against the Chams, a Muslim minority unsympathetic to the revolution"—a false imputation until the genocide began in 1975. He avers that DK, as he puts it, treated the Chinese "poorly," but that China may have helped protect them. And he notes that a Central Committee directive ordered the execution of ethnic Vietnamese residents in Cambodia. Yet Chandler concludes: "By and large, the regime *discriminated* against enemies of the revolution rather than against specific ethnic or religious groups" (Chandler, 1991, p. 285, italics added). He reveals no basis beyond DK's own for regarding these victims as "enemies of the revolution."

Nevertheless, there is scholarly agreement that the Khmer Rouge committed crimes against humanity. Eventually, a consensus on the genocide also emerged. Legal authorities Steven Ratner and Jason Abrams (1997) write in *Accountability for Human Rights Atrocities in International Law* that

> the existing literature presents a strong *prima facie* case that the Khmer Rouge committed acts of genocide against the Cham minority group, the ethnic Vietnamese, Chinese, and Thai minority groups, and the Buddhist monkhood. While some commentators suggest otherwise, virtually every author on the subject has reached this conclusion. (p. 244)

Meanwhile new evidence has continued to accumulate. The archive of 100,000 pages obtained by the Cambodian Genocide Program in 1996 includes a vast amount of secret correspondence and other documents from the highest levels of the Khmer Rouge regime, including its security organ, the *santebal*. (Note: this archive has been microfilmed by Yale University's Sterling Library Southeast Asia Collection.)

Since 1997 the CGP's website (www.yale.edu/cgp) has cumulatively published the Cambodian Genocide Data Bases, which now include over 19,000 biographical records of Khmer Rouge figures from Pol Pot down to local district chiefs, 5,000 photographs of victims, and 3,000 catalogue records on Khmer Rouge-era documents, many of them digitally displayed. These and other primary materials ensure that scholarly research and debate will long continue on the nature of the genocidal practices of the Pol Pot regime.

Eyewitness Accounts

Oral accounts of the Cambodian experience under the Khmer Rouge regime were difficult to collect after 1975, when that regime established itself and immediately closed the country to outside visitors (except for occasional short guided tours by foreign diplomats). Along with the broadcasts of the official DK radio station, the accounts of refugees who managed to flee to Thailand, Laos, or Vietnam were nevertheless the major source of information reaching the outside world. In 1979, after the Vietnamese destruction of the Khmer Rouge regime, Cambodia was opened to journalists and researchers, and many more refugees also found their way to foreign countries. Thousands of refugees and others who remained in Cambodia have now told their stories of the 1975–1979 years, and some literate Cambodians have published books on their experience. Relatively few, however, have been published in English, and even fewer narrate the experiences of the Khmer peasant majority, of ethnic minorities, of women, or of children. The accounts that follow have been chosen to fill that gap.

These testimonies were collected by Ben Kiernan and Chanthou Boua in 1979 and 1980, in the immediate aftermath of the overthrow of the Khmer Rouge. Kiernan, then a graduate student in Southeast Asian History at Monash University, Melbourne, Australia, was conducting his dissertation field research on 20th-century Cambodia. One of the interviews took place in a Cambodian village, one in a Lao refugee camp in Thailand, and two in a Buddhist monastery inside Thailand. The interviews were conducted in Khmer without an interpreter and in the absence of any person exercising authority over the interviewees. The conversations were tape-recorded and translated as accurately as possible by Kiernan and Boua. The details recounted are reasonably typical of hundreds of other interviews recorded by Kiernan in 1979–1980 and do not conflict with anything known from other sources about Cambodia in the 1970s, though the mass of material is for logistical reasons difficult to corroborate on all specific points.

Account 1: "The Chams are Hopeless" by Nao Gha

Nao Gha, a minority Cham Muslim woman, was interviewed by Kiernan in her village in Takeo province on August 26, 1980. The translation from the Khmer is by Kiernan.

I am 45 years old. I was born in Smong village, Smong subdistrict, Treang district, Takeo province. I first met the Khmer Rouge in 1972–1973, when they came here. In 1973, they called all of us Chams to the mountains. We went to Kampot province, to Ang Krieu in Angkor Chey district. We spent a year there. They still treated us well, let us work and fend for ourselves. They spoke well to us. They called us "deported base people" [*neak moultanh phniaer*]. They did not persecute us. Our leaders were chosen from among us Chams. In 1974 they sent us back home. Everyone came back from Angkor Chey, over 100 families, but religion was no longer allowed.

In 1975, after liberation, the persecution began. Some Chams came from Phnom Penh to live in a nearby Cham village. We had to work on irrigation non-stop, day and night. Killings of Khmers began in 1975. In 1976–1977 they killed someone every one or two months, for small infringements.

Then in 1976 they dispersed the Chams. The ten villages of Chams in this area were all dispersed, for instance to Samrong, Chi Khma, and Kompong Yaul subdistricts. We were not allowed to live together.

Our village was also dispersed. They burnt our village down. Four to eight families were sent out to each of eight villages. I went with five families to Kantuot village, in Tralach subdistrict. There I had to grow dry season rice, far away, and would return to the village only after seven months.

Our Cham leaders were dismissed in 1976, and replaced by Khmers. We were not allowed to speak Cham. Only the Khmer language was allowed. From 1977, they said: "There are no Vietnamese, Chinese, Javanese [Chams and Malays]—only the Khmer race. Everyone is the same."

No Cham women joined Pol Pot's revolution. A few men had but the Pol Pot regime did not trust us. They did not let us do anything; they did not let us into their kitchens. When we went to eat [in the communal mess halls established in 1976] we could only go to the tables, we weren't allowed to go into their kitchens or anything. They were afraid we would poison the food or something.

They hated us. They brought up the issue of the Chams being "hopeless." Soeun, the district chief of Treang [and son-in-law of the Southwest Zone commander Mok], said this several times in meetings of people from the entire district, beginning in 1977 and also in 1978. He also said at every meeting that the Chams had "abandoned their country to others. They just shouldered their fishing nets and walked off, letting the Vietnamese take over their country." [Soeun was referring to the 17th-century Vietnamese takeover of the kingdom of Champa, after which many of the Chams fled central Vietnam and settled in Cambodia. On this, Nao Gha volunteered the following comment:] I don't know anything about that. It happened long ago. I don't know which generation it was when the Vietnamese invaded and they shouldered their fishing nets and ran off to live in another country. I don't know, I don't know which generation that was.

All the Chams were called "deportees," even the base people. [In DK those who had lived in the Khmer Rouge areas before the 1975 victory were called "base people," or "people of the bases." They were distinguished from the urban evacuees, or "deportees." The Cham base people were denied this status; after being dispersed, they too were called "deportees."] The Khmers were called "full rights" and "candidate" people. We were called "minority" and were all classified as "deportees." Deportees were the most numerous, followed by candidates. The full rights people were relatives of cadres. The deportees, the candidates, and the full rights people all ate together, but lived separately and held separate meetings. They met in one place and studied politics; and the other two categories had meetings elsewhere.

1977 and 1978 were years of hard work and the greatest persecution. 1978 was the year of hardest work, night and day. We planted from 4 A.M. to 10 A.M., then ate a meal. At 1 P.M. we started again, and worked until 5 P.M., and then from 7 to 10 P.M. There was some education, for young children to learn the alphabet. It was about one hour per day, from 12 to 1 P.M.

There was not enough food, and foraging was not allowed. Rations consisted of yams and *trokuon* [a leafy Cambodian water vine]. Twice a month in 1978 we were forced [against religious beliefs] to eat pork on pain of execution. People vomited it up. My three brothers died of starvation in 1976, 1977, and 1978. My other relatives are still alive. Of the five families with whom I went to Kantuot village, one person died of illness. In four other villages, one or two others were killed for refusing to eat pork. They were accused of being holy men [*sangkriech*] in the old society. There was starvation in Samrong subdistrict, mostly in 1977, and one or two killings. In 1978 they killed four entire families of Chinese in my village. I don't know why. Also in 1978, they killed our former Cham leaders who had joined the Khmer Rouge but had been dismissed in 1976.

Account 2: "They Did Nothing at All for the Peasants" by Thoun Cheng

Thoun Cheng, a Cambodian refugee who fled the Pol Pot regime in June 1977, was interviewed in the Khmer language by Boua and Kiernan at the Lao refugee camp at Ubon Ratchathani, northeast Thailand, on March 13–14, 1979. His story has been arranged in sequence by Boua and Kiernan, with occasional editorial comments in brackets.

I was born in 1957 in the village of Banteay Chey, in Chamcar Loeu district, Kompong Cham province, Cambodia. My father was a carpenter, but with the help of just his family, he also worked his 6 hectares of *chamcar* [garden farmland] growing pineapples and bananas. My mother died when I was small; I had three older brothers.

During the 1960s, Banteay Chey was populated by about 3,200 ethnic Khmers, who mostly worked *chamcar*, and about 400 Chams, who grew rice. There were four Buddhist *wats* [Buddhist pagodas] and one Muslim mosque. Land was unevenly distributed: an elderly landlord owned 30 hectares in the village and an unusually large holding of 770 hectares in other parts of the district, including one large pineapple plantation. Poor farmers usually owned from 1 to 3 hectares.

I studied in primary school in the village; my education was interrupted by a three-year stay with relatives in the town of Kompong Cham, and six months in Phnom Penh.

The overthrow of Prince Norodom Sihanouk in 1970 was greeted with some disappointment by the villagers of Banteay Chey. I remember some of them traveling to Kompong Cham to take part in protest demonstrations. Soon after, fighting took place in the area between troops of the new Lon Nol Government and revolutionary Khmer Rouge claiming loyalty to the Prince. The Lon Nol troops retreated and were not seen in the area again.

As Banteay Chey itself was free of fighting, my relatives from Kompong Cham, a bus driver and his family, came to live in the village in 1970.

The war put an end to supplies of medicine to the village. Schools were closed, too, and I never got the opportunity of a secondary education. So from 1970, I made furniture and tilled the soil with my father.

Vietnamese Communist troops began making frequent visits to Banteay Chey. They paid for supplies that they needed and did not mistreat villagers. We first saw indigenous Khmer Rouge troops (who spoke like people from Kompong Cham) when they entered the village in 1972 and left again without causing upset. They lived in the forest and visited the village frequently over the next three years; life went on as before. The Khmer Rouge never stayed in or recruited from Banteay Chey and were busy fighting the Lon Nol troops all the time.

In 1973, the Vietnamese stopped coming; in the same year, the village had to withstand three months of intense bombardment by American B-52s. Bombs fell on Banteay Chrey three to six times a day, killing over 1,000 people, or nearly a third of the village population. Several of my family were injured. After that, there were few people left to be seen around the village, and it was quiet. Food supplies remained adequate.

Later in 1973, the Khmer Rouge temporarily occupied most of Kompong Cham City and evacuated its population to the countryside. Seventy-four people from the town came to Banteay Chey and took up a normal life there. Some of the evacuees had died of starvation and bombardment by Lon Nol planes along the way.

The Khmer Rouge victory in April 1975 and their evacuation of Phnom Penh city brought 600 more people to Banteay Chey. The newcomers were billeted with village families. Relatives of ours, a couple and their three children, and one single man, stayed in my father's house. They had set out on foot from Phnom Penh 15 days earlier and arrived tired and hungry, although unlike some others they had not lost any of their family members along the way. [The single man, Kang Houath, was eventually to escape from Cambodia with Cheng. Houath took part in one of the interviews with Cheng in Ubon. He said that some village people along the way had given the evacuees food, and others had exchanged food for clothes and other goods offered by the Phnom Penh people. The bulk of the people traveling the roads at the time, however, were former peasants who had taken refuge in Phnom Penh during the war and had been instructed or allowed to return to their villages by the Khmer Rouge, Houath added.] In return for food and shelter, the new arrivals in Banteay Chey helped the locals in their work in the fields.

Also in April 1975, Khmer Rouge troops came to live in the village. It was not long before they began imposing a very harsh lifestyle on the villagers. Everybody was now obliged to work in the fields or dig reservoirs from 3 or 4 A.M. until 10 P.M. The only breaks were from noon till 1 P.M. and from 5 to 6 P.M. [This compared to an average 8-hour day worked by the *chamcar* farmers in the preceding years.] One day in ten was a rest day, as well as three days each year at the Khmer New Year festival. Land became communal.

Also from 1975, money was abolished and big houses were either demolished, and the materials used for smaller ones, or used for administration or to house troops. The banana trees in the *chamcar* were all uprooted on the orders of the Khmer Rouge and rice planted in their place. Production was high, although some land was left fallow and rations usually just consisted of rice porridge with very little meat. After the harvest each year, trucks would come at night to take away the village's rice stores to an unknown destination.

In 1975, the Khmer Rouge also began executing rich people, although they spared the elderly owner of 800 hectares. They also executed college students and former government officials, soldiers, and police. I saw the bodies of many such people not far from the village. Hundreds of people also died of starvation and disease in the year after April 1975, when medical supplies were lacking.

At this time, the Khmer Rouge, led by "friend Sang," claimed that they were "building Communism"; they occasionally mentioned a Communist Party, although its local (and national) members were unknown to us. The soldiers did not work in the fields but mounted an armed supervision over those who did; nonmilitary members of the Khmer Rouge worked unarmed alongside the villagers. There were no peasant organizations formed or meetings held about work; every decision concerning the work to be done and how to do it was made by the supervisors, with no participation on the part of the workers.

There was a large number of Khmer Rouge troops in the village, in the hundreds; they lived separately from the people in a big hall which no one else was allowed to visit. I never chatted with any of the soldiers in the two and a half years I lived with them in Banteay Chey.

Everyone, including my father, disliked the Khmer Rouge in Banteay Chey—the work was simply too hard, the lifestyle too rigid, and the food too inadequate. The Khmer Rouge occasionally claimed to be on the side of the poor, the peasants, but they did nothing at all for them. On the contrary, sometimes they said: "You were happy during the war, now is the time for you to sacrifice. Whether you live or die is not of great significance."

I managed to hide two radios buried in the ground. The batteries were precious so I listened to the radio only once or twice a month. Traditional village music was banned; the Khmer Rouge theatre troupes that visited the village about once in three months were the only form of entertainment.

In the April 1976 elections, only the very big people [i.e., the leading officials] voted in Banteay Chey. Also, by that stage, the *wats* and the mosque in Banteay Chey were empty. Saffron-robed Buddhist monks were nowhere to be seen. The Muslim Chams were obliged to eat pork on the occasions it was available; some adamantly refused, and were shot.

During 1976–1977 most of the Khmer Rouge leaders in the village changed six times. More than 50 Khmer Rouge were executed in these purges. Sang's position was finally assumed by Friend Son.

Then, from January 1977, all children over about 8 years of age, including people of my age [20 years], were separated from their parents, whom we were no longer allowed to see although we remained in the village. We were divided into groups consisting of young men, young women, and young children, each group nominally 300-strong. The food, mostly rice and salt, was pooled and served communally. Sometimes there was *samlor* [Khmer-style soup].

The Khmer Rouge soon began attacking the Vietnamese Communists in speeches to these youth groups. These speeches were propaganda.

Also in early 1977, collective marriages, involving hundreds of mostly unwilling couples, took place for the first time. All personal property was confiscated. A new round of executions began, more wide-ranging than that of 1975 and involving anyone who could not or would not carry out work directions. Food rations were cut significantly, leading to many more deaths from starvation, as were clothing allowances. Three sets of clothes per person per year was now the rule. Groups of more than two people were forbidden to assemble.

1977 was easily the worst year of all. Many people now wanted to escape, although they knew it was very dangerous. My mind was made up when it became clear that I would remain unable to see my father and brothers. It was June 1977.

Houath, a neighbor, one other man, and I took three baskets of dry rice. [Cheng did not say how this was acquired.] Avoiding everyone along the way, we headed north and east for Thailand. Laos was closer but I had heard on the radio that Laos was "building Communism" too and I didn't want to go there. As it turned out, however, the four of us lost our way to Preah Vihear province and hit the Lao border at Kompong Sralao. Although Khmer Rouge troops were thinned out because of the conflict with Vietnam, we were spotted by soldiers who fired immediately, killing two of my companions. Houath and I were separated but arrived safely in Laos, where we met up again in a local jail on the banks of the Mekong.

I noticed that the Lao soldiers behaved differently from the Khmer Rouge I knew. They asked questions first, before apprehending people they suspected, whereas the Khmer Rouge were much more inclined to shoot suspects on the spot. I also gained the impression that living conditions in Laos were considerably better than in Cambodia.

Houath and I spent a total of 37 days in two Lao jails. I was given rice to eat, much more than I had had for a long time in Banteay Chey. I was not ill-treated, but when I was told that Vientiane was being asked for instructions whether to send me back to Cambodia, I escaped with Houath, and we fled to Thailand on 8 September 1977.

I spent another ten months in a Thai jail, before being transferred to the Ubon refugee camp.

Account 3: "Peasant Boys in Democratic Cambodia" by Sat and Mien

These are accounts of the experiences of two teenage Cambodian peasant boys (Sat and Mien) during 1975–1978. Boua and Kiernan interviewed them in a Buddhist *wat*, near where they were tending their new master's horses, in Thailand's Surin province, on March 7, 12, and 19, 1979. The text includes every detail recounted by the boys, translated and arranged in sequence by Boua and Kiernan. Occasional points added appear in brackets.

"They Were Killing People Every Day" (Sat). I was born in 1966 in the village of Lbaeuk, Kralanh district, Siemreap province, Cambodia. The village is a long way from Siemreap town, and I have never been there. My father, Kaet, was a rice farmer. He had married again after my mother died. I had five brothers and sisters; I was the third oldest.

In the years 1975 and 1976, they were killing people every day. Killings took place at some distance from the village. I heard that victims were bound and then beaten to death. They were usually people found to be fishing illegally or who had failed to inform the Khmer Rouge of all their activities. Also during 1975–1976, food was scarce in the village; rice porridge with banana stalks was the usual meal.

I can't remember when the Khmer Rouge first came from Oddar Meanchey province and took rice from the people of Lbaeuk. They soon began ordering the demolition of half a dozen big houses in the village, and the building of a large number of smaller ones to house the villagers. Many of the new houses became flooded in the subsequent rainy seasons. They were built in a circle around the outskirts of the village; to provide communal dining facilities, a large "economics hall" [*kleang setakec*] was constructed in the now empty centre of the village.

The Khmer Rouge recruited a large number of volunteers in Lbaeuk, mostly youths about 20 years old. They were attracted by the much larger food rations that Khmer Rouge received, and by the fact that they did not have to work, and could kill people. On some occasions Khmer Rouge members who had committed some transgression were executed by their fellows.

The village *wat* was also demolished; several people were killed in an accident that occurred in the process. The large statue of Buddha from inside was thrown in a nearby stream. The local Khmer Rouge leader had given orders for this to be done, without giving a reason; he was obeyed out of fear. From that time on, monks were no longer seen around the village.

The year 1976 was worse than 1975. By now, no one in Lbaeuk dared complain or question the regime. My father was temporarily jailed by the Khmer Rouge. I don't know the reason.

In 1977, all young children no longer breast-feeding were taken from their parents and cared for permanently by female members of the Khmer Rouge. The reason given was to enable the mothers to work more effectively. Boys of my age [11] and older were taken together to a forest locality called Lbaeuk Prey. There were over 100 boys in all. Our task was to plant rice, supervised by about 20 armed Khmer Rouge in their early twenties. We worked there for five months, during which time more than 20 of us were taken away to a nearby mountain top. I never saw them again. I believe they were killed.

They were boys who had not worked hard or had missed work or played games, and had ignored three warnings to this effect. [More minor infringements of the rules, Sat says, were punished with a spell breaking rocks to make roads.] Or, they were people who didn't reply when asked what were their parents' occupations.

Morale was low among the young workers. Laughing was permitted, but there was no singing while we worked and no dancing or other entertainment afterwards. Every night there were meetings, in which we boys were urged to work harder; there were no political speeches or discussion at these meetings, and nationalism was mentioned only in the context of the Vietnamese "attempt to take over our land." There were no references to China.

Other tasks we performed were removing weeds from the rice fields and making fertilizer. The job I preferred was tending crops such as watermelons, cucumbers, and other vegetables. I was able to spend a lot of time doing this because I was ordered to. Khmer Rouge leaders on bicycles and with guns [both possessions were a sign of office] occasionally inspected my work. I was never allowed to eat any of the fruits of my labor, all of which were carted away by truck; I don't know where. The food rations I received varied from rice porridge with salt, to rice porridge with fish.

At night we were obliged to mount guard duty. I was taught how to use a gun but never considered becoming a Khmer Rouge soldier when I was older.

Many of us missed our parents badly. Some of us cried with grief at times; the Khmer Rouge would then beat them with sticks until they stopped crying. One month after commencing work at Lbaeuk Prey, we were permitted to visit our parents in Lbaeuk. Some of the parents broke into tears on seeing their sons. My father told me he had now been assigned the task of catching fish for the village communal dining hall; he was forbidden to use any of his catch for his or his wife's consumption. My brothers and sisters had all been taken elsewhere and were not at home. After this visit, which lasted several hours, I returned to Lbaeuk Prey and never saw my family again.

In late 1977, all the boys from Lbaeuk Prey were taken in trucks to Samrong in Oddar Meanchey province. As before, the workers there were all teenage boys. I do not know where the teenage girls from my village had been taken.

In Samrong we began building a road that was to go to Preah Vihear [through hundreds of kilometers of uninhabited forest]. We were told that the road would be used to transport food and supplies. We all worked at the rate of 2 or 3 meters of road per day, using locally made buckets to shift the earth; some boys threw up the soil, while others packed it down into a road surface. By the time I left this site five months later, no vehicles had yet been seen on the road.

There was nothing enjoyable about this experience. We boys were not taught to read or write or to sing any songs; we were never shown any radios, books, or magazines, although I noticed that some of the Khmer Rouge had such things.

Later we boys were taken to a place in the forest called Ken, also in Oddar Meanchey province. We were again put to work building a road. We worked from 6 A.M. to 10:30 A.M., had a short lunch break and then worked until 6 P.M., when we had another short break and a wash and then worked until 10 P.M. There were no rest days. The work was so exhausting that some of the boys fell down unconscious at the work site.

Then, early in 1979, a Khmer Rouge leader arrived on a bicycle and announced that the Vietnamese were in Kralanh. We were told to walk to nearby Paong; when we arrived we were led towards the Thai border on foot for three or four days, carrying our own food and sleeping when tired.

I crossed into Thailand. However, one group of boys came across some Thai tanks; never having seen such things, they ran frightened back into the jungle, where they were killed by Khmer Rouge soldiers.

Now, I am not allowed to walk around or talk to people. When I become an adult, I want to live with other people.

The Khmer Rouge Leader Was a Kind, Easygoing Person" (Mien). I was born in 1965 in the village of Samlaeng, Roang subdistrict, Preah Vihear province, Cambodia. My parents, who were rice farmers, called me Daung.

[In early 1970, troops of the new Lon Nol regime retreated from Preah Vihear and from that point the province was under undisputed communist control.] During the next few years, Vietnamese Communist troops passed through Samlaeng, on one occasion, provoking a lot of interest but no hostility. They didn't steal anything from or harm the villagers; after paying for what they wanted, they moved on.

Also during the war, Samlaeng was bombed "many times" [by U.S. or allied aircraft] over a long period. I don't know if any of the people were killed.

In 1975 [after the Khmer Rouge captured and evacuated Phnom Penh], a number of people arrived in Samlaeng on foot after walking from Phnom Penh. Some people had died along the way; the villagers helped the newcomers settle in to their new environment.

During 1975–1976, life went on as before. My parents were happy during this period. Khmer Rouge troops lived in the village but did not cause any upset; I never heard any mention at all of any actual or suspected executions. Food supplies were adequate.

Then, in 1976, the revolution began. Its purpose was "to build up the country," I was told. The entire village was now obliged to eat in a communal dining hall. Rations were tight—usually only rice porridge. In late 1976, I heard that a Phnom Penh evacuee had disappeared from the village and was thought to have been executed. This was the only such case I knew of while living in Samlaeng.

In 1977, myself and three other village boys my age were taken away from our parents. The Khmer Rouge who escorted us away said that they would come back later to take away the other boys in the village, in groups of four at a time. I was taken to Samrong in Oddar Meanchey province, joining a work group of about 30 boys, the oldest of whom was 17. Our job was to clear the forest for *chamcar*, or garden farmland. Each morning we got up at 4 A.M. and worked around the house we lived in, tending fruit and vegetable crops, until 6 A.M. Then we would go into the forest and work there until 10 A.M. when we ate our lunch. This consisted of a carefully rationed bowl of rice porridge, sometimes with salt, sometimes with *samlor*. It was not tasty but I was always hungry and would eat it all. At 6 P.M. we would stop working in the forest and return to our houses. Every night we boys were assigned a small plot of land to tend near the houses we lived in. When we finished this task to the satisfaction of the overseers we were allowed to go to sleep.

While living with my parents, I had only been accustomed to doing household chores, and I found it difficult to adjust to the new lifestyle. The work was not enjoyable; each boy was allocated an area of forest to clear and we worked some distance from each other. We were not taught to sing songs or dance, or to read or write. I was never allowed to visit my parents again.

Nevertheless, the leader of the Khmer Rouge where I worked was a kind, "easygoing" person who never got angry and did not physically mistreat the children. The Khmer Rouge leader was about 30 years old.

After many months at Samrong, all the boys were sent to a place called Phnom Phtol, or Phnom Seksor. There we spent a few months looking after herds of water buffaloes. In early 1979, with Vietnamese troops approaching the area, we were told to go to Paong; we crossed the border into Thailand, followed by a large number of Khmer Rouge soldiers and children, not long after.

Notes

1. "Report to the Economic and Social Council," United Nations, July 2, 1985, 4/SUB, 2/1985/6, at 10 n. 17. "We agree with that assessment," the U.S. Department of State conceded in 1989.
2. S. Heder and B. Tittemore portray the UN experts as hesitant on the genocide issue: "They cautioned that it might be a 'difficult task' to prove that the CPK carried out acts 'with the requisite intent' to destroy such ethnic and religious groups 'as such'" (Heder and Tittemore, 2001, p. 14, n. 24).

Selected Bibliography

Amin, Samir (1977). *Imperialism and unequal development*. Sussex: Harvester Press.

Amin, Samir (1981). The lesson of Cambodia. *Conference on Kampuchea*, Tokyo, May–June, pp. 4, 8–9.

Asia Watch, & Physicians for Human Rights (1991). *Land mines in Cambodia: The cowards' war*. New York: Author.

Australian Department of Foreign Affairs and Trade (1990). *Cambodia: An Australian peace proposal*. Canberra: AD FAT, pp. v–7.

Barnett, Anthony (1983). Democratic Kampuchea: A highly centralized dictatorship. In David. P. Chandler and Ben Kiernan (Eds.) *Revolution and its aftermath in Kampuchea: eight essays* (pp. 212–229). New Haven, CT: Yale Council on Southeast Asia Studies.

Boua, Chanthou (1991). Genocide of a religious group: Pol Pot and Cambodia's Buddhist monks. In P.T. Bushnell, V. Schlapentokh, C. Vanderpool, & J. Sundram (Eds.) *State-organized terror: The case of violent internal repression* (pp. 227–240). Boulder, CO: Westview Press.

Boua, Chanthou, Kiernan, B., & Barnett, A. (1980, May 2). Bureaucracy of death: documents from inside Pol Pot's torture machine. *New Statesman*, pp. 669–676.

Boua, Chanthou, Chandler, David P., & Kiernan, Ben (Eds.) (1988). *Pol Pot plans the future: Confidential leadership documents from democratic Kampuchea, 1976–77*. New Haven, CT: Yale University Southeast Asia Studies Council.

Burr, W., & Evans, M.L. (Eds.) (2001). Text of Ford–Kissinger–Suharto discussion, U.S. Embassy Jakarta telegram 1579 to Secretary State, December 6, 1975. In *East Timor revisited: Ford, Kissinger and the Indonesian invasion, 1975–76*. National Security Archive Electronic Briefing Book No. 62. Retrieved from: www.gwu.edu/~nsarchiv/NSAEBB/NSAEBB62/doc4.pdf

Chandler, David P. (1985). Cambodia in 1984: Historical patterns reasserted?. In Institute of Southeast Asian Affairs, *Southeast Asian Affairs 1985* (pp. 177–186). Singapore: Heinemann.

Chandler, David P. (1991). *The tragedy of Cambodian history*. New Haven, CT: Yale University Press.

Chandler, David P., & Kiernan, Ben (Eds.) (1983). *Revolution and its aftermath in Kampuchea: Eight essays.* New Haven, CT: Yale University Southeast Asia Studies Council.

Cohen, Nick (1991, May 10). Oxfam activities censured as too political. *Independent,* London: n.p.

Dunlop, Nic (1999, April 30–May 13). KR torture chief admits to mass murder. *Phnom Penh Post,* pp. 1, 10.

Evans, Richard J. (1989). *In Hitler's shadow.* New York: Pantheon.

Guangxi People's Publishing House [Guangxi ren min chu ban she] (1985). *Jianpuzha*i [Cambodia]. Nanning: Author.

Heder, Stephen and Tittemore, Brian D. (2001). *Seven candidates for prosecution: Accountability for the crimes of the Khmer Rouge.* War Crimes Research Office, American University. Retrieved from: www.wcl.american.edu/warcrimes/khmerrouge.html.

Jackson, Karl (Ed.) (1989). *Cambodia 1975–1978: Rendezvous with death.* Princeton, NJ: Princeton University Press.

Jennar, Raoul (1991). *The Cambodian gamble.* Jodoigne, Belgium: European Center for Far Eastern Research.

Kiernan, Ben (1983). Wild chickens, farm chickens, and cormorants: Kampuchea's eastern zone under Pol Pot. In David Chandler & Ben Kiernan (Ed.) *Revolution and its aftermath in Kampuchea* (pp. 136–211). New Haven, CT: Yale Council on Southeast Asia Studies.

Kiernan, Ben (1985a). *How Pol Pot came to power: A history of Communism in Kampuchea, 1930–1975.* London: Verso.

Kiernan, Ben (1985b). Kampuchea and Stalinism. In Colin Mackerras & Nick Knight (Eds.) *Marxism in Asia* (pp. 232–249). London: Croom Helm.

Kiernan, Ben (1986a). *Cambodia: Eastern zone massacres.* New York: Columbia University, Centre for the Study of Human Rights.

Kiernan, Ben (1986b). Kampuchea's ethnic Chinese under Pol Pot: A case of systematic social discrimination. *Journal of Contemporary Asia, 16*(1), 18–29.

Kiernan, Ben (1986c). William Shawcross, declining cambodia. *Bulletin of Concerned Asian Scholars, 18*(1), 56–63.

Kiernan, Ben (1988). Orphans of genocide: The Cham Muslims of Kampuchea under Pol Pot. *Bulletin of Concerned Asian Scholars, 20*(4), 2–33.

Kiernan, Ben (1989a). The American bombardment of Kampuchea, 1969–1973. *Vietnam Generation, 1*(1), 4–41.

Kiernan, Ben (1989b, February 27). Blue scarf/yellow star: A lesson in genocide. *Boston Globe,* p. 13.

Kiernan, Ben (1990a). The genocide in Cambodia, 1975–1979. *Bulletin of Concerned Asian Scholars, 22*(2), 35–40.

Kiernan, Ben (1990b). The survival of Cambodia's ethnic minorities. *Cultural Survival, 14*(3), 64–66.

Kiernan, Ben (1991a). Deferring peace in Cambodia: Regional rapprochement, superpower obstruction. In George W. Breslauer, Harry Kreisler, & Benjamin Ward (Eds.) *Beyond the Cold War* (pp. 59–82). Berkeley, CA: Institute of International Studies, University of California.

Kiernan, Ben (1991b). Genocidal targeting: Two groups of victims in Pol Pot's Cambodia. In P.T. Bushnell, V. Shlapentokh, C. Vanderpool, & J. Sundram (Eds.) *State organized terror: The case of violent internal repression* (pp. 207–226). Boulder, CO: Westview Press.

Kiernan, Ben (1992). The Cambodian crisis, 1990–1992: The UN plan, the Khmer Rouge, and the State of Cambodia. *Bulletin of Concerned Asian Scholars, 24*(2), 3–23.

Kiernan, Ben (ed.) (1993). *Genocide and democracy in Cambodia: The Khmer Rouge, the United Nations, and the international community.* New Haven, CT: Yale Council on Southeast Asia Studies.

Kiernan, Ben (2000). Bringing the Khmer Rouge to justice. *Human Rights Review, 1*(3), 92–108.

Kiernan, Ben (Ed.) (2002a). Conflict and change in Cambodia. *Critical Asian* Studies, 34(4), 483–621. (Special Issue.)

Kiernan, Ben (2002b). *The Pol Pot regime: Race, power and genocide in Cambodia under the Khmer Rouge, 1975–1979* (2nd ed.). New Haven, CT: Yale University Press.

Kiernan, Ben (2003). The demography of genocide in Southeast Asia: The death tolls in Cambodia, 1975–79, and East Timor, 1975–80. *Critical Asian Studies, 35*(4), 585–597.

Kiernan, Ben (2008a). *The Pol Pot regime: Race, power and genocide in Cambodia under the Khmer Rouge, 1975–1979* (3rd ed.). New Haven, CT: Yale University Press.

Kiernan, Ben (2008b). *Genocide and resistance in Southeast Asia: Documentation, denial, and justice in Cambodia and East Timor.* New Brunswick, NJ: Transaction Publishers.

Kiernan, Ben, & Chanthou, Boua (Eds.) (1982). *Peasants and politics in Kampuchea, 1942–1981.* London: Zed Books.

Leopold, Evelyn (1991, September 22). Western nations want former Cambodian leader to leave country. Reuter Cable, UN (NYC).

Migozzi, Jacques (1973). *Cambodge: faits et problémes depopulation.* Paris: Centre National de la Recherche Scientifique.

Mommsen, Hans (1991). National socialism: Continuity and change. In Hans Mommsen, *From Weimar to Auschwitz: Essays on German History* (pp. 141–162). Cambridge: Polity Press.

Murdoch, Lindsay (1991, October 24). Evans backs Pol Pot trial. *Melbourne Age,* p. 1.

Mysliwiec, Eva (1988). *Punishing the poor: The international isolation of Kampuchea.* Oxford: Oxfam.

New York Times (1991, August 28). Sighted in Cambodia: Peace. *New York Times,* p. A20.

Pilger, John (1991a, May 17). In defence of Oxfam. *New Statesman and Society,* p. 8.

Pilger, John (1991b, August 1). West conceals record on Khmer Aid. *Sydney Morning Herald,* n.p.

Pilger, John (1991c, September 27). Culpable in Cambodia. *New Statesman and Society,* n.p.

Pilger, John (1991d, November 1). Organised forgetting. *New Statesman and Society,* n.p.

Pol Pot (1978, March 23). Interview of Comrade Pol Pot … to the Delegation of Yugoslav journalists in visit to democratic Kampuchea. Phnom Penh: Democratic Kampuchea, Ministry of Foreign Affairs.

Ratner, Steven, & Abrams, Jason (1997). *Accountability for human rights atrocities in international law: Beyond the Nuremberg legacy.* Oxford: Clarendon Press.

Shawcross, William (1979a). *Sideshow: Kissinger, Nixon and the destruction of Cambodia.* New York: Pocket Books.

Shawcross, William (1979b, September 26). *Sunday Telegraph,* n.p.

Shawcross, William (1980, January 24). The end of Cambodia. *New York Times Review of Books, 26*(21–22), 25–30.

Shawcross, William (1984). *The quality of Mercy: Cambodia, holocaust and modern conscience.* London: André Deutsch.

Shenon, Philip (1991, October 24). Cambodian factions sign peace pact. *New York Times,* p. A16.

Stanton, Gregory (1993). The Khmer Rouge genocide and international law. In Ben Kiernan (Ed.) *Genocide and democracy in Cambodia* (pp. 141–161). New Haven, CT: Yale Council on Southeast Asia Studies.

Thion, Serge (1983). The Cambodian idea of revolution. In David P. Chandler and Ben Kiernan (Eds.) *Revolution and its aftermath in Kampuchea: Eight essays* (pp. 10–33). New Haven, CT: Yale Council on Southeast Asia Studies.

Thion, Serge (1993). Genocide as a political commodity. In Ben Kiernan (Ed.) *Genocide and democracy in Cambodia* (pp. 163–190). New Haven, CT: Yale Council on Southeast Asia Studies.

United Nations (1999, March 16). General Assembly, Security Council, A/53/850, S/1999/231, Annex, *Report of the Group of Experts for Cambodia Established Pursuant to General Assembly Resolution 52/135.* New York: Author.

United Nations Subcommission on Human Rights (1991, August 23). 1991/8 situation in Cambodia: UN Subcommission on Human Rights Resolution.

Van Leur, J.C. (1955). *Indonesian Trade and Society.* The Hague: W. Van Hoeve.

Vatikiotis, Michael (1988, August 11). Smiles and soft words. *Far Eastern Economic Review,* pp. 28–29.

Vickery, Michael (1984). *Cambodia 1975–1982.* Boston, MA: South End Books.

Vickery, Michael (1988). Violence in democratic Kampuchea: Some problems of explanation. Paper distributed at a conference on *State-Organized Terror: The Case of Violent Internal Repression,* November, East Lansing: Michigan State University.

Vickery, Michael (1989). Cambodia (Kampuchea): History, tragedy and uncertain future. *Bulletin of Concerned Asian Scholars, 21*(2–4), 35–58.

Vickery, Michael (1990). Comments on Cham population figures. *Bulletin of Concerned Asian Scholars, 22*(1), 31–33.

Vickery, Michael (1998). *Society, economics and politics in pre-Angkor Cambodia: The 7th–8th centuries*. Tokyo: Centre for East Asian Cultural Studies for UNESCO.

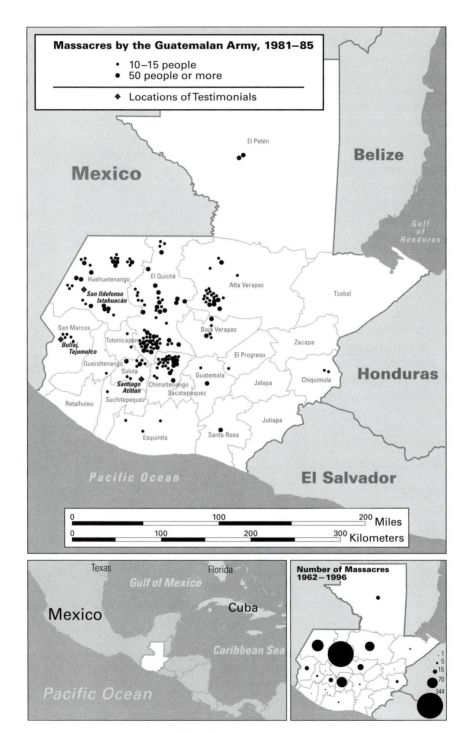

Map 10.1 Guatemala

CHAPTER 10

Guatemala: Acts of Genocide and Scorched-earth Counterinsurgency War

SUSANNE JONAS

There is no more painful chapter in the history of modern Guatemala than the events of 1980–1983 and their sequel in the mid-1980s. At the human level, it is a tale of wholesale slaughter and acts of genocide by the counter-insurgent state security forces, carrying out extra-judicial violence without any facade of legal constraints. That these genocidal acts were almost unknown in many Western countries, certainly in the United States, is a testament to the silence about Guatemala during the most brutal years. It was an indifferent, and, at times, complicitous silence. The victims were overwhelmingly Mayan indigenous civilians living in Guatemala's western highlands or *altiplano*. At that time, Mayan peoples (in over 20 sub-groups) constituted well over half of Guatemala's population of eight million.

Background: Heightened Identity Awareness and Resistance in the Mayan Highlands

Structural transformations of the 1960s–1980s changed the overall situation of Guatemala's indigenous highlands' populations in their class definition, and profoundly affected their self-conceptions and identities as indigenous peoples; here lay the basis for the widespread Mayan uprising in the late 1970s and early 1980s. (For a much more detailed account of the early history of the conflict and antecedents to the genocide, see Jonas [1991] and sources cited therein.) Economic growth followed by economic crisis broke down the objective barriers that had kept the Mayas relatively isolated in the highlands. This was greatly intensified by the economic and political crises of the 1970s and 1980s (including a major earthquake in 1976), when growing numbers of Mayas were forced to migrate to the

355

Southern Coast as seasonal laborers, and to Guatemala City in search of jobs. These changes and displacements brought them into increased contact with the *ladino* (non-Maya), Spanish-speaking world. Rather than "ladinizing" or acculturating the Mayas, however, this experience reinforced their struggle to preserve their indigenous identity, although in new forms—as Guatemalan Jesuit priest/anthropologist/activist Ricardo Falla (1978) put it, to discover "new ways of being Indian." As will be seen below, these factors explain why Guatemala's Maya peoples became one of the powerful social forces driving the insurgency of the 1970s and 1980s—and the principal victims of the army's brutal response.

In the countryside, structural contradictions—the crisis in subsistence agriculture, compounded by the massive 1976 earthquake—uprooted and displaced thousands of indigenous peasants, causing them to redefine themselves in both class and cultural terms. As producers, they were being semiproletarianized as a seasonal migrant labor force on the plantations of the Southern Coast, meanwhile often losing even the tiny subsistence plots of land they had traditionally held in the highlands. The combination of their experiences of being evicted from their own lands and their experiences as a migrant semiproletariat radicalized large numbers of highlands Mayas. Even the more developmentalist influences (that is, assisting the Mayas by providing them with land and thus a livelihood other than indentured servant) were contradictory in that they raised hopes and expectations in the 1960s, only to dash them in the 1970s. The clearest examples of this dynamic were those peasants who received land from the government's colonization programs in the 1960s, only to have it taken away again in the 1970s as the powerful army officers grabbed profitable lands in colonization areas.

Culturally, throughout the 1960s and 1970s highland Maya communities were being transformed and redefined as they "opened up" to contact with the *ladino* world. Increased contact had the paradoxical effect of reinforcing their defense of their ethnic/cultural identity, as expressed in their languages, customs, community and religious practices, claims to land and other rights, and their overall worldview. These elements of their identity became a factor in mobilizing their resistance to the *ladino*-dominated state. Politically as well, "reformist" parties such as the Christian Democrats came into indigenous communities, raising expectations of change—only to leave those hopes unfulfilled for most people. Meanwhile, indigenous organizations were defined by the government as "subversive" and excluded from the minimal forms of political expression that other sectors were permitted.

Furthermore, increased army repression against indigenous communities—incursions into villages, shooting indiscriminately, sometimes massively, and other forms of attack—had contradictory effects. Rather than terrorizing the Mayas into passivity, by the late 1970s it stimulated hundreds, later thousands, of them to take up arms (or seek to do so) as the only available means of self-defense against state violence. All of these paradoxical experiences of the 1970s coincided with the transformation of grass-roots organizations of the Catholic Church, the rise of Christian Base Communities, and the gradual emergence of a "Church of the Poor." This was expressed most concretely by village priests interacting with their communities, but they also eventually influenced the official Church hierarchy (*Conferencia Episcopal Guatemalteca*) to shed earlier conservative positions and alliances, and align itself with social justice movements. These new religious currents became central to the radicalization of the indigenous highlands, and led the army to identify actors (that is, individuals) representing the Catholic Church (including some bishops) as part of the "subversive" movement.

By 1978 these various strands were woven together in the emergence of the *Comité de Unidad Campesina* (CUC) as a national peasant organization, including both peasants and agricultural workers, both Mayas and poor *ladinos*, but led primarily by Mayas. From the viewpoint of the army and business elites, the CUC was by definition a "subversive" organization. The CUC came into the limelight after a major army massacre at Panzós, Alta Verapaz, in May 1978 (see Grandin, 2004), and the January 1980 massacre at the Spanish embassy in the capital, where Guatemalan security forces burned alive 39 indigenous protesters from the town of Nebaj, Quiché—including Vicente Menchú, father of the 1992 Nobel Laureate Rigoberta Menchú. In February 1980 the CUC staged a massive strike of workers on the Southern Coast sugar and cotton plantations; from the viewpoint of both the landowners and the army, this strike was their worst nightmare come true.

Also important in the growth of a politicized indigenous movement was a change in the stance of Guatemala's revolutionary armed insurgents vis-à-vis the Maya population. The leftist movement, which by its own definition was fighting for a socialist revolution, had begun in 1960, operating in eastern Guatemala, primarily a *ladino* (non-Maya) area. The movement (*Fuerzas Rebeldes Rebeldes*; FAR) had undergone a strategic defeat during the army's massive counterinsurgency campaign of 1966–1968, with U.S. military forces and advisors directly training the Guatemalan army (see below). That campaign, directed primarily against unarmed civilians, also introduced the phenomena of death squads and "disappearances" to Guatemala—and, via Guatemala, to all Latin America. The late 1960s saw the consolidation of the counterinsurgency state that was to dominate Guatemala for decades.

These events of the late 1960s led to a broad reevaluation of strategy and goals by the insurgents, and an organizational recomposition within the movement from 1968 through the early 1970s, following several splits from the FAR. Most important, the insurgents concluded that they had to rectify having virtually ignored the indigenous population during the 1960s. By the time of their resurgence in the early 1970s, two of the three major organizations, *Ejército Guerrillero de los Pobres* (EGP) and *Organización del Pueblo en Armas* (ORPA), had spent several years being educated by the indigenous population (about Mayan languages, customs, and rights struggles) and organizing a political support base, primarily in the western highlands, before renewing armed actions later in the 1970s.

The guerrilla armed uprising reached its height in 1980–1981, gaining 6,000–8,000 armed fighters and 250,000–500,000 active collaborators and supporters (Adams, 1988, p. 296), and operating in many parts of the country. By the early 1980s, entire Maya highlands communities were turning to the insurgents for arms to defend themselves from army incursions and massacres—although in reality the insurgents were totally unprepared to provide these communities with the means to defend themselves, and subsequently lost support from these communities. The new wave of armed struggle was taken very seriously by Guatemala's elites and army as heralding a possible seizure of power by the insurgents. In early 1982 the various guerrilla organizations united in the *Unidad Revolucionaria National Guatemalteca* (URNG), overcoming years of sectarian divisions. Even as unity was proclaimed, however, and even as the revolutionary movement achieved its maximal expression during 1980 and 1981, a change in the balance of forces between the insurgents and the army began during the second half of 1981, as the army initiated an unprecedented counter-offensive against the civilian support base of the insurgents.

The "Guatemala Solution": Total War at the Grass-roots, Acts of Genocide, and Crimes against Humanity

To those of us who have studied this history in detail on the basis of interviews and primary documents, what is most striking is the unity and single-minded determination of all those (both within the Guatemalan government and those serving on the behalf of the government) who were involved in the campaign against "*la subversión*." Inherent within this vision was the assumption that a scorched-earth counterinsurgency war was necessary to establish "social peace." Within this context, human rights crimes, including massacres and acts of genocide, were simply beside the point, since the Maya population was viewed as "subversive" by definition.

The stepped-up military counter-offensive was initiated in mid-1981 under the leadership of General Benedicto Lucas, brother of military President Romeo Lucas García (1978–1982). The campaign began in Guatemala

City, with a fall 1981 lightening swoop against the urban infrastructure of the guerrilla organizations, as well as urban popular movements.

The major thrust of the counterinsurgency campaign, however, was the scorched-earth war in the highlands, which began in 1981 but became even more brutal in 1982–1983 under the regime of General Efraín Ríos Montt (who took power through a military coup in March 1982 and was displaced by another coup in August 1983). As the army openly acknowledged, the goal was literally to "drain the sea" in which the guerrilla movement operated and to eradicate its civilian support base in the Maya highlands. The principal techniques included depopulation of the area through "scorched earth" burnings of entire villages, and massacres and large-scale forced relocations of the village inhabitants. Entire sectors of the Maya population became military targets, leading many scholars to identify these policies as genocidal. Falla (1984) called it genocide "in the strict sense," because it involved massacres of people such as the elderly and children who did not yet have the use of reason and therefore could not be considered guerrilla collaborators: "The ideological bridge is the concept that guilt and crime are transmitted biologically. It is racist" (p. 116).

The dozens of scholars who reached the same conclusions about the genocidal nature of these policies were joined by national, international, and inter-governmental human rights organizations in judging that the army's policies *were systematically directed to destroy some ethnic subgroups in particular, as well as the Maya population in general.*

Additionally, the UN General Assembly overwhelmingly passed Resolutions in 1982 and 1984 condemning the Guatemalan regimes responsible for these policies; the UN Human Rights Commission assigned Special Rapporteurs on Guatemala for many years, and hearings were held by the UN Committee for the Prevention of Discrimination and Protection of Minorities. In 1984 Pope John Paul II denounced the Guatemalan regime. (In addition to my own interviews and specific sources cited in the references for this chapter, numerous reports were issued by organizations such as Amnesty International and Americas Watch.)

The statistics are staggering: Some 440 villages were entirely destroyed (and that is according to the army's own figures). In the period 1981–1983 alone, 100,000–150,000 (primarily Maya) unarmed civilians were killed. There were over one million displaced persons (one million internal refugees, 200,000 refugees in Mexico). Accompanying these massive population displacements was the deliberate destruction of huge areas of the highlands (burning of forests, etc.) to deny cover to the guerrillas, and to assure that the region could never again serve as a theater for revolutionary operations. The environmental devastation was irreversible, even modifying climate and rainfall patterns (Perera, 1989).

In a subsequent analysis of the 1981–1983 period by the insurgents, the goal of the genocide and scorched-earth policies went beyond elimination of the insurgents' support base and the material base of the local economy. The deeper objective was to

> fracture the very bases of the communal structure and of ethnic unity, destroying the factors of reproduction of culture and affecting the values on which it rests ... understanding that the possibilities of survival and reproduction of the indigenous culture are directly linked to the prospects for revolution. (*Opinión Política* [*OP*] #2 and #3, 1985)

As one indicator, many Mayas in the highlands subsequently stopped wearing *traje* or traditional dress. In short, the very *identity* of the indigenous population was at stake; in this sense the war took on the character of an assault by the *ladino* state against the Maya civilian population. Further, the scorched-earth policy had the goals of destroying all forms of economic autonomy in the Maya communities (Smith, 1990)—and of "provoking such a degree of communal impoverishment as to destroy this form of peasant organization and place the producers at the mercy of capitalist economic laws" (*OP*, 1985). It was, in short, the most violent form of proletarianization—through military means.

A striking example of village massacres has been recounted by Ricardo Falla (1984) in his 1983 testimony at the Permanent People's Tribunal in Spain:

> The best documented massacre under the [1982–1983] Ríos Montt regime was perpetrated by the army at the totally indigenous village-farm of San Francisco in Nentón, Huehuetenango on July 17, 1982. An estimated 352 people were killed, of whom we have 302 names, 220 of them with the person's age and/or parentage. This village [is] ... not far from the northern border of Huehuetenango with Chiapas, Mexico.
>
> The survivors have been interviewed by the Christian Committee of the Diocese of San Cristóbal de las Casas in August 1982, by myself [Ricardo Falla] at the beginning of September 1982, by members of the Guatemalan Committee for Justice and Peace, and by Alan Riding, a reporter from the *New York Times* for an article published on October 12, 1982. On different dates, to different interviewers, the two main survivors have given absolutely consistent versions of the events.
>
> The pattern of the massacre, as in other massacres, was as follows. The soldiers separated the men off to one side, telling

them that there was going to be a meeting, and locked them up in the courthouse of the village-farm. The soldiers then rounded up the women from their various homes and locked them up at another location along with their children, both those having the use of reason and those not yet having it (the survivors make this distinction very clearly).

At about 1:00 p.m., the soldiers began to fire at the women inside the small church. The majority did not die there, but were separated from their children, taken to their homes in groups, and killed, the majority apparently with machetes. It seems that the purpose of this last parting of women from their children was to prevent even the children from witnessing any confession that might reveal the location of the guerrillas.

Then they returned to kill the children, whom they had left crying and screaming by themselves, without their mothers. Our informants, who were locked up in the courthouse, could see this through a hole in the window and through the doors carelessly left open by a guard. The soldiers cut open the children's stomachs with knives or they grabbed the children's little legs and smashed their heads against heavy sticks.

Some of the soldiers took a break to rest, eating a bull—the property of the peasants—that had been put on to roast. Then they continued with the men. They took them out, tied their hands, threw them on the ground, and shot them. The authorities of the area were killed inside the courthouse.

It was then that the survivors were able to escape, protected by the smoke of the fire which had been set to the building. Seven men, three of whom survived, managed to escape. It was 5:30 p.m.

The massacre continued, and when about six people were left, the soldiers threw grenades at them, killing all but two. Since it was already night, these two escaped through the window, covered with blood but uninjured. One of them was shot [and killed], the other lived. He is the surprise witness of this horrible deed. It is said that he arrived in Chiapas, Mexico, at 11 a.m. the following day, but because he had such a darkness in his soul, he did not even notice that it was daytime (pp. 112–114).

Institutionalization of the Counterinsurgency Apparatus

The next phase of the counterinsurgency campaign, from 1983 to 1985 (under the military regime of General Oscar Mejía Víctores), was also violent and devastating for the highlands Mayas. The most obvious goal was to consolidate military control over the population through a series of coercive institutions. Among these were:

- mandatory, involuntary paramilitary "civilian self-defense patrols" (PACs), designed to force villagers to participate in the eradication of the guerrilla movement, and generally to eliminate political activity in opposition to the government. Anyone who refused service was fined or, much worse, treated as a "subversive" himself. At one point, the PACs involved one million peasants—one-eighth of the entire population, *one-fourth of the adult population*;
- rural resettlement camps known as "model villages," concentrated in "Development Poles"—in essence, forced resettlement camps in which every aspect of people's lives was subject to direct military control; and
- Inter-Institutional Coordinating Councils, which centralized administration of development projects at every level of government (local, municipal, provincial, national) under military control. This created a military structure parallel (superior) to that of the civilian administration—a striking example of the militarized state. All of these institutions were subsequently legalized in the new Constitution of 1985, which provided the juridical framework for the elected civilian governments, beginning in 1986.

The purposes of the PACs went far beyond having auxiliary paramilitary forces, or even a captive labor force to construct roads and other infrastructure needed by the army. The goal was

> to construct new and massive forms of counterrevolutionary local power; ... to compromise a growing number of people in repressive activities, creating indestructible barriers between them and the rest of the civilian population—and irreversible levels of compromise of the patrol members with the army. (*OP*, 1985)

even in carrying out massacres of fellow-villagers. Villages and ethnic groups were turned against each other in an attempt to create "civil war" (Arias, 1985, p. 117). One anthropologist who observed PAC operations closely was struck by

> the degree of guilt and shame that people had internalized as a result of their participation in the civil patrol system. Apparently people had such guilt because the army entered the region like an angry father, accusing the Mayas of being rebellious children

who were responsible for the civil damage and strife created by the guerrilla movement. In its early stages, the army presented the formation of the civil patrols to the Mayas as a way of extricating themselves from any association with the guerrillas. During this period, when the civil patrols were being formed, the army forced Mayas to go on *rastreos* (hunts for guerrillas) and sometimes to stone or machete to death fellow villagers who were suspected or accused of being "subversives." Many of those who refused to participate in these acts or who tried to escape from civil patrol duty were punished by local authorities or sent to the regional army base for punishment. (Davis, 1988, p. 28)

The Development Poles were the major institution for the army's policies of population reconcentration from their original villages, following massacres and village destructions. These were intended, in the first instance, to deprive the revolutionaries of their support base; but longer term they were intended to centralize the new forms of counterinsurgent local power. These settlements, designed according to a military logic, brought the displaced populations under total army control. Particularly since the war had destroyed local supplies of food, firewood, etc., the displaced became dependent upon the army for food, as well as for work, shelter, and other "benefits," in a program called "Beans and Guns" (later "Shelter, Work and Tortillas"). This was a striking example of the systematic use of hunger as a weapon of social control.

Architects of these programs—including civilian counterinsurgents, those who, in the army's words, "had the vision to get involved" in the army's pacification programs—insist that they had a political as well as a military goal: to overcome the historic alienation between the state apparatus and the population by (forcibly) "winning it over" to the army's side, to create a real social base "among the people." According to one army document (cited in Manz, 1988, p. 18), military officers sought to mirror structures of the *Ejército Guerrillero de los Pobres* (EGP) in order to mobilize the population against the EGP. Military authorities even described the PACs as instruments of "participation"— as if they involved voluntary activity. In reality they were the product of extreme coercion, with resisters becoming targets of repressive retaliation.

Such coercion has been at the core of the relationship of the *ladino* army to the Maya population since the 19th century: "The military came to see rural Guatemala as its particular preserve, and reveled in its dominant position there. Any attempt to alter that position and organize peasants or rural workers into independent associations" was, therefore, an intolerable challenge (Handy, 1986, p. 407). In this sense, the genocide of the early 1980s was a logical extension of preexisting Maya/*ladino* relations (Adams, 1988, pp. 283–284). At the root of this system of institutionalized violence lay the fear of an indigenous uprising "coming down from the highlands" (Arias, 1985, p. 115); the uprising of the early 1980s came closer than any other experience to realizing that great fear.

Genocide Revisited: The Post-war Truth Commission or "Historical Clarification Commission"

Among the most controversial underlying issues of the Guatemalan Peace Accords negotiated over the course of six years (1991–1996) to end the 36-year war was justice for the victims of the war. (For a complete account of the negotiation of the Peace Accords and the subsequent struggles for their implementation, see Jonas [2000]). The issue of justice for the victims, including investigations of the massacres in the highlands, was addressed in several accords, the main one being the June 1994 Truth Commission Accord. Despite many weaknesses built into the Accord (e.g., not naming individual names, not automatically having judicial consequences), the Truth Commission (formally the "Historical Clarification Commission" [*Comisión de Esclarecimiento Histórico*] or CEH) itself was constituted and began functioning with great energy on July 31, 1997, six months after the signing of the Peace Accords on December 29, 1996. The CEH was headed by German human rights expert Dr. Christian Tomuschat, who had previously served as the UN's human rights monitor (Rapporteur) on Guatemala; the other members were two moderate Guatemalans, indigenous educator Otilia Lux de Cotí, and *ladino* lawyer Alfredo Balsells Tojo, both highly respected across the spectrum of Guatemala's organized social movements and political parties.

During the next year, the CEH took testimony from 9,000 war victims, who came forward in large numbers to tell their stories—as had been the case with the report authored by the Catholic Church Archbishop's Office of Human Rights (ODHA), entitled *Guatemala: Nunca Más* ("Never Again"). (The major coordinator of that report, Auxiliary Bishop Juan Gerardi, was brutally assassinated two days after the report's release in April 1998; this became Guatemala's highest profile post-war political crime.) In May 1998, the CEH conducted a public forum to get input from civil society organizations, including testimony from "binational" Guatemalan individuals and communities living in the United States. The CEH also sought written documentation from all domestic and foreign players in the war; while getting cooperation from the former insurgents of the *Unidad Revolucionaria Nacional Guatemalteca* (URNG), it ran into stone walls in attempting to gain access to Guatemalan army documents.

The CEH received an extension of its mandate in order to fully prepare its report, "Memory of Silence," which was finally presented on February 25, 1999, to a packed audience of 10,000. No one—not even the many interviewees, human rights groups, and analysts who had contributed to sections of the report—was prepared for the magnitude and scope of its findings. Among the highlights of the report were the following:

- Both the magnitude and proportionality of the crimes were even more overwhelming than previously known: The long debate over the number of people killed during the 36-year war was put to rest as the CEH report—like the 1998 report of the Catholic Church's Archbishop's Office—concluded that over 200,000 had been killed or "disappeared" during the course of the 36-year civil war (1960–1996). State forces were found to have committed 626 massacres, the URNG 32. Of the total atrocities documented, *93% had been carried out by state security forces and paramilitary groups linked to them (e.g., PACs)*; the URNG was responsible for 3%; and the remaining 4% was carried out by unidentified "other" forces.
- Although the entire war (1960–1996) was marked by acts of extreme brutality and cruelty, it was primarily during the "scorched earth" war in the indigenous highlands (1981–1983) that state forces committed *acts of genocide, as defined by international law (indiscriminate extermination of indigenous groups as such, elimination of entire Maya communities, including babies)*; furthermore, these were carried out as part of state policy, and not the result of simple "excesses." This particular finding was central, given that genocide was excluded from the 1996 amnesty accord and therefore, according to the CEH, could (i.e., should) be prosecuted.
- Rape and sadistic acts of sexual assault and torture against women were routine and systematic—part of soldiers' instructions; in an interview, Tomuschat called this the most "frightening" part of the report.
- As with the army, responsibility for URNG atrocities was attributed to the top leadership, and could not be dismissed as "excesses" or "errors" by rogue elements.

- The report made a strikingly harsh indictment of U.S. policy, beginning with its active involvement in developing the counterinsurgency capabilities and policies of the Guatemalan army during the 1960s. During the 1970s–1980s dirty war, the U.S. government directly and indirectly supported some of the Guatemalan state's illegal operations (although with some ambivalence under the Carter Administration, 1977–1980). During the 1980s, the U.S. government was fully aware of the massacres and other atrocities during that period of "scorched-earth" warfare and did nothing to stop them; in fact, it indirectly enabled and signaled approval of their actions (see below).

On the basis of its findings, and in order to begin meeting the massive challenges of reconciliation, the report made far-reaching recommendations to be undertaken by the two parties. By far, the bulk of these obligations fell on the governmental side, but successive governments, beginning with the one that had signed the Accords, under President Alvaro Arzú (1996–1999), rejected them directly or indirectly and considered them non-binding. Above all, until 2011, the government explicitly rejected the CEH finding that acts of genocide had been committed by state security forces. Despite the government's refusal to implement its recommendations, the Truth Commission Report remained alive in numerous ways. In the popular imagination, the CEH report, together with the ODHA report, was very broadly viewed as the authoritative interpretation of the war. A broad range of civil society organizations maintained public pressure on the government, and insisted that the report's recommendations were binding.

The U.S. Role: Not Simply Bystander, but Enabler

Many treatments of genocide omit the Guatemalan case altogether—one of the most celebrated being the Pulitzer Prize-winning book by Samantha Power (2002), in which Guatemala does not even appear in the index. Additionally, it is most common to portray the U.S. role as failing to act in time to prevent genocide (a sin of omission). In the Guatemalan case, however, the U.S. government, under most administrations during the second half of the 20th century, did not fail to act, but rather was a major enabler of systematic repression and, eventually in the 1980s, acts of genocide.

The active U.S. role began with the decisively documented 1954 Cold War anti-communist intervention by the Central Intelligence Agency (CIA) to overthrow the democratically elected, nationalistic government of Jacobo Arbenz (1951–1954). During the mid- to late 1960s (1966–1968), the U.S. government responded to Guatemala's leftist insurgency (formed in 1960) by directly retraining and transforming the Guatemalan army into a disciplined, counterinsurgency "killing machine," accompanied by death squads, etc. U.S. responsibility was documented at the time by U.S. participants (e.g., in *Time Magazine*, January 26, 1968, p. 23); it was definitively confirmed when a 1968 memo by then-U.S. Ambassador Viron Vaky surfaced (decades later), expressing regrets about the U.S. role in establishing the Guatemalan counterinsurgency state.

During the genocidal phase of the war in the early 1980s, the United States under the Reagan Administration, which was constrained by Congressional human rights legislation from sending direct military aid to Guatemala, found many indirect ways to signal its approval for the Guatemalan army's scorched-earth war. To cite just a few examples: in 1981, the administration sent top envoy/advisor General Vernon Walters to Guatemala to let the Guatemalan regime know that it was seen as a "friend"—and subsequently to Capitol Hill in Washington to lobby for a renewal of U.S. military aid. Assistant Secretary of State Thomas Enders, and even President Reagan himself, defended the regime of General Ríos Montt as "improving human rights," even as the latter presided over the genocidal policies of 1982–1983. In late 1982 Reagan (unsuccessfully) lobbied Congress to stop giving him a "bum rap" and to renew U.S. military aid, while accusing U.S.-based human rights organizations of spreading "disinformation" about Guatemala.

Perhaps the most compelling statement about U.S. responsibility in the Guatemalan case came from a public admission by U.S. President Bill Clinton—despite his administration's ongoing collaboration with the Guatemalan army. Three weeks after the release of the CEH report, during his (pre-scheduled) March 1999 trip to Guatemala, Clinton made the historic gesture of acknowledging responsibility for U.S. actions and complicity with human rights crimes in Guatemala over the previous 40 years. Meeting with an assemblage of Guatemalan civil society organizations, Clinton stated,

> For the United States, it is important that I state clearly that support for military forces or intelligence units which engaged in violent and widespread repression of the kind described in the [Truth Commission] report was wrong, and the United States must not repeat that mistake. We must, and we will, instead, continue to support the peace and reconciliation process in Guatemala. (March 16, 1999)

The Guatemala Genocide Case in Spain, and the Ongoing Search for Justice

Although the CEH report itself was restricted from naming individual military officers who had ordered or carried out acts of genocide and could not prescribe judicial consequences for them, it did not preclude survivors, including victims' families, from filing criminal suits against specific military personnel or "intellectual authors" of war crimes. Furthermore, in a separate operational law related to the final Peace Accords, the Guatemalan Congress passed a "National Reconciliation" law in December 1996. Most importantly, this law did not provide for an all-inclusive, blanket amnesty to the perpetrators of war crimes. More specifically, it exempted from amnesty the crimes of genocide, torture, and forced disappearances, as well as crimes involving the undue use of force against persons being held in military custody. However, extrajudicial executions not falling within those categories would not be exempted from amnesty. In practice, many issues would be decided by Guatemala's judicial system, which remained institutionally very weak, vulnerable to threats and chronic impunity—although the court system itself was slated for reform under the Peace Accords. Not surprisingly, then, while these accords and laws created spaces for pursuing justice, the road to the actual achievement of justice in post-war Guatemala remained a minefield, with obstacles at every turn.

Given this situation within Guatemala, in 1999, Guatemala's Nobel Laureate Rigoberta Menchú, with support from a legal team and human rights organizations, launched the first comprehensive complaint on behalf of survivors in Spain, initiating the "Guatemala Genocide Case." The case was broadly defined, charging wartime Presidents Lucas García (1978–1982), Ríos Montt (1982–1983), Mejía Víctores (1983–1985), and five other top former government officials with terrorism, genocide, and systematic torture. The Spanish National Court accepted the case under the principle of "universal jurisdiction" contained in the Geneva Convention, stipulating that the most heinous atrocities such as genocide, crimes against humanity, and torture can be prosecuted outside the country where these crimes occurred.

Even in Spain, when first invoked in 1999, this principle was challenged for several years on the grounds that legal remedies in Guatemala had not been fully exhausted. "Universal jurisdiction" with regard to the Guatemala Genocide Case finally became fully operational in 2005. Even then, the willingness of the Spanish Court to take on this case was necessary but not sufficient. The witnesses and their lawyers bore the burden of proving that acts of genocide had occurred and that the atrocities committed against their communities, as well as the preplanned "disappearances" of individuals, constituted state policy, and implicated the army's top command, rather than being simply abuses by soldiers. To make the case that there was a communications flow from top army commanders to soldiers would require both live testimony by survivors and hard data files from the war era. The live witnesses were represented by Almudena Bernabé of the U.S.-based Center for Justice and Accountability (CJA), which, in 2006, became the lead counsel and designed the entire strategy for the case, including the legal principles that would implicate the army's top command as intellectual authors.

In defiance of whatever dangers they might personally face, the survivors, most from the Maya highlands, persisted for years in keeping the investigations alive. These witnesses were assisted by Guatemalan human rights organizations such as the Rigoberta Menchú Tum Foundation (RMTF), the Center for Human Rights Legal Action (CALDH), and the Forensic Anthropological Foundation of Guatemala (FAFG), among many others, and the quasi-official Procuradoría de Derechos Humanos (PDH—Human Rights Ombudsman's office). But these Guatemalan organizations could not act effectively by themselves; they also required and obtained extraordinary support from international players. In addition to the Spanish Court, and international human rights organizations, these included the Inter-American Commission on Human Rights of the Organization of American States, which accepted Guatemalan massacre cases (e.g., Rabinal, Baja Verapaz) to be heard before the Inter-American Court of Human Rights. The Dutch government also provided funding to pursue ten "paradigmatic" cases of war crimes committed against Guatemalan communities or individuals.

In regard to written documentation beyond what was in the CEH and ODHA reports, a major breakthrough came with the discovery of a crucial wartime database. The abandoned and decomposing files and reports that the army-controlled National Police had maintained for decades during the war—the collection that came to be known as "el Archivo" ("El Archivo Histórico de la Policía Nacional")—was accidentally discovered in 2005 by the PDH. The entries in "el Archivo", once restored to usable condition, would become crucial evidence, particularly in the cases of individual "disappearances" carried out by the National Police. The work of making the records usable—cleaning, systematizing, digitizing, and releasing the information from "el Archivo"— was organized by the National Security Archive (NSA), working together with the PDH. As a U.S.-based organization, the NSA has specialized primarily in obtaining and publishing previously secret intelligence information from U.S. government agencies through Freedom of Information Act (FOIA) requests.

The Guatemalan armed forces had maintained equally detailed wartime records about their specific targets and the brutal methods used against communities and individuals, but systematically attempted to hide all records from public view. Such information would be essential to legal actions against military personnel involved in particular massacres and high-profile individual "disappearances." In 2000 Guatemala's highest judicial institution, the Constitutional Court, had ordered available military records to be turned over to civilian authorities. But it would be many years before any secret army records were located in military installations, extracted from army control, and eventually made public, as post-war Guatemalan governments capitulated to fierce army resistance and stonewalling. Finally, in 2008, President Alvaro Colom undertook to make military archives public (despite resistance from his Minister of Defense), and in 2011 inaugurated them as a "Peace Archive."

Using the "universal jurisdiction" won in 2005, Judge Santiago Pedraz had initiated the Spanish National Court's proceedings, and in 2006–2007 issued warrants for the arrest and extradition of the eight defendants. Guatemala's Constitutional Court initially accepted this instruction, but backed down at the end of 2007, denying the validity of the arrest warrants and extradition orders. At that point, during 2008–2009, the Spanish Court called several group delegations of survivors to testify in Spain, represented by CJA attorney Bernabé. Guatemalan experts also testified, including Fredy Peccerelli, the director and lead forensic anthropologist of the FAFG. Among the foreign experts who testified were Christian Tomuschat, former chair of the CEH, and Kate Doyle, the veteran investigator from the NSA, whose testimony focused on the paper trail of the army's "Operación Sofía," launched in mid-1982 by Ríos Montt in El Quiché. The Spanish Court broadened the case in 2011 to hear testimony about nearly 1,500 individual cases (representative of over 100,000 cases) of rape and other gender-related violence as a systematic instrument of counterinsurgency (35% of these victims being girls under 18 years of age).

Also in 2011, the Spanish Court issued an arrest warrant for the army officials responsible for the December 1982 massacre in Dos Erres, Petén. This provided evidence for a Dos Erres case filed in Guatemala, among the first such legal actions *in* the country itself. Four regular Kaibiles (the most brutal elite unit soldiers) were convicted and sentenced, as absurd as it sounds, to over 6,000 years in prison each, but the intellectual authors of the massacre, two Kaibil army officers, were not prosecuted in Guatemala. One was arrested in Canada and extradited to the United States, where he was charged with immigration infractions rather than genocide; the other was in Guatemala, where his trial began in 2011 but was subsequently suspended. Once again, the weaknesses of Guatemala's judicial system and the deeply engrained tradition of impunity precluded justice.

As of December 2011, Guatemala's top military command, the ultimate intellectual authors of the genocide, had not been brought to justice. Ex-President Efraín Ríos Montt had been a Congressman, enjoying parliamentary immunity from prosecution; he and the other seven defendants lived (or died) as free men, both inside and outside Guatemala, preventing any closure for the survivors. Nor did the survivors receive reparations even remotely commensurate with their losses; in fact, the ex-PAC members received far more reparations than their victims.

By late 2011, the process also faced a major new challenge, with the election of retired General Otto Pérez Molina as president. Before he even took office, Pérez Molina began appointing a number of wartime counterinsurgency officials to key positions—some of them, including Pérez Molina himself, linked to the 1980s scorched-earth policies and acts of genocide. Despite his preliminary promises not to interfere in ongoing investigations and cases – including his decision not to remove Attorney General Claudia Paz y Paz, the key figure in the prosecution of Ríos Montt in Guatemala once he lost his parliamentary immunity in January 2012 – overall process of seeking justice for survivors faced new uncertainties. International pressure, including the genocide case in Spain, would be as important as ever.

Despite endless barriers to justice in thousands of *individual* cases, the Guatemalan genocide investigation taken as a long-range *collective* enterprise has had great worldwide significance. Even in a country plagued by poverty, racial discrimination, injustice, impunity, widespread trauma, and fear, the courage and persistence of the war survivors, most from poor Maya communities, pushed forward an extraordinary and ongoing collective project of testimony and revelation.

Eyewitness Accounts

The following eyewitness accounts are based on testimony delivered at the Permanent People's Tribunal (a spin-off from the earlier Bertrand Russell Tribunal) held in Madrid in January 1983. The accounts were originally published in Spanish by the Institute de Estudios Políticos para America Latina y Africa (IEPALA) in *Tribunal permanente de los pueblos: Sesión Guatemala* (Madrid: IEPALA, 1988). They were translated and published in English in 1984, in the volume co-edited by Susanne Jonas, Ed McCaughan, and Elizabeth Sutherland Martínez, *Guatemala: Tyranny on Trial* (1984, pp. 82–86, 87–92, 100–106, 130–133, 154–161).

Testimony of Guillermo Morales Perez (Indian Peasant)

My name is Guillermo Morales Pérez, and I am here as a witness for my people in Guatemala. My residence is Bullaj, Tajumulco, department of San Marcos. I live between two villages: Monte Cristo and Bullaj. Today I am going to tell everything that is happening in Guatemala under President Ríos Montt.

As a witness I am going to testify before the public and the members of the jury as to how we have spent the months of 1982. When Ríos Montt became President, he announced that he was going to be democratic, but how long did the democracy of Ríos Montt last? Only 20 days, no more. After 20 days, he began to massacre, kidnap, and torture, according to the radio, and we heard that our brothers were being kidnapped and tortured.

The army entered the village of Bullaj the first time quietly, voluntarily, with affection, and what did they do? They deceived the people, they deceived us, they did what Ríos Montt ordered. He sent his army to trick us, and what happened when they entered? They killed two men. On May 15, 1982, the army entered and killed two men, dragging them out of their homes. The army men do not love their brothers, they think of us as animals. It's the same as when we go to kill a chicken. The army men no longer have mercy for Christians; they no longer have sympathy; they only think of us as animals. But it is they who have become animals, these government employees, this government, because it is the government that has declared a law to kill us for being peasants.

The army returned on July 20, and what did they do to us? They committed an injustice, because they came to the edge of these two villages, surrounded them, and started firing bullets to kill all the people who lived in the two villages. They succeeded in entering the village, and they set up camp. And out of fear, we fled. We went about 50 meters away from the houses because while we were inside, they had continued to fire at us. We left at night, without cover, dragging the children along. Women, 25 and 30 years old, pregnant, crept out of their houses. Others had just given birth only two days before. Even in their situation, they had to leave their homes, and they were very bitter, what with the bullets and all. Filled with fright, we had to leave, with the army on top of us, and we, what could we respond with? We are nobody, and they called us guerrillas.

And what type of guerrillas are we if we have nothing, if we only work in the fields? Our struggle is to work enough to be able to feed and maintain our families and to live through the year. Because if we do not work, we cannot live. The condition of the land where we live is bad. We don't have 300 or 1,000 *cuerdas;* we have scarcely one, five, or 10 *cuerdas* [one *cuerda* is the equivalent to 350 square meters—Eds.]. There is nowhere to put any livestock, or any other type of animal. We don't have that possibility. Thus, we can only work the land; it's the only way we can earn a living....

The shooting lasted from July 20 to July 22, almost three days. Then we returned to our houses. We proclaimed that we had not committed any crime because all we do is work in the fields. This is what we did. But what did they do? The set up camp in the village of Bullaj; we remained in our homes and continued working. On July 24 they began to bombard, bombard, bombard. They shot bullets all over, it was a noise like one hears when it rains on the coffee trees, like one hears in the *charunales* [trees that are used to provide shade for the coffee trees—Eds.]. We heard the shots very well, and they fell like a light rain. We ran away in fright, in terror, because we had never heard so many shots before.

Two more men were killed: Marcos Cash, 65 years old, and Luciano Chávez, 35 years old—they killed them, they hung them up. This evil army hung them, they knifed them in the neck, and at the same time they stuck them in their sides. They did all this the way they wanted, just like killing an animal to eat. This is what they did to our brothers.

We ran from the fear that we felt, with this constant bombardment that lasted two more days, July 24 and July 25. The following day, July 26, they camped in the village again. On July 27, they began burning all the houses. They burned the houses, they burned everything that was inside them—clothes, beds, our personal documents, money—all these things were burned. And at the same time, they ate all the animals, and what they could not eat, they shot full of holes. It lasted almost seven days, ending on August 2. From July 20 to August 2, 1982, 45 houses in all were burned. During this period, 300 or more army soldiers were in the village.

They returned November 24. And they returned in another way, trying to deceive us again. What did they do? They entered the village without making any noise, they came without firing a shot, very quietly, and we trusted them. Perhaps they were not going to do anything. Perhaps everything was over. Because according to what Ríos Montt said on the news, everyone was supposed to return to their homes and to rebuild them. The army was not going to continue burning; he said, "I repent for having burned your homes." In a note sent to the mayor of the Tajumulco he said, "Rebuild your homes, don't be afraid of the army, when they come, they will come in peace, they will not repeat their acts."

We felt safe and trusting, because we really felt that we had not committed any crime. We thought that we had not wronged Ríos Montt; we only claimed our rights to live well with what we earn from our own work. What did the army do on November 24 in the village of Monte Cristo? That afternoon, around 4:00 p.m., they divided up to go to the houses of the village, and captured four families, little boys and girls, teenagers, old men and women. They took them to where the army was camped and brought them before their commander. What did the commander of the army say? "Kill these lazy good-for-nothings, because they are with the guerrillas." They were then killed with machetes and knives, without using firearms. They cut off the head and arms of one of the women; they left her without head and arms, and they cut open her chest with a knife. Her name was Luisa Martin. And in this manner, they finished off all members of the four families, 18 people in all. The names of the dead people are: Joaquín Martin, Emiliano Martin, Juventino Hernández, Felipe Chávez, Jesús Ramos, Lucía Martin, Chavela Martin with three children, María Ramos, Esperanza Ramos, Oracio Martin and four other children from two to five years of age.

The following day, they continued burning houses and robbing whatever they found, things that the people had worked for. There were around 150 soldiers who entered the village on November 24 and 25.

We have heard the news that Ríos Montt wants to end the war with "Beans and Guns." There in our village, we see very clearly what the army does—bombard, shoot, burn houses, kill people, and destroy all the food supplies in the village. We have never seen this offer of beans that the news speaks of....

So many of our friends and family have died, and in addition to this, Ríos Montt has given orders for the creation of groups to patrol under his orders. On December 23, these patrols killed Santiago López, 55 years old; Rafael Chávez, 35 years old; and Rosalía Chávez, a 14-year-old girl. What did they do to this girl? They raped her and then killed her. They killed her 10 meters inside the Mexican border, but they took her out again and buried her 10 meters inside the Guatemalan border. This is what the patrol did under orders from the army....

The landowners have also acted in an evil way toward us. They give us a task which takes two days to do, and we only earn one *quetzal*, 50 *centavos*. Meat with bone is one *quetzal* for half a kilo, and pure meat costs one *quetzal*, 65 *centavos* for half a kilo. To be able to buy this half kilo of meat, we must work for two days. In reality, we do not eat any meat, and our families eat only a little tamale with salt. We cannot eat anything else the way the rich people can: milk, meat, eggs, vegetables, avocados— all the things that are at the market, that the land produces.

The rich people have all of this. And they have us like slaves, like animals, like beasts of burden, and they ride us. We carry them on our backs and give the rich man what he wants—we do everything.

Our personal dignity is dominated; and because of the lack of schooling and food, our children are the way they are, like me, with little schooling, even to explain this message I am giving. The majority of the country is also like this. We have no teachers, and at the same time, we do not have enough time to learn. There is much injustice in Guatemala. This is what I came to testify here in this country of Spain, so you will help us, because we can no longer stand the situation in Guatemala. Just as we are together here today, all together, we are brothers. We believe in this brotherhood and for this reason we plead for help and aid, to help our Guatemala be healed, that we may live in freedom and tranquility, and that we may all live together as brothers. Thank you.

Testimony of Regina Hernández (Guatemalan Committee for Justice and Peace, Refugee Program)

My name is Regina Hernández, and I am a member of the Guatemalan Committee for Justice and Peace (Comité Pro-Justicia y Paz de Guatemala). I have come before the Permanent People's Tribunal to give testimony about the displaced persons, or refugees, inside Guatemala. Before leaving Guatemala, I spent several months with these refugees, sharing their life and anguish.

They are the survivors of massacres perpetrated by the army in the villages in the highlands of Guatemala. They are those who managed to escape when their houses and crops were burned. Many of them witnessed the murders of their parents, brothers and sisters, spouses, and children.

Some are entire villages or communities who scattered to hide in the mountains when they heard that the army was near, to avoid being massacred like neighboring villages.

Others discovered earlier that the army was approaching, and because of the terror sown by the soldiers wherever they go, these people preferred to seek refuge in the capital or in other regions of the country, with the idea of returning to their villages when things settled down.

Others are families who have some relative or relatives connected with the opposition or "people's organizations" in Guatemala, and are thus "guilty by association."

The majority have no place to go and continually flee from one place to another. In their letter celebrating Holy Thursday, the bishops of Guatemala calculated the number of these refugee or displaced persons inside the country as more than one million. They also said that more houses have been destroyed by the current repression than were destroyed in the earthquake of 1976. The number of refugees has grown, because the repression—instead of decreasing—has become more acute.

How the Displaced Persons Live

The conditions of our lives are very bad. If once we lived in misery, under inhuman conditions, today our situation is worse—it is indescribable. We try to survive by imitating little wild animals, fleeing constantly in self-defense like hunted rabbits or deer. But the difference is that we are people, and it is difficult for us to move around—the colors of our clothes, especially the *huipiles* [traditional blouses, known for their beauty—Eds.] of the native women, make us targets, and we travel from place to place in groups of hundreds and sometimes thousands.

There are families with five or six children, small children who must be carried. To see a woman with one child on her back and one at her waist is very sad. Children who can walk carry a few clothes or a little food.

You fall and scramble up again. You hurt yourself on the thorns along the path, and then salty perspiration runs down into these cuts. This burns, as you can imagine! Then, when you decide to rest a little, the mosquitoes and flies crowd around to suck up your blood.

It is incredible how the children tolerate this without crying. What they can't stand is knowing that the army is near. I remember when we were in a small village and it was rumored that the soldiers were corning. All the children began to shout with fear and anguish.

When we found a place away from the soldiers, we would sit down to eat and share whatever we were able to bring along. We were so hungry that a cold corn tortilla and a little salt (if we had any) tasted wonderful. When we ran out of tortillas, we would go a day with only half a glass of corn meal mixed with water; this was all we had for the whole day.

We would also search for herbs we recognized and eat the leaves. This was during the winter, the season when the herbs grow. Sometimes all we had was a raw ear of corn that we found in those places where the crops had not been destroyed by the army. In the mountains, the refugees eat anything to survive.

Imagine what disease you find in these places where everything is lacking, where we must sleep exposed to the rain and wear our clothes wet until they dry out again. So many children have died of diarrhea, measles, pneumonia! If they don't die at the hands of the army, they die from disease.

So we move on, in growing numbers. In the mountains there are places that resemble the settlements constructed after the earthquake, where you find 1,500 to 2,000 families, places where you might eat only tortillas once or twice a day. Sometimes you wait a long time before getting to taste a little salt. There are places where people have gone to the extreme of drinking their own urine, because the rivers might be poisoned. We have also quenched our thirst with the dew that forms on the leaves of the plants.

Nevertheless, in the middle of all the anguish and terror that the army causes us, we try to encourage and inspire each other, to cheer each other up. One time we organized a little party, with guitars and violins, sharing with each other some of what we had left. We do this to have a few joyful moments and not to go crazy from anguish.

It's during these times that we live the Gospel—with deeds, not only with words. When we get to a place, we look around and check to see that everyone has arrived, that someone has not gotten lost along the way, that none of the children are missing. We all worry about each other. If we plan to stay in a spot for some time, we share what we have brought along to eat, and the few blankets or plastic covers that we managed to carry along to cover us at night. This is how we celebrate our faith, by sharing everything: sorrow, grief, suffering, and joy.

The Fear of Model Villages

All the things our people need are, for the government, a means of pressure to force us to turn ourselves in. They trick the international press into believing that the government is a savior, regrouping people and offering them "shelter, food, and work." But you don't know how much sorrow there is in the hearts of the people that the government has relegated them to living in "model villages." How can people agree with a government that has murdered their families and burned everything they had? If they are living in these "model villages," it is because they are there under threat. Men must be part of the civilian patrols; if they don't do it, they are killed.

Days of Anguish in Chimaltenango

I would like to tell you what happened on July 16, 17, and 18, 1982, when the army entered the village of San Martin Jilotepeque in the department of Chimaltenango. They entered the village on July 16, at 11:30 a.m., accompanied by civilian patrols. That day I was with a friend who had asked me to come to her house. We couldn't get there, because in the road we met all these people running away from the soldiers. It began to pour down rain that afternoon. We ran from the village and regrouped in a village nearby, with about 400 others, while the soldiers went from house to house, killing chickens to eat and trying on the men's clothes. The soldiers had also gotten wet in the rain and they were nonchalantly changing their clothes.

Meanwhile, in the next village, we got an enormous pot and prepared food for the children. We couldn't sleep because of the shots we heard throughout the night. The next day the soldiers approached the village where we were staying and all of us had to flee again. I remember the dawn of July 17, when we heard the cry, "Run, the soldiers are coming!" The children began to cry, terrorized, but after we started walking, they calmed down some. Each person carried his belongings, his poncho, some tortillas, corn meal, or whatever he could find. Each child who could walk also carried something.

The people of three villages came together in one place. We were resting when we again heard shots nearby. Once again we fled. Finally we came to another place farther away, where we found more people from other villages. There we rested again and shared what we had. We ran out of water and ate dry corn meal. We became nauseated from the lack of water. There were too many of us, so we decided to divide up into smaller groups. Each group went to a different village where we knew there were no soldiers. But in all this activity, families got divided up. In my group, there was a child carrying his mother's clothes and a poncho, while his mother went off in a second group carrying their tortillas. Her oldest child was in a third group, and the father—with the rest of the ponchos—went with yet a fourth group. I also saw a little girl about five years old who had lost her parents. But there we were!

We found a little orange tree loaded with oranges. We picked them all. They were very acidic, but they helped a lot. After a long walk—all day long—we came to another place about 9:00 p.m., and slept there. At this place they gave us hot tortillas, water, and a little salt.

On July 18 at 5:00 a.m., we were all up and ready to go. We washed with the dew from the plants. We found yucca and some other food and we each ate a little. We gave the leftover tortillas to the children. We were busy doing all this when we heard shots. We had to run again. Minutes later we saw the soldiers come running down a road. We had separated into groups of 20. What hurt me the most was seeing the old people with their canes, but thank God we managed to get away. From a distance, we saw the village burn.

When we heard that the soldiers had left our village, we returned home. We got there at 4:00 p.m. It was so sad, watching families find their houses and possessions reduced to ashes!

Help for the Refugees

All this suffering has forced me to leave my country to seek help. We need your help to cry out and denounce what is happening in

Guatemala, where they try to smother our cries with massacres. We need your help to survive and to resist this war.

Inside Guatemala, the service that I performed for my people was to bring them a little medicine, some food and clothes that I got from my friends. By sharing I have learned much from them. This little assistance meant risking my life; I knew that if I was found delivering these things, I would disappear forever. Many times I have been on the edge of death, sometimes from bullets and sometimes from flames, when they set fire to the forests. I have had to cross burning forests, practically suffocating from smoke inhalation.

What sadness! In Guatemala, the assassins of the Ríos Montt regime can go everywhere. And we, who have not stained our hands with blood, who have only tried to help, to defend ourselves, and to survive, must travel oh so carefully, hiding as if we were thieves. We are certain that someday there will be justice and that peace will come to Guatemala, with the help of all the people of the world.

The Committee for Justice and Peace has made a promise to bring help to 11 departments of Guatemala. It is one of the urgent tasks that we as Christians must undertake now, in this moment of struggle for our liberation.

Testimony of Juan Velázquez Jiménez (Indian Peasant and Mineworker)

My name is Juan Velázquez Jiminéz from the municipality of San Ildefonso Ixtahuacán, department of Huehuetenango. I come as a representative of the people of Guatemala to tell what is happening with the Ríos Montt government. But before that, I would like to speak of what has made my people famous: the problems of the mines at San Ildefonso Ixtahuacán, and the four-day march to the capital of Guatemala that my people made to hold a demonstration.

Work in the mine began when the government signed a 40-year contract with a gringo man [i.e., foreign—Eds.] named René Abularach. The people protested with a demonstration saying that they did not want the mine. A lawyer came, but the government showed no respect to him. Then the army troops began to arrive at the mine. The army had no respect for the people, but instead began to beat and slaughter them. The municipal mayor was immediately informed of what the army was doing but the mayor did not come, out of fear of the army. Later, the army arrested 15 men from the village, whom they took away. They also took prisoner a priest and a catechist and brought them by truck to the Huehuetanango department seat.

The army charged that the priest was guilty because he was giving guidance to the people. The priest responded that the people were only seeking their rights. The soldiers told the priest that he should not get involved in politics and let him go. The other men were struck, beaten, and kicked, and then were allowed to return to their village.

Later the gringos came to work in the mine and extracted tons of minerals in trucks. The people did not want the mine to continue because it was dangerous for the community. People thought that the community was going to cave in because the miners dug tunnels under people's homes. Tunnels were dug 4 kilometers under people's houses and some of the land in the community did cave in. Then, many people left to go to other, more faraway towns: to Cuilco, Ixcán, and La Costa. We were afraid, thinking that the whole town was going to cave in at once. We also did not want the mine because the lifeblood of the land, a very valuable mineral called tungsten, was being taken to another country.

People formed a union and went to demonstrate at the capital, walking on foot. For four days, they walked to the capital to demonstrate against the mine. Later, the same problems with Mr. Abularach continued. He claimed that the mine was not worth anything, while he was really trying to keep the miners from unionizing.

Now I would like to continue telling about what is going on with the Ríos Montt government. On May 6, 1982, the soldiers left Huehuetenango, and arrived in my town of San Ildefonso Ixtahuacán at noon. Along the road, they grabbed one of my brothers, took off his shirt and his pants, and left him naked. The soldiers tied him up and stuck him in a car. A red truck was in front and two olive green trucks were in back. They arrived at a crossroads where the trucks remained. They also left my brother there tied up in the car, with five soldiers to watch him.

Later, the soldiers arrived at a church where we were having a celebration. They started kicking us around and made us leave. At the celebration there were 45 adults and our children. The soldiers then gathered us together in the basketball court. Later, more soldiers arrived and surrounded the whole village. They began to drag people out of their homes until 10:00 p.m. Then they put us in a school, locked us up and told us to stay there while they ate, saying they were exhausted because of us. They locked the door real well and went to eat.

When they got back, the soldiers began to talk to us: "Now we sure did catch you today, you subversive thieves, you disgraceful Indians, you savages." We answered, "We are not stealing. We are celebrating the word of God." The second lieutenant said, "There is no God here who will bless you." They grabbed a 22-year-old peasant, and the second lieutenant told him: "All of you are bums and gossips. You are the teachers of all the subversive people here." Then one of the soldiers threw a lasso around the peasant's neck, and they hung him right there from a beam in the school. But the rope broke and the peasant fell to the ground. The second lieutenant kicked him, told him to get up, and then they tied him up again. They hung him again, and beat him all over until he died. Then the soldiers laid his body down.

The second lieutenant asked, "Where are the catechists?" The soldiers grabbed two of them and then three more people. Outside the school, the soldiers began to fire their guns, and those soldiers who were inside the school began to steal watches and money from the people. Then the soldiers took the dead man's body from the school and they brought some bombs inside, saying to us, "Be careful that you don't leave, because you will die." They grabbed 11 people from among those at the school, and took them to prison. My brother, whom they had left in the truck, also was killed. Five soldiers remained at the school, but then they left, with us locked inside. We stayed there crying. At 7 a.m. we broke down the doors of the school, and went home.

The soldiers went to Cuilco but later they returned to Huehuetenango, to the settlement called Laguneta, Aldea Alta in the municipality of San Ildefonso Ixtahuacán. I was working in the cornfields when they came. There were two peasants from the village of La Cumbre Papal, going to work in Chiapas. The soldiers grabbed them and searched their bags; they took away some hats that the peasants had, and then the soldiers tied them up by the neck. Five soldiers pulled at them from one side, and five soldiers from the other. The peasants were left there dead, tied to a tree. The soldiers cut off a piece of flesh from their legs, pants and all, and they left it hanging on a stick. They did that to both of these men.

Then they climbed up on a building and began to shoot. I was trembling with fear. When they arrived at the village of La Cumbre, they began to burn houses. I went to Laguneta and there I found a municipal employee. I told him that the soldiers had already killed two peasants. "We are not aware of it," said the employee. This happened on June 12, 1982. On June 13, 20 of us got together and went to see the bodies of the dead men. We took off the rope, dug a hole, and we buried them. And this I saw with my own eyes, because it is not good to tell lies.

On June 15, 1982, I was buying medicine in San Ildefonso Ixtahuacán when the airplanes went over. There were two in front and one behind, another two and then one, two and then one. There were a lot of planes and I was not able to count them all. I counted only eight. That day they went to bomb Nentón and San Pedro Necta, in the department of Huehuetenango. On the 16th, they were still bombing. The next day, one of my cousins arrived who had escaped death in the bombings; he was crying. Many people were killed in the bombings. There were many children killed, my cousin said.

On August 18, 1982, the soldiers came to organize civilian patrols in the village of Akjel, in the municipality of San Ildefonso Ixtahuacán. They ordered the assistant mayor to convene the people. When people arrived, the second lieutenant began talking, saying that by order of the Efraín Ríos Montt government, they were going to organize the civilian patrols. People asked him, "What are these civilian patrols for?" The second lieutenant answered, "To take care of the people so that the guerrillas don't come in." Then people asked: "Well, what are these patrols going to defend themselves with?" He answered, "You are going to carry machetes, rope, and a piece of wood. And if there are a lot of guerrillas, you are going to ring bells, sound horns, and yell, so that people come to grab the subversives."

People then said to the second lieutenant, "Second lieutenant, but we have to work on the farm. How are we going to eat?" He answered, "If you do not want to patrol, then you are subversives. You are going to respect the law, because it comes from the government. And if you don't respect the law that I have announced to you, I will kill your entire village." Then he showed us some bombs, and told us: "Here are your avocados, we are going to use them on your family." The people became very frightened and they agreed to patrol under the barrels of the soldiers' guns.

The second lieutenant said that the patrols had to receive identification cards that he himself, and the commander of the San Ildefonso patrols, would issue. On November 3, people from the village presented themselves in town and 100 identification cards were given out. The second lieutenant announced that all youth of 18 years old or over would have to go away to serve in the army. He also said that every patrol group had to bring its flag and identification cards when it was patrolling. "If you don't carry your flag and your identification cards, then you are guerrillas, and the army will kill you." That is how the civilian patrols in my town were organized.

On October 5th, I went to sell some oranges and bananas to the village of La Cumbre Papal. The civilian patrols were there, together with the soldiers. The soldiers asked for my papers, and told me that I had to go with them to the village of Papal. While I was in the village, the soldiers removed a man named Juan Ordoñez from his house, and another neighbor, and they set both of their houses on fire. The houses were made of straw. As the houses were burning, they threw both men, who were tied up very tightly, into the fire. And then they took me down farther, and we ran into two children who were eating corn on the cob in their homes. One ran off and hid in the *tamascal* [a steam bath used by the Indians—Eds.], and the other, a five-year-old, stayed inside the house. The soldiers set the house on fire, and burned it down with the child inside. The dead child was left in the house. The other child who had hidden in the *tamascal* was also killed. The soldiers then began to burn the other houses in the village. I could not count them all. I counted at least 20 houses that were burned by the soldiers. Then they let me return to my home.

In the month of November, a white pickup truck arrived. When it came to the Sevillaj bridge near the Cuilco mound, it stopped in front of Sr. José Lopez's house. Soldiers from the truck set his house on fire and then they machine-gunned Sr. Lopez, who was 60 years old, and all of his family. They killed a total of 10 people in that house. There was not one single person from José Lopez's family left. Then they forced the civilian patrol, who were accompanying the soldiers, to bury the dead in 6-foot ditches.

Throughout Guatemala, in various places and towns, our people cannot stand so much repression any more. People find dead bodies thrown at the side of the road. We find dead bodies without heads, without hands, without legs. We do not want anymore killing. We cannot stand Ríos Montt's repression, his misery, any more. We cannot work, we cannot do business, we cannot eat, because of everything that Ríos Montt is doing. And now we peasants want Ríos Montt to resign. We cannot stand him any more. I hope that you ladies and gentlemen can help us so that this Ríos Montt government will resign, along with his army, which is finishing us all off in Guatemala.

Testimony of Juan José Mendoza (Indian Community Leader)

A high point of this testimony was the story, which follows, of a community organization in the well-known tourist town of Santiago Atitlán, whose population of about 25,000 spoke Maya-Tzutuhil—Eds.

In Santiago Atitlán, a group of Atitecos who had suffered and knew the pain and suffering of their people organized in 1966. They were catechists of the Catholic Church. With the help of the parish priest, Father Ramón Carlin (a missionary from Oklahoma, USA), they began a campaign to teach reading and writing to the population. In 1970, with 300 members, we organized the Radio Association of the Voice of Atitlán. All the villages on the banks of Lake Atitlán participated; together we would seek a just and humane life.

We organized groups to teach reading and writing. We organized cooperatives: handicrafts, agriculture, and savings and loans offices. We began programs of health information and adult education, cultural programs and religious programs preaching the Christian gospel. We had a radio station to transmit the programs to all neighboring villages. Peasant children, young people, women, men, and the elderly participated. We all respected the sacred right to life of our relatives and neighbors; we shared our grief and our suffering as well as our happiness. All of the members of the Radio Association of the Voice of Atitlán voluntarily worked together to bring happiness and well-being to the lives of our oppressed people. Then, for trying to come out of our life of misery, the hatred of the government and the wealthy landowners destroyed us.

In June 1980, the army set up camp in the village of Cerro de Oro, eight kilometers from the town of Santiago Atitlán, with seven truckloads of soldiers, 50 soldiers in each truck. They interrogated the villagers of Cerro de Oro, to find out who were the collaborators in the Radio Association of the Voice of Atitlán and who were the influential people of the village. But the villagers did not give any information. So the army moved their camp to Cantón Panabaj, two kilometers from the village of Santiago Atitlán, on September 5.

On September 30, at 7:30 p.m., a paramilitary squad in a red car, coming from the department of Sololá, kidnapped the catechist Juan Ixbalán on a public street of the town of Santiago Atitlán. On October 10 they kidnapped another catechist, Manuel Coché. They tied his hands, beat him up, and dragged him from his house. Then the army forced the population to attend a meeting on October 15, at 11:00 a.m. They announced that the army had been sent by the government of Lucas García to protect and take care of the town of Santiago Atitlán. The people were prohibited from walking on the streets after 7:30 p.m., were forced to return from their work in the fields early in the day, and were forbidden to go very far from the town.

On October 24, at 4:30 p.m., the army and the national police surrounded the building of the Radio Association of the Voice of Atitlán, leaving after half an hour. But at 1:30 a.m., on the 25th, a group of soldiers, dressed in civilian clothes and well armed, kidnapped Gaspar Culan Yataz, director of the Radio Association; he was beaten savagely and shot in the head. His wife and daughter were also beaten. The soldiers carried the unconscious Mr. Gaspar to the camp; nothing more was heard of him.

The building of the Association was searched and plundered by the army on November 12. They stole radios and office machines, destroyed doors and windows. They hid a bag of firearms inside the building. The following day, Father Francisco, who had been the parish priest of Santiago Atitlán since 1969, told the mayor what had happened. The mayor called the army and, together with the army, he entered the building. The colonel ordered the soldiers to search the building, and they found the sack containing firearms. The colonel told those present that the Association had used arms and that they were accomplices of the subversives.

Four members of the Association were kidnapped on November 15, and savagely tortured. Three were buried in Chimaltenango in graves marked "XXX." The body of the youngest was found by his relatives, whose names are Nicolás Ratzan Tziná, Juan Pacay Rujuch, Diego Sosof Coché, and Esteban Ajtzip R. We had to hide in the ravines and hills and could not work. Many of our houses were ransacked, we were victims of persecution. Ever since the kidnapping of the director, we have had to abandon our work as the Radio Association of the Voice of Atitlán....

The murderous army was always looking for ways to terrorize the population of Santiago Atitlán. In September 1981 there was new persecution of ex-members of the Radio Association of the Voice of Atitlán. The army sent letters to every one of the ex-members telling them to give themselves up at the camp. If they did not turn themselves in, their houses would be burned, their families would be killed, and they would be prosecuted according to the law of the army. To save their families, 15 ex-members of the Association turned themselves in.

They were held in the camp for 15 days. They were threatened and forced by the Minister of National Defense to declare to the international and national press and to Guatemalan television that they were collaborators or members of the subversives and that all of them had gone to the camp to seek refuge and ask for protection by the army. On November 18, the army gave the interview to the press and television in the camp of Panabaj, Santiago Atitlán; they also forced many people to go to the camp and pretend to be subversives seeking shelter and refuge in the camp. All of these lies hide the crimes of the Lucas Garcia regime from the eyes of the world.

In the face of this difficult situation, many of us had to flee to Mexico at the end of November 1981.

Following the coup d'etat of March 23, 1982, Mendoza returned to Guatemala hoping to find more peace but instead found even greater insecurity. He came to live in the community of Nahualá where the following incident took place: an example of the Guatemalan people's indestructible defiance.—Eds.

The military commander had received an order from the army saying that the civilian patrol should not go out at 7:00 p.m., as was the custom, but should wait until 10:00 p.m. for that night only. However, the civilian patrol disobeyed the military commander and went out at 7:00 p.m. At that moment, the army was about to kidnap someone.

A group of well armed soldiers dressed in civilian clothes passed by, accompanied by a person with his head covered who was going to point out the house where the kidnapping would take place. The civilian patrolmen recognized the voice of the hooded person, and when the two groups met, a member of the civilian patrol unhooded the person. At that point, the soldiers machine-gunned the civilian patrolmen and also killed the hooded person. But members of the civilian patrol had prevented the kidnapping and unmasked the army as the author of the kidnappings and massacres of the indigenous population.

Testimony of Carmelita Santos (Indian Catechist)

My name is Carmelita Santos. I am an indigenous catechist and a member of the Guatemalan Committee for Justice and Peace.

I present my testimony to this People's Tribunal in the name of my Guatemalan brothers and sisters who are unable to lift up their voices today, and who suffer under the military dictatorship of General Efraín Ríos Montt. I wish to speak in the name of all the men, women, children, and elderly people of my country, so that the world will know about the terrible injustices that we suffer there, and so that our right to live on this earth as people and as children of God will be recognized.

My Work as a Catechist

I work in communities, talking to the people about God, and the people like that. I also teach people how to sing. People like to sing or to shout, because they fill their lungs with air and it makes them happy.

In 1970 and 1972, some good priests came here, who were honestly committed to helping their brothers in need. They weren't like the ones before them, who only talked to the "ladinos" in the village. They took care of us all. They came to our village to evangelize us but on seeing our communal lands where we all ate the same corn, they were the ones who were evangelized. When there was happiness, we all shared in it. And we all shared the same sorrows.

The priests wanted to improve our plight, but because we were many, two priests alone could not carry out improvements for all. The best thing they did was to set up schools, to train community leaders. These schools were established in various regions of Guatemala, since the priests could not cover every town. They and the nuns would visit each school, and then return two weeks or a month later. Those of us who were trained were called catechists, or community leaders.

The catechist works with the community, spreading the Word of God, allowing everyone to participate. The Word of God leads us to organize and make our demands together, because we will not be listened to on an individual basis. We organized a demonstration, protesting our oppression by the rich. But they said: "What's going on? The downtrodden Indians are acting up. Those who open their mouths will be killed."

Health Education

The nuns taught us the importance of hygiene. When children have rashes or intestinal parasites or diarrhea, it's because of bad health conditions. But there are even worse problems in villages like Canchún Chitucán, where there is no water because it sank after the earthquake. There is hardly enough to drink. Where could the people go? A priest said: "Let's dig a well."

But the religious people's love for the poor and their total devotion were not well-received by the rich. Neither they, nor the police, nor the judges, nor the soldiers like it when someone is concerned about the poor. They accused the priest of being a "guerrilla chief" and tried to capture him and kill him, but he managed to escape. He had to leave the country.

The Church, Threatened and Persecuted

First they threaten the community leader. If he doesn't leave immediately, he is kidnapped during the night and killed in the ravine. This has been done to catechists and to people who have listened to their sermons. Now we cannot hold our masses, or recite the rosary or the Novena of the Sacred Heart of Jesus, because we are being watched. In our village there are two strange men; they are not from the village, but they appear and disappear in the evenings.

Who persecutes the Christians? The big judges, paid by the governor or the ex-governor of Salamá; the soldiers stationed in the town of Rabinal; the national police; an employee of the city who is a friend of the soldiers or the national police; or a military commander.

This happened during the time of Lucas García, who said that there was freedom for the Church but who really persecuted it. They watched the villages and took away our leaders, killing them one by one. Oh! But Lucas went too far, and it was known that he was an assassin. The rich say that there was a change in government. They put in Ríos Montt, saying that he was "better," but he has the same heart as Lucas, and sharper nails. He's "democratic" but he's smarter than Lucas. Oh! "The envoy of God," Ríos Montt calls himself. Is he like God, powerful and merciful with the poor?

Testimony of the Communities Suffering in the Genocide Carried Out by the Ríos Montt Government

Ríos Montt shows his power to the poor. When he took over, he ordered his soldiers to eliminate from the map of Rabinal, Baja Verapaz, several villages that no longer had inhabitants. The people there had been slaughtered by soldiers and 10 commando squads from Xococ: Río Negro, Camalmapa, Canchún, Buena Vista, and the village of Chichupac, where there were only about 20 survivors.... In each of these villages there had been 300, 400, 500 or more inhabitants, not counting children. I say this because I have been in these communities many times, singing, praying, and celebrating the Word of God, or we would dance to the *son* of San Pablo or Rabinal. It hurts me that my people have left me alone. And I say this because I burn inside from the injustice of Ríos Montt against my poor people of Rabinal and against all the other poor people of the indigenous regions of Guatemala. Let them kill me for speaking the truth. I am not afraid.

Ríos Montt says that he is governing in the name of God. For those who believe in him, he is a Christian and belongs to an evangelical sect. But the repression got much worse for the poor with the arrival of Ríos Montt.

1 Plan de Sanchez, July 18, 1982

It was Sunday. Before, no one would go to the town to do their shopping. But that day, July 18th, in various villages—Concul, Irchel, Xeciguan, Chiac, and the whole village of Plan de Sánchez—the people decided to come with their baskets on their heads, filled with *macuy*, and *chiquiboy* [foods—Eds.] to sell and exchange for corn. Women came with chickens, or baby pigs, to trade for food to feed their families. Other women from the mountains brought cheeses to exchange for corn from Rabinal. Some merely wanted to go to Sunday mass. It was around 10 a.m. The soldiers stationed there had mortars and began to fire bombs on the villages around the town of Rabinal. Then a helicopter flew over us and dropped more bombs. There were two little planes, very high up, some distance from the helicopter, and we had the impression that they were watching over the helicopter.

When everyone saw this, and heard "boom! boom! boom!" they all got up. Some were crying because they had left their children in their village, children of 3 or 4 years who were too little to run away. Others said, "Mine are 8 and 10 years old; maybe they've run to the ravine." "But what about the elderly, who can't run?" So they decided to go to the villages.

But down the path, a village called Plan de Sánchez was surrounded by soldiers who would not let the people go by, telling them to wait for the captain, who was going to tell them something. Some, seeing the crowd from a distance, returned to the town. Others hid in the ravines and the hillside. Meanwhile, the soldiers were searching the houses in Plan de Sánchez, taking away the good clothing and the valuable old jewelry, stealing it all. Then they set the houses on fire and rounded up the children and the old people, all in one group.

In the afternoon, they began raping the women and torturing the men. What terrible screams could be heard two mountains away! Then they piled everyone up, poured fuel on them, and set fire to the people. Women, old people, and children were turned to ashes. One of the burning people managed to escape, and ran around like a cat until she finally fell into the ravine. The soldiers howled when they saw this naked person doing that; it was just a joke for Ríos Montt's soldiers.

Then they piled up the dead bodies and went to get Lorenza, the woman who had survived the fire. They sat her in the middle of all the bodies, they cut her lips, and made her watch the soldiers as they placed the burnt children at their dead mothers' breasts and the men's heads between the women's legs.

Lorenza was a preacher in the village, along with Narcisa. They belonged to the church choir and gave sermons. Narcisa had been burnt alive. But Lorenza had survived, and the soldiers asked her if she believed in God. "Let's see if He saves you!" they shouted. Lorenza, lying in agony, heard but remained quiet.

On Monday, July 19th, the soldiers went down to their barracks, taking with them some pigs, chickens, clothes, and jewelry from the dead people's homes. Some of the villagers managed to sneak down and bury some of the dead, and they found Lorenza dying. Jacinto, Lorenza's father, came and took his daughter to the health center. But the soldiers caught on immediately and they captured Jacinto and Lorenza. They said, "Hand over that shit, let's burn it some more." And Jacinto yelled that he would not hand over his daughter to the soldiers. At last he managed to get into the health center. A nurse wanted to help, but a soldier stopped her from doing anything. He took a needle out of his bag and gave Lorenza an injection. She died, leaving behind a baby girl 11 months old. In just one afternoon, 225 men, women, babies, and elderly people were killed, all burnt to death.

2 The Siege of the Church

One day we were working in my village. I can't remember the exact date, but it was a bit before what happened in Plan de Sánchez. In the afternoon a group of soldiers entered, shouting, "Well, well, what's going on with the Indians? Yours is a happy life. Why are you quiet? Where are the *marimbas*, your drums and *chirimía*? Eli? Go on with your customs, go to the chapel, celebrate the Word of God. Sing, and pray for peace." They told us a date, and said they would return, to see if we had done what they told us. We all asked each other, "Should we do it? My God, would they kill us during the mass? Maybe we shouldn't." "But they'll kill us anyway if we don't," said someone else. "Just yesterday they bombed a village." So we decided to do what they had said.

We took the *marimbas*, but played only one song, because almost all of us cried when we heard our song. We began the celebration of the Word of God, and we sang. When we had finished, our chapel was completely surrounded by soldiers.

The captain entered and came to us. "Well, folks, we want peace," he said. "But if you make trouble, we have this for you," and he showed us a big rifle in his hand. "This is for you if there's trouble." Our Bibles were on the altar. And he went up to the altar, took the Bibles and set them on fire. (For the soldiers, the Bible is subversive literature. Many people have buried theirs.) He took a hymnal, opened it and read a song which says:

> It is not enough to pray.
> Many things are needed
> for there to be peace.

The captain was furious, and he shouted, "Subversives! It's true, we have to kill all the Indians. And it doesn't matter if they are all gone. Don't worry, the village won't be empty—we can bring foreigners to live in your villages. There are plenty of people in the world!" I wanted to answer him, but I knew I would have been killed on the spot. I said to myself, "No foreigner could live in our village. We have no beds in which to sleep, all we eat is corn, we have no nearby water, no baths, no latrine, no electricity. No foreigner could live in our villages." And I wanted to answer, "They could not stand to live like we do, and work so hard. But riches do not fall from the sky, as my mother says, so we must work hard." I was so angry, but I didn't say a word, thank God.

The captain had a notebook, with a list of names in it, and he began to call out the names of all the members or Delegates of the Word of God. They were all poor peasants. When they heard their names being called, they humbly stood up, took off their hats and said "Here, I am here." They didn't understand why their names were being called. Quickly, the soldiers stood behind each person who answered. There were many men, each one with a soldier behind him. Some people thought maybe they were being called to form a commission. Some of the women had packed lunches, and went up to their husbands to tell them to take the food with them. The soldiers got very angry and almost kicked the women out. Then the men were taken outside. Their hands were tied and they were lined up below a pole near the chapel. The children cried out to their fathers, wanting to go with them, but the soldiers dragged the children away without pity. "Do you want us to kick you?" they asked. But the children did not understand what the soldiers were saying, and they continued crying. The mothers consoled their children.

The soldiers took the men down to a creek. They tied them with a rope around their necks and hung them from the trees, beating them with sticks and branches. At first, we heard screams, but little by little the voices grew fainter because the ropes cut off the men's breathing. Night fell, and the men had not died. The soldiers stayed, sitting there shouting and laughing. Who knows what they were laughing about. Maybe Judas knows. This is the story of Christians from the base communities and how they were killed. That day, 32 men died.

Jesus preached and helped the needy. He was persecuted to death, nailed to a wooden cross. Jesus still suffers today on the heavy cross of Guatemala, from the terrible repression by Ríos Montt. The Christian base communities represent Jesus, and they are killed, dragged out of their churches for celebrating the Word of God.

3 Chichupac, April 19, 1982

On the 18th of April, soldiers entered the village of Chichupac, telling the people not to be afraid. "We are defending the country," they said. "You must trust us. We want to talk to you in a group. The government we have now is good. We will return tomorrow, but we want everyone to gather together in the church. If you have old people who are sick, take them to church tomorrow, because we will bring two doctors with us. If they have problems with their lungs, or a toothache, they will be cured tomorrow. Take the children as well: we will bring them toys to make them happy."

Some people believed the soldiers, and they went to church. Many soldiers arrived and they passed out used plastic toys. There was no doctor.

After the toys were handed out, the soldiers did not respect the statue of Christ that the catechists had put on the altar. They began to destroy the statue with their machetes. The people were surrounded and could not leave the church. Then the soldiers called out people's names, including children, and took them to the clinic nearby. All the names were of people who had learned how to read and write. (During the time of Lucas García, all peasants had been ordered to learn how to read. People signed up to learn, and the catechists signed up to teach, but the soldiers killed them. One catechist was killed while carrying a notebook with the names of the people who were studying, including the names of children who could not go to school but who had signed up to learn.)

The women were raped before the eyes of the men and the children in the clinic. The men and the boys had their testicles cut off. Everybody's tongues were cut out. Their eyes were gouged out with nails. Their arms were twisted off. Their legs were cut off. The little girls were raped and tortured. The women had their breasts cut off. And the soldiers left them all there in the clinic, piled up and dying. Those who were not on the list were prohibited from burying the victims. I only remember that 15 children were killed. I cannot remember how many adults were killed. A woman who was there told me all this.

References

Note: This chapter is based primarily on knowledge gained through direct interviews conducted with a wide range of Guatemalans (and others involved), from virtually all political persuasions and social strata, over the course of several decades (since 1967). The following list of written sources is primarily from the 1980s, during the historical period discussed in this chapter, and it includes sources actually cited in the chapter. Unfortunately, considerations of space preclude an all-inclusive list of the 1980s literature—or of current scholarship that is interpreting and reinterpreting the historical era chronicled here, and that constitutes a vibrant new genre of scholarship.

Adams, Richard (1988). Conclusions: What can we know about the harvest of violence?. In Robert Carmack (Ed.) *Harvest of violence* (pp. 274–291). Norman, OK: University of Oklahoma Press.

Americas Watch, reports on Guatemala (almost yearly throughout the 1980s).

Amnesty International, reports on Guatemala (almost yearly throughout the 1980s).

Arias, Arturo (1985). El movimiento indigena en Guatemala: 1970–1983. In Daniel Camacho & Rafael Menjivar (Eds.) *Movimientos Populares en Centroamerica*. San Jose: EDUCA.

Comisión para el Esclarecimiento Histórico (CEH) (1999). *Guatemala: Memory of silence*. Guatemala: CEH.

Davis, Shelton (1988). Introduction: Sowing the seeds of violence. In Robert M. Carmack (Eds.) *Harvest of violence* (pp. 3–38). Norman, OK: University of Oklahoma Press.

Falla, Ricardo (1978). *Quiché Rebelde*. Guatemala: Editorial Universitaria.

Falla, Ricardo (1984). We charge genocide. In Susanne Jonas, Ed McCaughan & Elizabeth Sutherland Martinez (Eds.) *Guatemala: Tyranny on trial* (pp. 112–119). San Francisco, CA: Synthesis Publications.

Grandin, Greg (2004). *The last colonial massacre*. Chicago, IL: University of Chicago Press.

Handy, James (1986). Resurgent democracy and the Guatemalan military. *Journal of Latin American Studies, 18*, 383–408.

Jonas, Susanne (1991). *The battle for Guatemala: Rebels, death squads and U.S. power*. Boulder, CO: Westview Press.

Jonas, Susanne (2000). *Of centaurs and doves: Guatemala's peace process.* Boulder, CO: Westview Press.

Jonas, Susanne, McCaughan, Ed, & Sutherland Martínez, Elizabeth (Eds.) (1984). *Guatemala: Tyranny on trial.* San Francisco, CA: Synthesis Publications.

Manz, Beatriz (1988). *Refugees of a hidden war: The aftermath of counterinsurgency in Guatemala.* New York: State University of New York.

Oficina de Derechos Humanos del Arzobispado de Guatemala (ODHA) (1998). *Guatemala: Nunca Más.* Guatemala: ODHA.

Opinion Política (OP) (1985) Número 2 (Enero-Febrero) y #3 (Marzo-Abril). Guatemala/Mexico. (This was the analytical publication of a group of dissidents who had split from the EGP in 1984.)

Perera, Victor (1989, November 6). A forest dies in Guatemala. *The Nation,* n.p.

Power, Samantha (2002). *A Problem from hell: America and the age of genocide.* New York: Basic Books.

Smith, Carol (Ed.) (1990). *Guatemalan Indians and the state: 1540–1988.* Austin: University of Texas Press.

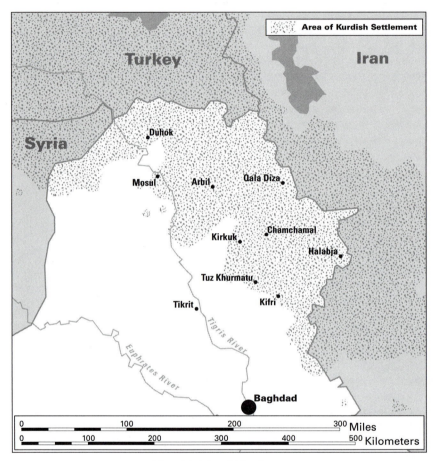

Map 11.1 Iraqi Kurdistan

CHAPTER 11

The *Anfal* Operations in Iraqi Kurdistan

MICHIEL LEEZENBERG

Introduction

The 1988 *Anfal* ("Spoils") operations, conducted by the Iraqi regime
against part of the Kurdish population and other minority groups living
in Northern Iraq, are among the best-documented cases of genocide.
Ostensibly a counterinsurgency measure against Kurdish rebels, they in
fact involved the deliberate killing of large numbers of non-combatants.
Captured documents prove the regime's genocidal intent: they make
abundantly clear that the government aimed at killing (Kurdish) civilians. Estimates of the number of civilians killed in the operations vary
from 50,000 to almost 200,000; the number of displaced or otherwise
affected persons is far greater. Over 1,000 Kurdish villages were
destroyed in the operations, as were their livestock and orchards. The
operations are characterized by an unusual degree of secretive bureaucratic organization and centralized implementation, rather than by the
mobilization of popular antagonisms. Because they are documented not
only by eyewitness and survivor testimonies, but also by a vast number
of captured Iraqi government documents, they provide one of the juridically most strongly and unambiguously established cases of genocide.

Although there is abundant and publicly accessible documentary evidence on the *Anfal*, little substantial research has been published since
the publication of the Human Rights Watch 1993 report *Genocide in
Iraq*, which was republished in 1995 as *Iraq's Crime of Genocide*. This
all-important study was based on extensive interviews with survivors,
but also on an incomplete (and possibly imbalanced) archive of documentary evidence made available by some of the Kurdish parties. In the
absence of more recent studies, it is impossible to assess whether any

documentary evidence that was later recovered might necessitate a revision of its main findings. Hence, the factual account of the operations given below is largely based on this, for now, indispensable study.

Underlying Causes of the *Anfal*

Three main historical trends may be seen as leading up to the *Anfal* operations: the so-called "Kurdish question"; the character of Saddam Hussein's Baath regime; and the Iran–Iraq war that broke out in 1980. First, there was the failure of successive Iraqi governments to find an adequate and enduring settlement of the Kurdish question (ever since the formation of the independent state of Iraq, there had been disagreements about the precise relationship between the central, Arab-led government in Baghdad and the predominately Kurdish-inhabited regions in the north of the country; put another way, the precise political, economic, and cultural status of the Kurdish regions of Iraq was an ongoing point of contention). During the 1960s, episodes of diplomatic activity between the Baghdad government and the political leadership of the Kurds had alternated with Kurdish armed uprisings and their suppression by Iraqi military force; in March 1970, an agreement between the Kurdish leadership and the Iraqi government had been signed, but this was quickly seen as a dead letter. In 1974 a full-scale war broke out between the Baghdad regime and the Kurdish movement led by Barzani, and it was not until Saddam Hussein signed an agreement with the Shah of Iran, which involved, among others, the latter withdrawing all support for the Iraqi Kurds, that the Kurdish front collapsed.

A second underlying trend was the Baath regime's character, in particular its harsh ways of dealing with any kind of opposition or treason, whether real, suspected, or imaginary. For example, during the 1970s, the regime engaged in the violent persecution of not only Kurds, but also Shiites living in the South of Iraq, and of members of the Iraqi Communist Party, with which the Baath Party had earlier, in 1972, formed an alliance through the establishment of a National Front.

The style of Baathist rule was based on Eastern European and, more specifically, Stalinist models. Not only was the Kurdish autonomous region unilaterally established in 1970 by the Baghdad regime modeled on the autonomous *okrugs* that had been established in the early Soviet Union; more generally, Saddam carefully modeled his rule after Stalin's government-by-terror. As a result, Saddam Hussein's rule over Iraq, effective since the early 1970s and officially consecrated after a 1979 coup in which Saddam ousted president and fellow Baathist Ahmad Hasan al-Bakr, systematically relied on purges, show trials, disappearances, and collective forms of punishment against whole families, tribes, villages, or population groups. It also relied on a considerable overlap between party organization and security apparatus, aimed at strengthening its total control of the country. Baathist policies toward the Kurds in the wake of the 1975 collapse of resistance had involved, among others, the forcible resettlement of several hundred thousand Kurds in the south of Iraq; the settlement of Arabs in predominantly Kurdish-inhabited areas; and the establishment of prohibited zones with a shoot-on-sight policy along the borders with Iran and Turkey. Collectively, these measures went far beyond counterinsurgency; they also aimed at changing the ethnic balance of the region, and at weakening, if not destroying, Kurdish ethnic identity.

The third long-term trend that led to the *Anfal* was the 1980–1988 war between Iran and Iraq. Repeatedly, the course of this protracted war in time made the Baath regime fear for its very existence; moreover, the Iraqi Kurdish parties played an ambiguous role, alternatively entering into negotiations with Baghdad and siding with the Iranians, not to mention the frequent infighting and realignments among the various opposition groups. Iraq's predicament was especially bleak in 1987, as Iran appeared to be regaining momentum after reopening its northern front in March in collusion with Iraqi Kurdish guerrillas. Moreover, in the course of 1987, the major Iraqi Kurdish parties, including the Kurdistan Democratic Party (KDP), headed by Massoud Barzani, and the Patriotic Union of Kurdistan (PUK), headed by Jalal Talabani, decided to join forces, ending their long-standing differences and years of infighting. The Kurds' tactical alliance with Iran posed a new threat to the Iraqi regime, which reacted by implementing increasingly drastic counterinsurgency measures. In response, on March 29, Iraqi President Saddam Hussein promulgated decree No. 160, making Ali Hasan al-Majid director of the Baath Party's Directorate of Northern Affairs, which was responsible for the autonomous Kurdish region in northern Iraq. Al-Majid, until then the director of General Security, was granted sweeping powers over all civilian, military, and security institutions of the region. He wasted no time in making use of them. In April he ordered the first attacks, including chemical bombardments, not only against the PUK mountain headquarters but also against the Kurdish villagers and villages that could provide the PUK with shelter and supplies. During this campaign, at least 703 Kurdish villages were destroyed.

After a few months, however, these operations were discontinued, possibly because the Iraqi army was too preoccupied with Iranian offensives. But al-Majid's June 1987 directives present a clear indication of what was to come. His order, Document 28/3650, dated June 3, imposed both a total blockade and a shoot-on-sight policy on the areas outside government control: "The armed forces must kill any human being or animal present within these areas." Document 28/4008 of June 20 provides a standing order for the summary execution of all (male) captives: "Those between the ages of 15 and 70 shall be executed after any useful information has been obtained from them." In part, these documents reaffirmed, and probably reinvigorated, standing Iraqi policies that had been in place since the late 1970s. (Note: both documents are reproduced in Human Rights Watch/Middle East's *Bureaucracy of Repression* [1994].)

The next organizational step toward *Anfal* was the nationwide census that was held on October 17, 1987. According to Human Rights Watch, this census was (at least in the Kurdish North) less a registration of population data than a sweeping government directive that not only identified the target population of the future operations, but also indiscriminately marginalized and criminalized it. All traffic to and from areas outside government control was forbidden, and relatives of alleged saboteurs were expelled from government-held areas. All individuals who consequently failed to participate in the census were stripped of their citizenship and were considered deserters or saboteurs who deserved the death penalty. It has not yet, however, been established beyond doubt precisely where these forbidden zones outside government control were located, how they were defined, and whether they coincided with the areas where the *Anfal* did in fact take place. At the time, only a few stretches of land in inaccessible mountain areas and along the border with Iran were wholly out of government reach.

Apart from this gradual escalation of counterinsurgency violence, there are two well-documented precedents or cases—not, strictly speaking, related to the *Anfal*—that indicate the Iraqi regime's readiness to resort to the killing of Kurds, as such: the 1983 disappearance of Barzani clansmen and the 1988 chemical attack against Halabja. The background of both incidents crucially involves not only to the armed Kurdish insurgency, but also the Iraqi war against Iran. After the 1975 collapse of the Kurdish front, hundreds of thousands of Kurdish villagers had already been deported to relocation camps or *mujamma'at*, their traditional dwellings having been destroyed and declared forbidden territory. Thousands of members of the Barzani clan had been deported to southern Iraq in 1976. In 1981 they had been relocated in the Qushtepe *mujamma'a* just south of Arbil; and then, in 1983, after Iran had captured the border town of Haj Omran with the aid of KDP guerrillas, the Iraqi government took its revenge on the Barzani clan. According to the then speaker of the KDP, Hoshyar Zebari (at present Iraq's foreign minister), over 8,000 men were taken from the Qushtepe camp and never seen again; the remaining women were reduced to a life of abject poverty. Apparently, government policies not only aimed at the physical elimination of Kurds associated with disloyal elements, but also aimed at the symbolic destruction of the honor of both the male and female members of the proud Barzani tribe.

It is the March 16, 1988 chemical attack against the town of Halabja, in which an estimated 5,000 Kurdish civilians died a gruesome death, rather than the *Anfal*, that has entered collective memory as a symbol of the Iraqi repression of the Kurds. The attack was captured, if not symbolized, in the indelible image of a Kurdish father clutching his infant son, both killed by poison gas, shot by the Turkish-Kurdish photographer Ramazan Öztürk. Although the Halabja attack was not part of the *Anfal* operations proper (which only targeted rural areas, not cities), it certainly followed the same destructive logic. It was prompted by the Kurdish–Iranian occupation of the city as an attempt to ease the pressure on the PUK headquarters, which at the time was bearing the brunt of the first *Anfal* operation. The chemical attack does not appear to have had any clear strategic aim, however; rather, it was in all likelihood meant as a warning—or, it was possibly conducted as an act of revenge. After the attack, nothing happened to Halabja for several months. It was not until July 1988 that Iraqi troops reoccupied the city, which they then proceeded to demolish. The remaining population was relocated to "New Halabja" *mujamma'a*, a few miles down the road.

The Course of the Operations

As for the *Anfal* operations proper, they did not begin until February 1988; presumably, by then, the Iraqi regime felt that Iranian pressure had eased sufficiently to allow for the redeployment of large numbers of troops to the north. The *Anfal* operations were conducted on a much larger scale and were of a much more systematic character than the spring 1987 operations: several army divisions participated in them, together with personnel of general intelligence and the Baath Party—along with Kurdish irregulars (also referred to as *jash*). In the course of the 1980s, the Baath government, whose military forces were drawn to the frontline with Iran, had established Kurdish irregular troops to maintain control in the rural areas of the north. Numerous *jash* leaders, though, maintained contacts with the Kurdish insurgents.

The first *Anfal* operation, starting February 23, was primarily directed against the PUK headquarters near the Iranian border, but it also extended to surrounding villages. Most villagers, however, appear to have escaped into Iran or to the larger cities of the Kurdish region in Iraq. Thus, whether by accident or design, the first *Anfal* does not appear to have involved the large-scale disappearance of civilians. This, however, was to change in the following operations.

In the following months, seven further operations were carried out, systematically targeting the different areas that had remained under Kurdish control. The attacks were generally carried out in the same way: typically, they started with surrounding the target area, which was then exposed to massive shelling and air attacks, including the use of chemical weapons. Apparently, these attacks were intended primarily to destroy the morale of the villagers and guerrillas (who had long become used to conventional bombardments). Next, with the target population dislodged, government forces would gradually encircle it and mount a massive ground attack by army troops and irregulars—or, alternatively, irregulars would persuade the villagers to surrender.

The Kurdish captives were first brought to local collection points, mostly by Kurdish irregulars; subsequently, government personnel took them to centralized transit camps at military bases near Kirkuk, Tikrit, and Duhok. Here, they were divided by age and gender, and stripped of their remaining possessions. The vast majority of captured male adults were loaded onto windowless trucks and taken to execution sites in central Iraq. Several people, however, survived these mass executions. All of them report having seen rows of trenches dug by bulldozers, each holding hundreds of corpses. It is more than likely that tens of thousands of Kurdish male civilians were massacred in this way, merely on account of their Kurdish ethnicity and of their living in an area declared out of bounds by the regime of Saddam Hussein.

Unknown numbers of women, children, and elderly are also believed to have been massacred. More typically, however, women were left alive and relocated. There also is credible testimony that many younger women were sold off as brides, or rather into virtual slavery, to rich men elsewhere—not only in Iraq, but also in Kuwait and Saudi Arabia. These reports were corroborated by a December 1989 document, which the Kurds claimed to have captured from Kirkuk's Directorate of Intelligence following the 2003 ousting of Saddam Hussein's regime by the U.S. government. The memorandum to the Baghdad General Directorate of Intelligence, marked "Top Secret," states that a group of girls aged between 14 and 29 had been captured during the *Anfal* operations, and "sent to the harems and nightclubs of the Arab Republic of Egypt." (Note: A copy of the document and a partial translation can be found at www.kurdmedia.com/news.asp?id=4057.)

Many elderly captives were initially resettled in the Nuqrat al-Salman concentration camp in southern Iraq. In the appalling living conditions there, up to 10% of the inmates may have died in the space of a few months. Often, corpses did not receive a proper burial and were left exposed in the summer heat (see Account 5, below).

On August 20, 1988, a cease-fire between Iran and Iraq came into effect. The Iraqi army now had its hands free to finish its campaign against the Kurdish insurgents. On August 25 it initiated the final *Anfal*, directed against what remained of the traditional KDP strongholds in the Badinan region bordering on Turkey. This area was not entirely sealed off, however, and over 60,000 Kurds managed to escape to Turkey. Following this exodus, substantial eyewitness reports about the Iraqi regime's continuing chemical attacks against its Kurdish civilians reached the international community, along with earlier journalistic reporting on the Halabja attack (see below). Press coverage led to some minor and inconsequential protests by Western governments. Among others, the U.S. government failed to act on reports published by one of its own officials—U.S. Senate Foreign Relations Committee member Peter Galbraith. In international forums like the UN Security Council, the Iraqis avoided condemnation by cleverly manipulating remaining Cold War cleavages and existing fears of Iran.

The violence against the Kurdish civilian population did not end with the successful completion of the final *Anfal*. Numerous refugees were lured back by the September 6 announcement of a general amnesty for all Iraqi Kurds, but many of them disappeared upon returning. The fate of the returning members of minority groups like the Yezidis and Assyrian Christians deserves particular mention. Unbeknown to themselves, these groups had been excluded from the amnesty by the government, which considered them Arabs rather than Kurds. Upon returning to Iraq, they were separated from the Muslim Kurds, and many of them, including women, children, and elderly, were taken to unknown destinations and never seen again.

After the amnesty, the surviving deportees were brought back to the north and simply dumped on relocation sites near the main roads to the region's major cities, surrounded by barbed-wire fences. Unlike the victims of most earlier deportations, they were not provided with any housing, construction materials, food, or medicine (let alone financial compensation), but just left to their own devices.

There were significant differences in the execution of the successive *Anfal* operations. In the first *Anfal*, few non-combatants disappeared. In later operations, adult males were taken to mass execution sites far away from the Kurdish region. In the final *Anfal*, captured men were often executed on the spot. Likewise, only in the operations in the Kirkuk region do women and children appear to have been executed. It is not clear whether such variations reflect an escalating logic of violence, a differentiated reaction to the degree of resistance encountered, or simply the whims of local field commanders.

The captured documents not only show a high degree of secrecy surrounding the operations, but also hint at an extreme concentration of power, and the bureaucratic structure that made them possible. There are indications, for example, that military intelligence did not know precisely what was going on and that lower army officers on various occasions balked at the standing order to execute all of the captives.

In the operations, the Kurdish irregular troops, or *jash* ("donkey foal") as they are disparagingly called among Kurds, played an important but ambiguous role. For many Kurds, enlisting as an irregular was a convenient means of escaping active front duty in the war with Iran (and of making a living). Other tribal leaders siding with the government, however, had their own accounts to settle with either the Kurdish parties or with tribes and villages in nearby areas.

The Kurdish irregulars appear to have had a subordinate status among the personnel involved in the operations. While they had a better knowledge of the mountainous territory than the regular security forces and could more easily persuade the population to surrender, not all of them were wholly reliable in the implementation of al-Majid's orders.

It is also unlikely that all irregular troops were equally well informed about the operations' true character. Apparently, many of them had merely been told to help in the rounding up of villagers for the purpose of relocation. Many, in fact, made a genuine effort to help the captives. Others, however, participated with glee in the rounding up of civilians and the looting of their possessions. In some cases, the irregular troops granted those Kurds they rounded up acts of clemency if provided a bribe to do so. A better appreciation of the role of the *jash* is hampered to some extent by the fact that after the 1991 uprising in the north, all (powerful) government collaborators were granted a general amnesty by the Iraqi Kurdistan Front, and most of them continued to wield considerable power under the new Kurdish rulers. In other words, their previous actions against their own people were conveniently overlooked.

In the spring of 1989, al-Majid resigned as the Baath Party's Northern Bureau chief. To all appearances, the Kurdish insurgency had been solved once and for all. The major Kurdish parties had been thoroughly demoralized, and indeed discredited, by the government's brutal actions, and they faced fierce internal criticism because of their tactics, which had left the civilian population exposed to the Iraqi onslaught. Virtually the entire surviving rural Kurdish population had been violently pacified and relocated to easily controlled resettlement camps.

In 1988, *Anfal* operations alone, an estimated 1,200 Kurdish villages were destroyed. The number of civilian casualties has been variously estimated: Kurdish sources, based on extrapolations from the numbers of villages destroyed, at first spoke of some 182,000 people killed or missing.

Human Rights Watch, a major international human rights organization, made a more conservative estimate of between 50,000 and 100,000 civilian dead. During the spring 1991 negotiations between the Kurds and the Iraqi government, the director of the operations, al-Majid himself, at one point exclaimed: "What is this exaggerated figure of 182,000? It could not have been more than a hundred thousand!"

Impact of the *Anfal*

The operations had a devastating effect not only on the Kurdish parties, ostensibly the main target of the operations, but also on the local population at large. In some of the operations, Kurdish forces had put up a fierce resistance; but they were unable to counter the demoralizing effect of chemical weapons, or to protect the local civilian population. After the end of the operations, some prominent members of the main parties called for soul searching and self-criticism, questioning if they had not exposed the population to unacceptable risks.

Among the Kurdish population at large, and also among Arab civilians and even among some government officials, there had been a few but significant episodes of resistance and of support for the victims. In the third *Anfal*, for example, the local population of Chamchamal rose up in revolt against the deportation of villagers. During the fifth, resistance of the *peshmergas* (Kurdish guerrillas) turned out to be so strong that two further operations against the same area were mounted, keeping government forces occupied for over three months.

Especially in Arbil, the local urban population, at times at great personal risk to themselves, made a prolonged effort to help the deported villagers. Several survivors of the executions, notably Taymur 'Abdallah from Kulajo near Kifri and Ako Izzedin Sayyid Ismael from Warani near Tuz Khormatu, were harbored by Iraqi army personnel or Arab tribesmen. (Note: for fragments of Taimour 'Abdallah's testimony, see Account 3 below; for Ismael's story, see www.globeandmail.com/servlet/story/RTGAM.20030403.unolen0405/BNStory/International.)

Among Iraq's Kurdish population at large, the operations instilled a pervasive fear of the regime. After the failure of the 1991 uprising, this fear caused a massive panic and the exodus of hundreds of thousands of Iraqi Kurds to the borders with Turkey and Iran. Following the establishment of a de facto autonomous Kurdish region in northern Iraq in late 1991, however, the *Anfal* became a symbol of the total delegitimation of Baathist—and, by extension, Arab—rule over Iraq's Kurds. No trials of former Kurdish collaborators were ever conducted, however; not even a truth commission was established, as had been done in other places with a similarly violent and traumatic past.

The *Anfal* operations have had a particularly traumatic effect on women. One significant aspect of the *Anfal* operations was their systematic differentiation by age and gender. Generally, though there were certainly exceptions, male youths and younger men would be rounded up for execution, whereas women and the elderly would be relocated either in the area or in the south of Iraq. In a recent study primarily based on interviews with female *Anfal* survivors, Choman Hardi (2010) stressed the need for a gendered view of the *Anfal* operations. She is particularly critical of the dominant representations of *Anfal* widows in the Kurdish media, which consistently depict them as mere victims with no life or agency of their own beyond mourning lost relatives. All too often, she notes, female survivors have been left to their own devices by the Kurdish authorities; not infrequently, survivors of chemical attacks have also been stigmatized as health hazards by their environment. Despite such difficulties, Choman emphasizes, female *Anfal* survivors have been "strong survivors," developing various strategies of coping with trauma, loss, poverty, and stigmatization.

Responses to the *Anfal*

The Iraqi regime made a sustained effort to keep the true nature of the *Anfal* operations entirely secret, or at least to maintain strict control over the flow of information. That said, throughout much of 1988, Iraqi radio proudly broadcast news of the "heroic *Anfal* campaigns," allegedly directed against saboteurs and collaborators of Iran; but these reports carefully avoided reference to the use of chemical weapons, the deportations and executions of civilians, and the razing of villages that accompanied the operations. On several occasions, victims of chemical attacks were dragged out of the nearby hospitals and disappeared; this may have been a form of collective punishment, but it is more likely that the regime was attempting to eliminate all eyewitnesses at this stage.

Despite several substantial investigations by journalists, academics, and parliamentary committees, the extent of international knowledge of, and indeed complicity in, Iraq's crimes still awaits assessment. Various European companies continued to supply Iraq with ingredients for chemical weapons, even at a time when its use of such weapons against the Iranian army was well documented. In the United States, the Reagan and Bush Sr. Administrations actively supported Iraq with military advisors, equipment, and atropin (a common antidote to mustard gas), and blocked international diplomatic initiatives against Iraq. It is by now certain that the U.S. government at that time had detailed knowledge about the campaign of destruction, of its scale, and of Iraq's systematic use of chemical weapons against its own civilians. In this regard,

Meiselas (1997) has reproduced a Joint Chiefs of Staff document from the National Security Archives, dated August 4, 1987, which speaks of a campaign coordinated by al-Majid, in which 300 villages had been destroyed, and of "the ruthless repression which also includes the use of chemical weapons" (pp. 312–313). Likewise, former U.S. military intelligence officer Rick Francona (1999), who served as a military advisor to the Iraqi regime in 1987 and 1988, asserts that the U.S. government was well aware of Iraq's use of chemical agents (in particular, nerve gas), both against Iranian soldiers and against its own civilians, but wished to prevent an Iranian victory at any price (cf. Hiltermann, 2007).

Prior to the 2003 Iraq war, the chances for prosecution of the perpetrators of the *Anfal* were slim. In fact, Iraq's well-established use of weapons of mass destruction hardly figured in the justifications for that war. That war itself was legitimized by Iraq's alleged (and as it turned out, imaginary) threat of weapons of mass destruction, rather than by its actual use of such weapons in the 1980s. Following the invasion and subsequent overthrow of the Baath regime, almost all senior members of the Iraqi regime went into hiding. In due course, however, most of them were captured, including the two who were held to bear primary responsibility for the *Anfal* operations: former Iraqi president Saddam Hussein and his cousin, Ali Hasan al-Majid. In late 2006 both were tried by a local tribunal rather than the International Court of Justice. Saddam was initially tried for his role in the 1982 Dujail massacre. Ultimately, he was condemned to death for the latter crimes and was executed in December 2006, before the *Anfal* trials had run their full course. In January 2010, al-Majid was executed as well, having been convicted of genocide for his role in the *Anfal*.

Interpretations of the *Anfal*

There is no definitive study of the *Anfal* operations as of yet; no balanced or comprehensive assessment exists of the documentary and other evidence currently available. What little substantial research there is seems to waver on how to qualify the attitude of the government that was responsible for them. As noted above, labels like "racist" or "fascist" have been used by Kurdish nationalist and foreign analysts; local Islamist voices point to the *Anfal* as evidence of the infidel (*kafir*) character of Hussein's regime. Such terms, however, are not very helpful in interpreting the operations, or even in characterizing the animus that drove them. One thing seems clear, though: The *Anfal* operations were not the culmination of any pervasive or long-standing ethnic antagonisms between Kurdish and Arab population groups in Iraq, but rather the result of centralized and highly secretive government policies. Regarding the finer points of the character and significance of the *Anfal*, too little detailed information is available at present to allow for anything more than informed guesses.

The *Anfal* operations cannot simply be explained away as a drastic form of counterinsurgency; but, then again, characterizing the mindset that made them possible is no easy task. The question of whether, and how far, the *Anfal* operations were driven by racist animosity has not yet adequately been answered. Racism does not appear to be a predominant feature of either Iraqi society, Baathist ideology, or the perpetrators' personalities. Although there have been, and are, occasional ethnic tensions among the different segments of the Iraqi population, there is relatively little grass-roots racial hatred between Kurds and Arabs in Iraq. Even after the 2003 war, whatever tensions there were between Kurds, Arabs, and Turkomans in the north paled in comparison with horrendous sectarian violence between Sunnis and Shiites in Baghdad (and this violence was mostly the work of urban gangs and militias, rather than of the population at large).

In official Baathist discourse, categories of loyalty, treason, and sabotage (which, ultimately, are of a Stalinist inspiration) are much more prominent than ethnic or racial categories; the latter appear to have been rather flexible items, given the Baath regime's at times rather arbitrary and voluntaristic way of creating and dissolving ethnic identities by bureaucratic fiat. When overtly racist language *was* used, this typically concerned Iranians and Jews rather than Kurds. Baathist ideology is of an undeniably Arab nationalist character, but it has always been ambivalent as to the inclusion of Iraq's sizable Kurdish population. There are indications, however, that in the course of the 1980s, even the act of stating one's Kurdish or other non-Arab ethnicity increasingly became treated as a criminal offence, if not an act of treason. For example, smaller ethnic groups, such as Yezidis, Christians, and Shabak, were forcibly registered as Arabs, and when they changed their ethnicity to "Kurdish" in the 1987 census, al-Majid had them deported and their villages destroyed.

It is even questionable whether al-Majid himself can be simply labeled a racist. On tape recordings of meetings with senior Party officials he can be heard speaking in a coarse and derogatory manner of Kurds, but his remarks hardly betray any generic hatred of Kurds as an inferior race; rather, he speaks of saboteurs and of uneducated villagers who "live like donkeys." But whatever al-Majid's personal motives and animosities, official discourse consistently proclaimed both Kurds and Arabs as equal parts of the Iraqi people or nation, on condition of their political loyalty.

Religious considerations do not appear to have been a prime motivating or legitimating factor either. The name *Anfal*, or "Spoils," which comes from the eighth sura of the Koran, has little specific religious significance here; rather, it appears to refer primarily to the right granted to the Kurdish irregulars involved in the operations to loot the possessions of the captured civilians. The Baath Party, which had ruled Iraq since 1968, is largely secular and was (and is) inspired more by 20th-century ideologies and practices of Nazism and Stalinism than by any specifically Islamic tradition.

Of the violent and indeed murderous character of Baathist rule in Iraq, however, there can be no doubt at all. After the conclusion of the *Anfal* operations, only 673 Kurdish villages still stood in the whole of Iraqi Kurdistan. Over the years, the regime had demolished 4,049 Kurdish villages in the north. After the end of the Iran–Iraq war and of the *Anfal* operations proper, state violence increasingly turned toward Kurdish cities.

In the late spring and summer of 1988, the largely abandoned town of Halabja was razed to the ground; and in June 1989, the city of Qala Diza, with a population of close to 100,000, which had not been targeted in the *Anfal* and was itself a site of relocation camps, was evacuated and destroyed. It is impossible to tell where this process of repression and destruction would have led if it had not been interrupted by the 1990 Gulf Crisis and the ensuing war and uprising.

Importance of and Current Interest in the *Anfal*

The *Anfal* operations formed the genocidal climax of the prolonged conflict between the successive Iraqi regimes and the Kurdish nationalist movement. As previously noted, they were the result of highly centralized and secret government policies rather than widespread ethnic antagonisms that could easily be manipulated or mobilized for political purposes. As a result, the full extent and genocidal character of the atrocities at first escaped public notice. The most notorious event of this period, the widely publicized attack on Halabja in March 1988, was not part of the *Anfal* proper; but it reflected the same mindset.

The full scale and bureaucratic nature, and indeed full horror, of the operations did not become widely known until the aftermath of the 1991 Gulf War. In the popular uprising against the Iraqi regime, literally tons of documents from various government institutions were captured: these provided ample, if partly indirect and circumstantial, evidence of the 1988 genocide. Although many questions remain unanswered, these documents, supplemented by the testimony of numerous eyewitnesses, provided compelling evidence in the genocide trial against Saddam Hussein and his aides, which opened in August 2006.

The authenticity of these documents has been contested by the Iraqi government, but it is extremely unlikely that they are forgeries. They not only form a complex network of interlocking texts of a highly bureaucratic nature, but, in many cases, they closely match the testimony provided by eyewitnesses and survivors. References to government actions are often quite indirect or opaque; thus, few documents openly refer to mass executions or chemical weapons. Even internal documents, as a rule, euphemistically speak of "special attacks" and "special ammunition" when referring to chemical warfare, or of "return to the national ranks" when talking about individual or collective surrender to government forces.

Taken together, the testimony and the documentary evidence provide detailed insight into the chain of command and, to a lesser extent, into the motives of the perpetrators. Among the personnel participating in them were the first, second, and fifth army divisions; General Security; and numerous members of the Baath Party (in particular, those associated with the Northern Affairs Bureau), as well as irregular troops mostly provided by Kurdish tribal chieftains (during the 1980s, the Baathist government had appointed local tribal leaders as *mustashars* or "advisors" to form irregular troops, and supplied them with arms and money to control the Kurdish countrywide).

The command was firmly in the hands of al-Majid, who acted as the head of the Baath Party's Northern Bureau, and who overruled all other authorities. It appears to have been the regional Baath Party apparatus, rather than the intelligence services, the police, or the army, that was at the heart of the operations. In all likelihood, the firing squads also consisted first and foremost of Party members.

The story of how Saddam's regime managed to get away with these crimes remains to be told. From 1988 to the present, the moral and legal significance of the *Anfal* operations has tended to be overruled by political interests. In 1988 Iraq enjoyed near-impunity on the international stage because of its war with the universally disliked Iran, and because of the strategic and economic interests that both Western and Eastern Bloc countries had in Iraq; the Baath regime cleverly played on such interests and on divisions within the appropriate UN bodies, and consequently managed to avoid any meaningful condemnation by the international community. Following the 1991 uprising, massive and detailed evidence of the *Anfal* became available; this included captured government documents, eyewitness accounts, and forensic evidence. For years, Human Rights Watch tried in vain to have a genocide case against Iraq opened at the International Court of Justice, but no country was willing to initiate legal proceedings—due, in part, to a fear of jeopardizing their chances both in regard to dealing with the Iraqi market (bound to be lucrative again once UN sanctions were lifted) and in the Arab world at large. In July 1995, U.S. Secretary of State Warren Christopher signed a communique declaring that the *Anfal* operations amounted to genocide, thus endorsing Human Rights Watch's attempts to initiate legal proceedings. As a result, the U.S. government undertook a campaign to have Hussein indicted for genocide and crimes against humanity, largely on the basis of the captured *Anfal* documents. It was, however, pursued erratically and appeared to reflect changing U.S. policies toward Iraq rather than any principled concern for the victims or for international law. Ultimately, no effective juridical steps were ever taken.

In 2003 the United States attacked Iraq, launching a war that was legitimated primarily by Iraq's alleged possession of weapons of mass destruction (which were never discovered, and which the Bush Administration had repeatedly been told by weapons experts would likely never be discovered since there was good reason to believe that Iraq did not possess them), and hardly, if at all, by Iraq's actual use of those weapons against Iraqi civilians. Moreover, the fact that some members of the George W. Bush (2000–2008) Administration in the United States had in the 1980s actively supported the Iraqi regime, and had continued to do so at the time it was committing its worst atrocities, made this administration's moral arguments for war unconvincing.

Information about the *Anfal* and about Iraq's use of chemical weapons had been gathered, in part at great personal risk, by authors like the Kurdish researcher Shorsh Rasool, the British journalist Gwynne Roberts, and the U.S. diplomat Peter Galbraith; but it was the capture by Kurdish guerrilla forces of some 18 metric tonnes of documentary evidence in 1991 that provided the most compelling evidence for both the extent of and the genocidal intent behind the *Anfal* operations. It is unclear how much additional material was captured from the archives of government ministries, security agencies, and Baath Party offices in the chaotic aftermath of the 2003 invasion, and in whose hands these documents ended up—especially the archives of the security office in Kirkuk, which appears to have been the *Anfal*'s nerve center, would seem crucial, both for legal proceedings and for further research into the precise conduct and character of the operations.

In August 2003 Ali Hasan al-Majid was arrested; in December of the same year, Saddam Hussein was captured by U.S. troops in Iraq, with the cooperation of local forces. Following some legal wrangling as to when, where, and how trials against members of the former Baath regime should be held, it was decided to have them stand trial in Iraq itself, even though the country's judiciary was hardly prepared for such a massive and complicated operation. In October 2005 court proceedings against Saddam Hussein were initiated. The first trial centered exclusively on an isolated incident, the massacre of 148 Shiite men in reprisal for an assassination attempt against Saddam during a visit to the village of Dujail. Although minor in comparison with numerous other accusations, the Dujail case was relatively well supported by documentary evidence and eyewitness testimony, and promised a speedy condemnation.

In August 2006, the *Anfal* trial started against Saddam Hussein, Ali Hasan al-Majid, and several other defendants. Court proceedings were often tumultuous, and even involved the removal of the chief judge for alleged bias in favor of Saddam. Numerous survivors, however, got a chance to testify against the former dictator. Although Saddam rarely denied the testimony brought against him outright, he repeatedly complained that he had not been given a chance to respond to the charges. It is true that he never did get to hear the documentary evidence.

In the Dujail trial, the death penalty had been demanded, and Saddam Hussein was executed in December 2006. As a result, the *Anfal* trial against him was left unfinished, much to the chagrin of numerous local and international observers; apparently, political pressures for a speedy execution of Saddam Hussein outweighed the demand for a full legal proceeding concerning the *Anfal*.

Subsequently, in June 2007, Ali Hasan al-Majid was condemned to death, together with two others, for genocide, war crimes, and crimes against humanity. Following an appeal procedure, al-Majid was executed in January 2010.

International human rights organizations not only expressed doubts about the fairness of these trials; they also bemoaned the fact that Saddam was executed before he could properly be called to account for his role in the *Anfal* operations. The *Anfal* trials had many other flaws, not least the fact that they were conducted under continuing U.S. occupation, which technically rendered them void under international law. Although there are few if any outright denials of the *Anfal*'s genocidal character, the murderous violence that emerged in post-2003 Iraq has likewise tended to distract attention from the enormity of the Baath regime's crimes. Because of these and other flaws, there is a risk that the *Anfal* trials may be remembered internationally, and especially in the Arab world, as a case of victor's rather than victim's justice.

There has been significant international judicial corroboration of the genocide claim, however. In December 2005, the Dutch merchant Frans van Anraat, who had sold chemicals to Iraq during the 1980s, was sentenced to 15 years imprisonment for complicity in war crimes, in particular the March 1988 attack against Halabja. Although van Anraat himself was cleared of complicity on charges of genocide, the court ruled that the Halabja attack did in fact constitute an act of genocide. The international juridical implications of this ruling may be substantial, given the obligations that genocide creates under international law.

Van Anraat's condemnation is only an isolated case, however; there are many other individuals, companies, and government officials in numerous countries who still have much to answer for. Thus, in *A Poisonous Affair*, Joost Hiltermann (2007) deplores the fact that the Reagan and Bush Sr. Administrations have never been called to account for their tacit approval, if not active encouragement, of Iraq's use of chemical weapons against both Iranian military and Iraqi civilians. The full extent of international complicity in Saddam's numerous crimes is still far from adequately known, and may never be completely revealed; but to uncover this complicity in more detail, a sustained and concerted international effort will be necessary. At present, however, there appears to be little will or popular pressure to call those responsible to account.

Eyewitness Accounts

To date, there is little available about the *Anfal* in the way of eyewitness evidence in Western languages. Important works, like Ziyad Abdulrahman's *Tuni Merg* (*Dungeon of Death*) and Shorsh Resool's *Dewlety Iraq u Kurd* (*The Iraqi State and the Kurds*), are available only in Kurdish. The main source for published accounts is Human Right Watch's *Iraq's Crime of Genocide* (1995), from which Accounts 2 and 5 below have been taken. In the future, further testimony that has served as the basis for this report may be made public. Other eyewitness accounts appear in Kanan Makiya's *Cruelty and Silence* (1993), especially the lengthy (and harrowing) interview with Abdallah, at first believed to be the sole survivor of the execution squads (see Accounts 1 and 3). More recent studies that make extensive use of testimony from survivors (mostly female) are Choman Hardi's *Gendered Experiences of Genocide* (2010) and a series of articles by German scholar Karin Mlodoch. Account 4 was recorded by the author and has not previously been published.

Account 1: The Chemical Attacks

This account, by Abdallah Abdel-Qadir al-Askari, who survived the attack on Guptepe (or "Goktepe" according to Human Rights Watch), provides a sense of the horrors of the chemical attacks. This is excerpted from Makiya's *Cruelty and Silence* (1993, p. 135). Note: for additional testimony from al-Askari, see Human Rights Watch's *Iraq's Crime of Genocide* (1995, pp. 118, 142, 154–155, 156–157).

On the evening of May 3 [1988] the situation in my village, Guptapa, was not normal. We had heard that the regime was preparing a chemical attack, but we didn't know when they would strike. It felt like there were unusual army maneuvers. Late in the afternoon with my brother-in-law and two friends—both teachers like myself—I climbed from our farm, which is on lower ground, to the highest point of the village. We wanted to see what was going on. Two inspection planes flew over. They threw out flares to determine the direction of the wind. Then another group of planes came, we think about 18 of them. The explosions were not very loud, which made me guess they were chemical bombs. When we raised our heads, we saw the sandy brown and grey clouds billowing upward. My background as a chemist left me in no doubt this was a chemical attack.

We climbed to the highest spot possible even though the wind was taking the gas away in the opposite direction. From there I shouted down to the people in the village: "This is a chemical attack! Try to escape! Come up the hill, come up here!" A lot of people did come to where we were and were saved. But a lot remained in the areas affected by the chemicals.

We discussed what to do. I thought we should wait 10 or 15 minutes, then go down. If we went at once, we too would be in danger and unable to help the others. But my friends wouldn't listen. So, we went down to the back of the village where the gases had not permeated and a lot of people were gathered. Some were very disturbed; one man shouted at me, "You have lost everybody; they are all killed. They have been bombing your house." This made me worried; I wanted to go back to my house but we hadn't waited long enough. Only three minutes had passed of the time I had fixed in my mind as the minimum.

The poison used in Guptapa in my opinion wasn't a single gas; it was composed of several gases. The combination affects the muscles, making them rigid and inflexible. In two minutes it can kill a person.

Finally I could run to my house. It was 20 minutes before sunset. When I got there it was entirely dark, but I found a small flashlight. First I put on a gas mask to protect myself. Then I went to the shelter which I had prepared for just such an eventuality. My wife knew that this was where the family should hide in case of chemical attack. Nobody was there. I became really afraid—convinced that nobody had survived. I climbed up from the shelter to a cave nearby, thinking they might have taken refuge there. There was nobody there, either. But when I went to the small stream near our house, I found my mother. She had fallen by the river; her mouth was biting into the mud bank.

All the members of my family had been running toward this stream because I had told them that water is good against chemical weapons. By the time they reached the stream, a lot of them had fainted and fallen into the water. Most of them had drowned. I turned my mother over; she was dead. I wanted to kiss her but I knew that if did, the chemicals would be passed on. Even now I deeply regret not kissing my beloved mother.

I continued along the river. I found the body of my 9-year-old daughter hugging her cousin, who had also choked to death in the water. Then I found the dead body of another niece, with her father. I continued along the stream. I found a woman who wasn't from our family and heard a child groan under her. Turning the woman over, I found the child; the water had almost reached him. I took the boy's clothes off, took him inside, and bundled him up in other clothes.

Then I went around our house. In the space of 200 to 300 square meters I saw the bodies of dozens of people from my family. Among them were my children, my brothers, my father, and my nieces and nephews. Some of them were still alive, but I couldn't tell one from the other. I was trying to see if the children were dead. At that point I lost my feelings. I didn't know who to cry for anymore and I didn't know who to go to first. I was all alone at night.

I saw one of my brothers: his head was tilted down a slope. My wife was still alive beside him, and my other brother was on the other side. My two daughters, the 6-month-old baby and the 4-year-old, were both dead. I tried to move them, to shake them. There was no response. They were both dead. I just knew they were dead.

My brothers and my wife had blood and vomit running from their noses and mouths. Their heads were tilted to one side. They were groaning. I couldn't do much, just clean the blood and vomit from their mouths and noses and try in every way to make them breathe again. I did artificial respiration on them and then I gave them two injections each. I also rubbed creams on my wife and two brothers. After injecting them, I had a feeling they were not going to die.

Our family has 40 members. I mean, it did. Now, of that big family we have only 15 left. Twenty-five of the beloved people of our family are dead. Among those were my five children.

Account 2: The Transit Camps

After being gathered at local camps, deportees were taken to centralized camps further south in Iraq. There, they were primarily in the hands of the security forces or the Party apparatus. This piece of testimony is excerpted from Human Rights Watch's *Iraq's Crime of Genocide* (1995, p. 147).

On the first morning, they separated the men into small groups and beat them. Four soldiers would beat one captive. The other prisoners could see this. About 15 or 20 men were in each group that was taken a little way off to be kicked and beaten with sticks and [electric] cables. They were taken away in the early morning and returned in the afternoon. The soldiers did not gather the men by name, but just pointed, you, and you, and so on. They were *Amn* [security personnel] from Tikrit and Kirkuk—butchers, we know them. When one group of beaten men returned, they took another and beat them. That night, I was in a group of ten or twelve men that was taken out and blindfolded with our hands tied behind us. They took us in three or four cars to somewhere in Tikrit. We drove around all night, barely stopping. They asked me no questions. The captured men could not talk to one another. Everyone was thinking of his own destiny. Of the ten or twelve they took out that night, only five returned.

The next night, when I was back in the hall, Amn came and asked for men to volunteer for the war against Iran. Eighty men volunteered. But it was a lie; they disappeared. A committee was set up by Amn to process the prisoners, who were ordered to squat while the Amn agents took all their money and put it in a big sack. They also took all our documents. The Amn agents were shouting at us to scare us. "Bring weapons to kill them," said one. "They are poor, don't shoot them," said another. And another: "I wish we had killed all of them."

Later that night the Amn came back and took all the young men away. Only the elderly remained. The young men were taken away in Nissan buses, ten or more of them, each with a capacity of 45 people. Their documents had already been taken. They left nothing but the clothes on their backs.

Account 3: The Execution Sites

This account comes from the extraordinary testimony of Taimour Abdallah, who was taken to an execution site near the Saudi border but managed to escape, albeit wounded. Although he did not speak any Arabic, he found refuge with a Shiite Arab family, and eventually managed to return to the Kurdish-held north. This excerpt is taken from Makiya's *Cruelty and Silence* (1993, pp. 185, 191–192, 195).

Note: part of his testimony also appears in Gwynne Roberts' 1992 BBC television documentary, *The Road to Hell*, which was aired in the United States as *Saddam's Killing Fields*. See chapter 9 ("The Firing Squads") in Human Rights Watch's *Iraq's Crime of Genocide* (1995, pp. 160–174). See also the story of another *Anfal* survivor, Ako Izeddin Sayyid Ismael from Warani near Tuz Khormatu (*The Globe and Mail*, April 3, 2003) (full text at www.fas.harvard.edu/~irdp/reports/taimour. html).

Q: What happened when you reached the prison of Topzawa in Kirkuk?

A: When we arrived, they put women and children in one hall and the men in another.

Q: In which group did they put you?

A: I was with my mother and my sisters.

Q: Did you see your father again after being separated?

A: I saw him once more in Topzawa and then I didn't see him again.

Q: What was happening when you saw him?

A: They were taking off his clothes except for the underclothes. They manacled his hands and then they put all the men in the lorries and drove them away.

Q: After that you never saw your father again?

A: No. [p. 185]

Q: What happened next?

A: … Just before reaching the place of the shooting, they first let us off the lorries and blindfolded us and gave us a sip of water. Then they made us go back inside. When we arrived, they opened the door, and I managed to slip aside my blindfold. I could see this pit in the ground surrounded by soldiers.

Q: Were your hands tied?

A: No.

Q: When they opened the door of the lorry, what was the first thing you saw?

A: The first thing I saw was the pits, dug and ready.

Q: … How many pits did you see?

A: It was night, but around us there were many.

Q: Four or five holes?

A: No, no, it was more.

Q: More than five, six, seven holes?

A: Yes, yes.

Q: Describe your pit.

A: The pit was like a tank dugout. They put us in that kind of a hole.

Q: They pushed you directly off the truck into the pit?
A: Yes.

Q: How high was it? One meter? Two meters? Could you stand up inside?
A: It was high.

Q: How high?
A: Up to the sash of a man.

Q: How many people were put inside?
A: One pit to every truck.

Q: And how many people were on a truck?
A: About 100 people.

Q: Was it just a massive hole?
A: It was rectangular.

Q: Was it cut very precisely by a machine?
A: By bulldozers as you would make a pit for a tank. [pp. 191–192]

Q: …Did you look into the soldier's face?
A: Yes.

Q: Did you see his eyes?
A: Yes.

Q: What did you see? What could you read in his eyes, in the expression on his face?
A: He was about to cry, but the other one shouted at him and told him to throw me back in the pit. He was obliged to throw me back.

Q: He cried!
A: He was about to cry.

Q: How far away was the officer who shouted?
A: He was close to him.

Q: The soldier who pushed you back into the hole, was he the one who shot you the second time?
A: Yes. This soldier shot me again after he received the order from the officer who was standing beside the pit. When he shot me the second time I was wounded here [he points] [p. 195].

Account 4: Deportations to Nuqrat al-Salman

This is the testimony of a 78-year-old man, originally from a village in the Qaradagh area, who had been resettled in Takiya *mujamma'a* near Chamchamal. From an interview conducted by Michel Leezenberg, Takiya *mujamma'a*, spring 1992; previously unpublished.

In our village alone, six people were executed on the spot by government troops; in the neighboring village, they shot 18 people. When they took us away from our village, we were not allowed to take anything with us—not even cigarette paper. After half a year, about 500 of us, mostly the sick and the elderly, were allowed to return. Here I have the document from the camp, saying that I am allowed to go back together with my wife and daughter. At the bottom, they have added "We have done what we had been told to do" in handwriting. Of another family of nine from our village, only the parents and a young daughter have returned. There is no news about the other six. Nobody knows what has happened to the children. They say that the truck drivers who brought them away have all been shot. Nobody knows whether there are still people in the Nuqrat al-Salman camp today, but they cannot possibly be alive after four years in that heat. People were too weak, too tired, and too hungry even to bury their dead. I've heard that sometimes corpses were left lying exposed, only to be eaten by stray dogs.

Now, we are in the Takiya *mujamma'a*, but we have nothing to live from. There is one cow here, but it is not ours; we can only use its milk. We are too old to work now, and all our belongings have been stolen by the government. After the 1991 uprising, the government in reprisal stopped the supply of cheap foodstuffs here. We are still afraid of them; the day before yesterday, they shelled the *mujamma'a* with their artillery fire. They can come back anytime they like. The *peshmergas* can't defend us against their heavy arms and armored cars. Some people tried to return to their villages near the front lines, but their houses have been bombed again soon after they had been rebuilt.

Account 5: Ali Hasan al-Majid

This interview is excerpted from Human Rights Watch, *Iraq's Crime of Genocide* (1995, p. 254). Note: the tape is dated May 26, 1988, but according to Human Rights Watch it is more likely from 1987.

Jalal Talabani asked me to open a special channel of communication with him. That evening I went to Suleimaniyah and hit them with the special ammunition. That was my answer. We continued the deportations. I told the *mustashars* that they might say that they like their villages and that they won't leave. I said I cannot let your village stay because I will attack it with chemical weapons. Then you and your family will die. You must leave right now. Because I cannot tell you the same day that I am going to attack with chemical weapons. I will kill them all with chemical weapons! Who is going to say anything? The international community? Fuck them! The international community and those who listen to them....

This is my intention, and I want you to take serious note of it. As soon as we complete the deportations, we will start attacking them everywhere according to a systematic military plan. Even their strongholds. In our attacks we will take back one third or one half of what is under their control. If we can try to take two thirds, then we will surround them in a small pocket and attack them with chemical weapons. I will not attack them with chemical weapons for just one day, but I will continue to attack them with chemicals for 15 days. Then I will announce that anyone who wishes to surrender with his gun will be allowed to do so. I will publish 1 million copies of this leaflet and distribute it in the North, in Kurdish, Sorani, Badinani and Arabic. I will not say it is from the Iraqi government. I will not let the government get involved. I will say it is from here [the Northern Bureau]. Anyone willing to come back is welcome, and those who do not return will be attacked again with new, destructive chemicals. I will not mention the name of the chemical because that is classified information. But I will say with new destructive weapons that will destroy you. So I will threaten them and motivate them to surrender. Then you will see that all the vehicles of God himself will not be enough to carry them all. I think and expect that they will be defeated. I swear that I am sure we will defeat them.

Selected Bibliography

Fischer-Tahir, Andrea (2003). *Wir gaben viele Märtyrer: Wiederstand und kollektive Identitätsbildung in Irakisch-Kurdistan.* Münster: Unrast Verlag.

Francona, Rick (1999). *Ally to adversary: An eyewitness account of Iraq's fall from grace.* Annapolis, MD: U.S. Naval Institute Press.

Galbraith, Peter (2006). *The end of Iraq.* New York: Simon & Schuster.

Hardi, Choman (2010). *Gendered experiences of genocide: Anfal survivors in Kurdistan-Iraq.* London: Ashgate.

Hiltermann, Joost (2007). *A poisonous affair: America, Iraq, and the gassing of Halabja.* New York: Cambridge University Press.

Human Rights Watch/Middle East (1994). *Bureaucracy of repression: The Iraqi government in its own words.* New York: Author.

Human Rights Watch/Middle East (1995). *Iraq's crime of genocide: The Anfal campaign against the Kurds.* New Haven, CT: Yale University Press.

Makiya, Kanan (1993). *Cruelty & silence: War, tyranny, uprising, and the Arab world.* New York: W.W. Norton.

Meiselas, S. (1997). *Kurdistan in the shadow of history.* New York: Random House.

Websites

www.hrw.org/reports/1993/iraqanfal. Human Rights Watch site from which the original 1993 report and other documents on the *Anfal* can be downloaded.

http://bbcnews.com. BBC news archive featuring timelines of Saddam Hussein's and Ali Hasan al-Majid's trials, background information on the *Anfal*, and much more about post-war Iraq.

http://ictj.org/search/node/anfal. International Center for Transitional Justice website; contains summaries of the court sessions during the different phases of the *Anfal* trial conducted in Iraq.

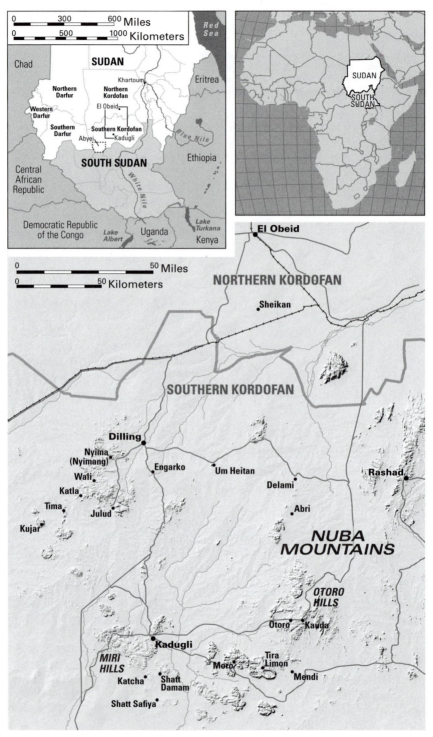

Map 12.1 Nuba Mountains, South Kordofan, Sudan

CHAPTER 12

The Nuba Mountains, Sudan

ALEX DE WAAL

Introduction

The assault on the Nuba Mountains of Sudan in 1992, at the height of Sudan's civil war, represents the most clear-cut case of genocidal intent in modern Sudan. It is a little-known episode that unfolded with no international attention at the time, with the Nuba completely cut off from humanitarian assistance and the focus of only a tiny advocacy effort. Cut off from the world by retreating to the hilltops, Nuba communities faced the threat of social dismemberment and cultural annihilation, and survived by their own efforts. Only three years later did the first international assistance arrive and human rights advocacy begin. Although the Nuba Mountains were the location of the first cease-fire in Sudan's war (in January 2002), the subsequent Comprehensive Peace Agreement (CPA) left the Nuba in a precarious position as the country divided into Sudan and South Sudan on July 9, 2011. Similar considerations applied to the people of the Blue Nile, also on the northern side of the north–south boundary but in strong solidarity with the south. A widely expected war erupted in the Nuba Mountains in June 2011, and spread to Blue Nile in September.

As an "African" people, many of whom were active supporters of the southern-based Sudan People's Liberation Army (SPLA), but who lived in northern Sudan, the Nuba were seen as an anomaly in a war (Sudan's second war, 1983–2005) defined as north versus south. Since the horrors of the Darfur war seized international attention in 2004, including massacre, man-made famine, and forced displacement, such a conflict is no longer an unfamiliar concept. In retrospect, the Nuba war foreshadows many of the features of the Darfur conflict.

This chapter provides a background to the Nuba people and charts how the war in the Nuba Mountains unfolded in three phases after the SPLA first entered the area in 1985. The concluding section discusses the incomplete resolution of the Nuba crisis and the prospects for the Nuba in the immediate future.

Background to the Genocidal Campaign in the Nuba Mountains

The Nuba Mountains lie in Southern Kordofan, a province (now state) in the geographical center of Sudan, just north of the north–south boundary, chiefly inhabited by a cluster of peoples indigenous to the area who are collectively known as "Nuba." This is not their own historical nomenclature—under different definitions of "ethnic group," the Nuba consist of anywhere up to 40 distinct groups with different languages. In fact, there is more linguistic diversity among the Nuba than in the whole of the rest of Sudan (Stevenson, 1984). They are remnant populations that took refuge in the hills for protection against slavery, practiced for centuries by states in the Nile Valley and the sultanates of Darfur.

The Nuba share Southern Kordofan with Arab cattle pastoralists, chiefly the Hawazma and Missiriya. The Nuba are farmers and typically inhabited the hills, while the pastoralists moved their livestock through the valleys. In times of peace and economic development, such as the first quarter-century after Sudan's independence from Britain in 1956, the Nuba expanded their farms into the fertile plains and both communities benefited from trade and exchange.

The British occupied Kordofan, including the Nuba Mountains, in 1900, and immediately typologized the people as "African," to be sealed off from the dominant Arab and Islamic cultures of northern Sudan. The Nuba Mountains became a "closed district" with entry and exit allowed only by permit, and insofar as the Nuba left their enclave, it was to work as unskilled laborers on the farming schemes of the Nile Valley, or as soldiers and household servants. Christian missions provided the few schooling opportunities open to the Nuba. While the majority of the Nuba adhered to traditional religions, as diverse as the "bewildering complexity" of their cultural traditions mapped by early ethnographers (Nadel, 1947, p. 2), many educated people converted to Christianity, while increasing numbers of those exposed to wider Sudanese society became Muslims.

In colonial and postcolonial Sudan, the Nuba possessed second-class status. They were discriminated against in employment and education. They also had the misfortune that the plains of Southern Kordofan are among the most fertile land in Sudan, and well-connected commercial farmers used the inequities of Sudanese land law to acquire land leases for mechanized agriculture in the area. Often, Nuba villagers would awake one morning to find a platoon of policemen accompanying tractors and contractors who were the new owners of the land, expropriating the existing smallholder farmers by force.

Nuba skill at music, dancing, wrestling, and body art has been celebrated by photographers, ethnographers, and cultural tourists, including George Rodger and Leni Riefenstahl. To the Western cultural critic, Riefenstahl's photo essays were an effort both in exoticizing the Nuba and celebrating a cult of primitive muscularity (Sontag, 1975). For many of the Nuba, however, these photographs represent a precious pictorial archive of their endangered cultural traditions. Briefly, in the 1970s, the Nuba achieved a balance between integration into a then-secular Sudanese state, and the opportunity to preserve and develop their own cultural traditions (Baumann, 1987). However, as successive Sudanese governments shifted toward a more Arab and Islamic orientation, the Western fascination with the Nuba as emblems of noble savagery embarrassed the northern Sudanese elites, who were increasingly candid about their "civilization mission" to extend Arab-Muslim culture to the peripheries of their huge and diverse country. The last thing they wanted was graphic depiction of nudity and sexually suggestive dancing among their citizenry.

During the hopeful years of the 1970s, Nuba students, teachers, and local government officers became political activists, promoting Nuba cultural awareness and political mobilization. Groups such as the youth organization Komolo became the nucleus of an underground movement, increasingly militant as the governments of Jaafar Nimeiri (ruled 1969–1985), Abdel Rahman Suwar al Dahab (1985–1986), and Sadiq al Mahdi (1986–1989) turned toward more exclusivist and Islamist political programs.

In 1983 Sudan's second civil war broke out, with military officers from the south forming the SPLA. Unlike the first Sudanese civil war (1955–1972), the manifesto of the SPLA's political wing, the Sudan People's Liberation Movement (SPLM), was not southern separatist. The SPLM leader, John Garang, propounded the philosophy of a "New Sudan"—a united, secular, and (in the early days of the movement) socialist country, in which the diverse African peoples of the Sudanese peripheries, including the south, the Nuba Mountains, Blue Nile, and Darfur, would band together and establish a political majority, reducing the ruling Arabized elite to a minority status. This program was attractive to the Nuba activists, and under the mentorship of a school teacher-activist, Yousif Kuwa Mekki, young Nuba joined the SPLA in large numbers.

Two years after the war began in southern Sudan, fighting spread to Southern Kordofan, and in 1987 Yousif Kuwa entered the Nuba Mountains at the head of an SPLA brigade.

On entering the Nuba Mountains in force, the SPLA scored one victory after another. Recruits flocked to its ranks. Its numbers, organization, and firepower overwhelmed the modest army garrisons and militia. Although an infantry force without vehicles, the SPLA gained ground and by 1989 seemed set to overrun the majority of Southern Kordofan, including several major towns. The government was close to panic.

From the outset, the government war in the Nuba Mountains was characterized by massacres of civilians and extra-judicial executions by military intelligence. Early government violence focused on identifying suspected collaborators with the rebels and ruthlessly eliminating them. Military intelligence headed the effort and its officers had *carte blanche* to detain, torture, and kill. Scores of educated Nuba disappeared during this period, many of them vanishing into the cells of military intelligence in the provincial capital Kadugli, and never reappearing. Several places near the town became infamous killing fields (see account 1, mek Defan Arno). The worst year for these killings was 1988.

Meanwhile, the government was severely constrained in its ability to use the regular army against the rebels. Bankrupt, the government decided to fight the war at minimal cost to the national budget by licensing tribally based militia as proxies. Immediately after the first SPLA incursions into Kordofan, the minister of defense, General Fadallah Burma Nasir, toured the area by helicopter and mobilized former army officers from the Arab tribes of the area to form militias to fight the SPLA, in effect giving them free rein to loot livestock, burn villages, and kill. The government did not trust the officer corps of the army, as many NCOs and rank-and-file were Nuba or from elsewhere in western Sudan, and many senior officers were opposed to the war and in particular the way they were instructed to fight it on the cheap. The politicians prevailed: the 1986 Armed Forces Memorandum brought the militias, known locally as *murahaliin* ("nomads") under the coordination of military intelligence, and in 1989 the militias were formalized into the "Popular Defence Forces." The militias committed the worst massacres of the war, often as reprisals for losses at the hands of the SPLA

The four years following the overthrow of President Nimeiri in a non-violent popular uprising in April 1985 constituted Sudan's third attempt at elected parliamentary government since independence. Within the capital, there was freedom of expression and association, and the elections of April 1986 were free and fair—though not held in many parts of the south, which were at war. The Nuba returned Members of Parliament (MP), including several for the Nuba-based Sudan National Party led by a veteran Nuba leader, Father Philip Abbas Ghabboush. In an augur of how parliamentary democracy was doomed by civil war, Nuba MPs' parliamentary immunity was violated by the security services when three were arbitrarily detained. Sudan's press was largely uncensored at the time, but reporters did not cover the unfolding atrocities in Southern Kordofan.

One of the immediate and foreseeable impacts of the war was famine. Nuba communities were rapidly reduced to destitution. Health services collapsed. The fertile fields in the valleys were abandoned and Nuba farmers retreated, as they had done historically in times of trouble, to the hills. Tens of thousands left for the cities. International humanitarian agencies did very little in response to this man-made crisis (African Rights, 1997).

The Perpetrators and how the Genocide was Committed

The June 1989 Islamist coup of Sudan brought a very brief period of respite to the Nuba, followed rapidly by an escalation of violence. The new assault took a different form: Senior cadres of the government's Arab and Islamic Bureau carefully planned an effort to go beyond mere counterinsurgency to try to enact a comprehensive program of social and political transformation. The Nuba assault was one part of a nation-wide revolutionary project intended to create a new Islamist Sudanese identity. The project went under different and overlapping guises during the years of Islamist militancy from approximately 1990 to 1996. One umbrella title was *al mashru' al hadhari* ("The Civilization Project"), a specific component of it was *al da'awa al shamla* ("The Comprehensive Call to God"), and in the case of the Nuba, it was also certified as *jihad* ("Holy War") (de Waal & Abdel Salam, 2004).

The Islamist government in Sudan was both secretive and confusing, and especially so during its most militant phase. The ambition and comprehensiveness of the program for Islamist transformation encouraged observers to believe in a carefully coordinated totalitarian project, directed by the *eminence grise* of the government and sheikh of the Islamists, Hassan al Turabi. From the first days of the coup, Turabi had played a characteristically deceitful role. The front man for the coup was a little-known brigadier, Omar al Bashir, who set up a Revolutionary Command Council of fellow officers. But real power rested with the civilian Islamists and their security-trained colleagues, who held no official positions in the new regime, but who met at night in their private residences to draft the decisions the loyal soldiers publicly took the following day. On issues central to national security, such as whether Sudan backed Iraq or Kuwait in 1990, Turabi clearly showed that he was in charge, overruling and humiliating the president.

With more knowledge about the functioning of the regime, it is now evident that the Islamists never managed to consolidate a single power center. Policy was always contested between the soldiers and the ideologues, with different factions among both and different coalitions holding sway on different issues at different times. The key division of labor was that President Bashir was tasked with keeping the government in power, intervening to make executive decisions only when regime survival was in danger, while the civilians under Turabi and his deputy, Ali Osman Taha, ran the government and the army ran the war. Unsurprisingly, the key conflicts within the regime arose when conventional precepts of national security and military strategy clashed with Turabi's revolutionary ambitions.

The campaign in the Nuba Mountains was exactly such an instance. The concept of *jihad* was developed in the Arab and Islamic Bureau, a quasi-official entity chaired by Turabi. The Bureau instructed the vice president, General Zubeir Mohamed Saleh, to conduct the Kordofan *jihad*. It planned the comprehensive relocation of the Nuba population to "peace villages," some of them in Southern Kordofan and some elsewhere, and the associated Islamization of the population. Those Nuba who already espoused Islam were considered too heterodox to qualify as fully fledged citizens of Sudan's new Islamist state, and would need to be cured of their various depravities (the medical metaphor was favored by Islamist social planners, many of whom were physicians, African Rights, 1997, pp. 202–203). It organized support for the military campaign in the form of international *mujahidiin*, who helped train the local militia, and instructed the religious leaders of Kordofan to issue a *fatwa* in its support. General Zubeir went along, though his agenda—and the army's—went as far as defeating the SPLA rebellion and no further. President Bashir's role appears to have been ceremonial—he blessed the militia commanders who graduated from a rally in the regional capital, el Obeid, in April 1992 and awarded them *jihadist* titles for the forthcoming campaign.

Following the el Obeid rally, six *ulama* (Muslim clerics) issued a *fatwa* in support of the campaign. Its most notable clause was one that excommunicated the rebels, on the grounds that fighting the Sudan government was equivalent to rebellion against Islam:

> The rebels in South Kordofan and Southern Sudan started their rebellion against the state and declared war against the Muslims. Their main aims are: killing the Muslims, desecrating mosques,

burning and defiling the Qur'an, and raping Muslim women. In so doing, they are encouraged by the enemies of Islam and Muslims: these foes are the Zionists, the Christians and the arrogant people who provide them with provisions and arms. Therefore, an insurgent who was previously a Muslim is now an apostate; and a non-Muslim is a non-believer standing as a bulwark against the spread of Islam, and Islam has granted the freedom of killing both of them according to the following words of Allah...[1]

No more disturbing manifesto was produced by Sudan's Islamists. One of its clearest sequelae was that government troops destroyed mosques in the SPLA-controlled areas (African Rights, 1995, chapter 4). The *fatwa* has been interpreted by some writers as a universal charter for *jihad* and as nothing less than a precursor of the declarations of war issued by Usama bin Laden (Bodanski, 1999, p. 111). The reality is more complex. The *fatwa* was demanded by the governor of Kordofan, General Sayed Abdel Karim el Husseini, who was not a leading Islamist but rather an army officer who found himself in an unexpectedly prominent position and who was keen to demonstrate his political credentials. When General Husseini first gathered the Kordofan clerics and ordered them to issue the decree, the most senior of them refused. The *fatwa* reflects an embarrassingly low level of learning and is manifestly the work of second-rate provincial clerics. Revealingly, it was made public only when the dignitaries from Khartoum had left Kordofan, while Turabi himself chose that very moment to go on an international tour (de Waal & Abdel Salam, 2004).

Vice President Zubeir personally directed the military assault. It was the largest offensive of the war, but severely underestimated the tenacity and skill of the SPLA forces, and failed to make provision for anything other than a quick victory. Ideologues are often let down by their neglect of practicalities, and especially tend to overlook the need for contingency planning when things go awry. The planners also paid little heed to the gap between the moral purity of the ideal *jihad* and the tawdry realities of counterinsurgency.

Military intelligence in Kordofan organized death squads which targeted community leaders and educated people. The younger brother of the governor and head of security for Kordofan, Khalid el Husseini, was so shocked by what he learned that he left Sudan and sought asylum in Europe in 1993.[2] He said that the government was "taking the intellectuals, taking the professionals, to ensure that the Nuba were so primitive that they couldn't speak for themselves."

Khalid el Husseini also explained that there was an official policy of segregating men and women in the "peace camps." More specifically, he stated that,

> The reason for the men and women being distributed in different camps is to prevent them marrying, the reason being that if the men and women are together and get married and have children, that itself is contrary to government policy ... the members of the Arab tribes are allowed to marry them in order to eliminate the Nuba identity. (Interview conducted by Julie Flint in June 1995 in preparation for her documentary, *Sudan's Secret War*)

The phrase "allowed to marry" amounts to "encouraged to rape" in the context of the absolute power held by the camp officials and guards over the females in their charge. Subsequent human rights investigations provided ample evidence for a policy of rape (African Rights, 1995; see account 2, "Fawzia").

A titanic plan for resettlement of the Nuba out of their homeland distinguished the campaign from the routine cruelties of Sudanese counterinsurgency. The government announced plans to resettle 500,000 people, the entire population of the insurgent area, and by late 1992 had relocated one-third of that number. An adjunct to this was a policy of starving the rebel-held areas into submission. The army and security disrupted trade and closed markets, destroyed farms and looted animals. Raiding, abduction, and rape prevented any movement between villages and to markets. Thousands died of hunger and disease, while the flow of basic goods (including soap, salt, and clothing) to the rebel areas almost completely dried up. The Nuba Mountains went back in time: people wore home-spun cotton or went naked, could no longer use currency and so instead reverted to barter, and relied upon traditional medical remedies.

The policy was genocidal in both intent and its possible outcome. But by the end of 1992 the military operation had clearly failed and the main tenets of the campaign were abandoned (de Waal, 2006). One reason for this was the divisions within the government, mentioned above. While some zealots were determined that there be a total social transformation of the Nuba, the army officers focused on the military objective of defeating the SPLA. There was a series of tussles over who was appointed to key positions in Southern Kordofan, with the military pragmatists winning the day.

Equally important, the SPLA resistance was sufficiently strong that the government forces simply could not prevail, and the agenda of social revolution faded along with the quiet withdrawal of the brigades. The

Nuba SPLA benefited from an inspired leadership. Commander Yousif Kuwa was a former teacher and cultural activist who believed that the strength of the rebellion lay primarily in popular support rather than military strength alone. In the SPLA-held areas, he encouraged a cultural revival, opened schools, convened a religious tolerance conference, and at the height of the *jihad*, organized a consultative assembly in which representatives of Nuba communities debated whether they could afford to continue the war. After five days of discussion, they voted to continue. Crucial in influencing their decision was the consensus opinion that any peace offer coming from Khartoum was not to be trusted (African Rights, 1995, chapter 5).

Lastly, the forced relocations caused a quiet but significant outcry among Sudanese citizens. The campaign involved rounding up women and children and transporting them, naked and starving, in market lorries to the outskirts of towns in Northern Kordofan where they were dumped in sites designated as "peace villages." Horrified by what they saw, townspeople rushed to help them with food and shelter, and were barred from doing so by Islamist cadres. Although the Sudanese press was very effectively muzzled, word spread about the atrocities, and undermined the standing and the morale of the Sudanese government leadership.

The Responses to the Genocide

The War Continues, 1993–2001

The immediate threat to the existence of the Nuba as a people faded after 1992. But the war continued for the next eight years. The Sudan government continued its counterinsurgency, repeatedly trying to uproot the SPLA forces. Every year there was a combined offensive involving regular troops and militia, and every year the SPLA struggled to hold its ground. The *jihad* had failed in its ideological and military aims, but it also left the SPLA as a defensive force, struggling to maintain the territory it controlled. Following a split in the ranks of the SPLA in the south in 1991, the Nuba forces were entirely cut off from resupply. Several efforts to bring in arms by foot and by air failed. The rebellion was essentially reduced to controlling the hilltops and to skirmishing over small garrison towns. The future of the SPLA's war would be decided in the negotiating chamber, not on the battlefield.

The government's political aim was defensive. By the mid-1990s, leading figures in Khartoum were privately warning that the war against the SPLA was unwinnable, and that there would need to be a negotiated settlement. Sudan's African neighbors, under the auspices of the Intergovernmental

Authority on Development (IGAD), established a negotiating forum and drafted a Declaration of Principles (DoP), which included the right of self-determination for the people of southern Sudan. The DoP was signed by the SPLM in 1994 but only by Khartoum, under pressure and with reservations, three years later. The pressure in question was the military involvement of three of the neighbors—Eritrea, Ethiopia, and Uganda—in supporting the SPLA and other Sudanese opposition forces, in retaliation for Sudanese sponsorship of terrorist and insurgent activities in their countries. Khartoum therefore reluctantly acknowledged the need for international mediation in the war in the south, but was desperate not to concede any further ground. In particular it did not want the Nuba and the people of Blue Nile (who were in a similar position) to be on the agenda. Therefore, while the continued war in the south was increasingly a matter of trying to improve the government's position ahead of any peace talks, in the Nuba Mountains it was a fight to the finish.

This war took on a different dimension that in some ways was just as destructive as the 1992 *jihad*. Under the rubric of *salaam min al dakhil* ("Peace from Within"), the government bought off SPLA commanders with cash and offers of positions, and promoted and rewarded loyal Nuba chiefs. A number of senior SPLA figures went over to the government side. They rarely emerged as significant rivals to the SPLA, but they took with them intelligence about SPLA organization and operations and their own coteries of followers, and they undermined morale. Meanwhile, the militia policy was broadened from the Arab tribes to include Nuba chiefs drawn from most of the diverse groups of the mountains. Under the elastic rubric of the Popular Defense Forces, individuals were given money, vehicles, status, weapons, and private retinues. Some ran their own prisons. As long as they did the government's bidding when required, they were allowed to act as local despots. Earlier in the war, the government had moved Nuba officers and troops away from Southern Kordofan, fearing that they would defect or mutiny. By the mid-1990s, it was moving them back, and a succession of commanders of the army and Popular Defense Forces in Kordofan were themselves from the area. One of the principal organizers of this strategy was a native of the area, of West African ancestry, called Ahmad Haroun, later to achieve notoriety when the International Criminal Court issued an arrest warrant against him for alleged crimes committed in his role as head of the "Darfur Desk" in 2003–2004.

The devastating consequence of this divide-and-rule strategy was that from 1993 onwards, the war was largely an intra-Nuba war. The majority of the forces on the government side were paramilitaries drawn from the Nuba Mountains themselves. Most of the battles were Nuba fighting

Nuba. It became easier for government patrols to infiltrate the SPLA-held areas. The co-option of Nuba irregulars, including former SPLA soldiers and commanders into government ranks, meant that hapless civilians often did not know who was who. The Nuba war became a war of attrition without clear front lines, characterized by skirmishes and small raids, with intermittent government offensives. In many cases, government garrisons consisted of the fiefdoms of chiefs and commanders and their militia, who gained a livelihood by extortion and raiding, and who abducted and held captive scores of young women, whom they sexually abused and forced to work as housemaids and farm laborers.

During the *jihad* period, the Nuba were almost entirely invisible internationally. Africa Watch published two newsletters, based on testimonies smuggled out of Sudan by Nuba activists, one of whom, Suleiman Rahhal, founded the Nuba Mountains Solidarity Abroad organization, which led a campaign to highlight the plight of the Nuba. In September 1992, following a visit to Sudan, Jan Eliasson, Head of the UN Department of Humanitarian Affairs, issued a public statement about the abuses in the Nuba Mountains, and in October 1992 the U.S. Congress passed a resolution that condemned the abuses. There was nothing more and the modest outcry had no discernible impact. The first significant publicity occurred following the African Rights mission to the SPLA-held areas in April 1995 (African Rights, 1995) and the BBC film by Julie Flint, *Sudan's Secret War*, screened in July that year. The airbridge established by African Rights in solidarity with the Nuba Relief, Rehabilitation and Development Organization led to a small but steady stream of journalists visiting the area, as well as small humanitarian operations by, among others, Christian Aid and Médecins Sans Frontières. The UN's Operation Lifeline Sudan, which operated under agreement with the Sudan government, only managed an exploratory mission in 2000.

The international attention undoubtedly helped the Nuba. Although modest, the humanitarian relief was a life saver. It put the Nuba on the political map, within Sudan and internationally, and paved the way for the scaled-up humanitarian programs that began in 2001–2002 and the cease-fire of 2002 (see below). However, some of the advocacy was polarizing. Among the international agencies that arrived in the Nuba Mountains were Christian evangelists whose insistence on distributing aid only to their co-religionists created tensions between followers of different faiths. Some of the foreign advocacy was uncritically supportive of the SPLM leadership and its agenda, which was primarily focused on southern Sudan. When some of the Nuba leaders began to explore compromise with the Sudan government, they were silenced by strident activists. This turned out to be to the Nuba's disadvantage.

The largest offensive of the post-*jihad* period occurred in May 2001. It followed shortly after the death of Yousif Kuwa from cancer in a British hospital and the return of his body for burial in the mountains. His successor as head of the SPLA forces was Abdel Aziz Adam al Hilu, one of the SPLA's most capable military commanders, particularly well known for his logistical skills (he had led the SPLA's abortive Darfur operation in 1991 and commanded the forces in eastern Sudan from 1994–1999). Having taken over from the ailing Yousif Kuwa some months before, Abdel Aziz had retrained and reorganized the demoralized SPLA forces, and succeeded in holding off a multipronged army attack. The denouement came close to the burial site of Yousif Kuwa, when he lured the army vanguard into a trap. Thinking that the SPLA forces had dispersed, the leading battalion made camp for the night, only to be surprised and overwhelmed by a sudden counter-attack in the darkness. Abdel Aziz collected the identity cards of several hundred slain soldiers, and noted that almost all of them were from western Sudan—Nuba, Kordofan Arabs, and Darfurians. He remarked to one of his lieutenants that the *Jellaba*—the ruling elites from Khartoum—were clever at staying in power by getting Sudan's Africans to kill one another. Among the identity cards was that of one of the Popular Defense Force commanders, a man who had been Abdel Aziz's close friend at university, whose family had hosted him during his studies.

A Precarious Peace

In retrospect, the May 2001 offensive was the last of the war, and the logic for peace on both sides was overwhelming. What made that more than an abstraction was the policy adopted by the incoming George W. Bush Administration in Washington, which had decided that it should work toward peace in Sudan. The main public steps in that direction took place shortly after the appointment of Senator Jack Danforth as Special Envoy on September 6, 2001, and the spur toward agreement that occurred just a few days later when the Sudanese leadership realized it could not afford to be on the wrong side in the "war on terror." However, in the previous months the newly appointed Deputy Administrator of USAID, Roger Winter (a Sudan veteran who had been the first American to visit the SPLA-held areas of the Nuba Mountains, in July 1995), had begun discreet negotiations for a humanitarian truce that would allow American food aid into the conflict-affected areas of mountains. The rationale for this was that the humanitarian need was immense and unmet by the UN, whose war-zones access permits only extended to southern Sudan, and that it was far cheaper to supply

Kordofan by road from the north than by air from faraway Kenya. Building on this, Danforth was quickly persuaded that he would make a cease-fire in the Nuba Mountains one of his first steps, both because of the humanitarian needs and because the SPLA forces there were unified and disciplined, unlike in many parts of the south.

In January 2002, at negotiations in the Swiss resort of Burgenstock, the Sudan government and the SPLA agreed a cease-fire for the Nuba Mountains. A small, unarmed monitoring team headed by a Norwegian brigadier was dispatched to oversee it. It worked. It was an illustration of how a small but energetic team, working with local commanders and community leaders, enjoying the confidence of all sides, could make a cease-fire work in extremely challenging circumstances (Souverijn-Eisenberg, 2005). It was also a turning point in the wider search for peace in Sudan, which then accelerated. The talks were formally convened by IGAD and were headed by a Kenyan mediator, General Lazarus Sumbeiywo, but his energy and creativity were backed by a formidable troika of the governments of the United States, Britain, and Norway.

Unfortunately for the Nuba, the search for political solutions to the Nuba predicament stalled for two years after the Burgenstock cease-fire. The Sudan government insisted that the cease-fire was *sui generis* and that the political substance of the peace talks concerned the south only. The SPLA and the troika also wanted the peace talks to prioritize the south, and argued that the issues in northern Sudan, including the Nuba, Blue Nile, Beja, and Darfur, and the civil opposition parties in the north and their demand for democratic representation, were secondary and would be resolved in due course after the main north–south issue had been settled. As the peace talks, held in the Kenyan towns of Machakos and Naivasha, slowly made progress, the Nuba leaders realized that their trust in the SPLA leadership to deliver an equitable deal for them was being compromised. When the Nuba and Blue Nile issues could no longer be ignored, a separate protocol was negotiated in the Nairobi suburb of Keren. The Nuba correctly saw this as a second-rate deal. The Sudan army had to withdraw entirely from the south and hand over security to the SPLA; the south would enjoy complete internal self-government under a "one country, two systems" constitution, and the southerners had won the right to vote for secession in a referendum six years after the peace was signed. The Nuba, located in northern Sudan, would see the SPLA withdrawn to south of the internal boundary, would only enjoy limited autonomy within northern Sudan, and would not have the right to self-determination. They did not have an option of "going south" to join their erstwhile comrades in arms. Their political future was to be decided by a "popular consultation" consisting of a vote in the Southern Kordofan state assembly on whether or not to continue with the quasi-autonomous status.

These provisions were signed into effect by the Comprehensive Peace Agreement of January 2005. Nuba concerns were slightly assuaged when the SPLM leader, John Garang, made his first ever visit to the Nuba Mountains shortly afterwards and promised that he would now hold the Nuba issue in his right hand, as a central agenda in his drive to create a "New Sudan." The Nuba SPLA leadership had always feared the secessionist tendencies of the southern majority in the SPLA, which would leave them isolated as a small "African" minority within a truncated northern Sudan more strongly identified with Arabism and Islam. They placed their faith in Garang, whose commitment to a whole-Sudan strategy they never questioned. The limits of this approach were painfully illustrated when Garang died in a helicopter crash on July 31, 2005, just three weeks after he was sworn in as the country's First Vice President.

For the first four years of the CPA-mandated Interim Period, the Nuba Mountains languished. Southern Kordofan became cantonized: the SPLM maintained its administration of the areas it controlled under the Burgenstock cease-fire, and replaced its soldiers with well-armed policemen. The government controlled the remainder, and maintained its well-armed paramilitaries. The two parties scarcely cooperated. Checkpoints controlled traffic on the roads passing from one zone to another. The two zones followed different forms of local administration and different educational curricula (the government side in Arabic, the SPLM side in English). The SPLM-controlled areas refused to cooperate with the national census, fearing manipulation. Agreement was not reached on constituencies for the elections or how to conduct the "popular consultation." Both sides rearmed, and violent incidents began to recur. Ordinary people in the Nuba Mountains spoke fatalistically about a new war, fearing that it would truly be a fight to the death and that it would surpass its predecessor in its ferocity.

Unexpectedly, the appointment of Ahmad Haroun as governor in 2009, with the SPLM's Abdel Aziz al Hilu as his deputy, led to a marked improvement in the running of Southern Kordofan. Despite being ideologically polar opposites, the two men had many similarities. Both were natives of Kordofan but had ancestry elsewhere; both were military men with a reputation for efficiency and problem-solving; both were also aware that Southern Kordofan was one of the potential flashpoints for a new war between north and south, and that the state would likely be destroyed in any new war.

Tragically, their partnership unraveled in early 2011, and the two ran against each other in state elections in May. According to the official count, Haroun won the governorship by a slender margin. Al Hilu disputed the result. Meanwhile, the two parties had failed to come to agreement on the future of the SPLA division in the Nuba Mountains, leaving more than 15,000 Nuba fighters with two unattractive options, contained in the CPA, of demobilizing or redeploying within South Sudan. With their political aspirations unmet, the SPLA forces moved toward Kadugli. The chief of staff of the Sudan Armed Forces demanded that they disarm or withdraw by June 1. Fighting broke out four days later, and rapidly spread to most of Southern Kordofan. On June 13, the African Union convened peace talks in Addis Ababa which led to an agreement on political partnership, governance arrangements, and security arrangements, signed on June 28. Unfortunately that was repudiated by President Bashir within days. In September the fighting spread to Blue Nile. At the time of writing (December 2011) the prospects for a negotiated settlement seem remote.

Why the Case of the Nuba Mountains is Important to Understanding Genocide

In comparison with the war and atrocities in Darfur a decade later, the campaign of massacre, destruction, rape, and forced relocation in the Nuba Mountains in the early 1990s garnered a tiny amount of attention and still more modest responses. The Nuba survived their ordeal almost entirely unaided. There was neither human rights advocacy nor humanitarian action, let alone any coercive measures such as sanctions or dispatch of peacekeepers with a mandate of civilian protection.

The significance of the Nuba case lies first and foremost in the importance of putting this neglected story on the historical record, for the sake of those who died, and those who suffered and survived. The story is also an essential component of any history of contemporary Sudan, and is important to any appreciation of the future prospects for peace.

The origins of the genocidal onslaught on the Nuba by the Islamist military regime lie in a combination of ideological extremism and fear of catastrophic military reverse, along with a routinized response to insurgency, of targeting the civilian population thought to be sympathetic to the rebels. The project of refashioning Nuba society in an Arab-Islamic image reflected a recurring tendency in Sudanese national politics. However, the ambition of the 1992 *jihad* and forced relocation was exceptional, the product of an Islamist revolution at the height of its hubris.

Just as significant as the origins of the Nuba genocide was its conclusion. The 1992 campaign failed, due entirely to internal factors within Sudan. International pressure or intervention played no role. What followed was a nasty internal war, marked by gross human rights abuses, including killing, rape, and the destruction of villages, and in turn an incomplete and fragile peace. At the time of writing, the relative peace that the Nuba enjoyed for nine years following the 2002 cease-fire has vanished, and the area is once again the location of a nasty war that threatens humanitarian disaster and serious human rights violations.

Eyewitness Accounts

Account 1: Mek Defan Arno Kepi

Mek Defan Arno Kepi was son of a famous Otoro chief and an important community leader in his own right (mek is a chiefly title). He lived in Eri, on the southwestern slopes of the Otoro hills. He was interviewed by this author (Alex de Waal) author on May 22, 1995 at Tira Limon in the SPLA-held areas of the mountains. His testimony illustrates the massacres committed by military intelligence officers in reprisal for the SPLA entry into the Nuba Mountains early in the war.

In July 1988 many sheikhs and omdas [district administrative chief] in the Nuba Mountains were called for a conference in Kadugli. When we were summoned, we were afraid. The SPLA had come among us, and we were hiding the SPLA in our area. The Governor, Abdel Rasoul el Nur, had warned us that he will deal with anyone who has SPLA in his area.

We were already fed up with our treatment from the government. Some sheikhs had already been killed—in that year they had already killed Sheikh Habil Ariya, Sheikh Adam Khidir and Sheikh Tamshir Umbashu, and two other sheikhs, I can't remember their names. Many others had been arrested. Two of our villages had already been burned: Kelpu was the first, destroyed by the Murahaliin, and Shawri the second, destroyed by the army.

We were 36 sheikhs and omdas who went, and one teacher. We were from all parts. Twelve were from Kadugli itself. We were seven from Otoro. Three were from Rashad and Delami, two from Shatt Safiya, two from Shatt Damam. There was only one from Moro, as the Moro people were very suspicious. Others were from Abri and other places. I also went with money to buy some goods for my shop while I was there. But we were all arrested and taken to prison. They took from me 46,000 Sudanese pounds and the clothes, blankets, watches and things I had bought for my shop.

I spent 59 days in prison. Colonel Ahmed Khamis was responsible for our interrogation there. Another one who was responsible is Sheikh Ismail Dana, he was sheikh of Debi but he became a government informer in Kadugli.

While we were in prison, some of us were taken out at night, and killed. A group of seventeen was taken. Ours was the second group, numbering six. We were taken to a place near Katcha at about 11 p.m. by a group of soldiers. There were six of them, plus the driver.

We were tied with our hands behind us, and lined up, with our backs to the soldiers. They were close, some ten meters away. Ahmed Khamis was supervising the procedure. Then they shot us—ta-ta-ta-ta-ta-ta. Immediately, with automatic guns. I was hit here [in the back of the head] and the bullet exited here [through the jaw]. I fell on my face. My face was all blood. I fell but I didn't die. I knew that if I made any move, they will come and finish me off. I heard more shots as they were poking about, finishing off the others. While I heard this final shooting I pretended to be dead. The soldiers came and kicked me with their boots. They even stood on me with their boots. I held my breath and just pretended to be dead.

One said, "This one is not yet dead." The other said, "Let's leave him, he's dead." The first fellow was not convinced and shot at me with a pistol. The bullet fell just in front of my face on the left side. The one who shot at me personally was [corporal] Ahmed Gideil, who is half Shawabna and half Arab.

They went back to their lorry. I heard the door shut and the engine start, and the sound of it driving away. When the sound of the lorry died away, I got up, to a sitting position. Because I was tied with my hands behind my back, I cleaned the blood from my face by wiping my face on my knees. I looked around and found that all my colleagues were dead. Then I left. I walked for a long distance in the wilderness until I found a small hut, all on its own, in the fields. I called out, "Salaam alekum." I said, "You people inside, come out and help me. Don't be afraid when you see me, I am a Nuba like you."

A woman looked out. She was frightened and went back inside and spoke to her husband, "There is someone outside who seems to have been knifed."

When the man came out he was also frightened and about to run away. I told him, "Please don't run, I am a Nuba like you."

He asked, "Which Nuba [tribe] are you?"

I said, "I am a Nuba from Eri."

He said, "Then why are you here?"

I said, "I was brought by the army and shot."

He said, "Are the shots we heard earlier this evening the ones you are talking about?"

I said, "Yes."

He said, "The army comes every night and shoots people in this place. The smell of the dead bodies is disturbing us and we cannot even stay here."

I said to him, "I do not want anything from you except for you to come and untie my hands." Which he did.

I thanked the man and said, "As far as you have freed my hands, now I will not die." Because the ropes were very tight and painful, the blood was not moving in my veins. The blood even burst one vein [higher up] on my left arm.

The farmer immediately took me to his sheikh. The sheikh said, "It is better that you stay here with us for ten days, and we look for medicine. Then we can take you back to your own people." But after four days, the sheikh came and said they had received a message from the army in Kadugli, saying that they had shot six but only found five [bodies], and if the one who is alive is being kept hidden in your villages, we are coming to burn all the villages in your area.

I told the sheikh, "I cannot be the cause of all your villages being burned and you being killed. Take me away. Throw me into any forest and I will see what will happen to me."

They took me that night to the bush. It was August and it was raining. I spent four days in the bush, eating only dust mixed with water. Some of this would go inside, down my throat, and some would spill outside, because my jaw was open [on account of the bullet wound]. After four days I reached Eri. I was already exhausted. I had no energy to walk all this way. Since we had been in prison we had been underfed—we were given just one [piece of] bread every day, and you eat one third for breakfast, one third for lunch and one third for supper, with only water.

I arrived in Eri and found my family. They did not recognize me. When I called my mother, she said, "Who is that who is calling me like that, in a strange voice?" By that time, the damage to my tongue and my jaw had disturbed my speech.

I said, "It is your son, Defan." My daughter recognized my voice. After they recognized me, they came to me crying.

I said, "Don't cry, I am already with you." I immediately asked my wife and daughter, "Did any soldiers come here?"

They said, "Yesterday there were three soldiers in the house, two on the veranda and one patrolling around the house." When I heard this I went immediately to the SPLA camp in the mountains, to Juma Kabbi.

After I left the house, eight soldiers came to the house. I left a message with my family not to tell anyone of my whereabouts. Messages had come from Kadugli to the police post that they had to find me.

My wound has healed. But even today I cannot eat proper food, I can only take soup and other liquids.

Account 2: Fawzia

Fawzia (not her real name) was a seventeen-year-old Otoro girl from a village south of Kauda, who spent three months in Mendi garrison "peace camp." Her voice was very quiet and she held her head in her hands throughout the interview. Her village was attacked at dawn on January 31, 1995. She was interviewed by the author in Kauda in the SPLA-held areas of the Nuba Mountains on May 12, 1995, the day after she escaped from the garrison.

Very early in the morning the enemy came and surrounded the whole village. Our family has two compounds—they took sixteen people from just our family. The soldiers said, "You will come with us to Mendi. If you refuse, you will be killed."

When we had all been gathered, we had no alternative but to go with them so we started to move with the soldiers. We were carrying bags of clothes—the soldiers took all the good clothes, leaving us just with the rags. They gathered us under a tree for the morning, with no food and no water, while they were burning the houses. It took three-and-a-half or four hours. All the houses and most of the furniture were burned. They took cows and goats in large numbers, I don't know the total. They looted the best furniture and other possessions. By the end of the morning we were about 25 women and girls under that tree.

After finishing their operation at midday, the soldiers started making us walk to Mendi. I was made to carry a bed. The sixteen of us were all carrying things looted from people's houses, like big dishes, plates, cups, and so on. On the way they said, "Something you have never seen before—you will see it in Mendi."

When we arrived in Mendi, we were taken to the garrison. All the looted properties were put in one place. The people were then divided. The older women were taken to one place, adult women who had one or two children were taken to another place, and unmarried girls were taken to another place. Before we were divided up, the officer said to us, "Now you have reached here, every one of you will be married. If any one of you refuses, you will be killed." Then we were given a small amount of flour to cook and told, "When you are married you will have enough food to eat."

Five of the women were already married. Three of them I knew: Khaltuma, Nura and Zeinab [not their real names]. Two of them I didn't know. Those of us who were still unmarried, the soldiers came in the morning and told us to work, carrying heavy things. Then they demanded sex. Those who refused to have sex were treated badly; they were forced to carry heavy things all day. In the evening, we were brought back to our place in the military camp to sleep. After dark, the soldiers came and took the girls to their rooms, and raped them. I was taken and raped, but I refused to be "married" to any of them. The girls who were "married" were treated better—they stayed in the rooms of their "husbands." But, when the soldier is transferred, the woman stays behind, whether she has a child by the soldier or not. I saw some women who were remaining behind, but I don't know their names.

When you have been taken, the soldier who has taken you will do what he wants, then he will go out of the room, you will stay, and another one will come. It continues like this. There is different behavior. Some lady, if she is raped by four or five soldiers, she will cry from pain. Then, if the soldiers are good, they will leave her. But others will beat her to keep her quiet, and they will carry on.

Every day the raping continued. It continued during the daytime and at night. My sister Leila [names have been changed], aged thirteen, was raped. My father's second wife, Asia, was raped. They wanted to rape my father's third wife, Naima, but she was heavily pregnant and she objected, and in the end nothing happened to her. Another lady, Umjuma, who has six children, was also raped.

It is impossible to count the men who raped me. It was continuous. Perhaps in a week I would have only one day of rest. Sometimes one man will take me for the whole night. Sometimes I will be raped by four or five men per day or night; they will just be changing one for another.

We were made to work. There were different types of work. Some of us were made to go to the garrison to clean the compound, the rooms and the offices. Sometimes we were sent to Ngurtu, which is one-and-a-half hours away, to bring sorghum. When we are carrying sorghum, each lady would carry two tins.

Older women with children were also made to work. Then, afterwards, they had to prepare food for their children. These women were taken to the peace camp, where they also had to build their own houses. All women, whether they have children or not, are given the same ration, of one cup of sorghum for breakfast and supper. So they worked for money or food. If there was no work available, they are forced to become prostitutes, so that they can get something to feed to their children. Many women were forced to sell themselves for money.

No clothes were distributed to us. But any soldier can bring clothes and use them as a bribe or a payment for sex. The only water in Mendi is from hand pumps that are just outside the garrison, about five or seven minutes' walk away. The women go with guards to collect water. On the way, or when women are going outside to collect firewood, the guards are saying, "Why are you talking about going back to the Anyanya

[SPLA]? Life here for you is comfortable. So don't refuse if one wants to marry you or sleep with you."

I did not see any people who had been in the peace camp for a long time. People are taken somewhere else after a while. But we heard that there are other peace camps where people stay for a long time.

Three men were taken from our village. One was carrying a bicycle on the way to Mendi. When we were inside, they were taken straight to the PDF for training. We never saw them again. Inside the town, men and women are completely separated. There is a school which teaches the Islamic religion only. All the Christians who are taken there become Muslims. There were some Christians with our group, and when we reached Mendi, they went to pray under a tree. The soldiers went and called them and said, "Don't repeat this. There can be no Christian prayers. There are only Muslims here." But the Christian women objected, and prayed again. The soldiers called again, and gave them a threat, "If you pray again you will be killed." The Christians didn't pray after that, but they also did not go to the mosque.

There is a hospital, but it was not for us. There is no medicine if you become sick. I stayed there three-and-a-half months, but I never saw any pregnant woman. It is unusual. Perhaps there were some at the early stages, before the stomach becomes big.

[By May 11, Fawzia had reached her limit of endurance. She knew the penalty of being caught while escaping, but took her chances.]

Yesterday, at 5 p.m., I thought about escaping. I talked to my younger sister Leila. I told her, "Let us escape."

My sister said, "How?"

I said, "We will try, God will help."

I told my sister, "Go to the hand pump as though you are going to bathe. After that, we will escape, because when you are bathing, you will not be monitored too much."

I went ahead with the bucket, my sister was to follow. But she delayed, and so I decided to go alone. I entered the bush there as though I was taking a bath, and escaped.

Account 3: Ahmed

Ahmed (not his real name) was a student from Nyima in the northern part of the Nuba Mountains, who went home during the summer vacation in 1992. His testimony, taken by a Nuba activist in Cairo in 1992, was one of the earliest first-hand accounts of the campaign in the Nuba Mountains.

There was a concentrated offensive on Wali, Tima, Katla and Julud [areas within the Nuba Mountains]. Nyimang was also attacked at the same time, and many people were killed in that area. The Tendiya and Salara people emigrated. Those who escaped are in the peace camp at Angarko, south of Dilling. There are about 3,500 people there, most of them women and old men. I spent ten days in Angarko looking for my relatives. The basic necessities are not there, the only food is sorghum distributed by the National Islamic Front youth organization, *Shabab al Watan* [literally, Youth of the Nation]. There is no grinding machine to pound the sorghum grains into flour, so people can only boil and eat it. This is causing many stomach problems and some people died. There is no health service. Most people were nearly naked.

They said the PDF had come and burned their villages and forced them to leave. Many were killed, they said. In fact, I saw lorries going from Dilling to el Obeid, and others coming from Kadugli bringing people from the southern areas.

I saw one mosque; inside they teach 360 children between the ages of four and eight. They are training the children so that they will become Mujahadiin.

The largest camp is Sheikan, which is fifty kilometers south of el Obeid. There are about fifteen thousand people there, including five thousand children. Many children are being taught in the *khalwa* [Koranic school] and trained to be Mujahidiin. People there are also suffering. In one day they buried 34 corpses. Most of the deaths were because of poor food—they give one quarter of a *malwa* [bowl] per day only. Only the *Shabab al Watan* are allowed in the camp, others are prevented.

People are transferred in trucks originally designed for cattle. They are trucks with trailers, with extended high sides. They stop sometimes for water, but people are not allowed off the truck to drink. Also the people are naked and don't want to get down naked. The transfer of people from these camps has started.

Dead bodies are an ordinary sight in these camps, and in el Obeid. Sometimes dogs will bring human parts to the house. The dogs have developed a taste for human flesh—there was one case where dogs attacked a living person who was lying under a tree. In Um Heitan, even the chickens are turning savage. Death is now something normal in the Nuba Mountains.

Account 4. Kaka

Kaka (not her real name), a farmer, is in her mid- to late fifties. She was born in Kadar, Kauda in the Nuba Mountains. She is a member of the

Toro tribe. The interview was conducted by Samuel Totten in January 2011. In this excerpt of the longer interview Kaka speaks about the abject hunger that she, her family, and fellow Nuba Mountains people suffered beginning in 1990 as a result of the Sudan government attacks on their villages.

When the government attacked us they burned down the entire village. Many of the homes had sorghum stored inside so the starving became great. Most of the tukuls had been burned, only here and there were tukuls still standing, not destroyed.

At night we made our way to Kujur and then on to Kadhar. It took us all night and into the morning. Even as we fled through the night we were shot at by the troops. There were no enemies in Kadhar and there were also caves there where we hid. We remained in Kadhar, in the caves, for one month. We remained there one month because the government remained in our area one month.

There were many, many people in those caves. All of the people from Kauda, between maybe 300 to 500, were up there.

When the government attacked us they knew we kept our sorghum in our tukuls and that our food supply would be destroyed, but they didn't care because [in actuality] they were targeting human beings, trying to destroy us. The soldiers got orders from the president, Omar al Bashir, to do this because he didn't want black people here.

People had nothing to eat so they had to eat the leaves from trees and roots. The leaves were no good, did not taste good but God gave us the strength to eat the leaves to remain alive.

We didn't just pull the leaves off and eat them, but ground them on a big flat rock, *krara*, and then we boiled it, stirred it up, and ate it. The leaves were still not rough, not fine. We just ate anything. Some people died from eating leaves—their bodies did not accept it as food or the leaves may have been poison[ous]—but we were starving so we ate anything. And if we died or lived it was according to God's plan.

There was a certain type of grass that used to spread [grow along] on the floor [ground], it's called *tirbibila*. We cut all the grass and then we dug the root out. We didn't eat the grass but just the root. We would cut it into small pieces and put the piece in the sun to dry and when it had dried we ground it up into flour. We boiled the water, mixed in the ground root and it became porridge and we took [ate] it when it was warm. It was tasteless. We were only taking [eating] it to be in the stomach.

We did not eat that grass because in the past we used the grass to place on injuries [as a salve], and when we took it in our mouths it was bitter and made the tongue ache.

We never ate that grass in the past but when people began starving they began taking that grass and when they did their tongues began getting big [swollen] and so did their ankles.

We also ate a fruit [*ngotank*], a small, sweet fruit that is plentiful in trees, and *nguebo*, a larger fruit [bigger than an apple, both the outside and inside are soft], which can be eaten from the tree when ripe or when it's not ripe, you pluck it, cut it into pieces, dry it in the sun, ground it and mix it with cool water and drink it.

There was also another grass we ate. It's called *kirthiti*. We plucked the grass, boiled it, and when it got soft we used a branch [to stir the grass and water] to make it more soft and then we drank it like porridge.

We had to go long distances searching for food but we never found enough. Even what we ate was not enough and we got very thin and began suffering greatly.

After we returned to our villages you could see people who were not well, weak, who could not work, not get around. Also, people's throats became swollen, tight, like something was pinching it. People could not swallow food and their tongues got swollen, too. People who suffered in this way plucked pods from a Kura tree and cracked them open and ate the seeds and also placed them in a kirta [a small bowl] with water and soaked them. After they were soaked they drank the water, which was very bitter.

When we returned we found nothing. Everything had been destroyed. My tukul had been burned down completely. Nothing was left.

Notes

1. *Fatwa* issued by religious leaders, Imams of mosques and Sufists of Kordofan State, April 27, 1992. (In some accounts this document is incorrectly dated to 1993.)
2. Interviewed by the BBC in Switzerland, June 13, 1995.

References

African Rights (1995). *Facing genocide: The Nuba of Sudan*. London: Author. Retrieved from: www.justiceafrica.org/publishing/online-books/facing-genocide-the-nuba-of-sudan.

African Rights (1997). *Food and power in Sudan: A critique of humanitarianism*. London: Author. Retrieved from: www.justiceafrica.org/publishing/online-books/food-and-power-in-sudan-a-critique-of-humanitarianism.

Africa Watch (1991). Destroying ethnic identity: The secret war against the Nuba. *News from Africa Watch, 3*(15), 1–13.

Baumann, Gerd (1987). *National integration and local integrity: The Miri of the Nuba Mountains in the Sudan*. Oxford: Clarendon Press.

Bodanski, Youssef (1999). *Bin Laden: The man who declared war on America*. New York: Forum.

de Waal, Alex (2006). Averting genocide in the Nuba Mountains of Sudan. *Social Science Research Council Webforum, How Genocides End*. Retrieved from: http://howgenocidesend.ssrc.org/de_Waal2.

de Waal, Alex, & Abdel Salam, A.H. (2004). Islamism, state power and jihad in Sudan. In Alex de Waal (Ed.) *Islamism and its enemies in the Horn of Africa* (pp. 71–113). Indianapolis, IN: Indiana University Press.

Nadel, Siegfried F. (1947). *The Nuba: An anthropological study of the hill tribes of Kordofan*. Oxford: Oxford University Press.

Sontag, Susan (1975, February 6). Fascinating facism. *New York Review of Books, 22*(1). Retrieved from: www.nybooks.com/articles/archives/1975/feb/06/fascinating-fascism.

Souverijn-Eisenberg, Paula (2005). Lessons learned from the Joint Military Commission, United Nations Department of Peacekeeping Operations, Peacekeeping best practices section. Retrieved from: www.peacekeepingbestpractices.unlb.org/PBPS/Library/JMC%20 Lessons%20Learned%20sum%20_past%20tense_26Aug.pdf.

Stevenson, Roland C. (1984). *The Nuba people of South Kordofan Province*. Khartoum: University of Khartoum Graduate Publications.

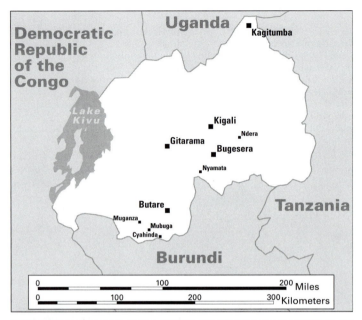

Map 13.1 Rwanda

CHAPTER **13**

The 1994 Genocide of the Tutsi of Rwanda

GERALD CAPLAN

Introduction

During 100 days in 1994, between 500,000 and 1,000,000 Rwandan Tutsi were systematically slaughtered in the swiftest genocide of modern times. Unlike many other atrocities, the deliberate, systematic attack against the country's Tutsi minority unambiguously fulfilled the definition of genocide as set down in the United Nations 1948 Convention on the Prevention and Punishment of the Crime of Genocide. Even worse, as indicated by the title of the report of the International Panel appointed by the Organization of African Unity to investigate the tragedy, Rwanda was *the preventable genocide.*

The title "preventable genocide" referred specifically to the events in the country around 1994. On the one hand, it is possible to isolate the key developments that led step by step from the earliest colonial period in Rwanda to the genocide a full century later. On the other, there was nothing inevitable about this process. At its heart was the deliberate choice of successive elites, both internal and external, to deepen the cleavages between the country's two main ethnic groups, the Hutu and the Tutsi, to dehumanize the group out of power, and to legitimate the use of violence against that group.

Before Independence

All history is open to interpretation, and conflicting interpretations can have major consequences. Rwanda is one such case. Broadly speaking, there is a Hutu and a Tutsi version of history that each has developed and exploited over the past century in its own interest. Foreign scholars have often reflected this division in their own work.

There are two essential issues in dispute. One is whether the Tutsi are native to Rwanda or relative latecomers, and therefore without the natural entitlements of the native Hutu (few take into account the tiny aboriginal Twa community). The second concerns the nature of Hutu–Tutsi relations prior to Rwanda becoming a colony of Europe. In regard to the first, virtually all authorities agree that the Tutsi were in Rwanda by the 15th century, which makes them natives by any rational calculation. As for the second, it serves the interest of some Tutsi to evoke a precolonial golden age of unmitigated harmony in which Tutsi were in charge yet the lines between Tutsi and Hutu were fluid to the point of being inconsequential. The version embraced by some Hutu is of severe ethnic discord going back to a time characterized by extreme brutality exercised by alien Tutsi rulers over ordinary Hutu. There is no reason to expect that these differing interpretations will be reconciled any time soon.

What seems to be largely accepted by all is that it was under *Mwami* (King) Rwabugiri, a Tutsi who ruled during the late 1800s, that certain key characteristics of modern Rwanda were fixed for the next 100 years. A powerful head of a centralized, highly organized state, he provided firm direction to an elaborate series of subordinate structures headed by chiefs and sub-chiefs. Under Rwabugiri, Hutu and Tutsi designations became rather less fluid, and those below the largely Tutsi ruling class were treated with much brutality.

In the colonial era (1889–1962), under German and then Belgian rule, Roman Catholic missionaries, inspired by the overtly racist theories of 19th-century Europe, concocted a bizarre ideology of ethnic cleavage and racial rankings that attributed superior qualities to the country's Tutsi minority. This racist fantasy held that the Tutsi 15% of the population were approaching, however gradually, the exalted level of white people, in contrast with the alleged brutishness and innate inferiority of the "Bantu" (Hutu) majority. Because the missionaries ran the colonial-era schools, these pernicious values were systematically transmitted to several generations of Rwandans along with more conventional Catholic teachings.

The alleged differences between ethnic groups were arbitrary and baseless. Hutu and Tutsi, after all, shared a common language, religion, geography, and, more often than is imagined, appearance. Intermarriage was far from unusual. Yet the ludicrous "Hamitic" proposition—that the Tutsi were descendants of Noah's disgraced son Ham—soon took on a life of its own.

From 1926 through 1932, the Belgian colonial rulers made the *mwami*'s complex structures more rigid and ethnically inflexible. They institutionalized the split between the two groups, culminating in the issuance to every Rwandan of an ethnic identity card. There would be no ethnic ambiguity in colonial Rwanda; all were to know their place. This card system was maintained for over 60 years until, with tragic irony, during the genocide in 1994 it became the instrument that enabled Hutu killers in urban areas to identify the Tutsi who were its original beneficiaries.

While it was to their benefit, the Tutsi elite were only too pleased to believe in their own natural superiority and to run the country for their Belgian patrons. The majority Hutu were treated with the harshness appropriate to a lower caste or an inferior race. Soon many Hutu came to agree that the two ethnic groups, distinguished mostly by vocation in prior centuries, were indeed fundamentally dissimilar in nature and irreconcilable in practice. The Tutsi came to be demonized as a foreign invading power; in other words, colonial settlers with no entitlements in Rwanda.

Once World War II ended in 1945, various African nations, Rwanda, included, demanded their freedom from colonial rule by Europeans and that it be replaced by majority rule. In Rwanda, a national independence movement emerged briefly in the late 1950s, an umbrella under which all citizens (Hutu and Tutsi alike) united to oppose colonial rule. But it failed to thrive in Rwanda. As a result voices of moderation and inclusiveness were drowned out by extremists advocating ethnic exclusivity. The tragedy of Rwanda is that the majority came to be defined by ethnicity alone. Since the Hutu were clearly the majority, they insisted on their right to rule

In their campaign in the late 1950s for an independent Rwanda under Hutu rule—which became known as the "Hutu Revolution"—Hutu politicians had two surprising allies. Both the powerful Catholic Church and the Belgian colonial administration, hitherto the leading proponents of Tutsi supremacy, now abruptly reversed their positions, both taking an active role in promoting the pro-independence, aggressively anti-Tutsi activities of a new generation of Hutu politicians.

This virtually unconditional support continued even when anti-Tutsi violence was organized before and after Rwanda gained its independence from Belgium in 1962. The Belgians, in a classic case of divide-and-rule, had used the Tutsi to run the machinery of colonial government. Many Hutu blamed their harsh treatment not on their Belgian overlords but on their direct Tutsi masters. Prompted by the emerging Hutu political leadership, vengeance was now wreaked on the country's Tutsi minority. In a series of attacks between 1959 and 1967, an estimated 20,000 Tutsi were killed and 300,000 fled in terror to neighboring countries, particularly Burundi, Zaire/Congo, and Uganda. When armed exiled Tutsi counter-attacked in an attempt to restore their rule, the penalty was paid by local Tutsi, who faced fearful retribution that resulted in the massive killing of Tutsi by the new Hutu army.

In the eyes of some Tutsi today, such pogroms constituted either a prelude to genocide or genocide itself. But no serious historian can accept this tendentious interpretation.

The First Rwandan Governments

Grégoire Kayibanda, a Hutu from the south of the country and a leader of the Hutu Revolution, became the first president of independent Rwanda in 1962. Like other Hutu who succeeded in obtaining a western education, Kayibanda had been a student at a Catholic seminary, where he absorbed the pernicious notion of the irreconcilability of Tutsi and Hutu. For him, the Tutsi were an alien race that had arrived in Rwanda belatedly and whose legitimacy in the country was very much in doubt. While he was not ready to cleanse them from his republic, he promoted the anti-Tutsi pogroms that characterized his decade in power.

Kayibanda's new government made its colors apparent from the start. As early as 1961, a United Nations Trusteeship Commission report stated that "the developments of these last 18 months have brought about the racial dictatorship of one party.... An oppressive system has been replaced by another one."

But Kayibanda had little idea how to conduct a modern government. His new all-Hutu administration failed to please even the large majority of their fellow Hutu. Daily life for the peasantry—the overwhelming portion of the population—remained precarious, while a small Hutu elite from the north and northwest grew increasingly dissatisfied with their marginal role in Kayibanda's southern-dominated government.

As pressure on President Kayibanda by aggrieved northern Hutu grew, he unleashed ethnic terror once again, hoping to save his regime by uniting the Hutu against the common Tutsi enemy. At the same time, ethnic cleavages were reinforced, not for the last time, by events south of the border in Burundi. There, unlike Rwanda, following independence from Belgium, the minority Tutsi continued to rule the majority Hutu. In 1972, after an appalling massacre by the Tutsi government of all educated Hutu, terrorized Burundian Hutu flooded into Rwanda, both inflaming ethnic tensions and joining in anti-Tutsi attacks.

But Kayibanda's exploitation of ethnic fears failed to save his regime. In 1973 he was overthrown by Juvénal Habyarimana, head of the Rwandan army, imprisoned, and apparently starved to death. Habyarimana became the new president. For the next 17 years, Rwanda enjoyed relatively good times and little ethnic violence. Habyarimana opened the country to the world and efficient, stable little Rwanda—"the Switzerland of Africa"—soon became a darling of the West's burgeoning development industry. As for the Tutsi, while they still suffered significant institutional discrimination, they were now physically safe for the first time in almost 15 years. They were allowed to play only a marginal role in politics, were largely shut out of the military and public service positions, and were limited by quota to 10% of education placements. Still, they thrived in the private sector and were successful in the liberal professions, including law and management. This naturally reinforced their ambiguous reputation as "the Jews of Rwanda"—a talented entrepreneurial group that could never quite be trusted to be "real" Rwandans.

Rwanda became an overwhelmingly Christian country, with more than 60% of Christians being Catholic. The Catholic Church remained a trusted ally and reliable bulwark of Habyarimana's Hutu-dominated regime, giving it legitimacy and comfort literally until the end of its reign. In common with the foreign governments and aid agencies that befriended Rwanda and its president, Church leaders rarely challenged the ethnic basis of public life or Habyarimana's one-party dictatorship; indeed, they embraced without reservation the notion of demographic democracy based on the Hutu's overwhelming majority.

By the late 1980s, however, economic progress stalled. Government revenues declined with the drop in the price of coffee and tea, Rwanda's two main exports. The World Bank and International Monetary Fund, indifferent to the social and political consequences of their policies, imposed ideologically driven programs that exacerbated inflation, land scarcity, and unemployment. Young men were hit particularly hard. The mood of the country was raw.

Invasion and Civil War

It was at this vulnerable moment, on October 1, 1990, that the adult children of the Tutsi refugees who had earlier fled into English-speaking Uganda reemerged as a rebel army, the Rwandan Patriotic Front (RPF). Thus, conflict-generated refugees led to refugee-generated conflict, with an unimaginable series of consequences.

Exiled Tutsi and their children remained unwelcome back home—a home some had never even seen. According to President Habyarimana, Rwanda was too poor, too crowded and had too little land to accommodate the exiled community—all plausible but provocative propositions. If the exiles who wanted to return were not allowed to do so legally, they figured they would have to find other means.

The RPF invasion of Rwanda in 1990 and the Hutu government's response constituted a giant step on the road to genocide. The RPF was not constrained by the knowledge that incursions by Tutsi exiles in the

1960s had led to great brutality against local Tutsi. As for Habyarimana, he had a choice in October 1990. Contrary to RPF expectations, few Tutsi welcomed these unknown "Ugandan" soldiers. A united front among all Rwandans against outside invaders was entirely possible. But an opportunistic and threatened Habyarimana chose the opposite course; with great deliberation, to further its own self-interest, the government chose to reawaken the sleeping dogs of ethnic division. All Tutsi were now portrayed as alien invaders, while class and regional divisions among Hutu were to be submerged in a common front against the intruders. Anti-Tutsi propaganda, largely muted over the previous 17 years, was unleashed anew. All Tutsi were denounced as fifth columnists, "*inkotanyi*," secret supporters of the RPF.

At the same time, Habyarimana called on his foreign friends for military help. The French, obsessed as ever with their rivalry with "anglo-saxons" in Africa (and since the refugees making up the RFP had been raised and educated in Anglophone Uganda, they were considered "anglo-saxons" by the French), responded most positively. Their forces prevented a swift RPF victory over the hapless Rwandan army, and French soldiers and advisors remained in the country, counseling Habyarimana's people politically and militarily on keeping the English-speaking insurgents from Uganda at bay. France was primarily responsible for ensuring that the Rwandan forces and militias were properly armed and trained. Habyarimana and his cronies learned that, whatever they did, they could count on the unconditional public and private support of the French government.

The impact of the RPF raid was devastating in every way. Its advances, together with government propaganda warning that the Tutsi were bent on restoring their cruel dictatorship, drove terrified Hutu into internal settlement camps. In a short time, close to 300,000 Rwandans, mostly Hutu, had been driven from or had fled their land to become internally displaced persons (IDPs). In early 1993, another large-scale RPF attack led to a further million, mostly Hutu, IDPs. Rwanda was in great turmoil. The ailing economy had little chance to recover. Anti-Tutsi violence, organized by the government or its allies, spread like wildfire, while the RPF insurgents similarly showed little restraint in dealing brutally with Hutu civilians in the areas they "liberated."

Within the Habyarimana government, real power increasingly resided with a small faction of insiders from the northwest called the *Akazu*, "the little house"; it was also widely known as "le Clan de Madame," as its core was comprised of the president's wife, her family members, and close associates, all of whom were the chief beneficiaries of the corruption that characterized the regime. As the economic collapse significantly reduced the available spoils of power and called into question the very legitimacy of the regime, the *Akazu* played the ethnic card with increasing cynicism to divert attention away from serious divisions among the Hutu, in particular the widespread resentment against the northwesterners who virtually controlled the Rwandan government.

This should not be taken to mean that planning of the genocide was initiated at a precise moment. Both physical and rhetorical violence against the Tutsi continued to escalate from the outset of the RPF invasion in 1990 until the genocide actually started in April 1994. Virtually all historians agree that this campaign was organized and planned and that at *some point* it turned into a strategy for genocide. But that exact point remains unknown. For Rwanda, the "smoking gun" that nails the perpetrators and their fanatical plot was not a single meeting or a particular document, but rather a cumulative series of events. While not definitive, the evidence most plausibly suggests that the idea of genocide emerged only gradually through 1991 and 1992, accelerating in determination after the Arusha agreement of 1993 (see below), and into 1994.

Later, after the genocide, a great international argument broke out over who knew what about the events unfolding in Rwanda. But there is little to debate here. The world that mattered to Rwanda—its Great Lakes neighbors, the United Nations, France, Britain, the United States, Belgium, the Vatican—knew exactly what was happening and that it was being masterminded at the highest levels of the state. They knew that this was no senseless case of "Hutu killing Tutsi and Tutsi killing Hutu," as it was sometimes dismissively described. They knew that a terrible fate had befallen Rwanda. They even knew that some Hutu extremists were actually talking openly of eliminating all Tutsi, although few could then conceive that an actual genocide was being plotted.

Anti-Tutsi violence, dormant for 17 years, was revived immediately after the RPF invasion on October 1, 1990, when organized anti-Tutsi massacres began, and ended only when the genocide itself ended in July 1994. Massacres of Tutsi were carried out in October 1990, January 1991, February 1991, March 1992, August 1992, January 1993, March 1993, and February 1994. On each occasion, scores of Tutsi were killed by mobs and militiamen associated with various political parties, sometimes with the involvement of the police and army, incited by the media, promoted by a burgeoning gang of Hutu extremists, directed by local government officials and encouraged by some national politicians.

As the terror heightened, the organizers learned that they could not only massacre large numbers of people quickly and efficiently, they could get away with it. Wholehearted backing of the Habyarimana regime by the French government and general indifference to the escalating racism by the Catholic Church and most of the other smaller

Christian denominations active in Rwanda reinforced this feeling. The general reaction of the West to the massacres was silence, even when exposed by human rights groups. A culture of impunity developed as the conspirators grew bolder. Extremist army officers colluded with the circles surrounding Habyarimana and the *Akazu* to form secret societies and Latin-American-style death squads known as *Amasasu* (bullets) and the "Zero Network."

But contrary forces were at work at the same time. With the end of the Cold War, pressure for democratization from both within and outside the country forced Habyarimana to accept multi-party politics. The apparent advance toward democracy, however, had several unanticipated consequences, all of them unwelcome. A host of new parties emerged, most of them Hutu. One of them, the Coalition for the Defence of the Republic (CDR), represented Hutu radicals and had links to the death squads. What was worse, parties organized their own youth militias, the most notorious being the *Interahamwe* (those who stand together, or those who attack together) formed by Habyarimana's own *Mouvement révolutionnaire nationale pour le développement* (MRND).

At the same time, new hate-propagating media sprang up, most infamously a private radio station calling itself *Radio-Télévision Libre des Mille Collines* (RTLM), which was financed and controlled by the *Akazu* faction. The sophistication and shrewdness of the anti-Tutsi propaganda was remarkable. The Tutsi were characterized as aliens who had no right to be in Rwanda at all (which was the basis of the fraudulent old "Hamitic" argument). At the same time, they were also dehumanized, branded the "other," non-persons, mere *inyenzi*—cockroaches—to be stamped out without mercy. Beyond all this, the Tutsi were purportedly plotting to kill the Hutu. For the Hutu, it was a case of kill or be killed. This multi-pronged propaganda attack proved hard to resist for many ordinary Hutu, as did the collateral benefit of stealing Tutsi cows, shelter, and other valuables.

While his militia terrorized opponents and beat up Tutsi and his radio station incited ethnic hatred and violence, President Habyarimana, with great reluctance, agreed to accept a coalition government. Immediately the newly appointed ministers joined with the Organization of African Unity (OAU) and several African and Western governments to pressure Habyarimana into negotiations with the RPF in Arusha, Tanzania. In August 1993, after long, drawn-out sessions, agreement was reached on a series of key issues. But the Arusha Accords were never implemented. Ultimately, Arusha backfired. The more it appeared that power and the limited spoils of office would have to be shared not only with other Hutu parties but also with the RPF, the more determined the *Akazu* insiders became in their desire to share nothing with anyone.

At almost the same time, a deadly new weapon was unexpectedly delivered from Burundi into the hands of the Rwandan Hutu. In October 1993, unwilling to accept the loss of Tutsi supremacy, Tutsi officers in Burundi assassinated Melchior Ndadaye, a Hutu who had become the country's first democratically elected president. Appalling massacres followed throughout the country. Many Hutu in both countries saw this catastrophe as final proof that power-sharing between Tutsi and Hutu was forever doomed. The Tutsi could never be trusted. The emergence of "Hutu Power" in Rwanda as an explicit and inflammatory organizing concept was the immediate consequence of the Burundi upheaval. Hutu Power meant the total repudiation of the Arusha Accords and any thought of power-sharing with the Tutsi. Large Hutu Power rallies across Rwanda attracted Hutu members of all parties, attesting to the new reality that ethnic solidarity trumped party allegiances. Political life, in these last turbulent months before the genocide, was reorganized strictly around two poles—on the one hand, Hutu extremists, on the other, everyone else—as each party split into a Hutu Power versus moderate faction.

As the conspiracy widened and deepened, so did knowledge of the conspirators' intentions. Virtually everyone in Rwanda associated with the United Nations, the diplomatic community, and human rights groups knew that Hutu extremists had developed death lists, carried out an ever-increasing number of massacres, purchased and stockpiled weapons, and issued threats to opposition politicians. In October 1993, the United Nations Security Council approved a military mission—the UN Assistance Mission to Rwanda (UNAMIR)—to oversee the implementation of the Arusha Accords (see below).

In January 1994, UNAMIR uncovered an apparent high-level *Interahamwe* informant whose revelations led Major-General Romeo Dallaire to send his famous January 11, 1994 "genocide fax" to UN headquarters in New York City: "Jean-Pierre," Dallaire reported, "has been ordered [by the extremist Hutu] to register all Tutsi in Kigali. He suspects it is for their extermination. Example he gave was that in 20 minutes his personnel could kill up to 1000 Tutsi." Dallaire's superiors at the Department of Peacekeeping Operations in the UN replied with the perverse instruction to inform President Habyarimana of this plan and to take no further action. Another opportunity to expose and perhaps end the conspiracy was lost.

When the genocide was finally unleashed only three months later, hours after Habyarimana went down with his plane, the violence, which was carefully organized and systematically coordinated, exploded first in Kigali, and then, progressively, across the country. A clique of extremist Hutu planned to mobilize the Hutu people with the explicit intention of exterminating all Tutsi in the country, including women and children. Many, including most of the foreign diplomats assigned to Rwanda, knew that a great disaster loomed for Rwanda, but few envisaged the possibility that the radicals would resort to outright genocide. It was a prospect simply too monstrous to contemplate. But for the radical Hutu leadership, no other response to their situation any longer seemed adequate.

The External Actors Before the Genocide

Several outside actors carried a heavy responsibility for the events that were now unfolding. Some were guilty of crimes of commission, others crimes of omission. But one way or another, as they had for the entire century, outsiders had great influence on Rwanda's fate, much of it malevolent.

Within Rwanda itself, the Roman Catholic and Anglican Churches and the French government were all active supporters of the Habyarimana government. Church leaders failed to use their unique moral position among the overwhelmingly Christian population to denounce ethnic hatred and human rights abuse. The French government was guilty of the same failure at the political and military levels. France's public backing of the Habyarimana regime constituted a major disincentive for the radicals to make concessions or to think in terms of compromise. At the same time, France continued to provide weapons and to act as senior political and military advisors to the government. The radicals drew the obvious lesson: they could get away with anything.

At the United Nations, the Security Council, led unremittingly by the United States, simply did not care enough about Rwanda to intervene appropriately. Aside from France's interest in Rwanda, there were no economic or strategic interests at play for any of the other members of the UN Security Council. As a result, they simply ignored what was taking place in Rwanda. What makes this betrayal of their responsibility even more intolerable is that the genocide was in no way inevitable. It could have been prevented entirely.

Even then, once it was allowed to begin, the destruction could have been significantly mitigated. What was required, military experts agree, was a relatively modest international military force, perhaps 5,000 properly trained troops, with a strong mandate to enforce, not merely monitor, the Arusha power-sharing agreements. Nothing of the kind was authorized by the Security Council before the genocide erupted, and the truncated force left in Rwanda during the 100 days was incapable of serious intervention.

In October 1993 UNAMIR was established, notable mostly for its weak Chapter VI mandate (peacekeeping versus peace enforcement) and minimal capacity. It was to monitor the implementation of the coalition government endorsed at Arusha, but had no mandate to prevent the killing of ordinary people. This constraint made the genocide more likely. The feeble UN effort convinced the Hutu radicals that they had nothing to fear from the outside world, regardless of their deeds. This assessment proved only too accurate. Once the genocide began, the United States, under the forceful leadership of its UN ambassador Madeleine Albright, backed automatically by Britain, repeatedly and deliberately undermined all attempts to strengthen the UN military presence in Rwanda.

Indeed, two weeks into the slaughter, with tens of thousands of lives being lost daily, and ignoring the opposition of the OAU and African governments, Ambassador Albright pushed the Security Council to cut the UN force by 90% at the exact moment it needed major reinforcement. For most of the 100 days of the genocide, General Dallaire commanded a force of only 400 soldiers, many of them inadequately trained or equipped. As horror stories accelerated week by week, the Security Council finally authorized a stronger mission, UNAMIR II, but once again the United States did all in its power to undermine its effectiveness. In the end, not a single reinforcement of soldiers or weapons reached UNAMIR before the genocide was ended by the victory of the RPF rebels in the civil war.

The Genocide

The two rockets that brought down President Habyarimana's plane on the evening of April 6 1994 became the catalyst for one of the great calamities of our age: a genocide and a civil war, separate but simultaneous. To this day, controversy reigns over the responsibility for this attack. Many experts believe the finger most plausibly points to Habyarimana's extremist allies, adamantly opposed to sharing power and spoils with the RPF as agreed at Arusha and openly threatening the President's life. Some, like British authority Linda Melvern, suspect the French might have cooperated with the plotters (Melvern, 2009). Others, including several historians, a French judge, and various genocide deniers, have insisted the RPF leadership was responsible, though without persuasive evidence for this counter-intuitive charge. A 2010 report by a Rwandan "Committee of Experts," followed by a 2012 report by a second French judge, together make a compelling case that the RPF could not have been responsible and that Hutu insiders alone could have fired the deadly rockets. This sensible conclusion will never satisfy genocide deniers; whether it will be accepted by reputable doubters is too early to know.

A certain chaos reigned for the few days following the shooting down of the president's plane, although the conspirators had control enough to begin the immediate and systematic search-and-murder missions against their leading opponents, both moderate Hutu and Tutsi. Soon enough, all sense of uncertainty ended. The government's military structure that had been expanding since 1990 was now utilized to execute the genocide as well as to fight a civil war. It was apparent that its creators had an overall strategy that they implemented with scrupulous planning and organization. It consisted of the control of the levers of government, highly motivated soldiers and militia, the tools to mobilize hundreds of thousands of ordinary Hutu, the capacity to identify and kill the victims, the means to kill vast numbers of people, and tight control of the media (specifically RTLM radio) to disseminate the ringleaders' messages both inside and outside the country.

Together, military leaders and the new interim government of Hutu Power supporters, which was sworn in after the plane crash, made the overall decisions, while Rwanda's elaborate governing structure—a carefully designed top-down administrative and political hierarchy ranging from the president himself on down through several levels to every hill or neighborhood in the country—implemented the genocide with remarkable efficiency. Local conditions also mattered. The Hutu leadership of the Catholic and Anglican Churches, with courageous exceptions, played a conspicuously treacherous role in these months, often directly complicit in aiding the *genocidaires*, at best remaining silent or explicitly neutral. This stance was interpreted by ordinary Christians as an implicit endorsement of the killings, as was the close association of church leaders with the leaders of the genocide. Perhaps this helps explain the greatest mystery about the genocide: the terrible success of Hutu Power in making so many ordinary people accomplices in genocide.

When the genocide ended little more than 100 days later, between 500,000 to as many as 1,000,000 women, children, and men, the vast majority of them Tutsi, lay dead. Thousands more were raped, tortured, and maimed for life. Women and children were not spared. Victims were treated with sadistic cruelty and suffered unimaginable agony. Thousands of moderate Hutu, those who had refused to cooperate with the Hutu Power radicals, had been systematically murdered.

This was very much a populist genocide. The calculated propaganda and mobilization worked only too effectively. To date, scholars disagree on anything like exact numbers, but it seems no fewer than 250,000 and perhaps as many as 750,000 Hutu were active participants in the genocide. Whatever the real number, the leaders could not have waged as efficient a slaughter as they did without such mass support.

As with other genocides, it is difficult to establish the exact numbers killed in Rwanda. The highest persuasive figure for Tutsi killed seems to be near one million, the very lowest perhaps half a million. Government spokespeople often use the phrase "more than a million." More research is needed to be certain. Even if the most conservative figure of 500,000 is used, it still means that over three-quarters of the entire population registered as Tutsi were systematically killed in just over 100 days. As well, millions of Rwandan Hutu became internally displaced within the country or fled in record-breaking numbers to become refugees in neighboring countries, above all Tanzania and Zaire/Congo.

The World During the Genocide

Until the day the genocide ended with the RPF's military victory, the UN, the governments of the United States, France, and Belgium, most African governments, and the Organization of African Unity all failed to describe the events in Rwanda officially as full-blown genocide and all continued to recognize members of the *genocidaire* government as legitimate, official representatives of Rwanda. All except the French government remained publicly neutral between a government that was executing the genocide and their RPF adversaries, the only force fighting that government.

Throughout the genocide, France supported the extremist genocidal government and remained openly hostile to the RPF. In mid-June, two months into the genocide, the French government, in a so-called humanitarian mission known as Operation Turquoise, shamefully endorsed by the Security Council, sent a well-equipped force to save what it could of their Hutu friends' preserve. In doing so, it created a safe zone in the southwest of the country, and while it may have saved the lives of 10,000–15,000 Tutsi, it jeopardized the lives of many others by giving them a false sense of security. Far more consequentially, as the RPF advanced, large numbers of *genocidaires* escaped to the safe zone and were then permitted by the French force to cross the border into eastern Zaire. Here they joined fellow *genocidaires* who had escaped through other routes, all of them ready to resume their war against the new Rwandan government formed by the RPF. As will be seen, this act was to have staggering consequences for the entire Great Lakes region of Africa.

The facts are not in question: A small number of major actors could have prevented, halted, or reduced the slaughter. This included France in Rwanda itself; the United States at the UN Security Council, loyally supported by Britain; Belgium, whose troops were withdrawn from the UN military mission with catastrophic consequences after 10 Belgian soldiers were murdered by Rwandan troops; and Rwanda's church leaders, perhaps including the Pope, had they demanded their followers to stop the killing. In the bitter words of General Dallaire, commander of UNAMIR, "the international community has blood on its hands."

In the years since, the leaders of the UN, the United States, Belgium, and the Anglican Church have all apologized for their failure to stop the genocide. Yet none has suggested that Rwanda is owed restitution for these failures, and in no single case has any responsible individual resigned in protest or been held to account for his or her actions. Neither the French government nor the Roman Catholic hierarchy (including the late Pope John Paul II) has ever apologized or accepted responsibility for its role in the genocide.

After the Genocide

Genocide never ends when the killing is ended. In a multiplicity of ways its consequences continue to be felt for years, decades, or generations. Much of Rwandan life today, and that of the entire Great Lakes region of Africa, is a product of the 100 days of genocide.

Reconciliation and Justice

When the civil war and the genocide ended on July 18, 1994, the situation in Rwanda was indescribably grim. Rarely had a people anywhere had to face so many seemingly insuperable obstacles with so few resources. Their physical and psychological scars are likely to linger for decades.

The country was wrecked, a wasteland. Of seven million inhabitants before the genocide, as many as 15% were dead, two million were internally displaced and another two million had become refugees. Many of those who remained had suffered horribly. Large numbers had been tortured and wounded. Many women had been raped, tortured, and humiliated, some becoming infected with HIV. Of the children who survived, 90% had witnessed bloodshed or worse. An entire nation was brutalized and traumatized. They were, in their own words, "the walking dead." Yet killers and survivors had no alternative but to resume living side-by-side on Rwanda's thousand hills.

This was the situation a new, inexperienced government had to confront. Its challenges were monumental and its strategies not always convincing. Although it has always called itself a government of national unity and included many prominent Hutu in high-profile offices, some believe real power in the land—political and military—has been exercised by a small group of the original "RPF Tutsi," the English-speakers from Uganda. Paul Kagame, leader of the RFP forces during the civil war and genocide, and vice-president and minister of defense until he became president in 2000, has always been the government's indispensable, if deeply controversial man. Today he can boast of his wholehearted friendship with many powerful business, political and religious leaders in the western world, yet many academics and human rights advocates, led perhaps by the late Alison des Forges of Human Rights Watch, consider him a ruthless dictator and even a mass murderer.

More balanced observers are awed by the country's almost miraculous post-genocide transformation over the past 18 years, but are disturbed by the continuing absence of a democratic political culture.

For some, Rwanda since 1994 has been a case of a government that was not trusted by its people and a people not trusted by its government. Under the circumstances, neither is surprising. A major insurgency into northwestern Rwanda by *genocidaires* based in the Democratic Republic of the Congo caused havoc through the late 1990s. The government, suspicious of all Hutu, responded with brute force, frequently failing to distinguish between *genocidaires* and ordinary peasants. In turn, Hutu who remained in Rwanda were reinforced in their belief that the RPF government was not theirs.

As with all societies in transition from tyranny and terror, among an endless host of problems that continue to bedevil Rwanda have been extremely complex questions and dilemmas of justice, guilt, and reconciliation. In the insightful words of scholar Mahmood Mamdani,

> The Tutsi want justice above all else and the Hutu want democracy above all else. The minority fears democracy. The majority fears justice. The minority fears that the demand for democracy is a mask for finishing an unfinished genocide. The majority fears the demand for justice is a minority ploy to usurp power forever. (Mamdani, 1996, p. 11)

Critics contend that the RPF will never allow the Hutu majority to regain control of the government out of a fear that they would then attempt to "finish the work" of 1994. Others consider this a perfectly legitimate fear. In the past decade the government and president have both faced elections, which they won handily, though some insist that the process was flawed.

Since hundreds of thousands of ordinary Rwandans had followed their leaders and actively participated in the 100 days of genocide, Rwanda faced an unprecedented situation in the aftermath: How to mete out justice. Largely to atone for its guilt, the UN Security Council set up an International Criminal Tribunal for Rwanda (ICTR) in Arusha, Tanzania, aimed at trying "the big fish." Rwanda itself resurrected the conventional judicial structure, wholly destroyed during the genocide, while adding a grass-roots institution known as *gacaca* (see below). In all of these, the process of trying accused *genocidaires* has been long, complicated, and frustrating. But if there are more effective ways to deal with this issue, they are not readily apparent.

The ICTR has been a source of controversy from its inception. Even its proponents have difficulty justifying its huge budget—since 1995, over $2 billion has been earmarked for its work. As of Spring 2012, after more than 17 years of work, the court has completed only 69 cases, convicted 59 while acquitting 10 others; 17 of the convicted have appealed their sentences. Nine of the most wanted men from 1994 remain at large, as do many hundreds of lesser fugitives.

Nevertheless, even within this seemingly derisory number, the ICTR's achievements are notable, even groundbreaking. The court interpreted the definition of genocide as presented ambiguously in the 1948 Convention for the Prevention and Punishment of Genocide, and used it to convict those guilty of genocide. In the Akayesu case it defined the crime of rape as a crime against humanity and, under certain conditions, as genocide. It convicted, for the first time, a leader of a government for the crime of genocide (Jean Kambanda). It ruled that the media can be a tool of genocide for which those in charge are responsible, even if they never themselves kill anyone. And it convicted Theoneste Bagosora, the man widely considered the ringleader of the *genocidaires*.

In Rwanda, a totally decimated judicial system had the responsibility for dealing with some 130,000 Hutu rotting in prisons in appalling circumstances, often without proper charges. The task defied capacity. When, in 2004, only some 6,500 had been tried, new measures were urgently needed. At this rate, it was estimated, it would take between two and four centuries to clear the backlog. The government resorted to two dramatic steps. To the chagrin of the genocide survivors' umbrella organization, Ibuka, the government released some 20,000 of those charged with lesser crimes or for whom no credible documentation existed.

Beyond that, it embarked on one of the most remarkable social-legal experiments of our time: local courts called *gacaca*, an attempt to blend traditional precolonial and contemporary mechanisms to expedite the justice process while promoting reconciliation. To clear the enormous backlog of cases, 11,000 *gacaca* courts were appointed, each made up of 19 locally elected judges. A staggering 170,000 Rwandans were trained for their roles. After some years of fine-tuning, the system was launched in 2005.

From the first, some human rights advocates were concerned that these grass-roots courts would operate as a kind of mob justice, with no properly trained professionals and no capacity to adhere to international standards. Yet most observers felt there was little practical alternative and began watching the *gacaca* panels with much interest. One unanticipated consequence was the naming of large numbers of new suspects, whose cases then had to be examined. Upon the conclusion of the *gacaca* process, some 1.5 million cases will have been tried. As in all things Rwandan, great controversy revolves around its success. Why were Tutsi accused of crimes during the genocide not tried? Has justice been done? Did the courts help or undermine the cause of reconciliation?

The Rwandan government believes the *gacaca* trials have been an unmitigated success, and a number of independent authorities more or less agree. Others are far more critical, even arguing that the reconciliation process has been set back. The best independent scholarship to date strongly suggests that the overall assessment of this bold experiment is far more positive than otherwise.

In the meantime, questions of justice and reconciliation, perplexing in any post-conflict situation, let alone a genocide, will remain to bedevil official actions and popular expectations. The government has created a series of structures and institutions designed to foster reconciliation and unity, but on its own terms. For example, the government has asserted that ethnicity can no longer be recognized except as a destructive aberration of the past. Furthermore, it has mandated that there can only be one identity—Rwandan—and any attempt to resurrect old ethnic issues is pounced on as unacceptable "divisionism." Essentially, that means citizens are no longer supposed to refer to themselves as Tutsi or Hutu. The government argues this is the only way to forge a united people. To its opponents, in and out of the country, it is merely a convenient excuse to suppress legitimate democratic opposition. The annual weeks-long commemoration of the genocide, some observe, concentrates solely on Tutsi victims, arguably implying that all Hutu were complicit.

The Regional Consequences of the Genocide

While these questions absorbed Rwandans internally, beyond its borders the genocide had created another monumental crisis. By the end of the 100 days, two million citizens had fled the conflict in every direction— more than 500,000 east to Tanzania, more than 250,000 south to Burundi, and, most dramatically, perhaps 1.2 million west to the eastern Kivu region of Zaire (now the Democratic Republic of the Congo, or DRC). As the fighting and genocide drew to a close, thanks to France's Operation Turquoise much of the Hutu leadership and many of the troops and militia behind the genocide had escaped from Rwanda into eastern Zaire, where they had a friendly dictator in charge and unlimited access to weapons.

The international media had first ignored, then largely misinterpreted the genocide as nothing more than another example of African savagery;

now they made the Kivu refugee camps a universal *cause célèbre*. Foreign aid and foreign aid workers flooded in, vastly more than went to Rwanda itself. Unfortunately, the *genocidaire* army and the *Interahamwe* militia had almost completely taken over the camps and were benefiting enormously from the work of the humanitarian community; genuine refugee needs could be met only when the NGOs finished meeting the demands of the military controlling the camps.

The goals of Hutu Power were transparent and well-known to everyone involved in dealing with the Kivu crisis: to overthrow the new RPF-led government in Kigali and return to power to "finish their work" of killing all remaining Tutsi. Almost immediately the Hutu began raids back into Rwanda, providing yet another major emergency for the new Rwandan rulers to deal with. Repeated demands from the new government of Rwanda for the international community to disarm the killers went nowhere. Once again, the leaders of the UN Security Council badly failed Rwanda.

The consequences for Africa itself of such international inaction were largely foreseeable and wholly disastrous. The post-genocide Rwandan government had long made it abundantly clear that it would not continue to tolerate the use of the camps in Zaire as launching pads for the *genocidaires'* return to Rwanda. By late 1996, the new government had had enough. Under the flag of an alliance of anti-Mobutu Zairians headed by the dissolute Laurent Kabila, and with the active support of Uganda, the RPF-led Rwandan army launched a vicious attack on the entire complex of Kivu camps in October and November. The cost in human life was enormous and a flood of refugees swarmed back into Rwanda. At the same time, substantial numbers of camp dwellers fled deeper into Zaire. Many of these were genuine refugees, some were *Interahamwe*, and some were members of Habyarimana's army, known as ex-FAR. Led by the new Rwandan army organized around the victorious RPF forces, the anti-Mobutu alliance pursued them all ruthlessly, killing large numbers including women and children. In the process they perpetrated atrocious human rights abuses whose actual magnitude is still not known. But the military action soon spread far beyond eastern Zaire. The emboldened anti-Mobutu alliance, still led by the Rwandan army and bolstered by the forces of Uganda, Angola, and Burundi, now set its sights on Mobutu himself. Within nine months, Mobutu fled and Kinshasa fell to the rebels. But there was to be no happy ending to the saga. Kabila, the new president of the re-christened Democratic Republic of the Congo, soon clashed with his Rwandan advisors, and in July 1998, little more than a year after they had helped him become president, Kabila threw the Rwandan and Ugandan military out of the DRC.

Within days, both armies returned to the Congo as an enemy force. The second Congo war in two years now began, but almost immediately escalated to continental dimensions. It became Africa's first great war. Directly or indirectly, more than a fifth of all African governments or armies from across the continent were involved, as well as perhaps a dozen or more armed groups. The alliances between and among these groups, with their varied and conflicting interests, were bewildering. Kabila's major military allies were Zimbabwe, Angola, and Namibia; facing them were the Rwandans, Ugandans, and Burundians. The situation was further endlessly complicated by the DRC's enormous mineral resources, an irresistible lure for governments, rogue gangs, warlords, and powerful foreign corporations alike, and by the continuing problem of arms proliferation sponsored by governments throughout the world as well as a multitude of unscrupulous private hustlers.

One year after the new war began, a cease-fire agreement and peace process was signed, but the cease-fire was repeatedly violated. In 2000 the Security Council sent a small peacekeeping mission (MONUC) to the Congo. Despite the deployment of MONUC, the violence continued. MONUC had little capacity, and, it sometimes seemed as though it had little will to deal with the complex realities on the ground. While most of the DRC remained beyond the control of its government, in eastern Congo full-scale anarchy and terror was unleashed. Rwanda and Uganda found the pursuit of mineral wealth at least as compelling as the destruction of the remaining *Interahamwe* fighters, and fought the DRC army and various armed gangs over these riches. Coltan, a metal ore used in cell phones and computers, previously unknown except to experts, became everyone's favorite plunder. Soon, open warfare broke out between erstwhile allies Uganda and Rwanda over control of territory and resources. As usual, ordinary Congolese were the greatest victims.

Through these years Congolese died in huge numbers. Including those killed in conflict, after being raped and tortured, or by famine and disease, they may now number close to five million (although all statistics are very rough approximations). By all accounts, this constitutes the greatest human-inflicted disaster since World War II. Those directly responsible include the governments of the DRC, Rwanda, and Uganda and an assortment of proxy gangs and warlords all competing for mineral resources. A controversial UN mapping report in 2010 concluded that in at least 104 documented incidents, the Rwandan Patriotic Army (RPA) probably killed "several tens of thousands" of victims in the Congo, the majority of whom were "children, women, elderly people and the sick, who were often undernourished and posed no threat to the attacking forces."

Those indirectly responsible are the Western countries backing the various belligerent governments and the international mining companies whose greed for the Congo's riches knows little restraint. Many have been named in UN investigative reports. What all have in common is a refusal to acknowledge the slightest responsibility.

Laurent Kabila was assassinated in 2001 and replaced by his son, Joseph. By the end of 2002, following extensive peace negotiations, Rwanda and Uganda claimed they had fully withdrawn from the DRC, although their murderous proxy militias remained. A greatly enlarged UN mission (MONUC II) is now deployed in the DRC, but its impact is ambiguous. At the same time, some 8,000–10,000 anti-RPF Rwandan rebels, including the remaining *Interahamwe*, still operate in eastern DRC under the umbrella of the *Forces Démocratique pour la Liberation du Rwanda* (FDLR). Relations between Kabila and Kagame have improved, but various militias and armies maintain low-intensity conflict and the hunt for mineral riches continues. No one knows how or when real stability for eastern DRC will be achieved. Until then, innocent Congolese, above all girls and women, pay the cost in suffering, rape, and death.

Rwanda Today and Tomorrow

Predicting the future of the Great Lakes region is a fool's errand. Looking at Rwanda itself, it is possible to be either quite optimistic or rather pessimistic.

In many ways, the progress the country has made since 1994 is remarkable. Major advances have been made in health care and in education at all levels. The ubiquitous devastation has completely vanished, manifested now only in the damaged walls of the National Assembly and the genocide memorial sites scattered throughout the country with their eerie corpses and skeletons. Yet, both the National Assembly and the sites have been left deliberately as memories of the genocide. Economic growth has been robust, although inequality remains severe. President Kagame has become a fierce advocate of a market economy and is also determined that the country becomes a leader in information technology in Africa. To visiting tourists or consultants, Rwanda is a country on the move—stable, safe, clean, orderly, bustling, modernizing. The police seem unbribable. Seat belts and motorcycle helmets are scrupulously worn. Visitors from elsewhere in Africa are often openly envious.

At best, however, that means Rwanda has returned to the status of being a desperately poor under-developed country, now ranked 166th of 187 countries on the UN's 2011 human development index. The gap between the small, privileged elite and its conspicuous consumption and the vast majority is huge and growing. Life expectancy at birth is 50 years and 60% of the population lives on less than $1 a day. Of the 10 million citizens in the country, more than 80% live in rural areas, most of them very poor. Poverty has been significantly reduced, but population growth is exceedingly high, with population density the highest in sub-Saharan Africa. Land scarcity is acute.

Beyond these conventional challenges of under-development, 18 years after genocide the direct financial burdens it incurred remain enormous for everything from assistance to survivors and violated women with HIV and AIDS, to programs for demobilizing and reeducating troops of the old regime.

Views on Rwanda today remain remarkably diverse. Hutu Power advocates, still thriving outside the country, continue perversely to deny the genocide with a series of self-contradictory propositions: It never happened. Or Hutu were enraged that the RPF shot down and murdered Habyarimana and spontaneously lashed out. Or people were killed in a civil war. Or if there was a genocide at all, it was perpetrated by the RPF both in Rwanda and in Zaire/Congo. Or there was a "double genocide." In France, former soldiers now insist that there was indeed a genocide in 1994, when the RPF murdered millions of defenseless Hutu. It would be useful to document and expose the network of European politicians, priests, soldiers, and academics who continue to fund and support this malignant force of deniers and who actively foment armed insurrection against the present government of Rwanda.

Hostility to the Kagame regime for its human rights abuses is also widespread. Some prominent former foreign friends of Rwanda have emerged as bitter critics, sometimes describing the country as virtually a totalitarian dictatorship. Instances of intimidated human rights activists, harassed reporters, and government opponents forced to flee the country are not hard to come by. The president, many charge, will brook no dissent of any kind, and the consequences for dissenters are severe. The presidential election of 2003, the first since 1994, was won by Paul Kagame with a ludicrous 95% of the vote. In the presidential election of 2010, Kagame "won" 94.3% of the vote.

The months surrounding this last election showed the world the Kagame government's worst aspects. In what sometimes seemed like an unending torrent, story after story poured forth of beatings, killings, attempted killings, harassment, arrests, abuse, and intimidation of politicians, journalists, and former comrades. All had in common their opposition to the RPF government. This display of the RPF's iron fist was accompanied by the government's adamant insistence that it was responsible for none of it. A new dimension was added when, on several occasions, bombs or grenades were thrown in parts of Kigali, which may or may not have been related to the flight from the country by two highly placed generals, once part of the inner clique, one of whom then barely survived an assassination attempt in Johannesburg, South Africa. This, too, the government insisted, was a coincidence for which it had no responsibility.

But the world reacted skeptically to the usual RPF denials. Even the RPF's good friends in the U.S. government publicly "expressed concern" about the atmosphere in which the election was taking place. "The political environment ahead of the election has been riddled by a series of worrying actions taken by the Government of Rwanda," declared the U.S. State Department, normally a reliable ally of Kagame, "which appear to be attempts to restrict the freedom of expression." Clearly the RPF had gone too far this time, as even some of its stalwarts had begun to realize.

More recently, initiatives have been taken to liberate civil society, to allow the media more latitude, and to modify the laws outlawing genocide denial to make them less exploitable for silencing critics. Whether these are serious reforms or mere public relations gimmicks will be clear soon enough.

Critics who consider themselves friends of Rwanda—those who fully grasp the trauma of the genocide and see the potential threat still looming from the Hutu Power militia based in eastern DRC—fear that certain policies of the government are counterproductive, likely to set back the goals of reconciliation and true long-term stability instead of enhancing them. They point, for example, to memorial services remembering only Tutsi victims, implicitly asserting mass Hutu guilt, and justice policies in which only accused *genocidaires*, always Hutu, are tried. All accusations of crimes against humanity allegedly perpetrated by RFP officers, many of them Tutsi; and agricultural reforms imposed by urban elites, seemingly Tutsi, are with token exceptions automatically ignored. Above all, such critics fear that the governing party is completely closed to all attempts at constructive criticism.

Yet, typical of Rwanda, other outsiders seem simply to ignore any negative aspect of President Kagame and his party. A remarkable array of prominent Western business leaders, politicians, and religious celebrities have embraced Kagame with apparent indifference to issues of human rights, democracy, and possibly misguided policies.

Still others see an unfair double standard imposed on the RPF government. Corruption in Rwanda is a great deal less widespread than among its neighbors. Suppression of free speech is hardly more ruthless. Security exists throughout most of the country. In elections for the National Assembly, opposition parties won a credible 25% of the vote. Beyond that, almost half the legislators are women, the largest proportion of any parliament in the world.

While some accuse Kagame and his government of exploiting the genocide for their own self-interest—"playing the genocide card"—others argue the opposite. Considering that it has been only 18 tumultuous years since the genocide, given the number of *Interahamwe* still active in eastern DRC and the uncertain feelings of the country's 85% Hutu majority, Rwanda remains surprisingly open, though within clearly circumscribed boundaries. But no one, on any side, doubts Kagame's steely determination to take whatever steps are necessary to keep his country secure and his government in power. But many friendly outsiders believe that the balance between security and liberty can now be safely redressed. As Kagame biographer Stephen Kinzer wrote after Kagame's reelection in 2010:

> he could look back with pride on his accomplishments. Rwanda has emerged from the devastation of genocide and become more secure and prosperous than anyone had a right to expect. The central task of his second seven-year term, which by law must be his last, is to add broader democracy to this security and prosperity (Kinzer, 2011)

Terribly poor, badly traumatized, deeply divided, a precarious entity in a fragile and explosive region, Rwanda is a country that is now bound to make history once again, as it did 18 years ago. Can it transcend its tragic past and move forward to defeat poverty and under-development as a united, secure and stable country? As has been true for more than a century, both Rwandans and outsiders will play central roles in determining the answer.

Eyewitness Accounts

The following accounts are used, with gratitude, from interviews with survivors carried out by Samuel Totten and Rafiki Ubaldo in Rwanda in 2008. For more in-depth interviews, see their book *We Cannot Forget: Interviews with Survivors of the 1994 Genocide in Rwanda* (2011).

Account 1: Julienne Mukumana, 2008, Born 1953

Prior to the genocide this interviewee resided in the hills of Huye, just outside of the university town of Butare. What she and her family experienced was nothing less than horrific, part of which is described herein. She and her family continue to suffer greatly from post-traumatic stress.

Around the 21st of April, at 3:00 in the morning, local officials and *interahamwe* told everyone—Tutsis and Hutus—to leave their homes. They were scattered all over the hills blowing whistles to wake us up, and as we looked out to see what was happening we were told to get out of our homes right away. The excuse they gave us was that the homes were not safe to stay in because there were robbers coming to rob us and take all of our belongings. We were told to go to Tonga where we would be safe, but that if we stayed we could be hurt. At Tonga the authorities checked everyone's identity card to see who was Tutsi and who was Hutu. Then, it was announced that Hutus had to go back home and Tutsis had to remain. Now that we were separated, we knew what followed, death.

So, we spent some days there. Then they—soldiers, *Interahamwe*, and other members of the local population—started to kill us. They had machetes, *agafuni* [hoes], guns, grenades, stones, spears, and *masusus* [clubs studded with spikes]. They were standing outside the fence and they said, "Those of you who do not wish to be hacked to death with a hoe or *masusu*, throw a goat or chicken over the fence, and you will be shot [instead of being killed by machete]." So everyone began running around grabbing goats and chickens to throw over the fence. It was a chance to get shot.

The doors and gates remained locked and as soon as there were no more goats and chickens to throw over the fence, the single shots stopped and they forced open the doors and gates and began killing people with machetes.

Frightened and shocked, we, many of us, laid down, and then they began to kill us. I was hit in the head with a *masusu*. It cracked my head open. I was also slashed with a machete on my left leg.

Some men stood up and began to fight, and I saw my husband struggling with a man with a machete.... I saw the man cut off my husband's arm from the shoulder. He was close to our children, and when he fell down, a soldier threw a grenade towards him. Our children, who saw their father being hurt, had taken a blanket and covered themselves with it. When the grenade exploded, it killed my husband and five of my children. One of my other children got hit with fragments of the grenade, but lived. One was not hurt. When the grenade was thrown, along with others that were thrown into the crowd, everyone, screaming and running, scattered everywhere, trying to find a way out of there.

I, too, ran, and as I was running towards the fence I fell into a garbage dump. It was about two meters [six feet] deep, but I could sit and see out of it. I spent the night there, not knowing where my children were or if they were even alive.

On Saturday, the military came with prisoners who wore pink caps with a red cross, and large tractors to collect dead bodies and bury them. I don't know how many were killed, but there were many, many people. Maybe up to 15,000.

Somehow, a soldier saw me and ordered me to get out of the garbage pit ... on my way out I saw the blanket we had brought with us and under there were decomposing bodies.... As I kept walking, I came to many children, and two of them were my children. So I ... think that some of those decomposed bodies were my other children. I could tell them by their clothes. One, who was two and a half, was covered with blood and the other one, who was four years old, was filthy and depressed and had been beaten with a club. At first, my children refused to hug me because my head and clothes were covered in blood.

I remembered that living nearby was the family of the teacher of my oldest son, and so we went over to them. This family was Hutu, but kind. The teacher, who was pregnant, brought holy water and started to clean the wounds of my youngest child believing that God would heal her. And she covered her wounds with a clean cloth.

We, my two surviving children and I, then continued on to the university hospital in Butare to get my wounds taken care of....

I went to see my brother-in-law, thinking he might help us to get another portion of food, but I learned that he had been killed that same night by soldiers.

I went back to the camp and there was a woman who had been slashed on both arms and she had bandages but it was smelling very bad because no one had changed the bandages. She had a baby six months old and couldn't care for it, and thus I told her I would do so. The woman with the baby had 70,000 Rwandan Francs and she helped us purchase food from kids selling it on the street. It was very difficult to find food, but she had money to buy it with and thus we were able to purchase some.

We spent two weeks at the hospital, but we were living in terrible conditions. The surroundings, the whole area, became like a large toilet and it became poisonous for the hospital.

During those two weeks, the *interahamwe* and soldiers entered the compound to locate men to kill. They came in the night with torches [flashlights] to find them. They also entered to find girls and when they found one they'd grab their breasts to see if they were still firm, not like older women, and if they were firm then they would take them to rape them.... [After two weeks we were transported back to our own villages].

[The bourgmestre and the councilors] held a meeting on how to kill us. In day light, in front of us, they held such a meeting. The discussion was right in front of us. Some were arguing they should kill us right there, but some said "If we kill them here in the commune then it will smell very bad in the commune." There was nothing we could do because the police were there with the *interahamwe*. So, one councilor said, "The best idea is to send every displaced person to his sector where the Tutsis could be killed and dumped in latrines...."

I suspected they would kill me in the night so I went down to Tonga with my children. When we reached the forest we went down a hill and tried to find a place to hide. That night it began to rain, pour down, and I was afraid my children would die because of the cold and rain. It rained until 3.00 in the morning or so. Torrents of water rushed down the hill and we remained wet all night long.

In the morning, the youngest, Jane, woke up and cried a lot because she was hungry. A man heard her and approached us. He asked us how long we had been there and if we had food to eat. I told him we arrived the previous night and that we didn't have any food. After a long time, about 50 minutes, he returned with a crowd of *interahamwe*. Before they reached us, one of the *interahamwe* climbed a tree so he could detect exactly where we were, and I called out to him, "You do not have to climb a tree, we are here."

There were about nine men. Two of them raped me and left me there. I was devastated, hungry and cold.... We then went to Nyanza. Once we got there I learned that two of my children, two of the boys, had escaped the killing in Matyazo. Jean Paul Uwimana was eleven years old and Augustin Kubwimana was eight years old. When they saw me they came running and hugged me and asked me, "Momma, you are alive?"

I asked them how they managed to remain alive, and they told me they had lived with a cow herder who took care of them. I told my boys that we should remain where we were and not run away, and if they should kill us at least we will be together. But the boys were frightened by what I had said, and ran away.

I then took my two little girls and I headed towards the nearest road-block and told those at the roadblock—the *interahamwe*—"I am tired of running so you can kill me." I had already lost my husband and five of my children and all of my other family members: my mother and father, six brothers and three sisters and all of their children.

There were ten *interahamwe* and I knew them all, as they lived on the same hill as I had at one time, and they told me, "Put your children in the trench so we can kill you alone." Then a man grabbed me and pulled me to the ground and raped me.

Clare, my older girl, saw me beg not to be raped, and then watched as I was raped. She was so traumatized by it that even after the genocide she would ask what those men had been doing to me. She had watched as I was raped the first time, too. In the middle of that, four men came up talking about how they had killed my two boys. And then the four men all raped me in front of my children.

Account 2: Anonymous, 2008, Born 1975

This account is by a Tutsi woman in her late twenties who came from a highly educated family. Her story is interesting on many levels, not least of which that her family was actually protected by a powerful Hutu who served as the warden of a prison near their home.

She asked that her name not be revealed as she feared possible retaliation from former Hutu and did not want to get on the wrong side of the current government in case she said something they might look askance at.

A big part of my extended family was killed. On my father's side only he and his sister were the ones left from his family. More than 50 of them I can remember, whose names I know, were killed in his family.

One of the most difficult aspects of this was that my grandfather was killed and thrown in a latrine, and after genocide my auntie returned to Kibuye and knew the place where he had been killed and put up some signs [of memorial] and left immediately because it was not safe. Later, she returned with my brothers in 1995, and the neighbors showed them where my grandmother was buried and my auntie placed some flowers there. In 2001, the family was ready to bury my grandmother in a dignified way with a ceremony and my auntie and two brothers and cousin bought a coffin to put the bones in and went to Kibuye where they dug up the whole area searching for the bones. The reason they waited until 2001 is because the area was not safe to return to, especially to search for your relatives [remains].

They dug all day, into the evening, when a neighbor came and told them that the killers had dug up the bones and threw them in a river so no one could dig them up and try to find out who the killers were. That was very hard on my father; he was not able to cope with that, not all the way up to the day he died. He talked about it over and over again, commenting on how very sad he was.

On my mum's side, close to 50 people, who I knew, were killed. One of the saddest aspects of that was that my grandfather was a pastor and helped many, many people but they killed him. He hid himself and his family in a church, and they entered and killed him and his family.

My uncle, my mother's brother, had both of his arms cut off before they threw him in a river. The killers first cut off one of his arms, and then told him to hold it with his other arm as they took him to the river. Then they told him to put both his arms over his head, and they cut off his other arm. They just wanted to torture him. Someone after the genocide told us what had happened to him.

After the genocide we were able to bury my grandfather and grandmother on my mum's side, along with five of my cousins who were killed with them.... Other relatives are buried in mass graves, but the neighbors of our relatives during genocide would tell us "they are buried here," and then "no, they were buried there," so we don't really know where they are buried. Others, cousins, were thrown in a river and a marker has been placed near the river and we go there [every year during commemoration] and have a small ceremony even though their remains are not there. We do not know what happened to many of them.

Just after [the] genocide, for a period of time, I feared people were following me, that someone was going to attack me, that someone was going to kill me. And during memorial period [April through early July] I also have had a hard time trying to understand what happened to us [the Tutsi people]. During commemoration I only see survivors and no one else, no other community members...

Many survivors continue to struggle, many are without adequate housing, have nothing.... For example, I know 24 students—12 males and 12 females—who are all living together in a very small house that is falling down. There is so little room they have to put their suitcases in the living room; the bedrooms are not big enough for their possessions. Also, they have no power and no water, and I don't think the government have plans to put it in there.

Africa is built around families, extended families. We lost so many family members it's like ... I, we, don't have a family anymore. We have our immediate family, but not our grandfathers, grandmothers, aunts and uncles so...

Selected Bibliography

Caplan, Gerald (2010, June 17). The politics of denialism: The strange case of Rwanda. *Pambazuka News*, n.p..

Clark, Phil (2010). *The Gacaca courts, Post-genocide justice and reconciliation in Rwanda: Justice without lawyers*. New York: Cambridge University Press.

Clark, Phil, & Kaufman, Zachary D. (Eds.) (2008). *After genocide: Transitional justice, post-conflict reconstruction and reconciliation in Rwanda and beyond*. London: Hurst Publishers.

Dallaire, Romeo (2003). *Shake hands with the devil: The failure of humanity in Rwanda*. Toronto: Random House.

Des Forges, Alison (1999). *Leave none to tell the story: Genocide in Rwanda*. New York: Human Rights Watch.

Habamenshi, Um'Khonde Patrick (2009). *Rwanda, where souls turn to dust*. n.p.: Iuniverse Inc.

Hatzfeld, Jean (2005) *Machete season: The killers in Rwanda speak*. New York: Farrar, Straus and Giroux.

Huggins, Chris (2009). Agricultural policies and local grievances in rural Rwanda. *Peace Review: A Journal of Social Justice, 21*, 296–303.

Independent Committee of Experts (2010). *Report of investigation into the causes and circumstances of and responsibility for the attack of 06/04/1994 against the Falcon 50 Rwandan presidential aeroplane*. Kigali: Republic of Rwanda.

Kinzer, Stephen (2008). *A thousand hills: Rwanda's rebirth and the man who dreamed it*. New York: Wiley.

Kinzer, Stephen (2011, January 27). Kagame's authoritarian turn risks Rwanda's future. *Guardian*. Retrieved from: www.guardian.co.uk/.../2011/jan/27/rwanda-freedom-of-speech.

Lemarchand, Rene (2009). The 1994 Rwanda genocide. In Samuel Totten & William S. Parsons (Eds.), *Century of genocide: Critical essays and eyewitness accounts* (pp. 482–504). New York: Routledge.

Mamdani, Mahmood (1996). From conquest to consent on the basis of state formation: Reflections on Rwanda. *New Left Review, 216*, 3–36.

Mamdani, Mahmood (2001). *When victims become killers: Colonialism, nativism, and the genocide in Rwanda*. Princeton, NJ: Princeton University Press.

Melvern, Linda (2004). *Conspiracy to murder: The Rwandan genocide*. London: Verso.

Melvern, Linda (2009). *A people betrayed: The role of the West in Rwanda's genocide*. New York: Zed Books.

Moghalu, Kingsley (2005). *Rwanda's genocide: The politics of global justice*. New York: Palgrave Macmillan.

Mushikiwabo, Louise (2006), *Rwanda means the universe: A native's memoir of blood and bloodlines*. New York: St. Martin's Press.

Omaar, Rakiya (1994). *Rwanda: Death, despair, and defiance*. London: African Rights.

Organization of African Unity (2000). *Rwanda: The preventable genocide*. Addis Ababa: Author.

Power, Samantha (2003). *A problem from hell: America and the age of genocide*. New York: Basic Books.

Prunier, Gerard (1995). *The Rwanda crisis: History of a genocide*. New York: Columbia University Press.

Rittner, Carol, Roth, John K., & Whitworth, Wendy (Eds.) (2004). *Genocide in Rwanda: Complicity of the churches?*. St. Paul, MN: Paragon House.

Stearns, Jason K. (2011). *Dancing in the glory of monsters: The collapse of the Congo and the great war of Africa*. New York: Public Affairs.

Straus, Scott (2006). *The order of genocide: Race, power and war in Rwanda*. Ithaca, NY: Cornell University Press.

Thompson, Allan (Ed.) (2006). *The Media and the Rwandan Genocide*. London: Pluto Press.

Totten, Samuel and Ubaldo, Rafiki (2011). *We cannot forget: Interviews with survivors of the 1994 genocide in Rwanda*. New Brunswick, NJ: Rutgers University Press.

Wallis, Andrew (2007). *Silent accomplice: The untold story of France's role in the Rwandan genocide*. London: I.B. Tauris.

Map 14.1 Bosnia and Herzegovina

CHAPTER 14

Genocidal Violence in the Former Yugoslavia: Bosnia Herzegovina

MARTIN MENNECKE[1]

For most Europeans, the term "genocide" used to be limited to the historical experience of World War II, Stalinist crimes, and the Holocaust—or to events happening in places far away, coming only as close as the evening news. This illusion of peacefulness was abruptly dashed when, in the 1990s, the multi-ethnic, Federal Republic of Yugoslavia dissolved into several wars of secession, with far more than two million people displaced and tens of thousands killed. As the result of certain actions in certain places, the terror of genocide had come back to haunt Europe.

Many of those in what once formed Yugoslavia are still marked by the traumatizing experiences of the 1990s. Whether living as internally displaced person in Bosnia Herzegovina, having returned to one's home-town or currently living somewhere else in Europe or North America, all remember the atrocities they have witnessed and suffered. The wars also continue to play a visible role in daily politics, be that in ongoing trials of former high profile politicians and military officers at the International Criminal Tribunal for the Former Yugoslavia (ICTY) in The Hague or the dispute still surrounding the independence of Kosovo.[2] Against this background, both scholars and students of genocide studies continue to wrestle with the questions of why and how genocidal violence emerged once again in Europe.

The Fall of Yugoslavia: Wars in Croatia and Bosnia Herzegovina

Yugoslavia's descent into war and genocidal violence began in 1991, when the republic of Slovenia and then the republic of Croatia declared their independence. The republic of Bosnia Herzegovina followed shortly thereafter, in 1992. While the war in Slovenia, where very few Serbs lived, lasted only 10 days and caused fewer than 50 deaths, the conflicts in Croatia and Bosnia were vastly more deadly and destructive.

In Croatia, Serbs constituted 12% of the population, and many of them feared that their status and security in an independent Croatia would suffer significantly. Assisted and armed by the Serb-dominated federal government in Belgrade, the capital of Yugoslavia, Croatian Serb military forces temporarily occupied approximately 33% of the territory in Croatia. The conflict lasted seven months and included—on all sides—the deliberate destruction of towns and cities, massacres of defenseless civilians, and the forcible removal of ethnic groups from their territory. This sort of campaign came to be known as "ethnic cleansing"—a term that tells little of the horror inflicted upon the affected civilians.

All in all, more than 10,000, maybe up to 20,000 people were killed; more than 200,000 people fled the country and more than 300,000 became internally displaced. Efforts by international negotiators helped bring the war to an end in December 1992, without, however, challenging the "Republic of Serbian Krajina," which had been erected by the Croatian Serbs on the territory they had seized during the war.

UN peacekeepers were deployed and the war zone remained divided until late summer 1995, when Croatian military forces, in a massive offensive dubbed "Operation Storm," retook the Serb-controlled territory. Today, some of the military leaders behind "Operation Storm" stand indicted before the ICTY and Croatian courts, where they are accused of being responsible for a scorched-earth campaign that led to the looting and burning of tens of thousands of Serbian homes and the unlawful killing of more than 100 civilians. "Operation Storm" is said to have forced more than 150,000 Croatian Serbs to flee their homes, an operation that constituted the single largest act of "ethnic cleansing" during the entire war in Bosnia (cf. Prosecutor *v*. Gotovina et al., 2011).

The war in Bosnia Herzegovina (Yugoslavia's most ethnically diverse republic, then comprised of approximately 44% Bosnian Muslims,[3] 31% Serbs, and 17% Croats), began only a few months after the war in Croatia ended. It was a complex, vicious conflict that lasted more than three years and resulted in the death of approximately 100,000 people, including many civilians.[4] Among the armed factions engaged in the conflict were Bosnian Serbs, Bosnian Muslims, Bosnian Croats, regular army and paramilitary forces from Croatia and Serbia, foreign mercenaries, United Nations troops, and NATO soldiers. As in Croatia, but on a much larger scale, atrocities were perpetrated widely and by all ethnic groups. These crimes included rape, massacres, the obliteration of villages, towns, and cities, and "ethnic cleansing," as a result of both Bosnian Serbs and Bosnian Croats attempting to remove the other, as well as Bosnian Muslims, from areas they claimed for themselves. The prosecutor at the ICTY has initiated proceedings against members of all ethnic groups, including soldiers and officers from all warring factions (cf. www.icty.org/action/cases/4). The majority of the indictments, however, are directed against Serbs, reflecting the fact that the Serb and Bosnian Serb forces were responsible for the largest number of criminal offenses.[5]

The scale and kind of atrocities committed in Bosnia and the "safe areas" (Bosnian Muslim enclaves designated as such and which were purportedly to be protected by UN peacekeepers) distinguishes the Bosnian war from the other Yugoslav wars. In April 1992, Bosnian Serb forces began an "ethnic cleansing" campaign in which many civilians were murdered; the rest were driven from their homes, the latter of which were systematically looted and destroyed. In addition, girls and women were raped as an instrument of spreading terror during the process of "ethnic cleansing," often in front of family members in their private homes or in the open in front of other villagers.

In the course of their "ethnic cleansing" campaigns, the Bosnian Serbs established numerous detention camps, where non-Serbs were confined under extremely inhumane conditions, frequently beaten or tortured. Some were subsequently murdered.[6] There were numerous cases where girls and women were held captive as sex slaves for weeks and months (see, for example, Prosecutor v. Kunarac et al., 2001). While the exact number never will be known, many studies report that thousands of rapes took place, ordered and authorized by Serb officials, and in many cases with the explicit purpose of impregnating the women (cf. Amnesty International, 2009, p. 5). While the International Criminal Tribunal for Rwanda (ICTR) has classified certain instances of rape during the Rwandan genocide as acts of genocide, the ICTY has not included sexual violence in its deliberations of the crime of genocide.

By mid-June 1992, Serb forces controlled two-thirds of Bosnia Herzegovina. In the course of the war, more than half of Bosnia's multi-ethnic population of 4.4 million people had been displaced. An estimated 1.3 million were internally displaced; another 500,000 had fled to neighboring countries and some 700,000 had sought refuge in Western Europe.

UN Safe Areas and the Fall of Srebrenica

In the spring of 1993, the UN Security Council declared that Sarajevo, Goradze, Srebrenica, and three other Bosnian Muslim enclaves in Serb-controlled territory were to be designated "safe areas," and thus guaranteed protection by a contingent of UN peacekeepers in order to provide shelter for the thousands of refugees who had fled already "cleansed" areas (see the resolutions by the UN Security Council in UN Doc. S/Res. 819, 824 and 836, 1993). These safe areas, however, soon became obstacles to international efforts to broker a peace agreement. The international community could not officially support any proposal handing the enclaves over to the Serbs via negotiations, as this could have been viewed as legitimating "ethnic cleansing" and rewarding aggression. At the same time, it was evident that the Bosnian Muslim enclaves could not continue to exist permanently in the midst of what had become Serbian territory without receiving external help. This constellation and the little trust the local Bosnian Muslim army units had in the small contingents of UN peacekeepers led to another problem, i.e. the lack of demilitarization of the safe areas. In addition, the safe areas developed into places of extreme suffering, as the refugees were subjected to frequent shelling, as well as shortages of food, medical supplies, and other necessities caused by Serb refusal to allow UN aid convoys to reach the areas (Ingrao, 2005).

Ultimately, in one of these so-called "safe areas," Bosnian Serb forces committed the largest massacre in Europe since World War II. It took place in Srebrenica, where approximately 40,000 people had eked out a bare existence, many since the spring of 1992. Encountering no significant resistance from either the members of the remaining units of the Bosnian Muslim army (the Army of the Republic of Bosnia and Herzegovina), who instead tried to flee the town into Muslim-controlled areas, or the tiny contingent of some 400 Dutch UN soldiers responsible for protecting the safe area, the Bosnian Serbs entered Srebrenica on July 11, 1995.

On July 13, women, children, and elderly people were put on buses and driven to the front line, to Muslim-controlled territory. Within 30 hours, the Bosnian Serb army deported more than 20,000 people from the enclave—but not the "battle-age" men. Instead, between July 13 and 19, more than 7,000 boys and men, mostly civilians, were systematically slaughtered in a carefully planned operation (cf. Prosecutor v. Popovic et al., 2010). Thousands were carried on buses to execution sites where they were murdered with automatic weapons and machine guns. After the mass shooting, killers walked among the corpses, looking for survivors, who they then shot with their pistols. After the slaughter, trucks were brought in to collect the bodies and haul them to mass graves.

The so-called safe area of Srebrenica had fallen without a single shot fired by its international protectors; in fact, the UN soldiers observed the deportations and supplied the fuel for the buses used by the Bosnian Serb army. A few days later, after the news about the events of Srebrenica began to spread in the international community, the Bosnian Serbs took another safe area, Zepa—again without encountering any serious international opposition. This safe area fell on July 25, two weeks after the Serbs had announced their plan to conquer it. Up to 2,000 Bosnian Muslim men of fighting age were in danger of experiencing the same fate as their compatriots in Srebrenica, but the Croatian offensive in the Krajina forced the Serbs to withdraw troops from Zepa (see the report of the UN Secretary General, *The Fall of Srebrenica*, 1999, paras. 394ff.).

Essential Factors Behind the Conflict

Some international observers, including political leaders who wanted to avoid direct forms of intervention, suggested that "ancient hatreds" stemming from centuries of conflict in the region were responsible for the outbreak of war and its barbarity. For example, Samantha Power quotes then U.S. Secretary of State Warren Christopher as follows: "The hatred between all three groups is almost unbelievable. It's almost terrifying, and it's centuries old. That really is a problem from hell." The logics of the "ancient hatreds" argument implied that the parties to the conflict had to "fight it out" and that international intervention could not stop the bloodshed.

However, there is a strong consensus among scholars of the region that the existence of any ancient hatreds was greatly exaggerated and in any case did not cause the war. Recalling the break-up of the Ottoman Empire and its violent repercussions on the Balkans—and in particular the gruesome inter-ethnic killings committed during and shortly after World War II—it was perhaps somewhat euphemistic to claim that "[s]ignificantly, all three communities in Bosnia-Herzegovina lived for centuries in relative harmony" (Cigar, 1995, p. 13). At the same time, it is important to remember that after World War II, under the leadership of Josef Tito (who ruled from 1945 until his death in 1980), ethnic politics and the revival of animosities from the past were discouraged. The official slogan of the communist government was "Brotherhood and Unity"; and indeed, despite the massive physical, social, and psychological traumas experienced by millions of Yugoslavs during World War II, "relative harmony" was largely restored in Europe's most ethnically diverse nation. In some cases, this only meant co-existence; in other communities, mutual mistrust persisted and, in still others, different ethnic groups lived together peacefully. This became, for example, evident in the high level of intermarriage among Serbs, Croats, and Muslims during Tito's regime (Bringa, 2002, pp. 217f.). Rather than "ancient hatreds," the wars of Yugoslav secession, and the Bosnian conflict and its atrocities in particular, reflect a cluster of factors, including ever-increasing economic instability, the rise of nationalistic leaders after Tito's death, the deliberate revival and exploitation of historical traumas from World War II, and the conflict in Croatia that preceded the war in Bosnia.

Having enjoyed the highest standard of living of any communist nation, Yugoslavia began to experience worsening economic problems in the 1980s. In part, its productivity declined due to mismanagement and technical obsolescence in many industries. Concomitantly, loans from international lenders that had helped support Yugoslavia's growth and standard of living had created a massive national debt. Unemployment increased, and many Yugoslavs worried about their economic futures. Robin Alison Remington (1984) described the Yugoslav economy as being "on the brink of collapse" and warned that Yugoslav politicians would be "trapped by the politics of scarcity for the foreseeable future" (pp. 370, 373).

As the national economic conditions deteriorated, tensions within and among the constituent republics developed and escalated. In 1981, less than a year after Tito's death, armed confrontations occurred between Kosovo Albanians and Serbs in the Yugoslav province of Kosovo. Then, in 1986, prominent academics published a lengthy memorandum in Belgrade in which they asserted that the very existence of the Serbian nation was under threat. The memorandum called on Serbia to "assess its own economic and national interests" and to wake up from its "four decades of passivity" to save the federal republic of Yugoslavia (Serbian Memorandum, 1986). Despite the latter reference to Yugoslavia as a whole, the memorandum was widely perceived as an open turn from the Yugoslav experiment to pan-Serbianism (Naimark, 2001, pp. 149f.). Tone Bringa (2002) argues that the failure to deal with the transition of authority and Tito's legacy were key reasons for the downfall of the old Yugoslavia (pp. 206ff.).

Tito's death created indeed a dangerous political vacuum. No leader emerged to replace his commitment to discouraging ethnic politics and promoting "Brotherhood and Unity"; just the opposite occurred. In May 1989, Slobodan Milosevic became president of Serbia, claiming the role as the "true defender" of Serb identity and the Serbian nation. He quickly consolidated power by purging the government and Yugoslav military of potential critics or rivals and assuming control of the powerful Serbian secret police. The Milosevic regime also took control of the media in Serbia (making particular use of television), and turned them into propaganda tools in order to inflame tensions between Serbs and other ethnic groups, both in Serbia and other republics. As it became clear that Slovenia and Croatia were moving toward independence, Milosevic and his agents began to provoke, organize, and arm Croatian

Serbs, who then began violent resistance against the Croatian government as it pushed for independence.

In 1990 Franjo Tudjman was elected president of the Croatian republic. He had been a general in Tito's Partisans during World War II and a major-general in the post-war Yugoslav National Army, but had been imprisoned by Tito during the 1970s and 1980s for advocating Croatian nationalism and separatism. Tudjman, the leader of the right-wing, nationalistic Croatian Democratic Union (HDZ), quickly instituted changes in the Croatian constitution that greatly increased his presidential powers and pushed through laws that were openly discriminatory against the Serbian minority in Croatia. Like Milosevic, Tudjman exploited the Croatian media to arouse tensions between Serbs and Croats.

Tudjman also played an important role in reviving historical traumas related to Yugoslavia's complicated and atrocious involvement in World War II. During that war, the Croatian "Ustasha" regime of Ante Pavelic ruled the so-called Independent State of Croatia, which at that time included large parts of Bosnia and parts of Serbia, as well as Croatia. Pavelic enthusiastically allied with Hitler and patterned his regime after Nazi Germany, from the official policy of racism to the details of his military's uniforms. The Independent State of Croatia willingly cooperated with the Nazi regime on the "Final Solution" against Jews and Gypsies, but went beyond it, launching a campaign of genocide against Serbs in "greater Croatia." The Ustasha, like the Nazis, established concentration camps and death camps. The most infamous of them was Jasenovac, in which captured Serbs were starved, tortured, worked to death, and killed. Between 1941 and 1945, more than 180,000 Serbs were deported, approximately 250,000 were forced to convert to Catholicism from Orthodox Christian faiths, and more than 300,000 were murdered (Lampe, 2000, pp. 210–214).

It must be noted that during World War II horrible crimes were committed by all sides (Serbs and Bosnian Muslims alike). For example, some historians assert that the Chetniks (Serb nationalists) committed genocide against the Bosnian Muslims, and, in fact, some large-scale massacres are well documented. Another aspect of Yugoslavia's complicated history under World War II is that there existed an SS division composed of Bosnian Muslim volunteers (Benson, 2004, pp. 79f.).

When World War II ended, over one million Yugoslav were dead. More than half of these are believed to have died as part of the inner-Yugoslav civil war. Even if exact numbers remain a matter of contention, it is estimated that 52% of the total war victims were Serbs, 19% Croats, 10% Bosnian Muslims, and the remainder from other groups (Benson, 2004, p. 77).[7] The victorious Socialist Partisans added to the toll by executing tens of thousands of Ustasha and Chetniks after the end of the war in 1945. Tito, the wartime leader of the Partisans and subsequent president of Yugoslavia, suppressed commemoration of this dark chapter in Yugoslav history, labeling all the dead "victims of fascism." The official memory did not distinguish between the different wrongs and responsibilities and silenced individual stories of suffering. Milosevic later used the government-controlled Serbian media to revive memories of the brutality meted out to the Serbs during World War II in order to suggest to Serbs that genocide against them was possible once again (for examples see Prosecutor *v.* Milosevic, 2002, pp. 10216–10220; MacDonald, 2002, pp. 138–140). Graphic documentaries of the Ustasha genocide were broadcast on Serbian television. Even mass graves of Serb victims of the Ustasha were exhumed and the bones ceremoniously reburied. Provocative, propagandistic books and articles on the genocide were also published. Additionally, academics were sent into areas of Croatia with high populations of Serbs to lecture on the atrocities of the past.

At the same time that Milosevic was resurrecting traumatic memories of Serb victimization under the Ustasha, Croatian President Tudjman instituted steps to "rehabilitate" the Ustasha regime (see, generally, Mac-Donald, pp. 98ff., 132ff.). In an important speech in February 1990, Tudjman referred to the Independent State of Croatia as "an expression of the historical aspirations of the Croatian people" (quoted in Stitkovac, 1999, p. 155). His government renamed streets and squares after leaders of the genocidal regime and selected, for the official insignia of the newly independent nation, a coat of arms very similar to that of the Ustasha government. Tudjman, an academic historian, also published a book in which he denied that the Ustasha regime had been guilty of genocide and drastically lowered the estimates of Serbs killed by the Ustasha. These actions, combined with new laws disadvantageous to Serbs in Croatia, fanned the flames of fear and anger.

Finally, the war in Croatia also contributed to the atrocious nature of the war in Bosnia. All major factions—the Yugoslav National Army, Croatian forces, and Croatian Serb forces—engaged in widespread and systematic atrocities and war crimes and thereby accelerated the escalating, reciprocal brutalization. In particular, the sieges of Dubrovnik and Vukovar, the execution of some 200 Croatian prisoners of war at Ovcara and the aftermath of "Operation Storm" stand out as appalling crimes committed during the war in Croatia. The practice of "ethnic cleansing," as noted above, began in Croatia when Serbs forced Croats from homes and villages, and vice versa. Some of the paramilitary units that later massacred Bosnian Muslims and destroyed their homes had begun their work in Croatia. Thousands of Croatian Serbs who had been "cleansed" from Croatia fled, as refugees, through Bosnia en route to relatives and refugee camps in Serbia, further frightening and angering Bosnian Serbs.

International Responses to the Conflict

From the moment the fighting broke out in Bosnia, the international community faced ever-increasing pressure from the media and from international human rights organizations to design a policy to stop the "ethnic cleansing" and bloodshed. In Europe and the United States, in particular, pictures of emaciated inmates detained behind barbed wire and hundreds of thousands of people being deported or fleeing their homes revived memories and images of World War II. Aware of these historical connotations, U.S. President Bill Clinton said at the time, "If the horrors of the Holocaust taught us anything, it is the high cost of remaining silent and paralyzed in the face of genocide" (quoted in Power, 2002, p. 275). No government, however, was ready to intervene in the war raging in Bosnia. The entire situation—the warring sides and the value of an intervention—appeared to be unpredictable, and many flinched at the potential cost of an intervention. The main focus of the international community was to deploy international mediators, an international arms embargo against Bosnia and the establishment of the ICTY—measures seemingly demonstrating engagement, but which were wholly insufficient.

UN Peacekeeping Operations

The UN Security Council authorized the deployment of UN peacekeeping forces—bringing nearly 40,000 soldiers from 39 different nations to Bosnia and Croatia. Their ability to protect endangered civilians and provide humanitarian assistance was, however, severely hampered by restricted rules of engagement, limited resources, and interference from the warring parties, as well as by a lack of political will to apply the military means available. Thus, for example, the peacekeeping force proved unable to prevent Bosnian Muslim forces from conducting raids from inside the safe areas on surrounding Serbian villages. Furthermore, both the governments that had sent the peacekeeping troops as well as their commanders on the ground proved unwilling to utilize NATO air power to defend the safe areas against Serb attacks. Due to a lack of political will both in the United States and the European Union—and despite a mandate "to deter attacks" on the safe areas—the UN and its member states did not prevent such attacks—and, as a result, several thousand people were killed in and around these areas.

At the same time, the international community maintained the UN arms embargo on Bosnia—which applied to all parties, but in fact only cemented the military advantage of the Serbs and, by implication, that of the Bosnian Serbs.[8] Only after hostilities between Croatia and Bosnian Muslims ended in 1994 (after diplomatic pressure from the West), along with increased U.S. military assistance in 1995, did the course of the war change. Following the Srebrenica massacre and another deadly mortar attack on Sarajevo, NATO initiated, on August 30, 1995, air strikes against the Bosnian Serbs. Ultimately, U.S.-led negotiations in Dayton, Ohio, ended the conflict in Bosnia in November 1995 and paved the way for more than 60,000 international troops that formed the NATO-led Implementation Force (IFOR) sent to Bosnia to maintain the cease-fire. One year later, IFOR was transformed into the Stabilization Force (SFOR), which still had around 31,000 troops. Today, there are still approximately 1,600 international troops under the framework of the European Union Force (EUFOR) left in Bosnia to oversee the implementation of the Dayton Agreement.

Questions of Responsibility: Official Reports on the Role of the United Nations and Individual States

The atrocious crimes committed in the Balkans—in particular, emerging reports about the massacres in Srebrenica and instances of mass rapes—led to harsh public criticism in numerous Western countries. Many queried how such crimes could be allowed to happen in Europe and, more so, in the presence of Western peacekeepers. Many felt that the international response to the suffering of the Bosnian Muslims during the conflict had been entirely inadequate (Cushman & Mestrovic, 1996). The question of political responsibility for this failure was evident and could not be ignored. Both the United Nations, the Netherlands (which had peacekeepers stationed in Srebrenica), and other countries instituted inquiries into why things had gone that wrong.

In 1999, at the United Nations, UN Secretary General Kofi Annan presented a comprehensive report reviewing the safe area policy and its failure at Srebrenica and Zepa. In its conclusion, the report criticizes the UN member states for not having done more to implement the different resolutions of the UN Security Council, and criticizes the Dutch battalion at Srebrenica—and the UN institutions involved in the area—for mishandling the available information prior to the massacre (Report by the UN Secretary General, 1999, paras. 467ff.). In November 2000, a commission of the French parliament began investigations into the events surrounding Srebrenica and the role of the French troops deployed to Bosnia. This was of particular interest, as there had been allegations of the French accepting the fall of Srebrenica in return for the release of French UN soldiers held hostage by the Bosnian Serbs. In the final report, the parliamentary committee of the *Assemblée Nationale* rejected the notion that there had been tacit French approval of the "ethnic cleansing" in the safe areas. At the same time, the French inquiry acknowledged that Srebrenica also constituted a failure of France based on manifest errors of certain French military officers.[9]

Most comprehensive were the Dutch efforts to shed light on the fall of Srebrenica—understandably so, given the particular role of the Netherlands: It had been a Dutch battalion that had turned over the safe area and with it thousands of refugees to the Bosnian Serbs. Furthermore, Dutch officers can be seen exchanging courtesies with the Bosnian Serb general Ratko Mladic in photographs and video footage. Ultimately, several official inquiries were instituted in the Netherlands, culminating in a 3,500-plus-page report published in spring 2002 by the Netherlands Institute for War Crime Documentation (NIOD; the report is available at www.srebrenica.nl). Requested by the Dutch government in 1996, the report mainly represents a historical account of the facts and, by and large, excuses the Dutch soldiers as under-equipped peacekeepers who had been deployed to a site where there was no peace to keep. NIOD, though, confirmed that some of the earlier Dutch investigations into the role of the Netherlands in regard to Srebrenica had turned into attempts to cover up the role of Dutch government officials and politicians. Furthermore, the NIOD report criticized the government responsible for sending the Dutch troops in the beginning of the 1990s for misjudging the situation on the ground.

As a response to this critique, the sitting Dutch cabinet jointly resigned in April 2002. Taking into account that only two of the acting ministers had been part of the government responsible for the deployment of Dutchbat (the Dutch peacekeeping force), this decision stands out as going beyond the sheer rhetorical recognition of political responsibility. Although other international and national bodies have acknowledged a shared responsibility for mishandling the safe areas and in particular Srebrenica, only in the Netherlands has this resulted in personal consequences. It should be noted, however, that this move came many years late and only a few weeks prior to already-scheduled national elections. In summer 2002, the Dutch parliament initiated yet another report, this time under the auspices of a parliamentary commission that interviewed some 40 political and military officials. The final report, a 1,600-page document, was presented on January 27, 2003, and provides for a detailed and candid critique of the Dutch decision-making process regarding Srebrenica. Its findings confirm that both the Dutch government and the United Nations mishandled the situation and bear the political responsibility for the lack of protection of the Muslim civilians at Srebrenica.

On the basis of the numerous international and national reports on the fall of Srebrenica and UN peacekeeping in Bosnia, it seems safe to conclude that the failure of the international community to protect the citizens of Bosnia was based on a combination of an unwillingness to become engaged, the mishandling of relevant information, and the ruthlessness of the warring parties, particularly the Bosnian Serbs' military and paramilitary units.

The International Criminal Tribunal for the Former Yugoslavia (ICTY)

While the conflicts were raging in the former Yugoslavia, some Western governments raised the question of criminal responsibility for those committing massive violations of human rights. In May 1993, the UN Security Council adopted a binding resolution establishing the International Criminal Tribunal for the Former Yugoslavia (ICTY) to investigate war crimes, crimes against humanity, and genocide committed in the Yugoslav wars since 1991 (for general information on the tribunal see www.icty.org). The ICTY became the first international institution to address atrocity crimes since the military tribunals after World War II and was therefore of truly historical significance. In particular, the establishment of the ICTY helped to finalize the negotiations at the United Nations vis-à-vis the creation of a permanent international criminal court as successor to the Nuremberg Tribunal. These negotiations had been dragging on, temporarily suspended by the Cold War, since the 1950s. Ultimately, the ICTY was joined by the International Criminal Tribunal for Rwanda (ICTR) and the International Criminal Court (ICC), which were established in 1994 and 1998, respectively, and a number of other, new transitional justice mechanisms.

The ICTY was placed in The Hague in the Netherlands and has a total of about 1,100 staff representing over 80 nationalities. The maximum sentence the ICTY can hand down is life imprisonment. Over the years, the tribunal has issued 161 indictments against persons allegedly responsible for serious violations of international humanitarian law in the Former Yugoslavia. As of December 2011, the tribunal has concluded proceedings against 126 persons: 13 were acquitted; 64 were sentenced; 13 were sent back to national courts in the Former Yugoslavia to be tried there; and 36 were deceased before their case could be concluded (including Slobodan Milosevic) or had their indictments withdrawn. The remaining 35 persons are currently in some phase of their trial at the ICTY—none remain at large. This tremendous accomplishment was achieved, when in summer 2011 Serbia surrendered Ratko Mladic, the person believed to bear greatest responsibility for the mass executions at Srebrenica and other crimes committed in Bosnia. The tribunal as such has no police force, thus turning political pressure on Serbia, for example in regard to Serb aspirations of becoming a member of the European Union, into a crucial instrument to turn over such suspects as Mladic.

In 2003 the UN Security Council decided that the ICTY (as well as the ICTR) was to design a so-called "completion strategy" and to conclude its work as, originally planned, by 2010. This decision came mainly as a result of a certain tribunal-fatigue among major states in the Security Council and was not the least linked to the immense costs incurred by the tribunals for the Former Yugoslavia and Rwanda. Subsequently, this deadline has been extended for a couple of years. Eventually, all remaining tasks will be placed under the International Residual Mechanism for Criminal Tribunals.

While there is no doubt that the ICTY's contribution to the development of international criminal law and justice has been seminal, there are vastly different opinions on how much it has contributed to the restoration of peace and reconciliation in the former Yugoslavia (see Orentlicher, 2008; Allcock, 2005). The number of actual cases tried by the ICTY is considered low compared to the money and time invested into the judicial process. Furthermore, from the very beginning various individuals, mostly from Serbia, have insinuated that the ICTY has an anti-Serb bias and was a political creation of the Western powers—a conspiracy theory that was also advanced by Slobodan Milosevic. Problems and criticism aside, it is important to remember that it was the ICTY, as a result of its indictments, that removed major war criminals such as Karadzic and Milosevic from the political scene. Additionally, the ICTY has created an indisputable record of the major atrocities committed during the Yugoslav wars which will help future generations to formulate a common history of the wars—something which notably was missing after the traumatizing events of World War II. Above all, the ICTY was at the time the only means to bring some measure of justice to the countless victims of atrocity crimes and to prosecute the main perpetrators—in the 1990s and early 2000s, neither Bosnia, Croatia, nor Serbia were capable of trying their own former or sitting state officials and military officers for alleged crimes against humanity or genocide.

Transitional Justice Efforts in Bosnia Herzegovina

Transitional justice is a term describing the process through which a given society seeks to address a violent past. This process is increasingly perceived as a necessary step toward rebuilding the rule of law, bringing about reconciliation and moving toward a transition to democratic governance. Transitional justice often involves any of the following instruments or a combination thereof: international or national criminal prosecutions; truth commissions; and reparations. The exact choice depends on a variety of factors, including the degree of interest the international community takes in the matter, the political will of the national elite and, of course, the availability of resources. In the case of Bosnia, the international community focused for (too) many years on the establishment and running of the ICTY.

When the warring parties under the supervision of the international community signed the Dayton Agreement to conclude the conflict, it was clear that the ICTY would only be able to prosecute the major war criminals. Low- and mid-level perpetrators would eventually have to face national criminal courts. In principle, there are many reasons for bringing justice home to the societies of the victims—and the perpetrators. The ICTY—being situated in The Hague, conducting its proceedings in English and French and prosecuting only a minority of the actual perpetrators—remained for many people in the Balkans a remote institution that meant little vis-à-vis their personal attempts to come to terms with the past. That said, international efforts to initiate national proceedings ran into a number of new problems. For example, there proved to be a strong bias among judges and prosecutors in the region for only prosecuting "the other side," i.e. Croatian trials for trying alleged Serb war criminals and vice versa. Moreover, the national institutions experienced severe difficulties in providing witnesses the requisite protection. For a number of years, therefore, the lack of political will and a lack of qualified personnel in Croatia, Serbia, and Bosnia hindered progress on this front.

A real turning point in terms of transitional justice was early 2005 with the establishment of the War Crimes Chamber in Sarajevo in Bosnia Herzegovina (www.sudbih.gov.ba/?jezik=e). With the help of the international community, this chamber's task was to handle the most serious war crimes cases in Bosnia. In fact, the ICTY soon began transferring cases to the War Crimes Chamber so as to empty its docket in order to meet its own deadline for shutting down operations. Similar special chambers have been opened in Croatia and in Serbia. This is a very positive development and has already led to a number of trials in Serbia, Croatia, and Bosnia. It has, however, proven difficult to transmit the message and significance of these trials to the general public and the local media. In addition, the new special chambers do not ameliorate the fact that many lower courts in all three countries still lack the will, resources, and expertise to conduct war crimes trials—and this is where the main bulk of the cases will have to be heard. Around 10,000 people living in Bosnia alone are suspected of having committed war crimes during the 1990s. According to the national strategy for the prosecution of war crimes adopted in 2008, all trials are to be concluded by 2024—some 30 years after they were committed (for more information on domestic criminal prosecutions in the region, see www.hrw.org/en/reports/2004/10/13/justice-risk and the websites of the relevant regional missions of the Organization for Security and Co-operation in Europe at www.osce.org).

In regard to other transitional justice measures, the Balkans have not yet seen much development. Vetting efforts concerning the army, police, and judiciary in Bosnia have attracted mixed reviews and are still ongoing. In terms of reparations and restitution there has not been a comprehensive government scheme for individual victims. Still, in an important decision in March 2003, the Bosnian Human Rights Chamber ordered the Bosnian Serb Republika Srpska to pay approximately €3 million (the official currency of the Eurozone in Europe) as a collective compensation award to the foundation overseeing the Srebrenica memorial and cemetery at Potocari (Selimovic et al. *v.* Republika Srpska, 2003). In June 2007, 10 survivors and the Mothers of Srebrenica Foundation, representing approximately 6,000 surviving relatives, launched a law suit in a Dutch court before The Hague against the Netherlands and the United Nations over the actions of the Dutch UN peacekeepers in July 1995. The plaintiffs sought a judicial declaration spelling out the responsibility of the Netherlands and the United Nations for what happened to the Bosnian Muslims at Srebrenica, as well as individual compensation (Fejzic et al. *v.* The State of the Netherlands and the United Nations, 2007; see also Clifford, 2007). In the following year, however, the Dutch court ruled that it could not hear the case because in its view the United Nations are immune from such proceedings before a domestic court. The proceedings took a new turn when, in July 2011, the Court of Appeals ruled that the government did have a responsibility to four particular victims; the matter is now expected to go on to the Supreme Court. It is important to note that the Dutch government continues to pay annually about $20 million in aid to Bosnia, one-third going directly to projects related to rebuilding Srebrenica; the surviving victims, however, have not yet received any compensation.

The process of establishing a commonly accepted narrative about the events of the Yugoslav wars and the atrocities committed in Bosnia in particular has been a cumbersome one. Over the years there have been numerous attempts to establish a Truth Commission for Bosnia, but this idea has not yet materialized—initially because of opposition from the ICTY (which feared overlap between such a commission and its own work), and later due to domestic politics. In the Serb entity of Republika Srpska (one of the two primary political entities of Bosnia and Herze-govina), the first official attempt at documenting the truth about Sre-brenica ended in blatant denial. Aiming at presenting the "whole truth," a 132-page government report claimed that most victims at Srebrenica had been Serbs and that the other casualties were 2,000 Bosnian Muslim soldiers who had declined Mladic's offer to disarm and instead fought against the Bosnian Serb troops. The report contended that "the number of Muslim soldiers who were executed by Bosnian Serb forces for per-sonal revenge or simple ignorance of the international law ... would probably stand at less than 100" (Republic of Srpska, Documentation Centre, 2002, p. 34). International pressure and the aforementioned deci-sion of the Bosnian Human Rights Chamber resulted in the establish-ment of a new commission at the end of 2002, which was to write a second, truthful report about the fate of those still missing in the after-math of Srebrenica. Initially, the commission failed to obtain access to critical information due to obstructionism by the Bosnian Serb authori-ties, but the Office of the High Representative in Bosnia, an international administrator in charge of supervising the implementation of the Dayton Agreement, fired several high-level officials, and the commission's report was published in June 2004. In this report, some nine years after the tragedy that befell Srebrenica, the government of Republika Srpska finally acknowledged the mass executions as historical truth and helped to locate 32 previously unknown mass graves (Republika Srpska, 2004).

Suing Serbia: Accountability as a State

Worthy of note is one other high-profile case focused on the responsi-bility for the atrocities and damages suffered by the victims during the conflict in Bosnia. Early in the conflict, in March 1993, the government of Bosnia Herzegovina attempted to address the "ethnic cleansing" and massive crimes committed against its civilian population outside the framework of international and national *criminal* courts by instituting proceedings against the government of Yugoslavia (which later was renamed Serbia and Montenegro) before the International Court of Justice (ICJ), the highest judicial organ of the United Nations. Different from the ICTY, the ICJ does not address the criminal responsibility of individuals, but focuses exclusively on questions of state conduct; that is, whether a state has violated rules of international law, such as the prohi-bition against genocide as it is set forth in the UN Genocide Convention on the Prevention and Punishment of the Crime of Genocide (UNCG). Therefore, the law suit, technically speaking, concerned nothing but the civil liability of an abstract entity—that is, the state Serbia.

On February 2, 2007, almost 14 years after Bosnia had asked the ICJ to act "immediately ... in order to avoid further loss of life," the ICJ finally delivered its long-awaited judgment.[10] The enormous delay was due both to successful litigation tactics by Serbia, as well as repeated requests by both parties to extend the time limit for submitting written pleadings. In its 175-page judgment, the Court determined that the massacres at Srebrenica in July 1995 constituted genocide, while the other crimes, including atrocities committed at detention camps, gross instances of sexual violence, and the "ethnic cleansing" campaign, did not. Notably, the ICJ agreed completely with the relevant case-law of the ICTY. With a view to Serbia's responsibility for the genocide at Srebrenica, the Court found that Serbia did not have the degree of direct control over the Bosnian Serb forces at Srebrenica, which international law requires if Serbia was to be held *legally* responsible for the genocide; *however*, it did find that Serbia, given its close relations to the Bosnian Serbs, could have done more to prevent the genocide at Srebrenica and because of that it had violated the legal duty to prevent genocide—a duty that never before had been recognized under international law. Furthermore, the Court concluded that Serbia had violated its duty to punish those responsible for the atrocities perpetrated at Srebrenica. This resulted in Serbia becoming the first nation to have been found in violation of the UN Genocide Convention since its adoption in 1948. Nonetheless, the ICJ ultimately rejected Bosnia's claim for compensation.

While the Serbs felt great relief that they had not been found directly (legally) responsible for the genocide, and immediately asserted everyone needed to move on,[11] Bosnian Muslims were extremely disappointed with the judgment. It was viewed as too little, too late. More specifically, the decision not to label the conflict as a whole to be a case of genocide resulted in extremely strong reactions as it did not correspond to the victims' own perception. In the days following the judgment there were angry demonstrations against the decision in Bosnia (see, for example, Reuters, 2007b). Survivors from Srebrenica and local politicians called upon the international community to at least abolish the status of Republika Srpska, as it was deemed unbearable that Srebrenica, as the site of genocide, should remain part of a Bosnian Serb entity. Nothing, however, came of the request.

As is so often the case with institutions of international justice, little was done to put the comprehensive judgment into plain words or to elucidate its complex legal findings for the affected society. In fact, the judgment and other relevant material were only made available in French and English, the Court's two official languages. Without an outreach strategy in place, many did not know that the case was limited to the framework provided by the UN Genocide Convention and that the judges could not issue any findings as to whether Serbia was responsible for war crimes and crimes against humanity committed in Bosnia. As a result, the judgment has led to intense discussions among international law experts, particularly in regard to whether the Court was right in not finding Serbia *legally* responsible for the crimes committed at Srebrenica. Former ICTY president Antonio Cassese called the judgment a "judicial massacre" and criticized the Court for establishing an "unrealistically high standard of proof for finding Serbia to have been legally complicit in genocide" at Srebrenica (Cassese, 2007). On the other hand, the judgment undoubtedly is of great significance in that it was the first time it was held that states (and not only individuals) can violate the UNCG and that there is a legal (not solely ethical) duty to prevent genocide (Mennecke & Tams, 2007). For many survivors, however, the judgment remains yet another example of the international community failing Bosnia. Tellingly, the president of a local non-governmental organization commented bitterly, "let Bosnia's blood and ashes rest on the hands of all those who made such a judgment" (quoted in Jelacic, 2007).

Genocide in Bosnia Herzegovina?

The question of whether the conflict in Bosnia Herzegovina as such, beyond the massacres at Srebrenica, could be characterized as genocide has occupied courts, scholars, and victims alike. The debate on this issue has been intense and at times polemical—and it is also, after the ICJ decision, far from concluded. Very early on in the conflict, the prosecutor at the ICTY expressed the view that the crimes committed by Bosnian Serb forces in Bosnia Herzegovina indeed should be labeled genocide (Karadzic & Mladic, Indictment, 1995), but the judges disagreed with this approach and dismissed the genocide charge in a number of proceedings, including cases against former detention camp guards and commanders and leading politicians (cf. Mennecke & Markusen, 2003, pp. 310ff.). Subsequently, though, the case against the Bosnian Serb General Radislav Krstic did lead to a conviction for genocide. More specifically, on August 2, 2001, he was found guilty of genocide for his role in the mass executions at Srebrenica, constituting the first genocide conviction by an international tribunal outside the context of the Rwandan genocide. After an appeal, however, Krstic was only found guilty for complicity in genocide (Prosecutor *v.* Krstic, 2004). In a subsequent decision, the Appeals Chamber confirmed that Bosnian Serb troops had committed genocide at Srebrenica, but found that certain officers of the Bosnian Serb army such as Vidoje Blagojevic did not act with the necessary genocidal intent (Prosecutor *v.* Blagojevic, 2007).

Later, though, in June 2010, the ICTY rendered a decision on Srebrenica convicting Bosnian Serb military officers for committing genocide and not merely being accomplices (Prosecutor v. Popovic et al., 2010). Many expect the same outcome for the ongoing case against the former political leader of the Bosnian Serbs, Radovan Karadzic. Karadzic was finally arrested in Belgrade in 2008, after 13 years in hiding. The trial commenced in October 2009 and is expected to last at least another year or two both because of the extensive scope of the charges against Karadzic, the complexity of the matter, and his decision and right to represent himself.

Why has the ICTY held that only the mass executions at Srebrenica constitute genocide versus atrocities committed in other parts of the former Yugoslavia? The answer lies in the legal definition of genocide pursuant to which the perpetrator has to act with "the intent to destroy in whole or in part" a group protected under the UNCG. According to the judges, only the evidence presented in regard to Srebrenica sufficed for the conclusion that there was specific genocidal intent to destroy a protected group in whole or in part. The ICTY judges found that in other instances the crimes in question aimed at terrorizing the civilian population and ultimately at removing all non-Serbs from what was considered Serb territory, but did not entail the intent to destroy a specific group in whole or in part. This view was later confirmed by the ICJ in the aforementioned case between Bosnia and Serbia. Only at the national level can one find courts that have put forward a different view on the character of the conflict in Bosnia as a whole. In Germany, for example, the Federal Constitutional Court has confirmed lower court convictions on the crime of genocide that were not related to Srebrenica, but other locations in Bosnia (German Federal Constitutional Court, 2000). The Bosnian War Crimes Chamber has since expressed the same view.

Outside the legal community, however, the picture is more ambivalent. For example, on the one hand, a number of monographs on the wars in the Former Yugoslavia do not refer to the conflict in Bosnia as a whole as genocide (see, for example, Lampe, 2000; Naimark, 2001; see also Burg & Shoup, 1999, p. 14). On the other hand, numerous other scholars and journalists writing about Bosnia speak of genocide and do so with great verve (see, for example, Cigar, 1995; Fein, 2000; Power, 2002; Lemarchand, 2003). Some proponents of using the term genocide in regard to the conflict in Bosnia have sharply criticized the legal discourse for its alleged "inability, as yet, to match reality authentically" (Charny, 2005, p. ix). Similarly, the aforementioned judgment of the ICJ has been rejected as a "travesty of justice," as a result of its engaging in judicial "hair-splitting" that has "made the definition of genocide so restrictive that the phenomenon of genocide effectively disappears altogether" (Hoare, 2007, n.p.). Another observer has called the judgment an "exercise in denial" and "perverse" (Shaw, 2007, n.p.). This being said, it seems easier to renounce the findings of the ICJ and the ICTY than to present a detailed and thoughtful argument as to why the conflict in Bosnia as a whole should be characterized as genocide.

Living with the Scars

Whether war crimes, crimes against humanity or genocide, any conflict involving atrocity crimes leaves the affected community in a state of deep distress and trauma.[12] The process of reconciling the different actors and of those of various ethnic, political, or other groups becomes even more challenging if the atrocity crimes were not committed as part of an inter-state conflict, but took place within one and the same society, in some cases pitching neighbor against neighbor. Along with other objectives such as rebuilding the rule of law and instituting democracy, any post-conflict effort is difficult and protracted—not to mention prone to setbacks. Bosnia is no exception in this regard. In fact, Bosnia can (and does) serve as an example of the fact that even in Europe, with the substantive financial and political support from various international organizations such as the UN, OSCE, and European Union, the rebuilding and reconciling of a post-conflict society remains a Herculean task.

To start with, there are a number of positive developments indicating that Bosnia is making progress toward becoming a stable, peaceful state and an active participant at the international level. For example, more than one million refugees have returned to their homes since the signing of the Dayton Agreement in late 1995. Significantly, more than 400,000 people returned to municipalities where they are, in terms of ethnicity, in the minority.[13] Another sign of progress is that around half of Bosnia's 500,000 war-damaged homes have been rebuilt. Nearly all property disputes have been resolved peacefully. Furthermore, the number of international peacekeepers has been reduced from more than 60,000 in the mid-1990s to less than 2,000 today. Moreover, the mandate of the High Representative of the international community in Bosnia is phasing out, which means that Bosnia will win back a great deal of sovereignty and responsibility over its own affairs. At the international level, Bosnia has entered into the so-called Stabilization and Association process, preparing the country for a future membership in the European Union. Furthermore, in 2007 Bosnia was elected to the UN Human Rights Council, and in 2010–2011 it was elected to serve as a non-permanent member of the UN Security Council.

These positive developments, however, cannot hide the fact that there are a number of persisting problems. At the political level, the scars of the war in the 1990s are impossible to overlook. Bosnia is composed of two "entities" established at Dayton: the Bosnian Muslim Croat Federation, which occupies 51% of the territory of Bosnia and Herzegovina, and Republika Srpska, the Serb entity that occupies the other 49%. Thus, Bosnia's internal set-up "recognizes" the logic of the "ethnic cleansing" campaigns carried out during the war; it even places Srebrenica as the execution site of more than 7,000 Bosnian Muslim men in the land of the Bosnian Serbs.[14] Srebrenica remains a troubled and physically battered place. Prior to the war, about 37,000 people lived in Srebrenica, 73% of them Bosnian Muslims and 23% Bosnian Serbs; today, some 6,000 Serbs and 4,000 Muslims live there. Moreover, the economic situation in the municipality is very poor, with few outside investors and a high rate of unemployment.

The relationship between the Bosnian Muslim-Croat Federation and Republika Srpska—which are compelled to work together in the multi-ethnic presidency of Bosnia—has been difficult and continues to complicate numerous important projects and hinder constitutional amendments (cf. International Crisis Group, 2009). The splits running through Bosnia do not only show as political and administrative borders on the map. Bosnian Muslims, Croats, and Serbs have also moved and changed their lives as a response to the war and the atrocity crimes committed throughout the early 1990s. Sarajevo, for example, prior to the war was home to more than 520,000 people and of these about 50% were Bosnian Muslims, 30% ethnic Serbs, 7% ethnic Croats, and 13% considered themselves as Yugoslavs or belonged to minority groups. Today, even if the exact numbers remain controversial, it is clear that the situation has changed drastically; Sarajevo's population has shrunk to around 400,000 and is dominated by Bosnian Muslims (nearly 80%). The few remaining ethnic Serbs (c.11%) live separated in what they call "Serb Sarajevo." Furthermore, Bosnia is also struggling with segregated schools where children take "national subjects" in which they learn the respective versions of "national history," leading to de facto discrimination and further separation. At elections, ethnic groups largely vote for parties of their own ethnicity. For future generations of Bosnians, it seems, Tito's slogan of "brotherhood and unity" will be little more than a historical reminiscence.

Despite the work of the ICTY and organizations such as the International Commission on Missing Persons (see www.ic-mp.org), thousands of Bosnians still do not know the whereabouts of missing family members. It is likely that many will never receive this information; and that is shocking when one realizes that more than 12,000 individuals are still missing after all of these years.

At Srebrenica, close to the former base of the Dutch UN peacekeepers at Potocari, a burial site has been established for those victims of the 1995 mass executions whose remains were found in one of the numerous mass graves in the region and which could be identified. In 2007, Potocari also became the site of a memorial called the Srebrenica Memorial Room (see www.potocarimc.ba/_ba/ssoba). Every year in July there is a commemoration to mark the anniversary of the fall of Srebrenica and to bury newly identified victims, bringing together tens of thousands of Bosnian Muslims and a small number of representatives from the international community. In the beginning the Bosnian Muslims could only visit Potocari under the protection of a strong police force as Bosnian Serbs would throw stones at their buses and harass them on their journey. Eventually the situation improved, but different opinions as to what and who to commemorate remain. In July 2005, for example, some Bosnian Serbs erected a seven-meter high cross in Kravica to mark the killing of some 40 Serbs by Bosnian Muslim forces in January 1993. The cross is placed at a highly visible spot which is along the main route that many of the buses bringing Bosnian Muslims to Potocari have to pass by. Kravica is also the place where an estimated 1,000 Bosnian Muslim men and boys were taken to be executed in July 1995.

Conclusion

In an earlier edition of this collection, Eric Markusen, one of the pioneers of genocide studies, wrote that he believed that the Bosnian Serbs and, on a smaller scale, Bosnian Croats did commit genocide (Mennecke & Markusen, 2004, p. 429). Our co-authored text continued, noting that

> Genocide scholars ... will in no way be bound by the final verdict of the ICTY or other legal institutions.... At the same time, genocide scholars will have to confront the fact that for the first time in history there is a legal body meticulously assessing the character of a conflict on the basis of a legal definition. The ICTY will make its final assessment after having heard and cross-examined thousands of survivors and expert witnesses and having analyzed tens of thousands of relevant documents, files and videos from the Balkan and other relevant countries. While law does not define reality, the work of the ICTY and other legal institutions should be scrutinized closely by any scholars interested in Bosnia and genocide (Mennecke & Markusen, 2004, p. 430).

The present author believes that this statement has retained its significance.

To scrutinize the legal proceedings also means to critically engage with their findings. This was, for example, not done by the ICJ in its aforementioned genocide case where the judges chose to limit themselves to citing and confirming the ICTY's findings without putting the relevant case-law through a critical analysis (Mennecke & Tams, 2007, pp. 73f.). Thus, there is more research to be done on the question of genocide. Scholars bear a responsibility that this research does not degenerate into polemics about the label "genocide"; instead, genocide scholars should recall that this "debate is not about whether the crimes ... actually took place; it is only about whether they are most properly described as crimes against humanity, rather than genocide" (Schabas, 2001, p. 288f.).

Eyewitness Accounts

The following accounts are excerpts from two testimonies given before the ICTY. The ICTY has on its website collected statements both by victims and perpetrators of the grave crimes committed during the conflict (www.icty.org/sid/105; www.icty.org/sid/203). The first witness cited below is Drazen Erdemovic, a former soldier in the Bosnian Serb army, who confessed to taking part in the Srebrenica massacre in July 1995. As discussed in more detail in the preceding chapter, the ICTY has held that of all the crimes committed during the conflict in Bosnia Herzegovina, only the Srebrenica massacre can be classified as genocide. Erdemovic was originally sentenced to 10 years in prison, but the sentence was later reduced and he was released from a Norwegian prison. The second testimony was given in the so-called Foca rape case, in which several Bosnian Serb men were eventually convicted of crimes against humanity for their systematic and repeated sexual abuse of captured civilian Muslim women. Numerous scholars have classified this type of sexual violence during the conflict as genocidal; for further references see the preceding chapter. The name of the witness, who was only 15 years old at the time of her serial rapes, was not disclosed to the public; she is known only as witness "87."

Account 1

Drazen Erdemovic, born on November 25, 1971, in Tuzla, appeared before the ICTY on Monday, May 22, 2000. The following is excerpted from transcript pages 3125 through 3135. Erdemovic is being questioned by Mark Harmon for the Office of the Prosecutor.

Q: What happened then?
A: Then Brano came back to us and told us that buses would come with civilians from Srebrenica on them. And I and some others started

objecting, saying, "What are we going to do there?" And he said that we would have to execute those people. In the course of this debate, the first bus was already arriving. This may have been 20 minutes later or half an hour later.... When the first bus arrived—I know about myself; I don't know exactly about the others, what they said—I said that I did not want to do that, that I cannot do that, that that is not the task of our unit. Brano told me then, "If you won't do it, stand up with them or give them your rifle, and you will see whether they will shoot you."

Q: Please continue.
A: When the first bus arrived, Brano told us that we had to deploy in a line from this garage here (indicates), from this building, in a straight line, perhaps 100 metres long. I don't know exactly.

Q: All right. Please continue, Mr. Erdemovic.
A: Then I saw two policemen taking men out, men who were in the bus, and these two men were probably the security for the transport of these men, and they reached Brano and Vlastimir Golijan [Ed. note: two other Bosnian Serb soldiers]. And the first group of people were brought behind this garage down there, maybe 100 metres away, maybe more, but roughly to such a position. Then Brano told us to form a line. The men in front of us were ordered to turn their backs. When those men turned their backs to us, we shot at them. We were given orders to shoot.

Q: Did Brano also shoot?
A: Yes.

Q: Did all of the members of your unit, the ten people who had been sent over there, did they all shoot?
A: Yes.

Q: What happened then?
A: The second group was brought, and they were lined up immediately behind those first group. Our backs were turned to the garage and we were moving in the direction of the garage. And that is how groups were brought in: Men again turned their backs to us and we shot that group of people who were in front of us.

Q: And then I take it another group was brought for execution, and they were executed as well?
A: Yes.

Q: And is that how the scene repeated itself throughout the day?

A: Yes, only I have to say that the last group of the first bus, or at the beginning of the second bus, I know that Aleksandar Cvetkovic [Ed. note: another Bosnian Serb soldier] and Brano had the idea to speed up the execution so that we could use a machine-gun, an M-84.

Q: What happened with that M-84 machine-gun?

A: Then Aleksandar Cvetkovic took this machine-gun, positioned it, and started shooting at the group of ten. However, because the ammunition was what it was, the people were just mutilated and wounded, and they begged to be finished off.

Q: Please continue.

A: Then a hot argument ensued between me, Brano, Slovenac, Goronja, and Aco, because some people could no longer listen to those men pleading to be killed, and we were saying if they have to die, why couldn't they die decently, peacefully, rather than being mutilated and hit and insulted and hurt? And then they put away that M-84 machine-gun.

Q: Now, Mr. Erdemovic, were any of these men who were brought down to be executed blindfolded, did they have their hands tied, or do you recall?

A: I can only remember that in the first bus they were blindfolded and their hands were tied, as far as I can remember.

Q: Now, approximately how many buses arrived at the Branjevo farm on the 16th of July, as best as you can recall?

A: As far as I can recall, because those were terrible moments for me, I think between 15 and 20.

Q: What time did the executions start in the morning of the 16th of July?

A: I think around 10:00.

Q: What time did they end on that same day?

A: 3:00 or 4:00 in the afternoon.

Q: Now, how many people do you estimate, Mr. Erdemovic, were executed at the Branjevo farm on the 16th of July?

A: I think about 1,000, 1,200.

Q: Your unit, the members of the 10th—all of the members who went on this assignment, including Brano, participated in those executions, did they not?

A: Yes.

Q: At some point in time, Mr. Erdemovic, did you have a conversation with one of the victims and attempt to spare him from the fate that awaited him?

A: Yes. That man, as soon as he got off the bus, started saying that he had helped some Serbs to get out of Srebrenica and reach the Federal Republic of Yugoslavia, and he was showing some pieces of paper with the telephone numbers of those people. I took him aside and told him, "Come here." He did. I started talking to him. We spoke about what had happened in Srebrenica. I let him light a cigarette. As there was a tap, a water tap not far, and I think I also gave him some water to drink. I was sorry and I wanted to save that man and others, but I selected him because he said that he had saved Serbs in Srebrenica and helped them to reach the territory of the Federal Republic of Yugoslavia, and I thought that I might save him thanks to that. However, not long afterwards, Vlastimir Golijan [Ed. note: another Bosnian Serb soldier] came, he took the man, and then Brano came too. And I said, "Why don't we investigate and see whether this man actually did what he said?"—to save him, and they said as one that they didn't want to have any witnesses.

Q: Was that man executed?
A: Yes. I think Vlastimir Golijan killed him.

Q: Now, Mr. Erdemovic, did you see Brano Gojkovic order the bus drivers, who were transporting these prisoners to the Branjevo farm, to do anything?
A: Yes, After the second bus, or the first—I don't know exactly—they started drinking and the spirits started to have their effect. And then Vlastimir and Brano were saying that the drivers could also be witnesses, and I know that one of the drivers did shoot at a man and Brano gave him a gun to do that. He shot at a man.

Q: Shot at him or killed him?
A: He shot at him. Now, whether that man died straight away, I don't know, I can't remember, I can't say. But he did shoot at him.

Account 2

Witness 87 appeared in the Foca rape trial on April 4, 2000. She is being questioned by an attorney for the Office of the Prosecutor. The following is excerpted from pages 1663 through 1675 of the trial transcripts.

Q: Thank you. Now, Witness, how old are you?
A: Twenty-three and a half.

Q: In April of 1992, how old were you?
A: About 15.

Q: Where did you live?
A: In Trosanj.

Q: Were there both Serbs and Muslims living there?
A: Trosanj was inhabited only by Muslims, the part up to the road, and a place called Mjesaja was inhabited by both Serbs and Muslims.

Q: What ethnicity are you?
A: Muslim.

Q: In 1992 whom did you live with?
A: With my mother, father, sister, and brother.

Q: In 1992 were you still in school?
A: Yes.

Q: What grade were you in?
A: Second grade of secondary school.

Q: Do you know when the war in Foca started?
A: I think it was on the 8th of April, though I'm not quite sure.

Q: At that time could you hear or see anything?
A: Yes. We could hear shooting, explosions, sometimes houses set on fire, and things like that.

Q: Did you see soldiers?
A: I didn't see soldiers until roughly the 3rd of July.

Q: Before the 3rd of July, how did the war affect your life? Did you continue to go to school?
A: No. The school work was suspended, I think it was at the beginning of April.

Q: Were you able to continue living in your house?
A: For a very short time. Afterwards we had to hide in the woods.

Q: Why did you have to hide in the woods?
A: Out of fear that we would be killed or something like that.

Q: Did you feel that you were targeted because you were Muslims?
A: Yes.

Q: Who else was in the woods with you?
A: My family and two other families. That was at the beginning. Later, a short while before we were attacked, there were several families in one group.

Q: What ethnicity were all these people in the woods with you?
A: They were all Muslim.

Q: When was your village attacked?
A: On the 3rd of July, 1992.

Q: Do you recall what time of day it was?
A: I couldn't tell the exact time, but it was about 6:00 in the morning. It was very early.

Q: Where were you when the village was attacked?
A: We were sleeping in a tent in the woods.

Q: What did you hear?
A: We heard shots.

Q: What did you do?
A: When we heard the shots there was panic, and the people started fleeing. Nobody knew where to go, in which direction. When the first man was hit or, rather, wounded, then we were swept by real panic.

Q: ...Did you see anyone else get shot?
A: Yes. I saw three persons who were shot. One was a man and two women.

Q: Do you know approximately how old the man was?
A: I don't know exactly. About 50 maybe.

Q: What else did you see the soldiers do?
A: When they started shooting at us, we were fleeing, and they ran after us. Then they surrounded a group of us, and they beat the men, demanding that they tell them where the weapons were, where they had hidden the weapons and things like that.

Q: Were there any weapons with you in the woods?
A: No.

Q: Was your father one of the men being beaten?
A: Yes.

Q: What did the soldiers do then?

A: They separated the men from the women and the children. They took us out of the woods to a meadow. It wasn't far. Then they lined us up, and then they asked whether we had gold, money, and the like. Then in our tents they found quite a number of old photographs and documents, and then they showed us those photographs, asking us who they were, where they were, and the like.

Q: In the meadow, was it women and children or men?

A: In the meadow were the women and the children. Though I don't remember very well, the men were not right next to us. They were separated from us, as far as I can recollect. They were not lined up in the same row, in any event.

Q: Could you hear what happened to the men?

A: After that, they told us that they were taking us somewhere, the women and children, and we hadn't moved far from the meadow when we heard shots, and I think—it is my opinion that those men up there were killed at the time.

Q: Did you ever see your father again?

A: No.

Q: Were you taken off at that time?

A: I was taken, but not for interrogation.

Q: Who took you?

A: I didn't know that man before, but his name was Pero. I don't know his surname. He took me away to a room. Well, it was a sort of room. But he didn't call out my name; he just came and took me by the hand and took me off.

Q: Did he tell you why he was taking you?

A: No.

Q: What did he do when he took you to this room?

A: When he took me to the room, he first of all ordered me to take my clothes off, and I didn't directly refuse, but I didn't take my clothes off. Then he did so. After that he raped me.

Q: Are you able to describe exactly what he did?

A: It's a little difficult for me. Well, what I mean is he had sexual relations; forcibly, against my will, he had sexual relations with me.

Q: Did he put his penis in your vagina?
A: Yes.

Q: What did he do after that?
A: I don't remember the exact details. I think somebody else came, who was in front of the door, who had been in front of the door, and who took me off again to where the others were, lined up to where the others were.

Q: What happened when you were returned to that group?
A: I don't think anything happened; that is to say, it was as if I wasn't present, conscious of it all, what was happening to me. Although not much time went by before two men turned up, who called me out by name, and the name of another individual, and we were asked to go to this so-called interrogation.

Q: That other individual, was it your sister?
A: Yes.

Q: What happened to you when you were taken out again?
A: They took me into a sort of room, not a big one; a small one, where there was a bed, a table, and a couple of chairs, and I think there were four soldiers in there, although people would be coming in and going out all the time.

Q: Do you know who those four soldiers were, or do you remember who they were?
A: I know two of them; that is to say, I didn't know one of them before, but I knew his name. I know the other one's name, because I knew him from before. Actually, I didn't know him, but I knew who he was. As for the other two, I didn't know their names.

Q: Can you tell us the names of the soldiers that you did know?
A: Dragan Zelenovic, nicknamed Zelja, and the other one was Veso Miletic.

Q: What did they do when you were brought to the room?
A: First of all they asked me questions.

Q: What kind of questions?
A: First of all they asked me about the other inhabitants of Trosanj, where they were, and where the inhabitants had hidden their weapons; do we know any of the places where the other inhabitants of Trosanj

could have escaped to and hidden. Then they asked me how old I was, my age, and whether I went to school or not.

Q: Did you answer those questions?
A: The first questions they asked me, I wasn't able to answer, because I didn't know. But I only answered the question—the last questions; that is to say, how old I was and whether I went to school.

Q: Did they ask you anything else about yourself?
A: They asked me whether I was a virgin, and I answered that I was a virgin until a few moments ago, or words to that effect.

Q: What was their reaction when you told them that?
A: I don't remember.

Q: What did they do?
A: After that Zelenovic told me to take my clothes off, and when I didn't do so, he did it. And then he raped me. And Miletic did the same, and the other two whose names I don't know.

Q: What happened after they raped you?
A: I don't remember exactly who it was, who took me out of that room, outside, to a bus where the other people were already sitting, except my mother, who was still outside, because she didn't want to leave without me. When I arrived, I got into the bus and then they took us off to the secondary school centre.

Q: Did you tell your mother what had just happened to you?
A: No.

Q: Why not?
A: I think that at that time I didn't have the strength to, to even look her in the eyes. Not only her, but anybody, to look anybody in the eyes.

Q: How did you feel at that time?
A: It's very difficult to describe that. I know that I was terribly frightened, I felt ashamed in a way, and in a way I felt very, very dirty, soiled.

Notes

1. The author would like to acknowledge the contribution of the late Eric Markusen, a great friend and mentor, who co-authored an earlier version of this chapter for the second edition of this book.
2. This chapter will focus on the events in Bosnia Herzegovina. For an overview of what subsequently happened in Kosovo and a discussion of whether the crimes committed in Kosovo amounted to genocide, see Mennecke (2009, pp. 529ff.).

3.   The Former Yugoslavia was a multi-ethnic federation including, among other groups, Serbs, Croats, and Bosnian Muslims. The latter were recognized by the Yugoslav constitution as a nation so that the term "Bosnian Muslim" did not refer to the religious affiliation, but to the "nationality" of a person. Starting with the war in the early 1990s, some Bosnian Muslims referred to themselves as "Bosniaks" to express their political aim of conserving Bosnia Herzegovina as an entity and to downplay the religious undertones of the term "Bosnian Muslims" which was utilized in war propaganda. Today, the term "Bosniaks" has become officially recognized by the state of Bosnia and Herzegovina. For the remainder of this chapter, we will in accordance with the language used by the ICTY retain the term "Bosnian Muslims." For a more comprehensive discussion of the complicated history of the different terms see Burg and Shoup (1999, pp. 18ff.).

4.   The number of victims of the war in Bosnia Herzegovina remains the subject of controversy among both scholars and citizens of the region. In 2005, following several years of research, the non-governmental Research and Documentation Centre (RDC) in Sarajevo produced a report listing the names of all known victims from all ethnic groups, which subsequently was confirmed by a team of international experts. The centre had established the personal data of more than 97,000 victims (of which more than 57,000 were soldiers and more than 64,000 were Bosnian Muslims) and estimated that the final result would not reach far beyond 100,000 dead. See the website of the RDC at www.idc.org.ba. For a discussion of the number of victims of the killings at Srebrenica see Prosecutor v. Popovic et al. (2010, paras. 607–664).

5.   This assessment of the tribunal is shared widely. See, for example, the Final Report of the UN Commission of Experts (1994, para. 251), Naimark (2001, p. 167), Bringa (2002, p. 199), Mennecke and Markusen (2003, pp. 293ff.), and Human Rights Watch (2001).

6.   The ICTY dealt repeatedly with massive crimes committed in Bosnian Serb detention camps. Bosnian Croat and Bosnian Muslim forces also established such camps, even if not as many. See, for example, the "Celebici Camp Case" about a prison camp near Konjic in central Bosnia, where Serb detainees were killed, tortured, sexually assaulted, beaten, and otherwise subjected to cruel and inhumane treatment (Prosecutor v. Mucic et al., Trial Chamber, Judgment, November 16, 1998).

7.   It should be noted that the Yugoslav Jews and Roma suffered proportionally the most grievous losses at the hands of Nazi Germany, its allies and the Croat Ustasha regime. Four out of five Yugoslav Jews perished (c.57,000) and one-third of the Roma population (c.18,000) were exterminated. See Benson (2004, pp. 77–78).

8.   The arms embargo was imposed by the UN Security Council in Resolution 713 (1991), before Yugoslavia dissolved. In the case against Serbia concerning alleged violations of the Genocide Convention, Bosnia argued before the ICJ that this resolution effectively kept Bosnia from stopping the ongoing genocide. For an interesting discussion of this matter, see Lauterpacht (1993, paras. 84–107).

9.   A French general, Bernard Janvier, had been in charge of the UN peacekeeping operations in Bosnia when Srebrenica fell. It was also a French General, Philippe Morillon, who, in 1993, famously promised the population of Srebrenica that they were "now under protection of the UN forces" (Report by the UN General on the Fall of Srebrenica, 1999, para. 38), and thus, presumably, had nothing to fear. For further information and a critical evaluation of the French proceedings, see the website of the French non-governmental organization Médecins Sans Frontières at www.msf.org.

10. Application instituting Proceedings, Bosnia Herzegovina v. Yugoslavia (Serbia and Montenegro), March 20, 1993, para. 137. All the relevant material concerning this case, including expert witness testimonies and the final judgment, with its separate and dissenting opinions, can be accessed at the website of the ICJ at www.icj-cij.org.

11. It should be mentioned though that Serbia's president called upon the parliament and the people of Serbia to accept the judgment and to condemn the genocide (Reuters, 2007a).

12. After 1995, many of the Dutch peacekeepers remained deeply marked by their experiences in the safe area. Many left the service, some suffered post-traumatic stress syndrome and an unknown number committed suicide. In the Netherlands the soldiers often served as scapegoats and were portrayed as having failed in their duty; in December 2006, the Dutch government attempted to ameliorate this by presenting the soldiers with an insignia. Even

though they did not receive a medal of honor, this move outraged survivors in Bosnia. A year later, some of the former peacekeepers visited Srebrenica, which again caused mixed reactions (Dzidic, 2007).

13. During the war in Bosnia, about two million people became refugees. With more than one million having returned to their homes, the remaining people are believed to be spread out over the Balkans and other countries. Around 100,000 live in Serbia and Croatia and an additional 115,000, including many Serbs, are still displaced within Bosnia itself. Information on the return of refugees to Bosnia can be found at the website of the UN Refugee Agency at www.unhcr.org.

14. This constellation—Srebrenica forming part of Republika Srpska which in turn forms part of Bosnia Herzegovina—also influenced the previously mentioned lawsuit of Bosnia against Serbia before the ICJ. Bosnian Serb politicians tried to obstruct this case, among others, by filing an application with the Bosnian Constitutional Court to stop the lawsuit. The Bosnian Serbs saw little to gain from a case that was aimed at establishing that Serbia had committed genocide in Bosnia, as it was obvious that this also would affect the political and possibly legal standing of Republika Srpska. The strange situation of Bosnia entailed the somewhat absurd possibility that the ICJ ultimately would rule in favor of Bosnia and sentence Serbia to pay reparations for her involvement at Srebrenica—and that such reparations would then partly benefit Republika Srpska, the entity that was established as a result of the crimes committed at Srebrenica. When, in February 2007, the ICJ ruled that Srebrenica had been the site of genocide committed by Bosnian Serb forces, survivors from Srebrenica demanded (without success) that the town be given a special, internationalized status and formally separated from Republika Srpska.

References

Allcock, John B. (2005). "The International Criminal Tribunal for the Former Yugoslavia." The Scholars' Initiative—Confronting Yugoslavia's Controversies.

Amnesty International (2009). '*Whose justice?' The women of Bosnia and Herzegovina are still waiting.* Retrieved from: www.amnesty.org/en/library/asset/EUR63/006/2009/en/8af5ed43-5094-48c9-bfab-1277b5132faf/eur630062009eng.pdf.

Assemblée Nationale (2001). *Rapport D'Information Sur Les Événements de Srebrenica.*

Benson, Leslie (2004). *Yugoslavia: A concise history.* Hampshire: Palgrave Macmillan.

Bringa, Tone (2002). Averted gaze: Genocide in Bosnia-Herzegovina. In Alexander L. Hinton (Ed.), *Annihilating difference: The anthropology of genocide* (pp. 194–225). Berkeley, CA: University of California Press.

Burg, Steven L., & Shoup, Paul S. (1999). *The war in Bosnia-Herzegovina: Ethnic conflict and international intervention.* Armonk, NY: M.E. Sharpe.

Case Concerning the Application of the Convention on the Prevention and Punishment of the Crime of Genocide, Bosnia *v.* Yugoslavia (Serbia and Montenegro), Judgment, International Court of Justice, February 26, 2007.

Cassese, Antonio (2007, February 27). A judicial massacre. *Guardian,* n.p.

Charny, Israel W. (2005). Foreword. In Samuel Totten (Ed.), *Genocide at the millennium: A critical bibliography* (Vol. 5, pp. vii–xi). New Brunswick, NJ: Transaction Publishers.

Cigar, Norman (1995). *Genocide in Bosnia: The policy of ethnic cleansing.* College Station, TX: Texas A&M University Press.

Clifford, Lisa (2007, June 9). Srebrenica survivors sue Dutch and UN. *IWPR Tribunal Update, 505,* n.p.

Cushman, Thomas, & Mestrovic, Stjepan G. (Eds.) (1996). *This time we knew: Western responses to genocide in Bosnia.* New York: New York University Press.

Dzidic, Denis (2007, October 31). Fury as Dutch soldiers return to Srebrenica. *IWPR Tribunal Update, 523,* n.p.

Fein, Helen (2000). Civil wars and genocides: Paths and circles. *Human Rights Review, 1*(3), 49–61.

Fejzic et al. *v.* The State of the Netherlands and the United Nations, Writ of Summons, District Court, The Hague, June 4, 2007.

German Federal Constitutional Court, 2 BvR 1290/99, Decision, December 12, 2000.

Hoare, Marko Attila (2007). The International Court of Justice and the decriminalization of genocide. *Bosnia Report, 55–56*. Retrieved from: www.bosnia.org.uk/bosrep/report_format.cfm ?articleid=3170&reportid=173.

Human Rights Watch (2001). *The Milosevic case: Questions and answers—Is there an anti-Serb Bias at the tribunal?* Retrieved from: www.hrw.org/news/2001/08/28/milosevic-case-questions-and-answers.

Ingrao, Charles (2005). "The safe areas (1992–1995)." The Scholars' Initiative—Confronting Yugoslavia's Controversies.

International Crisis Group (2009). *Bosnia's dual crisis*. Policy Briefing, Europe Briefing No. 57. Washington, DC. Retrieved from: www.crisisgroup.org/~/media/Files/europe/B57%20 Bosnias%20Dual%20Crisis.pdf.

Jelacic, Nerma (2007, February 26). Dismay and jubilation of Hague court judgment. *Balkan Insight*, n.p.

Lampe, John R. (2000). *Yugoslavia as history: Twice there was a country*. Cambridge: Cambridge University Press.

Lauterpacht, Elihu (1993). Separate Opinion, Case Concerning Application of the Convention on the Prevention and Punishment of the Crime of Genocide, Order of September 13, 1993, International Court of Justice, ICJ Reports, pp. 407–448.

Lemarchand, René (2003). Comparing the killing fields: Rwanda, Cambodia, and Bosnia. In Steven L.B. Jensen (Ed.) *Genocide: cases, comparisons, and contemporary debates* (pp. 141–173). Copenhagen: The Danish Center for Holocaust and Genocide Studies.

MacDonald, David Bruce (2002). *Balkan holocausts? Serbian and Croatian victim-centred Prosecutor v. Propaganda and the War in Yugoslavia*. Manchester: Manchester University Press.

Mennecke, Martin (2009). Genocidal violence in the former Yugoslavia: Bosnia Herzegovina and Kosovo. In Samuel Totten and William S. Parsons (Eds.) *Century of genocide: Critical essays and eyewitness accounts* (3rd ed.) (pp. 507–552). New York and London: Routledge.

Mennecke, Martin, & Markusen, Eric (2003). The International Criminal Tribunal for the Former Yugoslavia and the crime of genocide. In Steven L.B. Jensen (Ed.), *Genocide: Cases, comparisons, and contemporary debates* (pp. 293–359). Copenhagen: The Danish Center for Holocaust and Genocide Studies.

Mennecke, Martin, & Markusen, Eric (2004). Genocide in Bosnia and Herzegovina. In Samuel Totten, William S. Parsons, & Israel W. Charny (Eds.) *Century of genocide: Critical essays and eyewitness accounts* (2nd ed.) (pp. 415–447). New York and London: Routledge.

Mennecke, Martin, & Tams, Christian J. (2007). The genocide case before the International Court of Justice. *Security and Peace, 25*(2), 71–76.

Naimark, Norman M. (2001). *Fires of hatred: Ethnic cleansing in twentieth century Europe*. Cambridge, MA: Harvard University Press.

Netherlands Institute for War Documentation (2002). *Srebrenica, a safe area: Reconstruction, background, consequences, and analyses of the fall of a safe area*. Amsterdam: Boom Publishers.

Orentlicher, Diane (2008). *Shrinking the space for denial: The impact of the ICTY in Serbia*. New York: Open Society Institute.

Power, Samantha (2002). *A problem from hell: America and the age of genocide*. New York: Basic Books.

Prosecutor *v.* Ante Gotovina et al., Trial Chamber, Judgment, April 15, 2011.

Prosecutor *v.* Dragoljub Kunarac et al., Trial Chamber, Judgment, February 22, 2001.

Prosecutor *v.* Radislav Krstic, Appeals Chamber, Judgment, April 19, 2004.

Prosecutor *v.* Radovan Karadzic and Ratko Mladic, Initial Indictment, July 24, 1995.

Prosecutor *v.* Slobodan Milosevic et al., Transcripts, September 26–27, 2002.

Prosecutor *v.* Vidoje Blagojevic, Judgment, Appeals Chamber, May 9, 2007.

Prosecutor *v.* Vujadin Popovic et al., Trial Chamber, Judgment, June 10, 2010.

Remington, Robin Alison (1984). The politics of scarcity in Yugoslavia. *Current History, 83*(496), 370–374.

Republic Srpska, Documentation Centre (2002). *Report about Case Srebrenica (The First Part)*. Banja Luka: Author.

Republika Srpska, The Commission for Investigation of the Events in and Around Srebrenica Between 10th and 19th July 1995 (2004). *The Events In and Around Srebrenica Between 10th and 19th July 1995*.

Reuters (2007a, February 26). President tells Serbia: Condemn Srebrenica massacre. *Reuters* n.p.

Reuters (2007b, February 27). Bosnian Muslims protest against UN court ruling. *Reuters*, n.p.

Schabas, William A. (2001). Was genocide committed in Bosnia and Herzegovina? First judgments of the International Criminal Tribunal for the Former Yugoslavia. *Fordham International Law Journal, 25*(1), 23–53.

Selimovic et al. *v.* Republika Srpska, Decision on Admissibility and Merits, Case No. CH/01/8365 et al., Human Rights Chamber for Bosnia and Herzegovina, March 7, 2003.

Serbian Academy of Arts and Sciences (1986). *Memorandum.*

Shaw, Martin (2007, February 28). *The International Court of Justice: Serbia, Bosnia and genocide.* Retrieved from: www.opendemocracy.net/conflict-institutions_government/icj_bosnia_serbia_4392.jsp

Stitkovac, Ejub (1999). Croatia: The first war. In Jasminka Udovicki & James Ridgeway (Eds.) *Burn this house: The making and unmaking of Yugoslavia* (pp. 153–173). Chapel Hill, NC: Duke University Press.

UN Commission of Experts on Grave Breaches of the Geneva Conventions (1994). *Final report of the Commission of Experts on Grave Breaches of the Geneva Conventions and other violations of international humanitarian law committed in the territory of the former Yugoslavia established pursuant to Security Council Resolution 780 (May 27).* United Nations Document S/1994/674. New York: United Nations.

UN Secretary-General (1999). *Report of the Secretary-General pursuant to General Assembly Resolution 53/35, the fall of Srebrenica. November 15.* 54th Session, UN GA Doc. A/54/549.

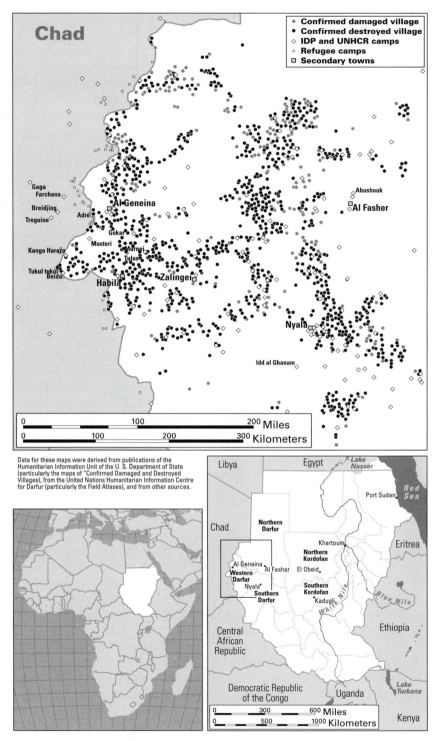

Map 15.1 Darfur region of Sudan

CHAPTER 15

Genocide in Darfur, Sudan

SAMUEL TOTTEN

Introduction

The mass killing[1] of black Africans of Darfur, Sudan, by Government of Sudan (GoS) troops and *Janjaweed*[2] (Arab militia) constitutes the first acknowledged genocide of the 21st century (2003 to present).[3] To date, it is estimated that between 300,000 to 400,000 people have been killed outright and/or perished as a result of "genocide by attrition" (meaning via starvation, dehydration, unattended injuries, and the purposeful withholding of humanitarian aid).

At the outbreak of violence, Darfur, a region in west Sudan, was comprised of three states (Northern Darfur, Western Darfur, and Southern Darfur).[4] The region is roughly the size of France (or Texas), and shares borders with Libya, Chad, and the Central African Republic. The vast majority of the people of Darfur, both the so-called "black Africans" and the Arabs, are Muslim.

Darfur is one of the most under-developed and isolated regions of Sudan, the latter of which constitutes one of the 25 poorest countries in the world. Over 90% of Sudan's citizens live below the poverty line, barely eking out an existence.

While much of the Darfur region consists of large swaths of hot and arid land (except during the rainy season when *wadis* swell with water), it also has lush grasslands where herds graze and areas where crops are cultivated. Up until fairly recently, the most productive land was largely occupied by sedentary farmers and cattle owners, who tended to be non-Arabs. By mutual agreement between the sedentary black Africans and Arab semi-nomadic and nomadic peoples, the pasture land was used at certain times of the year by the nomads to graze their herds. This resulted in a symbiotic relationship of sorts; that is, while the Arabs' animals were

513

allowed to feed and be watered, the herds fertilized the ground owned by the black Africans, thus renewing the soil for subsequent growing seasons.

When conflicts erupted in the not too distant past among individuals and/or groups (be it among individuals in the same village, different black African tribal groups, or between black Africans and Arabs), the disagreements were generally resolved by the intervention and mediation of local leaders (*umdas* or *sheiks*). While neither conflict nor violence were uncommon, it rarely resulted in wholesale violence that went on for months, let alone years. When called for, some sort of "blood money" was paid to the victim, be it for kin who were killed, animals stolen, or for some other transgression. The handing over of the blood money by the "guilty party" to the "victim" generally settled the grievance, and life went on as usual.

Notably, there was a certain amount of intermarriage among and between the various peoples of Darfur, including non-Arabs and Arabs. Thus, different groups of people cohabited as neighbors, friends, and even relatives—and not as sworn enemies due to ethnic, racial, or any other type of classification/category.

Who Committed this Genocide?

Both GoS troops and the so-called *Janjaweed* (Arab militia) are the actors carrying out the actual killing, mass and gang rape, and the wholesale destruction of black African villages. Ample evidence indicates that the vast majority of the attacks against black African villages from 2003 onward were undertaken, in tandem, by GoS troops and the *Janjaweed*. In most cases, the attacks involved bombings by GoS aircraft, followed by a ground attack involving hundreds of *Janjaweed* on camels and horses and four-wheel vehicles (some mounted with machine guns) carrying both GoS troops and *Janjaweed*.

The *Janjaweed* were largely semi-nomadic and nomadic Arab herders. Many had previously fought in one or more of the wars in the region, a good number serving as mercenaries. It is significant to recognize that many Arab herders were forced—upon the threat of death to themselves and harm to their families—to join in the attacks against the black Africans. It is also important to note that many Arab herders were not involved in the attacks, were not members of the *Janjaweed*, and did not necessarily support—and may have, in fact, looked askance at—the actions of the GoS and *Janjaweed*. In this regard, Julie Flint's (2004) observations are significant:

> It cannot be stated too often that the majority of Arab tribes in Darfur refused to join the government in its scorched earth and

genocidal actions in Darfur, despite blandishments, threats and inducements that range from sacks filled with cash to cars to development programs and homes in the capital, Khartoum.

In Darfur, the Rizeigat, Beni Halba, Habbaniya, Taaisha, Mahariya, Beni Hussein, Misseriya, and Maaliya tribes, to name only some of Darfur's Arab tribes, all chose either to cast their lot in with their African neighbors or endeavoured to remain neutral. (p. 1)

The Sudanese government readily admits that its troops responded to attacks on government facilities (including military bases) by black African rebels, but it has claimed, time and again, that the *Janjaweed* was responsible for the subsequent *and sustained* scorched-earth attacks against the black Africans and that it (the government) did not have the means to rein them in as they (the *Janjaweed*) were loose cannons. Such assertions are disingenuous, at best; again, ample evidence exists that the vast majority of the attacks on the black African villages were carried out by *both* GoS troops and the *Janjaweed* (Human Rights Watch, 2004a; Physicians for Human Rights, 2005; U.S. State Department, 2004).

There is also evidence that the GoS purposely hired the *Janjaweed* to join GoS troops in carrying out the attacks because GoS military troops were already overstretched in their war in southern Sudan and thus did not have enough soldiers available to address the crisis in Darfur (Human Rights Watch, 2004b).[5] Concomitantly, since many of the soldiers in the GoS military were black African, the GoS didn't trust the latter to carry out attacks on their own people's villages.

Who were the Victims?

As previously mentioned, the victims of the genocide in Darfur were various black African tribal groups. The main groups were the Fur, Massalit, and Zaghawa. That said, like many, if not most, of the issues surrounding the Darfur crisis, the composition of the population of Darfur is a complex one. Indeed, although "African" and "Arab" are common terms used in describing and, at least in part, explaining, the conflict, neither term does justice to the diversity of ethnic groups that make up Darfur nor to "the nuanced relationships among ethnic groups" (Human Rights Watch, 2004a, p. 1 of "The Background").

There are many, in fact, who claim that there is virtually no difference between the so-called black Africans of Darfur and the Arab population (Mamdani quoted in Sengupta, 2004, p. 1; de Waal, 2004a; de Waal, 2004c). Mamdani (2004), for example, asserts that "all parties involved in the Darfur conflict—whether they are referred to as 'Arab' or as

'African'—are equally indigenous and equally black" (p. 2). He has also
stated that "from the cultural point of view, one can be both African and
Arab" (Mamdani, 2004, p. 2). Such individuals assert that all the people
are black (and not necessarily "light" as the Arabs are sometimes purported to be), and that since all live in Africa they are all African. In this
regard, Alex de Waal (2004a), an expert on Sudan, has asserted that
"characterizing the Darfur war as 'Arabs' versus 'Africans' obscures the
reality. Darfur's Arabs are black, indigenous, African Muslims—just like
Darfur's non Arabs, who hail from the Fur, Massalit, Zaghawa and a
dozen smaller tribes" (p. 1). More specifically, de Waal (2004b) asserts
that

> The Zaghawa ... are certainly indigenous, black and African: they
> share distant origins with the Berbers of Morocco and other
> ancient Saharan peoples. But the name of the "Bedeyat," the
> Zaghawa's close kin, should alert us to their true origins: pluralize
> in the more traditional manner and we have "bedeyiin" or
> Bedouins. Similarly, the Zaghawa's adversaries in this war, the
> Darfurian Arabs, are "Arabs." In the ancient sense of "Bedouin,"
> meaning desert nomad ... Darfurian Arabs, too, are indigenous,
> black and African. In fact there are no discernible racial or reli-
> gious differences between the two: all have lived there for centu-
> ries. (n.p.)

Many also assert that there has been so much intermarriage between
various groups (and there are scores upon scores of various tribal groups
within Darfur) that it is almost impossible to definitively state whether a
person is from one tribe (or ethnic group) or another. Some also assert
that "where the vast majority of people [in Darfur] are Muslim and
Arabic-speaking, the distinction between 'Arab' and 'African' is more
cultural than racial" (United Nations Office for the Coordination of
Humanitarian Affairs, 2003, n.p.). Mamdani has asserted that "the real
roots of combat are not racial or ethnic but political and economic"
(quoted in Hill, 2006). Some have also noted that certain individuals
who have, over time, attained a certain amount of wealth have actually
chosen to become "Arab."

All that said, both the perpetrators and the victims themselves *do
make a distinction between* those who are purportedly "Arab" and those
who are purportedly "black African." One major report after another
(Human Rights Watch, 2004a; Physicians for Human Rights, 2005; U.S.
State Department, 2004) that includes first-person testimony by the
internally placed persons (IDPs) and refugees from Darfur contains vast
amounts of information in regard to the aforementioned distinctions

made by the very people involved in the crisis. For example, in its report, *Darfur Destroyed*, Human Rights Watch (2004a) reports that

> Especially since the beginning of the conflict in 2003, members of the Zaghawa, Fur, and Massalit communities have used these terms [black Africans and Arabs] to describe the growing racial and ethnic polarization in Darfur, perceived to result from discrimination and bias emanating from the central government. (p. 1, "The Background")

Such testimony also includes ample evidence that the *Janjaweed* frequently screamed racial epithets at their black African victims. The same is true in the scores of testimony this author has collected in interviews in refugee camps in Chad with survivors of the genocide. More specifically, one black African IDP and refugee after another commented on how the *Janjaweed* (and, for that matter, GoS soldiers) screamed such epithets as slave, slave dogs, and *zurega* (which is roughly the equivalent of "nigger") at them during the attacks on their villages. The victims consider all such terms extremely derogatory and vile.

Other comments that the perpetrators spewed at the black Africans include: "You are not a real Sudanese, you're black.... We are the real Sudanese. No blacks need stay here"; "We are going to cut off your roots"; "The President of Sudan ordered us to cleanse Darfur of the dirty slaves so we can have the beginning of the Arab Union" (quoted in Totten, 2006, p. 98). Emily Wax (2004), a *Washington Post* correspondent in Africa, reported that as a 22-year-old black African woman was grabbed and about to be raped by six *Janjaweed*, they spat out: "Black girl, you are too dark. You are like a dog. We want to make a light baby" (p. 1). Wax (2004) also reported that another young woman who was raped by militiamen was told, "Dog, you have sex with me.... The government gave me permission to rape you. This is not your land anymore, *abid* [slave], go" (p. 2).

Why was this Genocide Committed?

The causes of any genocide are extremely complex, and the Darfur genocide is no exception. No act of genocide is ever the result of a single factor; indeed, genocide results from a synergy of trends, issues, and events that influence the thinking and actions of potential perpetrators who, ultimately, intend to extirpate, in one way or another, those it perceives as enemies, dangerous and/or loathsome in some way (and thus "outside their universe of obligation"). In the case of Darfur, the issues/events that combined to make genocide possible were the following:

extreme drought; increased desertification; Arab supremacism; authoritarianism; extreme nationalism; an ever-increasing bellicosity in the region (within Sudan, Darfur, and beyond its borders); and the disenfranchisement of black Africans at the hands of the Sudanese government.

Extreme Drought and Desertification

Since the early 1970s, numerous droughts (including the "great drought" of 1984–1985), resulted in ever-increasing desertification within the Darfur region. Tellingly, as a result of a severe drought in the 1970s, sections of the Sahara Desert reportedly crept south by as much as 60 miles.

The desertification of the land in Darfur, accompanied by fierce sand storms, resulted in a dramatic decline in the yield of produce, loss of pasture land, and a loss of livestock. All of the latter, along with famine (some caused by nature, some by man—and some periods of famine lasting much longer than those of the past), increased tensions over land usage and access to water and, ultimately, resulted in ever-increasing conflict and violence between the nomadic/semi-nomadic Arab groups and the sedentary/farming group of non-Arabs.

Exacerbating the situation was the fact that drought affected other countries in the region as well, and nomads from Chad and Libya migrated to Darfur in extremely large numbers in search of grazing land, which put further pressure on the scant resources available.

Not only did nature force nomadic groups to sweep lower south to locate sustenance for their herds, it also resulted in their grazing of their herds for longer than usual. At one and the same time, farmers became ever more protective of the land. Some even resorted to putting up fences and establishing fees for land and water usage. What constituted protective efforts by the sedentary peoples/farmers were perceived by the nomads as stingy and unfair.

Arab Supremacism

Arab supremacism is an ideology that preaches, promotes, and sustains—in certain situations, at all cost—the notion that Arab beliefs and way of life are superior to all others. In that regard, it is an ideology that perceives all those who are not Arab as inferior. In Sudan this has led to both the demonization and disenfranchisement of certain groups. Essentially, and, ultimately, it calls for Arab dominance in all aspects of life—culturally, politically, economically, judicially, and socially.

The origins of Arab supremacism "lay in the Libya of Colonel Gaddafi in the 1970s" and "the politics of the Sahara" (Flint & de Waal, 2005, p. 50). Gaddafi, in fact, fantasized about establishing an "Arab belt" across Africa. To accomplish this goal, he created, with his oil riches, various mechanisms, including the *Faliq al Islamiyya* (Islamic Legion), which recruited Bedouins from Mauritania to Sudan; the *Munazamat Da'awa al Islamiyya* (Organization of the Islamic Call), which fostered Islamic philanthropy and evangelization; and sponsored the Sudanese opposition National Front, including the Muslim Brothers (or Muslim Brotherhood) and the *Ansar* (the *umma's* military wing).

Any mention of Arab supremacism and Sudan is incomplete if it neglects to comment on the role of Hassan Abd al Turabi—an Islamist, former law professor at the University of Khartoum, and a government official under Jaafar Nimeiri and then Omar al Bashir. Turabi was a major figure for decades in the Muslim Brotherhood, which originated in Egypt and had been active in Sudan since 1949. The group's primary goal in Sudan was to institutionalize Islamic law. In 1964 Turabi became the secretary-general of the Muslim Brotherhood, which was the year that the Brotherhood established its first political party. Turabi was closely involved with the Islamic Charter Front, which proposed that Sudan adopt an Islamic Constitution. The latter basically established that those Sudanese who were not Muslim would, from that point forward, be considered and treated as second-class citizens.

Over time, the Brotherhood established a close relationship with young Darfurians, convincing the latter that the Brotherhood's headlong push for the establishment of Islamic law was positive and that, as an organization, it was void of the prejudice and discrimination that was so rife within the Sudanese government when it came to ethnic and tribal differences. Understandably, these same young people came to trust and support Turabi.

Beginning as a peaceful civilian movement, the Brotherhood gradually morphed into a powerful and radical rebel group. More specifically, following a *coup d'état* in 1969, in which Colonel Jaafar Nimeiri became prime minister of Sudan, Turabi's Islamist Party was dissolved. Immediately, though, the Islamists began planning their own rebellion. The planned rebellion, however, was quashed by the Sudanese military in March 1970. The combined effort of the Sudanese air force and ground troops resulted in the deaths of hundreds of Islamist fighters. Many survivors sought exile in Libya, where they established military-like camps in preparation for a future attempt to dislodge the Nimeiri (who eventually became president) government. As Flint and de Waal (2005) note, "Their [the Islamists'] plan was an armed invasion of Sudan from bases in Libya, crossing Darfur and Kordofan to storm the capital. [Ultimately,] in July 1976, the Ansar–Islamist alliance very nearly succeeded … but the army counterattacked and the rebels were defeated" (pp. 22–23).

Turabi, a master at Machiavellian politics, found a way to disassociate himself from the failed invasion and to ingratiate himself with Nimeiri. In fact, Turabi became so close to Nimeiri that he became his attorney general in 1977. At one and the same time, in his quest to establish an Islamic state, "[Turabi] infiltrated Islamist cadres into the armed forces, including elite units such as the air force" (Flint & de Waal, 2005, p. 23).

Always intent on imposing his Islamist vision on Sudan, Turabi, in 1983, led the way in implementing *shari'a* (Islamic law) in Sudan. Due to a combination of disgust at being forced to adhere to *shari'a* and fear at the brutality (amputations and hangings) meted out by the government as a result of its *shari'a*-induced legislation, Nimeiri was overthrown in 1985. Parliamentary rule was subsequently reinstated. Almost immediately, Turabi helped to establish the National Islamic Front (NIF), a political party that was controlled by the Muslim Brotherhood.

For a short while, Sudan returned to parliamentary rule. However, in 1989, with Turabi in the shadows but playing an integral role as a power broker, the military overthrew the elected government, and Omar al Bashir was installed as president of Sudan. As Sudan entered a period of increased turbulence, Turabi is said to have virtually served as the real power behind the scenes.

In the early 1990s, the Sudanese Islamists began to inculcate Islamist thought throughout Sudan. At the forefront of the effort were Turabi and Ali Osman Mohamed Taha, an ardent Islamist and an on–off government figure. As part and parcel of this effort, Turabi, in 1990, had established the Popular Arab Islamic Conference (PAIC), which was basically a regional organization for political Islamist militants. In his position as secretary-general of PAIC, Turabi induced the Sudan government to create "an open-door policy for Arabs, including Turabi's Islamist associate Osama bin Laden, who made his base in Sudan in 1990–1996" (Human Rights Watch, 2002, p. 1). In order to accomplish their goals,

> Islamist cadres were dispatched to foment a new Islamist consciousness in every village. Islamist philanthropic agencies were mobilized to open schools and clinics, and to support the Popular Defence Forces. A raft of programmes aimed at building an Islamic Republic was launched. (Flint & de Waal, 2005, p. 28)

Ultimately, though, Turabi concluded that if he was to succeed in gaining power through the elective process, he needed to part ways with the Brotherhood for it perceived Islamism and Arabism as one and the same, while vast numbers of those residing in Darfur did not; and since Turabi believed he needed the votes of those in the West, he calculatingly cut his ties with the Brotherhood.

In 1999 Turabi set out to become the major power in Sudan. But, once again, his grand plans came to naught. Not only did Ali Osman break with Turabi as a result of looking askance at Turabi's ploys, schemes, and intrigues, but al Bashir—not about to be pushed aside—announced a state of emergency and removed Turabi from office (thus wiping out Turabi's powerbase within the government). The ramifications were immense for Darfur: "The Bashir–Turabi split lost Darfur for the government, but made it possible to make peace in the South" (Flint & de Waal, 2005, p. 41).

Authoritarianism

For over 20 years (1989–present) Sudan has been under the authoritarian rule of Omar al Bashir. His government controls virtually every aspect of Sudanese life. And when al Turabi was a power behind the scenes, it meant that the Islamists were, like puppeteers, largely directing all aspects of Sudanese life. Those living in what is commonly referred to as the "peripheries" in Sudan (that is, those areas far from Khartoum, the "center" or powerbase in Sudan), were (and are) perceived and treated as second-class citizens or worse.

As soon as the new al Bashir government, with its Islamist focus, took power in 1989, it began dictating what was and was not acceptable in the way of behavior, dress, speech, and assembly (or association) with others. Furthermore, individuals were arrested for any and all dissent, people "disappeared" into secret prisons, and many were tortured regularly and viciously Essentially, the judicial system answered only to al Bashir and his cronies.

Disenfranchisement

First, it is important to note that Darfur is not only one of the poorest regions in Sudan, but one of the poorest regions in all of Africa. Second, a single region of Sudan, the North (where Khartoum, the capital, is located), which comprises just over 5% of the population of the country, virtually controls all of Sudan. Put another way, it controls the wealth of the nation and it controls the politics of the nation. Almost all of those who hold major posts within the country have come from the North. Indeed, all of the presidents and prime ministers have come from the North, along with the vast majority of those who head-up important positions dealing with the infrastructure of the country, development, and banking. Third, it is the seat of advanced education in the nation. Fourth, for years on end, the black Africans of Darfur have requested the establishment of more schools, medical facilities, and roads—all of which are minimal in number, sorely underfunded, or, as is true in the case of roads, largely non-existent. Fifth, most, if not all, of the black Africans' requests for assistance have largely fallen on deaf ears in Khartoum.

For many years, the black Africans of Darfur decried the hegemony of the North, as well as the fact that they (those residing in the West) have suffered prejudice, discrimination, and disenfranchisement. Numerous examples of such disenfranchisement could be cited, but three that particularly irked the people of Darfur in the early 2000s shall suffice. (All of the following examples are in the present tense, exactly the way they were written, and thus readers need to realize that the statistics may well be different in relation to Sudan in 2012.) First, "infant mortality in the West (at 122.5 boys and 104.2 girls dying per 1,000 births) is strikingly different from infant mortality in the North (100.1 boys and 88.8 girls per thousand births)" (Cobham, 2005, n.p.). This difference was undoubtedly due in large part to the fact that adequate medical facilities and qualified medical personnel are available in the North but not in the West. According to the Justice and Equality Movement (2000), the rebel group that issued the *Black Book* that delineated the facts of disenfranchisement in Darfur,

> The entire State of Western Darfur has two medical specialists in the field of obstetrics and gynaecology, one in Geneina and the other in Zalengay. They are to serve a population of 1,650,000 aided by [a] few medical students who visit the area for training and for escaping mandatory military service. (p. 53)

Second, "water development is currently reserved for the ever-expanding capital Khartoum. The rest of the country is left out, dying of thirst as well as diseases like malaria, kalazar, bilharsiasis, and other water-borne diseases" (Justice and Equality Movement, 2000, p. 41).

Third, the development of the country (the construction of roads, bridges, water systems, hospitals, schools) is largely limited to the North. Even those other areas that have seen development largely benefit those who are from the North. As for the West, "the entire Western region now lacks a single developmental scheme which could support one province for a single week" (Justice and Equality Movement, 2000, p. 5).

In May 2000 *The Black Book* (the complete title of which is *The Black Book: Imbalance of Power and Wealth in Sudan*) mysteriously appeared in Khartoum. Copies were handed out outside major mosques following Friday prayers. Purportedly, many were even placed, brazenly, on the desks of key Sudanese officials, including that of al Bashir. As photocopies of the book were "spontaneously" produced, *The Black Book* began to appear throughout the country and abroad. *The Black Book*, was dedicated, in part, to "the Sudanese people who have endured oppression, injustice and tyranny."

The Black Book argues that ever since Sudan's independence those who control the political and economic power within the Sudanese government (frequently referred to as "the elite" or "the ruling elite"), and by extension, the entire country, are from northern Sudan. More specifically, it asserts that the vast majority of posts in the government, the judiciary, the military, and the police all come from the North (and primarily from three tribal groups, the Shaygiyya, Ja'aliyiin, and Danagla), and/or are appointed by the "center" or the ruling elite. It also states that the "peripheries" of the country (those in the West, South, and East) have been purposely denied fair representation in the government, and have been forced to lead a life of impoverishment. In the authors' introduction, it is asserted that at the turn of the millennium, Sudan remains "steeped in poverty, illiteracy, disease and lack of development" (Justice and Equality Movement, 2000, p. 1).

De Waal (2004b) argues that *The Black Book* essentially

> condemned the Islamist promise to Darfur as a sham. *The Black Book* was a key step in the polarization of the country along politically constructed "racial" rather than religious lines, and it laid the basis for a coalition between Darfur's radicals, who formed the SLA, and its Islamists, who formed the other rebel organization, the Justice and Equality Movement. (p. 8)

The Black Book may have constituted a key step in the polarization of the country along politically constructed "racial" lines, but it was hardly the first, or *the* major step. In light of the ongoing attacks from the early 1990s onward by various Arab groups (nomads, semi-nomads and then, collaboratively, by Arab herders and GoS troops) against black African villagers (during which racial slurs were a regular occurrence), it seems that the "racial divide" was evident, and being acted upon, many years prior to the appearance of *The Black Book*. In that regard, it seems that *The Black Book* was more the messenger versus the instigator of the polarization along "racial lines."

Ever-increasing Insecurity and Bellicosity in the Darfur Region

Beginning in the early 1990s, Arab herders started carrying out attacks against entire villages of sedentary black African farmers. Over time, such attacks began to involve both GoS troops and the Arab herders working in tandem. While vicious, such attacks were certainly not as systematic as the scorched-earth attacks that the GoS and *Janjaweed* carried out in 2004–2006 or the periodic attacks that have ebbed and flowed over the years, up through this writing (January 2012).

The initial increase in violent conflict within the region was due to a host of issues. For example, in the 1980s, the GoS, under President Nimeiri, abruptly replaced the tribal councils in Darfur, the traditional bodies that helped solve conflicts, with government oversight of the region. Nimeiri, however, failed to provide adequate resources to the regional government offices in order to carry out their work, and, as a result, the offices and expected services largely became hollow shells.

Making matters even more volatile, since riverine Arabs held the vast majority of positions in the government posts (including those as police and court officials), the black Africans of Darfur were automatically put at a distinct disadvantage. That is, disputes that were once dealt with, for the most part fairly and equitably, by traditional authorities and/or a combination of the latter and governmental authorities, were now handled by officials partial to the Arab sector of the population.

Furthermore, as certain groups of nomads increasingly bought into the beliefs of Arab supremacism, they began to act as if they were superior to the black Africans.[6] Along with the huge influx of weapons into Darfur (resulting, in part, due to the various wars in the region, three of which were the Libya/Chad conflict, the prolonged war in southern Sudan, and the Eritrean separatist war with Ethiopia (1961–1993)), more and more herders began carrying weapons. While this was likely done as a means of protection, they also had likely become accustomed to carrying them as a result of their having fought in one or more of the violent conflicts in the region. As the Arab herders increasingly engaged in conflicts with the black Africans over land and water usage, they (the Arabs) made it known that they were ready and willing to use their weapons. Thus, with the difficulties presented by the droughts and desertification of pasture land, the influence of Arab supremacism, and the Arab herders' experiences as mercenaries, it is not surprising that many of the Arab nomadic groups became increasingly cavalier and aggressive in their use of the sedentary people's lands in the early to mid-1990s.

Not only did the Arab nomads purposely neglect to seek permission to use the land, but when confronted by the black African farmers they refused to apologize for trespassing. And when confronted by the farmers, it was not uncommon for the nomads to threaten the lives of the farmers—and in many cases they carried out their threats.

Out of fear and anger over the constant assaults and attacks on their villages and a lack of protection from local and regional governmental authorities, along with the gradual realization that the Arab marauders had tacit approval from the local government officials to do as they wished, the black Africans began to form self-defense groups "on a tribal basis as opposed to based on local communities" (Fadul & Tanner, 2007, p. 301).[7]

The Initial Rebel Attacks and the Response by the Government of Sudan

By the early 1990s traditional dispute resolution approaches were proving to be inadequate. Arab nomadic attacks against black Africans were becoming more brazen, more frequent, more vicious and more costly in terms of lost lives and destroyed villages, farm land, and orchards. In August 1995, for example, Arab raiders attacked and burned the non-Arab village of Mejmeri in West Darfur, stealing 40,000 cattle and massacring 23 civilians. By late 1998 more than 100,000 non-Arab Massalit had fled to Chad to escape the violent attacks (Flint & de Waal, 2005, p. 69).

A great many of the attacks on villages were not one-time affairs. In fact, in the early to late 1990s, some villages were attacked up to three to four and more times. In certain cases, African villages were partially burned down by the marauders; in others, villages were utterly destroyed. Almost always, the villages were pillaged and then the black Africans' herds were stolen. Black Africans were often forced out of their villages only to be chased down in the desert and beaten and/or killed.

Desirous of remaining on their land, the black Africans more often than not returned to their villages once the marauders had left, rebuilt those sections destroyed, and carried on with life. However, as the attacks continued unabated, the black Africans began to look askance at the government. In light of the way the black Africans were being treated (a frustrating combination of being ignored and/or ill-treated by the government), it is not surprising that the following statement/critique of the Sudanese government made it into *The Black Book*:

> *Conditions for accepting the authority of the ruler/governing power:* The authority must demonstrate its commitment to maintain sovereignty of land against foreign intruders; treat its citizens equally; afford them peace and protection; guarantee dignified life; spread freedom and dignity, and must enable its citizens to fully participate in conducting their public affairs. All that is to take place within an environment that is conducive for participation of all without religious, ethnic, skin colour and gender discrimination.
>
> The state authority cannot implement that without commitment to its national laws that regulate and divide powers among

different state organs. Most important here is the separation between state powers, and in particular the political, the judicial and the legislative. (Justice and Equality Movement, 2000, p. 6)

Between 2001 and 2002, before the current conflict became widely known to the outside world, a rebel movement comprising non-Arabs emerged in Darfur. The first rebel group to appear called itself the Sudanese Liberation Movement/Army (SLM/A), and on March 14, 2003 it issued the following political declaration:

The brutal oppression, ethnic cleansing and genocide sponsored by the Khartoum government left the people of Darfur with no other option but to resort to popular political and military resistance for purposes of survival. This popular resistance has now coalesced into a political movement known as the Sudan Liberation Movement and its military wing, the Sudan Liberation Army (SLM/SLA). (The Sudan Liberation Movement and Sudan Liberation Army, 2003, pp. 1–2).

Within a relatively short period of time, the group splintered, and from the split emerged a rebel group that called itself the Justice and Equality Movement (JEM). According to Flint and de Waal (2005), within JEM there are "two main tendencies that dwarf all others: one is tribal, the other Islamic" (p. 89).

In addition to providing local security for the black African villagers of Darfur, the two rebel groups issued protests against the economic and political marginalization of Darfur. The aforementioned *Black Book*, the brainchild of the leaders of JEM, was one such protest; indeed, it constituted the most detailed critique of the government to date, as well as the protest that reached the greatest and most diverse audience (from the top officials of the country all the way to the illiterate population who learned about the contents of *The Black Book* as a result of having it read to them). Members of both rebel groups came primarily (but by no means exclusively) from three non-Arab tribes—the Fur, Massalit, and Zaghawa—that had been attacked for years by nomadic Arab groups and GoS troops.

By late 2003 a flood of black Africans had either been forced from their homes as a result of GoS and *Janjaweed* attacks or had left out of sheer fear. By September 2003 the UN reported that some 65,000 refugees from Darfur had fled to Chad.[8] By December 9, 2003 the United Nations estimated that there were up to 600,000 internally displaced people (IDP) in Darfur as a result of the attacks on the black Africans' villages. In November 2004, Médecins Sans Frontières (Doctors Without

Borders) estimated that some 1.8 million Darfurians had been displaced from their homes, with 200,000 of them in refugee camps in Chad (Médecins Sans Frontières, 2004, p. 1).

At one and the same time, the leaders of both rebel groups seemingly followed the ongoing peace negotiations between the GoS and the rebel groups in southern Sudan and realized that armed insurrection in the south had eventually led to important concessions by the GoS, including power-sharing and access to major economic resources. Whether such knowledge was the catalyst or trigger for the rebel initial attacks against the government only the leaders of the SLM/A know for sure.

Popular account has it that the GoS, alarmed by the rebel attacks and with its own military forces stretched thin by the north–south civil war, decided to recruit, train, and equip Arab militias (the so-called *Janjaweed*) to help suppress what it purportedly perceived as a black African rebellion in Darfur.[9] Any government whose military bases and/or other government facilities are attacked is going to retaliate and attempt to suppress future attacks. Governments will either arrest the perpetrators or, if the situation degenerates into violence, shoot and then apprehend them, or kill them outright. What the GoS did, however, was something vastly different and, ultimately, criminal. Using the argument that it believed that black African villagers were harboring rebels, the GoS (along with the *Janjaweed*) began attacking village after village after village of black Africans. Thus, instead of solely tracking down and attacking the black African rebel groups, the GoS and *Janjaweed* began carrying out a widespread and systematic scorched-earth policy against non-Arab villagers. In doing so, the GoS troops and the *Janjaweed* slaughtered men and boys (including infants), raped, mutilated, and often killed females, looted household goods and animals, and then burned the homes and villages to the ground (Physicians for Human Rights, 2005; United Nations Commission of Inquiry into Darfur, 2005; U.S. State Department, 2004). The attacks comprised bombings by aircraft, helicopter gunships, and *dushkas* (four-wheeled vehicles with mounted machine guns), as well as hundreds of *Janjaweed* on camels and horses. In a report of its findings, the United Nations Commission of Inquiry on Darfur (2005) stated that "the large majority of attacks on villages conducted by the [*Janjaweed*] militia have been undertaken with the acquiescence of State officials" (para. 125). As previously mentioned, the attacks led to the forcible displacement of, at first, tens of thousands, then hundreds of thousands, and, ultimately, over 2.5 million people in Darfur alone (and more than another 285,000 in Chad). All constituted early warning signals that something was vastly wrong in Darfur.

As early as spring 2002 (May 1, to be exact), a group of Fur politicians complained to Sudanese President Omar al Bashir that 181 villages had been attacked by Arab militias, resulting in hundreds of people killed and thousands of animals stolen (Flint & de Waal, 2005, pp. 77–78).

In what Flint and de Waal call a "pivotal point" in the conflict between the black African rebels and the GoS troops, the SLA and JEM forces struck the government air force base at el Fasher on April 25, 2003. In doing so, they killed at least 75 people, destroyed several airplanes and bombers, and captured the base's commander (Flint & de Waal, 2005, pp. 99–100). In quick succession, numerous other attacks were carried out: "the rebels were winning almost every encounter—34 out of 38 in the middle months of 2003. [At that point in time, the GoS purportedly] feared it would lose the whole of Darfur" (Flint & de Waal, 2005, p. 101).

Between 2003 and today, the GoS has repeatedly denied that its troops took part in the scorched-earth actions against the black Africans of Darfur. Furthermore, while the UN asserts that at least 300,000 have been killed in Darfur over the years (some scholars and activist organizations claim the number is closer to 400,000 or more), the GoS asserts that just 9,000 have been killed, mainly as a result of rebel actions. Ample evidence, though, from a broad array of sources (e.g., the black African survivors of the attacks; African Union (AU) troops deployed in Darfur as monitors; UN personnel based in Darfur; numerous humanitarian organizations working in the IDP camps; a number of human rights organizations—including Human Rights Watch, Physicians for Human Rights, and Amnesty International—who have undertaken studies in the region; and the investigations conducted by the United States in 2004, the UN in 2004/2005, and the International Criminal Court (ICC) between 2005 and 2008, respectively) have provided evidence that clearly and definitively refutes the GoS's denials.

By late 2003, various NGOs (non-governmental organizations) and the UN scrambled to help the IDPs and the refugees flooding across the Sudan–Chad border, and to get the word out about the escalating carnage in Darfur. In December 2003, Jan Egeland, UN Undersecretary for Humanitarian Affairs, asserted that the Darfur crisis was possibly the "worst [crisis] in the world today" (United Nations, 2004, p. 1). That same month, Tom Vraalsen, the UN Security General's Special Envoy for Humanitarian Affairs for Sudan, claimed that the situation in Darfur was "nothing less than the 'organized' destruction of sedentary African agriculturalists—the Fur, the Massaleit and the Zaghawa" (quoted in Reeves, 2003, p. 1).

In early 2004, one activist organization after another in the United States, Canada, and Europe began rallying around the Darfur issue, variously decrying the lack of action to halt the atrocities against the black Africans of Darfur, preparing and issuing reports, calling on the United

Nations, the U.S. government and/or the European Union to be proactive in addressing the crisis, and issuing calls for citizen action. On June 24, 2004, the United States Holocaust Memorial Museum (USHMM) took the extraordinary measure of temporarily shutting down normal operations to focus attention on the ongoing crisis in Darfur. U.S. Senators Sam Brownback and Jon Corzine, U.S. House of Representative Donald Payne (2004), as well as a Holocaust survivor and a member of the Darfurian community-in-exile, came together in a special program in the USHMM's Hall of Witness to highlight and discuss the unfolding conflict in Darfur. On the same day, the U.S. House of Representatives unanimously declared that the situation in Darfur constituted genocide.

On June 30, 2004, U.S. Secretary of State Colin Powell visited a refugee camp for IDPs and a refugee camp in Chad. While visiting the IDP camp, Abu Shouk, where malnutrition was rife among the 40,000 or so black Africans, Powell said: "We see indicators and elements that would start to move you toward a genocide conclusion but we're not there yet" (quoted by the BBC, 2004, p. 2).

In July and August 2004, the United States—in a joint effort involving the U.S. State Department, the Coalition of International Justice (CIJ), and the United States Agency for International Aid (USAID)—sent a team (the Atrocities Documentation Team or ADT) of 24 investigators to Chad to conduct interviews with Sudanese refugees from the Darfur region of Sudan for the express purpose of collecting evidence to help ascertain whether genocide had been perpetrated by the GoS and the *Janjaweed*. The ADT, which was the first ever official field investigation of a suspected genocide by one sovereign nation into another sovereign nation's actions while the killing was underway, conducted more than 1,000 interviews with Darfurian refugees in camps and settlements on the Chad side of the border with Sudan. Evidence collected by the ADT led U.S. Secretary of State Colin Powell, on September 9, 2004, in a hearing before the U.S. Senate's Foreign Relations Committee, to publicly accuse the GoS of genocide. It was the first time that one government accused another government of genocide during an ongoing conflict.

Ultimately, the U.S. State Department presented the findings of the ADT in an eight-page report, "Documenting Atrocities in Darfur." The analysis of the data collected in the 1,136 interviews by the ADT revealed "a consistent and widespread pattern of atrocities in the Darfur region of western Sudan" (U.S. State Department, 2004, p. 1). The data also suggested a "close coordination between GOS [Government of Sudan] forces and Arab militia elements, commonly known as the Jingaweit [*Janjaweed*]" (U.S. State Department, 2004, p. 2). Furthermore, the data indicated that there was a clear "pattern of abuse against members of Darfur's non-Arab communities, including murder, rape, beatings, ethnic humiliation, and destruction of property and basic necessities" (U.S. State Department, 2004, p. 3).

Sixteen percent of the respondents witnessed or experienced rape. Significantly, the ADT report suggests that the rapes were probably "under-reported because of the social stigma attached to acknowledging such violations of female members of the family" (U.S. State Department, 2004, p. 7). What makes the under-reporting even more probable is the fact that all of the interpreters and half of the investigators on the team were males, and many female victims were not inclined to mention such assaults in the company of males (strangers or otherwise).

During the course of his report on the ADP findings to the Senate Foreign Relations Committee on September 9, 2004, Powell remarked that the findings did not mean that the United States needed to do anything other than what it had already done. What that meant was this: While the United States had called on the GoS to cease and desist its ongoing attacks, submitted and supported various resolutions at the UN Security Council, applied sanctions against Darfur, and provided hundreds of millions of dollars for humanitarian aid and material/resource assistance to the AU contingent on the ground in Darfur, it was not about to carry out an intervention in Darfur.

With that said, the United States referred the Darfur matter, referencing Chapter VII of the UN Charter, to the United Nations. Subsequently, on September 18, 2004, the UN established the UN Commission of Inquiry into Darfur (COI), whose express purpose, as outlined in UN Security Council Resolution 1564, was to conduct its own investigation into the Darfur crisis. The COI conducted its inquiry in December 2004 and January 2005, and submitted its report to the Security Council in late January 2005. In its final section, "Conclusions and Recommendations," the COI report states:

> The Commission concludes that the Government of the Sudan and the *Janjaweed* are responsible for a number of violations of international human rights and humanitarian law. Some of these violations are very likely to amount to war crimes, and given the systematic and widespread pattern of many of the violations, they would also amount to crimes against humanity (United Nations, 2005, para. 603).

While many scholars agreed with the conclusions of the COI, others were taken aback that—based on the COI's own findings—it had not concluded that genocide had been perpetrated (see, for example, Fowler, 2006, pp. 127–139; Stanton, 2006, pp. 181–188; Totten, 2006, pp. 199–222; Totten, 2009, pp. 354–378).

Talk, Talk, and More Talk by the International Community

Between 2004 and today (January 2012), the UN Security Council has issued one resolution after another vis-à-vis the ongoing crisis in Darfur. The resolutions have addressed a host of issues, including but not limited to the following: the need by the GoS to halt the ongoing indiscriminate attacks on black African civilians and the forced displacement of hundreds of thousands of the latter; the need for the perpetrators of the atrocities in Darfur to be brought to justice without delay; concern over the GoS's failure to meet its obligations in ensuring the security of the civilian population of Darfur; disappointment regarding the constant cease-fire violations by all actors; the threat to issue various types of sanctions; the issuance of actual sanctions, including the freezing of certain actors' assets (including those of GoS officials, *Janjaweed* leaders, and a leader of a rebel group); and the referral of the Darfur conflict to the ICC, along with the names of alleged perpetrators of various atrocities.

The results of the resolutions have been, at best, mixed. Some were acted on, but most were not. Various resolutions were revised time and again, along with ever-increasing threats, but largely to no avail due to a dearth of action. Tellingly, in July 2006, a senior Sudanese government official was quoted as saying that "The United Nations Security Council has threatened us so many times, we no longer take it seriously" (cited in Nathan, 2007, p. 249).

After considerable debate, compromise, and dithering, the United States and the UN Security Council finally imposed some sanctions on Sudan. For example, on April 25, 2006, the UN Security Council passed a resolution imposing sanctions against four Sudanese individuals, all of whom have been accused of war crimes in Darfur. Those sanctioned were: Gaffar Mohamed Elhassan, an ex-Sudan air force commander; Sheikh Musa Hilal, a *Janjaweed* militia leader; Adam Yacub Shant, a rebel SLA commander; and Gabril Abdul Kareem Badri, a rebel National Movement for Reform and Development field commander. All four were to be subject to a ban on foreign travel, and any assets they had in banks abroad were to be frozen.

As for the United States, in May 2007 President George W. Bush ordered the imposition of sanctions that prevents 31 Sudanese companies (many of them oil-related) and three individuals (two high-level government leaders and a black African rebel leader) from doing business in the United States or with U.S. companies.

Realpolitik was at the center of the dithering, the watering down of certain sanctions, and the decision not to follow through on numerous resolutions and threatened sanctions. More specifically, various members of the Permanent Five in the UN Security Council (the United States, Great Britain, France, the Russian Federation, and China) have vested interests in Sudan and want to protect them.[10] China, for example, has an enormous petroleum deal with Sudan, and engages in significant weapons sales to it; Russia also has a major arms deal with Sudan; and the United States has, off and on, taken advantage of GoS's offers to help shut down terrorist cells within Sudan.

In June 2004, Sudan allowed the AU to deploy a small cease-fire monitoring team in Darfur comprised of representatives from the AU, the GoS, two (later, three) rebel groups, along with the European Union, the UN, and the United States. From a tiny force of 300 troops, the force slowly increased to—and eventually leveled off at (up through December 2007)—about 7,000 troops. "As violence against civilians continued, the African Union Mission in Sudan (AMIS) force's mandate was expanded in October 2004 to protecting 'civilians whom it encounters under imminent threat and in the immediate vicinity, within resources and capability'" (Human Rights Watch, 2007, p. 5). The new mandate, though, for all intents and purposes constituted little more than a paper tiger. The AU had neither the resources nor the capability to truly protect anyone, let alone themselves.

Between 2003 and 2008 the international community worked in various, though hardly effective, ways to bring the Darfur crisis to a close; and as it did, it continually decried the GoS troops' and *Janjaweed*'s attacks on innocent civilians and the GoS's support of the *Janjaweed* and its murderous behavior, and called on the GoS to rein in the *Janjaweed*. The GoS continued to vigorously and disingenuously protest the validity of the accusations made by the international community, but, periodically, also made lukewarm promises to bring the situation under control. Such promises, though, were quickly broken. In most cases, however, the GoS blithely ignored the international community's requests, demands, and threats.

When it became obvious that the AU troops were outmanned and outgunned, calls were issued by various actors to insert UN troops into Darfur. Initially, the AU adamantly rejected the offer, asserting that it wanted to operate an all-African operation. Al Bashir was also vociferous in his rejection of the calls for UN involvement in Darfur. Time and again, he asserted that any force that entered Sudanese territory without an invitation from the GoS would not only be a violation of Sudan's sovereignty, but would be perceived and treated as an enemy and dealt with accordingly. For example, on February 26, 2006 al Bashir asserted, and then warned, that "We are strongly opposed to any foreign intervention in Sudan and Darfur will be a graveyard for any foreign troops venturing to enter" (quoted in *Sudan Tribune*, 2006, p. 1).

Finally, after immense international pressure, Sudan, in mid-June 2007, agreed to allow the deployment of a special force into Darfur, the UN/AU Hybrid (UNAMID) force. Ultimately, that was followed, on July 31, 2007, by the passage of UN Security Council Resolution 1769 which authorized a combined AU/UN Hybrid force for deployment in Darfur. The resolution called for

> the immediate deployment of the United Nations Light and Heavy Support packages to the African Union Mission in the Sudan (AMIS) and a [AU/UN] Hybrid operation in Darfur [UNAMID], for which back-stopping and command and control structures will be provided by the United Nations.... [The] UNAMID ... shall consist of up to 19,555 military personnel, including 360 military observers and liaison officers, and an appropriate civilian component including up to 3,772 police per-sonnel and 19 police units comprising up to 140 personnel each.

In addressing the mandate of UNAMID, the resolution asserted that:

> Acting under Chapter VII of the Charter of the United Nations: ... UNAMID is authorized to take the necessary action, in the areas of deployment of its forces and as it deems within its capa-bilities, in order to: (i) protect its personnel, facilities, installa-tions and equipment, and to ensure the security and freedom of movement of its own personnel and humanitarian workers; (ii) support early and effective implementation of the Darfur Peace Agreement, prevent the disruption of its implementation and armed attacks, and protect civilians, without prejudice to the responsibility of the Government of Sudan.

Talk, Talk, and More Talk about Peace

Between 2004 and January 2012 the many and varied peace efforts attempted by the AU and the UN have virtually gone nowhere, and that is largely due to the intransigence of both the GoS and the various rebel groups. In various cases, either during or following a peacemaking effort, one or the other actors has either balked at something, walked away from the proceedings, or, in the case of various rebel factions, simply refused to acknowledge the efforts.

Many of the rebel groups are perceived as largely inconsequential by the international community, the GoS, and/or the major rebel groups—and, in fact, some are little more than bands of bandits—and have not been invited to participate in the peace talks. Many of those who have been rebuffed not only look askance at the peace talks but have stated that they will not recognize any agreement signed in their absence.

Unfortunately, it has not been unusual for peace agreements to be broken by one and/or both sides (meaning, the GoS and/or a rebel group) within days, if not hours, of their signing. The GoS has broken agreements both blatantly (attacking black African villages with Antonov bombers, helicopter gunships and GoS troops and *Janjaweed*) and surreptitiously (whitewashing planes, affixing UN insignias to the wings and sides of the planes, and using the planes to transport weapons and personnel into Darfur). Various black African rebel groups have not only reneged on agreements, but purposely prevented other rebel factions from taking part in the peace talks.[11]

Following seven rounds of contentious negotiations, a peace accord, the Darfur Peace Agreement (DPA), was signed in May 2006. However, as Fadul and Tanner (2007) aptly put it, the peace agreement was "stillborn" (p. 284). While the DPA was signed by the GoS and the Minni Arkoy Minawi faction of the SLA, it was not signed by the SLA faction led by Abdel Wahid Mohamed al Nur or by the JEM led by Khail Ibrahim. Shortly after the signing of the DPA, battles broke out between the non-signatories and the "government coalition," which included the SLA faction headed by Minni Arkoy Minawi.[12] Even greater violence was perpetrated by GoS troops and the *Janjaweed* against both black African rebel groups and black African civilians. As the attacks by the latter increased in number, there was a surge in the rape of girls and women and the murder of black African civilians. Thousands fled from their villages seeking sanctuary in IDP camps or refugee camps in Chad.

During the summer of 2006, the rebel groups that had not signed the DPA won a series of battles against the GoS, the *Janjaweed*, and Minni's SLA faction. This not only caused great consternation amongst GoS officials, but emboldened those rebel groups that had not signed the DPA.

Due to the endless violence that contributed to their ongoing insecurity, black African Darfurian civilians understandably looked askance at the DPA. As a result of the ongoing fighting and massive displacement of civilians, a vast number of black African Darfurians also began to look askance at the efforts and credibility of the African Union mission (AMIS) in Darfur. More specifically,

> Not only was AMIS weak but it was increasingly seen as partisan. The AU's role in imposing the DPA on the non-signatories compromised its neutrality in the eyes of those groups. In August, when the AU expelled the non-signatories from the AU-chaired Ceasefire Commission and AMIS was seen providing logistics to

the forces of SLA-Minni amid escalating violence, many Darfurians concluded that the AU had taken sides. (Fadul & Tanner, 2007, p. 308)

As Fadul and Tanner (2007) note, there were other issues as well in regard to why the black Africans found the DPA a dubious proposition. These included the lack of attention to "compensation [for the destruction of their villages and homes and the theft of their worldly goods], the rehabilitation of infrastructure, basic services, and reconciliation" (p. 286). The caveat, though, in regard to the latter statement was that "people always stressed these [compensation, rehabilitation of the infrastructure, reconciliation, et al.] were secondary to security" (Fadul & Tanner, 2007, p. 286).

As the violence continued unabated month after month in the aftermath of the signing of the DPA, many black African Darfurians argued that "there could be no peace unless the GoS military troops were forced to abide by it. In other words, peace depended on one of two things, a non-consensual deployment of Western troops or a rebel military victory—or both" (Fadul & Tanner, 2007, pp. 287, 288). In that regard, Fadul and Tanner (2007) observed that

[a]s late as 2004, many Darfurian intellectuals criticized the decision to take up arms against the government. The brutality of Khartoum's reaction was predictable, they argued, and the violence had cast the region back many decades. By late 2006, it was striking to hear many of those same individuals say they believed armed rebellion was the only solution to Darfur's problems, despite disenchantment with the shortcomings and human rights abuses by rebel groups on the ground. (p. 288)

In fact, beginning roughly in 2007 various rebel groups began treating their counterparts as enemies and engaging in battles with them. The disputes were over both significant matters (agreements and disagreements vis-à-vis the peace talks) and petty matters (e.g., personality clashes between rebel leaders). Not only that, but some rebel factions— the UN once estimated that there were up to 28 declared rebel factions in Darfur (Gettleman, 2007, p. A6) but today (January 2012), the number of rebel groups (declared and undeclared) is countless due to the fact that so many have split and split again—have attacked and killed civilians, raped black African women and girls, killed AU troops, and harmed and killed humanitarian aid workers.

Over time, and particularly from mid-2007 onwards, and despite the peace overtures, the lay of the land got even more dangerous in Darfur.

This was true for numerous reasons: throughout 2007, 2008, and 2009 the *Janjaweed* not only continued to attack black Africans but began fighting among and between themselves; throughout the same period various rebel groups continued to battle GoS troops and *Janjaweed* but also began fighting between and among themselves and attacking black African people in their villages and IDP camps (and the fighting between and among the rebel groups continues to this day, January 2012); and bandits roam the region attacking anyone and everyone, including IDPs and humanitarian workers. Disturbingly, and tellingly, a report entitled *Chaos by Design: Peacekeeping Challenges for AMIS and UNAMID*, Human Rights Watch (2007) asserted that "the [GoS] continues to stoke the chaos, and, in some areas, exploit intercommunal tensions that escalate into open hostilities, apparently in an effort to 'divide and rule' and maintain military and political dominance over the [Darfur] region" (p. 1). The latter continues to be true today despite the GoS's words and actions vis-à-vis their commitment to bringing peace to Darfur.

In early September 2007, UN Secretary General Ban Ki-moon announced a new round of peace talks, which were to begin on October 27, 2007 in Libya. Speaking of the peace talks, an article in the *International Herald Tribune* (2007) dryly observed:

> Darfur has a history of peace talks—their sheer numbers a testimony to their lack of success…. Since fighting began in 2003 between ethnic African rebels and the Arab-dominated Sudanese government, there have been over half a dozen cease-fires or peace deals of various formats—all quickly breached by both sides. (p. 1)

And, indeed, the peace talks in Libya ultimately resulted in nothing of substance.

Three months later, in early December 2007, the UN Under Secretary General for Humanitarian Affairs, John Holmes, informed the UN Security Council that

> 280,000 people had been forced to flee the violence in Darfur this year [2007], that attacks on aid workers and their convoys had reached "unprecedented levels" and that national authorities were closing off access to areas "where there are tens of thousands of civilians in severe need." (quoted in Hoge, 2007b, p. A10)

The Human Rights Council in Geneva reported that "from June 20 to mid-November [2007], at least 15 land and air attacks were carried out against civilian centers in Darfur by government troops and their affiliated militias and one faction of the rebel Sudanese Liberation Army" (Hoge, 2007b,

p. A10). Hoge (2007b) duly noted that the GoS was not the only guilty party; in fact, rebel groups were increasingly attacking IDP camps and threatening, stealing from, and seriously harming (beating, shooting, and killing) IDPs and aid workers.

To paraphrase Julie Flint (2009), between 2007 and January 2012 the situation in Darfur "gave way to periods of relative calm with spikes of extreme violence" (p. 11). And the peace talks have continued, but still not resulted in anything concrete. And that, unfortunately, appears to be how the rest of 2012 and beyond may play out as well.

The Later Years: December 2007 to January 2012

The deployment of UNAMID met one barrier after another. Well into December 2007, the GoS resisted the inclusion of non-African military personnel into the new force, the latter of whom were considered critical to the mission. The GoS also refused to provide land to the hybrid force, which was needed for supplying and housing troops. Likewise, the GoS refused to ease visa and travel restrictions, and was "blocking support staff and materials from the area through bureaucratic maneuvers" (Hoge, 2007a, p. A5). Additionally, the GoS asserted its right to "close down the [hybrid] force's communication's [channels] when its own army was operating in the area, and refused to give United Nations planes clearances to fly at night" (Hoge, 2007a, p. A5). In effect, the GoS was making a mockery of its so-called promise to allow for the deployment of the hybrid force; and in doing so, it drastically impeded the international community's efforts to provide African Darfurians with the protection they desperately needed.[13]

In January and February 2008, the GoS sent planes, ground troops, and the *Janjaweed* into West Darfur to attack four villages, all purported to be rebel strongholds, killing 115 people—including children, women, and the elderly—and displacing an estimated 30,000 people. The perpetrators looted and burned homes, shops, schools, and other edifices in the villages. In certain cases, civilians were burned alive in buildings.

A UNAMID report issued on March 20, 2008, asserted that the January and February 2008 attacks by the GoS troops and *Janjaweed* against black African villagers in Darfur constituted "violations of international humanitarian and human rights law" (n.p.). The report further claimed that "the scale of destruction of civilian property, including objects indispensable for the survival of the civilian population, suggests that the damage was a deliberate and integral part of a military strategy" (United Nations High Commissioner for Human Rights, 2008, n.p.).

UNAMID, though, was destined to struggle. It had been projected that UNAMID would gradually gear up and that by mid-year it would reach its full complement of 26,000 soldiers. In February 2008, by which time UNAMID numbered 9,000 troops, Balla Keita, the commander of the UN–AU Peacekeeping Force in West Darfur, decried the low numbers, asserting that more troops were urgently needed.

Over the years UNAMID attempted to be a presence in Darfur, but it was a thankless task as it continued to operate while being sorely under-manned, outgunned, and under-resourced. Exacerbating matters, UNAMID suffered its own fair share of attacks by the GoS, rebel groups and bandits roaming Darfur.

In their own ways, both the GoS and the international community also contributed to impeding the so-called peacekeeping mission in Darfur. The GoS established a rash of conditions and regulations, including the refusal to allow UNAMID to use helicopter gunships in Darfur. As for the international community, it continued to issue more lip service than help to the mission. As a result, UNAMID continued operating without badly needed helicopters and an adequate number of four-wheel vehicles to transverse the rough terrain. It was also without an adequate supply of mechanical parts to keep their machinery in good repair. Finally, in March 2008, Russia pledged several desert mobile heli-copters to UNAMID, which were added to helicopters donated by Ethiopia and Bangladesh. Be that as it may, the effectiveness of the UNAMID mission continued to be thwarted by the lack of an adequate number of helicopters, which were essential in such a large and hostile region (both in regard to the lack of roads and heat that took their toll on motor vehicles, as well as the constant and deadly threats posed by the GoS, *Jan-jaweed*, criminally inclined rebel groups, and bandits who roamed across the area).

In late July, the Darfur Consortium, a group composed primarily of African aid agencies and advocacy groups, lashed out at UNAMID, accusing it of failing to provide adequate protection for civilians in the area. A UNAMID spokesman agreed that the situation was unsatisfactory but countered that UNAMID had not received the resources it needed to do the job properly. He cited the fact that the mission did not have, for example, the helicopters and armored vehicles it needed to patrol such a desolate and huge area, and that some peacekeepers did not even have UN helmets and thus were using blue plastic bags in place of them to indicate that they were with the UN.

While also acknowledging that the report addressed a host of critical issues, the UNAMID force commander, General Martin Luther Agwai, retorted that too much was expected of UNAMID:

> For anybody to expect that 8,000 troops and under 2,000 police-men would police an area as big as France, that person [is]

daydreaming. With no roads, no means of communication and you expect UNAMID forces to be everywhere, I think is too much of an expectation. (Quoted by ABC News, July 28, 2008)

On July 8, the ICC Chief Prosecutor Luis Moreno-Ocampo announced that he had evidence to prove Sudanese President Omar al Bashir was guilty of genocide. In response, the AU issued a resolution calling on the UN Security Council to postpone the ICC case against al Bashir in order to avoid complicating matters on the ground in Darfur and jeopardizing the ongoing peace efforts. The AU further argued that "in the current circumstances a prosecution may not be in the interest of the victims and justice." In doing so, the AU invoked Article 16, which allows the UN Security Council to suspend prosecutions for a period of 12 months (and which can be renewed indefinitely). Not surprisingly, China, Libya, and Russia were in favor of the resolution but Great Britain, the United States, and France were not. Ultimately, a compromise was worked out. The United States abstained in the final vote, insisting that the language included in the resolution would send the wrong message to Sudan and al Bashir. (The ICC warrant for al Bashir's arrest is discussed in more detail below.)

On October 17, 2008, al Bashir traveled to Darfur and called for a national vision for peace. Rebel groups, including SLM/Unity and JEM, refused to attend, calling it a sham and an effort by al Bashir to avoid arrest and prosecution by the ICC.

Less than a month later, on November 12, 2008, continuing to try to appear the peacemaker, al Bashir called for an "immediate and unconditional cease-fire" in Darfur. The two largest rebel groups (SLM/A and JEM) asserted that they would continue fighting until the government agreed to act on their grievances. The very next week, GoS planes carried out bombing attacks on Kutum in northern Darfur. The UN reported that fighting was also taking place around Tine in Western Darfur and along the Sudan–Chad border with Chad.

In December 2008 the Darfur Consortium issued a report stating that hundreds, and possibly thousands, of black African women and children from Darfur had been kidnapped during the course of the Darfur crisis and forced into slavery by GoS troops and the *Janjaweed*. The women, the report noted, were kidnapped when the GoS and *Janjaweed* attacked black African villages, forced to walk to military camps where they were gang raped, and then made to work in the fighters' fields and homes. It was also claimed that other black African females were kidnapped and flown across Sudan and forced to marry GoS soldiers.

In late December, the head of UNICEF in Sudan charged that up to 6,000 children—some as young as 11 years old, and many against their will—were serving as soldiers alongside GoS troops and with the main rebel groups (including the SLM/A and JEM). This was clearly in violation of both Sudanese law and international agreements (United Nations Radio, 2008).

On February 17, 2009 the Sudanese government and JEM signed a declaration of goodwill in which each agreed to work toward bringing peace to Darfur (*Sudan Tribune*, 2009, n.p.). Qatar hosted the first peace talks to be held in almost two years between the GoS and JEM. During the course of the talks, both sides agreed to pursue "good faith" measures. However, in March, JEM called the peace effort off as a result of the Sudanese government's expulsion of 13 non-governmental organizations from Sudan (see below).[14]

On March 4, 2009 the ICC issued an arrest warrant for Omar al Bashir. Al Bashir was charged with seven counts of crimes against humanity (including murder, extermination, forcible transfer, torture, and rape) and war crimes (intentionally directing attacks against civilians and for pillaging), but not the charge of genocide, which ICC Chief Prosecutor Luis Moreno-Ocampo had requested. Notably, it was the first arrest warrant ever issued for a sitting head of state by the ICC.

Immediately following the issuance of the warrant, the GoS expelled 13 international humanitarian groups from the country and grabbed their assets. The various groups warned that as a result of their operations being shut down up to one million lives could be placed at risk.

Al Bashir vehemently rejected the ICC charges, and said as much during a rally in Khartoum. Then, on March 8, 2009, while in Darfur, al Bashir thumbed his nose at the ICC and the international community when he told cheering supporters in El Fasher (the capital of North Darfur) that Sudan would not allow the "recolonization" of Africa.

In an exclusive interview with the BBC on May 12, 2009, al Bashir denied, and rejected as propaganda, that his troops had targeted any civilians in Darfur. And, as he was wont to do, he cavalierly dismissed the international community's estimate of the number of dead (300,000–400,000) in Darfur as a result of the GoS's scorched-earth policy. This time, though, instead of claiming, as he usually did, that the number of dead was around 10,000, al Bashir declared that the number of dead was "less than one tenth of what has been reported [by the international community]" (Coalition for the International Criminal Court, 2009, n.p.).

In mid-June, a brouhaha broke out within the White House over how to describe the ongoing situation in Darfur. More specifically, on June 17, 2009, the U.S. Special Envoy to Sudan, Scott Gration, claimed that the Sudanese government was no longer carrying out a "coordinated" program of mass murder in Darfur, thus inferring that the United States no longer considered the situation in Darfur to be a case of ongoing genocide. "What we see is the remnants of genocide," Gration told reporters at a briefing in Washington. "The level of violence that we're seeing right now is primarily between rebel groups, the Sudanese government and ... some violence between Chad and Sudan" (quoted in Lynch, 2009, p. 1). Based on his reading of the situation, Gration advocated easing U.S. sanctions on Sudan and strengthening U.S. diplomatic relations with the GoS in order to bring about more cooperation.

Gration's assertion, however, was in direct contrast to comments made earlier in the month by both U.S. President Barack Obama and U.S. Ambassador to the UN Susan E. Rice. At a press conference in Germany on June 5, Obama had used the phrase "ongoing genocide" (ABC News, 2009) in speaking about Darfur. On June 15, just two days prior to Gration's assertion, Rice, while in attendance at the International Peace Institute Vienna Seminar in Austria, had said:

> [H]umanitarian requirements will often jostle with other legitimate policy concerns. It does no good to pretend that priorities do not sometimes compete—and even where they do not, even where our values and our interests fall neatly in step together, the answers are not always obvious. Again, consider Sudan, where we simultaneously face the genocide in Darfur, the recent expulsion of critical international NGOs, a faltering North–South peace process, and the risk of new instability in various parts of the country. The urgency and complexity of the overall situation can distract us from addressing adequately any single imperative, and indeed, the reverse is also a risk. (Quoted in Rice, 2009, p. 2)

Then, in August 2009, General Martin Luther Agwai, the commander of the UNAMID force, declared that the war between the GoS and rebels was over:

> "As of today, I would not say there is a war going on in Darfur," Gen Agwai said in Khartoum. "Militarily there is not much. What you have is security issues more now. Banditry, localized issues, people trying to resolve issues over water and land at a local level. But real war as such, I think we are over that." (Quoted in Pflanz, 2009, p. 1)

Both anti-genocide activists in the United States and various rebel groups in Darfur decried Agwai's comments. The activists basically condemned the comments as absurd; "This is incredibly premature. To say the war in Darfur is over directly contradicts what we see on the ground," said Colin Thomas-Jensen, policy adviser for Enough, the anti-genocide project based at the Center for American Progress in Washington. "There may be a lull in the violence, but you cannot say that it is over. There is no political settlement and no political process to resolve the conflict. Neither side is defeated and the government is building up its arms stockpile" (quoted in the Meldrum, 2009, p. 1). Corroborating Thomas-Jensen and providing a more realistic appraisal of the situation than Agwai, the International Crisis Group (ICG) (2007) declared that

> The Darfur conflict has changed radically in the past two years. While there are fewer deaths than during the high period of fighting in 2003–2004, the conflict has mutated, the parties have splintered, and the confrontations have multiplied. Violence again increased in 2008 while access for humanitarian agencies became more difficult. International peacekeeping is not yet effective and a political settlement remains far off. (p. 1)[15]

Indeed, despite the wishful thinking of UNAMID commander Martin Agwai and U.S. Special Envoy Scott Gration, the fighting in Darfur was far from over. In early September 2009, GoS troops and the *Janjaweed* carried out a major military offensive in the Korma region of North Darfur. Heavy fighting continued throughout September, resulting in the murder and displacement of thousands of black African civilians.

October and November 2009, however, proved to be relatively quiet. That is not to say, however, that there were not periodic clashes between rebel groups and the GoS and the *Janjaweed*, because there were.

In an October 27, 2009 report to the UN Security Council, the Panel of Experts Established Pursuant to Resolution 1591 Concerning Sudan stated the following:

> Most of the major armed actors in the Darfur conflict have continued to exercise their military options, violate the United Nations arms embargo and international humanitarian and human rights law, and impede the peace process. The Darfurian population continues to be victimized by the effects of attacks and counter-attacks involving most of the armed movements that frequently lead to the disproportionate use of force by the Sudanese Armed Forces (SAF) and their auxiliary forces, and result in killings, injuries and displacements. Internally displaced persons continue to suffer from the inability to return to their homes and from acts of banditry, as well as from the lack of adequate humanitarian services, partly caused by the expulsion of

international nongovernmental organizations on 4 March 2009.... The Government of the Sudan, while demanding respect for its privilege as a sovereign State, also falls short in exercising transparency and accountability. Government officials often object to inquiries made by the Panel under its mandate and offer lip service while committing sanctions violations.... The Government of the Sudan remains intransparent and unwilling to account for its efforts to disarm and control its various auxiliary and formerly affiliated forces, in particular combatants commonly referred to as members of Arab tribes or as *Janjaweed*.... Many individuals identified by internally displaced persons as *Janjaweed* continue to carry arms and engage in frequent violent behaviour against and harassment of internally displaced persons and, according to the Panel's findings, enjoy impunity for their offences....

In the aftermath of the issuance by the International Criminal Court of an arrest warrant against the Head of State of the Sudan, the Panel has received reports of severe violations of international humanitarian and human rights law, involving the harassment, persecution and torture of collaborators and individuals opposed to Government policies. (United Nations Security Council, 2009, p. 1 of Summary)

Tellingly, half a month later, on November 16, 2009, UN Secretary General Ban Ki-Moon issued a report ("Report of the Secretary-General on the African Union–United Nations Hybrid Operation in Darfur (UNAMID)") in which he asserted the following:

In the context of [the] ongoing violence, freedom of movement continues to be a serious concern for UNAMID and many of the agencies in Darfur. Since January 2009, there have been at least 42 incidents in which UNAMID patrols were denied passage by Government [of Sudan] officials, including incidents in which Government officials specifically threatened the safety of UNAMID staff and equipment. (United Nations Security Council, 2009, p. 3)

Just a week earlier, on November 10, 2009, the GoS made an announcement that only exacerbated matters; seemingly out of the blue, it issued a statement that it planned to begin closing down IDP camps in Darfur in 2010. Its plan, it said, was to build 20,000 housing units for the IDPs in the capitals of each of the three Darfur states. Purportedly, the IDPs were to move into the new houses or return to their villages.

Various Darfur rebel groups angrily rejected the idea. For example, Abdel-Wahid Al-Nur leader of the SLM asserted that "The [GoS] wants to send our people back to the same places they fled from so that they can get killed again under the whole world's eyes" (quoted in the *Sudan Tribune*, 2009, n.p.). Similarly, Ahmed Hussein, a spokesman for JEM, said the GoS's plan was a "cover-up for a new crime the government intends to commit similar to the one in Kalma camp [the August 2008 killings of IDP's by government troops].... It is classic of them to do so" (quoted in the *Sudan Tribune*, 2009, n.p.).

Not surprisingly, the violence in Darfur continued into 2010 and 2011. Bombings by GoS aircraft aimed at civilians in the Jebel Marra region of Darfur were daily occurrences throughout 2010 and well into 2011, with some 182 bombings in 2010 and an additional 84 by May 2011. There were also reports that land in the region had been freshly planted with landmines.

On February 23, 2010 the GoS and JEM signed a Framework Agreement for the Resolution of the Conflict in Darfur (which was to serve as the basis for additional negotiations), which basically signaled the end of seven years of fighting between them. Ecstatic over the agreement, Omar al Bashir declared that the war in Darfur was over. Two days later, though, fighting broke out once again in Darfur. The SLA, one of the dozens of rebel groups in Darfur, claimed that it had been attacked by GoS troops. While GoS military officials denied the charge and even declared that there had been no fighting in the region, Medecins du Monde, a French aid organization, confirmed that fighting had taken place, stating that the city of Deirbat had been attacked, though it did not say by whom, causing a "massive flight of people" and bringing the number of displaced in the region to 100,000 (Chick, 2010, n.p.).

In early February 2010, UNAMID (which was in its second year of deployment and had 15,000 troops on the ground, still 11,000 short of its full complement) announced that it was increasing its security presence in and around the region in order to attempt to prevent a further escalation of the violence that had broken out in Jebel Marra, South Darfur, and Jebel Moon, West Darfur and that had resulted in the deaths of many and the dislocation of thousands.[16]

In December 2010, Minawi, who had signed the Darfur Peace Agreement in 2006, virtually dismissed it. Furious at the comments of Ibrahim Mohammed Hussein, the GoS Minister of Defense, for asserting that SLA rebels were "a legitimate military target," Minawi abruptly severed his relationship with the GoS.

In a report issued June 2011, Human Rights Watch stated that as the result of an increase in violence in western Sudan between December 2010 and May 2011, approximately 70,000 civilians had been forced from their villages in Darfur by GoS militias. Dozens of villages and towns between El Fasher and Nyala had been affected, as well as various ethnic Fur areas in eastern Jebel Mara. An untold number were killed. In mid-May 2011 alone, aerial attacks by the GoS resulted in 20 people being killed. The report pointed out that

> the patterns of attack show that the assaults and arbitrary arrests were based on ethnic divisions.... The witnesses [interviewed] by the HRW investigators said the government militias composed mainly of Berti, Birgid, and Mima ethnic groups targeted the areas of Khor Abeche and surrounding villages in the Shearia in South Darfur where people from the Zaghawa ethnic group are based. The militias aligned to the government also attacked North Darfur Zaghawa particularly in Shangil Tobayi, Dar el Salam, and [nearby] areas.
>
> In a case documented by HRW, Sudanese soldiers after surrounding the house of a local leader asked him of his tribe and threatened to "kill all of them [Zaghawas] and rape all their women" (quoted in the *Sudan Tribune*, 2011, p. 1).

The same report noted that GoS forces had also attacked civilians in IDP camps and raped black African females. To make matters even worse, the GoS continued to block humanitarian aid from reaching the various areas under attack. For example, in May 2011, the GoS denied access to both humanitarian groups and peacekeepers to almost all of South Darfur, including two huge IDP camps.

In May 2011 the National Congress Party (the ruling political party of Sudan, which is headed by Omar al Bashir) approved a draft law allowing for the creation of two new states in Darfur, for a total of five. Under the plan, the territory currently under the administration of the states of South Darfur and West Darfur is to be divided into four states: Central Darfur, East Darfur, South Darfur, and West Darfur. The state of North Darfur is not to be divided. Purportedly, the goal of the law is "to ease the tribal tensions over pasturage and water" (*Sudan Tribune*, May 6, 2011, p. 1). Different rebel groups have different takes on the planned division, with some favor, some opposed. For example, the Liberation and Justice Movement is seemingly willing "to accept the solution proposed by the mediation as it creates a legislative assembly besides the executive body. But JEM rejects this option saying they want a 'government of Darfur' that represents the whole region at the level of the central government" (*Sudan Tribune*, May 6, 2011, p. 1). Only time will tell how this will play out and what it will mean for the civilians of Darfur.

On July 14, 2011 the GoS and the Liberation and Justice Movement, a relatively insignificant rebel group, signed a peace agreement in Doha, Qatar. Interestingly, the Doha Agreement called for the creation of a truth, justice, and reconciliation commission, individual and collective compensation, and the reinstatement of civil servants who had lost their positions in Darfur. While some touted the signing of the Doha Agreement as a major accomplishment, others were quick to point out that neither JEM nor the SLM/A signed it. JEM refused to sign the peace agreement since its leadership was displeased that such issues as security arrangements and power and wealth sharing had not been resolved.

Ibrahim Gambari, the UN–AU Joint Special Representative to Darfur, started a firestorm of sorts when he, in September 2011, asserted that the number of armed attacks in Darfur (all three states) had dropped by as much as 70% between 2008 and 2011. He also asserted that due to the decrease in the number of attacks, the number of displaced people had fallen from some 2.7 million people to roughly 1.7, as some one million individuals had purportedly returned to their land. Many, however, questioned Gambari's numbers and were not as sanguine as he was about what transpired in Darfur between 2008 and 2011. For example, in a fiery and detailed refutation of Gambari's assertions, Reeves (2011) argued, in part, the following:

> Recent statements by Gambari deliberately distort Darfur's realities as a means of claiming success for a failing UNAMID peacekeeping operation and justifying his own performance during a disastrous tenure as JSR [Joint Special Representative] of the United Nations and the African Union to Darfur. These statements—massively overstating reduction in the levels of violence in Darfur and offering a preposterously untenable figure for the number of returns by displaced persons—are demonstrably false and misleading; they have provoked deep anger among Darfuris, who have called for Gambari to apologize or resign.
>
> Gambari has also worked assiduously to appease the Khartoum regime, yet another motive for his recent lies about conditions on the ground in Darfur.
>
> Gambari and UNAMID use only the data for violent events that UNAMID itself is able to confirm; and it is clear from a range of sources that this is only a small fraction of events that occur. The same is true for UNAMID "mortality figures," which record only the deaths that UNAMID has confirmed from violence, and excludes those not confirmed.... Whatever claim Gambari was making, it flies in the face of conclusions by human rights organizations, humanitarians, and Darfuris themselves. He

is claiming success where there is none, and where conditions are in many ways deteriorating. It is hardly surprising that Darfuris in camps for the displaced responded with great anger to Gambari's remarks when they were reported (n.p.).[17]

Finally, in yet another move that created great consternation in Darfur, as well as other regions of Sudan, al Bashir announced on October 13, 2011 that Sudan would adopt an Islamic constitution. Such a move is bound to result in even more turmoil in Darfur and beyond in the years ahead.

ICC Arrest Warrants

On May 2, 2007 the ICC issued arrest warrants for Ahmad Muhammed Harun (Ahmed Haroun), Sudanese Minister of Humanitarian Affairs, and Ali Muhammed Ali Abd-Al-Rahman (aka Ali Kushayb), a senior leader of the *Janjaweed* since 2003 and a key figure in planning and carrying out attacks on civilian populations all across Darfur. The charges spelled out in the arrest warrant for Haroun state that he was responsible for murders, mass rape, torture, forced displacement of civilians, and outrages against the personal dignity of girls and women during the course of the attacks. The ICC warrant also states that Haroun was allegedly responsible for encouraging the aforementioned and illegal acts in public speeches he made during his tenure as Sudanese Minister of State for the Interior. The ICC warrant for Kushayb is based on the fact that he allegedly led several thousand militia members, and personally participated, in attacks against civilians that involved murder, rape, and inhumane acts. Not surprisingly, Sudan categorically refused to extradite Haroun and Kushayb. Then, in a move that not only added fuel to the fire and constituted yet another thumbing of his nose at the international community and the international criminal justice system, al Bashir, in September 2007, appointed Haroun co-chair of the committee appointed to hear victims' cases of human rights abuses in Darfur.[18] It was the proverbial case of assigning a fox to guard the hen house.

Clearly illustrating that he was not solely focused on GoS leaders, Moreno-Ocampo, on November 20, 2008, requested warrants of arrest for three rebel leaders (whose names were not released at the time to the press or public) allegedly responsible for rebel attacks on international peacekeepers in Haskanita, South Darfur on September 29, 2007. The attack resulted in the deaths of 12 peacekeepers and civilian police officers. Ultimately, the ICC only issued two warrants, one each for the arrests of Abdallah Banda and Saleh Jerbo, both of whom, as rebel leaders, are charged as criminally responsible co-perpetrators for three war crimes perpetrated in the Darfur region. Charges against the third rebel leader, Bahar Idriss Abu Garda, were dropped due to a lack of evidence.

Then, most notably, on July 14, 2008, following an extensive, multi-year investigation and having concluded that the GoS had committed genocide in Darfur, ICC Chief Prosecutor Luis Moreno-Ocampo applied for a warrant for the arrest of Sudanese President Omar al Bashir on charges of crimes against humanity, war crimes, and genocide. On March 4, 2009, following its examination, analysis and discussion of the prosecutor's application for the warrant, the majority of ICC judges (two out of three) in the pre-trial hearing case rendered a decision that resulted in the issuance of a warrant charging al Bashir with crimes against humanity and war crimes, but not genocide. One of the three judges, Judge Anita Usacka, wrote a powerful dissent in which she delineated why she believed that Chief Prosecutor Moreno-Ocampo's request for a warrant on charges of genocide made sense and should have been honored.

Upon receiving the majority's decision, Prosecutor Moreno-Ocampo filed an appeal on July 6, 2009, contesting the dismissal of his application for a warrant for the arrest of al Bashir on charges of genocide. In doing so, he spelled out why he thought the majority opinion/decision was incorrect.

On February 3, 2010, the Appeals Chamber of the International Criminal Court ruled that the ICC judges in the Pre-trial Chamber case had to reconsider the prosecutor's request and thus decide anew whether or not the arrest warrant should be revised to include the charge of genocide. In doing so, the Appeals Chamber made it abundantly clear that it was not concerned with the issue of whether al Bashir was responsible or not for the crime of genocide, but rather that its concern dealt with procedural law (i.e., whether the Pre-Trial Chamber applied the correct standard of proof when rendering its final decision vis-à-vis the prosecutor's application for an arrest warrant on the charge of genocide). Ultimately, on July 12, 2010, Pre-Trial Chamber I issued a second warrant of arrest against al Bashir, this time for the crime of genocide.

More recently, on December 2, 2011, Moreno-Ocampo requested an arrest warrant for Sudanese Minister of Defense Abdelrahim Mohamed Hussein. Hussein is wanted on charges of war crimes and crimes against humanity allegedly committed in West Darfur from August 2003 to March 2004.

Is there Agreement or Disagreement Among Legitimate Scholars as to the Interpretation of this Particular Genocide?

Various scholars, activists, politicians, individual governments, and others hold a wide range of views in regard to whether the GoS and

Janjaweed attacks on the black Africans constitute genocide or not. In mid-2004, various U.S.-based activists and some U.S. politicians declared that genocide had been perpetrated in Sudan. For example, in July 2004, the United States Holocaust Memorial Museum's Committee on Conscience, which uses "graduated categories of urgency" (e.g., "watch," "warning," and "emergency") to warn of potential genocidal situations, signaled an "emergency" (i.e., "acts of genocide or related crimes against humanity are occurring or immediately threatened"). On July 22, 2004 both chambers of the U.S. Congress adopted concurrent resolutions (House Concurrent Resolution 467 and Senate Concurrent Resolution 133) in which they condemned the atrocities in Darfur as "genocide." Then, as previously mentioned, following a U.S. State Department-sponsored investigation, on September 9, 2004 U.S. Secretary of State Colin Powell declared that genocide had been perpetrated and was possibly still being perpetrated in Darfur.

Also, as previously mentioned, a subsequent investigation (December 2004/January 2005), conducted by the UN Commission of Inquiry into Darfur concluded that "crimes against humanity," not genocide, had been perpetrated in Darfur. The UN left the door open that upon subsequent study of the crisis and/or additional investigations by other bodies (presumably the ICC), it was possible that genocide might be found to have been perpetrated. (For a discussion of the ADT and COI findings, see Totten [2006; 2009].)

In a May 7, 2004 report ("Sudan: Government Commits Ethnic Cleansing in Darfur") and later, in October 2007, in a paper ("Q & A: Crisis in Darfur"), Human Rights Watch declared that the GoS had committed both ethnic cleansings and crimes against humanity in Darfur. Amnesty International, another major human rights organization, has deemed the killings cases of crimes against humanity and war crimes, but has not taken a stand in regard to whether the atrocities amount to genocide or not. Following two on-the-ground investigations in Darfur (2004 and 2005) and an in-depth analysis of the data collected in such investigations (see, respectively, *Assault on Survival: A Call for Security, Justice and Restitution* and *Destroyed Livelihoods: A Case Study of Furawiya Village, Darfur*), Physicians for Human Rights declared that the GoS had carried out a genocide in Darfur.

Among those scholars who assert that the atrocities perpetrated in Darfur do not constitute genocide are, for example: Mahmood Mamdami (2007), who argues in an article entitled "The Politics of Naming Genocide: Genocide, Civil War, Insurgency" that the situation in Darfur appears to be more a case of insurgency and counterinsurgency versus genocide; Alex de Waal (see *Newsweek*, 2007), who sees the crisis in Darfur as basically a war and not genocide; and Gerard Prunier

(2005; 2007), who wavers between calling the crisis in Darfur "an ambiguous genocide" (2004), and, in a later article, both a genocide and a case of ethnic cleansing (2007).

On the other hand, such scholars as Kelly Dawn Askin (2006), Gerald Caplan (2006), Stephen Kostas (2006), Eric Markusen and Samuel Totten (2005), and Samuel Totten (2004) assert that the crisis in Darfur constitutes genocide. Furthermore, such noted anti-genocide activists as Jerry Fowler (2006) and Gregory Stanton (2006), both of whom are lawyers (Stanford Law School and Yale Law School, respectively), have also concluded that the atrocities committed in Darfur constitute genocide.

To establish whether a crisis/event is genocide or not, it is imperative to use the language of the UNCG as the means for examining the facts. Among the most critical words, phrases, and conditions set out in the UNCG are located in Article II:

> In the present Convention, genocide means any of the following acts committed with intent to destroy, in whole or in part, a national, ethnical, racial or religious group, as such:
>
> a. Killing members of the group;
> b. Causing serious bodily or mental harm to members of the group;
> c. Deliberately inflicting on the group conditions of life calculated to bring about its physical destruction in whole or in part;
> d. Imposing measures intended to prevent births within the group;
> e. Forcibly transferring children of the group to another group.

In asserting that the crisis in Darfur constitutes a genocide, many scholars argue that there is ample evidence that the attacks by the GoS and *Janjaweed* have clearly resulted in "a" through "c" of Article II of the UNCG. The group that is under attack, they have argued, constitutes a racial group, and the issue of intent can be inferred from the events on the ground (e.g., what has taken place during the course of the attacks on the black African villages). All of the aforementioned individuals have published analyses/rationales vis-à-vis their assertions that genocide has been perpetrated in Darfur by the GoS and the *Janjaweed*.

Stephen Kostas (2006), an International Bar Association Fellow at the Appeals Chamber of the International Criminal Tribunal for the Former Yugoslavia, discussing Colin Powell's finding of genocide based on the analysis of the data collected by the U.S. State Department's Atrocities Documentation Project (ADP), wrote:

> First, they [Powell and Pierre Prosper, former U.S. Ambassador at-Large for War Crimes, among others in the U.S. government] noted that villages of Africans were being destroyed and neighboring Arab villages were not. Large numbers of men were killed and women raped. Livestock was killed and water polluted. In IDP camps, the GoS was preventing medicines and humanitarian assistance from going in despite persistent international calls for access. Examining these factors, they concluded there was a deliberate targeting of the group with the intent to destroy it.
>
> Prosper recalls the group examining the concepts of unlawful killing, causing of serious bodily and mental harm, and "the real one that got us … was the deliberate infliction of conditions of life calculated to destroy the group in whole, or in part." Looking at the IDP camps, Prosper and Powell could not find any "logical explanation for why the Sudan government was preventing humanitarian assistance and medicine" into the camps "other than to destroy the group." The GoS was seen as offering unbelievable excuses, leading Powell to conclude that there was a clearly intentional effort to destroy the people in the camps who were known to be almost exclusively black African. (pp. 121–122)

Gregory Stanton (2006), a Yale Law School graduate and a genocide scholar, asks and then asserts,

> Was the killing [in Darfur by the GoS and *Janjaweed*] "intentional"? Yes. According to the elements of crimes defined by the Statute of the International Criminal Court, genocide must be the result of a policy, which may be proved by direct orders or evidenced by systematic organization. Was the killing in Darfur systematically organized by the al-Bashir regime using government-armed *Janjaweed* militias, bombers, and helicopter gunships? Yes. Were the victims chosen because of their ethnic and racial identity? Yes. Fur, Massalit, and Zaghawa black African villages were destroyed, while Arab villages nearby were left untouched…. Does this conclusion constitute the intentional destruction, in part, of ethnic and racial groups? Yes. In short, the violence in Darfur is genocide, and it continues. (pp. 182–183)

Jerry Fowler (2006), a Stanford Law School graduate and [then] Director of the United States Holocaust Memorial Museum's Committee of Conscience, argued the following regarding the issue of intent as it relates to the GoS and *Janjaweed*'s actions in Darfur:

> U.S. Secretary of State Colin Powell concluded that intent could be inferred from the Sudanese Government's deliberate conduct. Inferring intent from conduct in the absence of direct evidence is widely accepted. The International Criminal Tribunal for Rwanda (ICTR) has delineated numerous circumstances that are relevant to determining "intent" to destroy, many of which are present in the case of Darfur:
>
> - "The general context of the perpetration of other culpable acts systematically directed against the same groups"
> - "The scale of atrocities committed"
> - "The 'general nature' of the atrocity"
> - "Deliberately and systematically targeting members of some groups [black Africans] but not others [Arabs]"
> - "Attacks on (or perceived by the perpetrators to be attacks on) the foundations of the group" [especially, the rape of the girls and women, thus creating "Arab babies" and resulting in girls and women being considered "damaged goods" by their families and thus ostracized, which, in turn, generally, and automatically, precludes them from having children with their husbands or, if single, from even getting married and having children]
> - "The use of derogatory language toward members of the targeted groups"
> - "The systematic manner of killing"
> - "The relative proportionate scale of the actual or attempted destruction of a group" (International Criminal Tribunal for Rwanda, 1998, paras. 523–524; 2000, para. 166). (Fowler, 2006, p. 131)

Kelly Dawn Askin (2006), another lawyer, has noted the following:

> Rape as an instrument of genocide most often invokes subarticle (b) [of the UNCG] intending to "destroy a protected group by causing serious bodily or mental harm to members of that group," and (d) "imposing measures intended to prevent births within a group" .... The Akayesu Judgment of the ICTR [International Criminal Tribunal for Rwanda] is the seminal decision recognizing rape as an instrument of genocide. (p. 150)

Continuing, she argued that

> There is every indication that the official policy of the GoS and *Janjaweed* forces is to wage, jointly or separate, concentrated and strategic attacks against black Darfurians by a variety of means, including through killing, raping, pillaging, burning and displacement. Various forms of sexual violence regularly formed part of these attacks.... Rape crimes have been documented in dozens of villages [now, in 2012, it is more like hundreds] throughout Darfur and committed in similar patterns, indicating that rape itself is both widespread and systematic. (p. 150)

Askin (2006) also commented on the epithets made by the attackers during the course of the rapes, which indicates, in various ways, a desire to "deliberately inflict on the group conditions of life calculated to bring about its physical destruction in whole or in part" and "impose measures intended to prevent births within the group": "We want to change the color. Every woman will deliver red. Arabs are the husbands of those women" (quoted on p. 147); and "We will take your women and make them ours. We will change the race" (quoted on p. 147).

That which is delineated above is only a fraction of each individual's argument in regard to why the Darfur crisis constitutes genocide.

Do People Care about this Genocide Today? If so, how is that Concern Manifested?

Beginning in late 2003 and lasting for some four years or so, the issue of Darfur generated astonishing attention and concern among journalists, scholars, activists, university and high-school students, church people, movie stars, film makers, and others. While many different groups of individuals (including scholars and activists) still focus on the Darfur crisis, the attention by others has dropped off precipitously. Undoubtedly, that is due to people focusing on other crises in the world, of which there have been many.

For a good number of years numerous journalists wrote about the crisis in Darfur, and some consistently so. Most notably, Nicholas D. Kristof of the *New York Times* has made at least half a dozen trips to Darfur and the refugee camps in Chad, and has written extremely powerful and thought-provoking articles about what he witnessed, heard, and experienced. For his efforts, Kristof was awarded a Pulitzer Prize in 2006 for his series of articles on Darfur. Equally deserving of a Pulitzer Prize for her reporting on Darfur is Emily Wax, a journalist with the

Washington Post. Her columns, too, over the years, have been extremely powerful and thought provoking.

A whole host of organizations and sub-organizations have arisen over the years that address the Darfur genocide. For years, among the most active were Save Darfur and STAND: A Student Anti-Genocide Coalition. The Save Darfur Coalition comprised "over 180 faith-based, advocacy and humanitarian organizations, and represented 130 million people of all ages, races, religions and political affiliations united together to help the people of Darfur." The express purpose of the Save Darfur Coalition was "to raise public awareness about the ongoing genocide in Darfur and to mobilize a unified response to the atrocities that threaten the lives of two million people in the Darfur region." Eventually, the Save Darfur Coalition and the Genocide Intervention Network folded into the current United to End Genocide.

Students Taking Action Now: Darfur (which eventually changed its name to STAND: A Student Anti-Genocide Coalition, thus enlarging its focus, and now constitutes the student-led division of United to End Genocide) is comprised of student chapters in universities and high schools across the United States. The first U.S.-based STAND chapter was established at Georgetown University in Washington in 2004, shortly after President George W. Bush called Darfur "genocide." The students had attended a conference on Darfur at the United States Holocaust Memorial Museum and walked away thinking they had to do something to bring the issue of the Darfur genocide to the attention of the nation's students and beyond. That initial effort has expanded into an international network of student activism and now comprises more than 850 STAND chapters on university, college, high-school, junior-high and middle-school campuses around the globe.

STAND has been active on numerous fronts. For example, in January 2006 STAND initiated its Power to Protect campaign, which collected over one million postcards calling on President Bush to undertake more effective action vis-à-vis Darfur. In subsequent years, STAND successfully managed to get more than 25 states and eight universities to divest endowments and pension funds from companies doing business in Sudan; advocated for the successful passage of federal legislation, including the Sudan Accountability and Divestment Act (SADA), the Genocide Accountability Act (GAA), and hundreds of millions of dollars in peacekeeping and relief funds; and has raised more than $650,000 for the Genocide Intervention Network Civil Protection Program in Darfur.

Movie stars have also been drawn to the cause of Darfur. Among the most noted involved in bringing attention to the Darfur crisis are George Clooney, Mia Farrow, Don Cheadle, Matt Damon and, to a lesser degree, Brad Pitt. They have loaned their names to various efforts, have spoken at major rallies, helped to fund-raise, and, in the case of Cheadle, helped to produce a documentary and co-author a book on Darfur. Essentially, their "star power" has drawn immense attention to the crisis and in doing so has brought the issue to the consciousness of untold numbers of people.

Finally, between 2005 and 2007 numerous documentary films were produced about the Darfur crisis, including but not limited to the following: *All About Darfur* (2005); *Darfur Diaries* (2006); *Darfur Now* (2007); *On Our Watch* (2007); and *The Devil Came on Horseback* (2007).

At a minimum, all of the aforementioned efforts have helped to educate people about Darfur, and not allowed the international community to totally ignore the plight of the victim population. It hasn't though, at least thus far, resulted in pushing the international community to provide real protection for the black Africans of Darfur. That said, one has to pause and ponder whether many more black Africans would have been killed had there not been such a clamor made over the atrocities carried out by the GoS and *Janjaweed*. There is no doubt that the killing by the GoS and *Janjaweed* has waxed and waned, and the latter is likely, at least in part, due to the fact that the international community has focused fairly sustained attention on the ongoing crisis in Darfur.

What Does This Genocide Teach Us If We Wish to Protect Others from Such Horrors?

The genocide in Darfur has taught humanity, once again, as if it really needed another lesson along this line, the following: the international community is more wedded to *realpolitik* than it is to saving the lives of innocents; the UN Security Council is a group of disparate members whose primary focus is their own particular wants and needs and, as a body, it has no conscience to speak of; the UN Security Council's Permanent Five wield the power of life and death with their vetoes, but that doesn't constrain individual members from using their veto even when it will mean certain death to groups facing horrific atrocities, be they crimes against humanity or genocide; individual nations and leaders talk a good game but at one and the same time, and more often than not, lack the political will to act when it counts (be it due to *realpolitik*, politics at home, or simply a lack of concern or a dearth of real care); the time to act to save people from genocide is early on, when threats of and/or actual human rights violations far short of genocide are being carried out against a particular group; and the good intentions and efforts of activists can move many to action on the behalf of beleaguered others facing genocide but far too often, at least in today's world, they are overpowered by the *realpolitik* and the power of veto practiced by one or more of the Permanent Five members of the UN Security Council.

Conclusion

As the international community dithers, innocent people in Darfur continue to either be murdered, perish as a result of malnutrition, dehydration and lack of medical attention, and/or suffer rape at the hands of the GoS troops and hired militia, and, increasingly, members of various rebel groups. Nine long years have gone by since the start of the crisis in Darfur, and the international community continues to engage in talk over real action in an "effort" to ameliorate the problems that beset Darfur. Unfortunately, Darfur is a stark reminder that the world is no closer to solving, halting, let alone, preventing genocide than it was during the Ottoman Turk genocide of the Armenians (1915–1923), the man-made famine in Ukraine (1933), and the Holocaust perpetrated by the Nazis (1933–1945). The same is true, unfortunately, in regard to sexual assaults against girls and women during periods of violent conflict.

Eyewitness Accounts

Account 1

The respondent [name deleted for the sake of confidentiality] was born in 1972 in Andukeria, near Genenia in West Darfur. He is a Massaleit and had seven years of schooling. He first worked as a tailor and then a trader in produce.

This interview/oral history was conducted by Samuel Totten on June 10, 2007. It was conducted in the Gaga Refugee Camp in Eastern Chad. It was conducted under a lean-to within a larger compound with the respondent, interviewer, and interpreter sitting on multicolored rugs.

I lived in Goker during the attacks. Goker is between Habilia and Geneina. Its population was about 2,600. I left Goker about one month ago.

The trouble in Darfur started long ago, in 1994, and in Goker in 1995. Before, there were not a lot of camels in our area and then in 1995 more than 20,000 camels arrived. These camels, when they come along, they destroy everything. These camels were looked after by Arab people and the camels eat the plants that are growing and the Arabs say you can't do anything about it. When this happens, the people go and report it to the police and the police go and see the Arabs and the police come back and say, "These people are our people and we won't do anything to them." Because the head of the police are Arabs, and they have a program [an agreement] with the Arabs to destroy us. All of the farms were destroyed, including mine. They [the camels] ate all of the grain and plants.

After the rainy season, the farms were destroyed and the war between the Arabs and us began. In my own family, two of my cousins, both were farmers, were killed. They went to the market and they were returning and Arabs killed them, Arabs who had camels. The Arabs would stay in between villages and when our people visited friends or family members, the Arabs would rob and kill our people. They were criminals. This was the beginning of the *Janjaweed* [Arab militia who have conducted attacks, largely in conjunction with the troops of the Government of Sudan, on the villages of black Africans].

Because my cousins and others were killed at this time, all of our tribe members came together and fought the Arabs for six days and chased them way. Many of our people died and a lot of Arabs were killed. From our people, 190 were killed. All were fighters.

I, too, fought with those. We had no real weapons but we got weapons when we fought them. They had horses and camels and Kalashnikovs and Gems [shorter rifles than Kalashnikovs]. We fought in villages of the Massaleit and ate there and did not return home.

I was injured in the hand by a bullet. At the time I just salted the wound and bandaged it. I still do not have feeling in my thumb.

When we fought, the Arabs told us, "this country [Sudan] is not to be inhabited by slaves." When the Arabs were being beat, some started to run and others called out, "Don't run away from the slaves" and "This is a jihad against the slaves!"

After the battle, the government tried to help the Arabs and gave them horses, camels and money and weapons. And soon after, about one month, more Arabs came and attacked again. They came from different areas in Darfur, and Chad, and even Abeche [a major town in Eastern Chad, which the Gaga Refugee camp is located near]. And the fighting continued through 2000. There was no solution unless you fought. There was no security.

We would set up ambushes because we knew the Arabs would attack us again. So, we were ready. Mothers of fighters would often come out to where we were fighting and beg their children to return. Most of us, though, would tell our mothers we were going to a meeting and not tell them we were actually going to fight. We knew the Arabs would attack us in the village if we didn't ambush them and we didn't want that. The Arabs come from as far away as Libya, Mauritania, and Egypt and some are even Palestinians.

As for my mother, she told me "You must fight even if you die because you are defending your people." Everyone knew if something wasn't done the Arabs would sneak up and attack and kill everyone. Of course, my mother feared that I would die.

In 2000, General Mohammed Ahmed Mustafa Deby came to meet with representatives of Massalit and Arabs and said he was a representative of the President of Sudan, al Bashir. In the meeting the representatives of the Massalit told the general that we were here before the Arabs came to Africa and all the tribes came to our areas and they lived peacefully, but the Arabs came and started killing our people and so we fought them. The general said he was there to make a peace between us and the Arabs but he was deceiving us. Two months after this agreement, the Arabs started killing the leaders of the Massalit, and even some of the politicians inside Genenia.

After this, the Arabs started eliminating the educated people. There was a man named Ahmed Abdouffrag—an engineer and he went to Khartoum to ask the government to build roads in the Massalit area and he was killed in his home upon his return. This was in 2000. Some Arab people drove up to his home, called him out and shot and killed him.

Others who were killed were Ibrahim Darfouri, who was head of the legislative body in Genenia. His wife was head of the Women's Union in Genenia. They were both killed the same day. They shot and killed them both. This, too, was in 2000.

People outside Genenia, leaders of other villages, were also killed. Saleh Dakoro, *umda* of Morley, was killed in 2001. He went to Genenia and on his way back some *Janjaweed* shot and killed him.

Yacoub Congor, another *umda*, was also eliminated in 2001. He was in the *suq* in Habilia and about 35 *Janjaweed* came into the *suq*, searched for him and one shot and killed him.

In 2002, the Arabs established their own villages in our area. When our people were killed by the Arabs and went to the police, they said, "That's a tribal problem and we have nothing to do with it." But if a Massaleit killed even one Arab, the police would collect other police from other areas and even call the army and then come and attack the village [of the Massalit] where the Arab was killed.

The police would also go to other villages and arrest Massaleit [in retaliation for the one killing]. The police have a weapon called Fang, which is a rocket propelled grenade [RPG] and they would take the powder out of the shell and put it on the head of people and set it on fire and it would explode like diesel [gasoline]. I saw this with my own eyes.

You should know, all those people who were in Darfur and worked for the police, the army and security, were all taken out of Darfur and moved away to other parts of Sudan and they were all replaced by *Janjaweed*.

They had another weapon where they would tie you to two vehicles—your arms to one and your legs to another—and they would drive off in separate directions, pulling our body apart.

And many people were arrested and taken to the security office, and many of those people have never been heard from again. And it's the *Janjaweed* who run the security office. All were red people.

Possibly around May 2002, Arabs from different nationalities were brought into Idelganim to train them [the local Arabs] to help them establish a state comprised of Darfur, Chad and the Republic of Central Africa. al Bashir visited the camp and changed the name from Idelganim to Idelfoursan. He changed the meaning of the location, the camp, from "where goats live" to "where brave men with horses live."

Massalit from our tribe who are red like Arabs went into the training camps and posed as Arabs. Seven days after Omar Bashir visited the camp, Osama Bin Laden gave them [the Arabs] camels as presents. This place is east of Nyala in a village called Idelganim, near Kordofan. When these groups began moving about in Darfur, they were referred to as *gowat alsalam* (Peace Force). When they attacked, they would come in with 400 to 500 men on horses, surround the village and destroy it. And this was how our village was destroyed.

This day, about seven in the morning, in some villages near us, we saw horses, I cannot say the number, and three vehicles and helicopters. When the people were fighting at this time, the helicopters would land and take off but I don't know what they were doing. And we saw planes, all gray, Antonovs, come and go and we heard the dropping of bombs.

I left our village before it was attacked. We all fled right away, and I went to the police station and military in Goker [the regional headquarters of Goker]. The village was burned down, and I could see that as I was fleeing. We, many, many villagers, people from over 40 villages, about 6,000 people, stayed there [the aforementioned regional headquarters in Goker]. I stayed there from that time, until one month ago, when I came here [Gaga camp in Eastern Chad]. Some organizations came there and helped us—such organizations as Red Cross and Oxfam.

I never returned to my village. There was nothing I could do there. The huts were built of grass and thus nothing remained after the fire.

In the village, there were about 700 cows, nine camels, and more than 2,000 goats, and 19 horses. I personally lost 28 cows and 61 goats.

So, from November 2003 to last month [June 2007] I was in an internally displaced camp. While our IDP [internally displaced persons] camp was not attacked, it was not peaceful. For example, women could not go out to collect firewood. If a woman went outside the camp, the

Janjaweed would rape them. If they stayed inside, the government did not help provide wood for cooking. A man can't go out because if you go out yourself you'll receive one bullet [meaning a man will be shot and killed]. The government also interferes with the distribution of food. There are many different types of food handed out by relief groups and the *Janjaweed* tells them not to give us certain food just to make us angry.

The African Union troops had an office in the IDP camp but there were very few men—only about thirteen. But when there was, for example, a crime, such as the rape of a woman, we'd tell them and they would say they would look for the criminals but always came back and said they couldn't find them.

I think some of the African Union (AU) troops are on the side of the *Janjaweed* and the government of Sudan. I say this because the *Janjaweed* bring the troops sheep and milk. We can see with our own eyes they bring such things. What else they may bring we do not know.

It is also true, some of the African Union troops truly help us. For example, the Rwandese soldiers are very good and helped us. So did troops from Eritrea. But troops from Nigeria, Chad, Cameroon, Egypt, and Libya are working for their own benefit, not the benefit of Darfur.

So, again, for example, if a person like you comes to speak to me [in Darfur] during the day, the *Janjaweed*, GOS troops and members of the AU will come at night and take me and kill me. And if something happens to you [meaning black Africans], the Egyptian troops will even laugh.

Another time, in Mistere, where there are a lot of AU soldiers, the *suq* was attacked and two people, two traders, were killed and the market was looted, all by the *Janjaweed*, and all the AU soldiers did was take photographs during the attacks and nothing else.

One time, a journalist spoke to a person in our camp and that night some people—I'm not sure if it was *Janjaweed* or security people in the camp—went to his house. The man, though, thought there might be trouble so he had left his hut, but only after placing materials in his bed to make it appear he was sleeping there. Men burst into his room and fired four shots into the bed. The next morning we went to the African Union to report this, and the African Union soldiers went and got more soldiers, from all different countries, plus a man from a rebel group, JEM, to go to the man's house. When the soldier, who was from Egypt, saw the bullets he smiled. We told the one Rwandese soldier who was there that the killers would be back that night and asked him to take the man who was in danger to Genenia. The Rwandese soldier agreed but the Egyptian said no. We took the Rwandese soldier to the man who was hiding and when the soldier was about to take him to Genenia, the

Egyptian said, "No, he is not to be taken there." The Rwandese soldier said, "Yes, he will be. It's our job to protect people." So, the Rwandese soldier took him to Genenia and the Egyptian just stood there and allowed him to do so.

The problem is truly worse than before—that is, worse with the African Union troops. Before they came, everyone knew there was ethnic cleansing (*tathir irgi*) and mass killing (*ibada jamia*) but after the AU came, because they insisted on coming in order to show they were doing something to help, [but,] all they do is take photographs and talk, and the violence continues. So, it's worse now, because there was hope there'd be real help but there's not. The situation is the same but the hope is gone.

We stayed in the camp for a long time, and we hoped that with the African Union the situation would be better but it never was so we decided to leave and come to Chad.

Several small villages between Genenia and Mornei were attacked at 6:00 in the morning and I saw a lot of horses and dust and vehicles, Toyota Landcruisers. The people who were being attacked flew toward our village. Many rode horses and many came on foot. And the enemy, the *Janjaweed* and the GOS, was chasing them, and we, too, fled—with all of us were donkeys and they were running.

As we were fleeing the *Janjaweed* would halt women with babies and force the women to show whether their children were boys or girls. And when the enemy caught a man, the man was killed. And if they caught a woman and she had a child, if the baby was a boy, they would kill him. They would take the baby boy and throw him on the ground and step on his throat and kill him. In other cases, they would throw the baby boys into the fire to burn alive. If the baby was a girl, they would leave them. The same for little girls. But if the girls were 13, 14, 15 or older, they often took them away for three or four days, and they [the girls] would often come back. But some never came back and we still don't know what happened to them.

Not from our village but others, people I know were taken and made slaves. The attackers would say in front of the people, "You, I am taking as a slave!" They would force such people to watch their animals as herders. They don't take big people [adults] but young boys about eight or nine years old.

The last days before I came to Gaga, there was interference by the government [of Sudan] in the work of the international organizations. What I mean is that one organization was formed by the Sudanese government and when they distributed food to us they told us we wouldn't get any food unless we went back to where we came from. This began two months before we came here [Gaga camp in Chad]. Then, when you went to your village, they would come and take pictures and pass them around and say, "Everything is alright." They would bring food once or twice, but then the *Janjaweed* would come and kill you. I refused to go back, as did my friends.

When we refused to return to our villages, for 50 days we did not receive any food. And there were no other organizations providing food for any of us. The only way we were able to eat is that we knew the future could be worse so while we received three meals a day, we only ate two meals; and when we started receiving no food, we began to eat only once a day.

And during this time, just by accident, some journalists passed (three men and one woman) by our camp, and we told these journalists we had no food for 50 days and the journalists reported this to a human rights organization. A human rights organization came to see us after seven days and when we told them our problem, they reported it to the Red Cross, which brought us food, and three days later, the other organization [the Sudanese organization] packed up all their food and left and never came back.

This is my daughter [indicating a little girl sitting in his lap], and I named her Condoleezza Rice. Her complete name is Condoleezza Mahjoub Oumar. I want to give Condoleezza Rice [the U.S. Secretary of State] this girl, my daughter, who is two years [old]. Because Condoleezza Rice came to visit us in Darfur when we were in a very bad situation. I have no means to contact Condoleezza Rice to tell her that I want to give her my child, and I wish I did.

Many people work for Darfur—the African Union, the United Nations, Kofi Annan (at one point, however, he gave the *Janjaweed* three months to turn in their weapons; can you imagine how many people could be killed in that time?)—Condoleezza Rice and Colin Powell [the former U.S. Secretary of state] worked more than all these others to help us. So, we do not forget people who help us, who help Africa. I wish I had a boy and a girl, because then I would give the boy to Colin Powell and the girl to Condoleezza Rice. I also know that Condoleezza Rice has no child and thus I would like her to have my child.

Account 2

The respondent [name deleted for the sake of confidentiality] is about 30 years old (not sure of her date of birth, it is a guess). She was born in the village of Tolos in West Darfur, which is near the larger town of Mornei. She is a Massaleit.

This interview/oral history was conducted by Samuel Totten on June 10, 2007. It was conducted in the Gaga Refugee Camp in Eastern Chad.

It was conducted under a lean-to on which the interviewee, interviewer, and interpreter sat. Approximately 10–15 family members (e.g., her children, mother, sister, nieces and nephews, and others) sat and stood on the periphery listening in on the interview session.

When our village, Tolos, was attacked I was living with eight people in my home, my six children, me and my husband. Our village was attacked four years ago. I can't remember the month but it was about two months after Ramadan.

In the morning, early, we were taking breakfast, and we heard the planes. They are too loud, from far you can hear them.

The planes came first, then the trucks, and then the horses and camels. Some [Janjaweed] were on foot. The planes, Antonovs, flew over the village. They [the planes] were all white and the sides were red. They [three or four of them] dropped big things like binil [barrels], and they made fire. Everything caught fire, buildings, animals, people.

The planes dropped the big things, and about 20 minutes after the Landcruisers came. Some were green color, some were black and green [camouflaged]. There were many, I don't know how many because at the time I was scared, but it might have been about 100. They came from all directions. When we heard the big things falling and hitting, we ran out of the house but we didn't know where to go. The big things caused big holes, like wells.

Driving the cars were Sudanese soldiers. Most Janjaweed rode horses, camels and were on foot. On the trucks, they have a big gun [she is most likely referring to what are called doskas], and the soldiers held big guns, some red and some black [Bilgic, possibly of Italian make]. There were also modra [tanks] with men inside but you can't see them. Outside there is a big gun and everything was colored black and green. There were about ten modra. The camels and horses and Landcruisers were more than 400. They were crying loud as they came in, calling out "Nuba! Nuba!"

At that time, we were ten persons and we began running. I was with three of my sisters, my sister-in-law, my father's two sisters, and three were my neighbors. All of my children had run in fear and I didn't know where they were. My husband, too [was gone and she still does not know his whereabouts].

We ran outside the village to the west. There was a lot of shooting but none of us were hit.

I was so frightened, I left the village without my two babies and little four-year-old daughter who were inside our hut. I later found them because someone had grabbed them and run out with them.

As we were running I saw men from our village shot. They killed 27 men. They [the soldiers and Janjaweed] aimed at the men. I saw two of my fathers [her father's two brothers; in other words, her uncles, who are generally referred to as "fathers" by the black Africans] killed. We didn't have any guns in our village and they [the Government of Sudan troops and the *Janjaweed*] did all of the shooting.

I was looking and crying and running but what can I do? I was so fearful, didn't stop running and I was hysterical, crying and running. After the attack, we came back to our village and we found the dead bodies.

We ran for three days, to Habilia. No food and no water.

Not for 23 days did I find my one son [name withheld for the sake of confidentiality], in Mornei on the way out in the bush. On the way out, we came across my husband who had two of our other sons in the bush. Then we went to Habilia. We had nothing. Sometimes we went to the bush for firewood but we were attacked by the *Janjaweed*.

We returned to our village after ten days. We returned because it was safe. When we made it back, we did not find anything but bodies. There were about seven dead bodies.

Our animals, our cows, our sorghum, our millet, our clothes, nothing was left. Nothing. It was all burnt, destroyed. The whole village was destroyed.

We found three who were injured in a small valley, in different places. All three had been shot—one man in both arms and both legs and the other man in one leg and the other one in his hand.

We took the injured to Mornei on donkey and then they [the injured] were taken in automobile to Zallingi, east of Genenia. The people with the cars were black but I don't know if they were an organization or not. They were Sudanese, but I don't know where they were from. There was no hospital in Mornei and so they took them to Zallingi. The three are still living and one is here [in Gaga camp] in Block 7 and two are in Mornei.

When we left the village to return to Habilia, we came across the *Janjaweed* again, out in the bush. The *Janjaweed* were shooting guns and we began running. Because we are far away we could not hear what they were yelling at us. They followed us, but not too closely and then left.

In Habilia, we stayed without any work; sometimes we went into the bush to get firewood that we sold to buy food. We stayed there for two years, in an internally displaced persons camp.

Life was not good in the camp. There was not enough food and if you left the camp, the *Janjaweed* would sometimes beat us. There was not freedom.

I was attacked by the *Janjaweed*. We, men and women, were cutting firewood and they stopped us and beat us. They beat us with sticks for two hours. One person was injured very badly from the beating and he had head injures that left him feeling unwell.

Another time I was also out with five women and three girls (13 years old, 14 years old, and 15 years old) gathering firewood and the *Janjaweed* raped the three girls and a woman. We were about two hours from the camp, and we were on foot. When we first arrived at the area with the wood the *Janjaweed* about 20 of them, were on camels and horses and came up on us very quickly. Some of them said, "We already took your land, why are you around here? We use your land and now we are going to use you."

We all started running away and four of us got captured, three girls and one woman. One girl who was captured was my sister's daughter, who was 13 years old. From the morning until the evening the *Janjaweed* kept the girls and the woman.

When we reached the camp we told the mothers of the daughters about the capture of their daughters and the mothers went out and brought their daughters back on donkeys and took them to the hospital in Habilia. The four were badly injured because of the rape and the woman spent five days in the hospital and the girls were in for 10 days. The girls were raped by many men, some by five, some by 10.

From the four girls, one got pregnant and had the baby. She was the one who was 15 years. She is still in Habilia with the baby from the *Janjaweed*. When the girl's father heard about the baby from the *Janjaweed*, he got very angry and sick from his anger and died [possibly from a heart attack]. He was 50. He was not sick before that, but when he heard what happened he died.

We came to Gaga camp about one year ago. When we were in Habilia, there was no way you could go out without trouble from the *Janjaweed*. When we were in the Habilia camp, the *Janjaweed* came three times at night and attacked the camp. One time, they killed four guards, all [of whom] were Massaleit. So, it was not safe to stay there.

From Habilia, we, 16 of us (me, my mother, my mother's sister, my own sister, my husband, my father, my six children, my husband's sisters, my husband's brothers) went to Genenia and from Genenia to Adre, and from Adre [in Chad, along the Chad/Sudan border] to Gaga. In the *suq* in Habilia we found a car to take us to Genenia. We stayed for two days in Genenia, in the station of cars. Already we were forced out of Sudan [Habilia] and Genenia is in Sudan so we did not want to stay. From Genenia we found a direct car to Adre in Chad. In Adre we stayed for two days. In Adre there is no camp or organization to help so we did not want to stay there. We reached Gaga by car we hired.

In Gaga, it took one month and 10 days to get a tent. At that time, we lived outside the camp. Because there are many Massaleit in this camp, they would come out to see us and give us food.

The life in camp [the UNCHR camp in Gaga] is very difficult, but what can we do? There is no other way. When we first arrived, everything was fine, but now there is not enough food, not enough water, and not enough medicine.

With my husband and I live our four children and my mother. Before we got food every two weeks then it went to one month and now we have not had food for two months. So, now we have to go outside of the camp and work for Chadian people and they give us money and with it we buy millet. Sometimes, we buy sugar and sometimes okra and sometimes meat for our soup. We have had meat one time in months. We buy sugar more often because we like tea, so if we have money we can buy it every day, if not, then we don't. If we have money we also buy okra every day, if not we don't.

One day we get water and the next we don't. It's not regular. We don't know why this is so.

If we don't get water in the camp, we have to walk one hour on foot to get water out of the well. We get one *baka* [jerry can] of water from the well. I am the one who goes for the water and the *baka* with the water is very heavy so I can only carry one.

My baby [a little girl with a huge extended stomach], one and a half years, has had diarrhea for one year and we have seen a doctor here in Gaga ten times and he gave us medicine but it didn't do any good. We told the doctor and he gives more medicine and it doesn't do anything.

And when I make water [urinate] I feel very hot inside. This has gone on for three months. In Habilia I went to the doctor and got medicine for it and I felt better but here I go to the doctor and the medicine he gave me makes me feel no better.

I don't have a lot of hope. If the Americans bring peace to Darfur and bring security then maybe life will get better, but here, I don't think so. If the UN [peace force] goes to Darfur, we'd like to go back to our country.

Account 3

The respondent [name deleted for the sake of confidentiality] is 17 years old and resides in the Gaga Refugee Camp in Eastern Chad. She is a Massaleit.

This interview/oral history was conducted by Samuel Totten on June 10, 2007. It was conducted on a rug sitting in front of a UNCHR-issued tent with the sun beating down. A small makeshift fence made of tree branches surrounded the small, mostly dusty area which this woman and her family called home.

I was born during Ramadan but I don't know the day, month or year. I studied only one year in school. It was last year, here in Gaga.

I came to Gaga with my mother and my two sisters. One sister is 32 years and one is 20 years. In Masteri I lived with my mother and father and two sisters until three years ago. I met my husband, who is now 23, here in Gaga. I live with my husband and a baby girl, who is three months [old].

The government [of Sudan] used planes and trucks to attack us and the *Janjaweed* came on horse and camels and on foot. They came in the early morning just before sunrise and I was asleep. I first knew there was an attack because I heard the sound of weapons from the planes and the trucks. As soon as I heard the sounds I got up and ran from the hut. As we ran I heard some *Janjaweed* scream "Nuba *afnine*" ["Nuba shit"]. I don't know how many *Janjaweed* and soldiers there were but maybe it was around 200. So many I can't count. Maybe 20 green and black [camouflaged] Landcruisers and hundreds of horses and camels.

The soldiers and *Janjaweed* chased us and they kept shooting men and boys. Many were killed. They also caught men and slashed them with long knives on the legs and arms, cutting off their arms and legs, and sometimes both on men—and sometimes both arms. Some who had their legs cut off were able to move, some could not. Those who survived were later given a new leg and a stick [crutch]. But those who had different sides of their bodies cut off [such as a right arm and a left leg] could not continue on. They could not walk. All of the attackers were wearing black and green and white [camouflaged].

At such times you do not look around for other persons, you take care of yourself. We (my mother and my two sisters) made it to Goagor in one day. But for three months we did not see my father. He went another way and we did not know it. He went to Tabrie in Chad, and then he came to find us in Goagor.

In my village, the *Janjaweed* and soldiers killed my second "father" [uncle] and his two sons. The two were older than me, but I don't know how old they were. They were all shot and killed. My second father was shot and as we, my two sisters and I, were running we saw him. He had just been shot in the side of his body and his insides came out the other side. We picked him up and placed him under a tree. We were very young then and very frightened and so we left him and rushed off.

Later, some people went back to the village and they saw my second father under the tree, dead. And at this time they also found the two sons of my second father, dead.

We stayed in Goagor for two years. We stayed with the people in the village there. There were about 200 people from Darfur, from different villages. When we were there we asked to farm but they said "How could you farm, you are refugees and have no land." And then when we went to go to the well, the Chadians caused us problems and told us we could not get water before them because we are refugees. So, we had to wait until every Chadian got water before trying to get some ourselves. We stayed there because we had no other place to go.

We finally decided to leave Goagor because many other refugees were going to Hajar Hadid and Gaga and since we were refugees we decided to go, too.

From Goagor we went to Gaga. We wanted to go to Hajar Hadid but we were told that there was no room for new refugees at Hajar Hadid and so we came to Gaga.

Gaga is [a] bad life because there is not enough food or water. I hope life will get better, but I don't know. The food [though] is not the important thing; the important thing is that we get our country back.

Account 4

The respondent, Mohammed Abdullah Arbab, was born on June 15, 1977 in Baouda, West of Congo Haraza-Beida in West Darfur. He completed school through the eleventh year. He is Massaleit. He is the *umda* of the UNCHR refugee camp, Farchana.

This interview was conducted by Samuel Totten on July 12, 2007 inside the tent of the respondent in the UNCHR camp of Farchana. Sitting in the crowded tent, which contained all of the interviewee's earthly possessions, were the interviewee, the interviewer, and the interpreter. The initial interview lasted for just over two hours. At 4:50 p.m. the interview had to be terminated for the day since there was a regulation that all non-residents had to be out of the camp by no later than 5:00 p.m. It was agreed that the interviewer and interpreter would meet the interviewee back at the same place, the interviewee's tent, the next morning at 8:00 a.m. to resume the interview. Unfortunately, an emergency arose in which the interviewee needed to assist someone who had become sick in the middle of the night and had to be taken to the camp hospital. Since the interviewer and interpreter had arranged to be taken to a different camp the next day this remarkable interview was never completed. As it stands, though, it contains insightful and important information on a broad array of issues.

Before the first attacks on our area in May 2002, the relationship with Arabs and black Africans was very good. There was even intermarriage.

We had no rebel groups in our village. The rebels at that time were in the north.

We heard about attacks on other Massaleit prior to the attack on our village—about two months before we were attacked. Many villages in our area were attacked before ours was attacked. We had nothing to help with—nothing. The Government of Sudan had Antonovs and the *Janjaweed* had weapons and horses, and all we could do to assist was go and help bury the dead bodies.

Beginning with the first attacks on our area, the Sudanese government gave Hamid Dawai weapons, vehicles, and equipment for communication. Brought in to work with Hamid Dawai was Jamal (with *Shurta*, the Sudanese National Police) and Yasir (with the Sudanese Army), both with the rank of lieutenant. Then after this they attacked the first village, Kassia, on July 27, 2002. Thirteen huts were burned down and two villagers (Shiekha Dardama and Arbab Abou Koik) were killed. The attack was carried out in the early evening by both the *Jesh* (Sudanese Army) and the *Janjaweed*.

That night the dark came and the attackers returned to Beida. The villagers stayed in their homes for two days and then on Thursday the *Jesh* and *Janjaweed* attacked Kassia again. This time they killed seventeen people, destroyed the entire village by burning it down, stole all of the animals, and took the zinc roof of the school. Hamid Dawai's brother, Hasballa Dawai, was stabbed in the neck with a spear by a villager and killed. That was on Thursday, and then on Friday, three villages (Toucou/Toucoul, Migmesi, and Conga) were burned, totally burned down. In Toucou/Toucoul seven villagers were killed and in Migmesi one person was killed. The iman's brother was shot in the upper arm.

After the three villages were attacked and burned down, all of the villagers crossed the border into Chad, into such places as Amliona, Abassana, Matabano, Aboy, Sesi, and Berkangi. Then, on Monday, the *Janjaweed* and *Jesh* burned down villages called Andrig, Ajabani, Mermta, Temblei, Haraza, Bouta, Gobe, and Dim. The villagers from these villages could not go directly to Chad because right between their villages and Chad is a place, Aun Rado, where the *Janjaweed* are trained by the *Jesh*. So, the people, thousands, went to Kango Haraza in Darfur. They settled there for some days and the *Janjaweed* and the government returned and the area was burned down, and all the animals were stolen. And on the same day, several other villages, Awikar, Boukerei, Ararah, Megalo, and Kassedo were burned down. Out of this entire area, which is very big, only two villages remained—including Baouda, my village.

During many of these attacks, people were kidnapped and forced to work as guides to lead the *Jesh* and *Janjaweed* to important people.

In December 2002, they came and attacked Baouda and 25 people were killed. In Baouda, the attack was at 4:30 in the morning. The *Janjaweed* surrounded the village and before they started shooting they put fire on the houses, in the east part of the village. We didn't realize the *Janjaweed* had attacked the village, we just thought the village had caught fire. The houses were built of grass and we went to support and help the people with the fire. We heard about the fire because the owners were screaming. And when a man appeared to help with the fire the *Janjaweed* would shoot him. And when others heard the shooting they knew it was the *Janjaweed*. They were shooting with Kalashnikovs and Gem 4s. All the people rushed to their houses to get their wives and children.

Everyone began to run towards Chad and as people ran, the *Janjaweed* shot them. The *Janjaweed* and *Jesh* wanted to kill them all, but Chad was only one kilometer away. The government also brought more soldiers in government vehicles, Landcruisers, gray military Landcruisers, and all had *doskas* [large mounted automatic weapons] and they also had *animoks* [big trucks] that carry soldiers—up to 100 men. They chased people until they reached the *wadi*, which is at the border between Sudan and Chad. Then they [the soldiers and *Janjaweed*] returned and looted the village.

There were a lot of people who had sought refuge in our village from the other villages that had been destroyed, and many, many people were killed, so we don't know the number and since that day we have not returned to Sudan or our village.

I was on my way to help with the fire when I heard the sound of the shooting. The sound was very loud, and the *doskas* were firing, and the camels and horses were running into the village.

I returned to my house, got my wife and children (two girls, one two years and one four years), packed up my cart with a bag of clothes and some rugs to sleep on, hitched up my donkey, and when we were leaving the village, a leader of the *Janjaweed* called out to me. It was Algali Haron and he shot at me several times but the bullets didn't hit me. While on his horse, he grabbed me by the collar of my *gelabiah* and pulled me down from my cart and another *Janjaweed* called Salih Dardamo caught me from the back and held me as the other one stabbed me twice with a knife in the middle of the chest, just below the lungs. When he's stabbing me, my wife came up behind Algali Haron and hit him with an axe handle in the neck and knocked him down and my mother and my grandmother ran towards me and my father-in-law came to help me but he was shot by Salih Dardamo in the upper chest. (My father-in-law is now OK and is in Breidjing camp. He has two wives so you can find him in Breidjing and Triendi camps.)

Salih Dardamo, who was all alone and surrounded by my family members, ran to his vehicle and raced off. I then put my father-in-law on the cart. We then crossed the wadi into Chad. Many of the people didn't make it as they were shot and killed.

Another one of my uncles was slashed by a bayonet and he was so bloody we thought he was dead so we didn't pick him up. But somehow he managed to get on his knees and made it to Chad.

Across the wadi was a Chadian garrison and some of the soldiers helped to fight off the *Janjaweed* and *Jesh* and were killed. This was inside Chad. The commander of the soldiers, Battalion Commander Tadjedin, was shot and killed inside Chad.

The dress of *Jesh* and *Janjaweed* were exactly the same—camouflage shirts and pants. The only difference is the *Jesh* had insignias showing rank and the *Janjaweed* had none. The *Jesh* and police also had something over their pockets, but I could not see what it was as I was not close enough.

The *Janjaweed* and *Jesh* were screaming at the villagers, *Abid* [Arabic for "slave"] and *amby* [Arabic meaning "You have no religion"].

We settled across the *wadi* in Naclouta for one month. While there, the Chadian government tried by all means to protect us. But when people went to the *wadi* to get water or went to get their animals, the *Janjaweed* killed them. Sometimes the *Janjaweed* also stole our animals.

As we were escaping, I saw my cousin's husband, Alamin Idris, killed. He was shot in the *wadi*. There were many, many people who were killed. And nobody buried them, nobody returned there and thus they remained unburied. Some of them may have been carried away by the *wadi*, some may be buried by the sand, but many others have never been buried.

Other people in Kassia had tried to return and bury their dead and they were attacked by *Jesh* and *Janjaweed*. There, my father's brother, Khamiss Roy, was killed trying to do so.

After one month, the UNHCR came and picked us up in vehicles and took us to Farchana camp. When we arrived there were four blocks only and now there are 26. The first people arrived here on January 17, 2003, and we arrived in April 2003. Then in the beginning of 2004 I was selected to be *umda* of Farchana by the sheiks. The sheiks themselves nominated and elected me.

Before I was *umda* I was working with *Médécin Sans Frontières* in community service. I told the sheiks I didn't want to be *umda* but they insisted. At that time, we needed a person who could speak English and serve as a translator and they selected me as I know how to write and read. The most difficult aspect of the job is to make the people behave honestly.

The food we receive is not enough here [in the UNHCR refugee camp, Farchana], and there is a problem with water in April, May, and June; that is, there is a shortage. They give us a ration of twelve kilos of sorghum a month per person, but that is not enough. And we've never received meat. We have asked them to bring sardines [meaning fish in a can, not actual sardines] if they cannot provide us with meat, but they have not given us that either. They bring us sorghum only, every month. It's not ready to eat and so we have to bring it to the flourmill and when you take it there they take half of it because you have no money to have it milled. So, you end up with six kilos.

Nothing special is provided for the babies, the infants. And those at one year and above only get sorghum as well.

We all wonder if there is no solution. The United Nations, the Security Council, and the Secretary General, they all make resolutions but fail to force the Sudanese government to obey. Some people are shocked by this, when the decisions are continually reversed. It makes people lose hope.

Notes

1. The height of the mass killing of the black Africans of Darfur took place in 2004 and 2005. The attacks against the black Africans by the GoS and the *Janjaweed* continued unabated through 2009, but they ebbed and flowed across the years. Be that as it may, many black Africans were killed in the later years, and even more died of malnutrition, dehydration, starvation, and untended injuries. Many of the latter were a direct result of the GoS preventing humanitarian aid from reaching the victims. Finally, it should be duly noted that attacks by the GoS against those black Africans still residing in Darfur as well as those "housed" in internally displaced camps have continued through today (January 2012).
2. Colloquially, according to the black Africans of Darfur, *Janjaweed* means, variously, "hordes," "ruffians," and "men or devils on horseback."
3. The phrase "the first acknowledged genocide" is used here for it is possible that other genocides were and are being perpetrated in the early part of the 21st century but not detected yet by the international community. In fact, various scholars and political pundits have suggested that genocide could be underway in such places as the Democratic Republic of the Congo, and in far-flung areas across the globe where indigenous groups reside.
4. Civil war broke out in southern Sudan in 1983 and ended in 2005 as a result of a complex and prolonged international effort to bring the civil war to a close. It is estimated that some two million were killed during that 20-year period and another four million people were displaced. In fact, over the course of the war, at one time or another, about 80% of southern Sudan's people experienced displacement. The war began when the GoS implemented Islamic *Shari'a* law throughout the country. Both Christian and animist peoples residing in the south were adamantly against such a law, and made their disenchantment known. Ultimately, the GoS and rebel groups from the south (comprised of individuals from the Christian and animist groups) engaged in the lengthy and deadly fight—the rebels to wrest the south from the GoS in the north and the GoS to regain control of the south and to banish the Christian and animists from their homes and land. As one journalist put it,

    > When government planes are not bombing [the] homes, churches, and schools [of the people in the south in the areas controlled by the Sudan Peoples Liberation Army or SPLA], armed Arab militias on horseback spread terror throughout the villages, killing men, raping women and taking way their domestic animals. The conflict in Sudan is one in which all known rules of war have constantly been violated. (Achieng, 2000, p. 1)

    A December 1998 report issued by the United States Committee for Refugees asserted that

    > Sudan's civil war has been characterized by an incremental ferocity that has left untouched practically no one in southern Sudan.... The government has systematically

> blocked food supplies to the south, attacked villages and driven large groups of people to areas where they could not survive.... It's a very deliberate strategy on the part of the government of Sudan to depopulate large parts of southern Sudan. (Quoted in BBC, 1998, pp. 1, 2)

5. In May 2011, the National Congress Party, the ruling political party of Sudan, approved a draft law allowing for the creation of two new states (Central Darfur and East Darfur) in Darfur, for a total of five.

6. Arab nomadic groups were, and are not, of course, of a single mind and thus should not be painted as a monolithic group or movement.

7. In regard to the establishment of the self-defense groups by non-Arabs in Darfur, Fadul and Tanner (2007) comment:

> From the 1980s onwards, in Darfur and elsewhere, successive governments in Khartoum mobilized and armed Arab groups to do their bidding, mostly to attack and subdue populations considered hostile. The NIF [National Islamic Front] government furthered the tribal militia policy with the passage of the Popular Defense Act of 1989, making the PDF official. The government entrenched the policy in local government by elevating Arab traditional administrators above non-Arabs in the native Administration.... The Arab groups of western Sudan, Darfur, and Kordofan have been militarized for over two decades. By contrast, non-Arab communities mobilized along far more local lines, resorting to community-level strategies to try to ensure their protection. One such response was the establishment of self-defense committees. In the late 1980s and early 1990s, as Arab violence against non-Arab communities mounted, especially in western Darfur, and the state did not intervene, some of these communities started arming themselves.... These groups were poorly equipped and ill-coordinated, despite isolated attempts in the late 1980s and early 1990s to organize them.... They sold government sugar rations and livestock, and bought light weapons and ammunition from the Chadian military on the border....
>
> The important point here is that the locus of these groups was the village and its outlying homesteads. There was little if any tactical cooperation among the self-defense groups; if Arab militias attacked one village, the self-defense force in the next village would most often just stay put until it in turn was attacked. (p. 302)

8. In October 2006 the London-based Minority Rights Group International issued a report that asserted that United Nations' authorities were warned of ethnic tensions in Darfur as early as 2001 but chose to ignore the facts:

> As early as 2001, the UN Commission on Human Rights' Special Rapporteur for Human Rights in Sudan began paying particular attention to Darfur, visiting the region in early 2002. His August 2002 report highlighted the violence in Darfur and noted Masalit claims that "the depopulation of villages, displacement and changes in land ownership are allegedly part of government strategy to alter the demography of the region." Despite his concerns, the 2003 Commission on Human Rights removed Sudan from its watch-list and ended the mandate of the Special Rapporteur. (Srinivasan, 2006, p. 6)

Many argue that the international community was so intent on bringing the 20-year Sudanese civil war in the south to a close that it believed attention directed at Darfur might result in a "peace spoiler."

9. Tellingly, in interviews with black African Darfurian refugees in Gaga and Forchana refugee camps in eastern Chad during the summer of 2007, this author was told that Arab nomads had been provided with weapons and trained by the GoS as early as the mid-1990s. Furthermore, the so-called *Janjaweed* had been used by the Sudanese leadership since the late 1980s to supplement government troops in the fight against southern rebels (Prunier, 2005, p. 97), and it is certainly possible, if not highly probable, that many of them had roamed throughout Darfur and even joined nomadic groups as the latter herded livestock.

10. Each member of the Permanent Five of the UN Security Council can, alone, with a vote of "no" on any resolution defeat any motion or vote on an issue. The Permanent Five are the only members of the UN Security Council with such veto power.

11. Each rebel faction is eager to be involved in the peace talks and each no doubt has its own motives. Undoubtedly, many, if not most, are anxious to have their say regarding the fate of Darfur. And, as previously mentioned, all are undoubtedly cognizant of the new-found wealth and power that those residing in the south garnered upon the signing of the Comprehensive Peace Agreement, which finally brought to an end the 20-year war between north and southern Sudan and resulted in the establishment of the state of South Sudan.

12. The signing of the DPA by Minni Arkoy Minawi did not bode well for him or his faction. Not only did his faction lose battle after battle with the rebel groups that refused to sign the DPA, but his men began to defect to the other side. By September 2006, it was estimated that up to 75% of his men had joined the non-signatory rebel groups. Furthermore, and understandably, many Darfurians began to look askance at Minni's collaboration with GoS troops and the *Janjaweed*.

13. If the above was not enough of a hindrance to the deployment of the AU–UN hybrid force, by November 2007 not a single country had donated helicopters for the hybrid force. Without such equipment, the force's mobility and effectiveness were sorely restricted.

14. For a fairly succinct but detailed overview of the Darfur peace process, see "Darfur Peace Process Chronology" developed by the Sudan Human Security Baseline Assessment (HSBA) with the Small Arms Survey in Geneva, Switzerland.

15. In regard to the situation in 2008, the ICG (2009) noted that

> Attacks by both government and rebel forces continued throughout the entire year of 2008.... In turn, an assault on Khartoum by Justice and Equality Movement (JEM) rebels in mid-May 2008 left at least 200 dead and was a milestone in the Darfur conflict, constituting the first military strike on the capital in 30 years. (p. 1)

16 For information about the many attacks and counter-attacks in Darfur throughout 2010 and 2011, see the various articles and reports about such events in *The Sudan Tribune*, Human Rights Watch reports, UN Security Council resolutions and presidential statements, and UN reports.

17. For a detailed rebuttal to Gambari's assertion, see Reeves (2011).

18. Later still, Haroun was appointed the Governor of South Kordofan, where he remains to this day, having "won" an election in 2011 to remain governor.

References

Achieng, Judith (2000, August 25). Sudan's protracted war. *ICG News Desk.*. Retrieved from: www.hartford-hwp.com/archives/33/137.html.

Amnesty International (2004). *Darfur: Rape as a weapon of war—Sexual violence and its consequences.* London: Author. Retrieved from: http://web.amnesty.org/library.

Askin, Kelly Dawn (2006). Prosecuting gender crimes committed in Darfur: Holding leaders accountable for sexual violence. In Samuel Totten & Eric Markusen (Eds.) *Genocide in Darfur: Investigating atrocities in the Sudan* (pp. 141–160). New York: Routledge.

BBC (1998, December 11). Millions dead in Sudan civil war. Retrieved from: http://news/bbc.co.uk/1/hi/world/Africa/232803.stm.

BBC (2004, June 30). Sudanese refugees welcome Powell. Retrieved from: http://news/bbc.co.uk.

Caplan, Gerry (2006). From Rwanda to Darfur: Lessons learned?. In Samuel Totten & Eric Markusen (Eds.) *Genocide in Darfur: Investigating the atrocities in the Sudan* (pp. 171–179). New York: Routledge.

Chick, Kristen (2010, February 25). Darfur conflict flares after Sudan President Bashir declares war over. *The Christian Science Monitor.* Retrieved from: www.csmonitor.com/World/terrorism-security/2010/0225/Darfur-conflict-flares-after-Sudan-President-Bashir-declares-war-over.

Cobham, Alex (2005). Causes of conflict in Sudan: Testing the *Black Book*. Queen Elizabeth House, University of Oxford, Working Paper Series. Oxford: University of Oxford. Retrieved from: ideas.repec.org/p/qeh/qehw.ps/qehw.ps.

Coalition for the International Criminal Court (2009, May 28). Al Bashir with BBC "Hard Talk" Program. Retrieved from www.iccnow.org/?mod=newsdetail&news=3370

de Waal, Alex (2004a, July 25). Darfur's Deep grievances defy all hopes for an easy solution. *The Observer* (London), p. 1. Retrieved from: www.guardian.co.uk/sudan/story/ 0,14658,1268773.00.html.

de Waal, Alex (2004b). *Famine that kills: Darfur, Sudan*. New York: Oxford University Press.

de Waal, Alex (2004c). Tragedy in Darfur: On understanding and ending the horror. *Boston review: A poltical and literary forum*. October/November, n.p. Retrieved from: www.boston review.net/BR29.5/dewaal.html.

Fadul, Abdul-Jabbar, & Tanner, Victor (2007). Darfur after Abuja: A view from the ground. In Alex de Waal (Ed.) *War in Darfur and the search for peace* (pp. 284–313). London and Cambridge, MA: Global Equity Initiative, Harvard University, and Justice Africa.

Flint, Julie (2004, December 30). A year on, Darfur's despair deepens. *The Daily Star* (Regional, Lebanon), p. 1. Retrieved from: www.dailystar.com.lb/article.asp?edition_id=10&categ_ id=5&article_id=11388.

Flint, Julie (2009). *Beyond Janjaweed: Understanding the militias of Darfur*. Geneva: Small Arms Survey, Graduate Institute of International and Development Studies.

Flint, Julie, & de Waal, Alex (2005). *Darfur: A short history of a long war*. New York: Zed Books.

Fowler, Jerry (2006). A new chapter of irony: The legal definition of genocide and the implication of Powell's determination. In Samuel Totten & Eric Markusen (Eds.) *Genocide in Darfur: Documenting atrocities in the Sudan* (pp. 127–139). New York: Routledge.

Gettleman, Jeffrey (2007, October 31). At the Darfur talks in Libya, rebel unity is as scarce as the rebels themselves. *New York Times*, p. A6.

Hill, Monica (2006, December 7). U.N. troops are not the answer: Tragedy in Darfur—Unraveling the real causes. *Black Commentator*. Retrieved from: www.blackcommentator.com/209/209_ darfur_un_hill_guest_pf.html

Hoge, Warren (2007a, November 28). U.N. official criticizes Sudan for resisting peace force in Darfur. *New York Times*, p. A5.

Hoge, Warren (2007b, December 7). Lack of donated copters harms Darfur effort, U.N. leader says. *New York Times*, p. A10.

Human Rights Watch (2002). Biography of Hassan al Turabi. New York: Author. Retrieved from: www.hrw.org/press/2002/03/turabi-bio.htm.

Human Rights Watch (2004a). *Darfur destroyed: Ethnic Cleansing by government and militia forces in Western Sudan*. Retrieved from: hrw.org/reports/2004/sudan0504.

Human Rights Watch (2004b, July 20). Darfur documents confirm government policy of militia support: A Human Rights Watch briefing paper. Retrieved from: hrw.org/English/ docs/2004/07/19/darfur9096.

Human Rights Watch (2007). *Chaos by design: Peacekeeping challenges for AMIS and UNAMID*. New York: Author.

International Crisis Group (2007, November 26). *Darfur's new security reality: Executive summary and recommendations*. Africa Report No. 134. Retrieved from: www.crisisgroup. org/.../Darfurs%20New%20Security%20Reality.pdf

International Herald Tribune (2007, September 12). Success uncertain for new, U.N.-sponsored Darfur peace talks. Retrieved from: www.iht.com/articles/ap/2007/09/12/africa/AF-GENDarfur-Peace-Talks.php.

Justice and Equality Movement (2000). *The black book: The imbalance of power and wealth in Sudan*. Khartoum: Author.

Kostas, Stephen A. (2006). Making the determination of genocide in Darfur. In Samuel Totten & Eric Markusen (Eds.) *Genocide in Darfur: Investigating atrocities in the Sudan* (pp. 111–126). New York: Routledge.

Lynch, Colum (2009, June 18). Sudan's "coordinated" genocide in Darfur is over, U.S. Envoy Says. *Washington Post*, p. 1.

Mamdani, Mahmood (2004). How can we name the Darfur crisis? Some preliminary thoughts. *Black Commentary*, p. 2. Retrieved from: www.neravt.com/left/pointers.html.

Mamdani, Mahmood (2007, March 8). The politics of naming: Genocide, civil war, insurgency. *London Review of Books*. Retrieved from: www.wespac.org/WESPACCommunity/Discus-sionMessages/tabid/124/forumid/7/postid/408.

Mariner, Joanne (2004, October 27). *Rape in Darfur*. Retrieved from: http://writ.news.findlaw. com/mariner/20041027.html.

Markusen, Eric, & Totten, Samuel (2005). Investigating allegations of genocide in Darfur: The U.S. atrocities documentation team and the UN commission of inquiry. In Joyce Apsel (Ed.) *Darfur: Genocide Before Our Eyes* (pp. 48–59). New York: Institute for the Study of Genocide.

Meldrum, Andrew (2009, August 27). War over in Darfur? Not quite. *Global Post*. Retrieved from: www.globalpost.com/dispatch/africa/090827/war-darfur-over-not

Nathan, Laurie (2007). The making and unmaking of the Darfur peace agreement. In Alex de Waal (Ed.) *War in Darfur: And the search for peace* (pp. 245–266). Cambridge, MA and London: Global Equity Initiative, Harvard University, and Justice Africa.

Newsweek (2007, November 8). Dueling over Darfur: A human rights activist and an African scholar disagree—vehemently—on the best way to help Sudan. *Newsweek Web Exclusive*. Retrieved from: www.newsweek.com/id/69004/output.

Payne, Donald M. (2004, June 23). Rep. Payne urges action at Congressional Black Caucus Press Conference on the crisis in Darfur, Sudan—press release, p. 1.

Physicians for Human Rights (2005). *Destroyed livelihoods: A case study of Furawiya Village, Darfur*. Cambridge, MA: Author. Retrieved from: physiciansforhumanrights.org/sudan/news.

Physicians for Human Rights (2006). *Assault on survival: A call for security, justice and restitution*. Cambridge, MA: Author. Retrieved from: physiciansforhumanrights.org/library/report-sudan-2006.html.

Pflanz, Mike (2009, August 27). Darfur war is over, claims chief peacekeeper. *The Telegram*. Retrieved from www.telegraph.co.uk › ... › Africa and Indian Ocean › Sudan.

Reeves, Eric (2003, December 30). "Ethnic cleansing" in Darfur: Systematic, ethnically based denial of humanitarian aid is no context for a sustainable agreement in Sudan. *SPLMToday. com*, p. 1.

Reeves, Eric (2011, September 19). The UN'S man in Darfur: The expedient mendacity of Ibrahim Gambari. Retrieved from: www.sudanreeves.org/2011/09/19/the-uns-man-in-darfur-the-expedient-mendacity-of-ibrahim-gambari.

Rice, Susan (2009, June 15). Remarks [to the United Nations] by Ambassador Susan E. Rice, U.S. Permanent Representative, on the UN Security Council and the Responsibility to Protect. United States Mission to the United Nations.

Sengupta, Somini (2004, October 3). In Sudan, no clear difference between Arab and African. *New York Times, Week in Review*, p. 1. Retrieved from: www.nytimes.com/2004/10/03/weekinreview/03seng.

Srinivasan, Sharath (2006). *Minority rights, early warning and conflict prevention: Lessons from Darfur*. London: Minority Rights Group International.

Stanton, Gregory H. (2006). Proving genocide in Darfur: The Atrocities Documentation Project and resistance to its findings. In Samuel Totten & Eric Markusen (Eds.) *Genocide in Darfur: Investigating atrocities in the Sudan* (pp. 181–188). New York: Routledge.

Sudan Liberation Movement and Sudan Liberation Army (SLM/SLA) (2003, March 14). Political Declaration. Retrieved from: www.sudan.net/news/press/postedr/214.shtml.

Sudan Tribune (2006, February 27). "Darfur will be foreign troops' graveyard"—Bashir. *Sudan Tribune*, p. 1. Retrieved from: www.sudantribune.com/spip.ph?

Sudan Tribune (2009, February 17). Sudan and rebel Jem agree to sign declaration of good will. *Sudan Tribune*, n.p. Retrieved from: www.sudantribune.com/Sudan-and-rebel-JEM-agree-to-sign,30195.

Sudan Tribune (2011, May 6). Sudan's government endorses Darfur's division into five states. *Sudan Tribune*, p. 1. Retrieved from: www.sudantribune.com/Sudan-s-government-endorses-Darfur,38798.

Sudan Tribune (2011, June 8). Darfur's violence displaces 70,000 people in six months. *Sudan Tribune*, n.p. Retrieved from: www.sudantribune.com/Darfur-s-violence-displaces.

Totten, Samuel (2004). The U.S. investigation into the Darfur crisis and the U.S. government's determination of genocide. *Genocide Studies and Prevention: An International Journal, 1*(1), 57–77.

Totten, Samuel (2006). The U.S. investigation into the Darfur crisis and its determination of genocide: An analysis. In Samuel Totten & Eric Markusen (Eds.) *Genocide in Darfur: Investigating atrocities in the Sudan* (pp. 199–222). New York: Routledge.

Totten, Samuel (2009). The UN International Commission of Inquiry on Darfur: New and disturbing findings. *Genocide Studies and Prevention, 4*(3), 354–378.

United Nations (2004, March 22). Sudan: World's worst humanitarian crisis: press release, p. 2.

United Nations (2005). *Report of the International Commission of Inquiry on Darfur to the United Nations Secretary-General*. New York: Author.

United Nations Commission of Inquiry into Darfur (2005). *UN Commission of Inquiry: Darfur conflict*. New York: Author.

United Nations High Commissioner for Human Rights (2008). *Ninth periodic report of the United Nations High Commissioner for Human Rights on the situation of Human Rights in the Sudan attacks on civilians in Saraf Jidad, Sirba, Silea and Abu Suruj in January and February 2008*. New York: Author.

United Nations Office for the Coordination of Humanitarian Affairs (2003, December 31). In-depth: "Sudan: A Future without War?"—IRIN In-Depth on the prospects of peace in Sudan: SUDAN: the escalating crisis in Darfur. *IRIN Global*. Retrieved from: www.irinnews.org/InDepthMain.aspx?InDepthId=22&ReportId.

United Nations Radio (2008, December 12). Up to 6,000 child soldiers recruited in Darfur: UNICEF. Retrieved from www.unmultimedia.org/radio/english/detail/65273.html

United Nations Security Council (2009). *Report of the Panel of Experts established pursuant to Resolution 1591 (2005) concerning the Sudan -- S/2009/562*. New York: United Nations.

U.S. State Department (2004). *Documenting atrocities in Darfur*. Washington, DC: Author.

Wax, Emily (2004, June 20). "We want to make a light baby": Arab militiamen in Sudan said to use rape as weapon of ethnic cleansing. *The Washington Post*, pp. A01–02. Retrieved from www.washingtonpost.com/wp-dyn/articles/A16001-2004Jun29.html.

Appendix
UN Convention on the Prevention and Punishment of the Crime of Genocide

Adopted by Resolution 260 (III) A of the United Nations General Assembly on December 9, 1948.

Article 1

The Contracting Parties confirm that genocide, whether committed in time of peace or in time of war, is a crime under international law which they undertake to prevent and to punish.

Article 2

In the present Convention, genocide means any of the following acts committed with intent to destroy, in whole or in part, a national, ethnical, racial or religious group, as such:

a. Killing members of the group;
b. Causing serious bodily or mental harm to members of the group;
c. Deliberately inflicting on the group conditions of life calculated to bring about its physical destruction in whole or in part;
d. Imposing measures intended to prevent births within the group;
e. Forcibly transferring children of the group to another group.

Article 3

The following acts shall be punishable:

a. Genocide;
b. Conspiracy to commit genocide;
c. Direct and public incitement to commit genocide;
d. Attempt to commit genocide;
e. Complicity in genocide.

Article 4

Persons committing genocide or any of the other acts enumerated in Article 3 shall be punished, whether they are constitutionally responsible rulers, public officials or private individuals.

Article 5

The Contracting Parties undertake to enact, in accordance with their respective Constitutions, the necessary legislation to give effect to the provisions of the present Convention and, in particular, to provide effective penalties for persons guilty of genocide or any of the other acts enumerated in Article 3.

Article 6

Persons charged with genocide or any of the other acts enumerated in Article 3 shall be tried by a competent tribunal of the State in the territory of which the act was committed, or by such international penal tribunal as may have jurisdiction with respect to those Contracting Parties which shall have accepted its jurisdiction.

Article 7

Genocide and the other acts enumerated in Article 3 shall not be considered as political crimes for the purpose of extradition.

The Contracting Parties pledge themselves in such cases to grant extradition in accordance with their laws and treaties in force.

Article 8

Any Contracting Party may call upon the competent organs of the United Nations to take such action under the Charter of the United Nations as they consider appropriate for the prevention and suppression of acts of genocide or any of the other acts enumerated in Article 3.

Article 9

Disputes between the Contracting Parties relating to the interpretation, application or fulfilment of the present Convention, including those relating to the responsibility of a State for genocide or any of the other acts enumerated in Article 3, shall be submitted to the International Court of Justice at the request of any of the parties to the dispute.

Article 10

The present Convention, of which the Chinese, English, French, Russian and Spanish texts are equally authentic, shall bear the date of 9 December 1948.

Article 11

The present Convention shall be open until 31 December 1949 for signature on behalf of any Member of the United Nations and of any non-member State to which an invitation to sign has been addressed by the General Assembly.

The present Convention shall be ratified, and the instruments of ratification shall be deposited with the Secretary-General of the United Nations.

After 1 January 1950, the present Convention may be acceded to on behalf of any Member of the United Nations and of any non-member State which has received an invitation as aforesaid.

Instruments of accession shall be deposited with the Secretary-General of the United Nations.

Article 12

Any Contracting Party may at any time, by notification addressed to the Secretary-General of the United Nations, extend the application of the present Convention to all or any of the territories for the conduct of whose foreign relations that Contracting Party is responsible.

Article 13

On the day when the first twenty instruments of ratification or accession have been deposited, the Secretary-General shall draw up a proces-verbal and transmit a copy of it to each Member of the United Nations and to each of the non-member States contemplated in Article 11.

The present Convention shall come into force on the ninetieth day following the date of deposit of the twentieth instrument of ratification or accession.

Any ratification or accession effected subsequent to the latter date shall become effective on the ninetieth day following the deposit of the instrument of ratification or accession.

Article 14

The present Convention shall remain in effect for a period of ten years as from the date of its coming into force.

It shall thereafter remain in force for successive periods of five years for such Contracting Parties as have not denounced it at least six months before the expiration of the current period.

Denunciation shall be effected by a written notification addressed to the Secretary-General of the United Nations.

Article 15

If, as a result of denunciations, the number of Parties to the present Convention should become less than sixteen, the Convention shall cease to be in force as from the date on which the last of these denunciations shall become effective.

Article 16

A request for the revision of the present Convention may be made at any time by any Contracting Party by means of a notification in writing addressed to the Secretary-General.

The General Assembly shall decide upon the steps, if any, to be taken in respect of such request.

Article 17

The Secretary-General of the United Nations shall notify all Members of the United Nations and the non-member States contemplated in Article 11 of the following:

a. Signatures, ratifications and accessions received in accordance with Article 11;
b. Notifications received in accordance with Article 12;
c. The date upon which the present Convention comes into force in accordance with Article 13;
d. Denunciations received in accordance with Article 14;
e. The abrogation of the Convention in accordance with Article 15;
f. Notifications received in accordance with Article 16.

Article 18

The original of the present Convention shall be deposited in the archives of the United Nations.

A certified copy of the Convention shall be transmitted to all Members of the United Nations and to the non-member States contemplated in Article 11.

Article 19

The present Convention shall be registered by the Secretary-General of the United Nations on the date of its coming into force.

Index